A HISTORY OF NINETEENTH-CENTURY AMERICAN WOMEN'S POETRY

A History of Nineteenth-Century American Women's Poetry is the first book to construct a coherent history of this complex field. With contributions from some of the most prominent scholars of nineteenth-century American literature, it explores a wide variety of authors, texts, and methodological approaches. Organized into three chronological sections, the essays examine multiple poetic genres, consider poems circulated in various manuscript and print venues, and propose alternative ways of narrating literary history. From these essays, a rich story emerges about a diverse poetics that was once immensely popular but has since been forgotten. This volume confirms that the field has advanced far beyond the recovery of select individual poets. It is an invaluable resource for students, teachers, and critics of both the literature and the history of this era.

JENNIFER PUTZI is Associate Professor of English and Gender, Sexuality, and Women's Studies at the College of William and Mary. She is the author of *Identifying Marks: Race, Gender, and the Marked Body in Nineteenth-Century America* (2006), the editor of Elizabeth Stoddard's *Two Men* (2008), and the coeditor of *The Selected Letters of Elizabeth Stoddard* (2012).

ALEXANDRA SOCARIDES is Associate Professor of English at the University of Missouri. She is the author of *Dickinson Unbound: Paper, Process, Poetics* (2012) and the coeditor of *The Charles Brockden Brown Electronic Archive and Scholarly Edition, Volume 7: Poetry* (forthcoming).

A HISTORY OF NINETEENTH-CENTURY AMERICAN WOMEN'S POETRY

EDITED BY

JENNIFER PUTZI

College of William and Mary

ALEXANDRA SOCARIDES

University of Missouri

CAMBRIDGE
UNIVERSITY PRESS

One Liberty Plaza, 20th Floor, New York, NY 10006, USA

Cambridge University Press is part of the University of Cambridge.

It furthers the University's mission by disseminating knowledge in the pursuit of education, learning, and research at the highest international levels of excellence.

www.cambridge.org
Information on this title: www.cambridge.org/9781107083981

First published 2017

Printed in the United Kingdom by Clays, St Ives plc

A catalog record for this publication is available from the British Library.

ISBN 978-1-107-08398-1 Hardback

Contents

Illustrations

Contributors

FAITH BARRETT is Associate Professor of English at Duquesne University. With Cristanne Miller, she coedited *Words for the Hour: A New Anthology of American Civil War Poetry* (University of Massachusetts Press, 2005), and she is the author of *To Fight Aloud Is Very Brave: American Poetry and the Civil War* (University of Massachusetts Press, 2012). She has published articles on the poetry of Emily Dickinson, Herman Melville, George Moses Horton, and Abraham Lincoln.

PAULA BENNETT is Professor Emerita at Southern Illinois University–Cardondale. She is the author and editor of a variety of books and articles on nineteenth-century American women poets. Her current project is a book on nineteenth-century Southern women poets.

MONIQUE-ADELLE CALLAHAN is Assistant Professor of English at Emmanuel College. She is the author of *Between the Lines: Literary Transnationalism and African American Poetics* (Oxford University Press, 2011). Her translations and original poetry have appeared or are forthcoming in a number of journals and anthologies, including *Obsidian*, *Tupelo Quarterly*, *Bayou Magazine*, *OVS Magazine*, *The Healing Muse*, and *Stone Highway Review*. She has received fellowships from The Andrew W. Mellon Foundation, Cave Canem, Callaloo, and The Rockefeller Brothers Fund.

MICHAEL C. COHEN is Assistant Professor of English at UCLA and the author of *The Social Lives of Poems in Nineteenth-Century America* (University of Pennsylvania Press, 2015), along with many articles on nineteenth-century poetry, American literature, and the history of reading.

PÁRAIC FINNERTY is Reader in English and American Literature at the University of Portsmouth. He is the author of *Emily Dickinson's Shakespeare* (University of Massachusetts Press, 2006) and coauthor of

Victorian Celebrity Culture and Tennyson's Circle (Palgrave Macmillan, 2013). His next book, *Dickinson and Her British Contemporaries: Victorian Poetry in Nineteenth-Century America*, is forthcoming from Edinburgh University Press.

ERIC GARDNER is the author of *Unexpected Places: Relocating Nineteenth-Century African American Literature* (University Press of Mississippi, 2009), which won the Research Society for American Periodicals Book Award and was a *Choice* "Outstanding Academic Title" in 2010. Drafted with the support of an NEH Fellowship, his second book, *Black Print Unbound: The* Christian Recorder, *African American Literature, and Periodical Culture* (Oxford University Press, 2015), studies the African Methodist Episcopal Church's weekly newspaper during the Civil War era. A Professor of English at Saginaw Valley State University, Gardner has also edited three books and authored a score of shorter pieces on early Black print culture.

TAMARA HARVEY is Associate Professor of English at George Mason University. Her research focuses on women and early America, especially in a hemispheric context. She is the author of *Figuring Modesty in Feminist Discourse across the Americas, 1633–1700* (Ashgate, 2008) and coeditor of *George Washington's South* (University Press of Florida, 2004) and *Confronting Global Gender Justice: Women's Lives, Human Rights* (Routledge, 2010).

DESIRÉE HENDERSON is Associate Professor of English at the University of Texas at Arlington, where she specializes in early American literature and women's writing. She is the author of *Grief and Genre in American Literature, 1790–1870* (Ashgate, 2011), as well as essays published in *Early American Literature, Legacy: A Journal of American Women's Writing, Studies in American Fiction*, and *Walt Whitman Quarterly Review*. She currently serves as Features Editor for *Legacy*.

GARY KELLY is Distinguished University Professor at the University of Alberta, Canada, where he teaches English and Comparative Literature. He has edited the work of Felicia Hemans, Lydia Sigourney, Mary Wollstonecraft, and Sarah Scott, as well as female Gothic fiction, Newgate fiction, and Bluestocking writers. He has also published books and essays on Romantic fiction and women and the French Revolution, among other subjects. He is General Editor of the ongoing *Oxford History of Popular Print Culture*. His digital humanities projects include several online book-history databases using the "streetprint" application developed by his research team. Current projects include a history of the rise of the literary-academic industrial complex in Canada.

MARY LOUISE KETE is Associate Professor of English at the University of Vermont. Her scholarly and pedagogical focus is on eighteenth- and nineteenth-century American authors. Since publishing her first book, *Sentimental Collaborations: Mourning and Middle-Class Identity in Nineteenth-Century America* (Duke University Press, 2000), she has edited *Women's Worlds: McGraw Hill's Anthology of Women's Writing in English* (2007) and coedited (with Elizabeth Petrino) the collection of essays, *Reconsidering Lydia Sigourney: Critical Essays and Cultural Views* (University of Massachusetts Press, forthcoming). She is currently at work on a new book, *American Ekphrasis: Slavery and the Representation of the Free Self.*

MICHELLE KOHLER is Associate Professor of English at Tulane University. She is the author of *Miles of Stare: Transcendentalism and the Problem of Literary Vision in Nineteenth-Century America* (University of Alabama Press, 2014), and her essays on nineteenth-century American writers have appeared in the *Emily Dickinson Journal, Nineteenth-Century Literature, American Literary Realism*, and *Arizona Quarterly*. She is writing a new book about Dickinson and mid-nineteenth-century American constructions of time and timekeeping.

KERRY LARSON is Professor of English at the University of Michigan and is the author of *Whitman's Drama of Consensus* (University of Chicago Press, 1988) and *Imagining Equality in Nineteenth-Century American Literature* (Cambridge University Press, 2008) as well as the editor of *The Cambridge Companion to Nineteenth-Century American Poetry* (2011). He has published articles on Emerson, Hawthorne, and Whitman in *Raritan, ELH, Nineteenth-Century Literature*, and elsewhere.

MARY LOEFFELHOLZ is Professor of English and Vice Provost for Academic Affairs at Northeastern University. She is the author of *Dickinson and the Boundaries of Feminist Theory* (University of Illinois Press, 1991) and *From School to Salon: Reading Nineteenth-Century American Women's Poetry* (Princeton University Press 2004). She has also published essays on nineteenth-century American literature in venues including *American Literary History, The New England Quarterly, The Emily Dickinson Journal*, and *Legacy: A Journal of*

American Women Writers. She is the editor of Volume D, 1914–1945, of *The Norton Anthology of American Literature*, and she coedited (with Martha Nell Smith) *A Companion to Emily Dickinson* (Wiley-Blackwell, 2008).

JOANNA LEVIN is Associate Professor in the English Department at Chapman University. She is the author of *Bohemia in America, 1858–1920* (Stanford University Press, 2010) and coeditor (with Edward Whitley) of *Whitman among the Bohemians* (University of Iowa Press, 2014).

CRISTANNE MILLER is SUNY Distinguished Professor and Edward H. Butler Professor of Literature at University at Buffalo SUNY. Her publications on nineteenth-century American literature include *Emily Dickinson: A Poet's Grammar* (Harvard University Press, 1987), *Reading in Time: Emily Dickinson in the Nineteenth Century* (University of Massachusetts Press, 2012), and *Words for the Hour: A New Anthology of Civil War Poetry* (coedited with Faith Barrett, University of Massachusetts Press, 2005). She is also editor of *Emily Dickinson's Poems as She Preserved Them* (forthcoming), and she has published extensively on modernist poetry.

ROBERT DALE PARKER is the James M. Benson Professor in English at the University of Illinois. He has published *Changing Is Not Vanishing: A Collection of Early American Indian Poetry to 1930* (University of Pennsylvania Press, 2011) and *The Sound the Stars Make Rushing Through the Sky: The Writings of Jane Johnston Schoolcraft* (University of Pennsylvania Press, 2007), an edition of the writings of Jane Johnston Schoolcraft that includes a cultural biography. He is the author of two books on William Faulkner, a book on Elizabeth Bishop, *The Invention of Native American Literature* (Cornell University Press, 2003), and *How to Interpret Literature: Critical Theory for Literary and Cultural Studies* (Oxford University Press, 2015), as well as the editor of *Critical Theory: A Reader for Literary and Cultural Studies* (Oxford University Press, 2012).

ELIZABETH PETRINO teaches American literature at Fairfield University. She is the author of *Emily Dickinson and Her Contemporaries: American Women's Verse, 1820–1885* (University of New Hampshire Press, 1998), and has published articles on Emily Dickinson and her female literary peers in the *Emily Dickinson Journal*, *ESQ*, *Tulsa Studies in Women's Literature*, and *Legacy: A Journal of American Women Writers*. She has coedited (with

Jocelyn Boryczka) a prizewinning book on feminist pedagogy, *Jesuit and Feminist Education: Intersections in Teaching and Learning for the Twenty-First Century* (Fordham University Press, 2012). Currently, she is coediting (with Mary Louise Kete) *Reconsidering Lydia Sigourney: Critical Essays and Cultural Views* (University of Massachusetts Press, forthcoming).

JENNIFER PUTZI is Associate Professor of English and Gender, Sexuality, and Women's Studies at the College of William and Mary. She is the author of *Identifying Marks: Race, Gender, and the Marked Body in Nineteenth-Century America* (University of Georgia Press, 2006), the editor of Elizabeth Stoddard's *Two Men* (University of Nebraska Press, 2008), and the coeditor of *The Selected Letters of Elizabeth Stoddard* (University of Iowa Press, 2012).

ELIZABETH RENKER is Professor of English at The Ohio State University. She is the author of *The Origins of American Literature Studies: An Institutional History* (Cambridge University Press, 2007); *Strike Through the Mask: Herman Melville and the Scene of Writing* (Johns Hopkins University Press, 1996); the introduction to the Signet classic edition of *Moby-Dick* (1998); and an array of articles on poetics and poetic history, the history of American literature as a field, Herman Melville, and Sarah Piatt. Her book-in-progress, *Realist Poetics in American Culture, 1866–1911*, examines postbellum poetry in the United States in conjunction with the historical and disciplinary formations of American literary "realism."

ELIZA RICHARDS is Associate Professor in the Department of English and Comparative Literature at the University of North Carolina-Chapel Hill. She teaches and writes about American literature and culture before 1900, with a particular emphasis on poetry. She is the author of *Gender and the Poetics of Reception in Poe's Circle* (Cambridge University Press, 2004) and the editor of *Emily Dickinson in Context* (Cambridge University Press, 2013). She is currently completing a book on the relationship between poetry and journalism during the U.S. Civil War. She was awarded a National Humanities Center Fellowship in 2010–2011 to work on this project.

JESS ROBERTS is Associate Professor of American Literature at Albion College. She has published several articles on nineteenth-century print culture and Civil War literature, including "Sarah Piatt's Grammar of Convention and the Conditions of Authorship," which appeared in *The Cambridge Companion to Nineteenth-Century American Poetry*

(2011). She is the coeditor of Penguin's *Nineteenth-Century American Poetry* (1996). Her current projects focus on the richness of literature as a resource for creating and sustaining community.

ALEXANDRA SOCARIDES is Associate Professor of English at the University of Missouri, where she teaches American poetry and poetics as well as nineteenth-century literature and culture. Her first book, *Dickinson Unbound: Paper, Process, Poetics* (Oxford University Press, 2012), is about Emily Dickinson's compositional and material practices. She is the coeditor (with Michael Cohen) of *The Charles Brockden Brown Electronic Archive and Scholarly Edition, Volume 7: Poetry* (forthcoming) and is working on a new book about the conventions of nineteenth-century American women's poetry.

ANGELA SORBY is Professor of English at Marquette University. She is the author of *Schoolroom Poets: Childhood, Performance, and the Place of American Poetry* (University of New Hampshire Press, 2005) and three poetry collections: *The Sleeve Waves* (University of Wisconsin Press, 2013), *Bird Skin Coat* (University of Wisconsin Press, 2009), and *Distance Learning* (New Issues, 1998). She recently coedited (with Karen Kilcup) *Over the River and Through the Wood: An Anthology of Nineteenth-Century American Children's Poetry* (Johns Hopkins University Press, 2014).

CLAUDIA STOKES is Professor of English at Trinity University. She is the author of *The Altar at Home: Sentimental Literature and Nineteenth-Century American Religion* (University of Pennsylvania Press, 2014) and *Writers in Retrospect: The Rise of American Literary History, 1875–1910* (UNC Press, 2006). She is coeditor (with Michael A. Elliott) of *American Literary Studies: A Methodological Reader* (NYU Press, 2002). Her work has appeared in *American Literature, American Literary Realism, American Quarterly, ESQ,* and *Legacy: A Journal of American Women Writers*, among other places.

EDWARD WHITLEY is Associate Professor in the English Department at Lehigh University. He is the author of *American Bards: Walt Whitman and Other Unlikely Candidates for National Poet* (UNC Press, 2010) and the coeditor (with Joanna Levin) of *Whitman among the Bohemians* (University of Iowa Press, 2014). Since 2004, he and Robert Weidman have codirected *The Vault at Pfaff's: An Archive of Art and Literature by the Bohemians of Antebellum New York* (http://lehigh.edu/pfaffs).

SHIRA WOLOSKY was Associate Professor of English at Yale University before moving to the Hebrew University, where she is Professor of American Literature. Her books include *Emily Dickinson: A Voice of War* (Yale University Press, 1984), *Language Mysticism* (Stanford University Press, 1995), *The Art of Poetry* (Oxford University Press, 2001), *The Riddles of Harry Potter* (Palgrave Macmillan, 2010), *Poetry and Public Discourse in Nineteenth-Century America* (Palgrave Macmillan, 2010), and *Feminist Theory Across Disciplines* (Routledge, 2013), as well as other writings. Her awards include a Guggenheim Fellowship and fellowships at the Princeton Institute for Advanced Studies, NYU Law School, the Israel Institute for Advanced Studies, and the Drue Heinz Visiting Professorship at Oxford.

Acknowledgments

When Ray Ryan asked us to put a proposal together for *A History of Nineteenth-Century American Women's Poetry*, it took us less than an hour to go from worrying that we wouldn't be able to find enough work in the field to realizing we had enough scholars, topics, and ideas to fill ten volumes. We thank Ray for giving us this opportunity and for trusting us at every step along the way. His support of the project and of our partnership has been invaluable.

With the utmost gratitude, we would also like to thank the twenty-four scholars whose work appears in this volume. Each one of them approached this project with enthusiasm and dedication. They have written original essays on topics that we feel confident will push the field of American literary history into new realms.

To collaborate on an edition of essays while not residing in the same place involves thousands of emails, countless hours on the telephone and Skype, and multiple flights across the country. We would like to thank the partners, children, and stepchildren – Simon, Sam, Charley, Alex, Archer, Nate, Hallam, and Catherine – who, at crucial moments, have taken a backseat to our relationship. When we met at the National Humanities Center in the summer of 2008, we might not have been able to envision that together we would make such a book, but we did know that this friendship had special things in store for us. Working together to rethink women's literary history is, we hope, the first of many collaborations to come.

Introduction
Making History: Thinking about Nineteenth-Century American Women's Poetry

Jennifer Putzi and Alexandra Socarides

In July 1837, the noted Quaker writer, minister, and reform advocate, Joseph John Gurney, left his native England and made a series of trips to Canada, the West Indies, and North America. During his time in the United States, Gurney visited southern and northern cities alike, speaking widely upon prison reform, the abolition of slavery, and religious disunity in the Quaker church. On Gurney's departure from Philadelphia, a group of Quaker women presented him with a friendship album titled "The American Offering" as a gift for his seventeen-year-old daughter Anna, who had been left behind in England during her father's journey.[1] The album has 134 gold-edged leaves, and Anna's name is printed on its cover and title page. [Fig. 1] The rest of the pages contain approximately 100 poems, interspersed with prose excerpts and illustrations. While the selections are handwritten, the compilers also clearly had the conventions of print in mind, as they carefully inscribed the titles of poems and often added a relevant illustration.[2]

The opening poem, signed by Elizabeth Lloyd and titled "To Anna Gurney," declares that the album contains "a wreath" of the "native flowers" of the United States to serve as a "uniting bond" between Anna Gurney and her fellow Quakers. While "The American Offering" itself contains prose and illustrations as well as poetry, Lloyd indicates that it is the poetry in particular that will create and sustain this transatlantic "bond." In the final stanza, Lloyd marks exactly what Anna can expect to find in this collection of this "country's poesy":

> We will not twine in this bouquet, our country's gayest flowers:
> But the purest and the sweetest ones, that bloom in her bowers.
> There are no rare exotics here! Oh no – we only bring,
> To thee – an unpretending – simple – native, Offering!

Figure 1. Title page of the friendship album "The American Offering," 1838. Courtesy of The Winterthur Library.

Lloyd makes clear that this poetry is not remarkable because it is the "country's gayest," but because it is its "purest" and "sweetest." This purity and sweetness is referenced again, yet put differently, in the final line, where she marks the poems as "unpretending" and "simple." What accompanies this characterization is the insistence that the poems are wholly

American – they "bloom in her bowers," are "no rare exotics," and, most simply put, are "native." By employing the language and logic of flowers here, Lloyd suggests that while imported flowers/poems might distinguish themselves in external ways, it is the native ones that will smell the sweetest. What follows, then, are poems by the best-known American women poets of the day.

We open *A History of Nineteenth-Century American Women's Poetry* with this material artifact not to highlight, as Lloyd did, that nineteenth-century American poetry by women is "simple," nor to disagree with her, but to call attention to this community's act of compiling, framing, and implicitly narrating an emerging history of American poetry in which women writers play a vital role. While the poetry by women that is included in this album is interspersed with that of their male peers, women's poetry is clearly central to the compilers' project of representing the nation's creative output and moral standing in the world. The compilers of "The American Offering" were preceded in their historicizing of American poetry by Samuel Kettell's *Specimens of American Poetry* (1829) and George B. Cheever's *The American Common-Place Book of Poetry* (1831), both of which acknowledge the popularity and influence of women poets. Unlike these volumes, though, "The American Offering" devotes approximately half of its pages to the work of women, thereby quietly critiquing the history of American poetry as it is being constructed in American print culture. Lloyd's opening poem makes it clear that this volume represents a different kind of history, one shaped by women readers' and writers' sense of ownership over their "country's poesy."

When we look, more specifically, at how this community went about making this book – in other words, where they gained access to the poems by the women poets they included – we can see that they were culling from a variety of print sources. Two of their primary sources were anthologies of British and American women's poetry that had been recently published in America in 1837: Sarah Josepha Hale's *The Ladies' Wreath: A Selection from the Female Poetic Writers of England and America*, and D. F., Jr.'s *Selections from Female Poets: A Present for Ladies.* The compilers were not content, however, with only these selections and so turned to popular annuals (*The Atlantic Souvenir* and *The Token*) as well as local periodicals (*The Philadelphia Album and Ladies' Literary Portfolio* and *The Friend*). They also included poems by Quaker poet Elizabeth Chandler, which had been printed in *The Poetical Works of Elizabeth Margaret Chandler: With a Memoir of her Life and Character* (1836). These Philadelphia Quakers, in other words, clearly had access to a substantial amount of women's poetry and they were reading widely in the sources that printed this poetry. Yet they were not simply passive readers of this material: they were claiming it as their own and making editorial decisions about selections and transcriptions.

While the compilers of "The American Offering" seem confident in their efforts to set down poetry that "will never be forgot," we know now just how wrong they were about the future life of these poems. This forgetting – the cultural erasure of the work of numerous popular and influential women poets whose poems pervaded nineteenth-century America – has had a lasting impact on the shape of nineteenth-century American literary studies. Up until very recently most scholars of American literature would have claimed that a history of nineteenth-century American women's poetry was unnecessary, or perhaps even impossible. Nineteenth-century American women poets have long been regarded as too sentimental, too conventional, too popular – an undifferentiated mass not worthy of scholarly attention. This is, in part, a result of the ways in which they were framed in their own time. While women's poetry was widely published in nineteenth-century America and was read in the same context as the work of the male counterparts with whom these women poets were engaged (both in the marketplace as well as in the intimacy of the salon), this did not prevent contemporary critics such as Rufus Wilmot Griswold from distinguishing between them. Griswold's *The Poets and Poetry of America*, published in 1842, consisted primarily of the work of male poets, but it also contained biographical sketches of and selected poems by twelve women poets (with additional women included in a back section titled "Various Authors"). Yet his publication of *The Female Poets of America* six years later enabled him to remove many of these women poets from the next edition of *The Poets and Poetry of America*, thus drawing attention to them while at the same time removing them from conversation with the larger field.

Women poets were, Griswold contended, capable of emotional depth and expression unavailable – and, indeed, unnecessary – to men. Women's innate morality and spirituality, Griswold asserted, rendered them capable of "mirror[ing] in dazzling variety the effects which circumstances or surrounding minds work upon [their spirits]," but not of the "power to originate, [or] even, in any proper sense, to reproduce."[3] Such a reinforcement of gendered norms shaped later nineteenth-century approaches to this body of work, with Griswold's successors dismissing the idea that women poets of the early to mid-nineteenth century had anything of value to offer to a rapidly solidifying literary canon. Add to this both the early-twentieth-century New Critical reading practices that radically isolated poetry from the contexts in which it was written and consumed *and* the rise of Emily Dickinson to a position of exceptional prominence, and you quite quickly have a deeply entrenched perception of nineteenth-century American women's poetry as unsusceptible to study.[4]

The problem of Dickinson is worth addressing upfront, and readers will surely notice that while Dickinson appears in some of the essays collected here, we have deliberately assigned her space at the very end, where Mary Loeffelholz expertly tackles the conundrum that Dickinson has long presented for the construction of this field. Throughout most of the latter half of the twentieth century, Dickinson was widely regarded as writing against the work of her female peers, refusing to publish in order to avoid the compromises that even the very best of them were apparently forced to make. In recent years, however, scholars have reconsidered this approach. Initially, they reframed Dickinson scholarship so as to allow room for the ways in which her work was both embedded in the literary culture of her time and engaged in conversation with her peers.[5] As these "other" nineteenth-century American women poets began to constitute a field of their own, Dickinson's position was continually shifting. Should she inhabit the center and set the so-called standard by which her contemporaries might be judged? Should she hover as an ethereal presence, no longer dislodging these women poets from their places in literary history but bearing down on them nonetheless? Must she be excised entirely in order to give these women their due? While one might once have seen this critical conundrum as an impasse through which the field could not progress, the field has, in large part, been borne from it, as such questions have provoked a sustained evaluation of the historical, cultural, and literary significance of women poets who were once deemed, in the face of Emily Dickinson, to be wholly insignificant.

The recovery of this body of work began slowly, in part due to a lack of access to primary sources and in part due to its position in relation to women's fiction of the period. While women's fiction had received significant scholarly attention by the late 1980s and early 1990s, resulting in editions of the work of writers such as Catharine Maria Sedgwick, Harriet Beecher Stowe, and Louisa May Alcott, university presses were notoriously reluctant to reprint the work of relatively unknown women poets. It was only in the final years of the twentieth century that several anthologies of nineteenth-century American women's poetry were published, finally providing scholars and students access to this work – access that would later increase exponentially by the twenty-first century's user-friendly digital archives of books and periodicals.[6] Editions of work by individual poets and reprints of nineteenth-century volumes by women poets remain relatively rare, but in recent years scholarly editions have been published of the work of Lydia Sigourney, Sarah Piatt, Frances Ellen Watkins Harper, Adah Isaacs Menken, and Emma Lazarus.[7] While much of the work being done with women's fiction (and, to some extent, nonfiction) seemed to lend itself to the study of women's poetry, most critics focused entirely on fiction *or* poetry, rarely allowing the insights of one body of work to inform the other. Scholarly work on the sentimental novel, for example, was clearly relevant to women's poetry, given the central role of sentimental rhetoric in the work of many nineteenth-century American women poets, yet poetry often served as a foil for the woman's novel, representing a sort of excess of emotion that the novel was often purported to subvert or at least to use to more complicated ends. Similarly, although women's authorship and their negotiation of the nineteenth-century American literary marketplace were receiving scholarly attention, this work focused almost entirely on prose writers.[8]

As the field progressed beyond a state of dismissal, one of the most important (and contested) critical frames to emerge was that of the "poetess," a label often used to describe any woman poet writing and publishing in the nineteenth century. Early discussions of the poetess returned to primary sources, most notably to Griswold's *The Female Poets of America*, to reconstruct the way in which many women poets were received and read in the nineteenth century. Some scholars embraced the label of the poetess, demonstrating women's self-conscious but nonetheless often sincere adoption of its attendant expectations and conventions, a move that allowed women to succeed in a literary marketplace that had been otherwise hostile to them. Reading the figure in this way often led to the critical acknowledgment of the power of these literary and cultural contexts. Other critics, however, found the term unsuitable. They demonstrated the existence of a body of work that clearly did not fit into the stereotype that the label invokes – political poems, for example, or erotic verse – and often argued that the women poets most worthy of study (or the poems most worthy of study within a poet's larger body of work) only ever deployed the poetess figure subversively, making use of it as a mask of sorts for their "real" work. In 1999, Virginia Jackson and Yopie Prins cut through the terms of this debate by usefully connecting the "poetess" to a form of twentieth-century lyric reading in which women's poetry had become construed, incorrectly, as the very articulation of subjectivity. Instead, the poetess, they argued, "circulates from the late eighteenth century onward as an increasingly empty figure: not a lyric subject to be reclaimed as an identity but a medium for cultural exchange."[9] While the recovery of individual poets is important, they acknowledged, scholars' continued insistence on reading for subjectivity negates the equally important recovery of genre and convention. In a later development of this argument, Jackson insisted on the mutability of the poetess over the course of the nineteenth-century, asking "How could the Poetess of 1832 be the Poetess of 1891, when everything else about poetry (including the definition of the word itself) had changed in those seventy years?"[10]

The study of nineteenth-century American women's poetry began to thrive in the early part of the twenty-first century, with three book-length critical studies: Paula Bennett's *Poets in the Public Sphere: The Emancipatory Project of American Women's Poetry, 1800–1900* (2003), Eliza Richards' *Gender and the Poetics of Reception in Poe's Circle* (2004), and Mary Loeffelholz's *From School to Salon: Reading Nineteenth-Century American Women's Poetry* (2004). These studies represent crucial interventions in the study of nineteenth-century American women's poetry, as they drew on rich archives of previously untouched primary sources to demonstrate the rich potential of the field, to indicate the error of past neglect, and to point to the potential for future scholarship. Each of these scholars made deep cultural, political, and literary contextualization central to the recovery of and subsequent scholarship on American women's poetry and, as their essays in this volume prove, they continue to shape the field.

Given this evolving body of materials and scholarship, it certainly seems time to construct a history of sorts, one that can be used to provide a framework for this rapidly expanding field of study. Yet we recognize that to do so is to risk "making history" in a way that precludes new approaches to the field. Just as the histories made by anthologists, editors, and critics of the nineteenth and twentieth centuries in part contributed to the forgetting and neglect of American women's poetry, our focus on the poets, poems, topics, and approaches present in this book may prevent, for a time, those that we cannot yet see. We attempt this history here knowing that the process of recovery and recontextualization is far from complete. Revisions are both inevitable and welcome.

A History of Nineteenth-Century American Women's Poetry could have been organized in a variety of ways, one of which would have been to solicit and group essays under single-author categories. But readers of this collection will find that while certain poets continue to emerge across essays – there are more references to and treatments of Sigourney, Piatt, and Harper than to any other poets – there is no sustained argument for the recovery of any individual poet above the others. Neither will readers find stand-alone treatments of individual poets out of the context of their social and cultural surroundings. This was intentional. Guided by the proposed title of the volume, with its focus on "poetry" and not "poets," we solicited essays that would complicate an author-centered approach. Doing so allowed us to highlight the incredible diversity of these communities of poets, and therefore of the field itself. Due, in part, to the dearth of African American, Native, working-class, and southern women included in the nineteenth-century anthologies, and then to the twentieth century's critical focus on a singular upper-middle class woman poet from Amherst, this field has long been associated with well-off, northern, white women. Scholars have also tended to devote attention to writers who produced a significant body of work in print, thereby rendering unworthy of study those poets whose economic circumstances or racial identity precluded sustained creative output or access to publication venues. The privilege that has often been assumed to accompany the time and resources to write and publish poetry is challenged by an approach that puts genres, topics, and venues – instead of authors – at its center. Mary Louise Kete's focus in this volume, for example, on Lucy Terry Prince is a perfect example of the kind of scholarship that is facilitated by such an approach, as very little is known about Prince's life, her work was primarily oral, and only one poem, "Bars Fight," is extant. In a collection that highlighted authors, these facts would preclude any scholarly approach other than that which acknowledged Prince's existence as Phillis Wheatley's contemporary.

By highlighting a diversity of contexts for the production, circulation, and consumption of poetry, we include in this history women who were writing poetry from what we might otherwise call the margins: Native boarding schools, the factory, the plantation, and Bohemian communities, among other places and spaces. In their essay, for example, Joanna Levin and Edward Whitley argue that Bohemian circles offered women poets a location in which they might imagine their lives outside of – and often counter to – the mainstream. Jennifer Putzi shows how the space of the factory allowed female operatives access to print in *The Lowell Offering*, thereby enabling working-class women poets to position themselves as part of a much larger tradition of women writers. Outsider poets such as these become, in many ways, our insiders, as it is their stories that fill these pages.

Our focus on non-author-centered approaches also allowed us to acknowledge the diversity of material contexts within which this poetry was produced, circulated, and consumed. From the beginning of the century, Tamara Harvey explains, women poets were engaging in both manuscript and print cultures, often simultaneously, using their work to help shape a new American literature distinct from that of England. The essays that follow take into consideration this wide variety of material contexts, looking at manuscript sources as well as print sources, periodicals as well as gift books and anthologies. In doing so, they examine the ways in which context shapes composition and circulation for both amateur and professional writers. Michael Cohen, for instance, examines the importance of "scribal poetic cultures" in nineteenth-century America, looking specifically at the inscription of poetry in albums and the subsequent circulation of these albums among groups of young women. Elizabeth Petrino examines the work of Lydia Sigourney within the context of the gift book, arguing that Sigourney capitalized on both the technological advances that made gift books possible and the gift book's romanticization of preindustrial cultures. Michelle Kohler's work on *The Dial* also highlights the importance of publication venue, as she reconstructs a community of Transcendentalist women poets, focusing on the way in which editor Margaret Fuller enabled the publication of her own poems as well as work by Elizabeth Peabody, Caroline Sturgis, Ellen Sturgis Hooper, and Eliza Thayer Clapp.

This panoply of material contexts for women's poetry prompts questions about the long-held assumption that the single-author book was an important – in fact, was *the* important – kind of publication for any nineteenth-century poet. As Eric Gardner's essay on the circulation and publication of poetry within activist abolitionist circles indicates, such poetry is only visible to scholars the further they move away from "the venues that modern critics have valued and drawn from most." That does not mean that scholars should ignore the single-author book. As Faith Barrett's reading of Phoebe Cary's *Poems and Parodies* demonstrates, the space of the book allowed Cary to organize and present her poems in such a way that the conventions of sentimentality are laid bare. This exposure is crucial to Cary's rethinking of the ideologies that accompany poetic genres.

Barrett's interest in parody as a poetic genre calls attention to another concern of this book. Throughout these essays, scholars reveal a whole host of genres that were not just alive and well in nineteenth-century America, but that women writers took seriously *as genres.* As Kerry Larson's essay demonstrates, women writing poetry during this period were thinking critically about their relationship to poetry (or "Poetry") and their role as poets. They did so, however, in a variety of different genres. Elizabeth Oakes Smith, Larson argues, used the sonnet to express her sense of a "conflicted, often anguished relation to poetic form and the promises it seemed to hold." Whether they were writing sonnets, elegies, hymns, parodies, dramatic monologues, or epics, these poets registered that they were thinking about the history and conventions of the various poetic genres on offer, not collapsing them all into one monolithic "Poetry." And it is through attention to these genres that women writers often expressed praise, leveled critique, and contemplated the very nature of their work. For instance, in her essay on the friendship elegy, Desirée Henderson writes that it was through engaging with the tradition, history, and conventions of the elegy that these poets laid claim to the friendship elegy, "a subgenre of the elegy that demonstrates how generic conventions could be leveraged to promote the status of women's relationships and women's writing." Similarly, Jess Roberts examines what she calls the "doubleness" inherent to the dramatic monologue – "the subjective/internal and objective/external dimensions of the poem" – a characteristic of the genre that Sarah Piatt used to consider how "as mothers and daughters, as readers and writers, women possess and might exert agency to maintain or disrupt the things that restrict them."

A focus on the material circumstances of composition and circulation as well as on the history of the genres with which these women were engaged points out just how steeped in convention this poetry was. That's not to say it was "conventional," as that term has received a bad reputation over the course of the twentieth century. But it is to say that these women often took up the conventions available to them and used them to their advantage. This did not, as most narratives of convention want to espouse, always result in either complete capitulation or the articulation of a wholly subversive agenda or poetics. In fact, a deep and sustained engagement with these conventions often produced the very visibility – and, by extension, viability – that these women sought for their poems. What they did with these conventions – however they developed, warped, or reinstated them – is of great interest in these essays. Take, for example, Eliza Richards' treatment of flower poems, "a tradition spanning centuries" that nonetheless greatly attracted the nineteenth-century American woman poet. By taking a comparative approach to northern and southern women's poetry before and during the Civil War, Richards explores the different results of this "shared literary inheritance." Paula Bennett examines the way in which southern women poets fused a Gothic sensibility to the conventions of sentimental poetry in order to express their own apprehensions about race and gender, romance and reality.

Unsurprisingly, many of the essays here weave in and out of all of the issues explored above. Claudia Stokes' work on the hymn, for instance, brings together an emphasis on material context, genre, and convention, arguing that the hymn, which "reigned as one of the era's major poetic genres available to women[,] . . . imparted an authority to female hymnists that far exceeded anything otherwise available to women poets more generally." Using established conventions of the genre, female hymnists were authorized to "circulate their own exegetical interpretations of scripture, and influence the religious ideas of readers and worshippers." Alexandra Socarides's essay on the anthologies of the late 1840s that collected exclusively, and for the first time, poetry by American women shows how the conventions of anthology publication in particular came to play a major role in how both contemporary readers and later critics conceived of women's poetry.

While the nineteenth-century anthologies that sought to both define and contain the field had something at stake in explaining the Americanness of American women's poetry, the essays in this history push on the boundaries of the nation. American women poets not only imitated, responded to, collaborated with, and even visited their British counterparts, they also articulated their interest in global issues through their poetry. For Gary Kelly, one of the most important of these relationships was between two women who never actually met – the British Felicia Hemans and the "American Hemans," Lydia Sigourney. Kelly carefully reconstructs the print record of their coupling in the public eye, as well as how differing modernities on either side of the Atlantic dictated the survival in print of each poet. Páraic Finnerty is also interested in the ways in which print culture contributed to a female-centered transatlantic poetic tradition. He argues that the notion of such a network was a critical construction intended to highlight the gendered qualities of both British and American women's poetry. Thus, nineteenth-century women's poetry was simultaneously read within a national and a transnational context – a "fault line" that critics have long since struggled to address.

Other essays in this volume point to the importance of positioning nineteenth-century American women's poetry within a larger transnational framework, articulating new and innovative approaches to this body of work. For example, Monique-Adelle Callahan focuses on both the transatlantic and the transhemispheric in her work on Frances Ellen Watkins Harper, arguing that Harper deploys a "literary transnationalism" that allows her to reach beyond national borders in order to create a non-nation based African American poetics. In her close reading of Emma Lazarus' poetry, Shira Wolosky rethinks the theorization of the transnational along lines of "memberships" instead of "associations": "Instead of privileging a dissolution of borders that suspends identity," Wolosky argues, "Lazarus's texts open the possibility of multiple memberships as an ongoing unfolding of the self and its commitments."

While issues of material context, genre, convention, and transnationalism cut across many of the essays in this volume, we have structured the volume chronologically, in three sections: 1800 to 1840, 1840 to 1865, and 1865 to 1900. While it is worth questioning this kind of structural periodization – one that, we are well aware, begins and ends arbitrarily and hinges on the Civil War – it is within the essays themselves that such pressure on periodization is exerted. Some essays embrace their own historicization, as we see in Cristanne Miller's focus on the different kinds of verse forms that emerged in the postbellum period. Such an approach allows critics to use nineteenth-century American women's poetry to think, or perhaps rethink, literary history's narratives of development. Other essays push against the boundaries of history's categories: in Angela Sorby's exploration of children's verse, she invites readers to "traverse the nineteenth century twice" in order to examine two kinds of children's poetry: "poetry that reflects and promotes the interdependence of women and children, and poetry that idealizes childhood autonomy."

One might think that the construction of this history primarily requires attention to this history's details, in all their specificities. And it does. But, in the process of reconstructing that history, several essays here signal the need for continued revision to the broader paradigms that shape American literary history on the whole. These are interventions that originate in the specifics of nineteenth-century American women's poetry – an unlikely place, one might think, for the seeds of disciplinary change to reside. For example, Elizabeth Renker asserts that theorists of literary realism have neglected the contributions of women's poetry and points our attention to the ways in which realist poets such as Sarah Piatt, Emma Lazarus, Lucy Larcom, and Susan Coolidge used their work to interrogate the postbellum conflict between the real and the ideal. In doing so, she shows just how central these women's work is to the construction and definition of literary realism. Robert Dale Parker similarly exposes a flaw in existing approaches to women's poetry by constructing a literary history of Native women's poetry, almost all of which has been completely ignored by scholars. Often written in isolation from one another, these poems engage with similar ideas and traditions, Parker argues, creating a series of "braided relations." His approach demonstrates the necessity of reading and rereading this work, both on its own and in conversation with other poets and other traditions.

Throughout "The American Offering," Elizabeth Lloyd and her fellow compilers insist that they will be friends and "sisters" to Anna Gurney, with the tie between them symbolized by the very book in which they write. According to Lloyd:

> 'Tis not as strangers we would wreathe our native flowers for thee.
> Or on these pages, coldly breathe our countrys poesy.
> 'Tis not as strangers – though unknown – our gatherings we bring –
> Nor would we have thee deem our gift a stranger's offering!

The ability to connect with another human being in this way, Lloyd asserts in "To Anna," the poem that closes the volume, depends upon a shared language:

> This language, doubtless, thou canst read!
> And oh! 'tis beautiful indeed!
> Whether, in sound, its whispers be,
> Or whether offered silently!
> Its spirits too may be embalmed
> In leaflets from a distant land.

While Lloyd is ostensibly talking about the language of sympathy here, given the contents of "The American Offering" she could just as well be referring to poetry itself. These poems, many of which were first encountered in print and then lovingly and laboriously copied into this album, are assumed to be not only legible to others but also valuable. And so too are the poems by Lloyd, who claims a place in this tradition. There is no doubt that the field of nineteenth-century American women's poetry has advanced far enough to allow us to attempt to understand the language in which *all* of these women poets wrote, to articulate the aesthetics of their work as well as the rich reading, copying, publishing, and reprinting contexts of their time. We might, along with Lloyd, insist that this poetry "'tis beautiful indeed!," but we do so while also recognizing its culturally imbricated complexity.

Notes

We are grateful to Theresa Strouth Gaul and Patricia Okker for their constructive feedback on an earlier version of this introduction.

1. Anna Gurney (1820–1848) was the daughter of Joseph John Gurney and Jane Birbeck Gurney (1789–1833). Although the Winterthur catalog notes that Anna "presumably accompanied" her father on his journey to the United States, documentary evidence clearly demonstrates that she remained in England. See Eliza Paul Kirkbride Gurney, *A Brief Sketch of the Life of Anna Backhouse*

(Burlington: John Rodgers, 1852), 9–21. Many thanks to Winterthur Library, which, on two occasions, gave us access to this manuscript.

2. For more on the composition, copying, and circulation of poetry in Lloyd's circle of friends, see Michael C. Cohen, *The Social Lives of Poems in Nineteenth-Century America* (Philadelphia: University of Pennsylvania Press, 2015), 75–92.
3. Rufus W. Griswold (ed.), *Female Poets of America* (Philadelphia: Carey and Hart, 1849), 7.
4. See Virginia Jackson, *Dickinson's Misery: A Theory of Lyric Reading* (Princeton: Princeton University Press, 2005), for a fuller investigation of the twentieth-century reading practices of poetry referenced here.
5. See Elizabeth Petrino, *Emily Dickinson and Her Contemporaries: Women's Verse in America, 1820–1885* (Lebanon: University Press of New England, 1998) and Paula Bernat Bennett, "Emily Dickinson and Her American Women Poet Peers," *The Cambridge Companion to Emily Dickinson*, Wendy Martin (ed.), (Cambridge: Cambridge University Press, 1992), 215–235.
6. See Cheryl Walker (ed.), *American Women Poets of the Nineteenth Century: An Anthology* (New Brunswick: Rutgers University Press, 1995); Janet Gray (ed.), *She Wields a Pen: American Women Poets of the Nineteenth Century* (Iowa City: University of Iowa Press, 1997), and Paula Bernat Bennet (ed.), *Nineteenth-Century American Women Poets: An Anthology* (Malden & Oxford: Wiley-Blackwell, 1998).
7. Lydia Sigourney, *Lydia Sigourney: Selected Poetry and Prose*, Gary Kelly (ed.), (Peterborough, Ont. & Orchard Park: Broadview Press, 2008); Sarah Piatt, *Palace-Burner: The Selected Poetry of Sarah Piatt*, Paula Bernat Bennett (ed.), (Urbana: University of Illinois Press, 2005); Frances Ellen Watkins Harper, *A Brighter Coming Day: A Frances Ellen Watkins Harper Reader*, Frances Smith Foster (ed.), (New York: The Feminist Press at CUNY, 1998); Adah Isaacs Mencken, *Infelicia and Other Writings*, Gregory Eiselein (ed.), (Peterborough & Orchard Park: Broadview Press, 2002); and Emma Lazarus, *Emma Lazarus: Selected Poems and Other Writings*, Gregory Eiselein (ed.), (Peterborough & Orchard Park: Broadview Press, 2002).
8. For work on women's authorship, see Mary Kelley, *Private Woman, Public Stage: Literary Domesticity in Nineteenth-Century America* (Oxford & New York: Oxford University Press, 1985); Susan Coultrap-McQuin, *Doing Literary Business: American Women Writers in the Nineteenth Century* (Chapel Hill: University of North Carolina Press, 1990); Susan S. Williams, *Reclaiming Authorship: Literary Women in America, 1850–1900* (Philadelphia: University of Pennsylvania Press, 2006); and Melissa Homestead, *American Women Authors and Literary Property, 1822–1869* (Cambridge: Cambridge University Press, 2010).
9. Virginia Jackson and Yopie Prins, "Lyrical Studies," *Victorian Literature and Culture* 7 (1999): 523.
10. Virginia Jackson, "The Poet as Poetess," *The Cambridge Companion to Nineteenth-Century American Poetry*, Kerry Larson (ed.), (Cambridge: Cambridge University Press, 2011), 57.

PART I

1800–1840, American Poesis and the National Imaginary

CHAPTER I

Claiming Lucy Terry Prince: Literary History and the Problem of Early African American Women Poets

Mary Louise Kete

Of the millions of women who were stolen from Africa and sold into slavery in British colonial America, only two are remembered as poets: Lucy Terry Prince, who lived between about 1729 and 1821, and her much younger contemporary, Phillis Wheatley, who lived between about 1753 and 1784.[1] So many names lost. So few found. Prince and Wheatley beat the odds by being remembered at all; yet, they have posed an ongoing challenge to the project of tracing an African American literary tradition. Literary history, like any history, emphasizes consequence, narrative coherence, and affiliation. It yearns for beginnings, middles, ends or, at least, a series of "begats" tracing a lineage that helps us know who we are.[2] Prince and Wheatley would seem to offer a clear starting point to the story of African American literature and, particularly, to the study of African American women's literature. Both were abducted from Africa, both enslaved in British New England, both committed to the American Revolution and to evangelical Protestant Christianity. Both achieved manumission, married, and became mothers. Both were famous in their own times as poets. Yet, Prince's vernacular ballad recounting an event from the 1740s couldn't seem more different than the sophisticated, neoclassical poetry published by Wheatley in the 1760s and 1970s: affiliations between their poetic practices aren't that obvious. Nor has it been easy to find clear lines of influence between the poetry of either woman and that of the African American women poets who consciously attempted to forge a tradition in the aftermath of slavery. It shouldn't be that much of a surprise, then, that American literary history has had a hard time accommodating Wheatley and, to a greater extent, Prince.

The problem undoubtedly has to do with what April Langley calls the "dysfunctional relationship between Western- and African-centered theories" of black American and, generally, eighteenth-century aesthetics.[3]

It also has to do, as Vincent Carretta and John Shields have suggested, with the tendency for Americanists to approach eighteenth-century black authors from the vantage point of a present that assumes the existence of social formations, such as that of an American or African American national identity, that had not yet come into being.[4] One of the most important "corrections," as Henry Louis Gates' notes in his 2010 study of *Tradition and the Black Atlantic: Critical Theory in the African Diaspora*, was offered by Paul Gilroy's 1993 formulation of the "Black Atlantic."[5] Gilroy originally posited the "Black Atlantic" as an inherently hybrid and protean cultural formation that, as Philip Kaisary summarizes it, "was induced by the experience and inheritance of the African slave trade and the plantation system in the Americas and which transcends both the nation state and ethnicity."[6] As tastes have changed and scholarship has advanced along these lines, Wheatley has become more visible to both academics and poets. Scholars have begun to uncover the missing lines of influence and trace the poetic affiliations needed to weave Wheatley into the stories we tell about African American women's poetry and poetics. This has not yet been the case for Prince. It remains hard to appreciate what kind of a claim she may have had to the title of poet much less evaluate what's at stake in granting her that title now.

Although written more than forty years ago, Alice Walker's essay, "In Search of Our Mothers' Gardens," is still helpful for understanding why it has been so hard and yet so important to claim the earliest of black women poets for African American literary history.[7] Walker introduced readers to the names of Lucy Terry (Prince) and Phillis Wheatley as part of a personal analysis of the challenges presented by the scant traces of earlier African American women artists in the canon of American literature and American literary histories of the time. In 1974, neither the poetry of Prince, nor that of Wheatley, seemed any more or less helpful to Walker's personal search for a poetic ethos – the nature of her authority as a poet – than her own memories of gardens and songs. Ultimately, for Walker, the knowledge *that* Wheatley sang was of more consequence than the influence of *what* she sang. As Walker puts it in an apostrophe directed to Wheatley, "It is not so much what you sang, as that you kept alive, in so many of our ancestors, the notion of song."[8]

Mid-twentieth-century American literary history made it difficult for Walker to see much – or any – difference between Wheatley, who was the first black woman in America to publish any kind of book, and Lucy Terry Prince, who is known as the first African enslaved by the British to have composed poetry in English. Both were firsts, but both were still merely footnotes to what was considered the main, important story of American literature. And this story, as Walker so eloquently explains, didn't promise a place for someone such as herself, someone black and a woman. While Wheatley's poetry served as a haunting symbol of all she didn't want her own poetry to be, Prince remained just a precious – because rare – name. Neither one could provide a positive model of what it might mean to be a twentieth-century, African American woman poet; neither one could provide a positive model for what an "authentic" African American woman's poetry might look like. In the story Walker tells of her search for a matrilineage, both are equally mere epigraphs to a story that had not yet been written.[9]

More recently, though, the differences between Wheatley and Prince have tended to be magnified in the effort to craft a story of the development of African American literature that resulted from the calls for such a history made by Walker and others. Wheatley's poetry has become, for some, a problematic legacy that can't be relinquished, while for others the formalism of her aesthetic provides an important precedent for their own appropriations of conventional poetic genre and modes. As recently as 2003, it still seemed to Henry Louis Gates, Jr., that the majority of the critical reception of Wheatley continued to be shaped by the African American critics of his own and Walker's generation, for whom the "mastery of the literary craft" had been the "proof that she was, culturally, an impostor."[10] But, increasingly, academic criticism has come to recast Wheatley as "a pioneer of American and African American literature" for whom no apology is needed.[11] The sign that Wheatley's poetry is now secured in the canon of African American and American literatures is that the critical argument concerning her is no longer about whether or not her poetry had consequences for later artists or for our historical understanding, but about the nature or kind of consequence it has. Once sought, her direct influence upon the lives, if not the work, of mid-nineteenth-century black women poets, such as Frances Ellen Watkins Harper and Ann Plato, was found.[12] Young, black women in the post-Reconstruction era, such as Alice Dunbar Nelson, joined "Phillis Wheatley Clubs," which were centers for the project of racial uplift.[13] More recently, the "mastery of craft" that had once signaled Wheatley's co-optation by or collaboration with the cultural system that enforced the systematic and violent oppression of blacks has come to be viewed as an important precedent for formalist innovators such as Countee Cullen and Gwendolyn Brooks and contemporary poets such as Major Jackson and Natasha Trethewey.[14] Since the 1970s, that is, *what* Phillis Wheatley sang has become as important as *that* she sang, and she has an indisputable place in the history of African American poetry and poetics. But again: the same cannot be said of Lucy Terry Prince, and Phillis Wheatley has been left alone to shoulder the weight of beginning the tradition of African American women's poetry. Like the characters at the end of Toni Morrison's *Beloved*, a story about the haunting power of memory and dis-remembrance, we still don't know how to fit Prince into the still-evolving story of African American literature.[15]

"How can they call her if we don't know her name?" (*Beloved*, Toni Morrison)[16]

Of course, we do know Lucy Terry Prince's names. But to be able to claim her for literary history, we have to know more than her name. It could be that now it is more difficult for literary historians, much less poets, to make Prince and her poetry part of the usable past due to the degree to which she is not Wheatley: Prince lived in a rural, not urban, world; worked in oral, not literary, forms; and left only one poem, not many. The new light thrown on Wheatley seems to have deepened the obscurity of Prince. Rowan Ricardo Phillips contends that literary historians have burdened Wheatley by treating her as the sole "mother," the source, "ab ova" of the whole tradition of African American literature.[17] The iconicity of Wheatley, Phillips suggests, has paradoxically drawn attention away from the close, critical attention to her literary works.[18] Though Phillips may overstate the lack of current attention to Wheatley's poetry, "the insistent clamor of firstness" that her name invokes has also, I would argue, allowed scholars to avoid reckoning with her contemporary, Prince.[19]

Prince's only known poem – "Bars Fight" (circa 1746) – exemplifies many of the challenges posed by the poetry of Wheatley, but it also presents several unique problems. For one thing, in contrast to Wheatley, who not only engaged with an explicitly literary tradition but also actively pursued print publication, Prince worked solely in oral, vernacular forms. This meant that during her lifetime, the circulation of her stories, poems, and speeches depended upon her presence or the presence of those who had heard her in person. After her death, it would have been up to her community to keep her compositions and her memory alive. By the middle of the nineteenth century the currency of Prince's memory seems to have been limited to a few white New Englanders who preserved it in the oral and written stories they told to, and about, themselves as they indulged the antiquarian enthusiasm of the mid-nineteenth century.[20] The primary record of Prince's "Bars Fight" was first published in 1855 by Josiah Holland, in his two-volume *History of Western*

New Massachusetts. Holland was able to draw (directly and indirectly) on the recollections of older, white people from Vermont, Massachusetts, and Connecticut who claimed to have heard it performed by Prince, or from people who had heard it from people who had heard it from Prince. Holland's version reinforced legends of Prince that, especially in Vermont, were circulating (and still continue to circulate) between print and oral media. More problematically, it seems that Prince's ballad did not circulate, nor was it even known, in the black communities of later nineteenth-century New England or elsewhere. (This doesn't, of course, mean that it didn't have a place in black communities, only that one has not been found by scholars.[21]) If "Bars Fight" and Lucy Terry Prince belong in the history of African American women's poetry it is not because, so far, one can trace a line of direct influence through the nineteenth and twentieth centuries to today.

Here is the version provided by Holland:

"August 'twas the twenty-fifth,
Seventeen hundred forty-six;
The Indians did in ambush lay,
Some very valiant men to slay,
The names of whom I'll not leave out.
Samuel Allen like a hero fout,
And though he was so brave and bold,
His face no more shalt we behold
Eleazer Hawks was killed outright,
Before he had time to fight,
Before he did the Indians see,
Was shot and killed immediately.
Oliver Amsden he was slain,
Which caused his friends much grief and pain.
Simeon Amsden they found dead,
Not many rods distant from his head.
Adonijah Gillett we do hear
Did lose his life which was so dear.
John Sadler fled across the water,
And thus escaped the dreadful slaughter.
Eunice Allen see the Indians coming,
And hopes to save herself by running,
And had not her petticoats stopped her,
The awful creatures had not catched her,
Nor tommy hawked her on the head,
And left her on the ground for dead.
Young Samuel Allen, Oh lack-a-day!
Was taken and carried to Canada."[22]

Holland's version is the record of an oral composition as remembered by individuals who heard it performed, not a literary production. Yet, the ballad displays little stylistic or thematic affiliation with the vernacular spirituals and work-songs that play such a prominent role in African American cultural development. Tellingly, the most frequent adjective found in descriptions of Prince's verse is "doggerel." But neither the diction nor the prosody have posed as much of a challenge to readers as has the story told by "Bars Fight." It recounts an attack on the frontier settlement of Deerfield, Massachusetts, by the Abenakis and their French allies during King George's War of the mid-1740s. Prince, known in Deerfield as Lucy Terry, had been enslaved there since having been brought as a very young child by her putative owner in 1730. Composed soon after the events, and apparently sung by Prince over the course of her lifetime, the sympathy of the speaker lies with the white, English settlers and against the Abenaki attackers.[23] Like Wheatley's "On Being Brought From Africa to America," the speaker of "Bars Fight" seems not to critique her status as a captive of the English. The speaker seems to have no racial or political consciousness. This could, as was assumed about Wheatley, be the result of Prince's co-optation; or it could be a sign of the mediation by the white New Englanders who preserved both "Bars Fight" and the story of its author as relics of what they considered their own past. Holland's version of "Bars Fight," it must be admitted, doesn't readily suggest the kind of lines of direct influence, aesthetic quality, or topic that would make it easy to link Prince into the histories of African American literature that have been coalescing since the mid-twentieth century. "Bars Fight," that is, is a particularly vexing example of what Langley calls the "dilemma" posed to contemporary literary historians by "eighteenth-century African American literature": we want to claim it – after all, Prince is one of just two black women poets of this era whose names were passed on – but its claim isn't clear.[24]

"She has claim, but she is not claimed." (*Beloved*, Toni Morrison)[25]

The solution, as Langley puts it, is to discover or "liberate" additional "lenses through which Afro-British American literature . . . might be interpreted."[26] Seeing "Bars Fight" through additional lenses has allowed critics to qualify readings that would dismiss it as too damaged by the co-optation of its author, or by the exigencies of history, to be more than an "epigraph" to an indisputably African American tradition. Sharon M. Harris, for example, offers a "bicultural" reading of "Bars Fight" in which she reads the story as a satire of the captivity narrative that was so important to the Protestant, British colonists. Within the "American" cultural tradition the poem offers a validating tribute; but, Harris argues, read from the perspective of an "African America," the story reveals the hypocrisy of the slave-holding Puritans who interpreted stories of the captivity by, and redemption from, the "Indians" as a sign of God's Providence.[27] Langley contends with the problematic content of "Bars Fight" by situating the poem against a background of West African poetics, rather than against a conventional notion of African American experience. She resists Harris's notion that "Bars Fight" is satirical in the sense that the surface meaning of the text is contradicted by a latent meaning that is only visible from an African American perspective. Instead, Langley suggests that the relationship among the different levels of meaning is additive. Positing that "Bars Fight" undercuts the anti-Native American racism inherent in the captivity narrative by "depicting both sides of the skirmish valiantly, " Langley argues that storytelling allows the speaker to express the mourning of the white settlers who are her masters while personally mourning her own – and the collective – fate of being enslaved Africans.[28] For both of these critics, the problem posed by the content of "Bars Fight" (what is African American about it?) is at least partially resolved by information supplied by the context against which they read it. Most importantly, I would like to suggest, the location of "Bars Fight" within these different contexts allows readers to fix the ethos of the speaker and the speaker's audience so that, as contemporary readers, we can discern the import of the poem's content, which is otherwise unavailable.

Before I turn to "Bars Fight," I want to explore yet another context. When Lucy Terry Prince died in 1821 at almost one hundred years of age, one of western New England's newspapers of note published both an obituary and an elegy.[29] This was republished throughout the upper Connecticut River valley. As Lois Brown notes, this testifies to Prince's unusual social standing, as a black woman, in the cultural arena of early New England. Both the prose obituary and the verse elegy underscore that this standing derives from the power of her words – to what, that is, Lucy Terry Prince sang.[30] What is especially rare and important about the elegy is that it provides insight into how Prince was viewed by one of her younger, black contemporaries: the Reverend Lemuel Haynes (1753–1831).[31] As far as Haynes was concerned it was Prince's poetry – her metrical "feet" – that earned her the status of "sable mother" to an expanding, republican, and interracial America.[32]

According to biographer John Saillant, the "religious faith and social views" of Haynes "are better documented than any African American born before the luminaries of the mid-nineteenth-century."[33] Although Haynes is now obscure, he was once widely recognized as "a leading controversialist in the New England paper wars over politics and theology as well as a famed revivalist."[34] Unlike the African-born Wheatley or Prince, Haynes had been born in the colony of Connecticut to a black father and a white mother whom he never knew. Never enslaved, he was indentured as a baby to the West Hartford family who raised him and fostered his Christian convictions. Haynes labored for them until the fulfillment of his contract and returned to their home after fighting as a Minuteman and then as a soldier in the Continental Army, to prepare himself for ordination. He was as well and as broadly read as any of the revolutionary generation, including other future Vermonters such as Ethan Allen and Royall Tyler. And Haynes, like Allen and others who fought on the front lines of the Revolution, also gave theoretical consideration to the question of the principles for which he fought. Haynes began to lay out the foundations for his own theory of "True Republicanism" as early as 1776 in a privately circulated, political exegesis of the Declaration of Independence called "Liberty Further Extended, or Free Thoughts on the Illegality of Slave-Keeping."[35] His vision of the future political organization of the newly independent states was informed, as Saillant puts it, by an "ideal of interracial unity that Haynes and his peers had seen in the bible."[36] In the wake of the Revolution, Haynes became a successful and formidable Congregational minister in Rutland, Vermont, and he went on to participate actively on the side of the Federalists in the debate over the "boundaries of an emerging republican ideology" at the heart of which, as David Brion Davis argues, was the question of slavery and abolition. That Haynes, one of the most prominent revivalists of western New England, preached Prince's funeral sermon is itself a marker of Prince's consequence; but his elegy for her – part of his now lost funeral sermon and printed in the *Vermont Gazette* – suggests that he saw Prince as a fellow worker in the vineyard.[37]

The elegy bears pausing over, for it describes the claim, as Haynes saw it, that Prince had upon the memory of Americans, and predicts a place for her in the future, American imaginary:

> And shall proud tyrants boast with brazen face,
> Of birth – of genius, over Africa's race:
> Go to the tomb where lies their matron's dust,
> And read the marble, faithful to its trust.
> Let not within Columbia's happy bower,

Infested lungs pollute the sacred tower:
While Seargent, with his flagellating cord
Drives them away, as did our blessed Lord:
And Mallary, with his eloquence severe
Dispels the fog and purifies the air.
Shall drear Missouri's melancholy cell,
Caress the demon, emigrant of hell?
Shall there fell Slav'ry find a dark retreat?
And vagrant despots stalk about the street?
Then let our union be a fulsome name:
Our tongues shall hiss them from our courts of fame.
How long must Ethaopia's murder'd race
Be doom'd by men to bondage & disgrace?
And hear such taunting insolence from those
"We have a fairer skin and sharper nose?"
Their sable mother took her rapt'rous flight,
High orb'd amidst the realms of endless light:
The haughty boaster sinks beneath her feet,
Where vaunting tyrants & opressors meet.[38]

Her death, here, becomes an occasion for the kind of secular sermon Sacvan Bercovitch posited as peculiar to America.[39] Haynes specifies the risks posed by the falling away of his contemporary Americans from the republican values of the Revolution and he presents Prince as the key to recovering and surpassing the promise she embodied as a woman, a black, and as a poet. The elegy addresses not the dead Prince who has taken "her rapt'rous flight, / High orb'd amidst the realms of endless light," but the living Americans who have lost "their sable mother" and, thus, their way. Her verses, he hopes, will continue Prince's work of opposing the racism of the "haughty boaster" and the "vaunting tyrants & opressors [*sic*]" whose extension of slavery will give the United States a "fulsome" name. Prince's "dust" should be enough to shame the "brazen" faces of the "bold tyrants" who are figured as insolent children who betray their mother at their own risk. The insulting boast of white superiority ("'We have a fairer skin and sharper nose?'"), should be discredited by contemplation of "*their* matron's" tomb and the memory of "*their* sable mother" (my emphasis). Haynes' use of the third person, plural possessive here makes a remarkable claim about Prince and about America: the mother of the American authors of the Missouri Compromise, who boast of their "fairer skin," is both black and African. He invokes Prince's maternal, verbal, and American authority against the threat that "our union" is becoming a "fulsome name."

Haynes, in associating Prince with "Columbia" (the spirit of America) reminds the audience – the members of Prince's extended community – of the kind of claims she had to the ethos of their founding mother. She had, after all, actually been one of the earliest British settlers of Vermont, and her story was familiar across the upper Connecticut River valley where her obituary was published. A mother and grandmother, Prince had lived almost one hundred years, from her birth in some now unknown place in the western part of the African continent sometime in the middle of the 1720s, to her death in Sunderland, Vermont, in 1821. After having been stolen from her parents, she has been taken out to the frontier settlement of Deerfield, Massachusetts, by Ebenezer Wells, in 1730. Deerfield, in the upper Connecticut River valley, had been the site of contests over the borders between French and English North America for at least fifty years. It was from here that the Reverend John Williams, who wrote the second-most influential of the Puritan captivity narratives (*The Redeemed Captive Returning to Zion)*, was abducted with several of his children during the largest and most famous of the Deerfield raids in 1707. It was also from close by that the Reverend Jonathan Edwards set fire to what we now call the first Great Awakening. By the time of the 1746 raid on the meadows or "bars" of Deerfield, Lucy Terry was in her early twenties and had been working her entire life as a slave in the household and store of Wells and his wife. Even as a young girl, her powers as a raconteur had been remarked upon. Later – free and married to her husband, Abijah Prince – her Deerfield home became a popular gathering place for young townspeople eager to be entertained by the stories, poems, and songs of "Bijah's Luce."[40] Soon after, she and Abijah were among the earliest of British settlers in the land contested by colonies of New York and New Hampshire that became known as Vermont. Of her six children, two would fight, like Haynes, for the Continental cause. The aptness of Haynes' description of Prince as "their sable mother" thus rested on her active participation in the successive transformations of the upper Connecticut River valley into what Harriet Beecher Stowe would later call the "seed bed of this great American Republic."[41]

The validity of Haynes' association of Prince with the personification of America ("Columbia") also rested on her widespread fame as a fierce and successful orator who vigorously resisted aggressive and openly racist assaults on her family's rights to their property and privileges as Vermonters.[42] The success of this resistance has consistently been attributed to a level of rhetorical skill that seems to have matched, or even overmatched, that of trained lawyers. Gretchen Holbrook Gerzina and David

Proper have found archival evidence supporting and clarifying some of the oral legends surrounding her victories in the various courts that governed Vermont from the time it was part of a colony, through its period as an independent nation, and after it became the fourteenth of the United States of America. What is surprising, of course, isn't that race – or, rather, racism – was at the heart of each of these conflicts, but that Prince achieved the level of success that she did. But, as Brown points out, the white-authored obituary in the *Vermont Gazette* doesn't represent this political aspect of Prince; instead, it "effectively submerges her racial identity as it documents a life that could stand as a model white biography."[43]

The verse elegy, in contrast, asserts that Prince's "sable" color and her African origins were inseparable from her verbal genius as well as crucial to her role as a political mother to the kind of interracial republic Haynes hoped America could become. As the embodiment of republican motherhood, Prince's authority extended into the public realm and, Haynes implies, would extend beyond death by virtue of her words.[44] Haynes intertwines his lament for Prince with his anger at the direction the new country was taking with the passage of the Missouri Compromise of 1820. The speaker asks, "Shall drear Missouri's melancholy cell, / Caress the demon, emigrant of hell?" Haynes explicitly links Prince with two of the United States' Congressmen who had most vehemently opposed the entrance of Missouri as a "slave state." In the new state of Missouri, after all, not only was slavery legal, settlement by free blacks was illegal. The closing of Haynes' poem stresses the political nature of her verbal power with what Saillant points out is a typically Haynes-like, neoclassical pun hinging on the double meaning of the word "feet."[45] In this final apostrophe to the racist children of "their sable mother," Haynes asks them to consider the admonitory image of the "haughty boaster" who "sinks beneath her feet, / Where vaunting tyrants & opressors meet." Haynes not only pictures the apotheosis of Prince as a republican mother, but as an actual mother of the republic who has earned her status due to the role she had played through the closing years of the early republic. Prince's memory, Saillant proposes, would have been important to Haynes, personally, as a black intellectual, an author, and an American. In depicting Prince as his, and his audience's, "sable mother," Haynes' claims her as the figurative starting place of the story of himself as an American and the starting place he hopes will be America's story.

"The names of whom I'll not leave out." ("Bars Fight," Lucy Terry Prince)

Like Harris and Langley, Haynes perceived that it was crucial to understand Prince's personal ethos – that is, to recognize the character and nature of her authority as a poet. This allows Harris and Langley to look beyond the apparent content of "Bars Fight" to see what else Prince might be saying (as an African American or as an African in America) through her story of the ambush of some British colonists. Like them, Haynes figured Prince's ethos in political, gendered, and racial terms. Unlike them, Haynes' evocation of Prince directs our attention back toward her words, back toward the manifest level of what Prince sang. In 1821, the poem itself was already old-fashioned, a remnant of the past that was a product of a very different social arena to the one in which Prince was eulogized by Haynes. For in the 1740s Prince was living at the nexus of multiple border contests: political (French versus English), cultural (African versus English), and ontological (slave versus free). For Gilroy, the turbulence of this social arena is typical of the world of the black Atlantic, as is the fact that Prince produced two distinctively new forms out of this turbulence. One of these, the poem itself, is preserved in the version passed down to us. The other, Prince's poetic ethos, was, at least partially, the product of that poem. Within the frame provided by Haynes' elegy, Prince's "Bars Fight" comes into focus as a vestige of her effort to construct an ethos – a standing of authority within her community – despite the social forces bent on denying that she was person. To do so, let me suggest, Prince melded the vernacular tradition of the ballad brought by the English settlers with the oral traditions kept alive by the enslaved Africans who had been forcibly brought from various parts of West Africa into a new, syncretic, form.[46] As here, syncretism usually occurs at the joints where otherwise distinct cultural traditions touch or even overlap. In both the West African and the British traditions, the performance of narrative verse was used to commemorate remarkable events (current, historical, or mythical). In both traditions, such story-songs were entertainment that also served to honor, mock, chastise, or warn. But, especially in the West African traditions, such narrative verse was meant to perpetuate and define community values.

Like other English, topical ballads of the seventeenth and early-eighteenth centuries, "Bars Fight" opens in a journalistic manner telling us who ("Indians" and "valiant men"), what ("ambush"), when (August 25, 1746), and where (the Bars). As is typical of such ballads, "Bars Fight" does not attempt to answer the fifth journalistic question: why. The singer's focus seems to be on three sensationalistic subjects: the horror of the day, the names of the lost, and the grief of the survivors. As in other surviving versions of vernacular ballads from this era, the prosody can be – and has been, as I mentioned earlier – described as "doggerel." The verse is irregular, the rhymes strained, and the description of Eunice Allen's unfortunate struggle with her skirts that results in her being "tommy-hawked" certainly comes close, as Harris suggests, to slap-stick. Most broadsides could be sung to one or another of a small set of familiar tunes, but the tune Prince used (whether original or not) has been lost. The diction, like that of other English ballads, is straightforward and vivid; there is little imagery and few poetic devices are used to evoke the violent drama that begins with the "Indians" lying in ambush and ends with the kidnapping of "young Samuel Allen."

The "I" who in the fifth line announces a self-conscious goal for the story that follows is, however, one of two significant departures from the English vernacular ballad tradition. In contrast to the literary ballad that emerges with the Romantics, neither the authorship nor the authority of the English vernacular ballad was vested in an individual; these are anonymous productions, with license given to singers and communities to make changes as circumstances necessitated. The "I" of "Bars Fight" has more in common with that of the story-songs common to the West African tradition of the griot, one in which the persona of the speaker or singer enjoys a situated or pre-established position of authority within his or her community.[47] The griot, or griotte, has explicit and conventional responsibilities to maintain, add to, and circulate the stories by and through which a community forms and perpetuates itself. The griot's personal authority, as Thomas A. Hale explains, is established by training and, often, by birthright. The "I" of the griot, that is, underwrites the efficacy of the stories he or she tells: one should listen to and respect this poem because it is sung by a griot. Prince, abducted from Africa as a baby, had no recognized or conventional position of authority – no standing from which to speak for or by herself – within the predominantly white and English community in which she was a slave. She could have had no direct experience with this griot tradition, nor have had the conventional training needed to fulfill this role. However, as Proper and Gerzina recount, Prince was one of a significant number of enslaved Africans serving in the village of Deerfield and, despite the differences in natal languages and cultures, it is probable that the enslaved of Deerfield, like enslaved Africans throughout the Black Atlantic of the eighteenth-century, maintained vestiges of this West African practice.

Prince also seems to draw on the model of the griot's authority in line five, in which the speaker, pledging to "not leave out" the names of the "valiant men" caught in the fight, assumes an ethos quite different from that of the speaker of the English ballad. Part of this personal, not anonymous nor generic, task is remembrance. What follows is a catalogue of the names and fates of the very ordinary men and women who, though the speaker asserts that they "fout" like heroes, were actually routed and most likely would have been forgotten if not for Prince. The singer is clear that she has undertaken this task as a free expression of her agency, announcing this by the fiat "I'll" (I will or I shall). That this task is needed and will be ongoing is implicit, as is the assumption that the speaker already has the necessary authority and the ability. The act of pledging, in the manner of the griot, to personally keep and pass on these memories becomes, in this context, the constitution of a community bound by a shared experience of loss. That the speaker belongs to this community, which is simultaneously her audience, is marked by the use of the first person plural pronoun "we."

The open ending of the version we have of "Bars Fight" marks a second departure from the topical ballad tradition the English settlers would have brought with them. Such ballads are characterized by strong plots with clear beginnings, middles, and ends that are linked by consequence. The "Bars Fight" recorded by Holland, though it vividly recounts what happens in the brief moment of ambush in that meadow outside of Deerfield, gives no sense of what had come before or, most importantly, what will come after. It gives no summary meaning, no moral, for the audience to take away. It begins with the Indians lying in ambush and concludes with them having left the meadow with their captive, "young Samuel Allen." The survivors are left in a state of "grief and pain" in what the poem depicts as an incursion of irrational violence into a pastoral scene. Prince is known to have sung this ballad throughout her lifetime and, as Harris and Frances Smith Foster both note, she would have known the conclusion to this story: young Allen was eventually redeemed, and this proved to be the last of the Abenaki and French incursions into the English colony of Massachusetts.

Although parts of "Bars Fight" might be missing, oral transmission tends to preserve what the audience deems to be the most powerful elements of a composition. Prime among these is the catalogue of the ancestors of families (Allens, Amsdens, and Hawks) who still lived in and around the Connecticut River valley in the mid-nineteenth century when Prince's poem was printed. Second is the designation of these individuals as "heroes." Third is the expression of raw grief and dismay. In this sense, "Bars Fight" seems strongly inflected by two genres of the griot tradition, neither of which foreground narrative: the praise-song and the lament. In a praise-song, the singer's focus is on categorizing the actions of an individual or group as worthy of praise. Only as much story is told as is necessary to establish this. In the case of "Bars Fight," the singer's object is to grant heroic status to those who died or were captured. Yet, the object of "Bars Fight" also seems inflected by the griot tradition of the lament that not only preserves the memory of these settlers, but also publicly mourns the losses the community as a whole has sustained. The success of either or both of these goals implies the recognition of the ethos Prince has invented and deployed in "Bars Fight." And, in fact, Prince's name, as author, has remained attached to her composition.

Fusing English and West African verse traditions, "Bars Fight" repudiates the losses and threat of being forgotten that, in 1746, confronted not only the English settlers and their black slaves, but also the native peoples who were allied with the French. It speaks to the needs of a frontier people in a particularly precarious moment during which English hegemony over that specific geographic space was hardly guaranteed, but it also speaks to the need of the individual, Lucy Terry, to repudiate the denial of self implicit in her legal status as a slave and as a woman. By taking on the responsibility to maintain the memory of those frontier haymakers of Deerfield who died in an otherwise inconsequential skirmish, Prince invented an ethos for herself that was still "not forgot" by the black and white New Englanders of the Connecticut River Valley who marked her passing in 1821.

But this ethos – founded on the power of Prince's words – was later "forgot." Haynes' elegy for Prince is a helpful reminder that "Bars Fight" itself precedes the social formations of "American" and "African American" that would later coalesce in the new United States. It precedes, and is foundational to, the character (founded upon the ability to represent herself and her world on her mastery of language) to whom Haynes gave the title "sable mother." "Bars Fight," that is, is one of the warrants of the authority Lucy Terry Prince held by the end of her lifetime. Haynes' elegy also attests to a historical context in which Prince's poetry was understood to have had power and force. He speaks from within an indisputably American social arena in which someone who consciously identified himself as an African American claimed Prince as an African American poet and acknowledged her poetic legacy. What Haynes doesn't help us with is the nature of the challenge that Prince and Wheatley – like other black authors from the colonial and early national eras – continue to pose to the project of African American literary history.

Prince's "Bars Fight," however, does. First of all, it reminds us that the seemingly conservative task of remembrance, of finding a way to pass an account of the present on to the future, has a generative potential. In Prince's case, her promise to "not forget" laid the foundations for a new ethos, a position of authority, from which to speak to and for a new community. As a syncretic invention, "Bars Fight" reminds us that sometimes we have to invent new ways – new aesthetic forms – to meet the imperatives of history. The challenge posed by Lucy Terry Prince and Phillis Wheatley is that in changing our sense of the beginning of African American literary history, we can't help but change the nature of the rest of the story. But, finally, Prince's "Bars Fight" reminds us of how easy it is for that which has been remembered to be forgotten. After all, by the time Haynes died in 1833, he had come to realize that the moment was ending during which it was possible to imagine an America that could remember and honor women such as Prince as their "sable mother." If it has once again become possible to remember them through the practice of literary history, Prince and Wheatley challenge us to tell a story that "will not be forgot" again.

Notes

1. For a comprehensive, recent geography of the African diaspora, see David Ellis and David Richardson, *Atlas of the Transatlantic Slave Trade* (New Haven: Yale University Press, 2010). See Vincent Carretta, *Unchained Voices: An Anthology of Black Authors in the English Speaking World of the Eighteenth-Century* (Lexington: University of Kentucky Press, 2003), for a sense of the voices of Wheatley and Prince's peers. For a critical biography of Wheatley, see Vincent Carretta, *Phillis Wheatley: Biography of a Genius* (Athens and London: University of Georgia Press, 2011). For a standard edition of Wheatley's published and unpublished works, see Vincent Carretta, *Phillis Wheatley: Complete Writings* (New York: Penguin Classics, 2001). There is no standard edition of Lucy Terry Prince's one surviving poem, "Bars Fight," except for that published in Josiah Holland, *History of Western Massachusetts: The Counties of Hampden, Hampshire, Franklin, and Berkshire, volumes 1 and 2* (Springfield: Samuel Bowles and Company, 1855) and George Shelden, *A History of Deerfield, Massachusetts; The Times When and The People By Whom It Was Settled, Unsettled and Resettled, With a Special Study of the Indian Wars in the Connecticut Valley, With Genealogie* (Deerfield: Pocumtuck Valley Memorial Association, 1896). For authoritative biographies of Prince, see David Proper, *Lucy Terry Prince – Singer of History, A Brief Biography*

(Deerfield: Pocumtuck Valley Memorial Association & Historic Deerfield, Inc., 1997) and Gretchen Holbrook Gerzina, *Mr. and Mrs. Prince: How an Extraordinary Eighteenth-Century Family Moved Out of Slavery and Into Legend* (New York: Harper Collins, 2008).

2. See Maryemma Graham and Jerry W. Ward, "Introduction," *Cambridge History of African American Literary History* (Cambridge: Cambridge University Press, 2011), 2–16, for a survey of the problematics specific to the project of constructing an African American literary history. John Ernest, *Chaotic Justice: Rethinking African American Literary History* (Chapel Hill: University of North Caroline Press, 2009) also offers a challenge to early trends in African American literary history.
3. April Langley, *The Black Aesthetic Unbound: Theorizing the Dilemma of Eighteenth-century African American Literature* (Columbus: Ohio State University Press, 2008), 13.
4. Carretta, *Phillis Wheatley, Biography*. John C. Shields lays the groundwork for this argument in his "Introduction" to *The Collected Works of Phillis Wheatley* (New York and Oxford: Oxford University Press, 1989). He develops it more fully in his *Phillis Wheatley's Poetics of Liberation* (Knoxville: University of Tennessee Press, 2008).
5. Henry Louis Gates, *Tradition and the Black Atlantic: Critical Theory in African Diaspora* (New York: BasicCivitas, 2010). See Paul Gilroy, *The Black Atlantic: Modernity and Double-Consciousness* (Cambridge: Verso, 1993).
6. Philip Kaisary, "The Black Atlantic: Notes on the Thought of Paul Gilroy," *Critical Legal Thinking: Law and the Political* (September 15, 2014). Available online: criticallegalthinking.com/2014/09/15/black-atlantic-notes-thought-paul-gilroy/ [date of access unavailable]. I am indebted to Kaisary for drawing my attention to Gilroy's description of the utopian potential of the Black Atlantic.
7. Alice Walker, *In Search of Our Mother's Gardens: Womanist Prose* (New York: Harcourt Brace Jovanovich, 1983). The title essay of this collection was first published in 1974 in *Ms. Magazine*.
8. Ibid., 237.
9. See Rowan Ricardo Phillips, *When Blackness Rhymes With Blackness* (Champaign and London: Dalkey Archive Press, 2010), 17–22. I am indebted to Phillips for the notion of Wheatley and Prince and other early black authors as epigraphs – paregonal structures – to a distinctively African American literary tradition.
10. Henry Louis Gates, *The Trials of Phillis Wheatley* (New York: Basic*Civitas* Books, 2003), 82.
11. Carretta, *Phillis Wheatley: Biography*, ix.
12. In her seminal study, *Written By Herself: Literary Production by African American Women, 1746–1892* (Indianapolis: Indiana University Press, 1993), Frances Smith Foster notes the continued availability and influence of Wheatley upon nineteenth-century black authors. For a more recent discussion of the publication history of Wheatley's poetry, see Jennifer Rene Young, "Marketing a Sable Muse: Phillis Wheatley and the Antebellum Press," in

New Essays on Phillis Wheatley, edited by John C. Shields and Eric D. Lamore (Knoxville: University of Tennessee Press, 2011), 209–246.

13. For the history and discussion of the Phillis Wheatley Club movement, see Nina Mjagkij, *Organizing Black America* (New York: Garland Publishing Inc., 2001), 121–122.
14. For critical accounts of the development and trends in African American literary history, see Hazel Arnett Ervin, "Introduction," *African American Literary Criticism, 1773 to 2000* (New York: Twayne Publishers, 1999) and Rafia Zafar, "Introduction," *We Wear the Mask: African Americans Write American Literature, 1760–1870* (New York: Columbia UP, 1997). See also Keith Leonard, "Introduction," *Fettered Genius: The African American Bardic Poet from Slavery to Civil Rights* (Charlottesville and London: University of Virginia Press, 2006), which attempts to reclaim the "formalist poetic tradition" of black poets for the African American cultural tradition (6). Along with Leonard, Langley, *Black Aesthetic*, and Phillips, *When Blackness Rhymes*, offer different ways to extend assumptions about the "authenticity" of African American voices to include attention to form, engagement with multiple traditions, and literariness. For a provocative overview of the depth of the engagement of African American authors with the classical tradition, see William Cook and James Tatum, *African American Writers and the Classical Tradition* (Chicago: University of Chicago Press, 2010). Shields and Lamore, *New Essays on Phillis Wheatley*, features six essays treating Wheatley's classicism.
15. Toni Morrison, *Beloved* (New York: Vintage Books, 1987).
16. Ibid., 323.
17. Phillips, *When Blackness Rhymes*, 17.
18. Ibid., 29.
19. Ibid., 13.
20. Wheatley's poems, in contrast, circulated and continued to circulate via mass media throughout the English-speaking colonies and across the Atlantic to England and Europe. They remained available through print to later generations of black and white readers. See Carretta, *Biography of a Genius* and Young, "Marketing a Sable Muse."
21. The foundational studies of black New Englanders remain Lorenzo Greene, *The Negro in Colonial New England, 1620–1776* (New York: Columbia University Press, 1942); Sidney Kaplan and Emma Nogrady Kaplan, *The Black Presence in the Era of the American Revolution* (Amherst: University of Massachusetts Press, 1989); and William Pierson, *Black Yankees: The Development of an Afro-American Subculture in Eighteenth-century New England* (Amherst: University of Massachusetts Press, 1988). For a focus on the experiences of black women in early America, see Catherine Adams and Elizabeth Pleck, *Love of Freedom: Black Women in Colonial and Revolutionary New England* (Oxford and New York: Oxford University Press, 2010).
22. Holland, *History of Western Massachusetts*, Vol. 2, 360.

23. See Kenneth Morrison, *The Embattled Northeast: The Elusive Ideal of Alliance in Abenaki-Euramerican Relations* (Berkeley: University of California Press, 1989) for an extensive discussion of the wider context of the minor skirmish Prince recounts in "Bars Fight."
24. Langley, *Black Aesthetic*, 5.
25. Toni Morrison, 323.
26. Langley, *Black Aesthetic*, 1.
27. Sharon M. Harris, *Executing Race: Early American Women's Narratives of Race, Society and the Law* (Columbus: Ohio State University Press, 2005).
28. Langley, *The Black Aesthetic Unbound*, 144.
29. In concluding her discussion of Prince, Harris introduces the fascinating existence of the obituary of Prince and includes it in the appendix of her book. See also Lois Brown's full contextualization of this obituary in "Memorial Narratives of African Women in Antebellum New England," *Legacy* 20.1 (2003): 38–61. In an era when the deaths of few blacks were marked in so public a way, Prince was granted a double obituary: she is presented both from the perspective of a respected, black member of the community and from the perspective of the respected, white editor of the community's newspaper.
30. For a transcript of the prose obituary and the verse elegy see Harris, *Executing Race*, 183–184.
31. See John Saillant, *Black Puritan, Black Republican: The Life and Thought of Lemuel Haynes* (Oxford and New York: Oxford University Press, 2003). See also John Newman, *Black Preacher to White America: The Collected Writings of Lemuel Haynes, 1774–1833* (Brooklyn: Carlson Publishing, 1989).
32. I owe this dual reading of the word "feet" to Saillant, *Black Puritan, Black Republican*, 172.
33. Ibid., 3.
34. Ibid., 63.
35. See Ruth Bogin, "'Liberty Further Extended': A 1776 Antislavery Manuscript by Lemuel Haynes," *The William and Mary Quarterly* 40.1 (January 1983), 85–105.
36. Saillant, *Black Puritan, Black Republican*, 7.
37. Davis quoted in Saillant, *Black Puritan, Black Republican*, 78.
38. Harris, *Executing Race*, 183–184.
39. As Sacvan Bercovitch puts it in his "Preface" to the 2012 reissue of his landmark study of 1978, *The American Jeremiad* (Madison: University of Wisconsin Press, 2012), the "rhetoric of promise as threat, doomsday and millennium entwined – that vision of America as an unfolding prophecy – became in time the foundational national story" (xiii). See also David Howard-Pitney, *The African American Jeremiad* (Philadelphia: Temple University Press, 2005).
40. Holland, *History of Western Massachusetts*, 360.
41. Harriet Beecher Stowe, "Preface," *Old Town Folks* (New York: Library of America, 1982), 883.

42. Gerzina, in *Mr. and Mrs. Prince*, tracks down verification for the various legends of Prince's oratorical virtuosity. As Gerzina points out, focus on the success of her oratory has tended to obscure the racists acts against her family and property that occasioned her speeches (154–162).
43. Brown, "Memorial Narratives of African Women in Antebellum New England," 43.
44. Linda Kerber, "The Republican Mother: Women and the Enlightenment – An American Perspective," *American Quarterly* 28.2 (Summer, 1976), 187–205, introduces the notion of "Republican Motherhood" to describe the reformulation of the role of mother which accompanied the shift toward republican political and social theory in the late eighteenth century. See Ruth Feldstein, *Motherhood in Black and White: Race and Sex in American Liberalism, 1930–1965* (Ithaca: Cornell University Press, 2000). Prince may be a rare example of a black woman in early America described in this way.
45. Saillant, *Black Puritan, Black Republican*, 172.
46. This sense of the term "syncretism" derives from the work of the cultural anthropologist Melville Jean Herskovits, *Cultural Anthropology* (New York: Knopf, 1958).
47. See Thomas A. Hale, *Griots and Griottes: Masters of Words and Music* (Bloomington: Indiana University Press, 2007). See also Barbara Hoffman, *Griots at War: Conflict, Conciliation and Caste in Mande* (Bloomington: Indiana University Press, 2000).

CHAPTER 2

Before the Poetess: Women's Poetry in the Early Republic

Tamara Harvey

In January of 1790, *The Massachusetts Magazine; or, Monthly Museum* faced an embarrassing excess of Constantias. The magazine had been publishing poetry by Sarah Wentworth Morton under the name Constantia throughout its first year, but now the editors were adding Judith Sargent Murray to their list of essayists and poets and she asserted a prior claim to the pseudonym. The following notice appeared under the heading "To the FAVOURITES of the MUSES," immediately following the table of contents:

> The adoption of a signature already used by a justly admired writer, was rather delicately embarrassing to the Editors; they flatter themselves that their late, and early friend, will both feel themselves pleased at their attention to prevent mistakes. The authoress of Invocation to Hope; Philander, a pastoral Elegy; Lines to Euphelia, &c. will in future have her name decorated with a Star (*) at the end of it, unless one or other of the fair competitors in poetical fame, should be pleased to alter her signature, when due notice will be given, as we sincerely wish to be in the good graces of these valuable writers.[1]

Changing the pen name of Morton, a well-regarded poet who was socially prominent in Boston, was awkward enough; that she was understood by many readers to be using her poetry to mourn the suicide of her sister who had given birth to a child conceived with Morton's husband, Perez, may have made the editors and other contributors even more sensitive to her feelings. As Morton cycled through Constantia*, Philenia Constantia, and finally Philenia during the first half of 1790, the magazine published numerous encomia to her by the editors and other contributors, including Murray. Both the confusion over names and the effusive praise is evident in April, for instance, when Euphelia, a contributor who often framed her poems as responses to Morton's, addressed a poem "To CONSTANTIA*" while Murray, on the same page and using the name Constantia herself, contributed “LINES to PHILENIA.” The editors' delicacy did not, however, keep them from pitting the two Constantias against each other as “fair competitors in poetical fame,” and extravagant praise of both women kept alive the idea that one could be best.

Women poets whose work made it into print had long been described in superlatives rendering them exceptions that proved the rule of women's inferiority; Anne Bradstreet and Sor Juana Inés de la Cruz's shared title of “Tenth Muse” is perhaps the best-known example among colonial American poets. Vestiges of this condescension are at work in the pages of *The Massachusetts Magazine*, but the magazine's growing reliance on female readers and contributors and their interest in representing the full potential of the new republic informed new versions of old contradictions. The magazine had a strong editorial and financial interest in keeping their contributors happy, but it also wanted to display exceptional women as modern marvels. It supported pro-women agendas such as those expressed in Murray's “On the Equality of the Sexes” (published in the magazine soon after she asserted her right to the name Constantia), but also promoted narrow ideas about women's virtue, as in the excerpts from *The Power of Sympathy* published in their first issue that sensationalized and moralized about the scandal in the Morton household.[2] Herbert R. Brown describes *The Massachusetts Magazine* as “a shrine for literary ladies,” while Beverly Reed locates the representation of white women's bodies in this apparent veneration within an “exhibiting complex” meant to cement national identity on a global stage.[3] Both are right; as Mark Kamrath observes, the competing ideologies of the early republic gave rise to “dual and highly conflicted concerns of publishers: their desire, on the one hand, to do their patriotic duty and to help establish a virtuous citizenry and, on the other, to try to realize their own entrepreneurial ambitions and financial interests.”[4] For women writers this meant their literary and intellectual productions circulated as part of an emerging U.S. literary culture, but it also meant a kind of publicity that could be limiting and exploitive.

Women were not only at the mercy of publishers with contradictory interests, however; duality was also evident in the ways women navigated the literary landscape. In her “LINES to PHILENIA,” Murray writes of hoping that because of possible confusion “My growing name would be with musick fraught,” acknowledging her desire for fame, even at the expense of another.[5] Thus, her humility topos, a commonplace expression of inadequacy in poetry used by both men and women that was almost unavoidable for women, rests on wryly confessing her ambition while generously praising Morton. The acknowledgment of ambition itself might distinguish hers from most humility topoi by women in earlier generations, but more remarkable is the simple fact that she can frame this in terms of competition with another woman. Morton, for her part, replies by insisting that Constantia had been a perfect name for her "[w]hen press'd by ills, and sinking with despair":

> One *constant* state my hapless life has known,
> One *constant* love my changeless bosom moves,
> *Constant* to virtue tho oppression frown,
> And *constant* to the friend my soul approves.[6]

She praises Murray's happier genius and imagines her wreathed in myrtle. Then, for a moment, the sentiment teeters and the speaker entertains the possibility that envy would "tear those wreaths away! / And plant sad cypress where the laurel grew!" But envy is squelched and the poem ends somewhat ambiguously with praise either of the poet, to whom she will "Attentive listen," or of her name, upon which "timid grief" would "recline." Signing "PHILENIA CONSTANTIA," Morton leaves it to the reader to decide whether she loves Murray, her pen name, or the virtue constancy. Conventionally, both women use humility topoi that recognize the work of another as superior, but unlike previous poets they are able to cite a contemporary woman as that superior. More striking still, they both use humility topoi that draw on their own acknowledged ambition to retain a name that has become famous.

The early republic offered new opportunities for American women poets to assert their literary ambitions. Previous women poets had been equally concerned with politics, social issues, education, and literary recognition, but the need to forge a national literature with international significance along with a wider-reaching, more varied print culture meant that women poets were able to enter public debates about the meaning of the new republic and their place in it like never before. Between the publication of Phillis Wheatley's *Poems on Various Subjects, Religious and Moral* in 1773 and the works of the now less-canonical but enormously prolific Lydia Huntley Sigourney, whose first volume, *Moral Pieces in Prose and Verse* (1815), and the sixty-six other books that followed helped shape nineteenth-century perceptions of the poetess, a number of well-known women writers wrote, circulated, and published poetry, among them Morton, Murray, Annis Boudinot Stockton, Mercy Otis Warren, Milcah Martha Moore, and Susanna Rowson. This essay treats this post-Wheatley pre-Sigourney period, focusing particularly on Morton as a woman who self-consciously styled herself as a poet of the new republic. Morton wrote frequently for periodicals, and nine of her early poems were included in Elihu Hubbard Smith's 1793 volume, *American Poems* – the only contributions by a woman to be included along with works by John Trumball, Joel Barlow, Timothy Dwight, Philip Freneau, and other male poets of the early republic. She also published three long poems in which she styled herself as an American poet even more strenuously: *Ouâbi, Or the Virtues of Nature: An Indian Tale in Four Cantos* (1790); *Beacon Hill: A Local Poem* (1797); and *The Virtues of Society: A Tale Founded on Fact* (1799).

The study of American women's poetry (and, indeed, of American poetry generally) often takes a backseat to the study of American prose, and though recent scholarship has started to rectify this neglect, women's poetry of the early republic, a period of significant social, political, and literary change, continues to be largely ignored.[7] In recent years scholars have instead been drawn to the novels of the period, which are often seen to be more aesthetically, socially, and politically innovative while the poetry seems dated even by the 1840s, when one critic writing about Morton reminds his readers that "[t]here is a fashion in poetry" and, unfortunately, Morton wrote during a period that "was unfavourable to genius and good taste."[8] But poetry, like the novel, was the site of important transformations in literary culture. Women poets of the early republic, particularly elite women who had previously circulated their poetry in manuscript, were entering the realm of print publication in increasing numbers. Poets such as Morton and Murray helped to create a new literary culture for the United States as a whole, and in doing so altered a number of important literary conventions. Women actively participated in new public literary exchanges found in the magazines, created new educational materials aimed at both sexes, and imagined new epic visions for the United States. In their choices of topic and genre as well as their formulation of the inevitable humility topos, we see women poets of this period asserting their own literary authority by embracing the widely felt sentiment that the United States was inaugurating a new cultural moment with both national and global reach.

This essay attends to the ways in which American women's poetry during this messy, contradictory transition reflected the debates of the time as fully as the novel did. The first section focuses on women's changing opportunities to circulate poetry through the burgeoning magazines of the period and through book publication, both of which sought to represent America and engage Americans in ways that reflected the political debates and international ambitions of the new country. The second looks more closely at efforts by women poets such as Morton to assert themselves as *American* poets developing an *American* literature within their poetry.

"To Poetical Friends": Manuscript and Print Transformations

Some of the most significant recent recoveries of late-eighteenth-century American women's poetry rest on recognizing the importance of manuscript culture as an alternative form of publication, especially for elite women who would not or could not risk print publication. David Shields traces the emergence of literary coteries in eighteenth-century British North America as elites began to import the practices of single-sex "tea table" culture from England and mixed-sex salons from France.[9] Carla Mulford's edition of Annis Boudinot Stockton's poetry, drawn largely from a copybook of mostly unpublished works written between 1753 and the 1780s, illustrates the relationship between the voluminous occasional and impromptu poems that circulated privately and Stockton's much smaller print production.[10] Catherine La Courreye Blecki and Karin A. Wulf's edition of *Milcah Martha Moore's Book: A Commonplace Book from Revolutionary America* sheds further light on the circulation of manuscript literature among intimates.[11] Moore's commonplace book incorporated prose and poetry written by a small group of friends and, like Stockton's collection, focuses primarily on the revolutionary period. In short, some of the best and most influential poetry by women, particularly by elites, circulated in this way; once scholars knew where to look and how to look, a trove of neglected verse came to light.

Focusing on women's manuscripts illuminates women's literary communities and may suggest that their richest aesthetic productions or sharpest political critiques were kept out of the public eye. But this focus also risks reinforcing a familiar public/private split while making the practices of elite women the standard. Building on late-twentieth-century attention to early American women's manuscript poetry, scholars have started paying greater attention to interdependence between manuscript and print production. In particular, recent scholarship on Phillis Wheatley has led the way in thinking beyond the book/manuscript divide. Joanna Brooks has compellingly argued that Wheatley's many elegies were commissioned by and circulated among white women and that Wheatley capitalized on these connections to obtain the signatures that authorize *Poems on Various Subjects* and promote sales of that volume. Indeed, her poetry likely circulated in manuscript among those in Milcah Martha Moore's Pennsylvania coterie as well as among the elite women of Boston, with whom Wheatley interacted directly.[12] Karen Weyler likewise looks beyond the book, but stresses Wheatley's mastery of elegy in both manuscript and broadside form well before her book made it to press. Wheatley signed her name to her poems, becoming famous as "Phillis" in forms that reached both the drawing rooms of elite women for whom she wrote impromptu poems and a far larger and more socially diverse audience of broadside readers.[13] In short, understanding the various ways that her poems circulated gives us insight into Wheatley's poetic agency in a complex, changing publication climate. Both Brooks and Weyler recognize that coterie writing was highly class inflected, but Brooks pays attention to a symbiotic relationship between Wheatley and elite white women that allows us to see complicity and awareness on both sides, while Weyler sees Wheatley developing the elegy form in more public ways, with attention to a wide readership.

Relationships among literary women and a varied, rapidly changing publication climate continued to evolve in the years following the revolution. As Shields observes, "there can be no doubt that the relationship between sociable institutions and society at large (that is, the public) had changed with the creation of the United States."[14] Just as the rise of salon culture altered extant intimate manuscript circulation along enlightenment models, the turn into the nineteenth century brought political debates about elite affiliation and new formulations for women's ongoing concerns about their roles in public life. Angela Vietto, who has perhaps done the most to renew interest in Morton, aligns Morton's early contributions to *The Massachusetts Magazine*, including her exchange with Murray, with women's coterie culture of the eighteenth century, arguing that over the course of the following decades Morton's work would increasingly reflect a more "Romantic, individualistic notion of authorship that has come to dominate narratives of authorship in nineteenth- and twentieth-century America."[15] But while Vietto characterizes this transitional period as one of increasing individualism, Jared Gardner considers the ways in which manuscript coteries were echoed and transformed in magazines of the early republic for both commercial and political reasons. Magazines depended on readers who were also contributors to remain solvent while nurturing this network as a model of democratic polity. As Gardner observes, though editors seemed to pit Murray and Morton against one another, Morton was adept at engaging "the complex and potent chain of correspondence that is the heart of the magazine's enterprise," both by making her personal suffering public in her poetry and by participating in an array of literary exchanges, including the one with Murray, that elicit public praise and serve as a better rejoinder to *The Power of Sympathy* and similar attacks than a novel could have done.[16]

One of the best places to witness the odd mixture of public and private in *The Massachusetts Magazine* is in the notes section immediately following the table of contents. In the first number, these notes were split between those addressed to the public and those addressed to correspondents and patrons. Soon, however, the public was dropped from the heading and comments were instead divided between those for prose correspondents and those for poets. By publishing often opaque notes intended for pseudonymous or unnamed correspondents, the magazine seems to intentionally foster a more intimate scene of circulation that addresses readers who know the personal allusions while inviting other readers to imagine these associations. Favored contributors such as Morton were often extravagantly praised, as in December 1791 when the editors noted, "The insertion of *Philenia's* last composition, is a tribute of respect, due to the Sappho of America"; other "correspondents" found their submissions publically rejected, as in a note from the first issue that observed, "COSMOPOLITAN appears to be more an inhabitant of the town, than a citizen of the world."[17] Interestingly, both these notes signal the worldly ambitions of the magazine as they are played out among bantering intimates. As Gardner explains, magazines depended on readers who also saw themselves as contributors; this was necessary both to fill and sustain the magazine and to strike the right literary tone – something between private coteries and public literary display and without the rancor of party politics found in newspapers of the time.[18]

While Morton was able to draw on the sociable networks of correspondents undergirding magazines of the period for sympathy and accolades, this emerging literary space also exposed women writers to sexually inflected attacks that reveal the seamier side of print exchanges. For women writers, the coterie-like aspects of early magazines may have provided a semblance of respectability in the familiar wit and flirtation, but the anonymity of this semi-public discourse had its risks as well. At times the editors openly admonish correspondents who are too personal, as in August 1790 when they write, "Our poetical friends will please to remember, that *private letters* ought to be the vehicle of amorous compliment."[19] This and other efforts to discipline wayward contributors frequently hinge on appropriate gender relations in a periodical. In March 1789, the editors addressed a number of indecorous contributions particularly related to their regular "Enigmatical List" feature, publicly rejecting contributions entitled "*An Enigmatical Bill of Fare*" and

"*Wedding Supper*" for *double entendre* that "trespass[] upon the remotest bounds of decorum." The note following this one suggests that these and other contributions may have in part responded to "An Enigmatical List of Young Gentlemen in Boston" and "A Charade," by "Emma" and "Julia," published in the February number. This long note condemns the "ill-natured, illjudged, ungallant irony of a coxcomical newspaper scribbler." The editors go on to

> advise our fair young friends not to be intimidated, nor to relinquish those laurels of which they have a right to partake, but calmly to pursue the inclination of their genius, and *wish the man a dinner*. It is our design to vindicate the cause of those who are unjustly insulted, and make our Magazine a *retreat in which feminine delicacy may shelter itself*.[20]

Unfortunately this warning appears not to have been effective, for in the next issue another note explains that the piece signed "*Emma and Julia*" has been omitted because "its incorrectness and want of intrinsick merit" indicate that it is not the work of the two young women.[21]

While periodicals such as *The Massachusetts Magazine* tried to cultivate women writers and readers with mixed results, book publication offered still other opportunities for women poets that were more distinct from the intimacies of coterie writing. One of the poems from Milcah Martha Moore's manuscript book, "The female Patriots" (1768), probably written by Hannah Griffitts, gives us some sense of women's political poetry that circulated in manuscript during the revolutionary era. The poem's speaker calls for "Daughters of Liberty" to forego tea and embrace homespun, explicitly contrasting women's domestic resistance with the impotence of male efforts, "Since the Men from a Party, or fear of a Frown, / Are kept by a Sugar-Plumb, quietly down." She ends with a more explicit statement about the intervention she intends as a poet:

> But a motive more worthy our patriot Pen,
> Thus acting—we point out their Duty to Men,
> And should the bound Pensioners, tell us to hush
> We can throw back the Satire by biding them blush.[22]

Clearly a political poem, Griffitts' piece is also what Paula Bennett calls a "female complaint poem" that tacitly inveighs against male disregard for women's politics and pens.[23] The poet suggests in these closing lines that women's ability to shame men is even more important than their efforts to resist British taxation in the exercise of their domestic duties. Women do double duty, domestically and politically, and in doing so show men up as subordinates who mistake duty for blind obedience. In other words, the men are in typically female positions. It is not entirely clear whether "acting" in this passage refers to domestic duties or the work of "our patriot Pen." The confusion seems to be intentional: there is something arch in the political challenge, the gender inversions, and the allusion to competing satires that is particularly well-suited to the raillery of salon poetry.

Scholars today know Moore primarily because of her manuscript book, but in the 1790s she would have been far better known for her *Miscellanies, Moral and Instructive* (1787). Initially published in Philadelphia by Joseph James, it was reprinted a number of times in Burlington, Dublin, and London between 1787 and 1829. It is easy to join Blecki in finding this miscellany less compelling, in both its selections and its organization, than the manuscript book. Intended for school use, it is made up of prose and poetry chosen for didactic purposes, whereas the manuscript "preserved a significant body of work by American writers (chiefly women) and included material that reflects diverse issues of concern to American colonists."[24] Still, it is worth bearing in mind that Moore's published book also reflected issues of concern to Americans, now no longer colonists, principally the "improvement of young persons of both sexes."[25] While Blecki characterizes the collection as "patriarchal in its attitude toward women," its stress on patience, piety, and humility is perhaps better understood as appropriate for the moral education of children.[26] Aphoristic segments related to living a good and productive life are organized following the life cycle, beginning with "A Morning Hymn" and ending with poems about death. That Benjamin Franklin endorsed the volume as "highly useful to the rising generation" brings to the fore both the educational and national aims of the volume and Moore's ambitions and connections.[27] Moore was fitting her lifelong work as a compiler to new publishing opportunities and educational concerns. While the compilation of friends' poems and prose evokes an intimate community enriched through Moore's meaningful groupings, the miscellany aspires to shape the children of the new republic.[28] The popularity of the volume suggests that this mission resonated widely.

"The rapt bard's visionary dream": Morton's Visions of America

As we saw in the exchange between Morton and Murray, their humility topoi rested on expressions of ambition and competition among women writers. Women's literary expressions of humility frequently highlight anxieties, defenses, and critiques related to literary ambition; the changing opportunities for women writers during the early republic were reflected in their apologies. In their poetic exchange, Murray and Morton stress aspirations related to poetic recognition, but many humility topoi by women of this period stress instead the cultural needs of an emerging nation. In her apology at the beginning of *Miscellanies*, for example, Moore cites the unmet need for appropriate educational material as the occasion for her imperfect effort – an effort which she hoped would "prove an incitement to some person of greater abilities, to pursue this or a better plan, whereby our schools may be furnished with a book more deserving their acceptance."[29] In her preface to *Ouâbi*, Morton employs a highly conventional expression of humility, asking that her American topics be taken as justification for poetry otherwise hobbled by her limitations as a woman writer:

> The liberal reader will, I trust, make many allowances for the various imperfections of the work, from a consideration of my sex and situation; the one by education incident to weakness, the other from duty devoted to domestic avocations. And I am induced to hope, that the attempting a subject wholly American will in some respect entitle me to the partial eye of the patriot; that, as a young author, I shall be received with tenderness, and, as an involuntary one, be criticised with candor.[30]

In this apology, Morton's humility topos does not acknowledge ambition and envy as it did in her newspaper exchange with Murray. Instead, she insists on her "wholly American" topic and invokes duty and education, key terms in women's debates about their lack of suffrage and other political constraints in the emerging republic. What follows is a long poem that draws on centuries-old European myths of first encounter as well as a romantic version of the noble savage. Morton appeals to "the partial eye of the patriot" and, as in Washington Irving's representations of colonial and post-revolutionary New York, locates modernity in the United States rather than Europe while maintaining Indians as a premodern foil.[31] Thus, Morton participates in the bid to produce and define a world-class "American" literature for the United States while joining contemporary debates about women's place in that new republic.

Morton is just one of many women poets who suggest that their vision of America in some way made up for the limitations of their sex. In the seventeenth century, Anne Bradstreet and Sor Juana Inés de la Cruz emphasized new world resources and cultural wonders in their poetry.[32] By the mid- to late-eighteenth century, poets such as Annis Boudinot Stockton, Elizabeth Graeme Fergusson, Hannah Griffitts, and Susanna Wright began to write "political belles lettres" influenced by events such as the Seven Years' War and the American Revolution.[33] After the war, Stockton joins Morton and Moore in citing her American topic as an excuse for any failings in her poetry in her introduction to a poem defending Alexander Hamilton. Stockton explains that this poem, which appeared in the *Gazette of the United States* on March 13, 1793, "will express the sentiments of many of your readers, and by that redeem from censure, the rusticity of the verse. I am no politician, but I *feel* that I am a patriot, and glory in that sensation."[34]

In each of these cases, stress on American topics serves as an excuse for writing; evidently these poets were correct in assuming that American themes would draw readers. While Bradstreet and Sor Juana were celebrated as American wonders, female poets following the revolution could appeal to patriotism even as they exploited some of the same native material. Indeed, the nineteenth-century critic who bemoaned the want of poetic taste during Morton's time nonetheless celebrated her place in American literary culture, describing her as "next in succession" to Anne Bradstreet primarily because she introduced "the first Indian story," *Ouâbi*, to United States literature.[35]

Magazines were well-suited for poetry celebrating civic virtue and patriotic sacrifice as well as America's place in the world. For instance, Murray's first poem in *The Massachusetts Magazine*, "VERSES. Wrote at a period of the American contest, replete with uncertainty," was published in 1790 and treated a time in the revolution when "English America – with France combin'd."[36] In "A MONODY on the Death of *The Honorable Thomas Russell, Esq.*," Morton bemoans the death of Russell, a prominent Patriot and merchant, celebrating both his patronage "of every generous plan, / The public welfare to promote" as well as the sources of his wealth:

Fraught with the riches of each clime,
Thy ships advent'rous sail'd from either pole;
Their wealth, thy charity sublime,
Employ'd to sooth affliction's sinking soul.[37]

In this poem she highlights the development of a new government and civic culture while also situating American enterprise globally: Russell's ships make him wealthy and make the newly born United States a cosmopolitan and economic center. Morton takes care to note that Russell endeavors also "To raise thy country's growing fame." In other words, when Morton writes as an American, her observations reflect the concerns of a new republic seeking to establish a healthy state that also competes internationally.

Morton's elegy for Russell may be seen as a post-revolutionary version of what Wheatley was doing with her broadsides and manuscripts: a public elegy that capitalizes on Morton's social connections but also appeals to the patriotic civic impulses of the period. In *Beacon Hill* (1797), the poet is staking a stronger claim for her public position as poet, now a historian of the revolution rather than a promulgator of it. Here she actively claims a role akin to the Sappho of America; inspired by "the HISTORIC MUSE," she styles herself as "*Columbia's native minstrel*":

> What though no Genius, with enchanting power,
> Charm the coy MUSES from their classic bower,
> To wake with graceful art the slumbering line,
> And round *Columbia's native minstrel* twine
> One laurel wreath—yet shall her daring hand
> Sketch the bold trait, the living scene command,
> Till patriot glory all the strain inspire,
> And with the ray of TRUTH the coldest fancy fire:
> Then hence vain *fiction* from the deathless theme,
> And hence the rapt bard's visionary dream![38]

As "*Columbia's native minstrel*," she sketches patriotic truths, characterized as a "rapt bard's visionary dream" rather than a work inspired by genius. In denying genius, Morton refuses a single enchanted location as her source of inspiration, a "classic" poetic origin that by the end of this passage is associated with fiction. Instead she links her "daring hand" with the patriot's "bold trait." In this epic poem, her humility topos suggests that she is channeling a patriotic spirit that travels not only throughout the newly created states but also, eventually, around the world.

This vision in part reflects *Beacon Hill*'s origin as a prospect poem, one that Morton confesses could have "twenty other names" if she chose other locales and battles as her subject.[39] Christopher Phillips argues that Morton takes a fragmentary approach to epic, also found in Wheatley's works, adding that "the epic in pieces may be a particularly useful entry into the tradition for marginalized writers like Wheatley."[40] Certainly this kind of fragmentation requires less time and allows the poet to sidestep the risks of claiming too much authority in offering a totalizing history. But fragmentation also suits the politics and concerns of Morton's republic. In her apology, Morton asks that her verses be judged only on their intrinsic merits, insisting, like others before her, "that an author should be considered of no sex," but also taking care to note that "no party prejudice, no spirit of contention, has degraded the exalted theme."[41] In forestalling the criticism of prejudiced, hostile readers, she sees party politics and gender hierarchy as intermixed.

As though to reinforce her insistence that she is not motivated by party, she offers the possibility of substituting other locales in a gesture that unifies the former colonies, though she does not entirely eschew regional loyalties. Bunker Hill seems to serve in the role of first among equals when she writes, "Yet, when it is remembered, that the great events, which form the subject of the piece, originated within the view of this interesting eminence, the mind, by the natural association of ideas, will be easily led to contemplate every succeeding occurrence of the Revolution."[42]

The nature of the speaker's vision raises a number of questions. Morton reinforces her insistence that she is without party prejudice by framing the poem as a partial vision: by refusing to characterize the United States as a whole, she avoids regional bias. But we might also read her acknowledgment that the poem is not inspired by genius as a gesture of female humility: the sacrifices of the revolution and the prospect of the emerging United States are the true sources of her inspiration. And finally, her vision allows her to orient her history toward the future in ways that are both idealistic and imperial. Both the poet's and America's prospects rise over the course of the poem, the "rising empire from subjection free" that will in turn spread freedom:[43]

> From where the morning wakes her infant beam,
> And golden *Ganges* slopes his amber stream,
> To where the West a crimson robe extends,
> And o'er *La Plata*'s spreading mirror bends,—
> Till the full ray of EQUAL FREEDOM shine,
> And like the sun this genial globe entwine.[44]

Whereas in *Ouâbi* Morton asked that her American topic excuse her weakness, in *Beacon Hill* she is more confident in claiming the role of "minstrel."[45] And yet her authority is still drawn from her claims to being an American. The result is a significant reworking of a familiar strategy in women's poetry: Morton's vision allows her to gain authority by claiming first-hand experience, but it also orients that authority toward a future in which her authority would not need to be so self-consciously manufactured. Earlier women poets in the Americas joined providential inspiration with accounts of first-hand experiences of the New World. Morton offers a secular version of this in her vision of equal freedom spreading around the world. In both cases, the joining of idealism and self-authorization is further complicated by an appeal to the language of imperialism.

How Sarah Wentworth Morton is exhibited by others, how she begs "the partial eye of the patriot," and how she offers her own "rapt bard's visionary dream" provide useful insights into continuities between her and other well-known American women poets who preceded her while also showing significant transformations in how women poets of the early republic engaged a volatile, often contentious social and political landscape and a rapidly changing print culture. Women poets both represented the new republic and shaped it, finding in new publishing opportunities ways to influence readers young and old and project visions of American history and the future of the United States that reflected current political debates and global ambitions.

Notes

1. "To the Favourites of the Muses," *The Massachusetts Magazine; or, Monthly Museum* 2 (January 1790), n.p.
2. "On the Equality of the Sexes," *The Massachusetts Magazine* 2 (March and April 1790), 132–135, 223–226; "Beauties of 'The Power of Sympathy,'" *The Massachusetts Magazine* 1 (January 1789), 50–53.
3. Herbert R. Brown, "Elements of Sensibility in *The Massachusetts Magazine*," *American Literature* 1 (1929), 286; Beverly J. Reed, "Exhibiting the Fair Sex: The *Massachusetts Magazine* and the Bodily Order of the American Woman," *Periodical Literature in Eighteenth-Century America*, Mark L. Kamrath and Sharon M. Harris (eds.), (Knoxville: University of Tennessee Press, 2005), 229–233.
4. Mark Kamrath, "Eyes Wide Shut and the Cultural Poetics of Eighteenth-Century American Periodical Literature", *Early American Literature* 37 (2002), 498.
5. Constantia [Judith Sargent Murray], "Lines to Philenia," *The Massachusetts Magazine* 2 (April 1790), 248.
6. Philenia Constantia [Sarah Wentworth Morton], 'To Constantia," *The Massachusetts Magazine* 2 (May 1790), 309–310.
7. The turn of the millennium saw the publication of important studies that began to reframe the study of nineteenth-century American women poets, in part by attending to writing circles, political engagement, and modes of publication that do not fit modern assumptions about the circulation and cultural significance of prose and poetry respectively. See Eliza Richards, *Gender and the Poetics of Reception in Poe's Circle*. Cambridge and New York: Cambridge University Press, 2004; Paula Bernat Bennett, *Poets in the Public Sphere: The Emancipatory Project of American Women's Poetry, 1800–1900* (Cambridge: Cambridge University Press, 2004); and Mary Loeffelholz, *From School to Salon: Reading Nineteenth-Century American Women's Poetry* (Princeton: Princeton University Press, 2004). Angela Vietto, *Women and Authorship in Revolutionary America* (Aldershot: Ashgate Publishing, 2006), also offers an alternative to novel-centered

scholarship of the early republic, including a sustained discussion of Morton's poetry.

8. "Female Authorship," *The Monthly Miscellany of Religion and Letters* 3 (1840), 15.
9. David S. Shields, *Civil Tongues and Polite Letters in British America* (Chapel Hill: University of North Carolina Press, 1997), 119–120.
10. Annis Boudinot Stockton, *Only for the Eye of a Friend: The Poems of Annis Boudinot Stockton*, Carla Mulford (ed.), (Charlottesville: University Press of Virginia, 1995).
11. Catherine La Courreye Blecki and Karin A. Wulf (eds.), *Milcah Martha Moore's Book: A Commonplace Book from Revolutionary America*, Catherine La Courreye Blecki and Karin A. Wulf (eds.), (University Park: The Pennsylvania State University Press, 1997).
12. Joanna Brooks, "Our Phillis, Ourselves," *American Literature* 82 (2010), 9, 15.
13. Karen A. Weyler, *Empowering Words: Outsiders and Authorship in Early America* (Athens: The University of Georgia Press, 2013), 38–45.
14. Shields, *Civil Tongues*, 316.
15. Angela Vietto, "Sarah Wentworth Morton and Changing Models of Authorship," *Cultural Narratives: Textuality and Performance in American Culture before 1900*, Sandra M. Gustafson and Caroline F. Sloat (eds.), (Notre Dame: University of Notre Dame Press, 2010), 138.
16. Jared Gardner, *The Rise and Fall of Early American Magazine Culture* (Urbana: University of Illinois Press, 2012), 113–115.
17. *The Massachusetts Magazine* 3 (December 1791), n.p.; *The Massachusetts Magazine* 1 (January 1789), n.p.
18. Gardner, *Rise and Fall*, 96, 109–111.
19. *The Massachusetts Magazine* 2 (August 1790), n.p.
20. *The Massachusetts Magazine* 1 (March 1789), n.p.
21. Ibid.
22. "The female Patriots," *Milcah Martha Moore's Book*, 172–173.
23. Bennett, *Poets in the Public Sphere*, 10.
24. Catherine La Courreye Blecki, "Introduction," *Milcah Martha Moore's Book*, 69, 72.
25. Milcah Martha Moore, *Miscellanies, Moral and Instructive, in Prose and Verse* (Philadelphia: Joseph James, 1787), title page.
26. Blecki, "Introduction," 74.
27. Moore, *Miscellanies*, iv.
28. Blecki, "Introduction," 67.
29. Moore, *Miscellanies*, iii.
30. Philenia [Sarah Wentworth Morton], *Ouâbi: or the Virtues of Nature* (Boston: Thomas and Andrews, 1790), viii, italics in the original.
31. See Vietto, *Women and Authorship in Revolutionary America*, 110–111, for a fuller discussion of how *Ouâbi* attempts to establish a distinctively American literature while also commenting obliquely on Morton's family scandals.

32. Tamara Harvey, "'My Goods are True': Tenth Muses in the New World Market," *Feminist Interventions in Early American Studies*, Mary Carruth (ed.), (Birmingham: University of Alabama Press, 2006), 13–26.
33. David S. Shields, "British-American Belles Lettres," *The Cambridge History of American Literature, Vol. 1*, Sacvan Bercovitch (ed.), (Cambridge: Cambridge University Press, 1994), 337.
34. Mulford (ed.), *Only for the Eye of a Friend*, 174.
35. "Female Authorship," Female Authorship, 10.
36. "Verses," *The Massachusetts Magazine* 2 (February 1790), 120.
37. Philenia [Sarah Wentworth Morton], "A Monody on the Death of The Honorable Thomas Russell, Esq.," *The Massachusetts Magazine* 5 (May 1796), 292–293.
38. Philenia [Sarah Wentworth Morton], *Beacon Hill: A Local Poem* (Boston: Manning and Loring for the Author, 1797), 13–14.
39. Philenia [Sarah Wentworth Morton], *Beacon Hill*, vii.
40. Christopher N. Phillips, *Epic in American Culture: Settlement to Reconstruction* (Baltimore: The Johns Hopkins University Press, 2012), 59.
41. Philenia [Sarah Wentworth Morton], *Beacon Hill*, viii.
42. Ibid., vii.
43. Ibid., 49.
44. Ibid., 52.
45. In *Epic in American Culture*, Phillips explains that Morton takes the title "minstrel" from James Beattie's poem, *The Minstrel* (1771), a precursor to the Romantics whose poem treats a young man's budding poetic genius (60).

CHAPTER 3

The Passion for Poetry in Lydia Sigourney and Elizabeth Oakes Smith

Kerry Larson

One striking development in poetry of the nineteenth century is its intense idealization of poetry. Poets before and since wrote and would continue to write on the subject, but not, it would seem, with the same fervor. Particularly in the first half of the century in the United States, reverence for the muse can sometimes seem cult-like in emphasis. Unknown to prose, the exaltation of the medium pervades the theories of Edgar Allan Poe and Ralph Waldo Emerson, who take their inspiration from High Romantic texts such as Shelley's "A Defence of Poetry." Women poets of the time did not have occasion to issue prose manifestoes along the lines of *Eureka* or "The Poet," but in laying a wreath at the shrine of Poetry they, too, were no less impassioned and ambitious in their claims for verse. In the publications of Lydia Sigourney, the country's bestselling poet through the 1820s and 1830s, and Elizabeth Oakes Smith, author of the bestselling poem "The Sinless Child," first published in 1842, the link between poetry and a supreme Ideality is especially strong, albeit for very different reasons.

To explore such a link in these two authors is to ask, ultimately, what it is that they *value* about poetry. To the extent that such a question is entertained among scholars today, it tends to attract thematic considerations, as when Sigourney's commitment to republican motherhood is emphasized as a key motivation for her writing or when "The Sinless Child" is read as an attempt to reconcile Christianity and transcendentalism.[1] But this privileging of thematic content, while not unimportant, can only take us so far in understanding the author's relationship to her writing, and, indeed, after a certain point it runs the risk of reducing the verse to an instrument for the propagation of ideas or the encoding of messages. That Sigourney and Oakes Smith had a different understanding represents a point of departure for the discussion that follows. In Sigourney's writing the glorification of poetry is hidden in plain sight, intangibly but unmistakably conveyed through a style of rhetorical address whose manner draws upon an earlier period of literary history. In Oakes Smith, born almost a generation after Sigourney, the same glorification becomes a considerably more vexed affair that dramatizes a conflicted, often anguished relation to poetic form and the promises it seemed to hold.

I

Generalizing about Sigourney's art can be a challenge, given her remarkable versatility. Though commonly linked to domestic concerns, her writing does not shy away from topics drawn from world history, political causes such as slavery or prison reform, abstract meditations on vice, friendship and natural beauty, or retellings of Biblical stories or Native American lore. It is well-known that elegy figures prominently in her work, though not to the exclusion of satire, burlesque, loco-descriptive nature poetry, ekphrastic sketches, and closet drama. As a poet, Sigourney seems to have been at ease with hymn meter as much as blank verse, Spenserian stanzas as much as irregular variants of her own devising, ballads as much as odes, short epics or epyllions as much as light verse set to an anapestic gallop. She began an epic in five cantos, *Traits of the Aborigines of America* (1822), directly after the publication of her first volume of poetry, *Moral Pieces in Prose and Verse* (1815). A wide-ranging, indefatigable eclecticism sets her apart from contemporaries such as William Cullen Bryant and Maria Gowen Brooks, whose formal and thematic bandwidth is narrower in comparison. In the nineteenth century only Longfellow exhibits a comparable resourcefulness in exploiting such different verse genres.

Through these many variations, certain uniformities of style and tone do emerge. We can begin by noting that Sigourney is very much a poet of the second person. Speaking *to* predominates over speaking *of*. Be it a text on Africa, the Creator, the family rocking chair, the Susquehanna River, or George Washington's mother, Sigourney likes to accost her subjects. "Hail, beauteous and inconstant," begins a string of apostrophes entitled "To the Moon," "Queen of soft hours! How fanciful art thou / In equipage and vesture – now thou com'st / With slender horn piercing the western cloud."[2] The numerous poems written to something ("To a Wasp," "To a Fragment of Silk") are obvious instances of the use of direct address as a framing device, as are the countless elegies formed around appeals to an absent beloved or departed friend. The habit of saluting, summoning, commanding, exhorting, cajoling, upbraiding, and so forth calls attention to the status of the poem as a rhetorical event in which we do not simply behold an object but a speaker addressing an object. The immediate roots of this practice go back to a prior generation of poets such as Phillis Wheatley or Joel Barlow, whose commitment to poetry as a form of eloquent speaking draws, in turn, upon an older, oratorical-rhetorical tradition. Even in cases where we might expect simple description, Sigourney frequently brackets off the scene with a commanding injunction for the reader to "see," a mannerism ubiquitous in the volumes of Alexander Pope, James Thomson, and Edward Young that, according to her autobiography, she absorbed in her youth.

> – Morn is upon the city. See, how slow
> Its ponderous limbs unfold. On arid sands
> Thus the gorged boa, from some dire repast,
> Uncoils his length.[3]

> See! Where amid their cultured vales they stand,
> The generous offspring of a simple land.[4]

> Behold!—in glittering show,
> A gorgeous car of state!
> The white-plumed steeds, in cloth of gold,
> Bow down beneath its weight.[5]

The repeated practice of turning toward and facing the object imparts a ceremonial, stately quality to this verse, no matter what the subject matter. Even when playful, Sigourney's texts maintain a tone of high seriousness, as when she mock-heroically apostrophizes a crushed mouse, an insect, or a shred of linen. Although Romanticism's interest in humble or lowly subjects as legitimate sources of poetic interest clearly swayed Sigourney's own choice of topics, it is also clear that Romanticism's hostility to poetic diction – what Wordsworth called its "gaudiness and inane phraseology" – did not have the same impact.[6] Sigourney's affectionate panegyric, "The Ancient Family Clock," is typical not just in the homeliness of the subject, but also in the inclusion of words such as "garniture," "joyance," and "robeth," not to mention archaisms such as "I trow" and "Lo" or epithets such as "crystal-breasted truth and sky-reporting time."[7] Similarly, the speaker of "The Sunday School" bids its poorer charges to "look up, ye sad ones" at the school's "consecrated dome" and its pictured ceiling, where "more gorgeous robes ye see, and trappings rare / . . . the gaudier forms that daily rove."[8] Other common features of Sigourney's style – inverted syntax, frequent personification, periphrastic phrasing, and declamatory asides – further reflect the persistence of neoclassical standards of propriety.

Ordinarily, the combination of the lofty and the humble produces a comic or satirical effect. Sigourney did write many poems in this vein – sly reports on household mishaps or domestic upheavals told with humorous solemnity.

(The much-anthologized "To A Shred of Linen" is perhaps the best known of these.) Because these texts are meant to be taken ironically, the disparity between a high-minded, sententious rhetoric and the comparatively prosaic subject matter poses no problem for the reader. When the intended effect is not ironic, however, a different set of challenges can arise. Consider, for example, the first stanza of "The Death of a Beautiful Boy," a lyric in rhyming fourteeners that may serve as a fairly typical example of Sigourney's consolation verse:

> I saw thee at thy mother's side, when she was marble cold,
> And thou wert like some cherub form, cast in ethereal mould,
> But, when the sudden pang of grief oppressed thine infant thought,
> And mid thy clear and radiant eye a liquid crystal wrought,
> I thought how strong that faith must be that breaks a mother's tie,
> And bids her leave her darling's tears for other hands to dry.[9]

Picturing a baby boy next to his dead mother will seem in questionable taste to many – just the sort of thing that accounts for Sigourney's reputation as a maudlin poetess of sentimental mourning. And yet the stanza as a whole can hardly be said to wallow in emotion, sorrowful or otherwise. Poeticisms such as "marble cold" or "cherub form," like the metaphor of tears as "a liquid crystal," mediate and distance our response, while the shifting point of view, in going from the speaker to the boy, then the mother, and back again to the speaker, precludes identification with any figure in particular. As we go on to note that each of the four stanzas of "The Death of a Beautiful Boy" begins with the declaration "I see" and presents a tableau of motionless figures expressly posed for our consideration, we can see how Sigourney has adapted an older idiom, with its self-consciously stylized, magisterial mode of address, and transferred it to a scene of unassuming simplicity. The resulting sense of incongruity or excess is really more rhetorical than emotional. Or, to put the same point in a slightly different way, it is not a particular person or event that serves as a catalyst for feeling so much as a certain manner of speaking.

Wordsworth felt compelled to add a preface to the second edition of *Lyrical Ballads* in 1800 to explain why "low and rustic life" demanded "a plainer and more emphatic language" than past models of verse provided.[10] But through the early decades of the nineteenth century readers in the United States wanted their poets to sound like poets. Jay Fliegelman, Christopher Looby, and Sandra Gustafson have explored the fascination with oratorical performance in the early Republic – how "strains of eloquence refin'd," as Wheatley put it in her elegy to the evangelist George Whitfield in 1770, "[i]nflame the heart and captivate the mind."[11] More than fifty years later the same investment in the charismatic powers of formal speech may be observed in the first of William Cullen Bryant's "Lectures on Poetry" (1825), which ends by maintaining that the only difference between poetry and oratory "consists solely in metrical arrangement."[12] Bryant adds that "all that disgusts, all that tasks and fatigues the understanding, and all matters that are too trivial and common to excite any emotion whatever" – in short, all that "verse cannot raise into dignity" – are "unfit for poetry."[13] To treat the commonplace in a commonplace manner, Bryant suggests, is the province of prose. To treat the commonplace in a lofty, ennobling manner is the province of poetry.

In effect, Bryant tries to walk a line between upholding the distinction between poetry's elevated style and the commonplace while insisting that these need not be considered incompatible. The implicit clash of expectations is hard to miss, and to some extent poets of the time paid the price, Sigourney not excluded. Appropriating literary idioms from the past and pasting them onto remembrances of rocking chairs and Sunday schools is, after all, the very definition of cultural philistinism, and there's no point in denying that a fair share of Sigourney's output falls into this category. And yet, aside from the fact that this is as much a cultural as a personal problem (at least as I have presented it here), there's also no point in denying that as scholars we lack a critical vocabulary for approaching a generalized cherishing of aesthetic experience that is neither dismissive nor guilty of limiting its claim on our attention to the history and sociology of taste. In this connection it's crucial to acknowledge, I think, the extravagance and genuine immodesty in Sigourney's relationship to what she called "the pleasures of written thought," qualities that have been obscured by her reputation as a leading exponent of feminine propriety and middlebrow respectability.[14] Precisely because it is so warmly embraced and so liberally bestowed, literary decorum paradoxically becomes a source of indulgence. The sheer exuberance animating Sigourney's love of eloquence and decorum, that is to say, can often lift us past the blandishments of the philistine.

Although the qualities of exuberance and excess I have in mind tend to be diffused throughout Sigourney's work, some of the poems she wrote on poetry address them as an explicit subject of reflection. One, consisting of three stanzas, is simply entitled "Poetry":

Morn on her rosy couch awoke,
Enchantment led the hour,
And mirth and music drank the dews
That freshen Beauty's flower.
Then from her bower of deep delight,
I heard a young girl sing,
"Oh, speak no ill of poetry,
For 'tis a holy thing."

The sun in noon-day heat rose high,
And on with heaving breast,
I saw a weary pilgrim toil,
Unpitied and unblest;
Yet still in trembling measures flow'd
Forth from a broken string,
"Oh, speak no ill of poetry,
For, 'tis a holy thing."

'Twas night, and Death the curtains drew,
'Mid agony severe,
While there a willing spirit went
Home to a glorious sphere:
Yet still it sigh'd, even when was spread
The waiting Angel's wing,
"Oh, speak no ill of poetry,
For 'tis a holy thing."[15]

Who or what is speaking ill of poetry?, we may find ourselves asking. The poem doesn't say, which makes the refrain more free-standing than usual. But then that seems to be the point. Through morning, noon, and night; joy, tribulation, and agony; youth and old age, poetry remains "a holy thing." It's the fact that poetry is irreducible to any single context of use that proves its holiness. This is why it's a mistake to assume that these lines are telling us that poetry helps enrich our happiness when we're happy or lighten our sorrows when sad or embolden our faith when shaken. In fact, they say no such thing. Poetry is to be treasured for what it is and not for what it says or does.

Sigourney ends the poem with a "willing spirit" who, about to be escorted to heaven, "sigh[s]" in apparent regret at leaving behind the "holy thing" that is poetry. This seems a rather blasphemous conclusion, not unlike the declaration of the speaker of Emily Dickinson's "I cannot live with you" that Paradise seems "sordid" when set beside the radiant lover who has "saturated" her sight.[16] Here the lover is poetry itself, a connection developed in Sigourney's autobiography, *Letters of Life*

(1866), which recounts her earliest attempts at versification when prompted by nightly visits on the part of "Thought," who "sometimes brought me harmonies, and thrilled me to strange delight with rhythmical words." "So delightful were its visits," Sigourney continues, "that I waited for and wooed it . . . the echo of consenting and euphonious words allured me to these little exercises in composition more than any poetic impulse or original idea."[17] To explain her youthful passion to herself, Sigourney is moved to portray it as a compulsion, with "Thought" stealing into her bedchamber like a suitor in the night. But she also does not shy away from emphasizing her own role in the affair, her own waiting and wooing spirit. (A similar scene of seduction is played out in her delightful lyric "Thought."[18]) In the same way that "Poetry" suggests that its subject is to be treasured for what it is and not what it says, the "strange delight" of Sigourney's "little exercises" explicitly brackets conceptual content as a motivation for writing. Hers is an infatuation that compels "attention to style, and the import of classical words" such that it's no surprise for the reader of her autobiography to discover that in addition to compiling "a large and elaborate Commonplace Book" created to "multiply and illustrate different figures [of speech]," the young Lydia Huntley also "engaged in abridging, for private use, a treatise on Rhetoric, which had been among my favorite school studies."[19]

From early selections like "Desertion of the Muse" in *Moral Pieces in Prose and Verse* (1815) to "The Muse," written toward the end of her long career, Sigourney's poems on poetry often stage a rivalry between domestic responsibility and the "allure" of those "consenting and euphonious words" heard in her youth. Complicating the common perception among scholars that "for Sigourney, the authority to speak and write comes from her sense of sanction by moral cause and religious warrant," the drama in such cases depends upon the incompatibility between the role of teacher or mother and that of poet.[20] "While she slept on my breast, in the nursery fair," Sigourney writes of her first-born child in "The Muse," "A smothered lyre would arrest me there, / Half complaining of deep neglect, / Half demanding its own respect."[21] Personified as a lifelong companion for the speakers of these poems, the "holy thing" that is poetry, while not necessarily opposed to the precepts of Christian piety, isn't exactly reducible to them either. "Let her chant to my soul when I go to the dust," she writes at the end of "The Muse," repeating the ending of "Poetry" in its suggestion that Heaven will be a poorer place without this "strange delight." In fact, the conventional view that the office of poetry is to preserve and immortalize the beloved is turned on its head. Poetry is that companionable Presence that will, it is hoped, continue "to chant to" the self as it expires, as opposed to memorializing its deeds or expressing its inmost desires.

In the same way, it's safe to assume that the large readership Sigourney commanded in the prime of her career was not drawn to her poetry for its memorable characters. Remarkable only for their anonymity and indistinctness, the beautiful boys and grieving mothers who file past us, page after page and volume after volume, exist to be addressed and displayed, not immortalized. Even subjects with a name and history (Washington's mother, for example) are flattened out and rendered indistinguishable. The most consistently real thing Sigourney's writing offers to her reader is, rather, the pleasures of the literary. Her texts are not conceived to give pleasure so much as to access pleasures that are already part of literature's institutional heritage. Genre is traditionally assigned the task of managing and ranking this stock of associations, and, as I noted at the outset, Sigourney's collected works are notable for their fluency in transitioning among a broad variety of verse forms. Still, if a text such as "Poetry" is any indication, we can also begin to glimpse a different logic emerging in Sigourney's sheer love of rhetorical address, where "the literary" ceases to gesture toward an institutionalized past and starts to appear as a free-floating affect that transcends literary form itself. It is to this second development that we now turn.

II

In a stimulating article entitled "The Poet as Poetess," Virginia Jackson discusses the co-evolution of the figure of the Poetess and the lyric in nineteenth-century American poetry. She argues that the insistent spirituality of the Poetess, intensified by the gender politics of the time, plays an unacknowledged but pivotal role in "the history of the nineteenth-century lyricization of American poetry, a process in which ways of reading became more important than what one read, in which social relations indexed by genre became the social relations transcended by Poetry."[22] At stake in this process is the replacement of "hierarchies of genre" by "hierarchies of expression," which is to say the valorizing of poetry as "an ideal vehicle for 'natural and instinctive' vicarious personal expression."[23] The abstraction of gender evident in the figure of the Poetess corresponds, on this view, to the abstraction of poetry that occurs when the lyric emerges as the default category for any and all varieties of poetic expression.

Sigourney, with her regal, hortatory manner, would seem to straddle the divide between "hierarchies of genre" and "hierarchies of expression." In fact, these are more complementary than opposed, as I've suggested. By the same token, in the later stages of her career Sigourney's popularity began to wane, eclipsed by Longfellow's blockbuster, *Evangeline* (1847) and, before that, another bestseller that partly inspired Longfellow's text, Elizabeth Oakes Smith's "The Sinless Child" (1842). The latter, praised by Rufus Griswold for its "simplicity of diction" and by Poe for its "purity of style," reflects a movement away from the high oratorical-rhetorical mode practiced by Sigourney, Bryant, and Maria Brooks.[24] It also reflects, in the unreal, otherworldly saintliness of its hero, Eva, the onset of the kind of lyric abstraction described by Jackson. Though Oakes Smith herself took issue with the term, her creation epitomizes the figure of the Poetess as a vessel of pure feeling untouched by the conventionalisms of form.

But Oakes Smith's relation to poetry and form is much more complex than this brief summary indicates, as becomes apparent when we turn to a sonnet sequence that directly follows "The Sinless Child" in the 1845 edition of her *Poetical Writings*. Subtitled "The Poet's Life, in Six Sonnets," the sequence begins with "Poesy," a lavish tribute that flirts with the same blasphemous connotations of idolatry we found in Sigourney's "Poetry":

> With no fond, sickly thirst for fame, I kneel,
> Oh, goddess of the high-born art to thee:
> Not unto thee with a semblance of zeal
> I come, oh, pure and heaven-eyed Poesy!
> Thou art to me a spirit and a love,
> Felt ever from the time, when first the earth,
> In its green beauty, and the sky above
> Informed my soul with joy too deep for mirth.
> I was a child of thine before my tongue
> Could lisp its infant utterance to thee;
> And now, albeit from my harp are flung
> Discordant numbers, and the song may be
> That which I would not, yet I know that thou
> The offering wilt not spurn, while thus to thee I bow.[25]

The "numbers" may be "discordant" and "the song may be / That which I would not," but this is as it should be. "A spirit and a love," poesy is only secondarily a matter of representation. The sense in which poetry inheres in the very nature of things, a property of the earth and sky, makes it clear that poetry is here valorized as an expressive potentiality, unbound by a tradition of forms, just as Emerson makes it clear, in "The Poet," that insofar as "poetry was all written before time was," he is not interested in what can be found between the covers of a book.[26]

At the same time, we can see that "Poesy" is a Shakespearean sonnet, with a hexameter in the final line. The genre of the sonnet sequence not only recalls Shakespeare but, more particularly, what Stuart Curran has called "the rebirth of sonnet" that began with the publication of Charlotte Smith's *Elegiac Sonnets* in 1784 and continued through the next four decades with the sonnet collections of Mary Robinson, Anne Bannerman, and others.[27] Moreover, the reverential terms of address in "Poesy," together with its ritualistic acts of kneeling, offering, and bowing, suggest that, while the speaker may disclaim a "fond, sickly thirst for fame," the notion of fame itself, a perennial topic in a form dedicated to immortalizing the beloved, does matter a great deal. Finally, however much "Poesy" appears to imply that poetry is an expressive Ideal that pre-exists speech and is thus irreducible to generic categories, it's also important to note that its speaker regards her text as a material object, an "offering" to be left at the shrine of poetry.

It is indeed the assumption or taking on of form that's a crucial concern for Oakes Smith, something made inescapable by her commitment to the splendors of a poetry that exists despite, and not as the result of, her own "discordant numbers." This becomes especially clear when we turn from her panegyric to the "high-born goddess" of Poesy to the next sonnet in the sequence, "The Bard," where the overtones of a masculine poetics of prophecy and sacrifice seem to provide a counterpoint to the disembodied Ideality of the first poem. That Oakes Smith ends the poem by appearing to subvert the idealism she had just been affirming is only one of many strange twists in this extraordinary sonnet sequence.

> It cannot be, the baffled heart, in vain,
> May seek, amid the crowd, its throbs to hide;
> Ten thousand other kindred pangs may bide,
> Yet not the less will our own griefs complain.
> Chained to our rock, the vulture's gory stain,
> And tearing beak is every moment rife,
> Renewing pangs that end but with our life.
> Thence bursteth forth the gushing voice of song,
> The soul's deep anguish thence an utterance finds,
> Appealing to all hearts: and human minds
> Bow down in awe: thence does the Bard belong,
> Unto all times: the laurel steeped in wrong
> Unsought is his: his soul demanded bread,
> And ye, charmed with the voice, gave but a stone instead.[28]

One of the most familiar things said about the lyric is that it transmutes personal pain into universal feeling. Oakes Smith says this as well, only to veer away from it at the very end. The oddly placed observation about the bard demanding one thing but getting something else derails the theme of sublimation: instead of "deep anguish" triumphantly finding expression, we discover that the poem has turned on us, so that it becomes an open question whether the "wrong" in which the "laurel" is "steeped" refers to the general suffering of the human condition or to the clueless general reader who, like the father in the parable, gives stone where bread is needed.[29] The offering of "a stone" indeed seems a mockery of the earlier image of "our rock" of common suffering. What had seemed a celebration of the conversion of suffering into beauty – its conversion, that is to say, into an enduring form – abruptly detours into what seems an accusation of emotional voyeurism.

In contrast to the serene devotion of "Poesy," an agitated, restless spirit drives "The Bard" to the edge of coherence. From the first quatrain's theme of secret, inconsolable sorrow, a topos of the genteel Victorian lyric, we proceed to the garish image of Promethean punishment and its grim message of interminable suffering. The representation of bodily torment is so stark that its subsequent universalizing into song seems perfunctory. Indeed, it's not clear if Oakes Smith intends this implication: the volta and its triumphant declaration ("thence bursteth forth the gushing voice of song") occur a line too early, breaking up the abba rhyme and momentarily stranding the word "song." (More curiously still, Oakes Smith resumes the abba rhyme only to leave the word "wrong" similarly orphaned, like the last one standing in a game of musical chairs.) The impression of willful transgression culminates in the use of the Shakespearean couplet, traditionally assigned the task of summarizing the poem's concerns but here wrenching them out of focus by introducing a "ye" who, under the spell of poetry, confers immortal fame upon the bard when all he was looking for was simple comfort.

Sympathy at the expense of fame or fame at the expense of sympathy seem to be the two options presented, respectively, in "Poesy" and "The Bard." In both cases, characterizations of the Poetess as a vessel of "empty, idealized figures" tell half the story.[30] To cherish poetry as "a spirit and a love" – as a pure expressiveness that precedes representation – does not do away with form, but places a special pressure on its ability to mediate the relation between writer and audience – to perform the role that genre had once provided. "The Bard" registers the profound instability of that relation for Oakes Smith, where a proto-lyrical sensibility of intimacy grounded in shared sorrow vies with a proto-epical tradition of masculine heroism and sacrifice. In doing so, it also wreaks a kind of vengeance on poetic form, illustrating both the depth of Oakes Smith's hope for "pure and heaven-eyed Poesy" as well as her fear of its impending betrayal.

In her powerful chapter on Oakes Smith in *Gender and the Poetics of Reception in Poe's Circle*, Eliza Richards draws attention to the disillusion that overtook the poet after the success of "The Sinless Child." She quotes a passage from an unfinished autobiography where mention is made of "the great poem floating in my brain – spiritual – Miltonic – worthy to be preserved – to become a part of human thought" that never came to fruition.[31] Richards links Oakes Smith's love–hate relationship to poetry with her balked attempt to imagine an "alternative landscape" that does not "run up against the recalcitrance of gendered poetic traditions."[32] We may surmise that such traditions included not only Milton, but also predecessors such as Sigourney, and what could only have seemed to Oakes Smith an intolerably ephemeral mode of poetic production. Thinking again of Milton and "the desire at some time to write 'something which his countrymen would not willingly let die'," she writes elsewhere that "[N]othing can live that is not en-vased. The form must be beautiful, or the creation sinks with the old chimeras of rude chaos and dull night."[33] For Oakes Smith, to be concerned with form for form's sake is a mark of superficiality of a stereotypically feminine kind; it is to be like the hopelessly prosaic mother in "The Sinless Child," described as "accustomed to forms and content with the faith in which she has been reared."[34] But not to acquire a form means not "becom[ing] a part of human thought"; it is to suffer an incurable loneliness, like the Sinless Child herself, who, having no real identity (no shape, no form) can have no companions and thus no remembrance.

"Alone, yet not alone," the narrator of "The Poet's Life" finds herself caught between these two extremes.[35] "And is this life? And are we born for this?" the sonnet following "The Bard" asks. "To follow phantoms that elude the grasp" names one option; to discover that "whatsoe'er secured, within our clasp [is doomed] to withering lie" points to another.[36] In other sonnets of the sequence, the heroism of "the pilot, trackless through the deep" who charts a course by starlight or that of the eagle who "high above the darkling fir . . . take[s] his fill / Of that pure ether breathed by him alone" is drawn against the ambivalence of a speaker who "broods with a miser joy," hoarding a "hidden grief" while beholding "still unessayed, unknown . . . that pathway fearless."[37] What eludes our grasp is unreal – a phantom – while that which does not is all too familiar and banal. We feel keenly the wish for a form that would mediate this polarity; and in its absence we feel more keenly still the intensity of Oakes Smith's quarrel with poetry, as the initial lines of the sestet of "A Dream" suggest:

Fame, that the spirit loathing turns to ruth –
And that deluding faith so loath to part,
That earth will shrine for us one kindred heart![38]

Is it "fame" and its "deluding faith" that "the spirit" loathes? Or, rather, is the point that the spirit itself is the guilty party inasmuch as its "loathing turns [fame] to ruth?" Is fame's "deluding faith so loath to part" from the spirit, or is it the other way around? On such ambiguities does Oakes Smith's quest for the form that would "shrine" the spirit turn.

The apparent pathos of Oakes Smith's declining popularity and unfulfilled ambition should be tempered by an awareness that we not only lack a modern selection of her writing, but also a reliable bibliography of her publications over the course of her long career. Moreover, without discounting the special challenges gender occasions in a writer who would come to be known, in the decade following "The Sinless Child," for her outspoken feminism, it is worth noting that the struggles surrounding fame and form I have been describing are not necessarily dissimilar from those we find in the verse of contemporaries such as Poe and Emerson. Judged in terms of talent and ambition, Oakes Smith loses nothing in comparison with these two, whose poetry continues to attract scholarly monographs and articles. One therefore hopes to see the day when a broader community of Americanists turns to this remarkable figure and extends to her the recognition that she so richly deserves.

In thinking about the passion for poetry expressed in the verse of Sigourney and Oakes Smith, we discover significant differences in outlook. Initially it may seem as though these differences are dictated by a shift in taste from neoclassical correctness to a Romantic fascination with spontaneous expression. And yet Sigourney's very love of eloquent, decorous speech cannot help but alter the tradition she inherits, while Oakes Smith's relationship to the literary forms of her predecessors, both male and female, is much too conflicted even to appear to model the kind of lyric transparency conventionally associated with Romanticism generally and with the role of the Poetess in particular. To seek to understand why both authors valued poetry is to open new paths for literary history to explore, paths which in turn may help us to articulate more clearly the reasons why we should continue to value them.

Notes

I would like to thank Jennifer Putzi for her helpful feedback on an earlier draft of this essay.

1. See, for example, Gary Kelly's useful introduction to his edition, *Lydia Sigourney: Selected Poetry and Prose* (Peterborough: Broadview Editions, 2008). The reading of "The Sinless Child" referenced may be found in Emily Stipes Watts, *The Poetry of American Women from 1632 to 1943* (Austin: University of Texas Press, 1977), 100–105.
2. Lydia Sigourney, "To the Moon," *Poems* (New York: Leavitt & Allen, 1841), 218.
3. Lydia Sigourney, "Morning in Rural and City Life," *Poems* (New York: Leavitt & Allen, 1860), 137.
4. Lydia Sigourney, "Connecticut River," *Select Poems* (Philadelphia: Carey & Hart, 1852), 17.
5. Sigourney, "The Return of Napoleon," *Poems* (1860), 181.
6. William Wordsworth, "Preface to *Lyrical Ballads*," *Prose of the Romantic Period*, Carl R. Woodring (ed.), (Boston: Houghton Mifflin, 1961), 51.
7. Sigourney, "The Ancient Family Clock," *Select Poems*, 53–56.
8. Sigourney, "The Sunday School," *Select Poems*, 42.
9. Lydia Sigourney, *Poems* (Philadelphia: Key and Biddle, 1836), 86.
10. Wordsworth, "Preface," *Prose of the Romantic Period*, 51.
11. Jay Fliegelman, *Declaring Independence: Jefferson, Natural Language, and the Culture of Performance* (Stanford: Stanford University Press, 1993); Christopher Looby, *Voicing America: Language, Literary Form, and the Origins of the United States* (Chicago: University of Chicago Press, 1996); Sandra Gustafson, *Eloquence Is Power: Oratory and Performance in Early America* (Chapel Hill: University of North Carolina Press, 2000).
12. William Cullen Bryant, "Lecture First. On the Nature of Poetry," *Prose Writings of William Cullen Bryant*, Parke Godwin (ed.), (New York: Appleton, 1884), 13.
13. Ibid., 13.
14. Lydia Sigourney, *Letters of Life* (New York: D. Appleton and Co., 1866), 141.
15. Sigourney, "Poetry," *Select Poems*, 232–233.
16. Emily Dickinson, "I cannot live with you," *The Poems of Emily Dickinson*, Variorum Edition, 3 vols., R. W. Franklin (ed.), (Cambridge, MA and London: The Belknap Press of Harvard University Press, 1998), 674–676.
17. Sigourney, *Letters of Life*, 9.
18. Sigourney, "Thought," *Select Poems*, 84–85.
19. Sigourney, *Letters of Life*, 30.
20. Shira Wolosky, *Major Voices: 19th Century American Women's Poetry* (New Milford: The Toby Press, 2003), 30.
21. Sigourney, "The Muse," *Poems* (1860), 160.

22. Virginia Jackson, "The Poet as Poetess," *The Cambridge Companion to Nineteenth-Century American Poetry*, Kerry Larson (ed.), (Cambridge University Press, 2011), 68.
23. Ibid., 69, 68.
24. Griswold's comment may be found in the Preface to *The Poetical Writings of Elizabeth Oakes Smith* (New York: J. S. Redfield, 1845), 7. Poe's comment appears in his review of "The Sinless Child" and may be found in *The Complete Works of Edgar Allan Poe*, James Harrison (ed.), 18 vols. (New York: Thomas Crowell, 1902), 13: 79.
25. Elizabeth Oakes Smith, "Poesy," *Poetical Writings*, 95.
26. Ralph Waldo Emerson, *Essays and Lectures* (New York: The Library of America, 1983), 449.
27. Stuart Curran, *Poetic Form and British Romanticism* (New York: Oxford University Press, 1986), 31. For a thorough review of the sonnet revival in women's poetry in the United Kingdom during the late eighteenth and early nineteenth centuries, see Stephen Behrendt, *British Women Poets and the Romantic Writing Community* (Baltimore: Johns Hopkins University Press, 2009), 115–151.
28. Smith, "The Bard," *Poetical Writings*, 96.
29. See Matthew 7:9; Luke 11:11.
30. Jackson, "The Poet as Poetess," 69.
31. Qtd. in Eliza Richards, *Gender and the Poetics of Reception in Poe's Circle* (Cambridge University Press, 2004), 189.
32. Richards, *Gender and the Poetics of Reception*, 175.
33. Qtd. in Richards, *Gender and the Poetics of Reception*, 179.
34. Smith, *The Sinless Child, Poetical Writings*, 24.
35. Smith, "The Poet's Life," *Poetical Writings*, 98.
36. Smith, "The Unattained," *Poetical Writings*, 97.
37. Smith, "Religion," *Poetical Writings*, 98; Smith, "An Incident," *Poetical Writings*, 100; Smith, "Religion," *Poetical Writings*, 98; Smith, "An Incident," *Poetical Writings*, 100.
38. Smith, "A Dream," *Poetical Writings*, 99.

CHAPTER 4

Album Verse and the Poetics of Scribal Circulation

Michael C. Cohen

The vast majority of poems written in the nineteenth century were never published. While poems were major components of American popular media, appearing in newspapers, magazines, anthologies, schoolbooks, broadsides, and other print formats, they proliferated even more widely in an active culture of manuscript circulation by non-professional writers. Unlike novels, plays, lectures, and other literary genres, which can be said to come into existence (in a strict generic sense) only upon publication or performance, poetry has a long history of scribal production and informal modes of copying and exchange among coteries. The poems of John Donne, to give a canonical example, exist in more than 5,000 distinct seventeenth-century manuscript collations, far exceeding the number of printed copies that circulated in his lifetime. Because each collation had its own network of exchange, Donne's coterie audience was likely larger than the readership of his books, which were published only with his reluctant participation. Indeed, scholars now speculate that some of the most popular and influential poets of the seventeenth century were never "published," as that event is understood today.[1]

Over the course of the eighteenth century, literariness came to be associated with print publication, even for women writers, who had faced special prohibitions against it, while authorship, which had acquired new associations with originality and ownership, became more consolidated as a standard for judging literary value. Nevertheless, scribal poetic circles remained important in North America, and some of the most prominent eighteenth-century colonial poets, such as Henry Brooke, Lewis Morris, Susanna Wright, Hannah Griffitts, Jane Colman Turrell, Phillis Wheatley, and Annis Boudinot Stockton, wrote for coterie exchange.[2] As the publishing market for poetry expanded, manuscript composition increased as well, and through the nineteenth century poetry writing was an activity for people who had no ambition to become professional authors. Ralph Waldo Emerson noted as much in "New Poetry" (1840):

> [A] revolution in literature is now giving importance to the portfolio over the book. Only one man in the thousand may print a book, but one in ten or one in five may inscribe his thoughts, or at least with short commentary his favorite readings in a private journal. . . . This new taste for a certain private or household poetry, for somewhat less pretending than the festal and solemn verses which are written for the nations, really indicates, we suppose, that a new style of poetry exists. The number of writers has increased. Every child has been taught the tongues. The universal communication of the arts of reading and writing has brought the works of the great poets into every house, and made all ears familiar with the poetic forms . . . every day witnesses new attempts to throw into verse the experiences of private life.[3]

Emerson termed such work "*Verses of the Portfolio*," a phrase Thomas Wentworth Higginson would later adopt (notoriously) to characterize the poems of Emily Dickinson as peculiarly feminine, childish expressions of closeted genius. Higginson used the term in relation to poetry's intensified associations with childhood at the century's end.[4] Emerson, in contrast, viewed the "verses of the portfolio" as a sign of cultural democratization. He was ambivalent about the "democratical" tendencies of the new poetry, and he did not advocate for leveling hierarchical access to the publishing industry ("we should be loath to see the wholesome conventions . . . broken down by a general incontinence of publication"): portfolio verse was best in manuscript.[5] Still, he offered a canny diagnosis of the antebellum culture of poetry writing, which was linked, as he recognized, to expansions of literacy, education, and cheap print, as well as widespread changes to the structures of social life. Poetry writing had indeed become democratized, and, despite Emerson's gendered language, women, children, and others with limited access to literary culture were especially important producers of manuscript verse. Dickinson's fascicles are the most famous unpublished "books" of poems in the nineteenth century, but they are not unique.

Scribal authors are the hidden majority among nineteenth-century American poets, albeit their work is difficult to assess in the terms of literary history, which tends to move from major author to major author and is typically organized by groups or periods with shared aesthetic or political commitments (a lineage from Whitman to Frost, for example, or from the Croakers to the New York School). Manuscript verse is loopier and more difficult to historicize since it is often tied to older British sources, and therefore seems, almost by definition, out of joint with the moment of its inscription and out of keeping with narratives of literary development and innovation.[6] Manuscript verse is also more networked, imitative, and reiterative: poems written in albums or exchanged by letter were meant to sound familiar, to touch on literary commonplaces that both giver and receiver would recognize.

Scribal work is heterogeneous, and there are differences between exchanging poetry albums, circulating poems in letters, recording them in journals, or making manuscript books of them, among other possible actions. This essay will concentrate on a particular practice of manuscript verse and the literary culture that it derived from and that derived from it: namely, the composition and exchange of poetry albums. As will become clear, women primarily composed, compiled, and exchanged poems in albums.[7] Although men sometimes inscribed lines in the books of their female friends, they rarely (to my knowledge) owned these albums. The feminization of album poetics was recursively reinforced by the proliferation, beginning in the 1830s, of printed gift books and anthologies of elegant extracts, which were marketed overtly to women as source books for their album compositions. Most of the albums I discuss come from antebellum Philadelphia, which boasted one of the largest, most literate, and most literary populations in the first half of the century. My argument is meant to be modular, so while it will not account for all periods of the century or all regions of the country, its general contours and parameters can be useful to the study of other instances of nineteenth-century album verse culture.

* * *

"Roam where we will, where'ere our steps may tend,
The world is dull without a bosom friend
Though every hue thats pleasing to the eye,
And every sweet that breathes in nature sigh,
Though spring groves and shade orange bowers,
And all the luxuries of life, were ours,
Though blessed with days like those of golden times
And breathing airs like those of mildest climes;
Without a friend to whom we can disclose,
Our lovely pleasures, and our gloomy woes;
Still life would want its best its brightest part,
The dear the social feelings of the heart."[8]

Recorded by a woman named Carrie in the album of Rachel Matlack, who lived in southern New Jersey in the early 1840s, these lines celebrating friendship and "the social feelings of the heart" make a worthy introduction to the poetics of the album, for friendship was perhaps the most common theme in poems inscribed for and exchanged among friends.[9]

Carrie's poem was a gift intended to recall the giver, and it extolled an institution – female friendship – that in the antebellum decades had become a model for national sociability as such. Amicability underwrote the conditions that made album poems meaningful, and many poems accordingly put those conditions front and center. As one poem of 1830 put it, "And here o'er every consecrated page, / Friendship presides – her chosen heritage; / These simple flowers to her domain belong, / Who lives in feeling and who breathes in song."[10]

This poem's reflexive reference to the "consecrated page" where "Friendship presides" indicates both its position in the idealized milieu of female companionship (where women "live in feeling and breathe in song"), and also its more material location in a specific woman's album. A nineteenth-century album was an elegant folio or quarto-sized blank book, often printed with engravings and, eventually, chromolithographs, which began to be mass-produced after 1820, coinciding with the expansion of the American publishing industry. From what I can tell, these blank albums proliferated until about 1870, when smaller, pocket-sized "autograph books" mostly replaced them. The album blended the personal, handwritten sensibility of the coterie with the anonymity of mass-marketed print; it also complemented the annual gift book, one of the bestselling genres of the antebellum era that emerged at the same time. Writing a poem in another's album was similar to the practice of exchanging gift books, but gift books came with printed extracts and were not meant to be filled in or returned to the giver. Album exchanges were linked to the nascent practice of educating girls, and young women who compiled albums of verse often began to do so in school. Someone might receive an album as a gift from a friend, a parent, or a teacher, and would likely begin filling it by circulating the book among schoolfellows. The typical album that survives today contains poems written by various hands over several years; most women stopped exchanging albums around the time they married, though some kept it up for decades.

In the cultural and institutional context projected by the album, to appreciate poetry was to identify oneself as worthy of friendship, and to appreciate one's friends was to value their poems ("These simple flowers to her domain belong, / Who lives in feeling and who breathes in song"). Mary Potts, a fourteen-year-old Quaker girl living in suburban Philadelphia in the late 1830s, described her friend Jane Edge in terms that indicate how a love for people and poems could be intertwined.

> Jane is a lovely and talented girl I hope she may sometime be in print she has written several beautiful pieces and says she loves to write and wishes she had nothing else to do. she has some of the true poetic fire I believe she seems something like me only much more talented and lively. The words she copied in my album may apply to her –
>
> "How often is our path crossed by
> Crossed by some being whose bright spirit sheds
> A passing gladness oer it but whose course
> Leads down another current never more
> To blend with ours" – [11]

A friend "like me only much more talented," with "the true poetic fire," Jane was the star of Mary's circle of schoolfellows, most of whom wrote poems. These girls had many obligations in school and at home, yet still literary composition was a serious pursuit for them, and their acts of poetic exchange spoke both to the individual writers and to the social relationships secured by each inscription. As Mary explained, copying words in each other's albums recorded literary and personal affections. Because one person's "course / Leads down another current never more / To blend with ours," inscribing verse also sustained friendships over time and space. On one occasion, Mary noted how "Father was looking over my album and I was reading some out of it. I love to look over it and think of the lovely girls who have written in it and those happy times."[12] Even when the girls did not write original work, the verses still became "theirs" because the inscriptions spoke for them, calling them to mind as the album's owner reread the lines months or years later.

Potts and her friends were especially lively and active participants in the nineteenth century's scribal poetics, but they were also typical of a longstanding system of manuscript exchange and amateur authorship. Album inscription derives from an older tradition of commonplacing, or copying by hand key passages from selected and approved authors or texts, often on general, abstract topics (common places).[13] Commonplace books had been one of the principal tools of humanist scholarship since the medieval period, and the Lockean theories of education that informed American pedagogy helped to promote the practice in the early United States.[14] Copying was crucial to early American teaching, as well as to the habits of literacy inculcated among those who received even rudimentary training in reading and writing.[15] In the eighteenth century, the practice of copying or composing short poems on standard topics dovetailed with emerging theories of sensibility to establish poetic composition and manuscript circulation as key elements in the culture of politeness and civility.[16]

Such activities were sociable and refining; they cultivated bonds of friendship in the service of higher sentiments. In her usual charming manner, Potts linked her commonplace book with other daily pursuits of self-culture and improvement; in her diary she recorded how "some of the pieces in the commonplace book are beautiful. I have just been watching the beautiful clouds and repeating the piece to them. I do love beautiful poetry. read some pieces to mother."[17] Though it is not clear whether Potts's commonplace book was distinct from her album, it is clear that she "loved beautiful poetry" at least in part for the ways that it facilitated forms of aesthetic contemplation, filial piety, and personal introspection. Mary was usually specific about what she was reading, so her use of the generic "commonplace book" indicates that this kind of text helped her link "beautiful poetry" with the "beautiful clouds" (and beyond) by collapsing the difference between the personal and the conventional.

The ability to mediate, structure, or conventionalize personal experience through poetry is perhaps the most characteristic feature of albums, gift books, and "elegant extracts," the major mid-century formats in the scribal poetic culture outlined in this essay. Inscribing poems in such books, or exchanging them with friends, allowed writers to think of the poetry in them as "theirs," even when it was not original, while the scribal practices inculcated in such books enabled amateur poets to connect their worlds with the sentiments and ideals highlighted in their reading. The back-and-forth between the personal and the commonplace (or, between the handmade and the mass-produced) can be seen in the aesthetics of these different formats, which correlate closely, as three examples from the 1830s indicate. The hand-drawn cover of "Passages of Poetical Prose," a commonplace book compiled by Philadelphian Elizabeth Lloyd in 1832 [Fig. 2], carefully remediates the font and flourishes found in printed albums and "elegant extracts" of the period, such as the album printed in New York by J. C. Riker in 1835 that belonged to Elizabeth, a woman living in northeastern Massachusetts [Fig. 3], or *The Young Lady's Book of Elegant Poetry*, a compendium of extracts published by the Philadelphia firm Desilver Thomas & Co. in 1836 [Fig. 4]. In the latter two examples, Elizabeth's inscribed name personalizes the mass-produced album, giving her book an aesthetics of the hand that contravenes its mass-mediated anonymity, while the *Elegant Poetry* volume culls the passages and quotations that young women such as Lloyd and Elizabeth collected and exchanged with their friends.[18]

Antebellum literary culture offered a huge array of books like *The Young Lady's Book of Elegant Poetry*, which are challenging to categorize

Figure 2. Frontispiece to Elizabeth Lloyd's commonplace book "Passages of Poetical Prose," 1832. Courtesy of the Friends Historical Library of Swarthmore College.

bibliographically. They differ from schoolbooks, anthologies, and books of religious instruction; though "elegant extracts" could be didactic or based on religious themes, they lack an explicitly pedagogical or doctrinal purpose. They also differ from gift books, which were published on an annual

Figure 3. Title page of poetry album belonging to Elizabeth, c.1835. Collection of Michael Cohen.

cycle and tended to include newer (sometimes original) work. Books of extracts held more material, though little of it was original or new. Their contents ranged across genres and periods, going back to Shakespeare, though most matter came out of the eighteenth and early nineteenth centuries, usually from British authors. Extracts might be clustered around

PHILADELPHIA:

DESILVER THOMAS & Co.

Market Street

1836.

Figure 4. Frontispiece of *The Young Ladies Book of Elegant Poetry* (Philadelphia: Desilver Thomas & Co., 1836).

themes, or might not; the key feature of each gem was its brevity, which made it easier to memorize and copy, and many poems were represented by just a stanza or two, often without the original title or author listed. These printed collections subtended the scribal culture of album exchange: readers might peruse the books in depth, but more often they mined them for extracts that they wrote under their own names in others' albums. Entries could therefore be personal even when they were not "original." Poetry albums thus redact from the poetic culture at two removes, since they draw from collections, anthologies, and gift books that have already selected, condensed, and organized the literary field under the aegis of the extract, flower, gem, or beauty.

These extractive metaphors work their way back into the albums, informing the self-consciousness of the writers and their acts of inscription. Eliza Pusey's book *The Floral Album* is a good example. The humanist notion of the "florilegium" (or elegant extract) provided the metaphor of the "flower" that inflected popular American poetics through 1900; many compendia of refined quotations were entitled some variation of "Flowers and Poetry," and albums and anthologies often came with floral illustrations adorning their pages. Though *The Floral Album* was a mass-produced book, Pusey or a friend drew an elaborate, personalized frontispiece that precedes the colored, engraved title page. This interplay between the personal and the mass-mediated continues throughout the volume. "By the Owner," a poem presumably inscribed by Pusey, explains her book's purview:

> "My Album is a garden plot,
> Here all my friends may sow,
> Where thorns and thistles flourish not;
> But flowers alone will grow:
> With smiles for sunshine tears for showers,
> I'll water warm and watch these flowers."[19]

If *The Floral Album* deploys one of the basic metaphors for an antebellum album – the book as a bouquet of flowers – "By the Owner" adapts this metaphor to create a sense of special possession, in which the book is a garden cultivated by the sociable feelings and good wishes of Pusey and her friends. This claim on the personal comes through the inscription of a poem by someone else; "By the Owner" is the twelfth of British poet James Montgomery's "Mottoes for Albums." "Flowers" and "leaves" therefore do double-duty as metonymies for the book-as-object and metaphors for the inscribed poems that fill it, which nurture goodwill by particularizing the conventions of a sociable poetics.

The botanical motif is one of several self-referential tropes that enabled album poets to negotiate the paradoxical circumstances of a literary culture that combined the discourse of personal friendship with a mass-mediated system of poetry and printing. A poem inscribed to Mary Ann Hubbert in her album takes up a different metaphor for the album, this time as a miniature world inhabited by the owner's best virtues, features, and friends:

> As some fair mind does o'er these pages dwell;
> And read those feelings it has known so well,
> Perhaps a tear may startle in the eye;
> The breast may heave a fond impressive sigh.
>
> The album is a world, in which we trace
> A thousand joys, no sorrow may efface;
> Love, Friendship, Hope, with all their tender ties,
> Before the mind in sweet succession rise.
>
> And now, may no foul blot or stain appear,
> To blight the tributes that are offer'd here;
> But may the pledge, go round to every friend;
> And each his offering to the owner send.[20]

Entitled "The Album" and written beneath an engraved illustration within which the author inserted by hand the poem's title, this poem invests writing and reading with meaning by making each poem in the album a synecdoche for its writer: in rereading the book, Hubbert will experience the sentiments and somatic responses – tears, sighs, and so on – indicative of a properly socialized and engaged mind and heart. Her album is a book that outlines her life, allowing her to trace "A thousand joys . . . Love, Friendship, Hope, with all their tender ties." The album's bookishness is important; the clean pages and neat inscriptions demonstrate care and devotion on the part of her friends, just as a "foul blot" or stain might indicate a ruined relationship or hurt feelings. Thus, the author hopes to see the book well-traveled amongst Hubbert's friends, filled with the tributes that indicate a life well lived and an owner well loved.

The poem to Hubbert captures another common way of understanding the album's value, namely by emphasizing its relation to time: according to this theme, the book's purpose will be realized in the future, when its owner turns to it again and reflects on the memories inscribed in its entries. The motif of memory work operates through several conventions, including the "remember me" or "forget me not" refrain, the epitaph, and the anticipatory retrospect, which are condensed by the metaphor of the book as tombstone:

When the white marble tells where my ashes are lain,
And the willow droops gracefully over the spot,
Oh! sister, then seek it again and again,
That I, in thy memory may never be forgot.

When spring's early blossoms shall bid thee repair
To the dells, and the valleys, where oft we have strayed
Oh! Sister, dear sister, then let my grave wear
A wreath of sweet flowers, fresh culled from the glade.

And when thou art twining it round the green mound
Let it be at the shadowy twilight of even;
When the soft, balmy zephyrs are playing around,
My spirit shall waft the pure tribute to Heaven,

Oh! oft have I thought, when sweet health formed my brow,
That there would come a time when I might be forgot:
Oh! terrible thought! it even sickens me now:
Then sister, dear sister, I pray forget not![21]

These lines, written by Sarah H. Stevens to her sister Elizabeth, imagine a future when Stevens will be memorialized by an epitaph ("the white marble," which also figures for the poem) that will call on Elizabeth to remember her so "That I, in thy memory may never be forgot." The lines enlist many conventions of album verse, such as the "wreath of sweet flowers, fresh culled from the glade," which, as we have seen, is a standard metaphor for the extract. Placing such a "pure tribute" in Elizabeth's book, Stevens uses it to secure a memorial return that will ensure against "a time when I might be forgot": the poem thus guarantees a future with her sister that will endure beyond death. Many remembrance verses similarly imagine the poem or book as an inscribed tombstone: "This book shall soon be like the dwelling / Of the lamented dead: / Each page like the old marble tilling [*sic*] / Of some bright spirit fled."[22]

While marmoreal metaphors derive from the eighteenth-century Graveyard School aesthetic, their purpose in album poems is often different, since the album's owner is called upon not so much to recognize mortality as to remember loved ones. Futurity comes not from the poem itself, but from the ways that thc inscription of the poem in a treasured book will elicit remembrances of friends, by friends. As lines from Lydia Moore to Eliza Pusey put it:

When o'er this book thou casts thine eye
And think of names that once were dear,

May mine awake the pensive sigh,
While others claim the sorrowing tear.

Ah! will one wandering thought of thine
Rest in its rapid flight on me,
Nor to forgetfulness consign
The friend who loves to think on thee.

Ah! sure thy fancy oft will fly
To scenes that once were dear to thee,
Yes when these lines shall meet thine eye
Thou smiling will remember me.[23]

Seeking the "pensive sigh" rather than the "sorrowing tear," Moore imagines a future reading of her poem that will produce a mutual recollection – Pusey will not "to forgetfulness consign / The friend who loves to think on thee," but instead, "when these lines shall meet thine eye / Thou smiling will remember me." Her poem forestalls absence and loss by reinscribing memory as a reciprocal gesture, with her name recalling for Pusey "the friend who loves to think on thee." The memorial work of album verse depends upon this reciprocity, which tends to be absent from the one-way address of the epitaph. As John Pollock put it in his didactic inscription to Pennsylvanian Mary A. Williams in 1856,

> We delight not only to revel in present enjoyment, but in meditation to wander far back amidst the enchanting scenes of bygone days, so thrilling with interest even in recollection. While these are called up, one after another, we as it were select the choicest portions of lifes history, & thus live over again the periods around which memory delights to linger. As you have chosen this means, to strengthen the bonds of youthful associations, may you ever find in reading its sacred pages, those sentiments that have sprung not from base flattery or a perverse nature, but from the purest principles of the soul. May you ever prove that those who have herein inscribed their names, are not only your friends in name but in reality.[24]

Rereading the album's "sacred pages" in the future, Williams will reflect on whether "those who have herein inscribed their names" were friends "in reality" or merely "friends in name." Just as true friends choose the ideal gem or flower to "strengthen the bonds of youthful associations," Williams's future memories will "select the choicest portions of lifes history" to memorialize "the enchanting scenes of bygone days." In Pollock's view, Williams's book mediates her friendships by eliciting both careful writing and careful reading, two processes of selection that model the album as an ideal world. Jane E. Fleming made a similar point on the first page of her album:

"My Album is a mirror clear / Whence all my Friends appear / Reflected to affections sight/ In Memory's house of light." Here the comparison to a mirror enables the book to reflect metaphorically Fleming's friends by way of a future rereading in "Memory's house of light."[25]

Other poems reversed the metaphor of the book as an embodiment of its owner's life by imagining the owner to be an album herself:

> Thy mind is an album unsullied and bright
> Just opened – for angels and spirits to write
> Each thought and affection intent and desire
> That wisdom may sanction – that love may inspire.
>
> The book is immortal – Oh, guard it with care
> Lest demons should sully its pages so fair
> Repulse such intruders, nor shrink from the strife,
> And heaven will smile on "the book of thy life["].[26]

These lines, penned by an unknown writer sometime in the 1830s, conclude a small pocket album that belonged to a Massachusetts woman named Elizabeth. Here the metaphor of inscription opens Elizabeth to metaphysical connections with angels and demons, making her book's circulation among friends a model for imagining her relationship with heaven. The poem formalizes Elizabeth's spiritual life by comparing her to the book in which the poem appears; appropriately enough, the lines come from the poem "The Book of the Heart: Written in a Young Lady's Album" by the popular author Samuel Woodworth, whose poems (or extracts therefrom) occur repeatedly in albums of the 1830s and 1840s.

"To Mary," a poem written by H. E. Ludlow in a book belonging to Mary B. Swords, also metaphorically expands the act of writing in an album into a desire to leave an impression in the owner's mind:

> Here is one leaf reserved for me,
> From all thy sweet memorials free,
> And here my simple song might tell
> The feelings thou must guess too well.
> But could I thus, within thy mind
> One little vacant corner find,
> Where no impression yet is seen,
> Where no memorial yet has been,
> Oh, it should be my sweetest care
> To write my name for ever there –[27]

Like "Thy mind is an album," "To Mary" also comes from a printed source, Thomas Moore's "Written in the Blank Leaf of a Lady's Common-place

Book," and it too conflates book and owner in a metaphor for understanding the meaning of the poem's own inscription. Comparing the woman's book to her mind, the authors – both Moore and Ludlow – wish to write a memorial that will impress them forever in the owner's memory. "To Mary" expresses a desire to be remembered through writing a poem, and the gesture of recording the poem in Swords's book may indicate Ludlow's desire to leave a lasting memory with her friend. If so, taking lines from another author's text would seem ironically to contradict the wish for such a personal bond, since it asks to be remembered using someone else's words. However, it is important to recognize the secondariness and metaphoricity of Ludlow's "original" source. The "Lines written in a lady's album" genre flourished in the Romantic period (Moore, Woodworth, Montgomery, William Wordsworth, William Cowper, Robert Burns, and other widely read male poets wrote them), in reaction to the popularity of album composition and exchange. Whether or not Moore's or others' "Lines" originally went into someone's album, they were also published in books, magazines, and newspapers, and frequently republished in gift books, anthologies, and other condensed formats. Manuscript poetics thus inspired a print genre that was then re-inserted back into scribal culture, often replicating – with a difference – the imagined scene of original inscription. By copying male authors' "lines" to young women, other young women reframed the gender politics of poetry in the age of sensibility.

This kind of copying is not merely passive consumption, because the "author" – that is, the person writing the extract – assumes the literary authority expressed in the original writer's gesture of public intimacy. For instance, a poem dedicated "To Mrs Robert Adger" copies Wordsworth's "Written in an Album" and then adds a second stanza that redirects the original lines into a personal comment from writer to recipient:

Small service is true service while it lasts;
Of friends however humble, scorn not one:
The daisy, by the shadow that it casts
Protects the lingering dew-drop from the sun.

Thus writes the bard – thus breathes this heart
Which while thy wish it meets,
Would to thy soul that love impart
Which here so strongly beats.[28]

The writer affirms Wordsworth's Christian naturalism but transforms its one-way direction (daisy protecting dewdrop) into mutual reciprocity: the poem expresses the heartfelt wish of the writer ("thus breathes this heart") to impart a corresponding love in the soul of the recipient. Friendly service – in this case, inscribing the poem – inspires fellow feeling, so that copying the words of "the bard" enables a gesture of original friendship. Another example of an album poem copied from a printed poem pretending to be a manuscript poem written for a different album is "For Elizabeth's Album," which uses its source (in this case, a poem "Written on the First Leaf of a Lady's Pocket Book") to cultivate a Christian sensibility that makes the book a moral record of the young woman's experience.

> "While life's swift gliding-current steals away,
> And you here register each passing day,
> May this small book, by honest friendship given,
> Remind you of the record kept in Heaven.
> And, oh! may every hour of life afford
> Such themes as these, for conscience to record;
> Duties performed – time zealously employed,
> Talents improved, and happiness enjoyed,
> Errors corrected, sins and follies mourn'd,
> Blessings received, and grateful praise returned."[29]

This poem's reference to "this small book, by honest friendship given" recalls the materiality of the album in the service of a different reminder, "the record kept in Heaven," so that the print fiction of the "lines written on the first leaf of a lady's pocket book" enables a metaphorical transfer to the "book of life" and its attendant record of "duties performed." These duties are personal ("sins and follies mourn'd") as well as social ("Blessings received, and grateful praise returned"); pious contemplation by way of reading and writing serves the function of collective melioration, just as eighteenth-century theorists of the sentiments would have predicted. Of equal note, however, is the poem's own work as a reminder: inscribed on the front leaf (both in the original poem's title, and in the actual first page of this particular album), the poem anticipates future rereadings of the book by reiterating its primary purpose to "Remind you of the record kept in Heaven."

The strong conventionality of album poetry makes it a compelling source for reimagining nineteenth-century American women's culture. Poetry albums inculcated a kind of writing predicated on rereading and remembrance, where secondariness and not originality made poems valuable for giver and receiver. Attending to the manuscript circuits of the album might therefore help to revise widespread views about popular literature before the Civil War, which has tended to be understood according to the aesthetics and ideologies of cheap print and the passive consumption of mass-produced texts. Album verse, in contrast, allows us to consider nineteenth-century women's poetry as a participatory system of poetic culture, a culture of the hand as well as of the book.

Notes

For their help and generosity, I thank the staffs of the following libraries: The Quaker and Special Collections Library at Haverford College, particularly John Anderies and Ann Upton; the Friends Historical Library at Swarthmore College, particularly Chris Densmore; and the Historical Society of Pennsylvania.

1. Arthur Marotti, *John Donne, Coterie Poet* (Madison: University of Wisconsin Press, 1986); Arthur Marotti, *Manuscript, Print, and the English Renaissance Lyric* (Ithaca: Cornell University Press, 1995); Joshua Eckhardt, *Manuscript Verse Collectors* (Oxford: Oxford University Press, 2009).
2. David S. Shields, *Oracles of Empire* (Chicago: University of Chicago Press, 1990); Annis Stockton, *Only for the Eye of a Friend*, Carla Mulford (ed.), (Charlottesville: University of Virginia Press, 1995), 1–70; David S. Shields, *Civil Tongues and Polite Letters* (Chapel Hill: University of North Carolina Press, 1997); Catherine La Courreye Blecki and Karin A. Wulf (eds.), *Milcah Martha Moore's Book*, (University Park: Pennsylvania State University Press, 1997), 1–106; Joanna Brooks, "Our Phillis, Ourselves," *American Literature* 82.1 (2010), 1–28.
3. Ralph Waldo Emerson, "New Poetry," *The Dial* (October 1840), 220.
4. Angela Sorby, *Schoolroom Poets* (Durham: University of New Hampshire Press, 2005), 156–89.
5. Emerson, "New Poetry," 221.
6. Meredith L. McGill, "Common Places: Poetry, Illocality, and Temporal Dislocation in Thoreau's *A Week on the Concord and Merrimack Rivers*," *American Literary History* 19.2 (2007), 357–374.
7. Deirdre Lynch, *Loving Literature* (Chicago: University of Chicago Press, 2015), 137–144.
8. Carrie, "Roam where we will, where'ere our steps may tend" [untitled poem]; Rachel S. Matlack autograph album, 1833–1852, Am. 102802, Historical Society of Pennsylvania. Except where noted, I retain the manuscripts' original spelling and punctuation.
9. Laura Zebuhr, "The Work of Friendship in Nineteenth-Century American Friendship Album Verses," *American Literature* 87.3 (2015), 433–454.
10. R. D. [Dumont], "For Miss Swords's Album," Mary B. Swords poetry album, 1826–1833, LCP102, Historical Society of Pennsylvania. The poem is dated March 18, 1830, and the author's last name is identified in pencil, in a different hand.
11. Mary Potts, entry for April 26, 1838, unsigned diary, 1838–1839, Potts Family papers, MC. 1260, Special Collections, Haverford College, Haverford PA.

Though the diary is unsigned, internal evidence indicates that it belonged to Mary Potts.

12. Mary Potts, diary entry for March 16, 1842, Mary Potts diary, 1842, Potts Family papers, MC. 1260, Special Collections, Haverford College, Haverford PA.
13. David Allan, *Commonplace Books and Reading in Georgian England* (Cambridge: Cambridge University Press, 2010); Ann M. Blair, *Too Much to Know* (New Haven: Yale University Press, 2011), 62–116.
14. Jay Fliegelman, *Prodigals and Pilgrims* (Cambridge: Cambridge University Press, 1982), 9–35; E. Jennifer Monaghan, *Learning to Read and Write in Colonial America* (Amherst: University of Massachusetts Press, 2007).
15. Karen Sánchez-Eppler, "Copying and Conversion," *American Quarterly* 59.2 (2007), 317–322.
16. Shields, *Civil Tongues and Polite Letters*, 11–54.
17. Potts, diary entry for September 22, 1838.
18. Elizabeth Lloyd, "Passages of Poetical Prose" commonplace book, 1832, Morris Lloyd Family Papers, RG5/091 Box 1 Ser. 2, Friends Historical Library, Swarthmore College; Elizabeth poetry album, *Album*, 1835–1840, author's collection; *The Young Lady's Book of Elegant Poetry* (Philadelphia: Desilver Thomas, 1836).
19. "By the Owner," Eliza W. Pusey poetry album, *The Floral Album*, 1841, Am.12775, Historical Society of Pennsylvania.
20. J.O.G., "The Album. To Mary Ann Hubbert," Mary Ann Hubbert album, 1834–1836, LCP57, Historical Society of Pennsylvania. The poem is dated March 10, 1834.
21. Sarah H. Stevens, "When the white marble tells where my ashes are lain" [untitled poem], Elizabeth poetry album. The poem is dated "Newburyport [MA] July 3rd 1840. Heartland, Vt."
22. Anna M. Ewatt, "To Mary," Mary A. Williams poetry album, *Gems from Flora*, 1856, author's collection. The poem is dated October 25, 1856.
23. Lydia Moore, "When o'er this book thou casts thine eye" [untitled poem]; Eliza W. Pusey album. The poem is dated "London Grove, 3 mo 1st 1844," and is written on a tipped-in, folded paper. It is not clear whether it was originally part of the book.
24. John Pollock, "To Miss Mary A Williams," Mary A. Williams album. The extract is dated "Rainsburg [PA] June 13th 1856."
25. J.E.F., "My Album is a mirror clear" [untitled poem], Jane E. Fleming poetry album, author's collection.
26. Anon., "Thy mind is an album unsullied and bright" [untitled poem], Elizabeth poetry album. The owner of an album usually wrote the inscriptions on the front leaf, but in this case the poem's hand does not match that of the owner's name on the title page.
27. H. E. Ludlow, "To Mary," Mary B. Swords Poetry Album.

28. T. S., "To Mrs. Robert Adger," Jane E. Fleming album. The poem is dated "Charleston S.C. April. 1837." "Written in an Album" appeared in Wordsworth's 1835 volume *Yarrow Revisited, and Other Poems,* which was published that year in both London and New York.
29. L. Richardson, "For Elizabeth's Album," Elizabeth poetry album. The poem is dated "Andover, October 8th 1835." For an earlier printing of the poem, see T. D., "Written on the First Leaf of a Lady's Pocket Book," *Christian Observer* (March 1803), 158.

CHAPTER 5

Presents of Mind: Lydia Sigourney, Gift Book Culture, and the Commodification of Poetry

Elizabeth A. Petrino

In "Pocket Books and Keepsakes," published in 1828, British essayist and poet Leigh Hunt observes that a signature feature of gift books is their sumptuous binding and expensive construction. In parodying lines from Christopher Marlowe's *The Jew of Malta*, Hunt emphasizes the connection between wealth and literary annuals:

> Printed with ink with wine in it, and bound
> By fellows, as at operas, in kid gloves;
> Books bound in opal, sapphire, amethyst,
> With topaz tooling, Eden green morocco,
> That once was slippers to an emperor;[1]

An example of conspicuous consumption, gift books were sold as luxury commodities to middle-class readers who sought to demonstrate their wealth. Critics often condemned their poor literary merit and repurposing of both artwork and literary pieces, as Hunt implies:

> And full of articles of so great price,
> As one of them, indifferently written,
> And not ascribed unto a man of quality,
> Might serve, in peril of a writ of Middlesex,
> To ransom great bards from captivity.
> This is the sort of publishing for me:
> And thus, methinks, should noble booksellers
> Discrepate matters from the vulgar trade,
> And as their wealth increaseth, so inclose
> Infinite profit in a little book.

The pun on "articles" – both as valuable objects and literary works – underscores the solid earnings to be made for writers and publishers. Despite gift books' reputedly low literary value, an "indifferently written" literary work might save authors from a debtor's prison.[2] They might also allow "noble booksellers" to rise above the "vulgar trade" of commerce by promising to "ransom great bards" and securing their authors' reputations. His parody, then, satirizes the "infinite profit" to be made by writers and publishers; it also banks on the tendency of nineteenth-century readers to purchase expensive books as hallmarks of their class mobility and social status. As Samuel Goodrich explains about the books in his 1856 memoir, *Recollections of a Lifetime*, "public taste grew by feeding on these luscious gifts, and soon craved even more gorgeous works of the kind."[3]

Valued less for their literary merit than their surface appearance and opulence, gift books are truly presents of mind – not only do they reflect the giver's aesthetic taste, but they also bring to mind and make present to their readers an earlier era that resisted the shift to a more technological and commercial literary culture. As Manuela Mourão argues, gift books were "important historical artifacts of the then-present" and their authors were self-consciously preserving a society and literary aesthetic in transition, as printing technologies and social transformation were changing their world.[4] Despite the gift book's ultimate expression of capitalism, their literary works also resisted commodification by encouraging sentimental bonds. When Goodrich described gift books as the "age of annuals," he promoted their importance as "messengers of love, tokens of affection, signs and symbols of friendship."[5] Not only did sentimental bonds make gift books more personal and less commercial, but their illustrations and literary works also portrayed high Victorian views of gender, race, and class that centered on the expression of feeling. As much as the gift book reinforced emotional bonds between giver and receiver that went beyond mere commercial exchange, its writers and illustrators preserved a vision of a preindustrial world that was becoming part of the past.

In exploring the rise of gift book culture in America, I focus particularly on the writings of Lydia Huntley Sigourney (1791–1865), who capitalized on the gift book's popularity by contributing to a wide variety and compiling at least seven volumes herself.[6] Between 1828 and 1840, she published twenty-eight poems and two essays, "Martha Washington" in 1838 and "The Almshouse" in 1839, in *The Token* (1828–1834), and its successor, *The Token, and Atlantic Souvenir* (1835–1842). Placing her poems from a single annual against their accompanying illustrations affords us a unique perspective on Sigourney's desire to memorialize the antebellum era that was rapidly changing through industrialization. In this essay, I provide a general history of the gift book and its origins, and then turn to its conservative gender ideology and sentimentality, which Sigourney and other poets often used to their advantage. Sigourney's poems from *The Token*, such as "Flora's Party" (1828), "Connecticut

River" (1828), and "The Indian's Burial of His Child" (1831), provide a critique of the commercialism and social attitudes about women and Native Americans that the gift book embodied. Other poems, including "To a Fragment of Silk" (1833) and "The Ancient Family Clock" (1836), mourn the loss of individuality and the attendant sense of anonymity brought about by industrialization. In these poems, Sigourney shrewdly employs the gift book, with its wide distribution and sumptuous appearance, both for profit and to throw into high relief the difference between a spiritual economy she associated with a preindustrial, antebellum era and the often commercial values of a rapidly changing world.

"Infinite profit in a little book": The History of the Gift Book

The gift book (or literary annual, a term that is used interchangeably) originated in Europe and derived from other books, including the commonplace book, pocket book, and almanac. The commonplace book, usually handwritten, compiled information – proverbs, medical recipes, quotations, weights and measures, and other items – as a resource for later use. A precursor of the gift book, the pocket book was similar to the commonplace book and derived in the sixteenth century as *tavolette* (tablets), originally from Italy, made of slate or ivory, on which verses, household lists, and records were kept. Table books, as they were called in England, resembled the commonplace book or scrapbook filled with stray information, poems, excerpts of prose, and household lists. These table books also contained almanacs or calendars, until they were replaced by small, cheaply produced paper volumes, which proved lighter, more convenient to carry, and more affordable.

First appearing in England in the 1820s, gift books also evolved from French and German almanacs, such as *Almanach des Muses* (1765–1833) and *Musen-Almanach* (1796–1800). In 1828 Hunt commented that "[a] person may now have the old Pocket-Book, the old Almanack, and the old Tablets (in the shape of leaves of vellum) all confined in a Lilliputian book no thicker than a penny's worth of gingerbread."[7] The transition from pocket books to gift books accompanied a corresponding desire among publishers to produce expensive volumes for Victorian readers who sought decorative, tasteful gifts. As Mourão explains, the first gift book in England, *The Forget-Me-Not* (1823), was "inspired by ladies' pocket-books and almanacs of the eighteenth century – themselves a development of manuscript commonplace books owned by men and women since the Renaissance – and the first number actually contained a diary section."[8]

Whereas the older keepsake or pocket books often carried the traces of their original owners, the gift book became a popular literary anthology adapted to a mass market by eliminating the space for note taking in favor of providing a record of the previous year's literary work. In his 1912 *Literary Annuals and Gift Books*, Frederick Faxon notes that two more gift books appeared after the *The Forget-Me-Not* in 1824, and nine appeared in 1825. At the height of their production in England in 1832, sixty-three gift books appeared under different titles.[9] Laura Mandell argues about British gift books that "their short-lived status – roughly 1825–1860 – suggests that they performed the ideological work of distinguishing canonical from ephemeral poetry and then died when that distinction was finally well established."[10] By 1860, the gift book had almost entirely disappeared.

Between the 1820s and the 1860s, when gift books reached their peak of popularity in America, publishers, authors, and readers found their collaboration mutually beneficial. Although American publishers were slow to recognize the profit inherent in the gift book, their numbers eventually surpassed those in England and on the continent. *The Atlantic Souvenir*, the first literary annual in America, was published in 1826. While it is likely that the selling of British gift books competed with American volumes, their decreasing numbers in England led to a rise among gift books published in America. During their meteoric rise from 1846 to 1852, roughly sixty "gifts" appeared each year – in 1851, sixty-six were reportedly published, though by the end of the decade they had all but disappeared.[11] Among the most important annuals were *The Opal, Talisman, The Magnolia, The Gift, The Liberty Bell*, and *The Token*. American authors flocked to publish in their pages, and British authors lent prestige to American annuals and were courted for their work. As Meredith McGill argues, "while the United States held out the tantalizing possibility of a mass readership for British poets, Great Britain retained the power to confer status and prestige on American writers."[12]

Designed with elegant leather bindings and gold-embossed covers, and replete with hand-colored illustrations and engravings, gift books affirmed their owner's social class. Noting in particular the phrase Sigourney coined about the gift book, Ralph Thomson emphasizes their ornateness: "'Volumes of 'luxurious literature' (the phrase is Mrs. Lydia H. Sigourney's), they were even less a necessity than most books, and purchasers were willing to pay a good price for the luxury involved."[13] Appearing in the fall, gift books carried the date of the following year on the title page along with their actual copyright publication date – just in time for the Christmas gift-giving season. As Faxon explains, they were "gifts, tokens, souvenirs, mementos, keepsakes and offerings, or else they bore the name of some flower, plant or gem."[14] The earliest "gifts" began as duodecimos, then evolved into octavos, and finally quartos; the first gift books in America measured roughly 4.5″ to 2.75″ in size. The placement of the volume's illustrations or "embellishments," a list of which often appeared before the Table of Contents, suggested their prominence over the literary works themselves. These engravings or colored plates often evoked literary works, perhaps even served as their inspiration, and poets, such as Sigourney, occasionally illustrated the pictures with their poems.

An "inscription plate," usually colored or engraved, upon which the giver was expected to write the name of the recipient, also personalized the gift book and allowed the reader and giver to exchange messages. For example, *The Token, and Atlantic Souvenir, for 1838* contains a presentation page with a young man in a doublet with a Tyrolean hat and alpenstock, accompanied by a seated woman holding a large book and facing a lake. Framed by arching trees and a severed trunk on one side and embracing *putti* on a column on the other, the scene conveys both a Romantic landscape and the indebtedness of American authors to their European precursors. Similarly, *The Token for 1836* depicts an idealized garden with a couple in eighteenth-century dress and a fountain in the distance. An elaborate garden arch laced with climbing flowers and vines, draped with a banner and adorned with a neoclassical urn, lyre, and books, frames the scene. These presentation plates evoke Romantic or classical scenes that enshrine the past and literally "frame" the view for the reader, who gazes upon a space onto which the giver and receiver's names are inscribed. The idealization of the past in a classical era and the personal inscription allow the reader to understand that the gift book connects the reader with an era that bypasses modern commercialism.

If gift books were developed for profit, they were also meant to strengthen affective bonds among friends. Gifts – including attendant acts of sacrifice, love, generosity, and abundance – create social and emotional bonds and obligations that cannot easily be repaid. Following Marcel Mauss's seminal 1925 study, *Gift*, Hildegard Hoeller demystifies the notion that giving is purely disinterested, since it initiates a need to reciprocate that cannot be met by the receiver. On the other hand, she notes, "even while he sees the gift as self-interested, he distinguishes such self-interest from the one engendered by capitalism and commodity exchange. Thus Mauss, too, finds in the gift a hope, an antidote to capitalism's self-interested economic man."[15] Indeed, if gift books were exchanged as a token of affection, these sentiments were testified to by the frequent appearance with inscriptions of love and the personalization of their dedication pages. The older keepsakes often carried the traces of their original owners, since, as Hunt recommends, the "giver should mark his or her favourite passages throughout (as delicately as need be), and so present, as it were, the author's and the giver's minds at once."[16] Aligning the book with the giver's "mind," the book transcends its commodification by enshrining affection for the receiver.

Crucially, then, one major aesthetic shift was the emphasis on illustrations over literary works, and the inherent tension between text and image led to disparaging views about gift books among critics. Responding to the subordination of the literary text to the image, William Charvat observes that gift books "helped to give American verse a luxury status it had never had before. This was not a wholly fortunate circumstance, since it encouraged the common reader to think of verse as an appendage to sentimental pictures, but such cultural damage had begun back in the 1820s, when Philadelphia produced the first illustrated giftbooks."[17] Technological advances in printing made a mass-market audience and the commodification of poetry a reality. In the 1820s, steel engravings allowed the work of well-known artists to be reproduced: engravers scratched the design of a painting onto a black and white steel plate for twelve to sixteen hours a day by hand with a magnifying glass. Stereotype plates were reused without permission, and spurious "gifts" sprang up whenever a successful series ended, with the title changed, the date removed, and the old picture plates kept or replaced with newer ones.[18] In the face of such literary piracy, Fred Lewis Pattee suggests that "the literary morals of the fifties were loose indeed."[19] Responding to the gift book's sentimentalism and largely female audience, Pattee further disparages the gift book in terms that sexualize both its readers and the book's physical attractiveness: "the feminine buyers of books, and the masculine buyers of books for the ladies, were more concerned with the surface appearance than with their contents. The book to be bought must please the eye."[20] Sexuality – and the implicit eroticism in the gift book's lushness – combine in Pattee's description. Patricia Pulham argues that "at the heart of the annual form there lies a latent eroticism that compromises their probity," and female authors occupied a morally ambiguous place within the gift book's "implicit sensuality."[21] Lorraine Janzen Kooistra also stresses the gift book's "immense appeal for middle-class consumers . . . who had the pleasure of viewing ideal reflections of themselves in its beautiful pages."[22]

To the extent that these volumes were associated with female readers, moreover, Sigourney and other female authors contended with the view that middle-class women played a similar role as gift books in adorning and decorating their households. The sheer popularity of these volumes ensured that predominant gender ideology would be widely reproduced, and women, who received them from their fathers and husbands, would be initiated into the cultural norms of womanhood. Many titles – such as *Mourner's Chaplet, Marriage Ring, Mother's Present, Young Maiden's Mirror, Young Man's Guide*, and *Pastor's Gift* – underscore the gift book's support for proper behavior of the sexes and connect them to domestic life.[23] Sentimental images of young women and children also abounded. Isabelle Lehuu explains that "the importance of female portraiture in gift books is particularly striking given the fact that, by contrast, men far outnumbered women in portrait collections of the nineteenth century."[24] "The Gift," an illustration for *The Token, for 1829*, portrays a young woman in a garden who is adorned with flowers in her hair and holds a basket in her elbow while displaying a rose in her hands [Fig. 5]. Associated with nature, youth, and fertility, the woman also offers a flower, a token of love, to connect with the reader. An anonymous poem, "The Gift," which accompanies the illustration, affirms the view that sentiments and gift books were meant to be exchanged: the speaker describes the flower as "a gift" that may "wile a weary hour" and "touch" the reader's heart, but its message will also serve as "[a] token of love from me to thee."[25] Similarly, middle-class women were meant to adorn the home and guarantee the values of love and domestic life outside the venue for exchange and commerce.

"To ransom great bards from captivity": Sigourney's Poems and Gift Book Illustrations

In turning to Sigourney's poems in *The Token*, we might understand her gift book publications as a way to preserve a white, middle-class New England culture during a time of rapid technological change. While Sigourney idealized the era and region of her youth, she also recognized that the gift book's advances in printing and illustrating would make her a tidy profit and expand her literary reputation. Gender and genre are central themes and consistent with the view that the gift book is the repository for women's and children's roles in the home. The portrayal of Native Americans, whose romanticized depictions appear frequently, also highlights race as a prominent theme of the gift book. Building on sentimental imagery throughout these works, Sigourney portrays nostalgia for the past and subtly

Figure 5. A. E. Chalon, painter, and G. B. Ellis, engraver, "The Gift," *The Token: A Christmas and New Year's Present*, Nathaniel Parker Willis, ed. (Boston: S. G. Goodrich, 1828). Yale Collection of American Literature, Beinecke Rare Book Room and Manuscript Library, Yale University.

registers the often tragic and alienating effects of capitalism and industrialization on her era.

Sigourney satirizes social posturing in "Flora's Party," from *The Token for 1828*, as part of her larger desire to preserve antebellum values. As Paula Bennett notes, in "Flora's Party" Sigourney wittily "makes pointed fun of the affectations of the class to which she – like her readers – belonged" – namely, the "nouveau genteel values" that made her an aspiring member of the middle-classes and a figure often satirized.[26] "Flora's Party" seems, in many ways, to be ideal gift book verse, since the floral images appear to endorse the sentimental association between women and flowers. Yet its light, satirical tone sends up the pretentions of middle-class society with which she was familiar; describing a tea party with flowers as guests, Sigourney attacks the characteristic attitudes of each of Lady Flora's visitors: "prudish Miss Lily, with bosom of snow," turns away from suitors and "retired in a fright," whereas others, "Dandy Coxcombs and Daffodils," flaunt their appearance in "their dazzling new vests, and their corsets laced tight."[27] By inviting flowers "of every degree," Flora ensures a display of avarice, pride, and ambition that Sigourney deploys to satirize the social posturing of her era. One entertaining scene appears in the guests' reaction to the artworks that decorate Flora's salon:

> There were pictures, whose splendor illumined the place
> Which Flora had finish'd with exquisite grace;
> She had dipp'd her free pencil in Nature's pure dyes,
> And Aurora retouch'd with fresh purple the skies.
> So the grave connoisseurs hasted near them to draw,
> Their knowledge to show, by detecting a flaw.
> The Carnation took her eye-glass from her waist,
> And pronounced they were 'not in good keeping or taste';
> While prim Fleur de Lis, in her robe of French silk,
> And magnificent Calla, with mantle like milk,
> Of the Louvre recited a wonderful tale,
> And said, "Guido's rich tints made dame Nature turn pale."

By contrasting Flora's "free pencil" and the tints of "Nature's pure dyes" with the works of old European masters, Sigourney makes the critical remarks of social dames and their artifice all the more ridiculous and mocks the "grave connoisseurs" who apply their narrow, prudish standards to Flora's art. While she aims to make their social affectations laughable, she also partakes of an important ongoing debate within American art. In his "Preface", published in *The Token* in 1830 Samuel Goodrich highlights his decision to use six "original paintings" by American artists and endorse the use of "American talent only."[28] Clearly, Sigourney echoes Goodrich's nationalist aims in her satirical choice to elevate the natural composition of Flora over Fleur de Lis and Calla's rendition of Guido's painting in the Louvre.

In contrast to Sigourney's rejection of the social climbing satirized in "Flora's Party," "Connecticut River" (and its accompanying illustration) memorialize and celebrate the past. Democratic antebellum values are typified, albeit idealized, in Sigourney's portrayal of the river and its inhabitants:

> FAIR river! not unknown to classic song,
> Which still in varying beauty roll'st along
> . . .
> Though broader streams our sister realms may boast,
> More ancient cities, and a bolder coast,
> Yet from the bound where hoarse St. Lawrence roars
> To where La Plata laves the tropic shores,
> From where the arms of slimy Nilus shine
> To the blue waters of the rushing Rhine,
> Or where Ilissus glows like diamond spark,
> Or sacred Ganges whelms her votaries dark,
> No brighter skies the eye of day may see,
> Nor soil more verdant, nor a race more free.[29]

By invoking six ancient and New World rivers on four continents – the St. Lawrence on the border of the United States and Canada, La Plata in Uruguay, the Nile in Egypt, Rhine in Germany, Ilissus in Greece, and Ganges in India – Sigourney connects America to its "sister realms" abroad and, as Gary Kelly notes, conspicuously avoids mentioning that the Connecticut River was heavily used for commerce.[30] An illustration, "Scenery on the Connecticut River," also captures the idealized values of an earlier time. [Fig. 6] Two boats travel down the river, without any steamship or industrial commerce evident, flanked by hills and cliffs on both sides, while a man with a wooden leg and crutch and wearing a tricorner hat, a reminder of the war, walks with his dog. A note in the "Preface" acknowledges the composition's fantasy nature as "rather a Study from scenery on Connecticut River than a real view."[31]

Sigourney and *The Token*'s illustrators were self-consciously promoting an image of a utopian landscape that bypassed the commercialism of her era, yet in "Connecticut River" a distinct tension exists between commercial life and antebellum values. Thrift, industry, and a lack of affectation are extolled in "a race more free." Women and men share

Figure 6. A. Fisher, painter, and G. B. Ellis, engraver, "Scenery on Connecticut River," *The Token: A Christmas and New Year's Present*, Nathaniel Parker Willis, ed. (Boston: S. G. Goodrich, 1828). Yale Collection of American Literature, Beinecke Rare Book Room and Manuscript Library, Yale University.

equal responsibility and opportunity to thrive financially, as the farmer enlists "his thrifty mate, solicitous to bear / An equal burden in the yoke of care, / With vigorous arm the flying shuttle heaves, / Or from the press the golden cheese receives." Signs of temporality emerge as part of industrialization: here, the passage of time appears as "the warning clock its summons swells" for children to go to school. Their forgetfulness in nature disappears when "Till by some traveller's wheels aroused from play, / The stiff salute, with face demure, they pay, / Bare the curl'd brow, or stretch the ready hand, / The untutor'd homage of an artless land." Visitors from outside the community threaten its ideal existence. Similarly, the lack of memorial for the Native Americans highlights their absence ("Lo! here they rest, who every danger braved, / Unmark'd, untrophied, 'mid the soil they saved"). Emigration westward has led to a changing landscape, as the poem ends with an "exiled man" and "sad mother" who nostalgically recount their early lives on the river to their children. Sigourney's "Connecticut River" depends on her recollection of those whose lives have been erased by historical progress and her awareness that the utopian setting she describes had largely disappeared.

Other poems of Sigourney's, and their coupling with particular illustrations, reflect the desire to construct a counter-national narrative, supplanting the colonization of America by Europeans with Native American origins. In "The Indian's Burial of His Child," which appeared in *The Token, for 1831*, Sigourney portrays a father who consigns his child to join his recently buried mother, who died in childbirth, as he reasons that his child may suffer in a nomadic life: "Fate bids me wander wide, / Far from my home and thee; / Where'er the wild deer seeks to hide, / There must my covert be."[32] Much as the "life-stream perished at [the child's] birth" with his mother's death, the speaker argues, would not the child do better to consign himself to his "bed of earth" before "Famine's blight is shed" upon him? The speaker, who is doubly bereft, bemoans the thought of his child suffering from hunger: "How could I see thee pine, / And yet no aid bestow? / Nor flock nor cultured field are mine, / How could I bear thy wo?" Sigourney acknowledges the demise of the Indian – a fact that she underscored by providing an epigraph from an ethnographical study of Native Americans contending that nursing children were occasionally buried with their mothers. It is perhaps not surprising that Sigourney's poem invokes sentimental bonding between mothers and children as the gift book often depicted maternal love, yet the emphasis on shared feelings encouraged her middle-class readers to immerse themselves in a contested political debate about Indian removal and connect with the fate of Native Americans.

The illustrations in *The Token* depicting Native Americans also disrupt the predominant nationalist narrative of America, as technology invades and offers evidence of a culture in transition. In "The First Steamboat on the Missouri," an engraving from the *The Token for 1839* from a painting by John Gadsby Chapman, one Native American sits on a rock disconsolately and the other has his arms upraised in warning or supplication toward a distant steamship, as if predicting the destruction to their people that colonization would bring. [Fig. 7] The steamship appears at a distance and embodies the technology that made commerce and travel, as well as the gift book and other forms of print culture, possible. Situating the illustration's viewer from a point on the coast behind the figures, we are encouraged to consider their viewpoint, rather than that of those aboard the commercial steamboat, and to act as witnesses to the tragic scene unfolding before us. In fact, the Native Americans offer two contested – and distinctly opposing – positions with respect to the invading white settlers: submit or rebel. The nostalgic

Figure 7. J. G. Chapman, painter, and J. Andrews, engraver, "The First Steamboat on the Missouri," *The Token and Atlantic Souvenir: A Christmas and New Year's Present*, Samuel G. Goodrich, ed. (Boston: American Stationer's Association, 1838.) Yale Collection of American Literature, Beinecke Rare Book Room and Manuscript Library, Yale University.

view of Native Americans acts as a fitting harbinger to Sigourney of the disappearance of Native Americans and registers the impact of technology on her generation.

In "To a Fragment of Silk" and "The Ancient Family Clock," Sigourney's nostalgia for an earlier era also offers a critique of capitalism in a form that middle-class readers could purchase. "To a Fragment of Silk," published in *The Token* in 1833, aptly summarizes her concerns about a rapidly industrializing age and the commercial interests that drove the economy. Accusing the scrap of idleness, she chides it for being silent: "Well, radiant shred of silk, is it your choice, / Here on my carpet, thus at ease to lay? / I've heard the veriest trifles have a voice / Unto the musing mind; what can you say?"[33] Tracing its origins to "those unsightly worms, with tireless maws / And such a very marvelous digestion," she claims that their own manufacture of silk and sericin (a naturally produced substance that hardens into threads once in contact with air) predicts their own demise: "Their spinning wheels, no doubt, their health supply; / But lo! in cone-like urns they fold themselves to die."

Gary Kelly has noted that this poem, along with several other "rag" poems including "To a Shred of Linen" and "To a Fragment of Cotton," wittily traces the fragment from its European origins to its agricultural roots and early manufacture in America.[34] Sigourney would have been familiar with the sericulture in Mansfield and later Manchester, Connecticut, both located near her home in Hartford. Ezra Stiles, a minister, physician, and the President of Yale from 1778 to 1794, promoted sustainable agriculture of mulberry trees to encourage the silkworm industry and distributed seeds to each parish in the state, anticipating 5,000 trees eventually would be grown, yielding, in twenty years, one and a half million pounds of silk per year.[35] In Mansfield, sericulture grew in the 1780s as a home-based industry, until a mill was built that turned and twisted silk thread and mechanized the process in 1829.[36] In Manchester, silk production became an industrial venture through the efforts of Frank and Ward Cheney, two brothers who patented a machine for doubling, twisting, and winding silk; they eventually grew silk production into a profitable industry that allowed one girl to monitor three machines simultaneously.[37]

"To a Fragment of Silk" foretells the alienating effect of capitalism. "Bound on a voyage o'er the boisterous ocean" and "snugly packed in bales," the silk originated in Italy and partakes of the same transatlantic exchange that enabled the rise of commerce and manufacture in the New World:

> What was your destiny in this New World?
> In dazzling robe to make young beauty vain?
> Or for some waning lady pranked and curled
> To hide time's ravage from the giddy train?
> Or bid pale Envy's pang the bosom swell,
> That erring deems true bliss with outward show doth swell.
>
> Your history's not complete. Your second birth
> Is in bank-paper, to allure the eyes,
> Making the rich o'erprize the gifts of earth,
> And the poor covet what his God denies:
> Man's vanity from a vile worm may grow,
> And paper puff his pride; go, gaudy fragment, go!

Sigourney ponders the results of the silk manufacturing process in America: is its "destiny" to flatter the young with a "dazzling robe"? Or to let "some waning lady pranked and curled . . . hide time's ravage from the giddy train?" As a luxury item, silk might well have appealed to a "waning lady" or a "young beauty" of means, its popularity ensuring, Sigourney feared, the demise of the previous generation's republican values. Not incidentally, the gift book's origins in Europe also prefigure its appearance in America and appeal to its readers through its appearance. While she holds out the possibility for change – "Your history's not complete" – silk has a "second birth" in "bank-paper, to allure the eyes / Making the rich o'erprize the gifts of earth." Similar to the gift book's attractive exterior, silk tempts its admirers with a gaudy show, and its ornate surface leads the wearer to focus on material wealth, much as writing might increase an author's vanity within the literary marketplace: "Man's vanity from a vile worm may grow, / And paper puffs his pride; go, gaudy fragment, go!" "Puffing" implies that the work of authors has similar potential to gain value within a material economy of industrialization and commercialization. A review of *The Token* from 1836 condemns editors and publishers for falsely praising gift books: "It is a pity that some efficient method could not be adopted to do away with the present system of indiscriminate puffery."[38] When authors such as Sigourney wrote for gift books that relied on "puffs" to sell, they were subject to the same market forces that encouraged rapid publishing to meet their readers' demand, often at the expense of their literary reputation.

Finally, Sigourney's "The Ancient Family Clock," published in *The Token, for 1837*, memorializes the passing of an era through a machine – a fitting subject for the gift book, which saw its rise based on mass-produced printing. In the opening lines, the speaker personifies the clock, an "old friend" with its "honest face" and "gilded figures," reminiscing about her youth and listening to its "busy heart beat on."[39] Although she recounts family highlights – the meeting of young lovers, birth of children, and growth of young adults – that occurred in the home, the machine has remained unchanged. Through Sigourney's use of echoic phrases, such as "'*tick, tick*,'" the clock takes on a life of its own, and its very presence warns the listener of the passing of time. Sigourney suggests that the clock influences our view of human beings as automatons and machine-like, and, at the same time, she invokes the clock as a symbol of an older, more authentic kind of manufacture, similar to that which she extols in "To a Fragment of Silk." In "The Ancient Family Clock," timepieces offer evidence of both human skill and an older spiritual economy. The new-born's hearing catches the "quick vibrations" of the clock, which "didst wake the new-born thought," extending an analogy between the clock's machinery and the child's body, as the nurse observes "the body's growing wealth, / And prais'd that fair machine of clay." Similarly, the clock has witnessed tales that "lovers told / Into the thrilling ear, / Till midnight's witching hour wax'd old" and the clock sounds "to warn how Time / Outliveth Love, boasting itself divine, / Yet fading like the wreath which its fond votaries twine." Heralding the arrival of a new child or impending marriage, the clock becomes part of its family's celebrations and outlasts all its inhabitants. In doing so, she implies that art, like the clock, surpasses the creator who made the object:

> Thou has outlived thy maker, ancient clock!
> He in his cold grave sleeps, – but thy slight wheels
> Still do his bidding, yet his frailty mock,
> While o'er his name, oblivion steals:
> Oh Man! so prodigal of pride and praise,
> Thy works survive thee, – dead machines perform
> Their revolution, while thy scythe-shorn days
> Yield thee a powerless prisoner to the worm –
> Thou darest to sport with Time, – while he
> Consigns thee sternly to Eternity.
> Make peace! – make peace with Him, who rules above the storm.

Presenting a sumptuous exterior to the world, the clock tempts us to value material wealth over spiritual values. Shira Wolosky contends that in "The Ancient Clock," "each object teaches its lesson, usually on the vanity of material things (even as the many precious objects attest to their allure)."[40] Precisely issuing a warning against the allure of capitalism, Sigourney animates the clock to remind her generation that "dead machines" may surpass their creators in a "revolution" that leads to the decline of spiritual values.

As my analysis of the history of the gift book and Sigourney's contributions to it suggest, Sigourney used the gift book both to contribute to the construction of a national identity and to memorialize the passing of antebellum, preindustrial America. With its sumptuous exteriors and finely engraved illustrations, the gift book promised its readers a corresponding rise in social class through its pages and its enshrined dominant views about the roles of women and children. While capitalizing on such features that made the gift book so popular, Sigourney challenged these views by promoting the values of an earlier era. The gift book's importance lay not only in solidifying the canon by supplying readers with tasteful verse, but also in recording the tensions that arose when literary production shifted to a mass-market audience.

Notes

1. Leigh Hunt, "Pocket Books and Keepsakes," *Spenser and the Tradition: English Poetry 1579–1830: A Gathering of Texts, Bibliography, and Criticism* (online database: http://spenserians.cath.vt.edu), David Radcliffe (ed.), (Virginia Tech University, February 2006). Christopher Marlowe's *The Jew of Malta* (1589–1590) recounts the story of Barabas, a merchant whose jewels and treasures entitle him "[t]o ransom great kinds from captivity . . . And thus, methinks, should men of judgment frame / Their means of traffic from the vulgar trade, / And their wealth increaseth, so inclose / Infinite riches in a little room" (I.i.33–37).
2. Hunt's reference to the Bill of Middlesex, a legal fiction beginning around 1550 in England, underscores the value of gift books in securing an author's finances. By claiming a person trespassed in the county of Middlesex, where the Court of King's Bench held sway, the accused could be taken into custody, the trespassing complaint dropped, and another charge of debt introduced.
3. Samuel Goodrich, *Recollections of a Lifetime: Men and Things I Have Seen, in a Series of Familiar Letters to a Friend, Historical, Biographical, Anecdotal, and Descriptive*, vol. 2. (New York and Auburn: Miller, Orton and Mulligan, 1856), 260–261.
4. Manuela Mourão, "The Remembrance of Things Past: Literary Annuals' Self-Historicization," *Victorian Poetry* 50.1 (Spring 2012), 108.
5. Goodrich, *Recollections of a Lifetime*, 260.
6. The volumes to which Sigourney contributed include *The Atlantic Souvenir, The Memorial* of 1827, *The Legendary*, and *A Present for All Seasons: The Waverly Garland* of 1853; religiously inclined ones, such as *The Religious Souvenir* (for which she served as editor in 1838–1839) and *Beauties of Sacred Literature* of 1848; and annuals for children, such as *Youth's Keepsake* in 1831, among others. Pattee notes that Sigourney compiled seven gift books in the 1850s, a decade he refers to as "a veritable swamp of furbelowed sentimentalism." Fred Louis Pattee, *The Feminine Fifties* (New York: D. Appleton-Century, 1940), 284.
7. Hunt, "Pocket Books and Keepsakes."
8. Mourão, "The Remembrance of Things Past," 107.
9. Frederick W. Faxon, *Literary Annuals and Gift-Books: A Bibliography with a Descriptive Introduction*, The Boston Book Company, 1912, xi.
10. Laura Mandell, "Felicia Hemans and the Gift-Book Aesthetic," *Cardiff Corvey: Reading the Romantic Text* 6.1 (June 2001). Available online: www.cf.ac.uk/encap/corvey/articles/cc06_n01.html [accessed May 26, 2015].
11. Faxon, *Literary Annuals and Gift-Books*, xii.
12. Meredith L. McGill, "Introduction: The Traffic in Poems," *The Traffic in Poems: Nineteenth-Century Poetry and Transatlantic Exchange* (New Brunswick: Rutgers University Press, 2008), 5.

13. Ralph Thompson, *American Literary Annuals & Giftbooks* (New York: H. W. Wilson, Company, 1936), 9.
14. Faxon, *Literary Annuals and Gift-Books*, xv.
15. Hildegard Hoeller, *From Gift to Commodity: Capitalism and Sacrifice in Nineteenth-Century American Fiction* (Durham: University of New Hampshire Press, 2012), 8.
16. Hunt, "Pocket Books and Keepsakes."
17. William Charvat, *Literary Publishing in America, 1790–1850* (Philadelphia: University of Pennsylvania Press, 1959), 35.
18. Faxon, *Literary Annuals and Gift-Books*, xvii–xviii.
19. Pattee, *The Feminine Fifties*, 285.
20. Ibid., 275.
21. Patricia Pulham, "'Jewels—delights—perfect loves': Victorian Women Poets and the Annuals," *Victorian Women Poets*, Alison Chapman (ed.), (Cambridge, England: D. S. Brewer, 2003), 15.
22. Lorraine Janzen Kooistra, "Home Thoughts and Home Scenes: Packaging Middle-Class Childhood for Christmas Consumption," *The Nineteenth-Century Child and Consumer Culture*, Dennis Denisoff (ed.), (Hampshire: Ashgate Press, 2008), 154.
23. Faxon, *Literary Annuals and Gift-Books*, xv.
24. Isabelle Lehuu, *Carnival on the Page: Popular Print Media in Antebellum America* (Chapel Hill: University of North Carolina, 2000), 93–94.
25. "The Gift," *The Token: A Christmas and New Year's Present*, Nathaniel Parker Willis (ed.), (Boston: S. G. Goodrich, 1828), 1–2. Lehuu describes the gift book as "a 'transvalued' object. ... Giftbooks held more than an economic value in the market economy of nineteenth-century publishing." Lehuu, *Carnival on the Page*, 91.
26. Paula Bernat Bennett, "Laughing all the Way to the Bank: Female Sentimentalists in the Marketplace, 1825–1850," *Studies in American Humor* 3 (2002), 14.
27. Sigourney, "Flora's Party," *Nineteenth-Century American Women Poets: An Anthology*, Paula Bernat Bennett (ed.), (Malden: Blackwell Publishers, 1998), 8–12. The poem originally appeared in *The Token, for 1828*.
28. S. G. Goodrich, "Preface," *The Token: A Christmas Present*, S. G. Goodrich (ed.), (Boston: Carter and Hendee, 1830), v.
29. Sigourney, "Connecticut River," *Lydia Sigourney: Selected Poetry and Prose*, Gary Kelly (ed.), (Peterborough: Broadview Press, 2008), 141–145. The poem originally appeared in *The Token, for 1828*.
30. Kelly, *Lydia Sigourney: Selected Poetry and Prose*, 141n5.
31. S. G. Goodrich, "Preface," *The Token; a Christmas and New Year's Present*, S. G. Goodrich (ed.), (Boston: S. G. Goodrich, 1828), v.
32. Lydia Sigourney, "The Indian's Burial of His Child," *The Token, for 1831*, S. G. Goodrich (ed.), (Boston: Gray & Bowen, 1830), 184–186.
33. Lydia Sigourney, "To a Fragment of Silk," *The Token, for 1834*, S. G. Goodrich (ed.), (Boston: Gray & Bowen, 1833), 335–336.

34. Kelly, *Lydia Sigourney: Selected Poetry and Prose*, 107n2.
35. Kim MacDonald, "Silk in Connecticut," *Northampton Silk Project*, Smith College, 26 August 2002. Available online: www.smith.edu/hsc/silk/papers/macdonald.html (accessed December 21, 2015).
36. MacDonald, "Silk in Connecticut."
37. Ibid.
38. Anonymous, [probably by Park Benjamin], Review of *The Token* for 1836 *New England Magazine* (October 1835): 294.
39. Sigourney, "The Ancient Family Clock," *The Token, for 1837*, S. G. Goodrich (ed.), (Boston: Gray & Bowen, 1836), 208–211.
40. Shira Wolosky, "Modest Claims," *Cambridge History of American Literature*, Sacvan Bercovitch (ed.), vol. 4 (Cambridge: Cambridge University Press, 2004), 169.

CHAPTER 6

The Friendship Elegy

Desirée Henderson

A stock image from nineteenth-century visual culture shows a female mourner graveside: head bent, face veiled, clothed in black – setting, posture, and dress serving to encapsulate the predominant cultural view that grief was a feminized emotional experience and mourning an activity appropriately performed by women. [Fig. 8] Female poets of the period might have understandably felt constrained by this image and the expectations it represented, yet, for the most part, they embraced the gendered associations of mourning, turning stereotype into a vehicle for entrance into the esteemed literary tradition of the elegy. Changing cultural practices around death provided women writers with an opportunity to promote themselves as authorities on grief and commemoration, taking up sentimental tropes to represent women's experiences. In doing so, they necessarily rewrote many of the conventions of the elegy, turning elegiac modes to their own purposes and developing new criteria for evaluating the work of literary memorial.

These interventions are pronounced in the friendship elegy, a subgenre of the elegy that demonstrates how generic conventions could be leveraged to promote the status of women's relationships and women's writing. The friendship elegy is characterized by a wide temporal range, treating the event of death as a prompt to re-examine the past of the deceased and to imagine the future of her mourners. The friendship elegy highlights the different forms that women's relationships with other women could take and offers up a variety of roles for its characters and readers to inhabit. Though focused principally upon the dead, the friendship elegy could also turn the occasion of loss into an opportunity to address social issues, including the ways in which gendered norms threatened female friendships and inhibited the expression of female same-sex eroticism. What is offered as consolation is authorship itself. The friendship elegy invokes the mirror-sameness of a shared gender identity to not only communicate the deep kinship between speaker and deceased, but to enable a process of

Figure 8. "The Soldier's Memorial," Currier and Ives, 1863. Library of Congress, Prints & Photographs Division, LC-DIG-pga-05018.

substitution whereby the poet symbolically takes the place of her deceased friend. In this way, the friendship elegy engages in a self-reflexive form of literary criticism that makes the female poet and her writing into a living memorial for the dead.

Although nineteenth-century women's elegiac writing took many forms – including tributes to beloved family members, encomiums for prominent political leaders, pastoral portraits of memorial spaces and monuments, and psychologically complex depictions of the experience of death from the perspective of the dying or deceased – the child elegy is the most commonly recognized of these forms, considered by many to exemplify the sentimental mode that dominated both women's writing and cultural mourning practices in the period. For example, Joanne Dobson cites Lydia Sigourney's "Death of an Infant" as exhibiting the principle themes of sentimental literature: the terrifying threat of separation and the durability of human bonds despite such threats.[1] Sigourney's poem portrays the moment that a child's death occurs, a moment so terrible that even a personified Death recoils from his work. Other child elegies from this period focus on the effect of such losses upon mothers and their struggle to accept the divine hand behind the seemingly senseless deaths of their children. In "'Twas but a Babe," for example, Sigourney exhorts a mother to "trust / Your treasure to His arms, whose changeless care / Passeth a mother's love."[2] Yet, in many of these poems, the surviving mother is caught in a temporal bind between the rupturing moment of death, from which she cannot move on, and what Dana Luciano calls the "future-directedness" of Christian consolation.[3] While child elegies present a comforting picture of familial reunion in the afterlife, this promise is often unrealized as the poems themselves remain fixated upon the moment of loss. According to Elizabeth Petrino, this vision of heavenly reconciliation also promotes a conservative message with regards to gender roles, limiting the speaker of the poem to the singular and permanent identity of mourning mother.[4] Although the complex structure and socio-political content of child elegies has gained new appreciation from contemporary feminist critics, for many readers and scholars these poems embody the worst aspects of early women's poetry – a critical evaluation that all too often prevents a full appreciation of women's elegiac writing.[5]

While the child elegy is a significant form of elegy, it represents only a fraction of the multi-generic body of consolation literature that proliferated during the height of the sentimental cult of mourning, including mourning guidebooks, posthumous biographies, portraits of the afterlife, and more.[6] These texts teach us that although the death of a child was recognized as a tragic loss, it was no more worthy of literary commemoration than many other kinds of loss, including the death of a friend. S. Irenaeus Prime's *The Smitten Household*, an 1856 mourning manual, was divided into five categories of loss – child, wife, husband, parent, and friend – that clearly ranked the death of a friend as equivalent in significance to the deaths of family members and children.[7] Anthologies of mourning literature are also full of poems and other devotional texts about the deaths of friends, advising readers on the proper etiquette for expressing grief in such instances. Thus, both literary history and cultural practice point us toward the conclusion that the elegy was called upon to serve many purposes, and among these was to commemorate the loss of friends. My discussion of the friendship elegy over the following pages seeks to reconsider this form of the elegy tradition and particularly how it presented women writers with literary, rhetorical, and socio-political opportunities that are not evident within the child elegy, notably in its promotion of a wide range of temporalities and female identities.

Whereas many child elegies are fixed upon the singular moment of death, elegies on the loss of female friends display a temporal expansiveness – an ability to range across the life of the deceased and to project forward past the moment of death, toward a future act of memorial. From the moment of death, most friendship elegies turn back and look over the friend's life from childhood before following her through what were understood to be the defining moments of female experience (marriage, motherhood, etc.). In this sense, the friendship elegy partakes of the conventions of the funeral sermon and the eulogy, both of which depict the deceased individual's actions and achievements in life as testament to why she is worth remembering in death. For example, Sigourney's "The Lost Friend" opens with an account of her friend's birth and idyllic childhood, then follows her through her "maturer years."[8] Sigourney praises the deceased for her fulfillment of conventional gender roles, writing that she made "her household, and her own sweet life / Alike a model" and claiming for her the status of an "angel-presence shrin'd in clay" even while she lived. The poem turns at the end from this extended encomium of the living woman and toward the fact of her death with a simple "but": "But now her pleasant mansion . . . is desolate." The close proximity of life and death is reinforced by the poet's transformation of the deceased's possessions into keepsakes: "The chair / Is vacant, where so oft we saw her sit / . . . There are her garments as she laid them down." This poignant invocation of home turned memorial allows Sigourney to arrive at the consolatory promise of the afterlife. However, the poem closes with a move typical in friendship elegies: projecting the poet herself into the future. The loss of the friend prompts not only a look back at the deceased friend's life, but also a look forward to the life of the poet and fellow mourners: "So in our hearts some blessed trait to keep / Of her example, that we may not lose / The teachings of her life, or of our tears."

The proliferation of time begun by the process of remembrance exceeds the span of the deceased individual's life, creating a temporal gap that is filled by the living poet-mourner.

The friendship elegy also places emphasis upon the variety and variability of female friendships. Instead of restricting its female characters to singular roles, such as the mourning mother depicted in many child elegies, friendship elegies celebrate the diverse forms that women's relationships with other women might take: sororal, tutelary, erotic, textual. The first of these is sisterhood, a commonly referenced bond that was intended to legitimize the relationship between poet and deceased, rewriting what may have been seen as mere friendship as a profound, familial bond. This invocation of sorority frequently takes the form of flower imagery, depicting speaker and subject as intertwined plants: British poet Felicia Hemans, who was widely read and influential in the United States, writes of "sister flowers of one sweet shade / With the same breeze that bend."[9] Similarly, Amelia Welby writes that "Like flowers that softly bloom together … So were we linked unto each other / Sweet sisters, in our childish hours."[10] Such botanical imagery simultaneously invokes the pastoral conventions of the traditional male elegy and the feminized "language of flowers" that pervaded nineteenth-century women's writing in order to naturalize the sisterhood of women.[11] For instance, Sarah Helen Whitman's "She Blooms No More" characterizes the relationship between speaker and subject as one consecrated by their shared childhood in an imagined natural setting. The poet addresses the deceased as "one who shared with me in youth / Life's sunshine and its flowers," an image of kinship that blurs the line between biological sisterhood and friends who are close enough to be sisters.[12] However, the speaker's attitude toward the allure of nature has been altered by loss: "I dread to see the summer sun / … And early pansies, one by one / … They speak to me of one who sleeps in death." The poem ends on a surprisingly pessimistic note that resists the scenes of natural beauty that are portrayed throughout:

> They speak of things that once have been,
> But never more can be:
> And earth all decked in smiles again
> Is still a waste to me.

Although the botanical imagery of the poem reinforces the strength of sororal ties between speaker and deceased, nature fails to provide consolation. Instead, environmental cycles of growth, decay, and rebirth stand in opposition to the permanence of human death. Although in many poems seasonal renewal allegorizes the mourning process, in Whitman's poem the promise of consolation is blocked by the poet's persistent state of loss, effectively communicating the depth of grief that the death of the sister-friend provokes.

Another commonly invoked female relationship that appears within the friendship elegy is that of teacher and student. As with the language of sisterhood, the tutelary relationship serves to affirm the significance of the bond between speaker and deceased, characterizing the speaker according to a familiar and accepted social position in order to legitimate her right to mourn for and represent the dead. Departing from the characteristic hierarchical distinction between teacher and student, these poems depict the relationship as one of intimate and guiding friendship. For example, in the early years of the nineteenth century, Susanna Rowson penned several elegies for students of her young ladies' academy. Rowson's "On the Death of Miss Juliana Knox" imagines a personified, female Religion who marks the names of the deceased in a "magic volume" as confirmation of their entrance into heaven, a symbolic reference to the poet's work to preserve the memory of the dead.[13] Tributes to deceased students also form a substantial subset of Sigourney's writing, such as the section titled "My Dead" in her *Letters to My Pupils*, which includes biographical sketches of and elegies for twenty-six deceased students.[14] Sigourney's poem "Attending a Former Pupil to the Grave" opens with a direct address of the dead – "Daughter, I will not leave thee" – that layers a mother–child relationship across the teacher–student bond.[15] The poem looks back to the earliest days that the pupil inhabited the teacher's schoolroom before moving on to the time that she grew to be the speaker's friend. The special status of their relationship is evident in the depiction of the funeral at which "Stranger and friend sweep on / In long procession," while the poet proclaims "I am near." This condemnation of hurried, indifferent mourners elevates the poet's commitment to fulfilling the rites of remembrance: "I'll be the last to leave. O, be first / To welcome me above." The poet's tender care of the dead facilitates a promised reunion in the afterlife, concluding with an image of a future that is defined by the poet rather than the elegiac subject. Mary Loeffelholz argues that Sigourney's sense of herself as a teacher-poet granted her the authority to instruct and advise her readers, long after she was no longer in the classroom.[16] As this poem demonstrates, the role of teacher also extends beyond the boundary of the grave. Within the friendship elegy, sister, teacher, and friend are among the complimentary roles that enable the poet to fulfill her commitments to the deceased through acts of dedication and self-sacrifice that constitute a new identity as representative for the dead.

By centering on women's relationships with other women, the friendship elegy transforms mourning into an opportunity to represent the gendered and eroticized dimensions of those relationships. Indeed, the ways in which the friendship elegy was employed to comment upon heterosexual marriage and to represent homosexual desire recasts the genre as a whole, revealing an engagement with the cultural contexts that shaped women's friendships. The use of the genre for socio-political purposes comes into focus in mock-elegiac poems that adapt the language of elegy to describe the metaphorical "death" of a friendship because one friend marries, thereby equating marriage to death. In such poems, heterosexual marriage is depicted as tragically and irrevocably altering the homosocial link between poet and subject, an occasion of loss as deep and profound as a death. For instance, Annis Boudinot Stockton's commonplace book contains two poems titled "Tears of Friendship"; the first is subtitled "Elegy . . . to a friend just married, and who had promised to write, on parting, but had neglected it."[17] The second poem depicts the "pang severe" and the "tender falling tear" provoked by the friend's failure to honor her ties to the poet after she has married. Similarly, Emma Embury's "Stanzas, Addressed to a Friend on her Marriage" mourns for a friend's marriage in elegiac terms:

> Could I hear thy deep vow spoken
> Without a thought of pain,
> When I felt the best link broken
> In friendship's golden chain?[18]

The speaker struggles to appropriately align her emotions to the joyful occasion, acknowledging that her sorrow is "selfish" and exhorting herself to remember that "thou are happy!" Yet, when the speaker bids farewell to her friend, it is with a finality that evokes the grave: "Farewell, farewell, beloved one." The use of such heightened language to describe the end of female friendship serves as commentary upon heterosexual marriage and particularly the laws of coverture, which resulted in the "social death" of a woman whose legal identity was replaced by her husband's. If these poems tell us something about marriage, they also tell us something about the friendship elegy as a genre in which the special unions between women could be represented and celebrated. Even as they mourn for relationships lost, they present a vision of same-sex intimacy formed by shared lives and emotional connection. Embury writes,

> I've loved thee in thy sorrow,
> I'll love thee still in joy:

Time could not change our friendship, –
Shall absence it destroy?

The question mark at the end opens up the hopeful possibility that female friendship may survive despite the losses occasioned by marriage.

The affirmation of homosocial bonds in the friendship elegy also speaks to the homoerotic or homosexual nature of some female friendships. The deep intimacy portrayed in the elegies above is revealed to have a sexual and erotic dimension in poems such as Grace Greenwood's "To –, In Absence," which invokes the elegiac language of loss to represent the end of a love relationship.[19] Following the conventions of the friendship elegy, the poem begins by looking back upon an idyllic past, in this case when the poet first met her beloved. Greenwood's imagery evokes female eroticism as she writes of how the lover "didst smite the cold, defying rock, / And full and fast the living waters gushed."[20] The use of coded, natural language to represent sexual experience was common in nineteenth-century women's poetry, as Greenwood here signifies female genital response through the image of gushing waters. Although the gender identities of both poet and beloved remain unspecified, the absence of phallic or masculine imagery and the repeated references to water, tides, and blooming gardens Suggest that the poem depicts a lesbian experience.

If the poem portrays a joyful, same-sex union in the opening stanzas, the jubilant tone is short-lived, as an unspecified shadow falls across the lovers:

The cloud that darkened long our sky of love,
And flung a shadow o'er life's Eden bloom,
Hath deepened into night, around, above, –
But night beneficent and void of gloom, –

The images of darkness, shadow, and night move the poem more explicitly into an elegiac register. "Yes, we are parted," states the poet, writing of the "time of farewells" that have irrevocably separated them. However, the poem makes a surprising turn from this sense of separation: "Yet no, *not parted.* Still in life and power / Thy spirit cometh over wild and wave / . . . A ready help, a presence strong and brave." The poem moves from the embodied eroticism of the opening stanzas toward a disembodied spirit who remains with the poet as an inspiration, comfort, and companion. However, this imagined love still possesses a sexual component as the poet writes: "It falleth as a robe of pride around me, / A royal vesture rich with purple gleams." The lines again appear to be a symbolic reference to female genitalia and perhaps to autoeroticism, as the anaphoric structure of the middle stanzas builds toward a climatic rhythm. The poem concludes, addressing the beloved and her possession of a concrete token of the speaker's love:

> Yet shalt thou fold it closer to thy breast,
> In the dark days, when other loves depart,
> And when thou liest down for the long rest,
> Then, O beloved, 't will sleep upon thy heart!

Here the poem redoubles the sense of loss; the unspecified separation from early in the poem now projects forward toward the death of the beloved, though it remains suspended in the future as an event that has not yet occurred. When it does, the poem proposes an eternal union materialized in the multilayered image of gravesite and shared bed. This intertwining of sexual and elegiac imagery has implications for the representation of female homosexual relationships, as well as for our understanding of the friendship elegy as a genre. The language of elegy emphasizes the depth and significance of their love, thereby celebrating (even as it mourns) intimate same-sex relations. At the same time, placing a sexual relationship at the heart of a friendship elegy draws attention to the blurred lines between friendship and desire that can be tracked across the genre as a whole. The passionate declarations of love which are common within the friendship elegy can be seen to represent an eroticism which, though often only subtext, nevertheless characterizes female friendship more broadly and demarcates same-sex relationships in opposition to conventional gender roles and compulsory heterosexuality.

Whether metaphorical or literal, death is the primary threat to female friendships in the friendship elegy. Yet, these poems present a solution in the form of authorship – in effect, promoting the poet herself as an effective substitute for the deceased friend. As we have seen, the friendship elegy projects the continued existence of the speaker past the boundary of the poem and into a future position as author. It is by virtue of her ability to commemorate the deceased in a textual form that the poet gains the privilege of continued existence. And it is by virtue of her ability to write the life of the deceased that the poet functions as her replacement, the poet's voice taking the place of the absent dead. These tropes of substitution and inheritance are evidence of the friendship elegy's indebtedness to the traditional pastoral elegy. Ann Messenger has described the pastoral elegy as the most "professional" poetic genre for the ways in which the form serves as a platform for the self-promotion of the poet who seeks to succeed the deceased.[21] As Paula Backscheider writes, "The elegy form has been powerfully and eloquently identified with male bonding, power production, authorial self-identification, and the establishment of a hegemonic lineage that is male and owned by male poets, who by association become cultural heroes."[22] Although critics such as Celeste Schenck and Kate Lilley have argued that one of the defining features of the female elegy is its rejection of the masculinist jockeying for status that characterizes the elegy tradition, the friendship elegy demonstrates how women writers in fact adapted this feature of the elegy in order to lay claim to an authorial identity.[23] This is most evident in the characterization of poetic composition as a form of memorial that sustains the poet's identity in the aftermath of loss. A turn of focus from the deceased and toward the work of literary remembrance enables the friendship elegy to serve as a site for both defining female authorship and engaging in a self-reflexive form of literary criticism.

This emphasis upon the role that authorship plays in the mourning process is notable in poetic responses to the deaths of other women writers, such as the outpouring of elegiac writing provoked by the deaths of Felicia Hemans, Elizabeth Barrett Browning, and Charlotte Brontë. Even when no actual friendship existed between poet and subject, these poems imagine a friendship-like relationship, its intimacy derived from the speaker's admiration for the author and familiarity with her works. For example, Anne Lynch Botta's tribute to Browning acknowledges "I have not met thee in this outward world," but nevertheless claims "I have seen thy spirit face to face."[24] This mirror imagery sets the stage for the poem's dual meaning: as Botta praises Browning, she implicitly promotes herself as a figurative inheritor of the deceased's authorial role, partaking of her reputation for literary genius. A similar invocation of mirroring can be seen in Elizabeth Eames's "The Picture of a Departed Poetess," which describes the experience of viewing the portrait of an unspecified author. The poem opens with a question: "This still, clear, radiant face! doth it resemble / In each fair, faultless lineament thine own?"[25] At the heart of this question is the issue of likeness, in which physical resemblance between the speaker and the portrait's subject sets the stage for a more symbolic pairing. When Eames writes, "Sweet poetess! thou surely didst inherit / Thy gifts celestial from the upper skies," the praise reflects back upon the speaker and elevates her poetic skills as well. In both poems, it is the poet's ability to recognize and value the achievement of the deceased author's writing that confirms the poet's own position as author.

The emphasis upon poetic composition as an act of mourning that valorizes both the deceased and her figurative representative (the poet herself) can also be seen within the material history and diverse textual forms of nineteenth-century women's writing, particularly the popular practice of authoring and circulating verse in manuscript through albums and commonplace books. Networks of mostly amateur poets would pass an album amongst themselves, each adding new poems or copying lines from published verse, a writing practice that served as a way of constituting relationships through the act of sharing, commenting upon, and responding to the poetic process. As scholars such as Susan Stabile and Mary Louise Kete have shown, manuscript verse was also a central mechanism for mourning: elegies were among the most common forms of poetry to appear in these friendship albums but, more importantly, the composition and circulation of elegies was a means by which friends mourned for each other.[26] Kete's account of Harriet Gould's 1830 manuscript album demonstrates the multiple functions of privately authored verse; not only did a circle of friends write numerous elegies within the album, but when one member of the circle died, she was commemorated in the album as well.[27] In other words, collaborative composition constitutes both the friendship and the act of mourning for the loss of that friendship. Manuscript verse was not just functional, however; the collection and production of poems in these forums constitute a critical position on female authorship, as the women who collaborated through commonplace books participated in the construction of a literary culture that was openly appreciative of the feminized aesthetics of sentimental mourning.

The meta-critical role of the friendship elegy as literary commentary may be most conspicuous in the host of posthumous tribute volumes published for female poets during the nineteenth century. Works of these kind include *The Literary Remains of Miss Hooper* (1842); *The Poetical Remains of the Late Lucretia Maria Davidson* (1847); *Life Within and Life Without*, a tribute to Margaret Fuller (1869); and *A Memorial of Alice and Phoebe Cary* (1873). These works are simultaneously keepsake memorials, designed to participate in the mourning process, and anthologies of the author's works, designed to gather her writing into a coherent and recognizable oeuvre. In many cases the posthumous tribute was the means by which the deceased poet's literary reputation was secured, demonstrating the ironic fact that death was one of the primary ways a female poet could gain the critical significance to warrant the publication of a volume of her poetry. For example, Lucretia Davidson's untimely death at the age of seventeen provoked the publication of a collection of her verse that not only brought the poet to the notice of literary critics and a wide reading audience, but, as Loeffelholz has shown, constructed a particular authorial identity for the poet that hinged significantly upon the fact of her death.[28]

The posthumous tribute volume, then, is a friendship elegy writ large. While some volumes were arranged by family members or critics, they were typically the work of friends and were identified as such: a collaborative effort on the part of bereaved friends. In this sense, the posthumous tribute has much in common with manuscript albums: both genres sought to employ the collaborative process of composing, collecting, and circulating a set of poems as a way of mourning for the dead. This can be seen, for example, in *The Memorial: Written by the Friends of the Late Mrs. Osgood*, published in 1851. Frances Sargent Osgood was a well-known salon and periodical poet who died in 1850. The preface to *The Memorial*, authored by fellow poet Mary E. Hewitt, explains the circumstances that gave rise to its creation: a gathering of the departed Osgood's friends resulted in the decision to publish a "souvenir volume" in her honor and to use the profits to erect a monument over Osgood's grave in Mount Auburn Cemetery.[29] Interestingly, Hewitt acknowledges that not all the submissions were authored by Osgood's friends, or even by individuals who knew Osgood, but by authors that Hewitt solicited due to their social or literary significance (Nathaniel Hawthorne is an example). What makes this tribute volume stand out from others of its kind is the fact that it contains no poems by Osgood herself, except excerpts quoted in Rufus Griswold's biographical sketch of Osgood contained within the book. In other words, *The Memorial* concretely displays how the work of textual mourning had the effect of shifting focus from the literary reputation and career of the deceased to those of her symbolic successors. Specifically, in the case of *The Memorial*, the individual who emerges as the guiding authorial figure is Mary Hewitt, who is the author of six poems within the volume, more than any other contributor. Hewitt's opening "Proem" describes Osgood's demise as "Her sister angels missed her long from heaven / . . . [and thus] They bore her to their glorious home on high."[30] This sisterhood of angels is then compared to a living sisterhood of writers:

> And now, O tearful sisters of the lyre,
> O bard, and sage, raise we "the stone of fame"
> To her who wrought the lay with minstrel fire,
> And left to hear her song and blameless name.

In positioning the "sisters of lyre" before "bard" and "sage," Hewitt privileges the female community of authors that she clearly saw herself and Osgood as inhabiting. The poem imagines a future in which Osgood's fame will be preserved through the commemorative work of her fellow poets as both literal monument (the gravestone) and textual monument (the tribute volume). Moreover, Hewitt reprinted this poem under the title "To the Memory of Mrs. Osgood" in her 1853 volume *Poems: Sacred, Passionate, and Legendary*, one of three poems about Osgood that form a cluster in the collection. Hewitt's positioning of herself against Osgood in these various ways is consistent with elegiac tropes of substitution and inheritance. By working collaboratively with other authors to commemorate Osgood's loss, Hewitt affirms her own place within a prominent literary circle. By laying claim to her status as Osgood's friend, Hewitt extends the association and implies a shared literary significance. The language of elegy provides Hewitt and other authors of friendship elegies the opportunity to present themselves as the living, surviving representatives of the dead.

This feature of the female elegy has long opened it up to censure and denigration. Mark Twain's satirical portrait of the elegist Emmeline Grangerford in *Adventures of Huckleberry Finn* was driven not just by the poor quality of her compositions but by her self-serving impulse to transform the pain of another's loss into her own gain. Much feminist re-evaluation of the female elegy defends the genre from this accusation by claiming, in Schenck's words, that many female poets refuse to "capitalize on the friend's death" and "refrain decorously from substituting [their] own face for [their] friend's."[31] Yet, my reading has suggested a different way of interpreting how the elegiac conventions of substitution and inheritance are deployed in the friendship elegy. As I have shown, the forward temporal projection of the friendship elegy imagines a future moment when the poet's productions are not only valued, but are necessary for the preservation of the memory of the dead. This is the twinned work of remembrance and recovery, a means of keeping friends alive in memory while simultaneously creating a textual space wherein women's writing can be preserved and valued. Rather than an act of appropriation, these moves constitute a canny form of professionalization. The friendship elegy imagines a time when the poems that spring from a collaborative network of readers, writers, and critics will result in women's poetry being recognized as constituting a legitimate and laudable literary tradition that honors the memory of the poetesses who have come before.

Notes

1. Joanne Dobson, "Reclaiming Sentimental Literature," *American Literature* 69.2 (1997), 270.
2. Lydia Sigourney, "'Twas but a Babe," *Select Poems* (Philadelphia: F. W. Greenough, 1838), 190.

3. Dana Luciano, *Arranging Grief: Sacred Time and the Body in Nineteenth-Century America* (New York: New York University Press, 2007), 66.
4. Elizabeth A. Petrino, *Emily Dickinson and Her Contemporaries: Women's Verse in America, 1820–1885* (Hanover: University Press New England, 1998), 93–4.
5. On the child elegy, see also Diana Pasulka, "A Communion of Little Saints: Nineteenth-Century American Child Hagiographies," *Journal of Feminist Studies in Religion* 23.2 (2007), 51–67; Jessica F. Roberts, "'The Little Coffin': Anthologies, Conventions, and Dead Children," *Representations of Death in Nineteenth-Century US Writing and Culture*, Lucy Frank (ed.), (Burlington: Ashgate, 2007), 141–154; and Jennifer Thorn, "Seduction, Juvenile Death Literature, and Phillis Wheatley's Child Elegies," *Atlantic Worlds in the Long Eighteenth Century: Seduction and Sentiment*, Toni Bowers and Tita Chico (eds.), (New York: Palgrave MacMillian, 2012), 189–203.
6. On the diverse forms of the elegy across American literary history, see Max Cavitch, *American Elegy: The Poetry of Mourning from the Puritans to Whitman* (Minneapolis: University of Minnesota Press, 2007); Jeffrey Hammond, *The American Puritan Elegy: A Literary and Cultural Study* (New York: Cambridge University Press, 2000); Jahan Ramazani, *Poetry of Mourning: The Modern Elegy from Hardy to Heaney* (Chicago: University of Chicago Press, 1994); and numerous essays in Karen Weisman, ed., *The Oxford Handbook of the Elegy* (New York: Oxford University Press, 2010). On other nineteenth-century consolation genres, see Desirée Henderson, *Grief and Genre in American Literature, 1790–1870* (New York: Ashgate, 2011).
7. S. Irenaeus Prime, et al., *The Smitten Household: or, Thoughts for the Afflicted* (New York: Anson D. F. Randolph, 1856).
8. The poem is identified as a tribute to Mrs. Faith Wadsworth. Lydia Sigourney, "The Lost Friend," *The Weeping Willow* (Hartford: Henry S. Parsons, 1847), 120–124.
9. Felicia Hemans, "Kindred Hearts," *The Young Ladies Offering; or Gems of Prose and Poetry*, Lydia Sigourney, et al. (ed.), (Boston: Phillips & Sampson, 1848), 5.
10. Amelia B. Welby, "My Sisters," *The Female Poets of America*, Rufus Griswold (ed.), 2nd edition (Philadelphia: Henry C. Baird, 1854), 330–331.
11. On the language of flowers, see Petrino, *Emily Dickinson and Her Contemporaries*, 129–160.
12. Sarah Helen Whitman, "She Blooms No More," *Female Poets*, 174.
13. Susanna Rowson, "On the Death of Miss Juliana Knox," *Miscellaneous Poems* (Boston: Gilbert and Dean, 1804), 142.
14. Lydia Sigourney, *Letters to My Pupils*, 2nd edition (New York: Robert Carter & Bros., 1852).
15. Lydia Sigourney, "Attending a Former Pupil to the Grave," *Poems, Religious and Elegiac* (London: Robert Tyas, 1841), 159–160.

16. Mary Loeffelholz, *From School to Salon: Reading Nineteenth-Century American Women's Poetry* (Princeton: Princeton University Press, 2004), 32.
17. Annis Boudinot Stockton, *Only for the Eye of a Friend: The Poems of Annis Boudinot Stockton*, Carla Mulford (ed.), (Charlottesville: University Press Virginia, 1995), 252–254.
18. Emma Embury, "Stanzas, Addressed to a Friend on her Marriage," *American Women Poets of the Nineteenth Century: An Anthology*, Cheryl Walker (ed.), (New Brunswick, New Jersey: Rutgers University Press, 1995), 85–86.
19. Grace Greenwood is the pseudonym of Sarah J. Lippincott. On Greenwood's intimate female friendships, see Paula Garrett, "Grace Greenwood (Sarah Jane Clarke Lippincott) (1823–1904)," *Legacy: A Journal of American Women Writers* 14.2 (1997), 137–145.
20. Grace Greenwood, "To –, In Absence," *Poems* (Boston: Ticknor, Reed, and Fields, 1851), 159–162.
21. Ann Messenger, *Pastoral Tradition and the Female Talent: Studies in Augustan Poetry* (New York: AMS Press, Inc., 2001), 97.
22. Paula R. Backscheider, *Eighteenth-Century Women Poets and Their Poetry: Inventing Agency, Inventing Genre* (Baltimore: Johns Hopkins University Press, 2005), 311.
23. Celeste M. Schenck, "Feminism and Deconstruction: Re-Constructing the Elegy," *Tulsa Studies in Women's Literature* 5.1 (1986), 13–27; Kate Lilley, "True State Within: Women's Elegy, 1640–1700," *Women, Writing, History, 1640–1700*, Isobel Grundy and Susan Wiseman (eds.), (Athens: University of Georgia Press, 1992), 72–92.
24. Anne Lynch Botta, "To Elizabeth Barrett Browning," *American Women Poets of the Nineteenth Century*, 146–147.
25. Elizabeth J. Eames, "The Picture of a Departed Poetess," *Female Poets*, 249.
26. See Susan Stabile, *Memory's Daughters: The Material Culture of Remembrance in Eighteenth-Century America* (Ithaca: Cornell University Press, 2004) and Mary Louise Kete, *Sentimental Collaborations: Mourning and Middle-Class Identity in Nineteenth-Century America* (Durham, North Carolina: Duke University Press, 2000).
27. See, for example, the case of Lucy Howard, who contributes a poem to Gould's album and then is memorialized several pages later by Gould in a prototypical friendship elegy. Kete, *Sentimental Collaborations*, 191, 201.
28. Mary Loeffelholz, *From School to Salon*, ch. 1.
29. Mary E. Hewitt, "Preface," *The Memorial, Written by Friends of the Late Mrs. Osgood*, ed. Hewitt (New York: Putnam, 1851), v. In this goal, the volume was unsuccessful, as evidenced by the fact that the book was reissued in 1854 under the title *Laurel Leaves: A Chaplet Woven by the Friends of the Late Mrs. Osgood* and advertised by the publishers as a gift book appropriate for the Christmas season.
30. Hewitt, "Proem," *The Memorial*, 11.
31. Schenck, "Feminism and Deconstruction," 20.

CHAPTER 7

Gendered Atlantic: Lydia Sigourney and Felicia Hemans

Gary Kelly

The British poet Felicia Hemans, already celebrated in her own country, began to be published in the United States in 1826, just as the American writer Lydia Huntley Sigourney was achieving national recognition. Sigourney was soon being called "the American Hemans," and continued so for the rest of the century on both sides of the Atlantic. There were reasons for this: both writers achieved prominence during the onset of modernity as a field of struggle between different interests in the Atlantic world, and their work participated in this struggle, at a time when the roles of women and women authors continued to be controversial. This essay examines that participation in terms of the circulation of Hemans's and Sigourney's poems in the nineteenth-century Atlantic world and representative comment on it on both sides of the Atlantic in the nineteenth century.

For present purposes, I understand modernity as a relentlessly changing social-cultural discourse and set of practices that mediated and enabled modernization. Modernization I understand as an accelerating social, economic, cultural, and political transformation that was a field of struggle between contending interests, from social groups through regional formations and nation-states to empires. Modernity centered on a model of self-reflexive personal identity that was ostensibly created, nurtured, and repaired in "pure" or disinterested relationships of intimacy, domesticity, sociability, community, and nation. This modern subject was supposedly better able to manage modernization's more intense relationships of risk and trust, to disembed from customary relationships and networks and re-embed in modern ones, to manage the increasingly abstract systems from banking to government and education to empire, and to negotiate modernization's new chronotopes or representations of time and space.[1] But if the Atlantic world was the cradle of modernization, it was also the cockpit, as different versions of modernization contended for domination within nations and within the Atlantic world as a whole – versions serving different forms of state organization, from European absolute monarchies through British constitutional monarchy to American constitutional republic. Their differing interests and forms of modernization periodically impelled these Atlantic states into wars, notably the American War of Independence, the French and Napoleonic wars, and the British-American war of 1812–1814, which in turn intensified modernization within the combatant nations. The same differences kept the Atlantic states in constant economic and cultural competition, since commercial-industrial modernization necessarily linked artistic, technological, and commercial innovation. Both Hemans and Sigourney commented directly and indirectly on these conflicts, and both contributed significantly to the modernization of literature as a modern artistic commodity and a major vehicle for communicating and promoting contending modernities.

During the onset of modernity, historic roles of women in familial, cultural, ideological, and commercial economies were, controversially, refashioned in and for modernity in various ways, particularly as presumed or professed specialists by "nature," experience, and education in central elements of modernity. In literature and the print record more broadly, these specialties were often represented as fostering self-reflexive personal identity, pure relationships, domesticity, and the extended "domestic affections" of family, friendship networks, and community. Women were also frequently represented as specialists in humanitarianism, a humanized natural world, and "lore" or knowledges of everyday life, including "national" or communal lore. All of these themes recur frequently in Hemans's and Sigourney's work. But attitudes toward women's roles in modernity were also contradictory. Such roles were typically regarded as distinct from and probably inferior to men's roles, especially in professional and public life. Literature and the print record often represented women's roles as, on the one hand, assisting and supporting modernization within and from their own sphere, and, on the other hand, mitigating, palliating, or even opposing modernization, especially versions regarded by some as excessive, mistaken, or hostile, such as social and economic exploitation, ecological degradation, militarism, genocide, and so on. Women were also perceived as experiencing or representing a tension or conflict between private and public roles in modernity.

The intensity of concern over this perception was indicated by the frequency with which it was represented and exemplified in literature as it, too, underwent modernization in the developing cultural-industrial complex that produced and was produced by Atlantic modernity through a convergence of technological, commercial, managerial, infrastructural, and cultural innovation. Print culture in general and "literature" in particular constituted a major medium for imagining, representing, performing, promoting, contesting, and distributing different versions of modernity. "Literature" was used in several senses, including written and printed information of many kinds; what were then called the "belles-lettres" of poetry, fiction, drama, essays, and discursive prose; and forms of learning such as history, biography, autobiography, and natural history.

The thematics of modernity enabled increasing numbers of women to take a greater role in this emergent modern literary-industrial complex by exploiting their supposed expertise in modernity's central aspects.[2] In the Atlantic world, two women frequently named approvingly and compared as examples and proponents of such literary modernity were Lydia Sigourney and Felicia Hemans. Each fashioned a literary persona as feminine and domestic. Both were rumored or known at the time to have experienced conjugal alienation or domestic loss. But Hemans affected to be ignorant of domestic craft, while Sigourney proclaimed her mastery of it. Sigourney wrote in many literary and practical genres, "high" and "low," Hemans almost exclusively in verse and verse drama. Both essayed many verse forms to exhibit literary mastery, achieve literary authority, and succeed in a novelty- and fashion-driven literary market. Sigourney preferred plain-style effects in her poetry, minimized reference and allusion, and restricted her poems to the compass of a middle-class woman's education and reading. Hemans's poetry was often intricate, and dense with poeticisms and literary and learned references and allusions. Both wrote much poetry of loss and consolation. Sigourney published down-, mid-, and upmarket, Hemans mainly upmarket. Both were adept at marketing their work.[3] In addition to many volumes, both published often in periodicals, an increasingly important and remunerative medium for the diffusion of modernity. In the Atlantic world Sigourney was seen as "American" and Hemans as "British" or "English." But Sigourney also associated herself at different times with her home state of Connecticut, her region of New England, the eastern states as distinct from the frontier West, the North rather than the South, and the "civilized" rather than the "uncivilized" world. Hemans associated herself at different times with Europe, England, Wales, and Ireland, and she assumed perspectives of southern Europe, the New World, and beyond. Hemans became widely and frequently republished in the United States, where she was generally regarded as imaginatively, spiritually, and sympathetically American. Such was the nature of contending American and British modernities within the Atlantic world, however, that Sigourney and Hemans also came to be seen and represented – especially in the United States, and at times controversially – in relationship.

Comparisons between Britain and America were commonplace on both sides of the Atlantic. Many Britons realized that the United States would inevitably overtake Britain as a world power, at least in certain respects, and anxiously sought ways in which Britain might prolong at least a partial advantage. Since the mid-eighteenth century, leaders in the onset of modernity proclaimed that the arts, culture, manufacturing, and commerce were intertwined powerful forces in domestic and foreign trade. By the early nineteenth century many Americans, as self-conscious citizens of the pioneering modern constitutional nation-state, looked for ways in which the United States was challenging, equaling, or surpassing nations across the Atlantic, especially Britain. Modern political economists pointed out the relationship between modern technology and design and the defense of domestic markets against foreign competition, penetration of foreign markets, and national status and self-confidence. Accordingly, attention to "national" artistic achievement in the press and elsewhere was constant and intense, though often couched in aesthetic, moral, and intellectual rather than commercial or political terms.

Defining the "nationality" of art was problematic, however. When Sigourney was nicknamed "the American Hemans" there was already an American Hemans, and it was Hemans. Readers, not texts, make meanings, and Americans were reading Hemans in their own way.[4] Hemans's poems were republished by various firms in various places in the United States throughout the century in five main forms: frequent single- and multi-volume editions claiming to be "complete" or "entire" and "from the latest London [or English] edition"; less frequent volume-collections of major works; occasional themed collections (religious faith, nature, childhood, the "domestic affections"); selections in collections with other authors; and single shorter works in periodicals or for public and private occasions. Republication and reception of Hemans in the United States suggest that many Americans read Hemans in terms of their own identity and interests, which were diverse.

Hemans's poetry was first promoted in the United States in the mid-1820s by New England Unitarian intellectuals led by Andrews Norton, who found her work expressive of their version of modernization, requiring demystified religion and disestablished churches, and who accordingly arranged for Boston editions of her work. Other American readers and publishers soon found their own uses for Hemans, and earlier and new works were quickly republished. Her poem "The Landing of the Pilgrim Fathers" was distributed at celebrations of the founding of Massachusetts colony, and became almost a de facto American national anthem in New England. In 1831, *The Poetical Works of Hemans, Heber, and Pollok* was published by the Philadelphia firm of John Grigg, suppliers of modern knowledge manuals in the professions, technology, sciences, national and world history, and educational fundamentals, as well as guides to what we might now see as modern subjective self-formation, social relations, and sociability.[5] Hemans's death in 1835 occasioned British biographies and further editions, which were then quickly republished in the United States. Sigourney herself was commissioned to write "an essay on [Hemans's] genius" for one such edition, the seven-volume 1840 Philadelphia edition from the prominent literary publisher Lea and Blanchard.[6] This edition included the 1839 Edinburgh Blackwood edition's memoir by Hemans's sister Harriet Owen.[7] Owen countered previous biographies by suppressing Hemans's liberal political and religious views, tendency to satire, and affectation of worldliness. Rather, Owen represented her sister as the embodiment and poetic voice of pure relationships – essentially private, domestic, feminine, maternal, pious, Wordsworthian, religiously orthodox, and promoting of religious hope and consolation. This portrayal confirmed the predominant American view of Hemans; in her own essay, Sigourney echoed Owen's version of Hemans and thereby appropriated her for the version of American republican modernity that Sigourney professed to embody herself and that she promoted in her writing as "the American Hemans."

Male literary authority periodically validated this version of Hemans for a growing and diversifying reading public. Norton's initial promotion of Hemans was followed by the anonymous preface to successive Grigg editions and by Rufus Griswold and Henry Tuckerman's 1845 "complete" *Poems*.[8] By the 1840s, illustrated editions appeared, "furniture" books for display as well as or more than for reading.[9] Unlike Sigourney, Hemans did not deign to compile anthologies and school readers, so this was done in her name by the education writer Timothy Stone Pinneo in *The Hemans Reader for Female Schools*, which was published in New York and Cincinnati in 1847, perhaps prompted by an earlier London work entitled *Mrs. Hemans's Young Woman's Companion; or, Female Instructor*.[10] Pinneo's *Reader* included numerous selections from Sigourney's poems and Sigourney's 1840 essay on Hemans from the Lea and Blanchard edition. This essay's assertion that settlers were carrying Hemans westward in their household effects was apparently confirmed in 1850 by publication of a stereotype edition of Hemans's *Songs of the Affections* at Cincinnati, hub of an expanding canal network linking the frontier and the east.[11] The American Civil War prompted broadside and sheet music editions of poems such as "The Soldier's Deathbed," "The Rock Beside the Sea," and "The Graves of a Household," and more editions of *Songs of the Affections* including similar poems of loss. In America, as in Britain, Hemans was marketed from mid-century in "elegant" but inexpensive series of "classic" and "standard" works, such as the "Brilliant Editions" of New York firm Leavitt and the "vest-pocket series" of Boston firm Osgood and Co. In the 1870s, the often-republished Griswold-Tuckerman edition was supplanted by American editions of the 1850 English selection introduced by William Rossetti, English critic and original member of the Pre-Raphaelite Brotherhood.[12]

Such was Hemans's presence in American culture and its literary marketplace throughout Sigourney's career from her emergence in the 1820s as a national figure and identification as "the American Hemans." I find no record of Hemans being called "the British Sigourney." Sigourney acquired a smaller, narrower, and more down-market presence in Britain. This began in the mid-1830s with the London religious publisher Thomas Ward, who published a volume of Sigourney's work titled *Lays from the West* (1834). The book was edited by the Baptist clergyman Joseph Belcher, who also introduced an edition of Sigourney's *Letters to Young Ladies* (1834).[13] Ward also republished fiction and moral instruction for youngsters by Sigourney. Leading and minor London and Glasgow publishers of religious and moral instructional literature republished these and similar works in the 1830s and 1840s, when Sigourney arrived to tour Britain and France and promote new work, including London editions of her verse and prose travelogue *Pleasant Memories of Pleasant Lands* and *Pocahontas, and other Poems*.[14] The selection of "other poems" in the London edition of the latter was more religious in orientation than in the almost simultaneous New York edition, suggesting that Sigourney's London publisher, and perhaps Sigourney herself, saw her readership in Britain as likely more receptive to such work. Nevertheless, there followed London editions of her *Scenes from My Native Land* and selections in tourist-oriented anthologies on Niagara.[15] The evangelical-oriented down-market transatlantic firm Thomas Nelson and Sons then took her up with a *Poetical Works* (1854) and books for youngsters, followed by *Poetical Works* (1863) from the major down-market firm Routledge of London, and *Great and Good Women: Biographies for Girls* (1860s to 1880s) from the similar Edinburgh firm,

William Nimmo.[16] In contrast, American editions of Sigourney were few after her death, apart from her well-prepared posthumous autobiography, *Letters of Life* (1866).[17] Ironically, her name was kept before the American public as much by her essay on Hemans in periodic reprints of Hemans's work as by reprints of her own work. Her role in American modernity seems to have been almost extinguished by the cataclysm of modernization that was the American Civil War and its ghastly demonstration of the destructive power of modern technologies. Sigourney's role as a poet of religious modernity continued in Britain, whereas Hemans's role in Atlantic modernity persisted until the cataclysm of modernization that was the first World War.

Bibliographical evidence, then, indicates that Hemans had a larger presence in the Atlantic literary world than Sigourney, that Hemans and Sigourney had readerships of several kinds in Britain and America, that they acquired somewhat similar readerships on each side of the Atlantic, and that these were created by specialist publishers who republished and promoted their work. Both Hemans and Sigourney had editions of more or less complete "poetical works" on both sides of the Atlantic, but editions of particular works, editions of selections, and inclusion of selections in anthologies with other writers indicate that they were predominantly perceived and read as respectable female writers of religious poetry of modern subjectivity; relationships of family, community, nation, and humanitarianism; and the national chronotope of nature and lore. Evidence from commentators on Sigourney's identity and literary practice as "the American Hemans" confirms the idea that, while the two writers exemplified women's and women writers' roles in particular versions of Atlantic modernity, Sigourney exemplified these roles for a distinctively – if also diverse – American modernity.

As early as 1829, development of this role was asserted as a literary-patriotic imperative in the three-volume *Specimens of American Poetry: With Critical and Biographical Notices*, edited by Samuel Kettell and published by Samuel Goodrich and Co. at Boston.[18] *Specimens* purported to formulate a historical national literary canon. Kettell's "Introduction" to *Specimens* deplored "the state of dependence as to literature, in which we have continued, to the writers of Great Britain" and declared that "the feeling of patriotism must prompt the desire that native genius should be conspicuous in every high career of human intellect, and that a national spirit in the liberal arts should be encouraged, as instruments to nourish the civic virtues and give scope to the energies of mind among our countrymen."[19]

Kettell's separate introduction to his selection of eleven of Sigourney's poems (more than was afforded any other contributor) enrolled her in this project. Kettell declared that Sigourney gained her "laurels" where her "talents" were "best adapted," in "fugitive poetry" or occasional verse published mainly in newspapers and magazines. For Kettell, the present was the "golden age" of such poetry, where "the highest living talent has been exerted, and found its recompense." Accordingly, Sigourney could "be classed with" writers both popular and esteemed, such as the Englishmen Isaac Watts and James Hervey, the Americans William Cullen Bryant and Fitz-Greene Halleck, and Hemans. For Kettell, Sigourney was "only less popular" than Hemans, whose "productions" have likewise "been widely wafted . . . on the wings of the periodical press." This statement referred to distinctions emerging in the Atlantic world between literature "popular" and elite, ephemeral and enduring, shoddy and accomplished, commercial and artistic, American and British. Though "fugitive poetry" was disparaged, Kettell declared that "There is indeed, no other shape, in which the widest popularity may so well be combined with the most permanent endurance," as evidenced by the "circulation" of Sigourney's poetic "treasures," "which, in this refined age" was "the best evidence of their sterling value." This punned on "sterling" as silver coinage, of intrinsic rather than ascribed value; as British currency, often considered stable in contrast to fluctuating or inflated colonial currency; as enduring standard value; and as reliably excellent in quality. Kettell implied that, whereas poetry in volume form enjoyed cultural prestige but seldom paid, newspaper and magazine poetry had little prestige but could pay well. Further, Americans were thought, especially in Britain, to overvalue their own productions, yet Kettell claimed that many Americans wrongly considered native productions, including literature, inevitably inferior to British. Kettell then urged Sigourney to pursue this vein, for, "so far from being exhausted, we venture to predict, that as she digs more deeply, the golden ore will be found more rich, and more abundant."[20] Kettell closed by asserting that "Had Mrs Sigourney written no more than our 'Specimens' exhibit, she would still possess undoubted claims to the proud title of the American HEMANS."[21] Whether or not the "claim" was "undoubted" and the "title" was "proud" was debated in succeeding decades, from the following different but representative perspectives within Atlantic and American modernity.

In 1835 Edgar Allan Poe discussed the issue in terms of an emergent Atlantic high culture of evaluative criticism validated through what would later be academically institutionalized as "close reading" and was designed to professionalize literature against commercialization and popularization by the modern literary-industrial complex. In his anonymous review in the *Southern Literary Messenger* of Sigourney's *Zinzendorff, and other Poems* (1836) and volumes by Hannah Gould and Elizabeth Ellet, Poe found the "American Hemans" nickname apt but derogatory for several reasons. Sigourney resembled Hemans in being "merely" popular, popular for the wrong reasons, and too prolific. Sigourney's popularity was acquired "merely by keeping continually in the eye, or by appealing continually with little things, to the ear, of that great, overgrown, and majestical gander, the critical and bibliographical rabble." Worse was the way Sigourney "acquired the title of the 'American Hemans'," for "Mrs. S. cannot conceal from her own discernment that she has acquired this title *solely by imitation*" of two kinds. One was "the character of her subjects": "the unobtrusive happiness, the sweet images, the cares, the sorrows, the gentle affections, of the domestic hearth"; "the 'tender and true' chivalries of passion"; "the radiance of a pure and humble faith"; the representation of "nature with a speculative attention"; and "the most glorious and lofty aspirations of a redeeming Christianity." Then there was form and style: "the structure of her versification"; "the peculiar turns of her phraseology"; "certain habitual expressions (principally interjectional,) such as *yea! alas!* and many others"; "an invincible inclination to apostrophize every object, in both moral and physical existence"; and the excessive and distracting use of epigraphs "prefixed to nearly every poem." Nevertheless, Poe declared, "as Americans, we are proud – very proud of the talents of Mrs. Sigourney," and specified "her many and distinguishing excellences" (distinguishing her from Hemans, presumably) as "an acute sensibility to natural loveliness – a quick and perfectly just conception of the moral and physical sublime – a calm and unostentatious vigor of thought – a mingled delicacy and strength of expression – and above all, a mind nobly and exquisitely attuned to all the gentle charities and lofty pieties of life."[22] Besides these general evaluative comments, however, Poe gave numerous instances of verbal and metrical effects, for better and worse, in Sigourney's verse.

A more representative American perspective for the time, that of modernized Atlantic and American Protestant evangelicalism, was offered in the anonymous 1835 review of *Zinzendorff, and other Poems* in the New Haven *Quarterly Christian Spectator*, which declared that Sigourney "has been called the American Hemans; and yet these two writers are, in our view, quite dissimilar." Sigourney's poetry "does not possess to so great a degree, the element of passion and feeling," yet it has "an equal if not superior exhibition of poetic taste" and "the arrangement of words, the striking epithets, at one glance placing the object before the eye, indicate poetic talent of a high description." Perhaps unsurprisingly, the *Christian Spectator* found, however, that the "crowning excellence of Mrs. Sigourney's poetry ... is its *evangelical* character," enabling her to "rank far above Mrs. Hemans, and more gifted ones of the other sex." "Mrs. Hemans seems indeed to favour religion, but there is nothing distinctive in her views," whereas "Mrs. Sigourney is not afraid openly to confess the Saviour" and "sets out with the intention never to sink the christian in the poet." More particularly, Sigourney domesticated Christianity for modernity: "Her poetry is the poetry of home-life; the affections clustering around the manifold objects of the domestic circle, and exhibiting in the varied scenes of man's changeful trial, the necessity and beneficial influence of virtuous feelings, and the piety of the gospel." Implying a contrast to Hemans, the reviewer declared "We have had lauding enough of military glory and the feats of reckless ambition." The reviewer goes on to insist "Still less does Mrs. Sigourney incline to the merely romantic fancies of genius" and "the ideal life"; and "love, as it dazzles in the lines of by far the greater portion of writers, is nowhere to be met with in her pages." Further,

> the dreamy raptures, and the fulsome adulation of those who seem to know nothing of, or care for, a permanent and rational attachment, whose verse is full of "angels," and "bright eyes" [terms found in various poems by Hemans], and the hues and drapery by which is expressed the idolatry of high-wrought, short-lived and bewildering passion, – they will here be sought in vain.

Rather, Sigourney represents "the deeper and holier fount of christian affection, the sweet inspiration of confiding hearts blent in the strictest union, and sympathizing together in the mutations of life." The explanation is that "Mrs. Sigourney's poetry is the poetry of one who evinces a familiarity with the sacred volume; and from its rich and holy pages she draws many of her finest thoughts, and the imagery in which she has clothed them." In fact, "it is to this too much abused and despised volume, that modern poets owe their truest and most sublime conceptions," including Byron, Moore, Southey, Burns, and Scott, as well as Shakespeare.[23]

The figure of Sigourney as the "American Hemans" was challenged in another way by the populist New York illustrated weekly *Brother Jonathan*, which claimed Sigourney for a democratic plebeian modernity. An irreverent 1843 overview in *Brother Jonathan* of writers published in the genteel *Graham's Magazine* of Philadelphia declared that Sigourney "has never had anything like justice done her by the people of this country – nor even by the newspapers." "By one class, we find her always called the *American* Hemans, just as Irving was called . . . the American Goldsmith, or Addison," but "we don't care a fig for *American* Addisons, or Hemans[es], while we can get *English*." Rather, "we take such language to be anything but complimentary to either of these writers, or to the American People": "Copies we don't want – originals we do," because copies "destroy our confidence in ourselves, beget a false and foreign standard of worth, and lead to all sorts of mischief and discouragement." "Another class, and among these, are a multitude of penny-ha'peny editors, have undertaken to say, that Mrs. Sigourney is never original – never sublime – nor ever anything better than a very adroit manager, worker-over, and hasher-up of other people's thoughts." For evidence to the contrary, *Jonathan* cited Sigourney's "lines to Niagara – a subject that had been written to death": "Now, we say, that a woman who has the courage to grapple with *such* a subject, must have a mind of her own and a will of her own too," and "we say moreover that she has treated the subject worthily." Thus "the poetry of Mrs. Sigourney, is of a kind that must make a profound impression upon the understanding of the People, whenever they shall become fully sensible of her worth: upon their *hearts* we would say, but – for the fact that no people on earth had ever a heart, for what is called poetry."[24] By "what is called poetry" *Jonathan* probably meant what was called poetry in *Graham's Magazine*, indicating that literature was differentiated by class as well as gender and nation.

Sigourney's role in formulating poetically a distinctively American literary modernity implicitly informed Henry A. Clark's 1852 essay "The Nationality of American Literature: Its Character and Inspiration," which appeared in the upmarket *Sartain's Union Magazine of Literature and Art* from Philadelphia. American literature's "character and inspiration," Clark argued, was a distinctive modernity, represented by writers such as Sigourney. Clark opened by declaring "A National literature, to be worthy of the name, must exhibit the strong, peculiar traits, embody the feelings, partake of the prejudices, and illustrate the originality of a people."[25] He denied that the United States lacked the material and talent to create a national literature: "we have much of a superior and peculiar excellence, which is either indigenous and exclusively pertaining to us, or found in original and striking combination here." European history comprised "records of civilization sinking into disastrous darkness, and almost extinguished by the leaden weight of stagnant ages," but "The themes for our muse are holier far, – themes that touch the heart with a *softer* influence, and waken *tenderer* feelings." If Europe had a long and rich history, American "Romance may revel in the dim walks of the forest, and in the struggles of advancing civilization, and find noble themes in the contests that separated us from the sway of European power."[26] American writers could make any material American: "He who in birth, education, habits, feelings, and principles, is a true American, if he have within him the powers of genius, may gather spoil of all people, and tongues, and nations, and it will be his own and his country's for ever." Clark dismissed the charge of American imitativeness, indicated in "some nicknames that are thought to be highly honourable, but are . . . almost too silly to be repeated": "Mr. Irving has been called the American Goldsmith, Mr. Cooper, the American Scott, Mr. Bancroft, the American Gibbon, and Mrs. Sigourney, the American Hemans."[27] In fact the relationship was this: "Mrs. Hemans is a poet, – so is Mrs. Sigourney." Clark closed by predicting that the United States, having already "risen to the elevation of a 'first-rate power,'" "will speedily be the commanding planet" in the universe of nations, "and the *American author* may find in that title a claim to the respect of the world."[28]

Clark's reference to Sigourney was purposeful; indeed, he seems to have written his essay with her work, and what was by now the commonplace association of her with Hemans, in mind. Certainly her work treated largely and predominantly the "holier . . . themes that touch the heart with a *softer* influence, and waken *tenderer* feelings," and for doing so she was routinely celebrated or denigrated, and associated with Hemans. But, as the *Christian Spectator* had pointed out, her predominantly positive treatment of such subjects contrasted with Hemans's. Sigourney also reveled "in the dim walks of the forest," with her poems on aboriginal subjects; "in the struggles of advancing civilization," with poems and prose on settlement, economic modernization, ecological degradation, the socially marginalized, and social and sectional divisions within America; and in the "noble themes in the contests that separated us from the sway of European power," with poems on events and figures in the American War of Independence. Sigourney dealt far less than Hemans with Europe's "records of civilization sinking into disastrous darkness, and almost extinguished by the leaden weight of stagnant ages." Sigourney did "gather spoil of all people, and tongues, and nations" with her long poem *The Man of Uz*, which was based on the Biblical book of Job, and some Wordsworthian narrative poems such as "Carlisle" in *Pleasant Memories of Pleasant Lands*, but she pointedly ignored themes and forms prominent in major British Romantic writers such as Scott, Byron, Shelley, Coleridge, and Southey.

Americans' association of Sigourney and Hemans as an indicator of transatlantic continuities and differences was well known in Britain and elicited comments there that were often recirculated in the United States. In 1834 the influential *Blackwood's Edinburgh Magazine* declared, "Mrs Sigourney has been called by the affectionate admiration of her countrymen, 'the American Hemans,' and she is rightly so called, inasmuch as she is the best of all their Poetesses."[29] This was soon republished in the Philadelphia *Museum of Foreign Literature, Science, and Art*, devoted to keeping Americans abreast of cross-Atlantic culture. In 1839, the weekly London *Athenæum*, reviewing *The Ladies' Wreath*, an anthology of twelve British and twelve American "poetesses," noted Sigourney's status in the United States as "the American Hemans, which, considering the great popularity of the latter in the United States, indicates a very high estimate of her power – too high we think."[30] In 1841, however, the London weekly *Spectator*, briefly noticing the London editions of Sigourney's *Poems, Religious and Elegiac* and *Pocahontas*, declared "The admiration and imitation of Mrs. Hemans has been deeply injurious to the American taste; but as very many admire the English poetess, we may say that Mrs. Sigourney is an *alter idem* – an American Hemans."[31] This, too, was republished in the *Museum of Foreign Literature*. But at least one commentator in the United Kingdom stated, in 1855, that "it is exceedingly questionable whether Sigourney would not gain from a comparison with her poetic sister, Felicia Hemans. Many would esteem her an equal in fancy, grace, and rhythmical beauty, while in vigor and range of comprehension she is most undoubtedly superior."[32]

The print record, represented by the commentaries considered here, suggests various major ways that Hemans and Sigourney could be put in relationship in an Atlantic context of debates over self-consciously differing and competing modernities, including "national" literature, and the role of female writers therein. But the print record has its limitations. From today's perspective and recent research, it can be argued that both writers addressed the onset of modernity where they lived, as they saw it, in the interests of people like themselves. As I have argued elsewhere, for Hemans this modernity was, until late in her career, an Atlantic cosmopolitan liberal constitutionalism opposing what she saw as an unmodernized British state and destructively modernizing French Revolutionary, Napoleonic, and post-Napoleonic European regimes.[33] For Sigourney, this modernity was a uniquely American republicanism opposing what she saw as unmodernity past and present around the world; destructive contemporary modernity represented by commercialism, industrialism, and ecological degradation; and unmodernizable aboriginal peoples, immigrants, and American plebeians and blacks. Similarities and differences in the Atlantic literary-industrial complex put certain works of Hemans and Sigourney before readers in various forms at different times and places, described here, while similarities and differences in Atlantic modernization likely enabled readers to create in their own interests similar and different meanings from the works offered to them, as modernization proceeded. Only part of that story is told here, and since those readers are dead much of it must remain speculative.

Notes

1. See Anthony Giddens, *The Consequences of Modernity* (Stanford: Stanford University Press, 1990).
2. See Gary Kelly, "Bluestocking Work: Learning, Literature, and Lore in the Onset of Modernity," *Bluestockings Now! The Evolution of a Social Role*, Deborah Heller (ed.), (Farnham and Burlington: Ashgate, 2015), 175–208.
3. See Paula R. Feldman, "The Poet and the Profits: Felicia Hemans and the Literary Marketplace," *Keats-Shelley Journal: Keats, Shelley, Byron, Hunt, and Their Circles*, 46 (1997): 148–176, and *Lydia Sigourney: Selected Poetry and Prose*, Gary Kelly (ed.), (Peterborough: Broadview, 2008), 316–319.
4. See Alec McHoul, *Semiotic Investigations: Towards an Effective Semiotics* (Lincoln, Nebraska: University of Nebraska Press, 1996); Roy Harris, *Introduction to Integrational Linguistics* (Kidlington: Pergamon Press, 1998).
5. *The Poetical Works of Hemans, Heber, and Pollok* (Philadelphia: John Grigg, 1831).
6. *The Works of Mrs. Hemans, with a memoir by her sister, and an essay on her genius by Mrs. Sigourney* (Philadelphia: Lea and Blanchard, 1840).
7. Harriet Owen, *Memoir of the Life and Writings of Mrs. Hemans* (Edinburgh and London: W. Blackwood and Sons, 1839).
8. *Poems by Felicia Hemans with an Essay on her Genius by H. T. Tuckerman*, Rufus Wilmot Griswold (ed.), (Philadelphia: Sorin and Ball, 1845).
9. Felicia Hemans, *The Poetical Works of Mrs. Felicia Hemans* (Boston: Phillips and Sampson, 1848), "illustrated with steel engravings."
10. *The Hemans Reader for Female Schools*, Timothy Stone Pinneo (ed.), (New York: Clark, Austin, & Smith, 1847; Cincinnati: W. B. Smith & Co., 1847); *Mrs. Hemans's Young Woman's Companion* (London: James S. Virtue, 1840).
11. Felicia Hemans, *Songs of the Affections* (Cincinnati: J. A. and U. P. James, 1850).

12. *The Poetical Works of Mrs. Felicia Hemans*, William Rosetti (ed.), (London: Ward, Lock & Co., 1879).
13. Lydia Sigourney, *Lays From the West: Poems*, Joseph Belcher (ed.), (London: Thomas Ward, 1834); Lydia Sigourney, *Letters to Young Ladies, With An Introductory Essay by The Rev. Joseph Belcher* (London: Thomas Ward, 1834).
14. Lydia Sigourney, *Pleasant Memories of Pleasant Lands* (London: Tilt & Bogue, 1832); Lydia Sigourney, *Pocahontas, and Other Poems* (London: R. Tyas, 1841).
15. Lydia Sigourney, *Scenes in My Native Land* (London: H. G. Clarke, 1845); William Barham, *Descriptions of Niagara; selected from Various Travellers; with Original Additions* (Gravesend: Published by the Compiler, 1847); Washington F. Friend, *The Falls of Niagara* (New York: T. Nelson and Sons; Toronto: James Campbell, 1860); John Quincy Adams, *A Souvenir of Niagara Falls* (Buffalo: Sage, Sons, and Co., 1864).
16. *The Poetical Works of Mrs. L. H. Sigourney* (London and Edinburgh: T. Nelson and Sons, 1851); *The Poetical Works of Mrs. L. H. Sigourney*, F.W.N. Bayley (ed.), (London: George Routledge, 1850); Sigourney, *Biographies of Great and Good Women* (Edinburgh: W. P. Nimmo, 1866; also 1871, 1872, 1874, 1877, 1885).
17. Lydia Sigourney, *Letters of Life* (New York: D. Appleton and Co., 1866).
18. *Specimens of American Poetry: with critical and biographical notices*, vols. 1–3, Samuel Kettell (ed.), (Boston: Samuel Goodrich and Co., 1829).
19. Kettel, *Specimens*, vol. 1, xlvii, xlviii.
20. Kettell, *Specimens*, vol. 2, 206.
21. Ibid., 207.
22. Edgar Allan Poe, "Critical Notices," *Southern Literary Messenger*, 2.1 (December 1835), 112–113.
23. *Quarterly Christian Spectator* (New Haven), 7 (December 1835), 671–673.
24. "The Graham Writers," *Brother Jonathan* 5.4 (Saturday, May 27, 1843), 107–108.
25. Henry A. Clark, "The Nationality of American Literature: Its Character and Inspiration," *Sartain's Union Magazine of Literature and Art* 10:1 (January 1852), 46.
26. Clark, "Nationality," 47.
27. Ibid., 51.
28. Ibid.
29. "The Moral of Flowers," *Blackwood's Edinburgh Magazine* 35 (May 1834), 807.
30. *Athenæum: Journal of English and Foreign Literature, Science, and the Fine Arts*, 585 (12 January 1839), 24.
31. "Publications Received," *Spectator* (London), 669 (23 April 1841), 402.
32. "The Poets of America," *Irish Quarterly Review*, 5:18 (June 1855), 210.
33. See Gary Kelly, "Introduction," *Felicia Hemans: Selected Poems, Prose, and Letters* (Peterborough: Broadview Press, 2002), 15–85.

PART II

1840–1865, Unions and Disunions

CHAPTER 8

Women, Transcendentalism, and The Dial: *Poetry and Poetics*

Michelle Kohler

On November 6, 1839, more than twenty-five women met in Boston, probably in the home of Mary Peabody, to participate in the first of a series of formal Conversations on classical literature and mythology led by the brilliant Transcendentalist Margaret Fuller. In attendance was Elizabeth Palmer Peabody, the eminent educational reformer and intellectual who would soon host subsequent sessions of Fuller's Conversations for women in her West Street bookstore, the most important Transcendentalist gathering-place in Boston. Also in attendance at Fuller's first Conversation were, among others, Caroline Sturgis and her sister Ellen Sturgis Hooper, both of whose poems would be featured in the Transcendentalist journal *The Dial*, and other women who were or would become prominent activists and writers, including Lydia Maria Child, Elizabeth Cady Stanton, and Caroline Healey Dall. At this point, Fuller's and Peabody's Transcendentalist activities were already in full swing – Fuller had accepted the job as editor of *The Dial* only days before – and the success of this inaugural Conversation and those that followed ensured many women's active participation in the growth of Transcendentalism and heralded their eagerness to be drawn into its intellectual and literary fervor.

American Transcendentalism was a movement formed by a loosely organized nexus of intellectuals, writers, and clergymen centered in Boston in the 1830s and 1840s. With the sense that they were fomenting a cultural revolution, they turned away from the Lockean empiricism and rationalism that dominated New England's liberal Christianity and fervently pursued their own version of German Idealism, embracing intuitive ways of knowing and positing the divinity of the human soul. From these ideas sprang a series of reform efforts in education, civil rights, and communitarian (or sometimes hermetic) living, as well as a new way of understanding the origin and function of poetic language. While many of our accounts of the movement and its literature have tended to prioritize the careers of men such as Ralph Waldo Emerson, Henry David Thoreau, Bronson Alcott, and William Ellery Channing, Peabody and Fuller's leadership was crucial not only to the inclusion of women in Transcendentalist circles, but also to the development of the movement itself, including its new conceptions of poetry and other literary forms. As the Americanist pendulum swings toward a renewed interest in Transcendentalism, scholars have begun to redress the broader gaps in our understanding of women's contributions to Transcendentalist thought, evidenced by the pace of work on Fuller and the recent publication of *Toward a Female Genealogy of Transcendentalism*, a collection of essays edited by Jana L. Argersinger and Phyllis Cole.[1]

Even so, aside from excellent work by Philip Gura, Kathleen Lawrence, and Jeffrey Steele, little attention has been paid to the important role women played in developing Transcendentalist poetry and poetics.[2] This essay describes these contributions by women during the heyday of Transcendentalism in the 1830s and 1840s, focusing especially on Peabody and Fuller, as well as Sturgis, Hooper, and Eliza Thayer Clapp, who were regularly featured in *The Dial*. The essay's final section turns briefly to two developments in women's poetry that were outgrowths of Transcendentalism in subsequent decades: the engagement of women's poetry with Transcendentalist thought in *The Una*, a feminist newspaper published from 1853 to 1855, and the poems of Emily Dickinson, whose work from the 1850s to the 1880s offers one of the century's most rigorous critical engagements with Transcendentalism.

While Elizabeth Peabody is perhaps best remembered for her work on education reforms, especially for introducing the German kindergarten to American schools, she was also actively involved in developing the most esoteric aspects of American Transcendentalism and its poetics, and she played a crucial role in their material distribution. Her West Street bookstore, which was also a library and publishing house, was arguably the single most important space for the actual physical convergence of Transcendentalists, who met there daily to exchange books and ideas. As the literal center of these exchanges, and as proprietor and sometimes publisher of the reading material Transcendentalists consumed, Peabody tangibly influenced the movement's intellectual contours. She had a special interest in the language philosophy that would shape Transcendentalist conceptions of poetry: she believed that poetic language derives universally from nature, and that such language signifies spiritual ideas because nature embodies spiritual truths. This was fundamentally at odds with Locke's empiricist account of language as a set of arbitrary signs and, indeed, was part of the Transcendentalists' broad repudiation of empiricism in favor of the intuition of spiritual truths. We commonly associate this concept of poetic language with Emerson's 1836 *Nature*, where he argues that "Words are signs of natural facts" and "Nature is the symbol of spirit."[3] Emerson, however, was likely influenced by Peabody, who was actively working out these ideas well before Emerson's *Nature*. In 1826, for example, she wrote an admiring review (not published until 1834) of Johann Gottfried von Herder's 1782 *On the Spirit of Hebrew Poetry*, which treated the Bible's truth as rooted in its poetics rather than its facticity. "Poetry," argued Peabody in her review, "is the expression of abstract and spiritual truth by sensible objects, by the forms, colors, sounds, … of external nature. The foundation of the possibility of such an expression is the fact, that the human mind … and the natural creation … are but different images of the same Creator."[4]

Peabody's formulation became central to Transcendentalist poetics, which cast poetry as less a craft than a divine transcription made manifest in nature to the poet's special eye (signified most famously by Emerson's transparent eyeball, "uplifted into infinite space" and able to "see all").[5] Metaphor, then, is not the arbitrary or deliberate yoking of two discrete objects, but, rather, identifies an intrinsic unity. The soul may be compared to a wave, that is, because the wave is *in fact* a symbol of the soul; the poet's task is to recognize and then record these likenesses with accuracy.[6] While Transcendentalists are best remembered for their prose works, this way of thinking about poetic language led them to hold poetry in especially high esteem, to regard it as the literary form best able to represent the deep correspondence between spirit and matter. The most active sponsor of this concept of language, Peabody taught it in her own school as early as 1820 and then with Bronson Alcott during the 1830s. She would go on to promote and publish related ideas from language theorists such as Charles Kraitsir, Horace Bushnell, and Roland Gibson Hazard for the next several decades, ensuring the emergence of a relatively coherent Transcendentalist poetics, one that casts poetry as revelation and the poet as a prophet-seer.

While we often give Peabody short shrift, scholars have increasingly acknowledged Margaret Fuller's central role in the development of Transcendentalism; she was an intensely brilliant, prolific writer who served as the first editor of *The Dial* and interacted extensively with Emerson, Thoreau, Alcott, and many others at the heart of the movement. She was directly responsible for bringing women into Transcendentalist intellectual and literary circles and for seeing their poetry into print, both by creating the Conversations for women and by publishing women poets in *The Dial* during her editorship between 1840 and 1842. A third of the poems in the first issue were written by women, including Ellen Sturgis Hooper, Ellen Emerson, and Fuller herself; in the second issue, nearly all of the poetry was by women – almost a dozen poems by Caroline Sturgis and more poems by Hooper and Ellen Emerson. Throughout her three years as editor of *The Dial*, Fuller continued to publish poetry by women, including Sarah Clarke and Eliza Thayer Clapp.

Fuller herself wrote over 100 poems that we know of, most of them between 1835 and 1844 during her most intense involvement with the New England Transcendentalists and before her moves to New York and Italy. The great majority of these poems were unpublished during her lifetime, in large part because she regarded her poetry as a private exercise for spiritual growth, part of the journaling that was so important to Transcendentalist practices of "self-culture." She did, however, print some of her own poems in the first issue of *The Dial* and within her major prose works, and she circulated others in letters. While many of her unpublished poems are of interest, in order to emphasize Fuller's public contributions I focus here on several of those she chose to publish or otherwise circulate.

Fuller likely included her poems in *The Dial*'s first issue somewhat reluctantly in order to fill space in the nascent journal, which was slow to gather submissions. Her poems are short and quintessentially Transcendentalist in thought, favoring spiritual ascent over the mundane or material and relying on natural imagery to make abstract claims. For example, "A Dialogue" is a brief conversation between a dahlia and the sun in which the seductive dahlia invites the sun to descend for an amorous encounter, a plea the sun rebuffs in order to pursue its aerial progress.[7] This allegory for the Transcendentalist admonition to "shun father and mother and wife and brother" when your genius calls you to follow a superior spiritual course is reiterated in a different form in the next poem, "Richter," which celebrates writer Jean Paul Richter's ascendancy over the "fond illusions of the youth and the maid" in favor of "Devotion's highest flight sublime."[8] Fuller follows this up with the poem "Some murmur at the 'want of system' in Richter's writings," in which she again privileges freedom of movement (via nature and aerial flight) and freedom from social restraint: "Nature's wide temple, and the azure dome, / Have plan enough for the free spirit's home!"[9]

Another important, and less cerebral, set of poems are among those from 1844, a particularly productive year for Fuller, during which she wrote thirty-seven poems and completed both *Summer on the Lakes* and *Woman in the Nineteenth Century*. The poems from this period demonstrate Fuller's increasing interest in mythological imagery, often focusing on goddess figures or other symbols of feminine power, a style of allusion central to the feminist Transcendentalism she constructs in *Woman in the Nineteenth Century*. While most of the 1844 poems remained unpublished, it is evident that she held some of them in high esteem and even circulated several to Emerson; she refers proudly to them in her correspondence with him, noting that she has been writing "flowers and stones" that have a "hieroglyphical interest for those of like nature with me" and an "unimpeded energy."[10] In one of these poems, "Sistrum," Fuller urges on the "ceaseless motion" of the rattle of Isis in incantatory trochees: "Triune, shaping, restless power, / Life-flow from life's natal hour." In this perpetual activity is the promise of divine "self-fed energy, / Nature in eternity."[11] Fuller's image is in line with the Transcendentalists' belief in the ceaseless presence of divinity within the self, but it is significant that Fuller relies on a feminine symbol and asserts her own access to this power: "Life-flow of my natal hour." She thus counters the more masculine images of, for example, the "Man Thinking" Emerson posits in "The American Scholar" and the unsocialized boy he idealizes in "Self-Reliance."[12]

Fuller's "Double Triangle, Serpent and Rays," another 1844 poem in pulsing trochees and apparently shared with Emerson, finds power in the incorporation of both the male and female rather than in the primarily feminine energy of "Sistrum":

Patient serpent, circle round,
Till in death thy life is found;
Double form of godly prime
Holding the whole thought of time,
When the perfect two embrace,
Male & female, black & white,
Soul is justified in space,
Dark made fruitful by the light;
And, centred in the diamond Sun,
–Time & Eternity are one.[13]

By merging the binaries of female and male, one is also able to merge material and spiritual space, "Time & Eternity." Importantly, this is not because female corresponds to material, and male to spiritual (or vice versa), but because recognizing the way female and male intrinsically circulate into each other allows full experience of the soul's divinity even in its material state. In "Winged Sphynx" Fuller casts the soul's power as an emergent (and, again, feminine) one, deriving gradually from a journey that moves her from immaturity toward revelation:

> Through brute nature upward rising,
> Seed up-striving to the light,
> Revelations still surprising,
> My inwardness is grown insight.
> Still I slight not those first stages,
> Dark but God-directed Ages;
> In my nature leonine
> Labored & learned a Soul divine;
> Put forth an aspect Chaste, Serene,
> Of nature virgin mother queen;
> Assumes at last the destined wings,
> Earth & heaven together brings;[14]

Here, a female "Soul divine" labors within her "leonine" animal nature and then gains her "destined wings." The rhyming of opposites "leonine" and "divine" is worth noting, for, as Stephen Cushman argues in his excellent essay on Transcendentalist poetics, most of the movement's poets favored rhymed poetry perhaps in part because rhyme marks a kind of correspondence.[15] The pairings of words accomplished by rhyme is, for the Transcendentalists, akin to the intrinsic likeness identified by metaphor: rhyme offers "the most suggestive verbal image of correspondence . . . bind-[ing] the natural to the spiritual."[16] If, as Peabody argued, the sounds of words are intrinsically meaningful rather than arbitrary, then aural similarity indicates inherent similarity. Just as Fuller argues rhetorically for the intrinsic link between "Earth & heaven," "Time & Eternity," she captures that link aurally here in the pairing of "leonine" and "divine," and perhaps, too, in pairings such as "hour" (time) and "power" (eternity) in "Sistrum" and "godly prime" and mortal "time" in "Double Triangle."

It is also worth noting here the place of meter in Transcendentalist poetry, given Fuller's repeated use of trochaic tetrameter in these 1844 poems, which are rhythmically effective but far more conventional in form than content. Indeed, while the Transcendentalists enthusiastically embraced new ideas about poetry, they are often surprisingly unimaginative in their use of meter and other elements of form. As Cushman notes, most of the poems are metrical (with little variation) and perfectly rhymed, with little enjambment or caesura to add tension to the line.[17] But, argues Cushman, much of what he calls their formal temperateness derives paradoxically from their less temperate ideas about poetry. They believed that "meter comes physiologically from the heart," that "to write in meter is not to defer weakly to tradition; it is to affirm and proclaim vitality" from an innate energy.[18] Meter, then, should not disrupt through variation but, rather, issue naturally like a pulse, reinforcing the sense that the poem is true rather than invented. In the case of Fuller's poems, the persistent trochees seem part and parcel of the "self-fed" "Life-flow" and the inevitable natural growth she describes.

While Fuller did not widely circulate her often-gendered revisions to Transcendentalism in poetic form, she did develop them elaborately that same year (1844) in her brilliant prose work *Woman in the Nineteenth Century*, which deftly uses Transcendentalist principles to argue for intellectual and social equality for women. Fuller perhaps felt the need for cogent argument rather than metered pulse in order to make her public case for women's intellectual capacities, but she does include several poems in the book. The main text of *Woman* concludes with an untitled poem in which she offers a short, rhythmic rallying cry for women, insisting that power "will come," even "if not now," and that, in the meantime, one must have faith in the divinity within oneself:

> For the Power to whom we bow
> Has given its pledge that, if not now,
> They of pure and steadfast mind,
> By faith exalted, truth refined,
> *Shall* hear all music loud and clear,
>
> . . .
>
> Though rabble rout may rush between,
>
> . . .
>
> Persist to ask, and it will come;
> Seek not for rest in humbler home;
> So shalt thou see, what few have seen,
> The palace home of King and Queen.[19]

As in "Winged Sphynx," the female soul's power may be belated, but it is surely coming, particularly if one will "Persist to ask" and "Seek not for rest." Fuller concludes the book with a longer poem, entitled "The Sacred Marriage." As the stanzas excerpted below make evident, she offers a more social argument here than we have seen in the poems discussed so far. She suggests that "another's life" may have a large enough scope to fuel one's own spiritual growth:

> And has another's life as large a scope?
> It may give due fulfilment to thy hope,
> And every portal to the unknown may ope.
>
> . . .

Twin stars that mutual circle in the heaven,
Two parts for spiritual concord given,
Twin Sabbaths that inlock the Sacred Seven;
. . .

The parent love the wedded love includes,
The one permits the two their mutual moods,
The two each other know mid myriad multitudes;[20]

The union between two individuals, argues Fuller, models the larger union that binds everything. She thus suggests that love can be a means to spiritual power, and, indeed, many Transcendentalists actively cultivated this kind of elevated – and elevating – intimacy. The poem's penultimate stanza revels in this notion of love: "With child-like intellect discerning love, / And mutual action energizing love, / In myriad forms affiliating love." "Love," repeated at the end of each line in the place of rhyme, comes to mean more than the specific love between two individuals, as the two lovers extend it to "myriad forms." This poem's idealization of love relies, however, on the more cautious argument Fuller makes in the main text of the book that women often "live too much in relations" and thus become "stranger[s] to the resources of [their] own nature[s]."[21] A "sacred marriage" is only possible, Fuller stipulates, if both parties are regarded as "souls, each of which ha[s] a destiny of its own"; such intimacy is thus precarious for women in particular, however desirable for Transcendentalists in general.[22]

Fuller in fact cultivated "sacred marriages" with several people during her twenties and thirties, most famously with Emerson, but also with Caroline Sturgis, a dynamic, freethinking young woman from an elite Bostonian family and an aspiring poet whose work Fuller ushered into print. Sturgis's father tried to prohibit her from socializing with the heretical Transcendentalists, but she nevertheless developed extremely close ties with Fuller and then Emerson, who looked to Sturgis for advice on his own poetry. While she would publish few other poems during her lifetime, her work was central to the conceptualization of Transcendentalist poetry; as many as twenty-five of her poems appeared in *The Dial*, largely under Fuller's editorship. Nearly all of the poems in the second issue were hers (most of them were signed "Z," in line with Fuller's preference for single-initial attributions and Sturgis's own desire for anonymity).

Sturgis and Fuller, through their extensive correspondence, together developed what Kathleen Lawrence has called "aesthetic Transcendentalism," or a belief in the spiritualizing capacities of visual art and other deliberately aesthetic forms.[23] Sturgis was in fact also a talented visual artist whose sketches Emerson and other Transcendentalists eagerly sought out, often using them as tools for spiritual contemplation. The notion of a relationship between spirit and beautiful material forms inspires much of Sturgis's work in *The Dial*, where she calls upon the artist to recognize that relationship. In "Art and Artist," a poem from the October 1840 issue, for example, Sturgis idealizes the artist's transcendent perception in terms that recall Emerson's transparent eyeball: she esteems the "dauntless eye" with which the "lofty" artist "sees the thought flow to the form."[24] In April 1841, her poem "The Angel and the Artist," too, reveres the artist's power, even if it seems at first to chastise him for pursuing it:

> Angel. Back back must thou go,
> Spirit proud and poor!
> To be in the Essence, to love and to know,
> Thou canst not yet endure.
> Artist. Ah! but I did in that glorious hour
> When all was mine. –
> Angel. No, not for a moment hast thou had power
> The Cause to divine.
> Why despise forms from which Spirit doth speak?
> Artist. I will obey.
> Beautiful forms! in you will I seek
> The All-shining Day.[25]

While the poem first casts the chastised artist as lower than the angel, the angel eventually comes across less as a wise being and more as a stodgy naysayer, insisting that the artist cannot access "the Essence" and must keep his attention on earthly forms. The artist's final claim, at once obedient and triumphant, suggests otherwise: he will indeed access the spirit by means of "Beautiful forms!" Thus, the poem distinguishes between mortal and immortal, between form and Spirit, while it also suggests that the artist mingles with angels and, indeed, has more power to reach the divine than the angel seems willing to admit. In "Give Us an Interpreter," which appeared in *The Dial* in January 1841, Sturgis issues a call for such an artist. Anticipating Emerson's and Walt Whitman's similar pleas, she looks for "A man who with power shall backward throw / The curtain that hangs o'er the infinite now," by whose "piercing light men shall see with surprise, / From their souls sprang the earth, the stars, and the skies."[26]

But Sturgis does not always extend her optimism about the capacity of the artist to herself or her speakers. In what is perhaps her bleakest poem,

"Light and Shade," she writes "I have only a part and oh! I long for the whole." Caught in mortality, she wonders "why did ye place me here?" There is, on the one hand, "the wide infinite," and on the other hand, "I! and I! I still must cry! / And I! oh! how I scorn this I!"[27] To read this beside her poems on the artist, one is reminded, in fact, of the striking juxtaposition in Emerson's 1844 *Essays, Second Series*, where the ecstatic, idealistic essay "The Poet" is immediately followed by the grief-stricken, skeptical essay "Experience," in which Emerson finds himself ineluctably caught in his own mortality. Fuller's ordering of Sturgis's poems in *The Dial* actually creates this dichotomy a number of times, several years before Emerson's essays; there are multiple instances where one poem expresses transcendental ecstasy while the next, usually on the same page, expresses despair. In the third issue of *The Dial*, for example, there is first Sturgis's jubilant allegory, "Love and Insight," which imagines the two eponymous characters "wandering mid the bursting spring," their "high harmony" unifying everything. Immediately below this poem is her glum "Sunset," in which "The sun's red glory vanishes amid complaining waves," illustrating that "Bright beings always go thus, sink down into dark graves."[28] These juxtapositions do not represent the dominant tone of Transcendentalism, but they are nevertheless an important counterpoint. Both the practices of self-culture and the special capacity of the poet, with his or her "dauntless" and transparent eye, are crucial precisely because of the struggle the Transcendentalists felt between human limitation and potential, between material form and spiritual power.

This interplay is manifest, too, in the poems of Ellen Sturgis Hooper, who, like her sister Caroline, was active in Transcendentalist circles and participated enthusiastically in Fuller's Conversations, and whose poems were also published regularly in *The Dial*. In the brief untitled poem that appeared in the inaugural issue in July 1840, Hooper meditates on the gap between the ideal and the actual:

I slept, and dreamed that life was Beauty;
I woke, and found that life was Duty.
Was thy dream then a shadowy lie?
Toil on, sad heart, courageously,
And thou shalt find thy dreams to be
A noonday light and truth to thee.[29]

Hooper's waking discovery anticipates Emerson's realization in "Experience," where he admits, "It is very unhappy ... the discovery we have made, that *we exist*."[30] Hooper's self-directed rallying cry, "Toil on, sad heart," also closely anticipates Emerson's "up again, old heart!" from the same essay, although Hooper's imperative is more plodding and workaday than Emerson's cheerful encouragement.[31] In January 1841, *The Dial* published Hooper's "To the Ideal," which similarly bemoans the fact that when she dreams of "life above me, and aspire[s] to be / A dweller in [the] air serene and pure," then, inevitably, she writes, "I wake, and must this lower life endure."[32] While Emerson's blithe solution to this fall from idealism into existence is "to live the greatest number of good hours," Hooper urges herself more somberly to get "To work!" and "with heart resigned and spirit strong" to "Subdue by patient toil Time's heavy wrong."[33]

Like Emerson and Sturgis, Hooper looks to poets for salvation. In her poem "The Poet," published in *The Dial* in October 1840, she describes a savior-like poet who descends from the heavens with such "secret strength" and "an inward brighter light" that others "Worship the presence": "Men gaze in wonder and in awe / Upon a form so like to theirs"; "Men laid their hearts low at his feet, / And sunned their being in his light"; "Humanity, half cold and dead, / Had been revived in genius' glow."[34] Hooper similarly praises Emerson as this kind of redeeming poet figure in her tribute poem, "To R. W. E.," unpublished during her lifetime: "Thou art the deep and crystal winter sky, / Where noiseless, one by one, bright stars appear"; we "cool our souls in thy refreshing air, / And find the peace which we had lost before."[35]

Some of the most formally interesting poems in *The Dial* come from Eliza Thayer Clapp, a Unitarian Sunday school teacher and religious essayist from Dorchester, Massachusetts. In "Two Hymns," for example, a long poem from July 1841 in blank verse, rife with enjambment and caesura, Clapp expresses her despair that "Alone, alone / The soul must do its own immortal work": "I shrink, I cling / Like a scared insect to this whirling ball" surrounded by "higher forms" that are "kindred linked / Yet most communionless," "nearest, yet most apart, / Moving in saddest mystery each to each."[36] In "Clouds," she offers a more typically ecstatic reading of the clouds as "pure and true," symbols of the "supreme infinitude of Thought," but this poem, too, is full of blank verse lines whose syntax is broken up by enjambment and caesura, which renders the poem more longing and personally expressive than we might first expect.[37] Like Sturgis, Hooper, and the Emerson of "Experience," then, Clapp displays the struggle underlying the push for spiritual ascension when one is ultimately caught in mortality.

Margaret Fuller died tragically in a shipwreck in 1850 at the age of forty, and her death marks, or at least coincides with, the dissipation of a coherent Transcendentalist movement. (Caroline Dall would claim, thirty years later, that "what is meant by Transcendentalism perished with Margaret Fuller," although other factors contributed, perhaps especially New England's turn toward more aggressive social reform, with abolitionism at the helm).[38] But if Transcendentalism did not retain its intensity after the 1840s, it nevertheless remained an important context for American literary culture in general and for poetry in particular, and women, including women poets, continued to find its standard of self-reliance and its affinity with feminist progress to be friendly and fertile ground for their work. One important outgrowth in this vein was *The Una*, a monthly women's rights newspaper published from February 1853 to October 1855 by Dall, a Transcendentalist who had attended Fuller's Conversations over a decade earlier, and Paulina Wright Davis, an admirer of Fuller. As Tiffany K. Wayne has emphasized, the newspaper included contributions by significant figures from Transcendentalist circles, including Hooper, Peabody, Elizabeth Oakes Smith (a poet and activist who spoke on the lyceum circuit with Emerson), and Cady Stanton, as well as poetry by women who embraced Transcendentalist ideas even if they had not participated in its social institutions.[39] Elizabeth Jessup Eames's 1853 poem "Universe," for example, encapsulates Transcendentalist notions of nature, spirit, and poetry, finding the natural world to be "A living outgrowth of Divine completeness," itself "An Epic Poem of existence flowing / In music from the Heart of the Eternal."[40] Her poem "Conjugal Love," which appeared in *The Una* in 1855, celebrates the kind of "sacred marriage" of equally elevated souls promoted by Fuller.[41] Other poems bear the clear stamp of Transcendentalist ideas, such as Mary Gove Nichols's "Dawn" (1854), which celebrates the truth in nature, where "Wisdom shines in all of beauty" because "Only thus dear Beauty lives," and Ann Preston's "The Ideal Is the Real" (1854), which argues that the recognition of the Ideal in the seemingly mundane, "Real" world is possible if one listens to "Nature's tongues."[42] In 1854, *The Una* also included Hooper's poem "The Wood-fire," which had appeared in *The Dial* and which Thoreau quoted in full in the first chapter of *Walden*.

Transcendentalism is also an essential context for understanding the poetry of Emily Dickinson, who began writing in earnest in the 1850s. An avid reader of Emerson and Thoreau, she also corresponded devotedly for several decades with Transcendentalist Thomas Wentworth Higginson, whose essays and poems she admired. Dickinson's intellectual self-reliance, her resistance to orthodox religion, and her attraction to nature and spiritual ideas all bear the imprint of Transcendentalism, and, indeed, when her poetry was published posthumously in the 1890s, many critics aligned her with the ethereal, independent Transcendentalists. Despite these affinities, however, contemporary scholars tend to find Dickinson's poems to be primarily critical of the Transcendentalists' confident epistemological claims and their conflation of nature and spirit.[43] She seems to mock the Transcendentalist affinity for aerial progress, for example, in her 1862 poem that begins "Of Bronze – and Blaze – " (Fr319):

Of Bronze – and Blaze –
The North – tonight –
So adequate – it forms –
So preconcerted with itself –
So distant – to alarms –
An Unconcern so sovreign
To Universe, or me –
Infects my simple spirit
With taints of Majesty –
Till I take vaster attitudes –
And strut opon my stem –
Disdaining Men, and Oxygen,
For Arrogance of them –[44]

Here, the speaker first describes the night sky as so distant and absorbed in its own glory that it cares not for "Universe, or me." But then she ironically makes herself akin to the sky by adopting the sky's self-absorption and disdain for "Men, and Oxygen," parodying the Transcendentalist penchant for aerial flight (which we have seen, for example, in Fuller's *Dial* poems and Emerson's floating eyeball). In becoming like the night sky, however, the speaker is not so much spiritually expanded as she is reduced to a strutting misanthrope holding her breath.

There remains much work for scholars to do toward understanding the role women played in the development and afterlife of Transcendentalism and its poetics. While scholars have been attentive to the careers of Fuller and Dickinson, there is more to say about the place of Peabody, Sturgis, Hooper, and other women and other women in the theory and practice of Transcendentalist poetics, as well as about the significance of poetry to Fuller's thinking and writing. We also have yet to understand what influence Dickinson may have had on second-generation Transcendentalists such as

Higginson, to whom she sent her poems, and others who read her poems via informal circulation in her mid-century letters. Transcendentalism was never tightly organized (indeed, it was rarely called "Transcendentalism," except by its bemused onlookers), and while it had intellectual leaders, the movement was ultimately constituted by many individuals, both prominent and obscure, who thought, read, journaled, corresponded, conversed, and wrote. It is thus essential that we turn our attention to as many of these voices as possible and understand the movement through its disparate parts.

Notes

1. See Jana L. Argersinger and Phyllis Cole (eds.), *Toward a Female Genealogy of Transcendentalism* (Athens: University of Georgia Press, 2014), as well as Megan Marshall, *The Peabody Sisters: Three Women Who Ignited American Romanticism* (New York: Houghton Mifflin, 2005). Recent studies of Fuller include Brigette Bailey, Katheryn P. Viens, and Conrad Edick Wright (eds.), *Margaret Fuller and Her Circles* (Durham: University of New Hampshire Press, 2013); Katherine Adams, *Owning Up: Privacy, Property, and Belonging in U. S. Women's Life Writing* (Oxford: Oxford University Press, 2009), 31–70; and Jeffrey Steele, *Transfiguring America: Myth, Ideology, and Mourning in Margaret Fuller's Writing* (Columbia: University of Missouri Press, 2001) and "Freeing the 'Prisoned Queen': The Development of Margaret Fuller's Poetry," *Studies in the American Renaissance* (1992), 137–175. Recent biographies include Megan Marshall, *Margaret Fuller: A New American Life* (New York: Houghton Mifflin, 2013); Charles Capper, *Margaret Fuller: American Romantic, Vol. 2: The Public Years* (Oxford: Oxford University Press, 2007); John Matteson, *The Lives of Margaret Fuller: A Biography* (New York: W. W. Norton, 2012); and Meg McGavran Murray, *Margaret Fuller, Wandering Pilgrim* (Athens: University of Georgia Press, 2012).
2. See, for example, Philip Gura, *The Wisdom of Words: Language, Theology, and Literature in the New England Renaissance* (Middletown: Wesleyan University Press, 1981) and "Elizabeth Palmer Peabody and the Philosophy of Language," *Emerson Society Quarterly* 23.3 (1977), 154–163; and Kathleen Lawrence, "The 'Dry-Lighted Soul' Ignites: Emerson and His Soul-Mate Caroline Sturgis as Seen in Her Houghton Manuscripts," *Harvard Library Bulletin* 16.3 (2005), 37–67, and "Soul Sisters and the Sister Arts: Margaret Fuller, Caroline Sturgis, and Their Private World of Love and Art," *ESQ: A Journal of the American Renaissance* 57.1 (2011), 79–104; and Steele, *Transfiguring America.*
3. Ralph Waldo Emerson, "Nature," *Emerson: Essays and Lectures*, Joel Porte (ed.), (New York: Library of America, 1983), 20.
4. Elizabeth Peabody, "Spirit of the Hebrew Scriptures," *Christian Examiner* 16 (1834), 175.
5. Emerson, "Nature," *Emerson: Essays and Lectures*, 10.

6. For related studies of literary Transcendentalism, see Lawrence Buell, *Literary Transcendentalism: Style and Vision in the American Renaissance* (Ithaca: Cornell University Press, 1973); Stephen Cushman, "Transcendentalist Poetics," *The Cambridge Companion to Nineteenth-Century American Poetry*, Kerry Larson (ed.), (Cambridge: Cambridge University Press, 2011), 76–93; and Michelle Kohler, *Miles of Stare: Transcendentalism and the Problem of Literary Vision in Nineteenth-Century America* (Tuscaloosa: University of Alabama Press, 2014), 1–51.
7. Margaret Fuller, "A Dialogue," *The Dial* 1 (July 1840), 134.
8. This admonition is from Emerson's "Self-Reliance," in *Emerson: Essays and Lectures*, 494, where he repudiates love that "pules and whines."
9. Fuller, "Richter" and "Some murmur at the 'want of system' in Richter's writings," *The Dial* 1 (July 1840), 135.
10. Qtd. in Steele, "Freeing the 'Prisoned Queen,'" 161.
11. Margaret Fuller, "Sistrum," *American Poetry: The Nineteenth Century, Volume 1*, ed. John Hollander (New York: Library of America, 1993), 587.
12. See Emerson, "American Scholar," in *Emerson: Essays and Lectures*, 53–71, and "Self-Reliance," in *Emerson: Essays and Lectures*, 261.
13. Fuller, "Double Triangle, Serpent and Rays," *Nineteenth-Century American Women Poets: An Anthology*, Paula Bernat Bennett (ed.), (Oxford: Blackwell Publishers, 1998), 60.
14. Fuller, "Winged Sphynx," qtd. in Steele, "Freeing the 'Prisoned Queen,'" 164–165.
15. Cushman, "Transcendentalist Poetics," 83.
16. Ibid., 90.
17. Ibid., 83.
18. Ibid., 89.
19. Fuller, *Woman in the Nineteenth Century*, Larry J. Reynolds (ed.), (New York: W. W. Norton, 1998), 105.
20. Ibid., 135–136.
21. Ibid., 70.
22. Ibid., 66.
23. See Lawrence, "Soul Sisters," where she traces what she calls this "undersung interdisciplinary and female-driven" strand of American Transcendentalism (79).
24. Caroline Sturgis, "Art and Artist," *The Dial* 1.2 (October 1840), 232.
25. Sturgis, "The Angel and the Artist," *The Dial* 1.4 (April 1841), 469.
26. Sturgis, "Give Us an Interpreter," *The Dial* 1.3 (January 1841), 306.
27. Sturgis, "Light and Shade," *The Dial* 2.2 (October 1841), 203.
28. Sturgis, "Love and Insight," "Sunset," *The Dial* 1.3 (January 1841), 305.
29. Ellen Sturgis Hooper, "[I slept, and dreamed that life was Beauty]," *The Dial* 1.1 (July 1840), 123.
30. Emerson, "Experience," *Emerson: Essays and Lectures*, 487.
31. Ibid., 492.
32. Hooper, "To the Ideal," *The Dial* 1.3 (January 1841), 400.

33. Emerson, "Experience," *Emerson: Essays and Lectures*, 479.
34. Hooper, "The Poet," *The Dial* 1.2 (October 1840), 194.
35. Hooper, "To R. W. E.," *The Poets of Transcendentalism: An Anthology*, George Willis Cooke (ed.), (Boston: Houghton Mifflin and Company, 1903), 136.
36. Eliza Thayer Clapp, "Two Hymns," *The Dial* 2.1 (July 1841), 42–44.
37. Clapp, "Clouds," *The Dial* 2.1 (July 1841), 55–57.
38. Caroline Dall, *Transcendentalism in New England: A Lecture* (Boston: Roberts Brothers, 1897), 38.
39. See Tiffany K. Wayne, *Woman Thinking: Feminism and Transcendentalism in Nineteenth-Century America* (Lanham: Lexington Books, 2005).
40. Elizabeth Jessup Eames, "Universe," *The Una* 1.10 (1853), 158.
41. Eames, "Conjugal Love," *The Una* 3.4 (1855), 53.
42. Mary Gove Nichols, "Dawn," *The Una* 2.10 (1854), 341, and Ann Preston, "The Ideal Is the Real," *The Una* 2.7 (1854), 304.
43. See Jedd Deppman, *Trying to Think with Emily Dickinson* (Amherst: University of Massachusetts Press, 2008), 75–108; E. Miller Budick, *Emily Dickinson and the Life of Language: A Study in Symbolic Poetics* (Baton Rouge: Louisiana State University Press, 1985), 133–162; and Kohler, *Miles of Stare*, 105–136. On gender and Transcendentalism, see Mary Loeffelholz, *Dickinson and the Boundaries of Feminist Theory* (Urbana: University of Illinois Press, 1991), 7–46; and Joanne Feit Diehl, *Dickinson and the Romantic Imagination* (Princeton: Princeton University Press, 1981) and *Women Poets and the American Sublime* (Bloomington: Indiana University Press, 1990), 1–43.
44. Emily Dickinson, "Of Bronze – and Blaze –" (Fr319), *The Poems of Emily Dickinson*, Variorum Edition, 3 vols.,: R. W. Franklin (ed.), (Cambridge, MA and London: The Belknap Press of Harvard University Press, 1998), 337.

CHAPTER 9

Poets of the Loom, Spinners of Verse: Working-Class Women's Poetry and The Lowell Offering

Jennifer Putzi

In her autobiography, *A New England Girlhood* (1889), Lucy Larcom attempts to articulate the aspirations that led her and her fellow "mill-girls" to publish their work in *The Lowell Offering*; she writes: "we did not set ourselves up to be literary; though we enjoyed the freedom of writing what we pleased and seeing how it looked in print. It was good practice for us, and that was all that we desired."[1] Reading this explanation is perhaps more confusing than it is enlightening. To begin with, what does it mean to "set [oneself] up to be literary," and why does Larcom insist that the factory operatives did not do this? Why did "writing what [they] pleased and seeing how it looked in print" give them such satisfaction? Finally, what exactly is print "good practice" for, especially in the case of women who worked for the Lowell textile factories and published in *The Lowell Offering* between its first appearance in October 1840 and its demise in December 1845?

These women were an integral part of the nineteenth-century American textile industry that flourished throughout New England. With the establishment of the Boston Manufacturing Company in 1814, Francis Cabot Lowell and his fellow "Boston Associates" constructed and operated a series of mills throughout Massachusetts. In order to avoid the European practice of employing families in the mills, as well as the employment of male workers who might demand higher wages, the Associates advertised for female employees, usually between the ages of fifteen and twenty-five. While parents were persuaded to send their daughters to the mills by mill owners' assurances of corporate paternalism and protection, the daughters themselves were drawn by the wages – higher than anything they could earn in other occupations – and the opportunities for independence and self-improvement. Operatives worked for twelve hours a day, but were encouraged to spend their spare time attending evening schools and lyceum lectures and enjoying free access to circulating libraries.

The literary interests of the operatives prompted the organization of improvement circles, often held in churches, in which they met to share their work with one another.[2]

Although other operatives' periodicals were proposed and even published, the *Offering* quickly became recognized as the only one entirely written and, eventually, edited by the mill girls themselves. It was first published in October 1840, by the Revered Abel C. Thomas of the First Universalist Church in Lowell, and appeared sporadically until January 1841, when it became a monthly magazine. In 1842, Thomas sold the *Offering* to William Schouler, editor and publisher of the *Lowell Courier*, and two factory operatives, Harriet F. Farley and Harriott Curtis, were engaged as co-editors. Farley and Curtis eventually purchased the periodical from Schouler, although he remained as publisher until its demise in late 1845.

By the time Larcom's *A New England Girlhood* was published, almost fifty years after the first issue of the *Offering*, the equation between writing, print, and publication had shifted, with the dramatic expansion of the literary marketplace on the one hand and increased opportunity and technology for individuals to privately print and circulate their work on the other. During the antebellum period about which she writes, however, to be "in print" would necessarily mean to be published. Many literate women of the period occupied themselves with various forms of "parlor authorship," as Susan S. Williams calls it, writing diaries, letters, and poems, and occasionally exchanging their work with one another.[3] While many sought to preserve their work and that of their peers in commonplace books, scrapbooks, and private collections, very few actually attempted to publish. Publication, as Larcom points out, usually required some measure of literary ambition, some sense of one's self as "literary." The Lowell factory operatives, however, found themselves in the rare position of having access to print without first having to imagine themselves as "literary"; any literary aspirations developed as a result of the publication of their work. It is for this reason that *The Lowell Offering* provides us with a unique opportunity to see working-class American women negotiating their relationship to print in public, as the interrelated processes of reading, composition, and publication are a central feature of the work of the periodical.

The relationship between print culture, labor, and the literary in the *Offering* is, I propose, particularly salient in the poetry written and published by the operatives, in that poetry was both the most literary of genres and, for nineteenth-century American women, one of the most accessible. Poetry plays a prominent role in the *Offering*'s mission, as articulated by editors Curtis and Farley in 1843, to demonstrate the "intelligence" and "self-culture" of factory girls and of "the mass of [the] country" in general.[4] While the relative brevity of poetry lent itself to the long working hours of the factory operatives, the genre's inherent intertextuality allowed the poets to demonstrate their "self-culture," particularly their familiarity with and mastery of a vast reservoir of poetry, primarily British and American. Their use of this reservoir has led to their being labeled imitative and therefore uninteresting by later scholars, but such dismissals are generally mired in either a modernist aesthetic that has room for only a select few nineteenth-century poets or an expectation of working-class poets that would label their consumption and production of mainstream literary texts as inauthentic. I argue, instead, that we should think about how these poets used an imitative poetics to make their lives and texts legible to a wider, primarily middle-class, audience. I focus on poems produced by factory operatives that use the work of other women writers as their model or inspiration, not because they represent the majority of poems generated by this imitative poetics, but because they represent the *Offering* poets' positioning of themselves in a wider tradition of female poetic authorship.[5] Claiming literary culture for themselves, these mill girls adapted it to the circumstances of the factory and insisted on their own participation in and contribution to nineteenth-century American poetics.

The poetry of the *Offering* has received little attention, and most of that disparaging; this is, perhaps, in part because most scholars who have looked at the *Offering* are historians who have tended to turn to the periodical for factual details about factory life and reform. Hannah Josephson established this critical precedent in 1949, when she wrote in *The Golden Threads: New England's Mill Girls and Magnates* that "[t]he poetry in the *Offering* was almost completely undistinguished."[6] Philip S. Foner's *The Factory Girls* (1977), a selection of writing by and about female factory operatives in New England, features a number of poems, but only those that protest the conditions of labor in the factories.[7] Only one poem in *The Factory Girls*, then, is from the *Offering*, and even this is included in the section of the book titled "The Genteel Factory Girls" (as opposed to "The Militant Factory Girls," which follows). Benita Eisler, whose *The Lowell Offering: Writings by New England Mill Women* (also 1977) remains the only available anthology made up entirely of selections from the *Offering*, includes just one poem in the volume and says this of the periodical's poetry in her introduction:

> Poetry was the least happy form of expression for *Offering* talents. Most selections, favoring elegiac subjects and form, are frank pastiches of women poets scarcely more gifted than their acolytes. As soon as they set out to "pen verse," the spontaneous, freshly observed detail, the felt experience, were abandoned for the dreariest poetic formulas of the day.[8]

Eisler's assessment of this body of work as "the least happy form of expression" for *Offering* contributors indicates her unwillingness to grant it any formal or thematic complexity or to read it as important precisely because it followed such a popular and wide-spread "formula." For Eisler, to "pen verse" is simply to replicate the work of female poets whose work appeared in mainstream magazines; it is, therefore, unworthy of study.

Eisler's dismissal of the *Offering*'s poetry as an imitation of an already formulaic original has, for the most part, shaped the critical response to this work, even by literary scholars. Sylvia J. Cook's study of working-class American women writers, *Working Women, Literary Ladies: The Industrial Revolution and Female Aspiration* (2008), does much to position the *Offering* within its nineteenth-century literary and social context, but her argument about what renders the material of interest to scholars is not very different from that of Eisler. Both clearly prefer the fiction and nonfiction of the *Offering* to the poetry, claiming that the prose work realistically depicts the lives of the factory workers themselves. While Cook does not entirely dismiss the value of convention, she is quick to prioritize literary innovation in the *Offering*: "While much of [the operatives'] writing is in the vein of religious idealism, and is conventionally decorous and imitative in both form and content," she writes, "they also begin the more radical process of developing imaginative literary modes that anticipate later realism."[9] Despite all that differentiates their approach to the *Offering*, both Eisler and Cook largely ignore the poetry in the periodical because it does not meet their expectations for working-class women's literature.

What I would like to suggest here, however, is that the *Offering*'s immersion in and response to antebellum print cultures is precisely what should render it of interest to scholars of nineteenth-century American women's poetry. Adelia's "'The Graves of a Household,'" published in the *Offering* in April 1841, is likely a poem that critics following Eisler would find formulaic and imitative: it is modeled on a poem of the same title by the British poet Felicia Hemans, whose "The Graves of a Household" was originally published in the *New Monthly Magazine* in 1825, reprinted in *Records of a Woman: With Other Poems* in 1828, and widely circulated in the United States. It therefore provides a good test case for the value of imitation for *Offering* poets and, by extension, the value of poetry in any study of the *Offering*. Adelia's poem does more than simply borrow its title from Hemans' original; the *Offering* poet also integrates three entire stanzas from Hemans' poem into her own. There is no deception here, no plagiarism as such, as the title itself is in quotation marks and the poem is preceded with a note that reads "The statements in the following lines are facts; but they were suggested by that beautiful little poem of Mrs. Hemans, from which the first verse and the last two verses are extracted." Adelia's parsing of her use of Hemans' poem – the "statements" in her own poem "are facts," merely "suggested" by Hemans' poem, from which she "extract[s]" three stanzas – is not intended as a defense; there is no sense that Adelia fears that her work will be seen as derivative or inauthentic. It is, it seems, a clarification, an explanation of the poem's form and the poet's creative project.

Adelia clearly does not intend to alter the meaning of Hemans' poem; instead, her borrowing reinforces the sentimental, domestic, and religious message of the original, doubling it, in effect, by emphasizing its applicability to her own life experience. Nine stanzas long (as compared to the eight stanzas of Hemans' original), a third of Adelia's poem is freely "extracted" from Hemans', and these parts appear in quotation marks. These "extract[s]" establish the purpose of the poem – the detailing of the speaker's loss of her siblings, initially through geographical dispersion and eventually through death. While both poems assert a belief in the afterlife (the final two lines proclaim, "Alas for love, if thou wert all, / And nought beyond, O Earth!"), the emphasis of both poems remains on the separation of siblings, the disruption of an essential family bond.

Adelia's use of Hemans' original demonstrates her intimate familiarity with the work of the British poet but also places her poem in conversation with that of Hemans, rendering her own losses (or those of her own speaker) as worthy of comment as those of Hemans's speaker. Adelia essentially claims the same importance for her poetic expression of grief that has been afforded Hemans' poem by publication in her book and public association with her name and public celebrity. Moreover, by writing stanzas to be sandwiched in between the opening and closing stanzas of the original, Adelia also claims Hemans' poem as her own, to some degree. Such fluidity might, in turn, extend to yet another reader of Adelia's poem or Hemans' original (or both), who might write a poem of her own on the same subject, with the same title, perhaps even quoting some of the same stanzas.

Rather than a simple, unimaginative theft, then, Adelia's "'The Graves of a Household'" can be seen as a democratization of literary property and a claiming of poetic authority and authorship. The poem thus lays bare the process of composition for *Offering* poets whose access to print came hand in hand with their employment in the mills. For middle-class women writers, amateur or professional, the parlor played a central role in the production of literary texts, providing women with a space in which they might read books and periodicals, clip items from newspapers and organize them in scrapbooks, and compose their own work and share it with others. Factory operatives may have used the public spaces of their boarding-houses in a similar way, but they had neither the time nor the space for the sort of parlor authorship enacted in private homes. Instead, they adapted the literacy practices of the domestic parlor to the public space of the factory. For example, given rules against bringing books (including Bibles) into the mills, many girls pasted poetry on the walls, clipping favorites from the newspaper and creating a scrapbook of sorts out of the environment in which they worked. As Larcom recalled in her autobiography:

> I made my window-seat into a small library of poetry, pasting its side all over with newspaper clippings. In those days we had only weekly papers, and they had always a "poet's corner," where standard writers were well represented, with anonymous ones, also. . . . I chose my verses for their sentiment, and because I wanted to commit them to memory; sometimes it was a long poem, sometimes a hymn, sometimes only a stray verse.[10]

The emphasis on memory here is essential: as these poems are read, clipped, pasted on the wall or the machinery, and reread, they are internalized to such a degree that they become the property of the operative herself and her larger community in the mills. The operatives are simultaneously readers, authors, and editors in this process, selecting poems based on their own tastes and preferences, and literalizing the notion of the newspaper's "poet's corner." These poems then inspire their creations, which go on to be privately circulated and finally published in the *Offering*. Toward the end of the century, former operative Harriet H. Robinson explains,

> We little girls were fond of reading these clippings, and no doubt they were an incentive to our thoughts as well as to those of the older girls, who went to "The Improvement Circle," and wrote compositions.
>
> A year or two after this I attempted poetry, and my verses began to appear in the newspapers, in one or two Annuals, and later in *The Lowell Offering*.[11]

The internalization of newspaper poetry, then, leads to imitation and publication – a process that, to Larcom at least, represented "good practice." And unlike many middle-class parlor authors who had no access to publication or saw publication as inappropriate for women, factory operatives such as Adelia had the venue of the *Offering* in which to present their work to a wider public.

The centrality of an imitative poetics to the literary success of the *Offering* is evident in "Factory Blossoms for Queen Victoria," a poem published in October 1842 by Harriet Farley under the pseudonym "H.F." Farley's co-editorship of the *Offering* began in this same issue and "Factory Blossoms" seems to be a statement of the editors' ambitions for the periodical. In "Factory Blossoms," Farley presents her poem to the queen of England. The poem begins:

> Lady, accept the humble flowers
> Which I now tender thee;
> They bloomed not in Parnassian bowers,
> Nor on some classic tree.
>
> Amid the granite rocks they grew
> Of a far-distant land;
> Ne'er were they bathed in Grecian dew,
> Or watched by sylphic hand.
>
> This claims no place amid the wreaths
> Which often strew thy way;
> Simple the fragrance which it breathes,
> *A factory girl's boquet.*
>
> But deem me not, when it meets your sight,
> Wanting in courtesy—
> This stubborn Yankee pen wont write,
> YOUR GRACIOUS MAJESTY.[12]

Farley emphasizes the "humble" nature of her gift, but her humility is called into question by her daring to address Queen Victoria in this poem as well as her carefully capitalized refusal to behave as the queen's subject. Similarly, Farley does not mask the origin of her "boquet" in the factory. Unlike the work of other poets, which is nurtured on "Parnassian bowers" or "on some classic tree," the verses of the *Offering* poet have bloomed and thrived in the austerity of the industrial workplace. While flowers were commonly associated with poems in nineteenth-century America, this metaphor becomes even more interesting here in light of the fact that, just as many operatives created libraries or scrapbooks of their window seats in the factory, others created small window gardens. As David A. Zonderman notes, "Female workers often traded cuttings with each other, or helped a new arrival start her own window garden. . . . Flowers became a medium of social exchange among workers."[13] Neither the growing of flowers or the reading and writing of poems was a solitary experience in the mills; rather, these were communal processes that brought the operatives together and sustained their sense of themselves as working women with lives prior to and outside of the mill. Farley's poem extends the offer of fellowship across lines of class and national identity. While it is unlikely that the queen of England would read her poem, then, "Factory Blossoms" represents the kind of "social exchange" between the mill and the outside world that Farley and her fellow operatives envisioned for the *Offering*. This exchange is framed as "simple," but it indicates the reach of the editors' vision for the periodical and registers their mockery of the idea that they might humble themselves in order to carry out that vision.

The radical potential of Farley's proffered gift to the queen is highlighted when "Factory Blossoms" is compared to the poem it was "suggested by": Hannah F. Gould's "American Wild Flowers, For Queen Victoria," published first in London in a gift book and reprinted in the United States in the *Christian Observer* on November 26, 1841.[14] Gould's poem, like Farley's, pays honor to the queen, but not to the monarchy. Gould writes:

> Not drawn by state or titles forth,
> My liberal heart would homage pay;
> But at the shrine of moral worth
> I bring these fresh wild flowers to lay.[15]

The poem concludes with Gould's offering of "the simple wreath I weave," begging the "Fair Queen, from o'er the deep receive, / A free-will offering of the free." Gould proudly asserts her national identity, but the placement of this poem in the *Forget-Me-Not*, one of the earliest and most popular British literary annuals, also emphasizes her desire to work within a transatlantic literary marketplace, to claim American superiority in some things while granting the value of British culture in others. While the title of the *Offering* plays on the popularity of the gift book, its strict refusal to publish work by readers not employed in the mills (or not able to prove themselves to be employed) indicates a pride in and a recognition of the value of the parochial. Both Gould and Farley claim their identity as American poets, but, in the distinctive context of *The Lowell Offering*, "Factory Blossoms" not only allows Farley to critique the queen, but also to frame her poem (and, by extension, the *Offering*) as the distinctive offering of the "factory girl" who "may say / What others leave unsaid."

Farley reserves her harshest criticism of the queen for the way in which she treats the neediest of her subjects, and she laments the fact that Victoria seems to lose her womanhood in her exercise of "regal power."

> There's better far than pomp or state
> To claim a sovereign's care—
> Goodness should always make her great,
> And kindness make her fair.

While Gould's gift of her "American wild-flowers" represents only her respect and love for Victoria, Farley's offering is a mild rebuke to the queen, some of whose subjects are "by wrongs oppressed / Beneath a woman's sway." Rather than benefiting from a woman monarch, whose seemingly innate capacity for "goodness" and "kindness" should render her better able to wield power more sensitively and humanely, the oppressed see no change in their situation. As an American working-class woman, Farley represents the potential of the working-class, in England as well as America, capable not only of thriving under the right kind of government, but of being Queen Victoria's equal in all of the qualities that matter – dignity, humanity, moral worth, and intelligence. The poem closes with Farley's subversive suggestion that:

> Lady, on earth we ne'er can meet;
> But when, in death, we're laid,
> Proud England's Queen, perhaps, may greet
> *The Lowell Factory maid.*

It is not clear whether it is impossible for the queen and Farley to meet in life because of geographical distance or the distance created by social class. Nevertheless, Farley clearly suggests that it would not be inappropriate for the two to meet after death; the only barrier to such an encounter would be Victoria's pride – a sense of superiority that is out of place on both heaven and earth.

By using Gould's "American Wild-Flowers" as the model for her own poem, it is also possible that Farley is claiming equality to Gould, an established American female poet whose work was published widely in a variety of periodicals and had also been collected several times throughout the 1830s and 1840s. In doing so, she demonstrates her membership and participation in a larger literary culture of both readers (who write poetry) and writers (who read poetry). Rather than hiding this imitative practice or using it to mask a lack of skill or originality, Farley highlights her use of the poem, adding a note to the inside front cover of the October issue to point her readers' attention to the imitation. The exchange between women enacted in this poem – Gould and Queen Victoria, Farley and Gould, Farley and Queen Victoria – demonstrates the ambition and potential reach of the *Offering*, as well as its subversive potential – a potential that is only visible if poems such as "Factory Blossoms" are read within the thriving antebellum culture of poetic imitation.

As "The Graves of a Household" and "Factory Blossoms for Queen Victoria" indicate, imitation is neither simplistic nor formulaic. Each of these poems uses a specific original and relies on the readers' knowledge of that original (and, to some extent, its publication and circulation). But each uses a different imitative method, one that shapes the reading of the text that is ultimately published in the *Offering*. Like the other two poems I've discussed in this regard, "To M. M. Davidson" by M. R. G. (Miriam R. Green), which was published in August 1845, similarly frames imitation as a worthy poetic project, one that demonstrates the familiarity of these working-class poets with their literary forebears and peers. Responding to the relationship between Margaret Miller Davidson and her sister, poet Lucretia Davidson, the poem also positions the *Offering* poets in a longer tradition of imitation, particularly among American female poets. While "To M. M. Davidson" is not an imitation of a specific original, as are "The Graves of a Household" and "Factory Blossoms for Queen Victoria," this poem is an example of the versatility of the poetics of imitation evident in and central to the poetry of *The Lowell Offering*.

While Margaret Miller Davidson's work had been celebrated throughout her young life, it was collected and published posthumously in *Biographical and Poetical Remains of the Late Margaret Miller Davidson* (1841), with a lengthy introduction by Washington Irving. Appearing the year following the publication of the first issue of the *Offering*, it is possible that this book had an impact on the mill girls, whose own manuscript writings had so recently been converted into print. Margaret Davidson was best known as the sister of Lucretia, a poetic prodigy who died at the age of sixteen, when Margaret was only two years old. According to Rufus Griswold, Lucretia's death shaped the course of Margaret's life, in accord, apparently, with their mother's wishes:

> [Margaret] loved, when but three years old, to sit on a cushion at her mother's feet, listening to anecdotes of her sister's life, and details of the events which preceded her death, and would often exclaim, while her face beamed with mingled emotions, "Oh, I will try to fill her place – teach me to be like her!"[16]

Margaret's self-imposed training to become "like" Lucretia, according to Griswold, was to read precociously and voraciously; to embark "on a general course of education, studying grammar, geography, history, and rhetoric"; and, of course, to compose poetry.[17] As Mary Loeffelholz points out, "The name and death of Lucretia authorize the appearance of her sister Margaret," and Margaret's reputation is thus part of "the productive family machine of [Lucretia's] posthumous reputation."[18]

Margaret makes no secret of what drives her desire to write and publish poetry; in fact, her connection to her sister and her imitation of her work and her career are important parts of her public image. In the dedication of a long poem to Lucretia titled "Lenore," Margaret claims that the relationship between the two goes beyond mere influence or imitation to a sort of cohabitation of the same creative spirit. Using the same "hallowed harp" as her long-dead sister, she imagines her work as a collaboration between the two:

For thee I pour this unaffected lay,
    To thee these simple numbers all belong;
For though thine earthly form has passed away,
    Thy memory still inspires my childish song.

Then take this feeble tribute! 'tis thine own—
    Thy fingers sweep my trembling heartstrings o'er,
Arouse to harmony each buried tone,
    And bid its wakened music sleep no more![19]

Here Margaret offers "Lenore" to her long-dead sister as "tribute," but also acknowledges Lucretia's part in the production of this and other poems. It is not simply that Lucretia's "memory inspires [her] childish song," but that the song actually seems to belong to Lucretia, despite its having been written down by Margaret. The creative process here – the evocation of emotion, the shaping of harmonies, the production of music – is assigned by Margaret to Lucretia. This sort of collaboration between reader and poet as well as between sister poets is exactly what Green intends to evoke in her own tribute to Davidson published in the *Offering*.

"To M. M. Davidson" is prefaced by a note that explains that the poem was written "after perusing and reperusing" Margaret Davidson's *Biography and Poetical Remains*, particularly the poem titled "To die and be forgotten," in which, Green states, "she gives sway to the ebullition of a full heart, with regard to literary fame, in an affecting manner."[20] As editor of the *Poetical Remains*, Irving explains that "To die and be forgotten" was inspired by a conversation with Davidson's mother in which Mrs. Davidson asked her daughter "whether she had no ambition to have her name go down to posterity."[21] While Margaret rejects any elaborate commemoration of her death, she admits the appeal of being "embalm'd in kindred hearts."[22] Yet as soon as she imagines this sort of afterlife for herself, she dismisses the possibility:

> To be, when countless years have past,
> The good man's glowing theme?
> To be—but I—what right have I
> To this bewildering dream?

In the remainder of the poem, Davidson rather unconvincingly insists that she will forget about literary fame, instead "toil[ing] to write my name within / The glorious book of life." Having essentially transferred the credit for her own poetry to her deceased sister, Margaret seems in this poem to struggle with how she herself will be remembered.

In "To M. M. Davidson," Green reassures the now deceased Margaret that she will not, in fact, "be forgotten":

> Yet thy memory shall live, and ages to come
> Shall love to repeat thy sweet name:
> O, the golden thread that thy genius has spun
> To weave in the web of thy fame!

While subtle, Green's emphasis on weaving here renders this poem, like Farley's tribute to Queen Victoria, a sort of "factory blossom," a gift that could only come from the mill girls themselves. Although the "golden thread" was created by Davidson and left to survive her after her premature death, it is Green – and perhaps her fellow factory operatives – who are said to have woven this thread "in the web of thy fame!" Therefore, just as Margaret's career is inspired by and enmeshed with that of her older sister Lucretia, the writing careers of the female factory workers are intimately intertwined with that of Margaret, extending its life beyond her death and even imitating it in their own rapid acquisition of cultural literacy.

One way in which Davidson, and by extension other poets, will live on after their deaths is the deployment of a vigorous poetics of imitation. After commending Davidson's poetry about nature and calling her Nature's "lost, her favorite child" (perhaps in contrast to her earthly family, in which Margaret seems always to have been a poor replacement for Lucretia), Green describes the broad range of Margaret's "fancy":

> Thy fancy explored the boundless waves,
> That roar for the mighty deep,

And down, far down in the coral caves
Where "the green-haired sea-nymphs" sleep.

Quoting from Davidson's poem "A Moonbeam," Green incorporates Margaret's work into her own; as in Adelia's "The Graves of a Household," this "extraction" is purposeful and is intended to be noticed by Green's readers. Similarly, later in the poem, Green insists that "The 'good man' often will wander forth, / By the purest reverence led, / From the scenes of fashion and festal mirth, / To seek thy lowly bed," thus responding directly to Davidson's desire in "To die and be forgotten" to be "The good man's glowing theme." Such borrowings reinforce the wish Green expresses in her next stanza:

Methinks 'tis a theme may well inspire
The heart with a kindred flame,
O, would, while *I* touch the tuneful lyre,
I could imitate thy strain!

While quotation is not strictly imitation, it does highlight a related engagement with and an incorporation of other poetic texts; as in Adelia's "The Graves of a Household," the original text becomes part of the new text, signaling a sort of posthumous collaboration. Imitation is regarded as a positive poetic project, one that is not just instructive for the poet but is productive of a superior "strain" of poetry, to which both Margaret Davidson and Green aspire.

While Green seems to lament her inability to imitate Davidson, her poem, like "To die and be forgotten," contains mixed messages about her own talent and her desire for fame. In imitating Davidson's modest dismissal of her own talent and ambition, Green may be seen as asking for a response similar to that she has given Davidson – some assertion that she is not to "be forgotten" herself. At the very least, her tribute has rendered her worthy of Davidson's attention: as a sort of reward for her own faithfulness to the deceased poet, Green imagines for herself a meeting of the two poets:

O, then may we meet in the heavenly choir,
Where eternal anthems ring,
And strike with thee the seraphic lyre
To the songs which *all* can sing.

In this rendition of an American women's literary tradition, Green effectively takes the place of Margaret's sister, striking the "seraphic lyre" with Margaret, just as Margaret herself imagined she and her sister making use of the same "hallowed harp." The ending frames Green as Margaret's poetic heir, just as Margaret was her sister's. By emphasizing "the songs which *all* can sing," Green also claims poetry for everyone, thus dissolving the boundary between audience and performer, establishing imitation as the way in which those who hear the song can become those who sing it. The *Offering* writers can then lay claim to a lineage of song (and poetry) that renders their own work worthy of attention.

Although the poetry in the *Offering* has largely been ignored by scholars, it might productively be seen as central to the project of the periodical. Poetry comes to stand, in many ways, as proof of the factory operatives' desire to engage with print culture. Speaking of all of the writers published in the *Offering*, Robinson insists in her memoir of 1898, *Loom and Spindle*, that "These authors represent what may be called the poetic element of factory life. They were the ideal mill-girls, full of hopes, desires, aspirations; poets of the loom, spinners of verse, artists of factory life."[23] For many scholars, this "poetic element" has been evidence of the factory operatives' lack of talent, and the work has been condemned for its aspirations – either to gentility or to literariness, with both seen as somehow inauthentic on the part of young working women. Rather than seeing these poets as aspiring to be middle class, however, I am suggesting that we see them as rejecting the idea that poetry and print culture are by their very nature middle class. Accessing a literary tradition usually denied them by class and education, the *Offering* poets claimed poetry for themselves, experimenting with its place in their own lives and their own periodical.

Notes

1. Lucy Larcom, *A New England Girlhood: Outlined From Memory* (Boston: Houghton and Mifflin, 1889), 221.
2. Histories of the New England textile factories include Hannah Josephson, *The Golden Threads: New England's Mill Girls and Their Magnates* (New York: Duell, Sloan, and Pearce, 1949); Caroline F. Ware, *The Early New England Cotton Manufacture: A Study in Industrial Beginnings* (New York: Russell & Russell, 1966); and David A. Zonderman, *Aspirations and Anxieties: New England Workers and the Mechanized Factory System, 1815–1850* (New York: Oxford University Press, 1992). Studies of women's work in the factories include Thomas Dublin, *Women at Work* (New York: Columbia University Press, 1979) and William Moran, *The Belles of New England: The Women of the Textile Mills and the Families Whose Wealth They Wove* (New York: St. Martin's Press, 2002). For collections of the writing of female factory operatives, see Philip S. Foner (ed.), *The Factory Girls* (Urbana and Chicago: University of

Illinois Press, 1977); Benita Eisler (ed.), *The Lowell Offering: Writings by New England Women* (Philadelphia: Lippincott, 1977); and Thomas Dublin (ed.), *Farm to Factory: Women's Letters, 1830–1860* (New York: Columbia University Press, 1991).

3. See Susan S. Williams, *Reclaiming Authorship: Literary Women in America, 1850–1900* (Philadelphia: University of Pennsylvania Press, 2006).
4. Harriot F. Curtis and Harriet Farley, "The Lowell Offering," *Christian Register*, 22.51 (December 23, 1843), 202.
5. My discussion of this imitative poetics is deeply indebted to Eliza Richards' argument about gender and mimicry in nineteenth-century American poetry. See *Gender and the Poetics of Reception in Poe's Circle* (New York: Cambridge University Press, 2004).
6. Josephson, *Golden Threads*, 189.
7. Foner, *Factory Girls*.
8. Eisler, *The Lowell Offering*, 113.
9. Sylvia J. Cook, *Working Women, Literary Ladies: The Industrial Revolution and Female Aspiration* (New York: Oxford University Press, 2008), 46.
10. Larcom, *A New England Girlhood*, 175–176.
11. Harriet H. Robinson, *Loom and Spindle, or Life Among the Early Mill Girls* (New York: Thomas Y. Crowell and Company, 1898), 46.
12. H. F. (Harriet Farley), "Factory Blossoms for Queen Victoria," *The Lowell Offering* 3 (October 1842), 1–4.
13. Zonderman, *Aspirations and Anxieties*, 67.
14. Eisler, *The Lowell Offering*, 3 (October 1842): inside front cover.
15. Hannah F. Gould, "American Wild-Flowers, For Queen Victoria," *Christian Observer* 20.48 (26 November 1841), 192.
16. Rufus Wilmot Griswold (ed.), *The Female Poets of America* (Philadelphia: Carey and Hart, 1849), 155.
17. Ibid., 155.
18. Mary Loeffelholz, *From School to Salon: Reading Nineteenth-Century American Women's Poetry* (Princeton, New Jersey: Princeton University Press, 2004), 14, 22.
19. Margaret Davidson, "Lenore," *Biography and Poetical Remains of the Late Margaret Miller Davidson*, Washington Irving (ed.), (Philadelphia: Lea and Blanchard, 1843), 217.
20. Miriam R. Greene, "To M. M. Davidson," *The Lowell Offering* 5 (August 1845), 181–182.
21. Washington Irving, "Biography of Miss Margaret Davidson," *Biography and Poetical Remains of the Late Margaret Miller Davidson*, 74.
22. Margaret Davidson, "To Die and Be Forgotten," *Biography and Poetical Remains of the Late Margaret Miller Davidson*, 74–75.
23. Robinson, *Loom and Spindle*, 117.

CHAPTER 10

Women's Transatlantic Poetic Network

Páraic Finnerty

Although still an emergent field, transatlantic scholarship has challenged the legitimacy of nation-based literary paradigms and shown that in nineteenth-century Anglo-American culture "the nation and the transatlantic are deeply implicated in one another."[1] Scholars have demonstrated that the often-stated concern of nineteenth-century American writers with the establishment of a distinctive national literature coexisted with a desire to create relations – whether competitive, hostile, ambivalent, deferential, or imitative – with their British literary heritage; and that British writers discovered in America an alternative political, social, and cultural arrangement that inspired, intrigued, horrified, or unsettled them. Evidence also exists that nineteenth-century American women writers, artists, reformers, and travelers forged professional, personal, and literary relationships with their British counterparts, with whom they shared social and moral goals as well as political and religious concerns. Whether they travelled to Europe or not, American women writers generated and sustained strong connections with this continent and its female inhabitants, and regarded themselves as part of a female-centered transatlantic "web" or "matrix" involving the circulation of ideas and texts and the creation of affective bonds.[2]

The question of how the poetic – and women's poetry in particular – functioned within this transatlantic world has yet to be fully addressed. One of the most provocative facts to have emerged is that an American, Edmund Clarence Stedman, first coined the term "Victorian poetry" and that his book *Victorian Poets* (1875) defined, theorized, and invented this field of study. Stedman's period-based, critical investigation of the nature of British poetry allowed him to conceptualize the distinguishing features of his own nation's poetry in his follow-up book, *Poets of America* (1885). In other words, Stedman recognized that a transatlantic framework was "fundamental to the articulation of national poetic traditions not because American poets borrowed from the British, but because comparable historical-material conditions in the two countries produced similar poetries."[3] Recent discoveries about the "presence of American poetics within Victorian poetics, and of Victorian poetics within American poetics" have also revealed the "centrality of women poets, women's poetry, and figures of women" within the nineteenth-century "traffic in poems" between the two countries.[4] The essays in Laura Mandell's *Romanticism on the Net* special issue on *The Transatlantic Poetess* and Meredith McGill's *Traffic in Poems: Nineteenth-Century Poetry and Transatlantic Exchange*, for example, show that in nineteenth-century poetry women are "not the exception – marginal figures who need solicitously to be brought back into national canons – but figures who make legible the extranational origins of national myths and make it possible to track the shifting currents of cultural exchange."[5] These essays indicate the comparable strategies adopted by women poets as they attempted to conform to, subvert, or transcend the expectations associated with their categorization by the sobriquet poetess. The poetess, a popular and later denigrated figure associated with excessive feeling and interiority, looms large in such scholarship and emerges as a personage who mediates and facilitates "trans-Atlantic [cultural] exchange."[6]

Such research, implicitly or explicitly, foregrounds the fact that nineteenth-century women poets such as Felicia Hemans, Elizabeth Barrett Browning, Lydia Sigourney, Lucy Larcom, Emily Brontë, Emily Dickinson, Letitia Landon, and Lucretia Davidson shared a similar cultural field and responded to it in ways that show their interconnectedness and, in certain instances, their exchanges with and influence on each other. Building on this work, this essay examines how such interconnectedness between women poets was culturally produced by exploring how women poets on both sides of the Atlantic positioned themselves and were positioned within an identifiable female poetic network. I will focus primarily on American print culture's frequent placing together of the poems and names of British and American women in periodicals, newspapers, textbooks, anthologies, and gift books, all of which emphasized these poets' associations and commonalities, as well as wider cultural debates about the interrelated construction of poetry and gender in Anglo-American culture. Two gift books, *Selections from Female Poets: A Present for Ladies* (1837), edited by D. F., Jr., and *The Ladies' Wreath: A Selection from the Female Poetic Writers of England and America* (1837), edited by Sarah Hale, will function as this essay's principal examples of texts that structurally and rhetorically locate women poets within a larger international female poetic community and connect their effortless occupancy of this field with their exceptional powers of sympathy and identification. In doing so, these texts disclose a general fault line within their conceptions of contemporary women's poetry: on the one hand, these poets symbolized and celebrated the affections associated with hearth, home, and nation, but, on the other, they were unsettling figures who emblematized cosmopolitanism and whose poetry embraced transnational subjects and topics.

Although culturally encouraged to write poems that offer consolation, celebrate the domestic and the spiritual, or focus on mourning, abandonment, and death, nineteenth-century American women poets were well aware that the precursors who authorized and legitimized their art were two controversial foreign women: Sappho and Corinne. In *Woman's Record; or Sketches of all Distinguished Women* (1853), Hale observes that Sappho's "morals have been as much depreciated, as her genius has been extolled," before noting that her suicidal leap from Leucate was a consequence of Sappho – a "far from handsome," older, "masculine" woman – desiring the much younger and "beautiful Phaon."[7] While Sappho's actions associate female creativity with transgressive desire, suffering, and death, Hale emphasizes Sappho's unmatched inventiveness and artistry, as well as the honors paid to her in her lifetime and after her death. Updating the Sappho story, the opening of Germaine de Staël's novel *Corinne, or Italy* (1807) presents its eponymous heroine, an Anglo-Italian *improvisatrice*, being crowned with laurel leaves in the Roman Capitol because she has sung of Italy's glory and happiness. Having shown the fame and honor Corinne achieved for her passionate impromptu performances of poetry, de Staël presents readers with what happens when Corinne falls in love with her Scottish Phaon, Oswald, Lord Nelvil: her creative talents decline; she is abandoned by Lord Nelvil (who, under pressure from his family, marries Corinne's more conventional half-sister, Lucile); her health fails; and she dies. Before dying, she composes a poem, "Corinne's Last Song," and listens as a young girl performs it at the Capitol. In the poem, Corinne asks her audience to remember both the songs she sang in praise of the beauty of Italy and those later songs that revealed her personal misery: "Remember my verses sometimes, for my soul is stamped on them. But deadly muses, love, and unhappiness have inspired my last songs."[8] Lord Nelvil, who is present, experiences "the violence of his emotion, [and loses] consciousness entirely"; as Corinne explains, only by listening to women's songs of personal suffering will "[m]en . . . realize what harm they do."[9] The success of this performance shows that an expression of sorrow can grant cultural authority, encourage acts of remembrance and repetition, and move listeners to feel.

Corinne provided generations of nineteenth-century British and American women with a model of the lyric poet as a figure of genius, inspiration, and sensibility; connected the woman artist's talent inextricably with her identity; and popularized the idea of Italy as a country where women and their creativity were honored and celebrated. More specifically, Patrick Vincent argues that the "romantic poetess's elegies on love or death also draw on the knowability of familiar images and affects directly or indirectly quoted from *Corinne* in order to weave a network of liberal sympathy from Britain across to Russia and the United States."[10] In this way, the poetess's generic poems of women's suffering (and men's complicity in this experience) promoted the idea of a collective female voice within the public sphere: poems of individual suffering merge into a poetry of communal sorrow that, ideally, transforms readers into a community of sympathizers. *Corinne*, with its focus on an Anglo-Italian poet-performer, also propagated the idea of the poetess as a figure who "signifies multiple and diverse nations and nationalisms" and "emerges, indeed, as a mobile category, always already in transit, signifying her patriotism paradoxically through devotion to nations not her own."[11] These associations of the poetess with female collectivity, the power of sympathy, and transnationality explain why in nineteenth-century women's poetry there is an "insistent figuring of movement across and between cultural boundaries, with its emphasis on travel," a search for or identification with the exotic other, "an attempt to transcend restrictions in fantasy, or an effort to discover a universal womanhood which transcends cultural differences."[12] Such trajectories are exemplified in Mary E. Hewitt's "The Last Chant Of Corinne" (1854):

By that mysterious sympathy which chaineth
For evermore my spirit unto thine;
And by the memory, that alone remaineth,
Of that sweet hope that now no more is mine,
And by the love my trembling heart betrayeth,
That, born of thy soft gaze, within me lies;
As the lone desert bird, the Arab sayeth,
Warms her young brood to life with her fond eyes.

Hear me, adored one! though the world divide us,
Though never more my hand in thine be prest,
Though to commingle thought be here denied us,
Till our high hearts shall beat themselves to rest;
Forget me not! forget me not! oh! ever
This one, one prayer, my spirit pours to thee;
Till every memory from earth shall sever,
Remember, oh, beloved! remember me!

And when the light within my eye is shaded,
When I, o'er-wearied, sleep the sleep profound,
And, like that nymph of yore, who droop'd and faded,
And pined for love, till she became a sound;
My song, perchance, awhile to earth remaining,
Shall come in murmur'd melody to thee;
Then let my lyre's deep, passionate complaining,
Cry to thy heart, beloved! remember me![13]

Hewitt changes the addressee of Corinne's song: whereas in the novel, Corinne asks her Roman audience to remember her, this poem's speaker pleads with an individual addressee to perform this function. The poem more closely resembles versions of Sappho's address to Phaon, including Hewitt's own "Imitation of Sappho" (1854), and within this context the speaker might be interpreted as a composite Sappho–Corinne appealing to a Phaon–Nelvil. By drawing attention to and writing a dramatic lyric from the perspective of these archetypal abandoned women, Hewitt aligns her poem with and yet subtly differentiates it from a poetic tradition of female suffering. Although within this poetic tradition the poem's "Thou," "Thee," and "Thy" address a male figure, read within the context of *Corinne* the speaker also pleads with a beloved audience to re-establish a "mysterious sympathy" with it and for communal commemoration. The poem's transhistorical and transnational trajectory, from Arabian desert songbird to Greek nymph through the legend of Sappho, calls on nineteenth-century American women readers and poets to memorialize and identify with this foreign woman who speaks for and "unite[s]" all who "pine for love." In this context, Hewitt is one such poet who has created a poem that enacts, in a comparable way to the Italian girl-performer in *Corinne*, Corinne's request for posterity to sympathize with and remember her.

The literary connections the poem maps between Sappho, Corrine, and Hewitt were explicitly signposted in American print culture. In newspapers, periodicals, elocutionary readers, and gift books, European and American writers were continually associated with or compared to one another, and were presented as part of a shared literary tradition. For example, in an 1847 essay in *The Ladies' Repository*, which argues that women's endowments "frequently rival and outshine, in brilliancy, those of the other sex," E. W. Merrill mentions Sappho, the "distinguished poetess . . . to show the antiquity of female celebrity," and then offers a "long line of famous females," including the novelists de Staël, Catherine Maria Sedgwick, and Maria Edgeworth, and the poets Hemans, Sigourney, and Hannah More.[14] In a similar manner, in an 1835 essay,

"Mrs. Sigourney and Mrs. Gould," published in the *North American Review*, the author begins by referring to Madame de Staël's representation, in *Corinne* and her other works, of the "perils" that beset the female writer who aspires to fame, but argues that in Britain and America there is a "difference in the state of female literature in our own day and the past."[15] Having discussed the writings of More, Edgeworth, Joanna Baillie, Harriet Martineau, and Mary Russell Mitford, and the "excellencies of Mrs. Hemans," the reviewer praises Sigourney as a "popular and useful writer" and Hannah F. Gould as a promoter of "the cause of morality and virtue," endorsing both as authors within a transatlantic field.[16] Despite their presence in the title, Sigourney and Gould are not the central focus of that essay; instead, it centers on the delineation of an international female literary coterie. The essay is typical of the way in which such publications underlined that which connected rather than separated women writers; in its most extreme cases, British and American poets are presented in a hodge-podge manner that doesn't differentiate between them. For example, William Baxter's 1844 essay "Poetry," from *The Ladies' Repository*, asks: "Who is there that can listen to the pensive breathings of Landon – to the deep, fervent, impassionate strain of Hemans, or the pure lessons of a Sigourney, without, in some measure at least, partaking of the spirit by which they were animated?"[17] Similarly, Mrs. N. S. Averill's essay "Favorite Authors," published in *The Ladies' Repository* in 1859, describes what she calls the "lovely sisterhood – Miss Landon bowing and weeping before the chill blasts of sorrow, Mrs. Sigourney, hopeful Eliza Cook, and Mrs. Osgood with her cheery lays; the sisters Davidson, whose wondrous genius beamed forth a few glowing rays . . . But fairest and sweetest of all the group is Mrs. Hemans."[18] Again, an 1852 essay in *Godey's Magazine* cites Hemans, Osgood, Sigourney, and Landon as showing the "truly worthy part [women have played] in the great world of literature," and notes "that, under propitious circumstances, [women] may acquire intellectual greatness."[19] In these and other examples, American commentators continually connect Hemans and Sigourney as comparable, interchangeable representatives of a transatlantic sisterhood; in 1842, Alexander H. Everett, writing in the *United States Democratic Review*, suggests that since the death of Hemans, Sigourney is not merely the "first of the lady-poets of our country," but is "at the head of the lady-poets of the day."[20] The near substitutability of these poets is emphasized in an 1849 essay, "Female Poets of America," in the *North American Review*, in which the writer pays tribute to Sigourney by applying to her the words she used about Hemans in "Monody on Mrs. Hemans":

every unborn age
Shall mix thee with its household charities;
The hoary sire shall bow his deafened ear,
And greet thy sweet words with his benison;
The mother shrine thee as a vestal flame
In the lone temple of her sanctity;
And the young child who takes thee by the hand
Shall travel with a surer step to heaven.[21]

Sigourney's poetic tribute to Hemans, which was included alongside Sigourney's "Essay on the Genius of Mrs. Hemans" in the 1840 American publication of *The Works of Mrs. Hemans*, balances the expression of mourning and melancholy with its celebration of Hemans's fame and genius. By using these lines, the essayist constructs Sigourney, who is still living, not merely as the heir of Hemans's poetic authority and power, but also as a poet who will be honored with a comparable Anglo-American legacy as guardian of the domestic, moral, and religious life of future generations.

Two contemporary gift books offer excellent examples of the transatlantic print space that British and American women poets cohabited, in which national designation, even when mentioned, is generally less important than shared gender identity. In *Selections from Female Poets*, the editor, D. F., Jr., suggests that he is offering something "entirely new": a poetical compilation of "the productions of female authors exclusively."[22] Although such a format was hardly novel and had already been popularized by George Coleman and Bonnell Thornton's *Poems by Eminent Ladies* (1755) and Alexander Dyce's *Specimens of British Poetesses* (1827), what was new was the editor's decision to include and intermingle British and American women poets and their poems, thereby creating a transatlantic network. In his preface, D. F., Jr. notes that his chosen poets share "a feminine cast of thought and style discernible in the productions of females; and this will perhaps render their perusal particularly grateful to readers of the same sex, [for whom] this little book is specially designed."[23] Without reference to the question of nationality, women readers are presented with a literary assembly comprising British poets, such as Hemans, Landon, Anna Laetitia Barbauld, and Caroline Norton, and American ones such as Gould, Sigourney, and Emma C. Embury.

Like later nation-based anthologies such as George W. Bethune's *The British Female Poets* (1848), Frederic Rowton's *The Female Poets of Great Britain* (1848), Caroline May's *The American Female Poets* (1848), Rufus Griswold's *The Female Poets of America* (1849), and Thomas

Buchanan Read's *The Female Poets of America* (1849), D. F., Jr.'s gift book underscores the demand for poems that show a "feminine cast of thought and style"; however, it, unlike these later collections, is not concerned with defining each nation's poetics. The marketability of women's poems signals one of the consequences of Romanticism's redefinition of poetry as inextricably associated with "the social, or relational, experience of feeling" and the idea of "emotion as social energy that moves through persons, speech, objects, places, and texts as they are viewed, read or remembered."[24] Such changes afforded a place for women – who were stereotypically associated with the affections, sympathy, and morality – within the previously male-dominated field of poetry. On both sides of the Atlantic, women's poetry became associated with Edmund Burke's category of the beautiful by embodying and producing affection and tenderness and by emblematizing the female body itself. Through this process, a feminine type of writing became culturally authorized and legitimized and women poets gained a public identity by performing the role of the poetess. Women poets made money by publishing poems in periodicals, annuals, and gift books that endorsed ideals of female piety, purity, and morality and presented standard topics of love, loss, and domesticity in a sentimental way. At first popular, influential, and admired for their excessive emotions, subjectivity, spontaneity, and artlessness, poetesses and poetess poetry became increasingly associated with overindulgence, sentimentality, and the commercialization of poetry.

Unlike D. F., Jr.'s gift book, Hale's *The Ladies' Wreath* engages with and counteracts emerging stereotypes that associate the poetess with a private, domestic, highly personal poetics; one of the ways she intervenes in this discourse is by positioning British and American women poets within a complex Anglo-American field. Hale, who was the editor of the *American Ladies' Magazine* and later of *Godey's Lady's Book*, presents her book which was published in the same year as D. F. Jr.'s *Selections*, as "prepared especially for Young Ladies, a gift book for all seasons," "a wreath, whose flowers will always bloom to give pleasure, whenever the heart is opened to their influence."[25] As with the magazines she edited, with the publication of *The Ladies' Wreath*, Hale sought to promote a "separate women's culture" by writing "for a specifically female adult audience."[26] Unlike D.F., Jr.'s, Hale's volume separates the English and American poets and includes an introduction to each poet that contains a summary of their central themes, specific style, and American reception. In part this separation allows Hale to better highlight that her "countrywomen" have "nobly won [a] high place in the literature of our country," owing to the powers of sympathetic feeling and rigorous thought that they share with their British counterparts.[27] Despite this nationalistically inflected division, Hale makes it clear that what unites these poets is that their poems aim to "promote the good of others" and improve the morals of society; because these are now the central goals of literature, according to Hale, it is an area in which "woman is morally gifted to excel."[28] Hale's gift book shows that one of the best ways of offering young ladies "a mirror, bright and polished, in which they may see reflected the beauty of virtue, the loveliness of the domestic affections, and the happiness of piety" is by presenting them with a transnational community of morally worthy and socially engaged women.[29] Hale's book holds up women's poems and lives as providing instructive paradigms for admiration and imitation. While Hale acknowledges that women poets do not have "such unlimited range of subjects as man," and that the "path of woman is very circumscribed," she draws on examples from her collection of British and American women poets to prove that the woman poet has a "freedom as perfect as his; and the delicate shades of genius are as varied and distinctly marked in the one sex as its bold outlines are in the other."[30] In fact, despite underlining the moral qualities that connect these women, she also stresses that all of these poets have "some peculiar stamp of individuality, which marked their genius as original"; she criticizes those "who always speak of the 'true feminine style'" as though "there was only one manner in which ladies could properly write poetry."[31]

Hale's introductions, like those found in later anthologies, offer biographical information with an awareness that, as she puts it, "the private histories of eminent persons are always sought after with eagerness; and were this passion for biographical literature, rightly fostered and directed, it would have a most powerful influence in promoting the intellectual and moral improvement of woman."[32] Readers are being encouraged to find such information as interesting and instructive as the poems. Although she offers biographical information about the poets, she unsettles the commonplace that women's poems grant readers access to their author's private thoughts and feelings. Undermining the illusion of such intimacy, for example, the reader is told that although Hemans was deserted by her husband and left to support their five young sons, she rises in her poetry above "scenes and sufferings that so tried and tortured her sensitive heart."[33] Even Landon, a self-styled improviser, is given credit for her artistry, and the reader is warned that although Landon has written "much pathetic poetry," she herself is sociable and shines among "the fair, fashionable and fascinating of the London world"; her reader should, in general, not confuse the "suffering heroines of [her] poems, with the accomplished writer."[34] In a context, as Eliza Richards puts it, where "her extreme typicality renders the poetess most vulnerable to oblivion," Hale is here endeavoring to stifle this tendency by stressing the particularity of these poets through reference to their distinctive biographies and poetic styles and the "variety" and diversity of their poems.[35]

To delineate such diversity, Hale distinguishes between women poets who appeal to readers' emotions to inspire morally and those who attempt to move readers with descriptions of personal suffering and hardship. At the center of Hale's Anglo-American poetic community are the recently deceased Hemans, who is highly praised for the compassionate "outpourings of her soul" that make her "pre-eminent among female poetic writers," and Sigourney, whose "fine perception of the harmonious and appropriate" make her the perfect "eulogist of departed worth" and elegist; the plight of others "awakens her sympathy" and then she, in her poems, "comfort[s] the bereaved [as if she were] beside them."[36] Standing in sharp contrast to these women, Landon, who was England's greatest living poetess and was also incredibly popular in the United States, is who is admired because "her imagination is vivid, varied, and fertile, and in depicting scenes of passionate love or sorrowful despair she is unrivalled by any modern poet."[37] Landon's poems excite sympathy by re-enacting the Corinne/Sappho story that connects women's poetry with grief, abandonment, and death; however, for Hale, Landon should, "like Mrs. Hemans, have extended the sphere of *love* to the conjugal, parental, filial, and fraternal feelings": "household affections, rather than the *tender passion*, should [have been] her theme."[38] Using these examples, Hale makes it clear that to be a great poet one must experience personal suffering; however, one's poetry must transcend such sorrow and seek to sympathize and identify with others.

Hale's volume typifies the contemporary fostering of "affinities" and "sentimental ties" among the "sister poets in [different] countries," the transformation of such poets into "morally exemplary domestic muses," and the circulation of poems within "the brisk transnational trade in feminine sentiment across Europe and between Europe and the United States."[39] She also differentiates these forms of affect-laden poetry from other kinds of poems written by women in Britain and America. For her, the predominance of "romance and sentiment" in poetry underestimates women's studiousness, reason, judgment, and cerebral powers.[40] Countering the way "[p]assion has too often usurped the place of reason, and a selfish sensitiveness been fostered" and the idea that women poets simply and spontaneously express their feelings, Hale advocates that poets should carefully craft their poems.[41] For example, Osgood is accused, as Landon is also, of "compos[ing] with great rapidity," but Hale hopes that in time Osgood (and, by implication, Landon) will "appreciate her own powers, or . . . cultivate them by careful study and critical revision."[42] She gives examples of women poets' reflective and intellectual qualities and their integration of the emotions and the intellect. As well as being a poet of affect, Hemans is praised for having the "highest gifts of intellect"; Joanna Baillie's poetic power derives from her "knowledge of the human heart," which she illustrates "with the cool judgment of the philosopher, and the pure warm feelings of the woman."[43] Although Mary-Ann Browne has a "bold and ardent imagination," she is "reflective, serious, and at times sublime"; "she condenses her thoughts, and this gives power and energy to her language," and she teaches "the reason as well as touch[es] the heart of the reader."[44] Similarly, Anna Peyre Dinnies is a "genius performing the office of a guardian angel," whose poetry is characterized by "vigor of thought, and delicate tenderness of feeling" and "intellectual power"; Elizabeth F. Ellet's poetry is scholarly and displays her "fervid and active mind."[45] More's poems "unfold and illustrate religious and moral truths"; her poetry is "an *amulet* as well as an ornament; and if it be not properly designated by a flower, it is because it deserves something less perishable – it is the evergreen Pine, the emblem of piety and philosophy."[46] Gould is praised for her wit at a time when women "almost scrupulously avoid ridicule and satire, even when the subjects treated of seemed to justify or demand these forms of expression."[47] Hale's gift book taps into the reality of women developing philosophical, intellectual, and religious literary traditions, as an alternative to, or in reaction against, the prevailing poetic discourse of affect and sentimentality.[48]

While Hale's choice of poems for inclusion within her gift book confirms her volume's transnational spirit, occasionally she stresses her nationalistic credentials. Hale includes poems written by British poets about Italy and France, as well as poems that focus on the representation of other races, such as the Moors and Jews, which encapsulate the movement in women's poetry beyond the domestic sphere and interiority to forge alliances with representatives of cultural or social otherness, and marginalized figures. Moreover, the recurring sea imagery and journey motifs in the selected poems suggest that home, for women, is a place of exile, and foreign locations are an escape from home. At points, there is a tension in Hale's introductions between a domestic or nationalistic focus and a global or international one; in part, this may be because she sought to underline "the reputation of my own sex and my own country."[49] Although she includes Hemans's poems "Washington's Statue" and "Landing of the Pilgrim Fathers," and Joanna Baillie's "Christopher Columbus" and "Tomb of Columbus," Hale does not include many poems in which Americans represent Europe or Europeans. One exception is Sigourney's previously mentioned tribute to Hemans, which Hale aligns with Landon's similarly elegiac "Stanzas on the Death of Mrs. Hemans," implicitly placing both within an emerging transnational tradition of tribute poems by women poets about their female precursors. Hale also mentions Osgood's time in Europe, where she "found friends, as one so amiable and gifted could hardly fail to do, who are fostering her genius with the 'warm breath' of praise, so very pleasant, when given by those we honor and love."[50] She tells her readers that articles by Osgood have appeared in London periodicals, and that there she is "receiving that attention from persons of taste and influence, which, we doubt not, will stimulate her to vigorous application – all that is wanting to insure her success and celebrity."[51] While Osgood's success in Britain, which reflects well on her native land and will benefit her, is celebrated, Emma C. Embury is reprimanded for her Europeanization. While Hale understands that it is "the natural impulse of poetic and ardent minds to admire the genius and glory of Italy, and to turn to that land of bright skies and passionate hearts for themes of song," she questions whether it is still the case "that our new world afforded no subjects propitious for the muses."[52] Despite Embury's "fine sensibilities, and [the pathos and tenderness of] her pictures of beauty," and her commitment to "improving her own sex" and female education, she failed to appreciate that in America "the wonders of nature are on a scale of vast and glorious magnificence which Europe cannot parallel" and "enterprise and change, excitement and improvement, are the elements of social life."[53] Countering her own transatlantic approach, Hale encourages American poets to "look into their own hearts, not into the poems of others, for inspiration, and to sing, in accordance with Nature and human life around them, 'The beauteous scenes of our own lovely land.'"[54] This nationalistic stance evokes a tension running through women's poetry between its emphasis on women's powers of sympathy, which expose them to alternative points of view and encourage them to cross geographical space and historical time to imagine the viewpoints of others, and a concomitant promotion of the hearth, home, and nation as setting the limits of women's imaginative range and conceptual outlook.

Although not included in Hale's gift book because she had yet to establish a reputation as a poet, Barrett Browning, from the publication of her collection *Poems* (1844) onwards, became the epitome of the intellectual, studious, philosophical, prophetic, formally inventive, and socially, morally, religiously, and politically engaged poet that Hale celebrates. In "The Editors' Table," from an 1847 issue of *Godey's Magazine and Lady's Book*, Hale mentions the different merits of the poets Hemans, Baillie, Norton, Landon, and Maria Jane Jewsbury, before declaring "we better love the high-souled devotion to humanity shown in the poems of the learned and gifted, and loving-minded Miss Elizabeth Barrett."[55] In *Woman's Record*, Hale calls Barrett Browning "one of the most distinguished female poets of the age"; she has an "energy and force of character truly rare," and has "brought out the powers of her mind, and cultivated its faculties." The "deep affection and true piety of feeling meet us everywhere [in her work]," making her "among those women who do honour to their sex, and uplift the heart of humanity."[56] From the moment she took up residence in Italy in 1846, Barrett Browning became the nineteenth-century's archetypal transnational poet, a reputation confirmed by the publication in the American abolitionist annual *The Liberty Bell* of "The Runaway Slave at Pilgrim's Point" (1847/8). The speaker of this dramatic lyric is a fugitive slave who has murdered her own child, a child who was the result of her being raped by a white man. Here, Barrett Browning, following the transnational spirit of women's poetry sketched in this essay, transcends the confines of her own subjectivity, middle-class white femininity, and domesticity to create a speaker who is denied the very privileges Barrett Browning enjoys:

> I am black, you see, –
> And the babe, who lay on my bosom so,
> Was far too white, too white for me;
> As white as the ladies who scorned to pray
> Beside me at church but yesterday,
> Though my tears had washed a place for my knee.[57]

The poem is one of the many literary outputs of a poetic network that encouraged women writers to see themselves as participating in an international community whose poems of sorrow and suffering inspired moral sympathy and cross-national affiliation and called for debate, resistance, and change.

Notes

1. Colleen G. Boggs, *Transnationalism and American Literature: Literary Translation 1773–1892* (New York: Routledge, 2007), 4.

2. See Brigitte Bailey, "Introduction: Transatlantic Studies and American Women Writers," *Transatlantic Women: Nineteenth-Century American Women Writers and Great Britain*, Beth L. Lueck, Brigitte Bailey, and Lucinda L. Damon-Bach (eds.), (Durham: University of New Hampshire Press, 2012), xiii, xv.
3. Michael Cohen, "E. C. Stedman and the Invention of Victorian Poetry," *Victorian Poetry* 43 (2005), 168.
4. Virginia Jackson, "American Victorian Poetry: The Transatlantic Poetic," *Victorian Poetry* 43 (2005), 159; Meredith L. McGill, "Introduction," *The Traffic in Poems: Nineteenth-Century Poetry and Transatlantic Exchange*, Meredith L. McGill (ed.), (New Brunswick: Rutgers University Press, 2008), 3.
5. McGill, "Introduction," 3.
6. Virginia Jackson and Yopie Prins, "Lyrical Studies," *Victorian Literature and Culture* 7 (1999), 522.
7. Sarah Josepha Hale, *Woman's Record: or, Sketches of all Distinguished Women, from "The Beginning" Til A. D. 1850* (New York: Harper & Brothers Publisher, 1853), 56.
8. Germaine de Staël, *Corinne, or Italy*, Sylvia Raphael (ed.), (Oxford: Oxford University Press, 2008), 402.
9. Ibid., 402, 403.
10. Patrick H. Vincent, *The Romantic Poetess: European Culture, Politics, and Gender, 1820–1840* (Hanover: University Press of New England Press, 2004), 22.
11. Alison Chapman, "The Expatriate Poetess: Nationhood, Poetics and Politics," *Victorian Women Poets*, Alison Chapman (ed.), (Cambridge: D. S. Brewer, 2003), 67, 59.
12. Isobel Armstrong, *Victorian Poetry: Poetry, Poetics, and Politics* (New York: Routledge, 1993), 325.
13. Mary E. Hewitt, "The Last Chant of Corinne," *The American Female Poets: with Biographical and Critical Notices*, Caroline May (ed.), (Philadelphia: Lindsay & Blakiston, 1854), 345.
14. E. W. Merrill, "The Proper Sphere of Woman," *The Ladies' Repository* 7 (1847), 337.
15. "Mrs. Sigourney and Mrs. Gould," *North American Review* 41 (1835), 433.
16. Ibid., 440, 446, 454.
17. William Baxter, "Poetry," *The Ladies' Repository* 4 (1844), 5.
18. N. S. Averill, "Favorite Authors," *The Ladies' Repository* 19 (1859), 225.
19. Henry E. Woodbury, "Woman in her Social Relations," *Godey's Magazine* 45 (1852), 336, 337.
20. Alexander H. Everett, "Mrs. Sigourney," *United States Democratic Review* 11 (1842), 246.
21. [Elizabeth F. Ellet,] "The Female Poets of America," *North American Review* 68 (1849), 422.

22. D. F., Jr. (ed.), *Selections from Female Poets: A Present for Ladies* (Boston: Samuel Colman, 1837), iii.
23. Ibid., iii–iv.
24. Julie Ellison, "Transatlantic Cultures of Sensibility: Teaching Gender and Aesthetics through the Prospect," *Approaches to Teaching British Women Poets of the Romantic Period*, Stephen C. Behrendt and Harriet Kramer Linkin (eds.), (New York: Modern Language Association of America, 1997), 85.
25. Mrs. [Sarah J.] Hale (ed.), *The Ladies' Wreath: a Selection from the Female Poetic Writers of England and America* (Boston: Marsh, Capen Lloyd, 1837), 4.
26. Patricia Okker, *Our Sister Editors: Sarah J. Hale and the Tradition of Nineteenth Century American Women Editors* (Athens: University of Georgia Press, 1995), 54.
27. Hale, *Ladies' Wreath*, 223. See also Paula Bernat Bennett, *Poets in the Public Sphere: The Emancipatory Project of American Women's Poetry, 1800–1900* (Princeton: Princeton University Press, 2003), 19; Isabel Armstrong and Joseph Bristow, "Introduction," *Nineteenth-Century Women Poets*, Isobel Armstrong, Joseph Bristow, and Cath Sharrock (eds.), (Oxford: Oxford University Press, 1996), xxiii.
28. Hale, *Ladies' Wreath*, 4.
29. Ibid., 4.
30. Ibid., 4, 225, 4.
31. Ibid., 4.
32. [Sarah Hale,] "Eminent Female Writers," *Ladies' Magazine* 2 (1829), 393.
33. Hale, *Ladies' Wreath*, 14.
34. Ibid., 118.
35. Eliza Richards, *Gender and the Poetics of Reception in Poe's Circle* (Cambridge: Cambridge University Press, 2004), 154–155; Okker, *Our Sister Editors*, 144.
36. Hale, *Ladies' Wreath*, 15, 13, 225–226.
37. Ibid., 116.
38. Ibid., 117.
39. Vincent, The Romantic Poetess, 75.
40. Hale, *Ladies' Wreath*, 385.
41. Ibid., 253.
42. Ibid., 326, 327.
43. Ibid., 14, 61.
44. Ibid., 187.
45. Ibid., 338, 374.
46. Ibid., 81.
47. Ibid., 254.
48. Bennett, *Poets in the Public Sphere*, 43–46, 137–138.
49. Hale, *Ladies' Wreath*, 385.
50. Ibid., 325.
51. Ibid., 325–326.
52. Ibid., 274.
53. Ibid., 275.

54. Ibid.
55. Sarah Hale, "Editors' Table," *Godey's Magazine and Lady's Book* 35 (1847), 154.
56. Hale, *Woman's Record*, 605–606.
57. Elizabeth Barrett Browning, "The Runaway Slave at Pilgrim's Point," *Aurora Leigh and Other Poems*, John Robert Glorney Bolton and Julia Bolton Holloway (eds.), (London: Penguin, 1995), 369.

CHAPTER 11

Making and Unmaking a Canon: American Women's Poetry and the Nineteenth-Century Anthology

Alexandra Socarides

At the end of the 1840s, American poetry – and American poetry by women in particular – was collected, packaged, and marketed to a wide readership in a way that it never had been before. Three anthologies of American women's verse hit the literary marketplace at the close of the decade: Caroline May's *The American Female Poets* in 1848, followed in early 1849 by Rufus Griswold's *The Female Poets of America* and Thomas Buchanan Read's *The Female Poets of America.* This situation invites certain questions: Why three big books of the same nature at the same time? What was the purpose of these endeavors? How did these books position the qualities and roles of women's poetry at mid-century? What effect did the publication of these anthologies have on the field of American women's poetry, then and now?

While answers to these questions will undoubtedly shed light on issues of American women's historical poetics and how that poetics was (and continues to be) read, I want to remind readers at the outset of the fundamental concern at the heart of this story: the production of books whose contents were meant to be read did not ultimately result in such reading, at least not in the long run. Subsequent editions of each of these anthologies appeared every few years up through the 1860s – proof that there was a steady contemporary readership and demand for them – yet not one of the 123 women poets showcased in these anthologies are read by general readers today, and only a handful have found their way into university classrooms and critical discussions of literary history. In this way, this is not simply a story about a watershed moment in the history of women's poetry – its unprecedented production, circulation, and reception – that now feels far away from us in the twenty-first century; it is also about how these anthologies themselves have long positioned these poets both everywhere and nowhere. A close look at these books shows just how vexed the placement of the woman poet in literary culture was, as each editor grappled with questions about women poets' visibility and invisibility, about their privacy and publicity. Such issues are charged in particular ways by the expectations that accompany the specific categorical umbrella that these anthologies strove to define – one that was based on the combination of nation, gender, and genre – and under which this work was, for the first time, being grouped.

While poetry anthologies began appearing in America as early as 1793, until the publication of these three anthologies no such book had yet limited its selection to poems by American women.[1] Earlier anthologies had primarily grouped poems together by theme, audience, or form – for instance, poems about flowers, poems for children, sonnets. But by the 1830s editors of poetry anthologies were beginning to make selections based on the category of nation. For instance, Samuel Kettell's *Specimens of American Poetry* (1829), George B. Cheever's *The American Common-Place Book of Poetry* (1831), and Rufus W. Griswold's *The Poets and Poetry of America* (1842) all collected the work of male and female American poets. In these collections the issues of genre and nation were foregrounded, as can be seen in Cheever's preface, where he explained the reason for his publication:

> The unexpected favor, with which the *American Common-Place Book of Prose* was received, encourages its publishers to hope that a similar volume of extracts from American poetry might be attended with the same success. It is true, that there are more good prose writers in our country than there are poets; but it would be strange, indeed, if enough of really excellent poetry could not be found to fill a volume like this.[2]

In positioning the volume's goal (and anxiety) as one that has to do with the relationship between genre and nation – is there "enough" of such a thing as "American poetry"? – gender is not an operative factor. When gender was placed front and center, the category of nation often fell away, such as in Sarah Josepha Hale *The Ladies' Wreath: A Selection from the Female Poetic Writers of England and America* (1837) and D. F., Jr.'s *Selections from Female Poets: A Present for Ladies* (1837), both of which collected the poems of British and American women. What does it mean, then, that in the late-1840s three simultaneous attempts were undertaken to create a new category for writers, readers, and publishers? What were the ambitions of these anthologies, and how did those ambitions contribute to what happened to these poets and poems?

Unlike the modern-day anthology, which, according to Joseph Csicsila, came about in the 1920s and was a kind of "literary textbook" primarily designed for teaching purposes, these mid-nineteenth-century anthologies were geared toward middle-class readers who would read them for pleasure in their homes.[3] Collected in such anthologies were texts that readers may have encountered elsewhere (primarily in newspapers), and the anthology now provided them access to these texts between hard covers and all in one place. Appearing in an anthology did not signal, as it often does today, that one had landed a place in the literary history of the future. As can be seen by the sheer number of poets included in these books and the very little space these editors gave to explaining their theories or practices of inclusion and exclusion, these anthologies were not interested in whittling the mass of women poets down to a special few through whom the nation could define its female poetic tradition. Instead, the result was three hefty and capacious books that attempted to both reflect the field and mark out the women who comprised it.

A close look at these three anthologies reveals that, unlike the group we think of them as today – unlike, in fact, the group I have presented them as here in these opening pages – each anthology was its own production with its own specific purpose. Each book faced similar questions that accompanied the pulling-together of so many poems by so many women, but each answered them differently: Would they reprint poems from newspapers or try to scare up unpublished manuscript productions? How would they position these poets in relation to their British female and their American male contemporaries? What resources would they use to present the life, work, and personhood of each poet? How early would their literary histories begin? Would they predominantly print certain kinds of poems, or poems on similar topics? While I will eventually address some of the specific poets and poems published in these anthologies, answering these questions requires that I begin by focusing on the character and quality of the anthologies themselves. As Natalie Houston has argued, "anthologies produce literary history and aesthetic conditioning not simply through their contents, which have generally been the focus of academic study, but also in their material design, which determines how readers relate contextual information to literary texts."[4] In the case of these anthologies, beginning with the para-textual and extra-literary details of the first editions of these books sets the stage for what they have to tell us about the history of nineteenth-century American women's poetry.

Caroline May's *The American Female Poets* (1848) included the work of seventy-three American female poets – beginning with Anne Bradstreet and ending with Mary J. Reed.[5] The book itself appeared as a kind of companion to *The British Female Poets: With Biographical and Critical*

Notices (also 1848), which had been edited by George W. Bethume and was produced by the same Philadelphia publisher. The two books have the same layout – the title pages are identical (except for the words "British" and "American," and the respective editor's name) and they both include a frontispiece and a preface. Despite this kinship, the character of each book is marked as different from the start, as the frontispiece in May's is a simple portrait of Frances S. Osgood looking straight at her reader, while the one in Bethume's is an ornate drawing of Caroline Norton. [Fig. 9 & Fig. 10] May might have been capitalizing on the success of the British anthology, but her use of Osgood's portrait to represent the face of American women's poetry here signals that the American book is modern and modest, where the British one is traditional and elaborate.[6]

The primary objective of May's "Preface" is to explicitly position her anthology in relation to the many other venues for the publication of women's poetry. She does so by referring to the fact that "fugitive pieces of various merit have been poured forth through our newspapers and other periodicals, with the utmost profusion," and she goes on to present her collection as one that brings such fugitives together.[7] Some reviews, such as the one that appeared in *The Literary World* in October 1848, celebrated this as a strength of the anthology. This reviewer proclaims that "Most of the lady poets to whom we are now introduced in their full gala costume, we have met before in the dishabille of the monthlies, or the street dress of the newspapers."[8] While the "full gala costume" made possible by the anthology format appealed to some (as it seems to establish, or re-establish, their respectability), the "dishabille" and "street dress" of these women poets' origins in print was enough to prejudice other reviewers against the anthology itself. For instance, one reviewer wrote, in *Holden's Dollar Magazine* in November 1849: "[May's] immortal names are gleaned – and that by a not very laborious search – from the corners of newspapers, from the pages of Lady's Books and Annuals."[9] The implication here is that May picked these women, largely at random, off the side streets and put them on the thoroughfare.

Despite the fact that Griswold's *The Female Poets of America* (1849) was the only volume to print the poems in columns resembling those of a periodical, this anthology of poems by ninety-five women poets was not interested in the relationship between women's poetry and the periodical press. Griswold, unlike May, was an established editor to whom many of these women gave, as he puts it, "permission to examine and make use of their literary MSS. without limitation."[10] In other words, because Griswold's resources were different – the image being created here is of

Figure 9. Frontispiece, portrait of Frances Osgood, *The American Female Poets*, Caroline May, ed. (Philadelphia: Lindsay & Blakiston, 1848). Courtesy, American Antiquarian Society.

Figure 10. Frontispiece, portrait of Caroline Norton, *The British Female Poets: With Biographical and Critical Notices*, George W. Bethune, ed. (Philadelphia: Lindsay & Blakiston, 1848). Courtesy, American Antiquarian Society.

an editor who was close to his sources – he did not need to acknowledge the history of many of these poems' previous lives in print. This freed him up to focus on a different issue entirely: how he might guide the public to think about poetry written by women. To this end, Griswold opens his "Preface" with a remark that addresses the problem of how to assess the poetical talents of women: "It is less easy to be assured of the genuineness of literary ability in women than in men."[11] With that as his challenge (to, in fact, *prove* how one might judge "the genuineness of literary ability in women"), Griswold goes on to make a number of statements about men's natures, women's natures, and the nature of "aesthetic ability."[12] His logic runs as follows:

> Among men, we recognize his nature as the most thoroughly artist-like, whose most abstract thoughts still retain a sensuous cast, whose mind is the most completely transfused and incorporated into his feelings. Perhaps the reverse should be considered the test of true art in woman, and we should deem her the truest poet, whose emotions are most refined by reason, whose force of passion is most expanded and controlled into lofty and impersonal forms of imagination.[13]

This theory of opposites – men who are true artists find a way to incorporate feelings into their mind; women who are true artists find a way to incorporate reason into their emotions – provides the basis for his assessment that the works by the women included in his book "illustrate as high and sustained a range of poetic art, as the female genius of any age or country can display."[14]

May was preoccupied with how to position American women poets in relation to British women poets and with the shift in venue that her anthology was enacting. Griswold, in turn, was preoccupied with justifying the very category of the woman artist. Thomas Read's *The Female Poets of America* (1849) was far less invested in this matrix of issues and was, instead, governed by personal interest. In the "Publishers' Advertisement" (there is no formal "Preface"), Read is presented as both a poet and a painter. His status as an artist in both respects guides all aspects of the book's presentation, as "the illuminated proem" was written and illustrated by Read, "the portraits are all from paintings made by him expressly for this work," and "the paper, and even the type on which it is printed, were made for this special purpose."[15] Read's book of seventy-two contemporary American women poets (unlike May and Griswold, he does not begin with Bradstreet but with Maria Brooks) is created as an aesthetic object in its own right, as is clear to any reader who opens onto the multicolored and lavishly illustrated proem, "The Fairer Land." [Fig. 11]

Proem.

THE FAIRER LAND

BY THE EDITOR

All the night, in broken slumber,
I went down the world of dreams,
Through a land of war and turmoil
Swept by loud and labouring streams:
Where the masters wandered chanting
Ponderous and tumultuous themes.

Chanting from unwieldy volumes,
Iron maxims stern and stark,
Truths that swept and burst and stumbled
Through the ancient rifted dark;
Till my soul was tossed and worried,
Like a tempest-driven bark.

But anon, within the distance,
Stood the village vanes aflame,
And the sunshine, filled with music,
To my oriel casement came;
While the birds sang pleasant valentines
Against my window frame.

Then by sights and sounds invited,
I went down to meet the morn
Saw the trailing mists roll inland
Over rustling fields of corn,
And from quiet hillside hamlets
Heard the distant rustic horn.

There through dasied dales and byways,
Met I forms of fairer mould,
Pouring songs for very pleasure—
Songs their hearts could not withhold—
Setting all the birds a-singing
With their delicate harps of gold.

Some went plucking little lily-bells,
That withered in the hand;
Some, where smiled a summer ocean,
Gathered pebbles from the sand;
Some, with prophet eyes uplifted,
Walked unconscious of the land.

Through that Fairer World I wandered
Slowly, listening oft and long,
And as one behind the reapers,
Without any thought of wrong,
Loitered, gleaning for my garner
Flowery sheaves of sweetest song.

Figure 11. "The Fairer Land," *The Female Poets of America*, Thomas Buchanan Read, ed. (Philadelphia: E. H. Butler & Co., 1849). Courtesy, American Antiquarian Society.

Despite the fact, then, that they all collected the same kind of texts (broadly speaking, poems by American women), that they were published at the same historical moment, and that they have oddly interchangeable titles, these three anthologies were driven by different concerns, preoccupations, and agendas. It is no wonder, though, that this history of their differences has been largely invisible, as almost immediately these books were treated as a single production, as a wave of American women poets come onto the scene together and all at once, in this new format. We can see this even before the publication of the first anthology, as a writer for the "Home Correspondence" column in *The Literary World* asked readers on April 19, 1848, "Have you heard of the simultaneous movement on the part of Philadelphia publishers, to do justice and honor to those who have genius as well as beauty?"[16] The idea that there would be multiple books of this kind was exhausting to some, as a reviewer in the December 1848 issue of *Godey's Lady Book* declared, when announcing the publication of May's anthology: "We shall be deluged with books of this sort, as no less than three different publishers are in the field already."[17] Not everyone was overwhelmed, though, and when all three anthologies were finally in the hands of reviewers, the *North American Review* ran the first piece about them collectively, declaring, in the end, that "The general interest in the subject, shown by the almost simultaneous publication of so many works related to them, is an encouragement for future efforts."[18]

Whether individual readers and reviewers were dismissive or supportive of this effort to publish American women poets in the anthology format, it is clear that they all treated it as a movement. This led, within four years, to satirical articles such as "The Female Poets of Every Age and Clime," which presented an image of the ubiquitous woman poet and the saturation of the market with her poetry:

> Most of our readers are probably familiar with Griswold's volume of the "Female Poets of America." This is a collection of ninety-four, only, of America's female poets, and we have no doubt many an attentive reader has perused its pages with delight. There can be scarcely a town or village in our broad country that cannot boast its female poet, who has seen her verses in print, and has had her large circle of admirers.[19]

This article goes on to excerpt from a fictional manuscript called "The Female Poets of every Age and Clime, edited by two who emulate a place among them," including, for instance, poems written by "Mrs. Noah" about her husband and the ark. While there is obviously meant to be humor in this satire, it also reflects a serious assumption about women's poetry at mid-century. The result of "Griswold's volume" (here functioning as a stand-in for all three anthologies and, by 1852, their multiple editions) was that the female poet, once she adorned the shelves of all middle-class literary households, could be imagined to reside everywhere – both physically and temporally. This is, in part, due to just how many of them there were, as is gestured at by the title "The Female Poets of every Age and Clime," but it is also a result of the fact that they all appeared in print together, no longer dispersed among newspapers, magazines, and gift books. By putting them in the company of so many other writing women, these anthologies (both individually and together) publicly showcased this community in a way that was largely incommensurate with standard protocols of gender and genre.

And the editors of these anthologies worried about these protocols. While Griswold was concerned about "the propriety of bringing before the world compositions produced amid humble and laborious occupations," May was particularly self-conscious about and apologetic for the potential problems that might arise from highlighting the fact that women, seemingly en masse, were producing poems that were now appearing in books that looked like those that usually contained men's poems.[20] As a result, May attempted to reprivatize these women in the very act of publishing them. "The themes which have suggested the greater part of the following poems have been derived from the incidents and associations of every-day life," May writes, and she goes on to define "every-day life" as "home, with its quiet joys, its deep pure sympathies, and its secret sorrow, with which a stranger must not intermeddle."[21] It is one thing to say that the poems were born in the private space of the "home," but May has a harder time explaining how these women could allow their biographies to be made public in her anthology's headnotes, for, in her words, "no women of refinement, however worthy of distinction – and the most worthy are always the most modest – like to have the holy privacy of their personal movements invaded."[22] The publicity required by the basic format of the anthology itself called these women's modesty into question, and May attempts to defend that modesty by relaying that some women responded to a call for biographical facts with the declaration "that they had not lived at all."[23] Denying their very personhood, it seems, was necessary if they were going to have their poetry appear in such a venue.

Given that over the first half of the nineteenth century women published poems in periodicals of all sorts (from daily newspapers to Christmas and New Year annuals), we might think that the publication of their poems in these anthologies would not have been so vexed, but it was.[24] The anthology, as a result of how it was constructed, declared itself as differently public than these other venues. The newspaper, because of its form as a media that was daily, discardable, and read by the masses, never encouraged its readers to imagine that it was a private space for personal absorption in its texts. But the anthology presented this possibility while also undercutting it, for the reader of the anthology was always aware of the presence of the anthologist (whose hand is everywhere) and of the community of other, imagined readers who were also holding these big books in their hands. The anthologist not only produced the para-textual materials (preface and biographical headnotes) that guided the way readers of the anthology read, he or she was also responsible for all selections, extractions, revisions, and ordering of the reading material itself. As Anne Ferry has argued, "discontinuity, a distinguishing feature of this kind of poetry book, is itself an ever-present reminder that someone along with the reader, or rather just ahead of the reader, is as it were turning the pages, pointing out poems and directing attention to how they act toward one another."[25] Framed within this format of discontinuity – where the reader jumps from woman poet to woman poet as well as from poem to poem, all of which are taken from multiple sources – these women were handed over to a reading public that was always aware that the anthologist's actions were taken in the service of that public. Because everyone was reading, say, the same two poems by Mrs. E. C. Kinney, "the book [was] by self-definition not designed for private discoveries," writes Ferry, "but to build a community of shared experiences."[26] In short, then, the anthology form both re-contained the woman poet in a space that its editors falsely presented as private *and* made her public in such a way that she seemed to be forever proliferating out into the world beyond the reader's grasp.

One can see already how, despite the differences between these books, their status as anthologies immediately raised similar concerns for readers and critics – concerns that allowed them to be collapsed into one kind of dismissible production. What adds insult to injury here is that the poets and poems collected in these anthologies showcase a diversity of women's historical poetics that have since been flattened out as a result. As we can see from the reception history sketched out above, most reviewers had nothing to say about the poems themselves. It should not be surprising, then, that later critics – many of whom, ironically, have sought to recover this poetry – have read the poetry as alike and, because alike, unremarkable and ultimately forgettable. For instance, Leah Price has argued that "over the course of the nineteenth century editors narrowed their generic range until the anthology-piece became tacitly synonymous with the lyric."[27] Paula Bennett, moreover, has argued more specifically that each of these particular mid-century anthologies "features only one kind of poem, whoever the writer: that which met the age's idealizing genteel standard."[28] Yet a closer look inside these anthologies reveals that the poems collected there actually reflected the generically and thematically diverse landscape of American women's poetry.

Out of the 123 poets that appear across these three anthologies, only forty-two of them appear in all three anthologies. Of those forty-two, many were the most widely published poets of the day, such as Maria Brooks, Lydia Sigourney, Sarah Josepha Hale, Emma Embury, Elizabeth Oakes Smith, Sarah Helen Whitman, and Frances Osgood. Others had died young – such as Elizabeth Margaret Chandler, the sisters Lucretia and Margaret Davidson, Sarah Louise P. Smith, Julia H. Scott, and Lucy Hooper – and had received posthumous fame stemming from editions of their poetry, letters, and memoirs. Not all of the overlapping poets were well-known, though, as these editors also made similar choices about which emerging women poets to include; all three books contained the poems of, for example, Anna Cora Mowatt, Emily E. Judson, Anne Charlotte Lynch, Sarah C. Edgartown Mayo, Mary E. Lee, Juliet H. Campbell, and Alice B. Neal. The many poets who only appeared in one, or sometimes two, of these anthologies were chosen, we might assume, based on the anthologist's aesthetic inclinations, personal interests, and source materials. In short, taken together, these three books introduced readers to a vast array of poets.

Of the more than 1,000 poems that were published in these anthologies, just over twenty of them appear in all three books.[29] While it is now impossible to say why a given editor chose a given poem, it is clear that these editors – like all editors – clearly had their own preferences. For instance, while May published diverse kinds of poems – her table of contents is filled with titles such as "Lines," "Hymn," "Song," "Stanzas," "Sonnet," "Ode," and "Ballad" – Griswold seems to have been most drawn to the sonnet, and he highlighted these poems within his individual selections of authors. Not only do their choices reflect different inclinations in terms of form and genre, the poems themselves – their topics, strategies, rhyme schemes, meters, lengths, metaphors, and figures – are anything but uniform.

If one wanted to read for sameness in this field, the logical thing to do would be to turn to the poems that all three anthologies printed, with an eye toward figuring out what they all have in common. There are a few general statements one could make about this, namely that many of these poems are about or address nature (Sigourney's "Solitude," Anna Maria

Wells' "The Future," Kinney's "A Winter's Night," Osgood's "To a Dear Little Truant," and Judson's "My Bird"), three of the poems celebrate American places (Sigourney's "Niagara," Hale's "The Mississippi," and Elizabeth F. Ellet's "Sodus Bay"), and two of the poems are about poetry itself (Kinney's "Spirit of Song" and Lee's "The Poets"). But equally as many of the poems chosen by all three editors do not fit into any of these categories. For instance, not all of these poems displayed American spaces, as can be seen in Sarah Louise P. Smith's "The Fall of Warsaw," and the pastoral narratives that emerge in the nature poems are accompanied by both Biblical (Whitman's "David") and classical (Sara Jane Clarke's "Ariadne") stories. In other words, even looking to the poems that all three editors included does not help to define the kind of poems that these anthologies set out to publish.

Instead of asking what all of these poems have in common, then, we might return to the diversity of poetics that these anthologies highlight, revisiting and revising the story of sameness that has long been told about these women poets. One way of doing this is to locate a poet who appears in all three anthologies but whose work has been selected from in different ways. For instance, poems by Emma Embury appear in each anthology: sixteen in May, sixteen in Griswold, and eight in Read. Yet of all of these poems, no one poem appears in all three anthologies, and only three poems appear in two anthologies: both Griswold and Read publish "The Aeolian Harp," "On the Death of the Duke of Reichstadt," and "The Widow's Wooer." This leaves thirty-four of Embury's poems that were only published in one of these anthologies, a fact that proves both how many poems of hers there were to choose from and how little consensus there was on what constituted an Embury poem worthy of anthologizing.

May publishes the most formally diverse selection of Embury's poems, as she includes poems written in 4-, 5-, 6-, 7-, 8-, and 12-line stanzas, all with a host of different rhyme schemes. There is not only a range of topics covered here – everything from poems about Christ to poems about love – but the poems are, at turns, historical ("Jane of France," which is written in quatrains of iambic septameter), consolatory ("Confidence in Heaven"), and pastoral ("Poor, But Happy," whose syntax feels directly indebted to Bryant's "Thanatopsis"). Griswold does not include any of the poems May used in her anthology and instead publishes, among others, linked sonnets ("Two Portraits from Life"), a tribute to a public figure ("Madame de Staël"), and a cautionary ballad ("Ballad"). Most strikingly, Griswold publishes two poems – "The American River: A Remembrance" and "The English River: A Fantasy" – as companion pieces, printing them side-by-side on the two columns of a single page. Placed thus, the poems become a study in contrasts, with "The American River" opening with the lines "It rusheth on with fearful might, / That river of the west / Through forests dense, where seldom light / Of sunbeam gilds its breast" and "The English River" beginning "It floweth on with pleasant sound – / A vague and dreamlike measure, / And singeth to the flowers around / A song of quiet pleasure."[30] Read's choices are, again, different than May's and only overlap with three of Griswold's. His most interesting choice of poem is the first of his book's section on Embury, "The Ruined Mill." This begins as a descriptive poem that studies how nature has overtaken an abandoned, man-made structure, yet in the last stanza it turns toward a reflection on the poet's process and work:

> So here, in this secluded spot,
> Beside the ruined mill,
> Came back the fancies long forgot,
> Which fain would haunt me still;
> That stream an emblem seemed to be
> Of mine own gushing poesy,
> Wasted with idle will,
> Without concentrate power to stay
> A leaflet on its loitering way.[31]

Whether or not Embury's poetry was actually "gushing" or not is not for us to say, but what we can say is that she produced enough of it that each editor had the opportunity to present her wide range of poetic strategies, preoccupations, and inclinations.

But to push the point about these anthologies' differences even further, it is worth calling attention to the poets who only appear in one of them. Doing so propels us to the opposite side of the "lyric sameness" assessment I discussed above, an approach that both collapses the women into one kind of poet and her poems into one kind of poem. There are, in total, forty-eight poets who only appear in one of these anthologies: ten in May, twenty-six in Griswold, and twelve in Read. May's choices include, among others, Amanda M. Edmond, a religious poet who wrote only between the ages of fourteen and eighteen; M. C. Canefield, who mostly wrote for children; and Anne M. F. Annan, who mostly wrote stories. Like May, Griswold includes little-known poets, but in his case, many of them were already dead, such as Lavinia Stoddard, Julia Rush Ward, and Katherine A. Ware. Like both May and Griswold, Read introduces readers to poets whom they may not have known as poets, but in so doing he expands the definition of the poet, for he includes the work of actress Charlotte

Cushman as well as that of Mrs. Margaret M. Davidson, the mother of Lucretia and Margaret Davidson. In Read's anthology, this mother's poems appear just before the entries by her daughters, both of whom appear in all three anthologies. Invested primarily in the family connection, Read states in the headnote that, "as the parent of these remarkable but fated children, Mrs. Davidson is regarded with sympathy, and her writings with interest."[32] One of the things that we can see from this eclectic span of poets is that not all of these anthologists had the same idea about who wrote poetry.

Our impulse to ignore the diversity of poetics that I have laid out above – to treat the anthologies themselves as three versions of the same project and to read their selections as articulations of a lyric sameness that we now read as characteristic of the nineteenth century – is to overlook the important role that editors, readers, and critics played in the construction of the category of American women's poetry. In other words, it may not be the poetry itself that is responsible for its erasure from literary history, but, instead, the form – in this case, the anthology – within which this poetry was contained, and the reception of that form. While, as I have shown, each of these anthologies took a different approach to defining the field, they all employed a structure that would allow contemporary reviewers, as well as later critics, to collapse and disregard it. By defining a specific type of author (one marked by gender, nation, and genre), by grouping together the poems of these individual authors, by producing biographies of these authors, and, in the case of Read, by reproducing these authors' visual likenesses as portraits that appeared alongside their poems, the emphasis fell on these women's identities, and the related anxieties about their publicity and proliferation. One reason, then, why it is so hard for us to see today that the nineteenth-century American woman poet produced a diverse poetry is because the anthology almost thoroughly obscures that fact from view.

The 1840s anthologies mark an important moment in the history of American women's poetry, but I hope to have shown that they do not do this in the way we previously thought, or wanted to think. Theirs is not an easy history, but is one rife with contradictions and disjunctions. The editors of these books presented a wide poetic field while at the same time containing it. They made these women visible, but too visible to be seen. They produced the kind of book that, on the one hand, highlighted the public, communal, and representative nature of women's poetry and, on the other hand, established the private and individual identity of the woman poet. Understanding the complexities of this history can allow us to rethink the form through which it circulated and can return us to the diversity of purposes, aesthetics, and genres of women's poetry that were alive and well in the nineteenth century.

Notes

1. See Elihu Hubbard Smith (ed.), *American Poems, Selected and Original* (Litchfield: Collier and Buel, 1793). Also, it is worth noting here that one book of exclusively American women's poetry predates the anthologies I discuss in this essay: Rufus Griswold (ed.), *Gems from American Female Poets* (Philadelphia: H. Hooker, 1842). I do not consider this an "anthology," though, because it is a pocket-sized book.
2. George B. Cheever (ed.), *The American Common-Place Book of Poetry* (Boston: Carter, Hendee and Babcock), 3.
3. Joseph Csicsila, *Canons By Consensus: Critical Trends and American Literature Anthologies* (Tuscaloosa: University of Alabama Press, 2004), xvi.
4. Natalie M. Houston, "Valuable by Design: Material Features and Cultural Values in Nineteenth-Century Sonnet Anthologies, *Victorian Poetry* 37.2 (Summer 1999), 250.
5. Paula Bennett states that May's anthology included the work of seventy-eight poets, but she may have been referring to a later edition. See Paula Bernat Bennett, *Poets in the Public Sphere: The Emancipatory Project of American Women's Poetry, 1800–1900* (Princeton: Princeton University Press, 2003), 17.
6. See Eliza Richards, *Gender and the Poetics of Reception in Poe's Circle* (Cambridge: Cambridge University Press, 2004), 62, for a reading of this portrait.
7. Caroline May (ed.), *The American Female Poets* (Philadelphia: Lindsay and Blakiston, 1848), v.
8. "The American Female Poets," *The Literary World* 3.90 (October 21, 1848), 749.
9. "Holden's Review," *Holden's Dollar Magazine* 3.11 (November 1849), 697.
10. Rufus Wilmot Griswold (ed.), *The Female Poets of America* (Philadelphia: Carey and Hart, 1849), 10.
11. Griswold, *Female Poets*, 7.
12. Ibid.
13. Ibid.
14. Ibid., 8.
15. See "Publisher's Advertisement" at the front of Thomas Buchanan Read (ed.), *The Female Poets of America: With Portraits, Biographical Notices, and Specimens of their Writings* (Philadelphia: E. H. Butler & Co.), 1849.
16. "Home Correspondence," *The Literary World* 3.65 (April 19, 1848), 245.
17. *Godey's Lady Book*, 37.12 (December 1848), 392.
18. "The Female Poets of America," *North American Review* (April 1, 1849), 435.

19. "The Female Poets of Every Age and Clime," *To-Day: A Boston Literary Journal* (January 17, 1852), 41. Note that this article says there are ninety-four poets in Griswold's anthology, when actually there are ninety-five. They may have counted one of the three sets of sister poets included as one instead of two poets.
20. Griswold, *Female Poets*, 9.
21. May, *American Female Poets*, vi.
22. Ibid., viii.
23. Ibid.
24. See Meredith L. McGill, *American Literature and the Culture of Reprinting, 1834–1853* (Philadelphia: University of Pennsylvania Press, 2003), for the most extensive treatment of poetry's appearance in periodicals in the antebellum period. See Bennett, *Poets in the Public Sphere*, for a study of women's poetry as it circulated in periodicals throughout the nineteenth century.
25. Anne Ferry, *Tradition and the Individual Poem: An Inquiry into Anthologies* (Stanford: Stanford University Press, 2001), 125.
26. Ferry, *Tradition*, 125–126.
27. Leah Price, *The Anthology and the Rise of the Novel: From Richardson to George Eliot* (Cambridge: Cambridge University Press, 2000), 5.
28. Bennett, *Poets in the Public Sphere*, 19.
29. This is a difficult number to be exact about, as Griswold's introductions were long and sometimes included parts of poems that he didn't print in full later. Also, some poems were published under slightly different titles. My number accounts for poems printed in full in the stand-alone sections of poetry.
30. Emma Embury, "The American River" and "The English River," *Female Poets*, Griswold, (ed.), 146.
31. Emma Embury, "The Ruined Mill," *Female Poets*, Read, (ed.), 87.
32. Read, *The Female Poets of America*, 379.

CHAPTER 12

"What witty sally": Phoebe Cary's Poetics of Parody

Faith Barrett

In 1854, the prestigious Boston house of Ticknor, Reed, and Fields published a first solo collection of poems by the Ohioan Phoebe Cary, then thirty years old. In the collection's title, *Poems and Parodies*, Cary points toward the dialogic nature of this project, whose first section is composed of 131 pages of seemingly sincere sentimental poems and whose second section is composed of 65 pages of parodies of many of the most acclaimed poets, both British and American, of the nineteenth century. All but one of the poets she parodies is male – Felicia Hemans is the sole exception – and some, including John Greenleaf Whittier, were her friends or acquaintances. From a twenty-first century standpoint, the volume is full of extraordinary contradictions. Why publish elegies, hymns, and parodies in the same volume? Why parody poets such as Whittier who were friends and admirers? And why parody some of the most influential editors and writers in the Northeast? How can we make sense of the varied rhetorical purposes of *Poems and Parodies*?

Because this collection marks its rhetorical contradictions so explicitly, *Poems and Parodies* might serve as a keystone text, one that enables us to better understand the relationship between sentiment and satire across a whole range of nineteenth-century poets' works, including, for example, the poles of sympathy and irony in Emily Dickinson and Sarah Piatt. Because Dickinson is freed from the pressures of print publication, she is also liberated from the obligation to maintain tonal or ideological consistency in her poems; she can thus experiment with contrasting positions, writing in a naïve, childlike voice in one piece and compressing complex axioms from the philosophy of language in another, expressing the desire to comfort the grieving in one poem and mocking the narrowness of conventional feminine roles in another. Piatt achieves tonal duality through her innovative use of dialogic structures, a rhetorical device in which mothers often address children, their words hovering on a knife-edge between irony and sincerity, a strategy that allows different readers to interpret the same poem in radically different ways. As Paula Bennett has noted, however, Piatt typically placed her most subversive pieces in the ephemeral medium of periodicals, building her published collections around more conventional poems.[1] Piatt's caution thus emphasizes Cary's boldness.

In folding both poems and parodies into one volume and in responding both seriously and parodically to sentimental poetry, Cary challenges her nineteenth-century readers to re-examine the rhetorical conventions of poetry in this era. Moreover, in *Poems and Parodies*, both the proliferation of different speakers and the dialogic relationship between the first and second sections unsettle twentieth-century critical assumptions about the centrality of "lyric" self-expression in nineteenth-century women's poetry.[2] In addition to troubling the idea of a unified speaker, the collection's two sections interrogate a range of binary oppositions, including some that have been central to the methods we have used in approaching nineteenth-century poetry; these pairings include not only the opposition between public and private spheres, coded masculine and feminine, but also the opposition between the lyric and the comic, the sincere and the parodic. The generic heterogeneity of *Poems and Parodies* reminds us that what we call poetry was in the nineteenth century an extraordinary versatile and capacious means of expression. Indeed, Cary's collection foregrounds the tension between innovation and convention that characterizes so much of the poetry of the mid-to-late nineteenth century. While the poems in both halves of Cary's collection are in many ways entirely conventional, the collection as a whole is innovative in the distinctive ways that it foregrounds the conventions of nineteenth-century poetry, making those conventions the object of its own critical inquiry.

Consider, for example, the way that Cary unsettles the workings of the sentimental elegy with the opening sequence in the "Poems" section. "The Life of Trial," a representative example from this sequence, likens the experience of embodied femininity to Christ's suffering through the crucifixion. The first two stanzas present the nameless heroine whose "trials" indelibly shape her identity:

> I am glad her life is over,
> Glad that all her trials are past;
> For her pillow was not softened
> Down with roses to the last.
>
> When sharp thorns choked up the pathway
> Where she wandered sad and worn,

Never kind hand pressed them backward,
So her feet were pierced and torn.[3]

Wraith-like, the female figure hovers in a place of unending and unspecified "affliction," suffering that will only be resolved by her crossing over into the next life and joining God. The last two stanzas compare that crossing over to the experience of giving birth, as the woman's body releases her spirit at the moment of death:

Long for her deliverance waiting,
Clung she to the cross in vain;
With an agonizing birth-cry
Was her spirit born again.

And her path grew always rougher
Wearier, wearier, still she trod,
Till, through gates of awful anguish,
She went in at last to God!

Representing femininity itself as suffering, this poem, like others in the opening sequence, takes the sentimental ideal of the angel of the house to its logical extreme. The sequence sketches in the outlines of that figure again and again, offering no less than thirteen elegies, twelve of which mourn the deaths of Christian women and girls. In *Poets in the Public Sphere*, Bennett argues that *Poems and Parodies* marks a crucial turning point in nineteenth-century American women's poetry – the moment when one woman skewered literary sentimentality so effectively that its cultural power could at last begin to wane.[4] Bennett contends that the relentless accumulation of dying solitary women in the collection's opening pages foregrounds the oppressive structure of nineteenth-century marriage, which locked women into lives of unrecognized domestic labor and financial exploitation.[5] While each individual poem seems sincere in its commitment to representing a woman as a model of Christian virtue, the litany of dead female figures across this sequence indicts the limitations of women's traditional roles, implicitly arguing that femininity itself is a form of martyrdom. By piling up no less than twelve sentimental elegies for martyred femininity, Cary exposes the erasure of female agency that underpins these literary conventions. The accumulation of dead female figures works to unsettle the elegies' commitment to tonal sincerity, thereby also destabilizing the conventions of the "sentimental" poem.

In the dialogue that it establishes between "poem" and "parody" and "sentiment" and "comedy," Cary's collection juxtaposes extremes in order to undo their opposition. The unspecified forms of suffering endured by nameless heroines in the opening "Poems" sequence appear in sharp contrast to the trials of the female characters in the parodies, who are situated in specific rural and typically Midwestern settings and whose names often emphasize their rustic origins. Still more importantly, the parodies often include detailed lists of different forms of women's labor. "The Wife," Cary's parody of James Aldrich's "A Death-Bed," is a representative example. Underlining the popularity of the poems she chose as source-texts, Cary did not need to include the originals in her collection. For the convenience of twenty-first century readers, however, here is the beloved Aldrich poem, followed by Cary's parody:

A Death-Bed

Her suffering ended with the day,
Yet lived she at its close,
And breathed the long, long night away
In statue-like repose.

But when the sun, in all his state,
Illumed the eastern skies,
She passed through Glory's morning-gate,
And walk'd in Paradise![6]

The Wife

Her washing ended with the day,
Yet lived she at its close,
And passed the long, long night away,
In darning ragged hose.

But when the sun in all his state
Illumed the eastern skies,
She passed about the kitchen grate,
And went to making pies.[7]

Typical in "The Wife" is Cary's close echoing of the rhyme scheme and rhythmic patterns of the original; here, as in her other parodies, she borrows enough exact phrasing that the nineteenth century reader can recognize her source. Though not all of her parodies are as explicitly comic as this one, what this parody shares with most is a commitment to the textured specificity of a woman's experience, including her "washing" and her "darning" of "ragged hose." The overt comedy is signaled by the replacement of the sublime walking in "Paradise" with the quotidian "making pies," a joke that is heightened by the slant rhyme of the two phrases. Introducing quotidian detail moves the representation of woman's experience from an exalted plane where she has no agency to an ordinary one where her agency is limited to performing household chores. Contemporary reviewers were typically dismayed by Cary's assault on such beloved pieces, however. Reviewing *Poems and Parodies* for the *Southern Literary Messenger,* John Reuben Thompson laments the Aldrich parody in particular, suggesting sarcastically that Cary is quick to parody other poets' death-bed scenes because she wants to corner the market on this theme herself.[8] But in her parody of "The Death-Bed," Cary mocks the sentimental ideal of the angel of the house, reminding readers of the excess of elegies in the opening "Poems" sequence.

The speakers in the parodies are clearly linked to the witty and ironic social persona Cary would go on to develop in the Sunday salons that she and her sister Alice began hosting in their New York home beginning in 1856.[9] In her adoring biography of the two sisters, Mary Clemmer Ames, their friend and contemporary, calls Phoebe "the disenchanter," a woman with a "keen sense of the ludicrous in the relation between words and things."[10] With *Poems and Parodies,* the Midwestern farmer's daughter talks back to the New York and Boston-focused centers of literary power in mid-nineteenth century America. Cary here uses imitation as a form of ironic deference, her means of joking entrée into Northeastern literary circles. Echoing the role of the court jester and some of the techniques of minstrelsy, Cary plays the affectionate buffoon. Turning idyllic New England landscapes into rustic Midwestern scenes, pastoral settings into working-class urban neighborhoods, and European ancestral halls into American farmhouses, the "Parodies" trade on her own performance of the country bumpkin. While that persona may have been successful in the salon setting or when isolated parodies appeared in newspapers or magazines, contemporary reviews of *Poems and Parodies* were decidedly ambivalent, with most reviewers – like Thompson – expressing particular dismay about the parodies. It's therefore no surprise that Cary never again published an explicitly titled group of them.

While Linda Hutcheon situates the term "parody" in the twentieth century, key claims of her study can help to illuminate the rhetoric of Cary's nineteenth-century project. Hutcheon defines parody as imitation with "a critical difference," yet she also emphasizes that parody's "transgression is always authorized."[11] Read from this angle, Cary's parodies are works of homage in their echoes of the nineteenth-century's great men of letters, even as they subvert the poetic conventions these writers follow. Cary uses imitative techniques in a fashion that is analogous to Dickinson's reliance on child voices; both approaches defuse the threat of female literary mastery. Reading the long history of parody starting in the classical era, M. M. Bahktin contends that "there never was a single strictly straightforward genre . . . that did not have its own parodying and travestying double."[12] Appearing mid-century, *Poems and Parodies* marks a moment when the figure of the poetess and the sentimental poetry she was linked with were perhaps at the height of their cultural power. Consider, for example, the 1848 publication of *The Young Ladies' Offering; or Gems of Prose and Poetry*, featuring work by acclaimed British and American women writers; the volume responded to the enormous popularity of gift books and annuals in this era. Through a series of literary lessons, the collection offers models of Christian piety, familial love, and feminine virtue. Cary's *Poems and Parodies* talks back to anthologies such as this one, which were marketed for explicitly didactic purposes for young female readers.

The competing rhetorical aims of *Poems and Parodies* foreground what looks, at first glance, like a paradox: it is Cary's facility with the conventions of sentimental models for femininity that enables her to make a living as a poet. But that facility enables her to write *both* poems that endorse sentimental conventions *and* poems that parody those conventions. In the nineteenth-century context in which Cary is writing, one in which poetry pursues an extraordinary range of rhetorical purposes, this dual set of aims does not represent a contradiction: rather, these dual aims emphasize Cary's remarkable skill at responding to the rules of the literary marketplace in such a way as to build a career for herself as a writer. Thus, what is extraordinary about Cary's *Poems and Parodies* is not that it presents a parodic double to *The Young Ladies' Offering*; rather, the collection's most extraordinary feature is that Cary writes into one collection *both* the originary sentimental model *and* her parodic double of that model, so that each illuminates the other.

Central to Cary's career, then, is her strategic use of imitation. Analyzing the relationship between genius and mimicry in nineteenth-century women's poetry, Eliza Richards draws on Judith Butler's and Luce Irigary's use of the term "mimicry" to suggest that women poets use such strategies to unsettle the relationship between original and copy, between originary genius and poetic imitation.[13] Because mimicry acknowledges its own inadequacy – the inevitability of its failure to reproduce the original – it can work to undermine the cultural assumptions of the original, exposing those assumptions as contingent. Thus, as Bennett argues, Cary's *Poems and Parodies* exposes the constructedness of the ideology of the angel of the house by reiterating, with a difference, the foundational assumptions of this discourse.[14] Analyzing the work of women writers in Poe's circle, Richards argues that mimicry is a crucial strategy for women poets of this period, relying as it does on subterfuge and constraint.[15]

What *Poems and Parodies* makes clear is that Cary is just as adroit at maneuvering in relation to male editors' and reviewers' expectations of female poets as she is at maneuvering in relation to the general reader's expectations about the sentimental poem. And for Cary, imitation is integral to this maneuvering. Thompson, for example, comments on the many death-bed scenes that open the collection, noting drily that Cary's muse must be "a fountain of tears."[16] Thompson can see the excess of the repetition but cannot recognize the critique that repetition offers. Rufus Griswold's strategic method of presenting the Cary sisters to the public in *Female Poets of America* offers still another instance of a male editor's misreading. In introducing the group of poems by Alice and Phoebe Cary, Griswold quotes Alice as saying "We write with much facility, often producing two or three poems in a day, and never elaborate."[17] Griswold goes on to note that "in the west, song gushes and flows, like the springs and rivers, more imperially than elsewhere."[18] In these passages, Griswold implicitly praises the sisters' poems as the unrevised outpourings of inspiration, though of course Alice's description of their process also reflects the financial exigencies that compel them to produce multiple poems per day. Such speed in composition also suggests that both sisters were adept at imitating the dominant poetic conventions. Emphasizing both their feminine virtue and their domestic work, Griswold insists that Alice and Phoebe's poems are "the fruits of no literary leisure," but rather "the mere pastimes of lives that are spent in prosaic duties."[19] By 1850, however, writing poetry had become a paying occupation for both sisters.

As I will go on to suggest, implicit in Cary's mapping of women's options in *Poems and Parodies* is a meditation on the challenges that the woman writer faces in the literary marketplace. This meditation comes close to the surface in "The Soiree," her remarkable parody of "The Arsenal at Springfield" by Henry Wadsworth Longfellow. In "The Arsenal at Springfield," first published in *Graham's Magazine* in 1844, Longfellow celebrates the terrible beauty of weapons, imagines the war-like histories of different peoples, and laments the bloodshed that results from the use of these "burnished arms."[20] Longfellow's poem opens by describing the terrible music weapons can make:

> This is the Arsenal. From floor to ceiling,
> Like a huge organ, rise the burnished arms;
> But from their silent pipes no anthem pealing,
> Startles the village with strange alarms.

Ah! what a sound will rise, how wild and dreary,
  When the death angel touches those swift keys!
What loud lament and dismal Miserere
  Will mingle with their awful symphonies.

In its opening stanzas, Cary's parody takes aim at the social rituals that lead women into marriage, rituals in which women exercise what little agency they have in the narrow paths open to them. Cary loads irony into her piece by comparing the women's motionless and initially silent bodies to the passivity of the weapons:

This is the Soiree: from grate to entrance,
  Like milliners' figures, stand the lovely girls:
But from their silent lips no merry sentence
  Disturbs the smoothness of their shining curls.

Ah! what will rise, how will they rally,
  When shall arrive the "gentlemen of ease"!
What brilliant repartee, what witty sally,
  Will mingle with their pleasant symphonies![21]

Comparing the women's lack of agency to that of the weapons, Cary's parody signals how the "music" of flirtation begins only with the arrival of the "gentlemen of ease." Lined up like mannequins, the "lovely girls" then spring into coquettish action; the poem compares their verbal play to the "rally" and "sally" of the battlefield. Given Longfellow's celebrity status, Cary may well have known that he and his young wife Fanny visited the Springfield arsenal while they were on their honeymoon in 1843; Longfellow told friends that he wrote the call for peace at his wife's request.[22] If Cary knew the anecdote, she surely relished the irony of rewriting a male-authored history of warfare – a poem inspired by a honeymoon trip – as a history of flirtation. Cary's first two stanzas suggest that flirtation, like war, wastes human potential.

Yet while the poem begins by focusing on the coquetry of "the lovely girls," by the third and fourth stanzas the focus shifts to include social talk in general. The third stanza evokes the "infinite sweet chorus" of "the evenings that have gone before us," while stanza four describes the comically varied accents of the participants: the "guttural" German, the "Italian clang," and the "Yankee twang." These details emphasize the remarkable mixing of national identities and social classes that could occur in an urban social setting. The poem next turns its satiric attentions to the occupations of the male attendees, first the editor who "sends out his paper, filled with praise and puff," and then the "holy priests" who "beat the fine pulpit, lined with velvet stuff." With these lines, Cary slyly turns the poem toward representation of her own social milieu. Given the sisters' authorship of poems and hymns, editors and ministers were precisely the kinds of male acquaintances they would have been eager to cultivate after their arrival in New York. In these later stanzas, then, Cary begins to reflect on the social position of the woman writer. Her send-up of social rituals becomes more ironic still if we consider the influential literary salon that she and her sister would go on to host in their New York home on Sunday evenings. In contrast with the "lovely girls" at the start of "The Soiree," Cary and her sister used their weekly salons to expand their network of ties in the literary world, a network that certainly furthered their efforts to support themselves as writers. By all accounts, the Cary sisters were gracious hosts, with Alice's warmth balanced by Phoebe's wit; the sisters thus put their social skills – their "witty sally" – to effective professional use.[23]

In her satiric representation of the woman writer's social circle, Cary sends up the "ancient dames with jewelry o'erladen" and the bluestockings with the same relish with which she mocks the "lovely girls" in the opening stanzas. Where Longfellow describes the "diapason" or great swelling harmony of the "cannonade," Cary's poem evokes the "diapason of some lady *blue*," the "tones of thunder" of the bluestocking's tirade. The line may be a droll self-portrait; after all, Cary would go on to serve as the editor of *The Revolution*, a paper published by Susan B. Anthony that lobbied for women's suffrage. Alternatively, the line may suggest a Margaret Fuller or an Elizabeth Peabody – women who were both known for their commanding intelligence and their outspokenness. The Oxford English Dictionary reminds us of three possible meanings for the "lady *blue*" in mid-nineteenth century America: the phrase suggests a learned woman, a tipsy woman, or a mournful woman, a delicious word play that makes this line function as the climax of the poem's humor.

That climax is extended in the eighth stanza, which Cary lifts almost verbatim from Longfellow's poem:

> Is it, O man, with such discordant noises,
> With pastimes as ridiculous as these,
> Thou drownest Nature's sweet and kindly voices,
> And jarrest the celestial harmonies?

Changing only the second line, she rewrites Longfellow's "such accursed instruments" (the weapons of war) to "pastimes as ridiculous." When the poem blames "man" for the racket of social chatter, having just inveighed against the long-winded bluestocking, it surely intends both the grandeur of the apostrophe and the generic use of the noun to register ironically. Drawing the irony out still further, the poem closes by declaring that if women devoted more of their time and money to "the home, the husbands, and the babies," they would not have time "to visit such a place" as the soiree. Yet in a collection that laments women's unrecognized domestic labor on so many of its pages, such advice can hardly be taken seriously. Moreover, one of this poem's most wickedly subversive arguments would seem to be that living in New York as a single, childless woman can really be a lot of fun; the piece is a marvelous antidote to the relentless and solitary despair of "The Life of Trial." The women at "the soiree" seem to enjoy themselves thoroughly in the absence of either "husbands" or "babies." Clearly Cary is spoofing the didacticism of so much of the advice directed at girls and women in this era. She is also talking back to Griswold, whose endorsement of the Cary sisters in *Female Poets of America* praised them for their domestic industry, the "prosaic duties" that he insisted took up so much of their time. Given the skill with which the sisters built paying careers for themselves as writers, it seems likely that they might have prioritized the hosting of social gatherings as an effective means of building a professional network. By representing social chatter as a "ridiculous" pastime, Cary downplays the sisters' social dexterity, suggesting that their networking is as inconsequential as the "witty sally" of the "lovely girls" with the "shining curls." By parodying Longfellow's call for peace as a witty injunction to women to stay home and do their housework, Cary defuses the threat of the woman writer's growing power – both in the salon and in the literary marketplace.

Cary's meditation on the challenges faced by women writers is more explicit still in the poem that immediately precedes "The Soiree," "'He Never Wrote Again'." In this piece, Cary rewrites Felicia Hemans' elegy for Henry I's son William as a mock-elegy for a male writer who can't find a publisher for his work. In sending up male writerly ambition, she heightens the irony by parodying a female poet. By likening the male writer's failure to the death of a prince, Cary signals the sea change that is taking place in the literary marketplace, as more and more women in both England and the United States see their work in print and take up positions as editors. In January of 1855, Hawthorne would famously complain in a letter to William Ticknor about the "damned mob of scribbling women" and the negative effects their success would have on the reception of his work.[24] Cary here portrays a man who shares Hawthorne's frustration. Further, in taking the Hemans poem as her model for parodic revision, Cary also underlines the strategies that Hemans used in establishing her writing career: in "He Never Smiled Again," Hemans memorializes the lives of an English prince and king, a judicious thematic choice for a female poet in the early part of the nineteenth century. Moreover, Hemans here practices the traditional art of the elegy, in which the poet makes a claim for his or her own immortality by representing the death of a powerful figure. The conventions of the elegy thus reveal the poet's ambition, even as they theoretically down-play the poet's presence. Hemans describes Henry's grief following the death of his son as an emotion that shatters the king's identity. He continues to observe the rituals of life at court, but he is irrevocably altered by his loss:

> He sat where festal bowls went round,
> He heard the minstrel sing,
> He saw the tourney's victor crown'd,
> Amidst the knightly ring:
> A murmur of the restless deep
> Was blent with every strain,
> A voice of winds that would not sleep –
> He never smiled again.[25]

Onto this refrain-driven narrative of a king's loss, Cary layers the narrative of a male writer who sees his chances of fame fade away with his failure to find a publisher.

Central to the comedic edge of Cary's parody is her reiteration of Hemans' weighty, memorializing tone. While that stately tone seems appropriate in Hemans' elegy for a dead prince, it quickly becomes ironic in Cary's depiction of a struggling nameless male writer:

> His hope of publishing went down
> The sweeping press rolled on;
> But what was any other crown
> To him who hadn't one?
> He lived, – for long may man bewail
> When thus he writes in vain:
> Why comes not death to those who fail:–
> He never wrote again![26]

Matching Hemans' poem stanza for stanza, Cary's poem represents the failure of the male writer's ambition as a tragedy of comically epic proportions. Moreover, by performing an ironic rewriting of Hemans' elegy, Cary exposes the male poet's overweening ambition, the motive force of the elegy. Cary writes the poet back into the genre of the elegy, making clear that writing for publication is a process inherently shaped by ambition.

The failed writer watches with dismay as books are published all around him. Cary's second stanza underlines the technological developments that made printing faster and cheaper in the mid-nineteenth century:

Books were put out, and "had a run,"
  Like coinage from the mint;
But which could fill the place of one,
  That one they wouldn't print?
Before him passed, in calf and sheep,
  The thoughts of many a brain:
His lay with the rejected heap:–
  He never wrote again!

Likening the printing of books to the minting of coins, this stanza underlines the monetary value of the published writer's work – and perhaps also the growing monetary value of famous authors' names – even as it also suggests that writers follow the herd, like "calf and sheep," a phrase that mocks their lack of individuality while also evoking the bindings of books. The final stanza blames a tearful female readership for shaping literary fashions:

Minds in that time closed o'er the trace
  Of books once fondly read,
And others came to fill their place,
  And were perused instead.
Tales which young girls had bathed in tears
  Back on the shelves were lain:
Fresh ones came out for other years: –
  He never wrote again!

In "'He Never Wrote Again'," Cary suggests that the male writerly ego knows no bounds, and that rejection is a calamity that leads the male writer to long for death ("Why comes not death to those who fail"). Yet the fragility of that masculine writerly ego was a luxury that Phoebe and Alice Cary could not afford. Rejection presumably taught them how best to shape their poems in relation to the tastes of the mid-nineteenth century. In representing books as following literary fashion, catering to "young girls" who might "bathe" the page with "tears," Cary displays her own canny sense of what the literary marketplace can support.

In mimicking most of the great male poets, British and American, of the nineteenth century, Cary surely intended her "Parodies" to suggest that these writers should not take themselves too seriously. In imitating poets as different from one another as Robert Burns, John Greenleaf Whittier, Edgar Allan Poe, William Cullen Bryant, Byron, and William

Wordsworth, Cary shows her range as a parodist, sending up long ballads, short elegies, sound-based poetry, and didactic postures with equal writerly aplomb. Indeed, by parodying such a diverse mix of writers, Cary seems to parody the concept of the poetry anthology itself. The middle of the nineteenth century saw an outpouring of successful anthologies including, among others, the two-volume *The Poets of America* (1839–1840), edited by John Keese, and *The Poets and Poetry of America* (1842), edited by Rufus Griswold. By parodying mostly male poets, with Hemans as the sole exception, *Poems and Parodies* slyly points to the gender imbalance in these kinds of anthologies. Appearing just six years after Griswold's *Female Poets of America*, a volume that included poems by Alice and Phoebe Cary, *Poems and Parodies* sends up Griswold's anxieties about the difficulties of ascertaining which female poets might be worthy of recognition by including sixty-five pages of parodies of the century's most beloved male poets. By poking fun at some of the leading male editors and writers of her day, *Poems and Parodies* signals that Cary has arrived on the literary scene.

Moreover, Cary's parodies also extend a particularly friendly invitation to readers whose educations, like her own, were hard-won. Whereas the "Poems" section relies on short lines and regular meters, in the "Parodies" section elaborate formal commitments are often central to the piece's parodic stance. Apart from underlining Cary's technical skill, the comic effects she achieves with form suggest that nineteenth-century readers were perfectly capable of finding humor in formal regularity, a laughter shaped by their highly developed ear for poetic sound. Multiple pieces in the "Poems" section remind us how frequently poetry was read aloud in this era, and the slow burn of the humor that gradually unfolds in Cary's parodies would have been a particular pleasure to listeners who knew the originals. When we consider the pedagogical centrality of poetry at this time, it's easy to imagine that Cary wants to give readers for whom education was a hard-won privilege a taste of a very specific kind of pleasure. Cary knows that readers like her will have encountered these poems in reading primers. These are much-loved favorites – but who doesn't love to mock the great works imposed on them in the schoolroom? By sending up such familiar chestnuts with the parvenu's exuberant confidence, Cary invites other readers not born into literary circles to laugh with her at the work of the masters.

Even as Cary upheld nineteenth-century norms for femininity, she also supported herself through the work of her pen. Having declared Cary to be the "wittiest woman in America," Ames goes on to note that "a flash of wit, like a flash of lightning, can only be remembered, it cannot be reproduced."[27] With her *Poems and Parodies,* Cary bottles up the lightning of her social wit, offering us a written version of her subversive imagination. Describing the cultural work performed by parody, Hutcheon argues that parody's "ambivalence stems from the dual drives of conservative and revolutionary forces that are inherent in its nature as authorized transgression."[28] Central to Cary's achievement is her deft mimicry of the dominant poetic conventions of her day. By folding both sentimental poems and parodic doubles into one project, Cary underlines what is at stake for women in the literary perpetuation of the angel of the house; in creating her own parodic anthology, she also propels nineteenth-century poetry forward by interrogating the limits of that ideology and by emphasizing the challenges faced by a woman writer. With its image of the bluestocking holding forth, "The Soiree" celebrates the growing power of women writers even as it also deploys a self-effacing humor to defuse the threat of this change. At the same time, in "'He Never Wrote Again'," Cary unequivocally announces the demise of a literary marketplace that is shaped and directed entirely by men. In *Poems and Parodies,* Cary represents not only the conservative genre conventions of her time, but also the revolutionary discursive freedoms that she and other women writers in this era would begin to claim as their own.

Notes

I am grateful to Jenny Putzi and Alex Socarides for their responses to an earlier version of this essay.

1. Paula Bernat Bennett, "Introduction," *Palace-Burner: The Selected Poetry of Sarah Piatt,* Paula Bernat Bennett (ed.), (Urbana: University of Illinois Press, 2001), xxxii.
2. Analyses by Virginia Jackson, Cristanne Miller, and Bennett have re-examined the term "lyric" in the context of the nineteenth century. While Jackson argues that use of the term is often anachronistic, Miller notes that it had a capacious meaning in this period. Rejecting the idea that every poetic speaker is an extension of the writerly self, Bennett contends that women poets addressed an array of political issues. See Virginia Jackson, *Dickinson's Misery: A Theory of Lyric Reading* (Princeton: Princeton University Press, 2005); Cristanne Miller, *Reading in Time: Emily Dickinson in the Nineteenth Century* (Amherst: University of Mass Press, 2012), 19–48; and Paula Bernat Bennett, *Poets in the Public Sphere: The Emancipatory Project of Women's Poetry, 1800–1900* (Princeton: Princeton University Press, 2003).
3. Phoebe Cary, "The Life of Trial," *Poems and Parodies* (Boston: Ticknor, Reed, and Fields, 1854), 10–11.

4. Bennett, *Poets in the Public Sphere*, 113–134. For analysis of Cary's place in recovery debates, see Lucia Cherciu, "Parody as Dialogue and Disenchantment: Remembering Phoebe Cary," *American Transcendental Quarterly* 20.1 (March 2006), 325–341. My reading of Cary is indebted to Bennett's and Cherciu's analyses.
5. Bennett, *Poets in the Public Sphere*, 124.
6. James Aldrich, "A Death-Bed," *The Poets and Poetry of America*, Rufus Wilmot Griswold (ed.), (Philadelphia: Cary and Hart, 1842), 383.
7. Phoebe Cary, "The Wife," *Poems and Parodies*, 192.
8. John Reuben Thompson, "Notices of New Works," *Southern Literary Messenger* 20.2 (February 1854), 126.
9. Alice Cary arrived in New York in 1850, and Phoebe joined her in the spring of 1851. Though the sisters had hosted gatherings in their home before, they bought a house in 1856, and the renown of their Sunday salons began to grow thereafter.
10. Mary Clemmer Ames, *A Memorial of Alice and Phoebe Cary with Some of Their Later Poems* (New York: Hurd and Houghton, 1874), 158. For further discussion of Cary's wit, see also 183–187.
11. Linda Hutcheon, *A Theory of Parody: The Teachings of Twentieth-Century Art Forms* (New York: Methuen, 1985), 26.
12. M.M. Bakhtin, *The Dialogic Imagination* (Austin: University of Texas Press, 1981), 53.
13. See Eliza Richards, "Introduction," *Gender and the Poetics of Reception in Poe's Circle* (London: Cambridge University Press, 2004), 1–27, esp. 19–20.
14. Bennett, *Poets in the Public Sphere*, 130.
15. Richards, *in Poe's Circle*, 22–24.
16. Thompson, "Notices of New Works,"126.
17. Rufus Griswold (ed.), *The Female Poets of America* (Philadelphia: Carey and Hart, 1849), 372.
18. Griswold, *Female Poets*, 372.
19. Ibid. 372.
20. Henry Wadsworth Longfellow, *Belfry of Bruges and Other Poems*, (Cambridge, MA: John Owen, 1846), 23–26.
21. Phoebe Cary, "The Soiree," *Poems and Parodies*, 179–181.
22. Quoting Longfellow's account of the visit to the arsenal, Thomas Wentworth Higginson tells this story in his 1902 biography *Henry Wadsworth Longfellow* (Boston: Houghton Mifflin, 1902), 173.
23. See, for example, Ames' discussion of their salon. For discussion of Horace Greeley's early visits to the sisters, see *A Memorial of Alice and Phoebe Cary*, 33–34. For a fuller discussion of the salon, see 59–69.
24. Letter, Nathaniel Hawthorne to William D. Ticknor, January 19, 1855, in *Nathaniel Hawthorne, The Letters, 1853–56*, Thomas Woodson (ed.) et al., *The Centenary Edition of the Works of Nathaniel Hawthorne*, vol. 16 (Columbus: Ohio State University Press, 1987), 304.

25. Felicia Hemans, "He Never Smiled Again," *Poems of Felicia Hemans* (London: William Blackwood and Sons, 1849), 346.
26. Phoebe Cary, "'He Never Wrote Again,'" *Poems and Parodies*, 177–178.
27. Ames, *A Memorial of Alice and Phoebe Cary*, 183, 184.
28. Hutcheon, *A Theory of Parody*, 26.

CHAPTER 13

Nineteenth-Century American Women's Poetry of Slavery and Abolition

Eric Gardner

> And your guilty, sin-cursed Union
> Shall be shaken to its base,
> Till ye learn that simple justice
> Is the right of every race.[1]
>
> – Frances Ellen Watkins Harper

Published in the February 23, 1861 *Anti-Slavery Bugle* and then reprinted in the March 8, 1861 *Liberator*, Frances Harper's "To the Cleveland Union-Savers" has much to teach us about the content, approaches, and reception (then and now) of nineteenth-century American women's poetry of slavery and abolition. The poem, whose final stanza opens this essay, only began to garner scholarly attention following its inclusion in a handful of anthologies at the end of the twentieth century.[2] Its neglect probably came partly from many twentieth-century critics' use of modernist and/or post-modernist aesthetics as the sole measures of poetic quality. If they knew of the poem's existence, such critics would likely have dismissed Harper's pronounced metrics and sometimes-expected rhymes – as well as her Protestant, sentimental, reform-centered ethos, images, and arguments – even though many of her nineteenth-century readers and listeners valued exactly these features. Its neglect may also be partly attributed to a hierarchy of genres: "To the Cleveland Union-Savers" works within traditions of occasional and podium poetry – both dismissed by many twentieth-century critics. This poem about the rendition of "hunted sister" Sara Lucy Bagby is also, of course, clearly political and topical – modes many twentieth-century critics assumed were opposed, in simple binary, to artistic creation. Even those who valued select political or topical poetry might have dismissed women poets – and especially women poets of color. Further, the poem was "newspaper verse": it was never published in a "major" periodical venue in the nineteenth century, did not appear in book form until after the Civil War, and even then appeared in a work of history (William Still's 1872 *The Underground Rail Road*) rather than a collection of poetry, making it a likely candidate for being labeled as of "historical interest" only – a New Critical kiss of death. If they knew of the poem, many modern critics might simply have ignored it because of the supposed ephemerality of its original publication venue; of course, many may never have seen the poem simply because they failed to look at such venues.

For all this, Harper's poem did matter: it helped inform the North of the events in Cleveland, argued that there could be no (moral) union with slavery, and did this work through the artistic demands and circumstances of poetry. Select Black readers during and after Reconstruction valued the poem as both (and simultaneously) activist argument and artistic creation. Still, for example, marked it as one of Harper's "best productions."[3] William Wells Brown called it "eloquent."[4] The poem continued to have a life in Black print and school culture – sometimes within rhetorical frameworks of sisterhood, and often within calls for the nation to, in essence, recognize that Black lives matter. Study of Harper's poem and its reception challenges us to ask not only who and what were valued, but who got to do the valuing.

The poem's nascent recovery highlights questions we must ask as we explore the ways diverse American women used poetry to engage with issues surrounding US chattel slavery.[5] Many of the poems treated in this essay call for action – whether simply praying for an expanded (if still limited) benevolent fellow-feeling (or a pronounced paternalism), or demanding that readers break the Fugitive Slave Law and aid enslaved people in ways Bagby herself must have prayed for – and they do so from gendered spaces through diverse venues. This essay emphasizes poetry printed in various book forms and concludes with a brief, speculative discussion of poetry circulated through periodicals and non-print modes. Rather than reify previous critics' fetishizing of the bound book, though, it seeks to differentiate various "book" venues as a way of aiming at where and how we might travel next. The essay's exploration of different "book" venues suggests that political radicalism, poetic experimentation vis-à-vis abolitionist viewpoints, and broader participation in such poetries often became more feasible as poets moved farther from the venues that modern critics have valued most – e.g. single-author books – toward venues such as those where "To the Cleveland Union-Savers" appeared.[6] This essay thus seeks to acquaint readers with some of what we know of American women's poetries of slavery and abolition, but also to consider less charted areas.

My approach is demonstrative, comparative, and speculative rather than comprehensive or definitive, and recognizes how much work remains necessary.[7]

Though published comparatively early, a likely part of current students' introduction to American women's poetry of slavery is popular white poet Lydia Sigourney's "To the First Slave Ship," a poem that came to us in large part because Sigourney included it in a crucial early collection. In its modern life, the poem made appearances – all citing Sigourney's 1827 *Poems* – in Cheryl Walker's *American Women Poets of the Nineteenth-Century* (1992), the more generalist *Columbia Anthology of American Poetry* (1995), and several editions of the *Heath Anthology of American Literature* and the *Norton Anthology of American Literature*. Each of these anthologies implicitly suggests that it was a major poem in Sigourney's oeuvre and/or that it represents a major strand of her worldview. In the Library of America's anthology *American Anti-Slavery Writings* (2012), the poem comes between works by white abolitionist Elizabeth Margaret Chandler and enslaved poet George Moses Horton, only a few pages before an excerpt from Black activist David Walker's fiery *Appeal*, which called for collective Black action (even revolution) in dialogue with some of the nation's founding documents.

Sigourney's poem, though, is a reminder that antislavery poetry need not be immediatist, antiracist, or particularly egalitarian or revolutionary; it lumps enslaved people together and addresses "the slave" as trope and type. The poem does do the important work of demanding that white readers listen: "Hear'st thou *their* moans whom hope hath fled?"[8] From that listening, the speaker concludes, "Our guilty land / Should tremble while she drinks" the "tears" of enslaved people. Functioning within what Paula Bennett identifies as "an epistemology of suffering that made a feeling imagination the primary source of moral knowledge and, hence, of civil action," the poem is nonetheless hesitant about just what specific public actions could or should happen.[9] It ends only by asking enslaved people to "Look to that realm where chains unbind" and "where the patient sufferers find / A friend, – a father in God." This vague call to wait, paired with calls for white folks to practice sentiment, means that, like much white antislavery verse, this poem is actually as much about white sentiment as about recording or imagining specific Black experiences or urging any specific public actions. Not surprisingly, the poem's brief pre-book periodical history places it far from radical or immediate abolition: it was first published in the October 1825 *African Repository* (the journal of the conservative American Colonization Society).

Sigourney's 1827 *Poems* certainly didn't call attention to the poem. Included on pages 176 and 177 of a 228-page volume, it was placed between the longer "Defeat of the Queen of Narragansett, in 1679" and "On the Death of An Accomplished Physician." While Sigourney did return to antislavery verse more often and sometimes more bravely than many white contemporaries, there is no indication that she thought of the poem or even its subject as "major." "To the First Slave Ship" cannot be found in her *Select Poems* (which had gone into its eleventh edition by 1856).

Like the few abolitionist poems in "mainstream" single-author books, Sigourney's abolitionist poetry was occasional at best and was almost always part of a kind of reform miscellany – one that also spoke to other causes addressed by some evangelical Protestants (Indian removal and temperance, for example).[10] Shira Wolosky calls such work Sigourney's "benevolent society poetry" and notes that it is often "poised between social and domestic roles," emphasizing a modest, teacherly voice.[11] Sometimes this mode and this venue even collapsed abolitionism and broader reform in individual poems, as in white poet Phoebe Cary's "The Christian Woman," which appeared in the 1850 *Poems of Alice and Phoebe Cary* and which joins, without much distinction, "the sad slave," individuals in "deep prison-cells," and "little children" praying.[12] While the venue of the "mainstream" single-author collection and the praxis of "benevolent society poetry" brought versions of antislavery ethos into the broader public consciousness within the framework of domestic action, these poetries often blunted abolitionism's sharpest critiques. Open almost solely to white middle- and upper-class women, this venue was also usually marked by the "modesty" Wolosky sees as key to nineteenth-century women's poetries, including a need to draw limits around egalitarian impulses.[13] Thus, such poetry often, in Janet Gray's language, featured a "rhetoric of sentimental condescension" flowing from white writers', editors', publishers', and readers' hesitance about extending a full empathy or sympathy to beings whose personhood they often found doubtful at best.[14]

These limits make a volume such as the 1836 *Poetical Works of Elizabeth Margaret Chandler* all the more striking. Its prefatory texts articulate a general reformist ethos – a life shaped by "the light of Christian philanthropy" – and the volume includes poems challenging Indian removal, bemoaning dueling, and pushing for Christian education.[15] But the book, a posthumous collection of the work of a white Quaker woman, repeatedly emphasizes antislavery engagement in ways that lean much more toward immediatism and egalitarianism. A dozen poem titles refer directly to slavery, and abolitionist editor Benjamin Lundy's biographical introduction claims that Chandler "was the first American female author that ever made this subject the principal theme of her active exertions."[16] Several other poems address slavery without title references, and these especially mark the book's reach. Chandler's poetics of social responsibility links inaction with complicity and demands much more of readers than most white women's antislavery poetry in single-author collections. The volume repeatedly calls on readers to, per the title of one poem, "Think of the Slave." The poem "To Those I Love" demonstrates Chandler's own commitment to that work and the tension that commitment caused:

> Oh, turn ye not displeased away, though I should sometimes seem
> Too much to press upon your ear an oft-repeated theme;
> The story of the negro's wrongs is heavy at my heart,
> And can I choose but wish from you a sympathizing part?[17]

Chandler's poetry often imagines slavery more fully than that of her other white contemporaries, albeit from her own cultural place as a white female Quaker in the North. While this work sometimes extends rhetorics of personhood to Black people, it more often illustrates the difficulties of such rhetorics in white women's verse. On the one hand, the poems that imagine specific Black and enslaved experiences illustrate, in Faith Barrett's language (considering Julia Ward Howe), that such poetries granted women poets the "freedom to assume roles they never could assume in life."[18] On the other, they highlight that such an assumption was often just that – and could slip into appropriation. Chandler's own poem on a slave ship does, for example, show an individual enslaved person, but can only imagine the type of the "noble savage" who, "once a chief, and a warrior," murmurs "in anguish."[19] The poem's resolution is more definite than Sigourney's: "madness was firing his brain" and he chooses suicide. Chandler takes public (poetic) voice through speaking for African Americans – simultaneously a brave gesture of linked identification and an assumption that she could know experiences far different from her own. These depictions challenge white readers to move beyond general reform sympathies; nonetheless, Chandler does not – and arguably could not – make her characters resemble complex living beings, much less empower them with any revolutionary agency.

This pushing of boundaries highlights that *Poetical Works*, while still a book, contrasted massively with, say, Sigourney's books. What was being memorialized in *Poetical Works* – by Lundy, a key early abolitionist editor – was a female abolitionist's consciousness and art; that is, Chandler's "poetical remains" were designed and received as antislavery argument. Chandler thus never garnered the attention some of her fellow women poets did, in part because mass "moderate" audiences did not really consider abolitionist texts as literature until *Uncle Tom's Cabin* (1852).

With few exceptions, the only bound books to approach Chandler's level of progressive antislavery emphasis were antislavery gift books. Developed concurrently with the slave narratives more contemporary readers are familiar with, these texts reached a sector of the (mostly Northern) public enlarged by the growing immediatism of the later 1840s and especially the wedge into popular culture created by *Uncle Tom's Cabin.* Physically and visually books, antislavery gift books nonetheless represent a venue that both embodies and troubles many senses of the "book" as an entity. Because these subject-specific edited collections of diverse voices appeared on a fairly regular schedule, for example, they also carry notable features of periodicals. Importantly, both better-known collections such as the almost-annual *Liberty Bell* (fifteen volumes between 1839 and 1858) and *Autographs for Freedom* (1853 and 1854) and lesser-known collections such as the 1841 *Star of Emancipation* were conceived, edited, and managed by women – the *Liberty Bell* by white Boston activist Maria Weston Chapman, *Autographs* by British abolitionist Julia Griffiths, and the *Star* by the members of the Massachusetts Female Anti-Slavery Society. Chapman spent two decades gathering contributions for the *Liberty Bell* (both texts and funds for printing), arranging and editing prose and poetry, negotiating with publishers, and moving books into readers' hands.[20] Among her breakthrough editorial choices, of especial note are the 1845 publication of the poem "Plegaria a Dios" by Placido (in the original Spanish with a headnote and translation by Chapman) and the 1856 publication of "A Curse for a Nation" by Elizabeth Barrett Browning. In the first of these, the *Liberty Bell* enlarged the audience of the poetry of the Cuban activist (who was key to figures such as Martin Delany) while emphasizing the important role select highly educated women could play as translators; in the second, the gift book continued to build a powerful transnational Romantic antislavery sense of, per Barrett Browning's opening, how "an angel" might say to British citizens "Write! / Write a nation's curse for me, / And send it over the western sea."[21] While not as long-lived, Griffiths' *Autographs* moved into wider distribution Black men's verse, such as James Monroe Whitfield's poem "How Long?" (1853) and George Boyer Vashon's epic fragment of the Haitian Revolution, "Vincent Ogé" (1854).

While scholars such as Karen Sanchez-Eppler and Mary Loeffelholz have done landmark work in thinking about abolitionist gift books, we desperately need fuller publication and reception histories of these texts.[22] Beyond the fact that these volumes represent a rich middle ground between books and periodicals – one that self-consciously avoided ephemerality but could include different voices from different moments – I note three additional critical features. First and foremost, these volumes represent women authors *and* editors creating spaces for sometimes more radical poetries of slavery and abolition – spaces many (white male) publishers were simply unwilling to foster. Second, they represent a fascinating blending of various domestic economies (both in terms of the nation and the home) because, while they were marketed alongside diverse hand-crafted and luxury goods at antislavery fairs, the capital exchanged for them went directly to socio-political action against US chattel slavery. "Gift" books though these were, the central (financial) acts tied to this venue were book purchase and antislavery activism. Finally, any "gifting" of these books outside of specific abolitionist circles (after purchase) might in itself be a challenging political act.

For all of these reasons, antislavery gift books are more diverse in terms of approach and subject matter than any other print venue – save perhaps periodicals. For example, Placido's poem is comparatively light in direct reference to chattel slavery, but Chapman labels Placido as "a man of color and originally a slave" who "wished to become the Spartacus, the Washington of his race."[23] This appears in the same volume as Eliza Lee Follen's paean to Cassius Clay, which focuses on white antislavery activism even as it opens (referencing Lovejoy's martyrdom) that "'Tis said they'll kill thee, Cassius Clay."[24] Both appear in the same volume as white Connecticut abolitionist Martha Hempstead's stunning poem "The Fugitive," which imagines a "weeping, bitterly weeping" enslaved woman carrying her child through the "tangled wild" trying to escape her master (also her child's biological father), who, after "a tale of wrong / Too grievous to be spoken" plans to auction off both the woman and the child, as he has a new "fair young bride."[25] This political diversity mirrored formal variety, with women poets exploring short and long narratives (a common mode in gift books) and revisions of lyric modes, including the sonnets contributed by Chapman's sister Ann Weston.

But while some of these collections – especially *Autographs* – began to include texts by Black men, the reach of the majority (like most "book" venues) did not extend to Black women. Two Black women's texts demonstrate both the difficulties of getting Black women's verse into book venues and the ways Black women poets might have to revise their work and/or the existing venues to reach publication: Ann Plato's 1841

Essays and Frances Watkins's 1854 *Poems on Miscellaneous Subjects* (she would not marry and take the name Harper until 1860). Plato's slim volume contains much more of its title genre than poetry, and little of the book considers US chattel slavery, even though it was prefaced by James W. C. Pennington, an important Black minister who would later pen his own slave narrative. The few poems echo Plato's broader emphasis on general reform. Her poem "The First of August" celebrates British emancipation, for example, but studiously avoids American chattel slavery, and these careful choices are part of her implicit argument that, as a young Black woman, she shared the literary world of her Hartford neighbor Sigourney. Though *Essays* had the cloth and boards of a book, it was a small, locally produced, and locally sold text "printed for the author" that was written by a Black woman who, according to Pennington's preface, hoped to find patronage. Plato's book was thus far from Sigourney's venues – as far as Harriet Wilson's *Our Nig* (1859) was from *Uncle Tom's Cabin*. Even getting that close may have circumscribed the volume's content and Plato's reach.

By the time the initial edition of Harper's *Poems* came out in 1854, on the other hand, its author was already an antislavery activist, and the collection was designed to work in conjunction with that activism. Meredith McGill usefully reminds us that, within the discipline of bibliography, the format of *Poems* "is more of a pamphlet than a book" – "three signatures (forty-eight pages) sewn in a stab binding with a pasted-on paper cover" and "published in small print runs in successive batches to be given away or sold at her antislavery lectures."[26] McGill is right that seeing *Poems* "through the lens of format instead of genre reveals its affinity with numerous texts that are similarly indexed to oral performance" or function "just outside of sanctioned institutions."[27] And Harper did at least sometimes combine lectures with poetry readings – as seen in a September 8, 1854 *Liberator* notice (by William Cooper Nell) of her "lecture on 'Christianity' and an original poem, which Miss W. recited from her recently-published volume."[28] Beyond the physical features and distribution modes McGill describes – that is, the look, feel, and placement of an abolitionist pamphlet – the brief preface by William Lloyd Garrison, the reprinting of poems that had previously appeared in the abolitionist press, the ordering of poems, and the abolitionist emphasis all place *Poems* firmly in the tradition of antislavery pamphlets, even though that venue had not been used (even with Chandler's poetry) to share a single-author collection of poetry for adults.

Simultaneously, though, *Poems* was spoken of at the time as "a book of poems" and, tellingly, "a little book of poems."[29] In this frame, Harper's

Poems actually talks back to single-author collections and general reform poetry. William Still, for example, told readers of the September 2, 1854 *Provincial Freeman* that Harper's volume was clearly in the general reform tradition, as its "various subjects" included "Christianity, Anti-Slavery, Temperance, and other kindred reforms." Scholars from Frances Smith Foster on have recognized that the book is true to the "Miscellaneous" of its title, and especially to the sense of a Protestant reform miscellany. *Poems* thus functioned at the nexus of an antislavery pamphlet and a single-author collection of reform-centered poetry and used a performative occasion to move a Black poet's "book" of poems (that did both activist antislavery and broader Protestant reform work) into readers' hands.

That nexus, a space of what Loeffelholz calls "tutelary community-building," created an essentially new and unique venue for the direct antislavery, antiracist, egalitarian politics that Harper clothed in (what initially seem) traditional poetics.[30] While a full reading of *Poems* is beyond my scope, three features demand some consideration. First, some of Harper's most notable revisions of previous abolitionist poetics focus on direct address and speaker. "The Slave Mother," for example, begins with "Heard you that shriek?" – a demanding question that throws readers directly into the terror of the poem, terror shared (albeit differently) by both speaker and main character.[31] Such moves complicate the ground Barrett studies in reference to Julia Ward Howe – a "unified nationalist 'we.'"[32] They also challenge the kinds of appropriation noted above – and even Bennett's often sound argument that "appropriation is inevitable whenever sympathy serves as the basis for political reform."[33] Harper is actually more hesitant than many white poets to offer first-person imaginings of slavery; many of her speakers are witnesses who pray, advocate, and demand from spaces just outside of slavery. In so doing, they place readers in those fraught, close, and potentially complicit spaces, too. McGill's recognition that Harper's "poems circulated in close proximity to her circulating body" takes on more and different power when we remember that the reader of the "you" in "The Slave Mother" in the 1850s could have been an audience member Harper gestured to when reciting.[34]

Second, Harper's pronounced metrics and rhymes remind us that on one level, as Keith Leonard points out, "cultural assimilation of poetic mastery was the abolitionist poet's greatest act of resistance."[35] But they also – and more so – remind us that many of Harper's poems were designed to function as *both* oral and written pieces – to be work, per Loeffelholz, that was "both immediately lucid and deeply allusive, in multiple registers."[36] If we study only medium or format, we can miss the multiple modes and locations of a given object – here, among others, not just single-author book or abolitionist pamphlet, or even a combination of the two, but also souvenir and record of oral performance and community event, written "proof" of Black poetics, written and oral reform argument, and tool for communal and individual reading.

Finally, *Poems* and its complex new venue used Protestant reform (specifically evangelical and arguably millenialist Protestant reform) – in ways that evoked and leapt beyond the approaches of Phillis Wheatley, early Black lecturer Maria Stewart, and Ann Plato – as a warrant for placing abolition *and* Black rights together at the center of faith practice. As Wolosky notes, "Harper's work powerfully projects the radical potential of religious piety."[37] That warrant places both the oral and printed manifestations of Harper's sermonic tone and heavy, almost-ceremonial metrics and rhymes – as well as her rich Biblical references – as natural responses to a sense that artistic work *must* be actively socially progressive. But as exciting as this venue was – and might have been – it was one that few Black women had access to; Harper's innovation was formed from her own very specific circumstances, including her careful building of both reputation and abolitionist connections.

Given both the limited number of women able to publish poetry through "book" venues and the limitations on the content and politics of many of these venues, periodicals may actually offer the fullest range of American women's poetries of slavery and abolition now extant. These venues – often as different from each other as the various "book" venues noted above – are only beginning to be fully studied: of the major anthologies of nineteenth-century women's poetry, only Bennett's shows sustained engagement with diverse periodicals. Scholarship has often been similarly reticent. I thus close with select suggestions to help guide this much-needed study and brief commentary on the equally necessary study of non-print venues.

First and foremost, as both white-run abolitionist and Black periodicals grew in number and size, the opportunities for Black women to publish poetry – including poetry on slavery and abolition – grew slightly, if nonetheless significantly. For example, Sarah Forten, daughter of James Forten, a wealthy African American and key early supporter of William Lloyd Garrison's *Liberator*, published poetry there and elsewhere in the 1830s, often under the pseudonym "Ada." This work offers fascinating comparatives to Sigourney and Chandler's poetry on slavery in terms of lyric modes, first-person speakers, and gendered imagery. Her poetry's emphasis on witnessing and on questions of nation and nation-building also makes it a key predecessor of Harper's verse. Toward the end of the period studied here, "Mistress and Slave," a poem published in the December 12, 1863 *Christian Recorder*, features as its speaker an unnamed enslaved woman who recounts her sexual assault at the hands of a white man nominally courting her white mistress. The poem ends with a sense of the Civil War's avenging potential: "Ere the wo[e]ful sheaves are garnered / And the bloody vintage trod."[38] Nothing is yet known of the poet, Ellen Malvin, though the fact that the *Recorder*, organ of the African Methodist Episcopal Church, was largely Black-authored offers the possibility that Malvin was African American. Forten and Malvin remind us that turning to periodicals will expand our list of women who wrote poetries of slavery and abolition and likely produce a roster more diverse in terms of race, location, class, and personal history. It will also push us beyond women who saw themselves as poets and make us consider diverse women who published perhaps only a single poem or a handful of poems, and it will expand our sense of women translators of poetry and women editors of poetry – not just Maria Weston Chapman or Julia Griffiths, but also, for example, Lydia Maria Child, who was a key force at the *National Anti-Slavery Standard.*

Turning to periodicals should also give us a fuller sense of texts and their circulation, as, for example, reprinting was a key feature of nineteenth-century periodicals. Sigourney's "Difference of Color," which originally appeared in the July 5, 1834, *Parley's* and later in her 1836 *Poems for Children*, took on a different tone when published in the August 11, 1838, New York City *Colored American*, where it was boldly bylined "By Mrs. Sigourney" and placed among arguments against racial discrimination written *by*, to quote the poem's first lines, "Afric's sons."[39] The reprinting of "To the Cleveland Union-Savers" moved Harper's poem from a more local venue to a larger national one, mirroring the ways the poem's direct address turned from Cleveland to a nation complicit by both action and inaction. As Elizabeth Lorang and R. J. Weir demonstrate in their work on the African American *Weekly Anglo-African* and the white abolitionist *National Anti-Slavery Standard*, text-sharing between periodicals was at times as crucial as permission-free reprinting.[40] Maria Lowell's 1849 *Liberty Bell* poem "Africa," for example, found new life not only when it was reprinted in the September 5, 1863 *Anglo-African* but also when it was then likely shared with the *National Anti-Slavery Standard*, which reprinted it in their September 12, 1863 issue. Abolitionist and Black periodicals published such poetry not only to concretely address the cause, but also, especially by sharing works by "well-known" white women, to mark "friends" and so to suggest that the movement had breadth and depth in terms of appeal, propriety, domesticity, and faith.

Features related to the timescale of periodicals and the ways different periodicals' politics and constituencies shaped these poetries are also key. Periodical and non-print outlets allowed possibilities for immediate "of the moment" poems such as Harper's "To the Cleveland Union-Savers"; such poems ranged from a mass of responses to *Uncle Tom's Cabin* to poetry tied to John Brown. Of particular interest here (but sometimes sorely missing from considerations of poetries of the Civil War) are the significant number of periodical poems by African Americans that commented directly on news of the War – such as the formerly enslaved Fanny M. Jackson (later Coppin)'s May 9, 1863 *Weekly Anglo-African* poem "The Black Volunteers," which speaks of how "Now, Freedom stands holding with uplifted face" and praises newly enlisted Black soldiers.[41] Jackson's poem is also an example of how a periodical's place in print culture and on the political landscape may have shaped its poetries of slavery and abolition: the *Anglo-African* campaigned actively for Black soldiers and became a venue they read and wrote for.

Periodicals were more than just stepping stones or staging grounds for poems of slavery and abolition on the way to book publication. They also – perhaps primarily – functioned as venues in and of themselves, with different writers, readers, communities, goals, structures, organizational schema, and content. Recognizing this will help us not only to better understand women's poetries of slavery and abolition in periodicals, but also to approach the much more nascent study of non-print circulation of such poetries – in primarily oral venues ranging from antislavery lecture recitations to interactions within small antislavery and other groups (such as those studied in Elizabeth McHenry's germinal *Forgotten Readers* [2002]). It should also push us, per Lauri Ramey's 2008 *Slave Songs and the Birth of African American Poetry*, to think about the nexus of poetry and song lyrics tied not only to enslaved people's singing but also the number of post-bellum collections and performances of songs tied to slavery (e.g., by the Fisk Jubilee Singers). We also have growing evidence of antislavery poetries within various manuscript cultures – ranging from a note in Chandler's *Poetical Works* about how a friend "copied '*The Slave Ship*' from my album" to the Library Company of Philadelphia's online presentation of the albums of Philadelphia African Americans such as Amy Matilda Cassey, Martina Dickerson, and Mary Anne Dickerson.[42] In short, many more and different women used poetry to engage slavery and abolition and to call for variations of Harper's "simple justice" in more and different voices and venues than historians of American poetry have suggested. We have much to do to recover their work.

Notes

1. Frances Ellen Watkins Harper, "To the Cleveland Union-Savers," *A Brighter Coming Day: A Frances Ellen Watkins Harper Reader*, Frances Smith Foster (ed.), (New York: Feminist Press of CUNY, 1990), 93–94.
2. The poem is included in the Schomburg edition of Maryemma Graham (ed.), *The Collected Poems of Frances E. W. Harper*, (New Yok: Oxford University Press, 1988), 213–214; *A Brighter Coming Day*, 93–94; Joan Sherman (ed.), *African American Poetry of the Nineteenth-Century*, (Urbana: University of Illinois Press, 1992), 118–119; and Paula Bernat Bennett (ed.), *Nineteenth-Century American Women Poets: An Anthology*, (Malden: Blackwell, 1998), 136–137.
3. William Still, *The Underground Rail Road* (Philadelphia: Porter and Coates, 1872), 764.
4. William Wells Brown, *The Rising Son* (Boston: A.G. Brown, 1873), 525.
5. This essay builds from efforts linking African Americanist inquiry and print culture studies ranging from Lara Cohen and Jordan Stein's *Early African American Print Culture* (Philadelphia: University of Pennsylvania Press, 2012) to P. Gabrielle Foreman's "A Riff, A Call, and A Response: Reframing the Problem That Led to Our Being Tokens in Ethnic and Gender Studies; or, Where Are We Going Anyway and with Whom Will We Travel?" *Legacy* 30.2 (2013), 306–322.
6. Some readers may assume my discussion centers on "medium." Alternately, readers of Meredith McGill's sophisticated study of "format" in Harper's work may see suggestions of that term; see "Frances Ellen Watkins Harper and the Circuits of Abolitionist Poetry," in Cohen and Stein, *Early African American Print Culture*, 53–74. I owe a debt to McGill's work, but emphasize *venue* to study differences within and between different media and formats tied to the places and powers of authors, textual middle-folks, audiences, and other entities, circumstances, and phenomena. I choose this term to emphasize not just the object-ness of "medium" but also a sense of performative spaces in which and through which "media" are constructed and disseminated.
7. I generally limit my scope to printed poetry, roughly beginning with David Walker's massively important 1827 *Appeal* and ending with the Civil War, recognizing a rise in immediatist abolitionism *c.*1845, and for reasons of space do not treat subjects ranging from Confederate women's pro-slavery poetry to verse on slavery written for children.
8. Lydia Sigourney, "To the First Slave Ship," *Poems* (Boston: S. G. Goodrich, 1827), 176–177.
9. Paula Bernat Bennett, *Poets in the Public Sphere* (Princeton: Princeton University Press, 2003), 56.

10. Clusters of abolitionist poetry in this venue are rare before the Civil War, with a notable exception being the group of five poems in Julia Ward Howe, *Words for the Hour* (Boston: Ticknor and Fields, 1857.)
11. Shira Wolosky, "Poetry and Public Discourse, 1820–1910," *The Cambridge History of American Literature*, vol. 4, Sacvan Berkovitch (ed.), (Cambridge: Cambridge University Press, 2004), 167.
12. Phoebe Cary, "The Christian Woman," *Poems of Alice and Phoebe Cary* (Philadelphia: Moss and Brother, 1850), 217–218. Cary did write more direct abolitionist poems; see Bennett, *Poets in the Public Sphere*, 102–103.
13. Wolosky, "Poetry and Public Discourse," 155.
14. Janet Gray, *Race and Time: American Women's Poetics from Antislavery to Modernity* (Iowa City: University of Iowa Press, 2004), 74.
15. Benjamin Lundy, "Preface," *The Poetical Works of Elizabeth Margaret Chandler*, Benjamin Lundy (ed.), (Philadelphia: Lemuel Howell, 1836), 3.
16. Lundy, "Memoir," *Poetical Works*, 13.
17. Elizabeth Margaret Chandler, "To Those I Love," *Poetical Works*, 66.
18. Faith Barrett, *To Fight Aloud is Very Brave: American Poetry and the Civil War* (Amherst: University of Massachusetts Press, 2012), 87.
19. Chandler, "The Slave Ship," *Poetical Works*, 136.
20. See Lee V. Chambers, *The Weston Sisters: An American Abolitionist Family* (Chapel Hill: University of North Carolina Press, 2014).
21. Elizabeth Barrett Browning, "A Curse for a Nation," *Liberty Bell* (Boston: National Anti-Slavery Bazaar, 1856), 1. Chapman had earlier secured a contribution from Browning for the 1848 *Liberty Bell*, "The Runaway Slave at Pilgrim's Point."
22. See Mary Loeffelholz, *From School to Salon: Reading Nineteenth-Century American Women's Poetry* (Princeton: Princeton University Press, 2004), 67–93, and Karen Sanchez Eppler, *Touching Liberty: Abolition, Feminism, and the Politics of the Body* (Berkeley: University of California Press, 1993), 14–49.
23. Headnote for "Plegaria a Dios," *Liberty Bell* (Boston: Massachusetts Anti-Slavery Fair, 1845), 67.
24. Eliza Lee Follen, "To Cassius M. Clay," *Liberty Bell*, 21.
25. Martha Hempstead, "The Fugitive," *Liberty Bell*, 209–214.
26. McGill, "Frances Ellen Watkins Harper," 57.
27. Ibid., 60. Johanna Ortner's rediscovery of Harper's first collection *Forest Leaves*, detailed in an article published as this volume was in press, reemphasizes the fact that Harper's verse came to early publics in pamphlet form; see "Lost No More: Recovering Frances Ellen Watkins Harper's *Forest Leaves*," *Common-place* 15.4 (Summer 2015). common-place.org/book/lost-no-more-recovering-frances-ellen-watkins-harpers-forest-leaves/. That said, scholars have not yet found direct ties between *Forest Leaves* and organized abolition, so Ortner's work also complicates some of McGill's conclusions.
28. Also see the September 29, 1853 *Pennsylvania Freeman* for a report of how "Miss F. Watkins, of Baltimore" "recited gracefully two anti-slavery

poems" – "Bible Defense of Slavery" and "Eliza Harris" – at an anti-colonization meeting at Philadelphia that also featured lectures by Robert Purvis and Mary Ann Shadd.

29. W[illiam] S[till], "To the Editor," *Provincial Freeman* (September 2, 1854), np (issue page 3), and W[illiam] S[till], "Correspondence," *Provincial Freeman* (March 7, 1857), 110 (issue page 2).
30. Loeffelholz, *From School to Salon*, 120.
31. Harper, "The Slave Mother," *Poems on Miscellaneous Subjects* (Boston: J. B. Yerrinton and Son, 1855), 6.
32. Barrett, *To Fight Aloud is Very Brave*, 88.
33. Bennett, *Poets in the Public Sphere*, 56.
34. McGill, "Frances Ellen Watkins Harper," 67.
35. Keith Leonard, *Fettered Genius: The African American Bardic Poet from Slavery to Civil Rights* (Charlottesville: University of Virginia Press, 2006), 21.
36. Loeffelholz, *From School to Salon*, 95.
37. Wolosky, "Poetry and Public Discourse," 224.
38. Ellen Malvin, "Mistress and Slave," *Christian Recorder* (December 12, 1863), np (issue page 1, consecutive page 197).
39. Lydia Sigourney, "Difference of Color," *Colored American* (August 11, 1838), 100 (issue page 4).
40. See Elizabeth Lorang and R. J. Weir, "'Will not these days be by thy poets sung': Poems of the Anglo-African and National Anti-Slavery Standard, 1863–1864," *Scholarly Editing* 34 (2013). scholarlyediting.org/2013/editions/intro.cwnewspaperpoetry.html.
41. Fanny M. Jackson, "The Black Volunteers," *Weekly Anglo-African* (May 9, 1863), np (issue page 1).
42. Chandler, *Poetical Works*, 12, and "Cassey and Dickerson Friendship Album Project" at http://lcpalbumproject.org. All three friendship albums are in the Library Company's print collection: the Cassey album is P.9764, the Martina Dickerson album is 13859.Q, and the Mary Ann Dickerson album is 13860.Q.

CHAPTER 14

Fever-Dreams: Antebellum Southern Women Poets and the Gothic

Paula Bennett

> It may be that the continual presence of darkness in human shape, as a tangible reminder of the fears and impulsions that it has come to symbolize, helped to create a sensibility which seems distinctively Southern, and which has been contributing more than its share to contemporary literature.[1]
>
> –Harry Levin, *The Power of Blackness*

> Explicit or implicit, the Africanist presence informs in compelling and inescapable ways the texture of American literature. It is a dark and abiding presence, there for the literary imagination as both a visible and an invisible mediating force.[2]
>
> –Toni Morrison, *Playing in the Dark*

When Sarah Piatt left New Castle, Kentucky, for Washington DC in 1861, she had already published close to 160 poems between the *Louisville Journal* and the *New York Ledger.* Appearing from 1854 to 1861, these early poems were stylistically worlds apart from the bitterly ironic, realist-based poems that had originally caught my eye, and, with a condescension I now deeply regret, I labelled them juvenilia in the introduction to my selected edition of her work.[3] Looking back, I think two factors accounted for my misreading of the poems. The first was indeed a matter of style. These poems were as lush as Piatt's later poems were spare. The second and more important was Piatt's choice of persona. In the florid words with which the *Louisville Journal* editor, George Prentice, introduced her poems, these were the poems of "a poetess": her heart a "soul-lyre," her poetry, like the song of the nightingale, a matter of nature not art.[4] When selecting sample poems for *Palace-Burner*, I chose only those I believed directly relevant to her later work, dismissing out of hand the many poems in which her persona mourned failed love affairs, all of them written, as I saw it, under the sign of the poetess.

But were the conventions of antebellum poetess poetry – the first-person lyricism, the emphasis on feeling, the privileging of suffering, the use of generic language and figures, and the overall literariness of the poems (that is, the way in which they echoed each other) – as limiting as I believed, or were there alternative ways for women writers to use these conventions that I did not consider?[5] This essay looks at three very different women poets – Louisa S. McCord (1810–1879), Sarah M. B. Piatt (1836–1919), and Catherine Warfield (1816–1877) – all of whom came from the planter class and all of whom adapted poetess conventions in ways that addressed their own culture and the darkness within it. Steeped in the classics and in British literature, most notably Byron and the British Romantics, these three women found in poetry a vital outlet through which to express their deepest anxieties. Reworking poetess conventions to suit the sometimes bizarre contradictions of their lives as upper-class Southern women, they layered the darkness of the Gothic onto the romanticism of a poetess sensibility, creating a poetics that was uniquely Southern in style and substance. Although these three women also wrote other kinds of poetry, from elegies and love poems to occasional verse, here I focus on their Gothic poems and on the role that slavery played in shaping this verse.

"'Tis sweet to deceive ourselves": Louisa McCord

No Southern woman poet more fully identified with the values of her class than Louisa McCord. Born in 1810 in Charleston, South Carolina, McCord came from the highest echelons of planter aristocracy. In 1819, her father, Langdon Cheves, was appointed President of the Bank of the United States by President Monroe, and the family moved to Philadelphia where McCord attended a school for young ladies, supplemented by home schooling in French and mathematics, the latter at her own insistence. Ten years later, the family returned to South Carolina and, in 1833, Cheves gave McCord a 1,530 acre plantation in Pendleton, South Carolina. In 1840, at what for the South was the advanced age of thirty, McCord married David James McCord, a politician and attorney, with whom she had three children. Virtually everything she published appeared between 1848 and 1856, after which her father's growing dementia led her to abandon writing for caretaking.[6]

Described by a female acquaintance as "a masculine clever person, with the most mannish attitudes and gestures, but interesting and very entertaining," McCord was born into a patriarchal society that had no place for a woman of her intellectual inclinations.[7] "A fiercely biting and intellectually gifted polemicist," she used writing to compensate for (and circumvent) her political-sidelining, initialing or publishing anonymously a series of essays on slavery, economics, abolition, and woman's rights that rank her today as one of the Old South's most articulate theorists.[8] While most scholarly interest in McCord has focused on these essays, she also published a highly-respected closet drama, "Caius Gracchus: a Tragedy in Five Acts." Taking as her subject the Gracchus brothers' failed land reform movement of 133–123 BCE, McCord uses her play to showcase the political role their mother Cornelia Africana played in their affairs – for McCord, evidence that women could be politically effective without leaving home. The privately printed *My Dreams* (1848) was McCord's sole poetry volume and, at least at first glance, her one apolitical work. It is also the one in which the tug and pull of her gender issues is least resolved. A formal and thematic mélange, *My Dreams* contains allegories, moral fables, religious meditations, meditations on life, satires, poems on dreams, and a number of personal poems invoking the poetess's "I."

In titling her volume *My Dreams*, and varying her forms, McCord may have hoped to open up a "feminine" space in her writing. But if so, her rigid allegiance to Southern principles of social and political order subverted her intentions from the start, as even a quick perusal of *My Dreams*' introductory "proem" on dreaming makes clear. Far from justifying dreaming as McCord meant it to do, the "proem" ends by disowning it. Not only is dreaming enjoyable, McCord argues, far more important, insofar as it helps "driv[e] away discontent," it is also useful. To do so, however, dreams must deceive, a contradiction that lands McCord squarely in a catch-22: "'Tis sweet to deceive ourselves, to fancy a Heaven, tho' we must at last wake to Earth. . . . Sleeping or waking 'tis sweet to forget the world and ourselves in airy visions which are not, which cannot be, which even as we dream, we know them false."[9] Understood thus, dreaming, far from making us "content," frustrates us further. And, finally, it is this message, not dreaming's "sweetness," that her poems teach one dreamer after another: "Where / Lingers now the magic ground / To my cheated sight so near?" asks the weary interlocutor in "To a Fly."[10] In the surreal "The Garden of Experience," a naïve speaker is crushed when every flower she admires withers at her touch.

For McCord, the inevitability of frustration is precisely why order was a social necessity. By their very nature dreams fail us, and when they do, they produce just the state of mind that the "proem" said they "distracted" us from: "Murmuring Discontent," which was "a sin against high Heaven." But God's ordained order – an order in McCord's mind identical to that of Southern patriarchy – could not fail. "Equality," she wrote in "Negro-mania" (1852), "is no thought nor creation of God . . . and abolition is a dream whose execution is an impossibility."[11] Ditto for "woman's-rights." Finally, male or female, slave or free, every person must accept his or her God-assigned place. Thus, in "Caius Gracchus," Cornelia tells her daughter-in-law to "stay within doors" and hide her "passions" if she cannot "smother them."[12] And in the allegorical "The Fire-fly," the lowly insect tells his female interlocutor to give up "fantastic hopes" and to her "earthy home returning, / ... Seek to be contented."[13] Faithful to her own logic, McCord lived by these same principles – not only publishing anonymously, but abandoning writing altogether when her father fell ill.

Leigh Fought, McCord's biographer, who makes "The Fire-fly" central to her interpretation of McCord's career, believes that she struggled throughout her life to subordinate what she construed as her inappropriate ambitions to her duty as a Southern woman.[14] But as Fought admits, there are no diaries or letters to support this interpretation.[15] There is, however, one poem, "The Spirit of the Storm," that in its Gothic texture and thematics suggests the price McCord paid for "smother[ing]" her dreams and "stay[ing] within doors." In this poem, McCord exploits the poetess lyric's emotional freedom and, with it, her largely repressed Romantic sensibility, to rail against the gulf that separated what she was from what she could be. Abjuring an embodied self, McCord's speaker identifies with the storm, introjecting the very rage and darkness that her efforts at self-sacrifice sought to suppress:

> Wild spirit of the storm, who rid'st the blast,
> And in the growling thunder speak'st thy rage,
> Would I could soar with thee!
> Untamed, unfetter'd, roaming through the vast
> Expanse of universe from age to age,
> 'Tis thine, thine! to be free!
> 'Tis mine, to lie, and grovel in the dust,
> And wonder at thy might,
> And in admiring amazement lost,
> To tremble at the terrors of thy fearful night.
>
> But no! with thee my spirit longs to rise,
> It doth not tremble. – Genius of the storm!
> Thou art but tameless, wild,
> As I would be, could I enfranchise
> My chain'd being, – cast off the grovelling worm.
> Nature's untamed storm-child,
> With thee the whirlwind in its might I'd ride,
> Revel in the howling blast,
> Play with the forked lightnings, and deride
> The timorous world, by thee with weary fears harassed.[16]

In the extremity of its vocabulary and emotions, "Storm" can fairly be called a Gothic poem, but what makes the poem's Gothicism unique – and to my mind unforgettable – is the bizarre and terrifying transmogrification of the speaker herself. Not only does the poem rip apart McCord's carefully structured argument for a hierarchically organized social order and for her own subordinate position within it; in exposing the seething anger beneath her submission, its multiple allusions to freedom and enslavement raise questions about McCord's own identity. For who is to say that the speaker of this poem, with all her rage and wildness, is white, let alone a surrogate for McCord herself? Indeed, if anything, the poem reads like a rewrite of Phillis Wheatley's "To Maecenas," a poem whose speaker depicts herself as groveling on the ground when she wishes to fly heroically in verse.

How could the tightly reined-in McCord, scion of the Southern aristocracy and dedicated defender of the South's "peculiar institution," translate her own situation so exactly into one that mimics not just Wheatley's, but also that of the iconic kneeling slave of the abolitionist emblem, merging herself with those in whose oppression she was so deeply complicit? And how deep did her identification with darkness go? There comes a point when "dream" turns into nightmare, a nightmare that McCord's "Spirit of the Storm," with its allusions to "rage," "terror," and "howling," gestures at without ever confronting. Building on the work of Harry Levin and Toni Morrison, I now want to turn to two poets, both of whom suggest – albeit very differently – that the unconscious (if not necessarily the conscious) minds of planter-class Southern women were indeed steeped in a (slavery-born) darkness that drew them, perhaps inexorably, to replicate itself in their verse.

Love Games and Gothic Lovers in Sarah Piatt

"Flirtation," Mary Chesnut wrote in December 1864, "is the business of society. That is, playing at lovemaking. It begins in vanity – it ends in vanity. It is spurred on by idleness and a want of any other excitement. . . . It is a pleasant but very foolish game."[17] Like McCord, Chesnut was a prominent figure in the South's planter aristocracy; unlike her fellow South Carolinian, however, she questioned many of her class's basic beliefs. In this respect, she came closer to another female writer of planter birth, one for whom society's "pleasant" games took, if anything, an even darker turn: Sarah Piatt. Descending on her mother's side from large slaveholding families, Piatt lost home, family, and marital prospects with her mother's death in the 1840s.[18] An outsider thereafter, she became a shrewd observer of the planter class's mating games, devoting the majority of her early poems to their dissection. These are the poems I discuss here, touching first on the games themselves and then on the dark dénouement Piatt gives them.

Piatt's view of "lovemaking" as a game, albeit a bitter one, becomes obvious if one reads the poems as a unified group rather than individually. In this game, as Susan Grove Hall observes, Piatt's speaker plays the "dreamer" and the poems trace her trajectory from wary hopefulness to utter disillusionment.[19] Opposite her is a cadre of male suitors who, if one ignores those unnamed, number at least eleven: Allan, Charlie, Percy, et cetera. Named or not, these suitors participate in a limited group of scenarios. Some are dead. Of these, the most important are "Allan," based on a cousin whom Piatt seems to have loved, and an unnamed other, who may also have biographical ties.[20] Both these men are key actors in Piatt's "lost [Southern] romance," and she mourns them on and off throughout her career, but most movingly in two elegies: "The Memorials" and "A Dirge by the Sea."[21]

Of the remaining lovers, only Charlie has a developed storyline, albeit a bleakly comic one. The rest, with one exception – the Gothic lover discussed later in the chapter – have scarcely more presence than their names. They come and they go, loved and then lost, typically although not always, in a poem or two. Significantly, they also come in only two physical types. Like Allan and Charlie they are idealized as blonde, blue-eyed, and "divinely fair."[22] Or, like the unnamed man in "The Memorials," who is said to have a "heart . . . blacker than his hair," they are figures of darkness drawn on a hyper-masculine Byronic template.[23]

Insofar as Piatt's typecasting and objectification of the suitors marks their fictional status, they are key to reading the poems themselves. As the speaker tells Charlie, whom she calls "half like my ideal," he is not a real person.[24] He is the projection of a fantasy, just as Shelley's ideal beloved is "the shadow of some golden dream" in the passage from *Epipsychidion* that Piatt uses as an epigraph to one of her Charlie poems.[25] A negation of a negation (shadow/dream), he is without tangible substance or agency. Rather, like the "fragrant flowers," "summer stars," and "myrtle bowers," which are also constitutive of the dreamer's romance, he is part of "the scenery of [her] soul," nothing more.[26] Like so many women in male-authored texts, that is, he is a poetic device. Emptied of personhood, his sole function is to serve as the occasion for the female speaker's complaints, with disillusionment – not poetess grieving – their true, if mocking, focus.

Piatt's rhetorical strategies – the many names, the limited storylines, and the stereotyping – ultimately destabilize the lyric identity of the lovers, the speaker, and the poems themselves, putting substantial distance between the poet and her poems. As Piatt would later call such tales, they are "love-stories," and they end where Piatt believed all such quests for the ideal in material form were bound to end: in bitterness and pain for those "foolish" enough to take them seriously.[27] As she told her sister, Ellen, in "To Ella," the pursuit of love was the pursuit of a "mira[ge] of the heart," which terminated not in "enchanted fountains" but in "showers of – dry and burning sands."[28] As Hall argues, this was the existential loss of faith that went to the heart of Piatt's love poetry, and it led her perhaps inexorably to love's dark side.[29] Understood in this context, the stakes in Piatt's "game" could not have been higher, as the poems devoted to the unnamed man whom I am calling "the Gothic lover" make clear.

Between April 1858 and May 1859, Piatt published a cluster of eight Gothic poems that are distinguished by the dominant role an unnamed lover plays in them.[30] First introduced in the *Ledger* in two closely interrelated works – "My 'Castles in Spain'" and "A Moon-Rise by the Sea" – this man is a shadowy and ambiguous presence whose toying with the speaker precipitates an emotional breakdown. In "My 'Castles in Spain,'" he first lures the speaker with his "blue and dreamy eyes," then with a "scornful smile" abandons her amidst the wreckage of her dreams, while in "Moon-Rise," he tempts her with the promise of "a palace in the deep," only to drown her.[31] The breakdown itself plays out in the *Louisville Journal* in poems that deploy multiple formal devices designed to replicate a disordered brain's chaotic movements: irregularly sized verse paragraphs instead of stanzas, asterisks that divide paragraphs from each other, erratic rhyming, irregular indentations, broken lines, and multiple pauses.

Together with these devices, Piatt also employs a vocabulary consisting of words and images with Gothic associations. Words that appear multiple times in various forms include burn, night, dark, wild, strange, fire, tears, haunt, red and crimson, blood, gloom, fear, pale, storm, sad, mourn, dead, and mad. Samples of images include "fearful gloom," "dread abys[ses]," "sulph'rous flame," "poisoned daggers," "desolating storms," and "the raven's wailing strain."[32] Many of the words if not the images – night, dark, sad, and so on – are also part of Piatt's customary poetic vocabulary, but only in the Gothic poems are they integrated into a primary discourse meant not just to supplant the Romantic discourse of her other poems but also to pervert it. Thus, for example, in "A Poet's Soliloquy" Piatt depicts nature as dead, barren, and diseased: "pale roses," "*dead myrtles*," "eternal wast[es] of sands," and "clou[ds] bathed in blood"; while in "Fragments" she makes it frightening, alluding to a "shrieking tempest . . . / . . . bea[ting] its black wings o'er the dead" and "snowy blooms" of the "myrtle-tree" gushing blood.

With these words, phrases, and descriptions, Piatt sketches out a mind haunted by the graves of the dead and lost in the chaos precipitated by its own despair. In "Fragments," the speaker records a series of horrific dreams. In one such dream, "fev'rish fires" threaten to "burn [her "Judas"/ lover's] life away," while in another an angel throws him into the "gloomy deeps" of "a dread abyss."[33] In "Idols – a Dream," the speaker stages the scene of her own damnation. Commanded by a stranger to look to God, she is unable to do so and seals her doom. Her eyes still fixed on the stranger whose beauty obsesses her, she descends to hell where "horrid things did swim / Below – around."[34] If in "To Ella" Piatt claims to have lost faith in "the Fairy land of love," in "What Seems," published four months later, she reprises the Gothic, describing her "bosom" as "an abyss of fire – / Thronged with lost Angels – who, in vain, aspire / To climb to heaven!" – suggesting she had lost faith in God and in herself as well. [35]

Obviously Piatt's use of darkness in these poems is essential to their Gothic mystique. But the speaker's overwhelming emphasis on personal guilt – her references to the abyss, idols, her inability to look to God, her staging of her own damnation, and her identification with lost Angels – also seems, like McCord's emphasis on carceral imagery in "Storm," to point to something deeper. In McCord's case, the speaker's language seems to suggest, however bizarrely, her deep-buried identification with the slaves she owned, an identification enabled by the restrictive social conventions under which this all-too-exceptional woman labored. In Piatt's case, it is not so much identity that is repressed as desire, desire so strong and at the same time so utterly unacceptable to the speaker that it emerges with the same explosive power as McCord's storm. Who the lover is in these poems (if anyone) we cannot know. But his darkness, beauty, power, and corruption, not to mention his "heartless pride," suggest that, to her, he was an avatar of the South and of the men of her own class who owned the vast majority of the South's agricultural land and the slaves who worked it.[36]

In "An Orphan's Adjuration," published the same month as "Idols," Piatt bewails her fate as a Southerner, bitterly complaining of her own corruption in a poisonous environment where "serpents hiss and roses fade and sounds of sadness swell."[37] In the postbellum "A Hundred Years Ago" these same serpents make it impossible for her to reconcile the "real" South with the "Fairy land" South she had believed in when "The world was full of dew and very fair" – that is, when she was young.[38] Like McCord's dream of a God-ordained slavocracy, Piatt's fantasy South was a "mirage of the heart," whose beauty she had mistaken for truth. The real South, the South of snakes and suffering, where the idle and vain few lived off the labor and heartbreak of the many, was far closer to a Gothic hell. Read in this context, Piatt's early poetry, far from being "juvenilia," contributes centrally to Southern literature, providing a social and psychological critique of Romanticism, and, by implication, Romanticism role in undergirding slavery, unequaled in nineteenth-century American women's verse.

Catherine Warfield: Apocalypse Southern Style

Catherine Warfield was born in Natchez, Mississippi, the offspring of elite slaveholders on both sides. Not long after the birth of her younger sister, Eleanor, in 1819, Warfield's mother, who suffered from a hereditary form of mental illness, was institutionalized. Possibly as compensation for their loss, the two girls became quite close, sharing a love of literature that eventually resulted in their co-authorship of two privately published poetry volumes, *The Wife of Leon* (1843) and *The Indian Chamber and Other Poems* (1846). Both volumes suggest that Catherine developed an early interest in the Gothic and, after Eleanor's death in 1849, her first literary venture was a Gothic novel, *The Household of Bouverie* (1860), to this day considered her strongest work. Like this later text, the poem I focus on here, "The Legend of the Indian Chamber," uses a Gothic setting to engage the issue of domestic abuse.[39] However, unlike the novel, this poem takes the issue well beyond one household, placing it in a global perspective. In legitimizing slavery, the South effectively supported the right of one class of persons to abuse another on whatever grounds it chose. Drawing on Indian and European settings, Warfield puts this "right" into question wherever it was claimed – including in the backyard of her own slaveholdings.

The plot of "The Legend of the Indian Chamber" centers on wife-murder occurring on two continents: in India through the ritual practice of suttee and in Europe, where the poem's villainous protagonist, a nameless Norman baron, kills his new bride and dumps her body in the Rhine River. The poem's action occurs sometime after this last event, and is confined to the "Indian Chamber" of the baron's castle. A sumptuous (if decaying) room, this chamber is the designated viewing space for the corpses of the baron's "illustrious line," and two of the chamber's furnishings play crucial roles in the narrative.[40] The first is an arras "wrought in symbols wild and weird."[41] Woven in India and enspelled by "Indian seers," this arras, which gives the chamber its name, depicts events in Hindu mythology mixed with scenes from Indian life. Among the latter are a Rajah's funeral pile and its sacrificial object, the Rajah's wife, on whom the plot will turn.[42] The second prop is a "plumed bed of state," whose "long and hearse-like hangings" bespeak "a silent history / Of departed funeral."[43] From behind these hangings the ghost of the baron's bride emerges to tell the baron's servant, Basil, how she was murdered. Predicting the baron's death that night, she asks the pious old man to say masses for her soul.

The bride's prediction comes true, but she is not responsible for the baron's death; the Rajah's wife is. Basil has barely finished cleaning the Indian chamber when the baron enters accompanied by "an eastern stranger" – pointedly a white colonizer, who says he lost "health and youth and blood" in getting "wealth and idle treasure" in India.[44] The baron has invited this man into his home intending to kill him with a chalice of poisoned wine he has prepared. However, his plan goes awry when the stranger, who has been perusing the arras, sees the Rajah's wife come alive. Ignoring the baron's proffered chalice, the stranger describes how the wife descends from the funeral pile and, going to "the Brahmin's sacred shrine" – also depicted on the arras – takes up a jewelled cup of flames and enters the Indian chamber itself.[45] At this juncture, the eastern stranger stops, disabled by terror; the poem's narrator picks up the tale, describing how the Rajah's wife, acting as a surrogate for the "victim bride" (that is, for the baron's murdered wife), forces the baron to drink his own poison:

> Chained and speechless, guest and servant
> Saw the baron drain the draught;
> Saw him fall convulsed and blackened
> As the deadly bowl he quaffed;
> Saw the phantom bending o'er him,
> As libation on his head
> Slowly, and with mien exulting,
> From the cup of flames she shed.[46]

In thus having the Indian wife enact the bride's revenge, Warfield fuses into a single hybrid figure the poem's two dark-haired female victims, made one by the abuse each has suffered. Just as the castle's "plumed bed of state" is the symbolic equivalent of the Rajah's funeral pile, so, for both of these women, marriage is death – death enabled in each case by marital laws that encouraged despotic power in men while denying recourse or redress to their wives.[47] Nor do Warfield's concerns with issues of differential distributions of power end here. While there are no black slaves in this poem, the baron does call his servant, Basil, "slave," thus including slaves within the poem's general category of the abused.[48] Add to this that one of two female victims is both colonial subject and a woman of color, and it seems clear that Warfield is not just critiquing overweening male power, as she does in her other Gothic works. She is placing this power explicitly within a context that relates it to an array of caste and class oppressions. That is, she is thinking about the politics of oppression generally, wherever it arises, be the victims male or female, slave or free, colored or white, Euro-American or Asian. Indeed, one can almost feel the narrator's own exultation as the Rajah's wife metes out justice. The poem's other males – guest and servant – are frozen in place. The abused victim(s) are triumphant. In the poem's apocalyptic last lines, darkness and cold wipe out everything: "And the lofty torches warring / For a moment in the blast, / In their sconces were extinguished, / Leaving darkness o'er the past!"[49]

Warfield could conceive of such identifications, I would suggest, because slavery, with all its inequities, was part of her reality – a reality whose fever-dreams were precisely the nightmares of revenge and apocalypse that the poem's conclusion adumbrates. If the poem's subject is the evils of giving unrestricted power to one class of persons over another, then, in this poem's imaginary, Rajah, baron, colonizer, and slaveholder are finally all the same and all will suffer the same fate. Given that Warfield owned many slaves and staunchly supported the Confederacy, it is unlikely that she was fully conscious of where her poem's logic was tending, but this is the inevitable conclusion it suggests. Of these three poets, Warfield was in this way the most representative. Like the many planter women who, on one level or another, recognized slavery's systemic evils, she did nothing to end them, instead rationalizing the necessity for slavery, and putting into her writing dreams whose full meaning she could not or would not own. It was of such dreams that the Southern Gothic was made.

Notes

1. Harry Levin, *The Power of Blackness: Hawthorne, Poe, Melville* (New York: Vintage, 1958), 233.
2. Toni Morrison, *Playing in the Dark: Whiteness and the Literary Imagination* (Cambridge, MA: Harvard University Press, 1992), 46.
3. Paula Bernat Bennett, "Introduction," *Palace-Burner: The Selected Poetry of Sarah Piatt* (Urbana: University of Illinois Press, 2001), xxiv. I owe a substantial scholarly debt to Susan Grove Hall for making me rethink my position. See "From Voice to Persona: Amelia Welby's Lyric Tradition and Sarah M. B. Piatt's Early Poetry," *Tulsa Studies in Women's Literature* 25 (2006), 223–246. Hall has deeply influenced my treatment of Piatt's early poetry throughout.

4. For the "soul-lyre," see Sallie M. Bryan [Piatt], "When We Parted," *Louisville Journal* 27 (September 4, 1857), 2. For nightingale, see Sallie M. Bryan [Piatt], "The Fated," *Louisville Journal* 29 (October 24, 1859), 2.
5. Eliza Richards discusses poetess conventions (echoing in particular) in *Gender and the Poetics of Reception in Poe's Circle* (Cambridge: Cambridge University Press, 2004), 16–20. Jess Roberts addresses them in relation to Piatt in "Sarah Piatt's Grammar of Convention and the Conditions of Authorship," *Cambridge Companion to Nineteenth-Century American Poetry*, Kerry Larson (ed.), (Cambridge: Cambridge University Press, 2011), 173–183.
6. The information in this paragraph is based on Lounsbury's detailed chronology in *Louisa S. McCord: Poems, Drama, Biography, Letters*, Richard C. Lounsbury (ed.), (Charlottesville: University Press of Virginia, 1996), 2–3 s.v. 1819, 1829, 1833; 5–10 s.v. 1840, 1848–1854, 1855, 1856–1857.
7. As quoted in Lounsbury, "Chronology," *Poems*, 8, s.v. 1851.
8. Elizabeth Fox-Genovese, *Within the Plantation Household: Black and White Women of the Old South* (Chapel Hill: University of North Carolina Press, 1988), 244.
9. McCord, *Poems*, 44, 45.
10. McCord, "To a Fly," *Poems*, 128.
11. Louisa S. McCord, "Negro-mania," *Louisa S. McCord: Political and Social Essays*, Richard Lounsbury (ed.), (Charlottesville: University Press of Virginia, 1995), 241.
12. McCord, "Caius Gracchus," *Poems*, 170, 171.
13. McCord, "The Fire-fly," *Poems*, 96.
14. Leigh Fought, *Southern Womanhood and Slavery: A Biography of Louisa S. McCord, 1810–1879*, (Columbia: University of Missouri Press, 2003), 10, 72–73.
15. Ibid., 4, 8–10.
16. McCord, "The Spirit of the Storm," *Poems*, 131.
17. Mary Boykin Chesnut, *Mary Chesnut's Civil War*, C. Vann Woodward (ed.), (New Haven: Yale University Press, 1981), 690.
18. In a poem for her dead cousin, Piatt writes of her situation after her mother's death: "You knew I lacked the golden gifts / Men prize so much – you knew … / My life was like a pale sea-flower that drifts, / … Lone on a lonesome wave." These lines address both her lack of dowry and her deracination. Sallie M. Bryan, "A Dirge by the Sea," *New York Ledger* 26 (December 29, 1860), 6.
19. Hall, "From Voice to Persona," 223.
20. In "Early Friends," Piatt's speaker mourns a loved cousin who died abroad, and in "Percy Godolphin," she calls him "Allan." Sallie M. Bryan, "Early Friends," *Louisville Journal*, 26 (August 18, 1856), 2; and Sallie M. Bryan, "Percy Godolphin," *Louisville Journal*, 27 (April 11, 1857), 2.
21. Sarah Piatt, "Over in Kentucky," in Paula Bernat Bennett (ed.), *Palace-Burner* (Urbana: University of Illinois Press, 2001), 37. Late poems

explicitly referencing early love affairs include "The First Party," "The Coming Back of the Dead," "My Other Gods," and "Confession."

22. Sallie M. Bryan [Piatt], "Visionary's Fancies," *New York Ledger* 24 (November 13, 1858), 3.
23. Piatt, "The Memorials," in Bennett, *Palace-Burner*, 158–160. This poem appeared in the *Ledger* in 1859.
24. Sallie M. Bryan [Piatt], "Memories and Musings," *Louisville Journal* 27 (November 4, 1857), 2.
25. As quoted in Sallie M. Bryan [Piatt], "Charlie," *New York Ledger* 24 (September 6, 1858), 7.
26. Sallie M. Bryan [Piatt], "The Broken Spell," *New York Ledger* 13 (June 27, 1857), 7
27. See Piatt, "Love-Stories," in Bennett, *Palace-Burner*, 35.
28. Sallie M. Bryan [Piatt], "To Ella," *New York Ledger* 15 (June 18, 1859), 3.
29. See Hall, "From Voice to Persona," 239–240.
30. Along with the Gothic poems I discuss, there are three others I include in this group: "Among the Shadows," *Louisville Journal* 28 (August 2, 1858), 2; "I Dreamed that I was Free," *Louisville Journal* 28 (September 21, 1858), 2; and "One Year Ago to Night," *Louisville Journal* 29 (May 18, 1859), 2. This category is elastic, however. See Hall, "From Voice," 237–239, for an alternative set.
31. Sallie M. Bryan [Piatt], "My 'Castles in Spain,'" *New York Ledger* 16 (April 24, 1858), 7; and Sallie M. Bryan [Piatt], "A Moon-Rise by the Sea," *New York Ledger* 16 (May 1, 1858), 3.
32. Sallie M. Bryan [Piatt], "Idols – A Dream," *Louisville Journal*, 29 (May 28, 1859), 2; Sallie M. Bryan [Piatt], "Fragments," *Louisville Journal* 29 (February 16, 1859), 2; and Sallie M. Bryan [Piatt], "A Poet's Soliloquy," *Louisville Journal* 29 (March 9, 1859), 2.
33. Sallie M. Bryan [Piatt], "Fragments," *Louisville Journal* 29 (February 16, 1859), 2.
34. Bryan [Piatt], "Idols."
35. Bryan [Piatt], "To Ella"; and Sallie M. Bryan [Piatt], "What Seems," *New York Ledger* 15 (September 24, 1859), 7.
36. Bryan [Piatt], "A Moon-Rise by the Sea."
37. Sallie M. Bryan [Piatt], "An Orphan's Adjuration," *New York Ledger* 15 (May 21, 1859), 7.
38. Piatt, "A Hundred Years Ago," in Bennett, *Palace-Burner*, 13.
39. Catherine Warfield, "Legend of the Indian Chamber," *The Indian Chamber and Other Poems* (New York: C. B. Richardson, 1866), 17. Although the two sisters did not sign their poems, "Chamber" appears under Warfield's name in an anthology whose editor was in direct contact with Warfield prior to publication. See Mary Forrest [Julia Deane Freeman] (ed.), *Women of the South Distinguished in Literature* (New York: Derby & Jackson, 1861), 116–117.
40. Ibid., 13.
41. Ibid., 14.

42. Ibid., 15.
43. Ibid., 20.
44. Ibid.
45. Ibid., 22.
46. Ibid.
47. Ibid., 15.
48. Ibid., 11. In the antebellum South, household slaves were usually referred to as "servants" and Warfield appears to be playing on that fact.
49. Ibid., 23.

CHAPTER 15

The Civil War Language of Flowers

Eliza Richards

During the Civil War, the idea of the "home front" signified differently in Union and Confederate literature. While northerners frequently contrasted peaceful home settings with battlefield violence, there was often little meaning to the distinction in the south, where the war enveloped farmland, towns, and cities, and the distinction between soldiers and civilians was blurred, even erased. Historians have begun to explore "the merger of home front and battle front in the experience of military occupation" during the war, particularly in relation to southern women.[1] If the home front for northern women poets signified a safe place at a remove from the fighting, in the southern states it was often the very site of violent conflict.

Critical studies tend to focus either on Union or Confederate literature, assuming that they function as discrete expressive systems.[2] A comparative approach offers insight into the gendered aspects of poetic-political participation in the conflict, spanning the sections that unilateral perspectives cannot. This essay demonstrates that women poets regardless of section took up topics and tropes from the antebellum period and adapted them to a radically different wartime outlook. Registering the urgency of civic issues, women writers turned away from staging dramas of private expression toward a more direct public address. Though many of the poems discussed here carry patriotic sentiment, they are more centrally preoccupied with war's devastation: massive death tolls, environmental damage, broken lines of communication. Above all, they register the encroachment of violence on the very poetic traditions they are using to address war's circumstances. As a result, the revisions they undertake differ according to the writer's regional sympathies; rather than reflecting and enforcing a clear boundary between sections, however, the poems form a continuum influenced by identification with place, as well as proximity to battlefield violence: the closer "home" is to a violent epicenter, the less relevant extant traditions prove to be.

This essay explores how northern and southern women responded to the Civil War by reworking a shared literary inheritance in divergent ways: "the language of flowers." A tradition spanning centuries, but taking the form recognized as "Victorian" in the late eighteenth and early nineteenth centuries, its possibilities particularly attracted popular American women writers in the 1840s and '50s. In her study of the history of the language of flowers, Beverly Seaton explains: "During its heyday in America, the language of flowers attracted the attention of many of the most popular women writers and editors, which gives the history of these books in America its main distinction from France and England – the association of the idea with upward mobility in the journalistic world almost exclusively for women."[3] A means of elaborating a "lady's" identity, with its accompanying associations of aesthetic and emotional sensitivity, the poetry of flowers served as a coded language for the communication of complex feelings that form an important part of what Milette Shamir identifies as an American obsession with privacy before the Civil War.[4] But Seaton and others don't address the fate of the language of flowers after the war begins. Flower poems of the "bellum" period demonstrate that war exerted stress on earlier forms of poetic expression; they offer a study of how these conventions could be adapted to explore a disoriented, shocked sensibility. Northern women poets tended to take flowers as a focal point for exploring how to feel about remote violence, while southern poets cast the language of flowers as corrupted and thoroughly compromised by the proximity of extreme violence.

In the early half of the nineteenth century, flowers undergirded the fantasy of a natural, embodied language whose purity derives from its divine origins. "The alphabet of the angels," flowers offered themselves to writers as a means of purifying poetic language and the sentiments it expressed.[5] In the introduction to her lavishly illustrated encyclopedia of floral symbolism, *The Poetry of Flowers and the Flowers of Poetry* (1841), popular poetess Frances Sargent Osgood offers a succinct formulation of the tradition's significance. An expression of "divine passion . . . flowers were ingeniously made emblematical of our most delicate sentiments; they do, in fact, utter in 'silent eloquence' a language better than writing; they are the delicate symbol of the illusions of a tender heart and of a lively and brilliant imagination."[6] It is a commonplace in the period that verbal language is a poor substitute for "silent eloquence," unmarred by human failings and imperfections. Because flowers are already "ingeniously made emblematical" by divine powers, they serve as a means for women to explore sentiments, including "the passions," with propriety. While

Osgood stresses the "emblematical" nature of flowers, a review of the many literary forms saturated with flower imagery reveals that there is no coherent tropic practice, no universal language. Seaton, who has conducted the most extensive review, found that vocabularies changed from book to book, and that there was "no agreed-upon set of meanings."[7] Dorri Beam complicates Seaton's presumption – shared by other critics – of a one-to-one symbolic equivalence between flowers and feelings. Instead, she stresses that the language of flowers offers not just a vocabulary, or a transparent equation among flower, text, and woman, but a versatile "grammar" with which to construct individualized expressive fields.[8]

Lydia Sigourney, one of the most popular and influential poets of the nineteenth century, "captures the essence of floral poetry, which sought to make every poem a living picture," in Elizabeth Petrino's words.[9] That the picture is "living" is crucial. Women poets sought to animate and naturalize their writings by communicating with blossoming plant life. In Sigourney's "Solitude," for example,

> the violet's eye
> Looked up to greet me. The fresh wild-rose smiled,
> And the young pendent [*sic*] vine-flower kissed my cheek.[10]

In her "living picture," Sigourney dramatizes the transfer of floral purity to the female speaker. The flowers' animated greetings transmit their purified passions to the speaker's verbal reverie.

Floral language in the nineteenth century purified a range of ideas about female sexuality and sensuality that might otherwise have come under scrutiny. As Beam and others have indicated, the language of flowers offered a means of articulating and exploring the more transgressive aspects of sexuality, in part because of the association of flowers with inherent spirituality.[11] Even when signifying homoerotic, autoerotic, or adulterous feelings, flowers could not themselves be corrupt. Osgood was particularly successful in eroticizing flower language in the antebellum period. In Rufus Griswold's posthumous collection of Osgood's work, for example, a daisy's innocence is violated because she allowed a "zephyr" to play with her until "the gem on her bosom was stain'd and dark." In another poem, a speaker explains that she tried to keep her "rosebud" intact by kissing it repeatedly, with the opposite effect; with a comic level of metaphoric transparency, she finally confesses that "I could not keep my bud from blowing!"[12]

Implicit in Osgood's exaggerated sexualized play is the suggestion that, by midcentury, some US women poets were growing tired of the language of flowers as they had been using it – to explore private sentiments – and were expressing their boredom with the figural system within its current terms. In a poem entitled "Clover Blossoms" from her 1856 collection *Forest Buds, from the Woods of Maine*, Elizabeth Akers Allen proclaims:

> I've read of roses till I tire of them,
> Of daffodils and myrtle-blossoms too,–
> I'd rather have a fresh, sweet gem
> Like this I hold, unhackneyed, pure and new;[13]

The speaker's exasperated homage to the homely clover blossom suggests the lengths she has to go to identify an "unhackneyed" subject. She turns to the uncultivated field for inspiration at almost exactly the same time that Walt Whitman turns to the grass. But it wasn't just boredom with conventions that transformed the language of flowers in the early part of the 1860s. The violence of the Civil War penetrated the fantastical world of private sentiments and altered it.

Though the antebellum poetry of flowers was adaptable to the particular practitioner's concerns and publication goals, one thing remained stubbornly consistent: it was deeply identified with the expression of private, apolitical feeling. From the early 1860s, with its urgent calls to support national war efforts, women poets of both sections demonstrated a new interest in expressing public, patriotic, politicized sentiments, sometimes in conjunction with previous formulations of private feeling.[14] Their adaptations and innovations differed, however, according to the proximity of war's violent disruptions. Working within the antebellum tradition, northern women actively defended the space of moral purity that previous poets had taken for granted. Feeling the pressure of war's encroachment, they questioned how the spiritual, moral, and sensual language of flowers could speak to disturbing news reports of unprecedented death tolls, advances in weapons technologies, and the devastation of regions – such as the Shenandoah Valley – traditionally depicted in song and story as the apex of pastoral tranquility.

Allen's "Spring at the Capital" exemplifies a trend in northern adaptations of the language of flowers during the war: the speaker registers the awareness of distant suffering from a safe vantage point. Born in Maine, Allen worked as a government clerk in Washington during the war; she also published topical poems in the *Atlantic Monthly* and elsewhere.[15] In "Spring at the Capital," Allen responds to the sounds of fighting beyond the reach of vision: "the clash of martial music" and the "jar of drums," which sets the flowers "atremble."[16] Never invaded, Washington was nevertheless close to many of the battles, and the city was full of hospitals that tended primarily to wounded Union soldiers. Turning to the flowers for reassurance, Allen's speaker notes the incongruity between the tranquil scenario before her and the violence she hears:

Down-looking in this snow-white bud,
How distant seems the war's red flood!
How far remote the streaming wounds, the sickening scent of human blood!

Stressing the ways the flowers put "war at a distance" only brings closer to home the "streaming wounds, the sickening scent of human blood."[17] Allen seeks in the flowers a remedy for war, but "battle-stains" and "blood red trouble" overwhelm the vision. What is not in the line of sight overwhelms a traditional meditation on a flower's purifying, "snow-white" influence.

By the end of the poem, Allen's apostrophic address ("O flowers!") substitutes symbolic abstractions for specific blooms, as if the speaker realizes that what she observes can do nothing to solve the problem of suffering. She overloads the address with the charge of ending the war and erasing its violence, of ushering in the

Dawn of a broader, whiter day
Than ever blessed us with its ray,–
A dawn beneath whose purer light all guilt and wrong shall fade away.

Then shall our nation break its bands,
And, silencing the envious lands,
Stand in the searching light unshamed, with spotless robe, and clean, white hands.

The speaker urges a return to purity, unity, and goodness, which will redeem democracy before the rest of the "envious lands" who are waiting for the experiment to fail. The immaculate whiteness of the final image, however, seems fantastically unattainable due to the blood-drenched images that precede it, especially given the slightness of the honeysuckle and hyacinths upon which the huge hope rests. Through juxtaposing war's carnage with the moral purity of the language of flowers, Allen charts – perhaps inadvertently – the tradition's painful inadequacies in the present moment.

If Allen's poem raises the question of how conscious her critique of floral grammars is, Adeline Whitney, another *Atlantic Monthly* poet, explicitly stages the question in "My Daphne."[18] Best known for her satiric best-seller *Mother Goose for Grown Folks* (1860), Whitney lived her entire life in the Boston, Massachusetts, area; she was primarily known for her novels and advice books for women, but during the war she published a number of topical poems in the *Atlantic Monthly*.[19] "My Daphne" offers a complex, encrypted meditation on the limitations and possibilities of the language of flowers in encountering war's violence. Rather than the woodland and garden flowers – the fringed gentians, violets, snow-drops, and irises that antebellum women poets spoke with and through – this speaker dwells upon her relation to a houseplant. By charting her vigilant care, Whitney's speaker suggests that even flowers are no longer safe outside the home and must be brought within the sheltered environment of the domestic sphere to survive the war. The need for shelter, however, does not arise from any imminent, physical threat. Instead, the speaker seeks to preserve "Daphne's" (the word is used as a proper noun throughout) mythological innocence. The naiad Daphne was transformed into a plant to thwart Apollo's amorous pursuit; the speaker in turn tries to protect the flower from the infringements of war. Only under protected conditions and special care can the flower serve as a symbol of hope for northern victory and the conflict's end.

Rootbound at the outset and "crippled" by the constraint, the Daphne is unable to "burgeon all her flowers of hope." The speaker goes about the "kindly task" of repotting her; immediately, "quick released // from earthen bound and sordid thrall, / My Daphne sat there, proud and tall." In spite of this success, the speaker's concern over whether the flower will bloom grows rather than diminishes, especially once she "learned, in accidental way, / A secret," which she declines to tell the reader until the end of the poem, as if fearful of even naming the thought. The secret transforms the speaker's understanding of the plant's growth as a sign of hope into "something ominous and strange," which spurs her to tend the plant "with anxious care, / Almost with underthought of prayer." She confides that her anxiety derives from imagining that Union victory depends on the flower's blossoming; if the plant thrives, she hopes to hear the "coming roll / Of pealing victory, that should bear / My country's triumph on the air." With so much depending on "the plant whose life a portent bore," the speaker devotes all her energies to its care, until she and the plant assume a common identity; they are "we" who "waited, day by day," until the Daphne blooms:

her fair buds outburst their bars,
And whitened gloriously to stars!

Above each stalwart, loyal stem
Rested their heavenly diadem,

And flooded forth their incense rare,
A breathing Joy, upon the air!

Embodying Union patriotism, the "loyal" Daphne takes on the qualities of a flag, her "fair buds" "whiten[ing] gloriously to stars." The stripes appear in the ghostly secondary meaning of the constraining "bars" from which the plant must break free. The botanical banner then transforms again, into a celestial being that presides over the righteousness of the Union cause.

The Daphne's transformation complete, the poem would seem to have reached its end. But after the narration methodically consolidates patriotic sentiment, the poem takes a sinister turn. In the midst of a meditation on the blossom's freight of "Peace," the speaker abruptly turns to the dirt in which the Daphne is rooted, and the container that holds it. In the final stanzas, the speaker reveals that the flower's burgeoning of hope had all the while been predicated upon the mandate to kill that characterizes all war:

> For all this life, and light, and bloom,
> This breath of Peace that blessed the room,
> Was born from out the banded rim,
> Once crowded close, and black and grim,
>
> With grains that feed the Cannon's breath,
> And brook his sentences of death!

In the pot's "banded rim" and soil, the speaker sees the circle of the "Cannon's" mouth, loaded with the black powder that fuels its explosion. Her vision emerges from her earlier epiphany, and the secret is now revealed to the reader: the "trim and tidy cask" that she had used to re-pot the Daphne is an empty powder keg. The container that allowed the Daphne to thrive also enabled the killing of countless men. Realizing this irony, the speaker posits an equation between the "breath of Peace" and "the Cannon's breath," the two images perfectly balanced. The twinned "breaths" simultaneously underwrite mass death and the end of violence. While it would be possible to interpret this logic as akin to resurrection – life born of death – the poem's reversed sequence undermines that comforting explanation: first we are asked to celebrate "life, and light, and bloom," then we are interrupted by a gruesome reminder of its origins, which "brook the sentences of death." Rather than trying to remove women's private meditations in the language of flowers from broader narratives of violence – like Allen's speaker – Whitney's speaker takes pains to implicate her Daphne, and therefore herself. There is no place for floral purity apart from war's "sentences of death"; for the language of flowers to remain vibrant, Whitney suggests, women writers must hold themselves accountable. While northern women sought to retain the power of moral purification associated with the language of flowers, they often professed failure, lamenting the infiltration of violence in what should be an arena of inviolate goodness.

Whereas the language of flowers remained a central, if problematic, means of communicating women's sentiments in northern poetry of the Civil War period, southern women more frequently turned away from the tradition entirely. In *The Southern Illustrated News, The Southern Literary Messenger*, and the various collections of southern wartime newspaper and magazine poetry that emerged during and soon after the war (there is no single periodical that can serve as a counterpoint to the *Atlantic Monthly* because publications in the southern section were far more decentralized and erratically issued), fewer poems engage in metaphoric play with floral figures. This is evident even though the tradition of floral poetry in the south was just as strong as it was in the north leading up to the war; indeed, the book credited with popularizing the language of flowers in the United States in 1829 was edited by a "Lady" from Virginia.[20] To a greater degree, flower poetry is displaced by the more direct task of consolidating and articulating Confederate nationalism, a more central necessity for the southern section since they were bringing a new nation into being.[21]

In spite of these nation-building exigencies, however, southern women also wrote in and about the language of flowers, identifying its limitations and possibilities in a time of war. If northern women worked on adapting the tradition to current circumstances so that the language of flowers expressed patriotic sentiments, lamented the loss of innocence and peacetime tranquility, and meditated on the ethics of thinking about violence from a distance, southern women more frequently charge the tradition with irrelevance and stage scenarios of total repudiation. Rather than shoring up floral powers of purification, southern women poets tend to stand witness to violence that destroys actual flowers as well as their emblematic counterparts. When southern women poets are not testifying to the total destruction of symbolic possibilities rooted in natural environments, they are repudiating the system entirely, presenting dead flowers to the reader, for example, or pointedly choosing plants that don't blossom when commemorating the dead.

In closer proximity – emotionally as well as physically – to mass death and environmental devastation, southern poets insist that flowers break under the enormous burden of maintaining or restoring moral order. Kentucky writer Agnes Leonard bluntly says as much in "After the Battle":

Thickly on the trampled grasses
Lay the battle's awful traces,
Mid the blood-stained clover blossoms
Lay the stark and ghastly faces[22]

"Battle's awful traces" overwhelm the clover blossoms, which are trampled, blood-stained, and upstaged by the "stark and ghastly faces" scattered among them. The image contrasts starkly with Allen's 1856 "Clover Blossoms," in which the poet turned to field flowers to refresh her poetic meditations. Her creative concerns seem trivial in comparison to Leonard's nightmarish scene, which is not a vision, like Allen's images of blood in "Spring at the Capital," but a reality within the frame of the poem. Under such circumstances the blossoms can only indicate that war's violence destroys everything that once enabled pastoral vision. Even the poem's meter – a leaden trochaic tetrameter – reverses the iambic norms of flower poetry (all the poems discussed thus far have been predominantly iambic) and underscores the ways that the expressive possibilities have been trampled on and perhaps stamped out.

Then-acclaimed (if now obscure) poet Rosa Vertner Jeffrey offers reasons for the differences between northern and southern perspectives on the war in the very language of flowers that she analyzes. Jeffrey was well-suited for such a comparative meditation. A resident of Kentucky born in Mississippi, before the war she published a book of poems with Boston's prestigious Ticknor and Fields, and a novel during the war that was read and reviewed in both sections.[23] Kentucky was a crucial border state, identified with the south (slavery was legal there), but officially neutral, and then later allied with the Union. Several battles took place there, including the Battle of Perryville, in October 1862.[24]

Jeffrey's "Lilies of the Valley – Inscribed to the Friend Who Sent Them" charts the ways that the devastation visited upon her "home beloved" alters her reception of a gift of flowers.[25] Stressing a rift in understanding between northern and southern women, she marks the flowers of the title as a gift from a northern friend. Though Jeffrey as well as her speaker is southern by birth and sympathy, she complicates the issue of location by identifying Rochester, New York, as the place of the poem's composition in the byline: in doing so, the author casts herself as displaced from home, a refugee of the war. Her affiliation with region, however, is independent of any nationalist sentiment – it is unclear whether she is pro-Union, pro-Confederate, or neutral. More evident are the ways that the violence in her homeland makes it impossible for her to accept the lilies of the valley within the terms of the antebellum language of flowers. She acknowledges the symbolism that they are traditionally invested with upon receipt: they are "modest, dainty, vestal." Once she iterates the gift's meaning, however, she refuses to accept it, and instead turns the occasion into a lecture on sectional differences in perspectives on the war. She tells her well-meaning friend that the flowers

> mind me of a home beloved, my home in by-gone years,
> Then beautiful beyond compare, now dark with blood and tears;
> They mind me that a storm of strife has strewn my native shore
> With wrecks of hope and happiness, lost, lost, forevermore.

Unable to enter into accord with the lilies' virgin purity (as Whitney identifies with her Daphne), the speaker can only locate those feelings in the past. The flowers remind her of a time before the war when they were representative of her southern homeland. Unavailable to her current emotional state, relevant only by contrast, the flowers pain her with the thought of all that she has lost. She instructs her friend on the difference between northern and southern perspectives on the war; northerners

> prate of battles, they tell thee of the war,
> And thou dost read of, nay lament, its horrors from afar;
> But oh! Thy heart would grieve like mine, did that red deluge flow,
> Dividing thee from cherished scenes, and friends of long ago.

While the northern "Lady" learns about war "from afar" by reading about it in newspapers and hearing about it secondhand, the southern speaker claims to have experienced "that red deluge." As a result, the torrent of blood has destroyed her connection to the tranquil past with its domestic affections. The poem's Rochester byline complicates Jeffrey's insistence on witnessing violence: perhaps she saw the carnage before seeking refuge in the north, or perhaps the speaker's witnessing does not depend upon actually being there. Either way, her emotional rootedness in place makes the carnage a material fact and a mental presence that displaces present pleasures. Jeffrey's poetic lecture to her northern friend on the occasion of receiving a bouquet makes the point quite clearly that the language of flowers has no place in the present moment; it is anathema to the violence taking place in southern regions, and therefore incapable of expressing the emotions of southern onlookers.

Other southern women are less direct in their evaluations of the language of flowers, but still they suggest that the annihilating capabilities of war can render even nature unnatural. The work of Margaret Stilling – the pen name of Virginian Mary Evans – offers a fascinating example. Evans was a teacher during the war, yet, according to Mary Tardy, "found the opportunity to cultivate the muses, to the pleasure of the blockaded Southrons, contributing her productions in poetry and prose to the 'Confederate' literary journals."[26] In "The Buds that Fall," published in 1863 in *The Southern Literary Messenger*, the speaker charts the redirection of her attention from the flowers that thrive to the buds that die before they bloom.[27] Without mentioning the war directly, the poem emphasizes the ways that mood and context alter one's outlook. The speaker begins by noting what she can no longer see; the lost vision is much like other antebellum floral fancies that emphasize nature's spiritual beauty:

A thousand blossoms mid the trees
Like clustering jewels shine,
And fragrant incense on the breeze
Comes like a breath divine.

Though she begins the poem with this scene of "Fruition's hope," the speaker finds she can do nothing with it, given the present circumstances, and therefore must

sadly turn from all
That swells with life around,
To watch the little buds that fall
Upon the waiting ground.

"The buds that fall" take on a sinister cast as the speaker watches them, first because the "ground is waiting" to receive young lives cut off before their prime, as if there were some strange force that welcomed the death of "Fruition." The scenario darkens further when the speaker introduces another unspecified presence that seems to be the buds' human counterpart – young men who also fall to the ground before maturity. "Above" the fallen buds

is the throb, and change
Of glad Fruition's tide,
While on the stained and trodden grass
They wither side by side.
And from among them seems to call
A voice both sad and strange,
"Come watch the little buds that fall
And Hope to Sorrow change."

Either the buds "wither side by side" in strangely organized rows suggestive of soldiers falling in battle lines, or something unnamed "wither[s] side by side" with the buds. Both possibilities suggest the unnatural harvest of young men, an unarticulated and perhaps unmentionable thought that is sustained by the "stained and trodden grass" surrounding them. The poem suggests the difficulty of justifying in spiritual terms the massive failure to thrive confronting the speaker, the sheer number of entities, both human and botanical, cut off before their prime.

Stilling's poem resonates powerfully with one by Emily Dickinson frequently interpreted in the context of the Civil War; the poems offer divergent perspectives on similar scenes that support the assertion that location makes a difference in writers' renovations of the language of flowers. Dickinson's poem begins by aligning three images in order to summon the mass death of young men. The force of the similes rest in the contrast between their loveliness and the horror they summon:

> They dropped like Flakes –
> They dropped like stars –
> Like Petals from a Rose –
> When suddenly across the June
> A Wind with fingers – goes –[28]

Like Stilling, Dickinson manipulates natural images of things falling to suggest apocalypse: if stars can fall as thickly as petals or snowflakes, the universe is catastrophically awry. But the poem concludes by returning to "God," who "can summon every face / On his Repealless – list." He may be a sinister force, pulling men up indiscriminately from earth to heaven by the handful, but he is still a figural presence. Stilling, in contrast, concludes with an unidentified "voice both sad and strange" that calls us to watch "Hope to Sorrow change" without offering any sort of explanation. The location of violence on the southern home front calls for the staging of the death not only of buds and men, but of the redemptive possibilities of the language of flowers.

Working within the established tradition of the Victorian language of flowers, both northern and southern women poets registered war's presence as an expressive challenge, formulating in the process ideas about the ways that extra-literary events can transform aesthetic practices. Their poetry of flowers form a continuum of responses to the Civil War that range from raising questions and exploring complex emotions about remote suffering to lamenting the environmental devastation and overwhelming tragedy of mass death in wartime. The kind of response is linked to the poet's proximity to the violence, emotionally as well as physically; the place a poet considers "home" and its orientation to the location of violence informs poetic responses to the war.

In spite of the varied stagings of frustration over the limitations of the language of flowers, the Civil War did not destroy this resilient tradition. In the years after the war, women poets from both regions went on to publish volumes steeped in the language of flowers that carried a set of transformed possibilities into the twentieth century. Adeline Whitney, for example, published a collection of poems entitled *Pansies "... for Thoughts"* in 1872.[29] Foregrounding the especially prickly transformation of the tradition for southern women writers, Georgia poet Elizabeth O. Dannelly published *Cactus; or, Thorns and Blossoms* in 1879.[30] In 1866, Dannelly had published an outraged epic poem on Sherman's burning of Columbia, South Carolina, that was based on William Gilmore Simms' eyewitness account. She pointedly includes that poem in her collection, along with others from her Confederate period, even though the war had been over for fourteen years by that time. In her preface to *Cactus*, Dannelly explains why she chose such a well-defended and not necessarily attractive plant, which blooms only rarely and briefly, to serve as the representative of her verse:

> Having, in 1866, consented to write for a weekly paper a series of satirical poems, I selected for my *nom de plume* "Cactus," the name of a plant bearing thorns, flowers, and fruit, as a signature suggestive of much liberty, under which might appear the variegated flowers of poesy, the mature fruits of sober thought, or the formidable thorns of satire. The same considerations have led to its selection as the title of my Poem.[31]

Taking "liberty" in hand, Dannelly stretches the language of flowers to include negative emotions, critical public commentary, and other forms of expression that could not be expressed through the language of flowers before the war. Dannelly connects her choice of a more versatile, variegated plant to the southern experience of the war: "It is, perhaps, only by Southern friends, so well acquainted with the life of a Southern woman before and since the War, and the marvelous changes of that life, that I can expect allowances to be made for defects which, under more favorable circumstances, might have been avoided."[32] Dannelly makes quite clear that she will not erase that experience or the "defects," even though she is glad that time is "healing the wounds inflicted by the late civil war." Nevertheless, she insists that "the past has Its history ... TO BE RECEIVED AS A WHOLE." The wholeness of history, and the history of pastness (a suggestive formulation), even with its immense pain, sorrow, and political complexity, affects her choice of "*nom de plume*," as well as the ideas expressed through it.

The language of flowers lost its innocence and purity during the war, along with its clear line to spiritual solace and the protective presence of divinity. This loss was also a gain that renovated the language and made it suitable for postbellum expressions of negative emotions that previously had no place. Louise Glück pays homage to the ongoing vibrancy of this language in her 1992 Pulitzer Prize-winning collection of poems, *The Wild Iris*. The speaker assumes the viewpoint of a bulb planted in the earth:

> Overhead, noises, branches of the pine shifting.
> Then nothing. The weak sun
> flickered over the dry surface.
>
> It is terrible to survive
> as consciousness
> buried in the dark earth.[33]

Bulbs, unlike "buds that fall," do grow and bloom, albeit via a strenuous process. The burial of thousands during the Civil War buried "consciousness" as well "in the dark earth"; the challenge for women poets was to find ways to find "Fruition" in that dark consciousness by renovating the language of flowers.

Notes

1. LeeAnn Whites and Alecia P. Long (eds.), *Occupied Women: Gender, Military Occupation, and the American Civil War* (Baton Rouge: Louisiana State University Press, 2009), 195, n6. The question of whether to capitalize the words "north," "south," "northerner," and "southerner" is a complicated one. To do so is to identify all people living in a section with either the Union or the Confederacy. I refrain from the capitalization so as not to assume the equation of one with the other. The allegiances are indicated by the poems themselves.
2. Daniel Aaron, *The Unwritten War: American Writers and the Civil War* (New York: Knopf, 1973). Recent work on the Civil War includes Faith Barrett, *To Fight Aloud is Very Brave: American Poetry and the Civil War* (Amherst: University of Massachusetts Press, 2012); Randall Fuller, *From Battlefields Rising: How the Civil War Transformed American Literature* (New York: Oxford University Press, 2011); Coleman Hutchison, *Apples and Ashes: Literature, Nationalism, and the Confederate States of America* (Athens: University of Georgia Press). Civil War historian Alice Fahs' *The Imagined Civil War: Popular Literature North and South, 1861–65* (Chapel Hill: UNC Press, 2001) is an exception to this trend; historians have long treated the Union and the Confederacy in comparative terms.
3. Beverly Seaton, *The Language of Flowers: A History* (Charlottesville: University Press of Virginia, 1995), 84.

4. Milette Shamir, *Inexpressible Privacy: The Interior Life of Antebellum American Literature* (Philadelphia: University of Pennsylvania Press, 2006), 1–3.
5. Qtd. in *The Poetry of Flowers and Flowers of Poetry*, Frances Sargent Osgood (ed.), (New York: J.C. Riker, 1841), 7. The quotation is broadly attributed to Benjamin Franklin.
6. Osgood, *Poetry of Flowers*, 23.
7. Seaton, *Language of Flowers*, 2.
8. Dorri Beam *Style, Gender, and Fantasy in Nineteenth-Century Women's Writings* (Cambridge: Cambridge University Press, 2011), 37.
9. Elizabeth Petrino, *Emily Dickinson and Her Contemporaries: Women's Verse in American Literature, 1820–1885* (Hanover: University Press of New England, 1998), 132.
10. Lydia Sigourney, "Solitude," *Select Poems* (Philadelphia: Parry and McMillan, 1856), 70–71.
11. Beam extends the work of Paula Bernat Bennett, "'Pomegranate-Flowers': The Phantasmic Productions of Late-Nineteenth-Century Anglo-American Women Poets," and Christopher Looby, "'The Roots of Orchis, the Iuli of Chesnuts': The Odor of Male Solitude," in *Solitary Pleasures: The Historical, Literary, and Artistic Discourses of Autoeroticism*, Paula Bernat Bennett and Vernon Roasario (eds.), (New York: Routledge, 1995), 189–213, 163–187. Bennett and Looby take up the question of later poets, but not in terms of their engagement with public, civic wartime feelings.
12. Frances Sargent Osgood, *Poems* (Philadelphia: Cary and Hart, 1850), 339, 355–356.
13. Elizabeth Akers Allen, "Clover Blossoms," *Forest Buds, from the Woods of Maine* (Portland: Francis Blake, 1856), 63.
14. The public address to the nation in Civil War poetry by both men and women is the subject of Barrett's *To Fight Aloud is Very Brave*.
15. Allen's best-known work, "Rock Me to Sleep Mother," was enormously popular during the war and gave rise to a controversy over authorship that Jennifer Putzi has explored in "'Some Queer Freak of Taste': Gender, Authorship, and the 'Rock Me to Sleep' Controversy," *American Literature* 84.4 (2012), 769–795.
16. Elizabeth Akers Allen, "Spring at the Capital," *Atlantic Monthly* (June 1863), 766–767.
17. Mary Favret, *War at a Distance: Romanticism and the Making of Modern Wartime* (Princeton: Princeton University Press, 2010).
18. A.D.T. Whitney, "My Daphne," *Atlantic Monthly* (August 1862), 164–165.
19. "Adeline D.T. Whitney," *Nineteenth-Century American Women Poets: An Anthology*, Paula Bernat Bennett (ed.), (New York: Blackwell, 1998), 122.
20. "A Lady," [Elizabeth Gamble Wirt], *Flora's Dictionary* (Baltimore: F. Lucas, 1829); Seaton, *Language of Flowers*, 85.
21. Hutchison identifies and discusses this trend in *Apples and Ashes*.
22. Agnes Leonard, "After the Battle," *War Poetry of the South*, William Simms, (ed.), (New York: Richardson and Co., 1866), 415.

23. Mary Tardy (ed.), *Living Female Writers of the South*, (Philadelphia: Claxton, Remsen & Haffelfinger, 1872), 33–34.
24. "Perryville," *Civil War Trust*. Available online: www.civilwar.org/battlefields/perryville.html?tab=facts [accessed December 20, 2015].
25. Rosa Vertner Jeffrey, "Lilies of the Valley," *The Southern Poems of the War*, Emily V. Mason (ed.), (Baltimore: J. Murphy, 1868), 355.
26. Tardy, *Living Female Writers of the South*, 400.
27. Margaret Stilling, "The Buds That Fall," *Southern Literary Messenger* (August 1863), 492.
28. Emily Dickinson, Fr545A, *The Emily Dickinson Archive: An Open-Access Website for the Manuscripts of Emily Dickinson* (Harvard University): www.edickinson.org/ [accessed December 20, 2015].
29. A.D.T. Whitney, *Pansies " ... for thoughts"* (Boston: Houghton Mifflin and Company, 1872).
30. Elizabeth O. Dannelly, *Cactus; or, Thorns and Blossoms* (New York: Atlantic Publishing & Engraving Co., 1879).
31. Dannelly, *Cactus*, viii.
32. Ibid.
33. Louise Gluck, "Wild Iris," *Wild Iris* (Hopewell: Ecco Press, 1992), 1.

CHAPTER 16

Poetry and Bohemianism

Joanna Levin and Edward Whitley

The February 6, 1864, issue of the *New York Illustrated News* included two artist's renditions of the nightly revels at Charles Pfaff's beer cellar, the saloon that had become famous as the gathering place of the United States' first self-described bohemian literary community. In the first image, a promiscuous gathering of men and women fills the air with pipe and cigar smoke as alcohol flows freely and all but one of the women in the picture find themselves in the amorous embraces of lusty bohemian men. In the second image, the men are alone, the air is virtually smoke-free, and a single bottle of wine sits on a table covered with literary works-in-progress as male writers soberly discuss their art in an environment free from the distracting presence of women [Fig. 12 & Fig. 13]. Period sources differ as to what actually took place on an average night at Pfaff's during its heyday from the late 1850s till the end of the Civil War, with some claiming it to be a site of intellectual discussion of the highest order, and others, such as an unpublished poem by Walt Whitman, describing it as a place "where the drinkers and laughers meet to eat and drink and carouse."[1] The debate was not local to the Pfaff's bohemians. As both Daniel Cottom and Joanna Levin have recently shown, following Henry Murger's popular account of the bohemians of Paris's Latin Quarter in his *Scènes de la vie de bohème* (1851), "the bohemian" became a contested figure whose values and ideologies were claimed by different groups for a range of purposes throughout the nineteenth century and across the Atlantic world.[2] Regardless of the various meanings ascribed to bohemianism in the nineteenth century, women poets played an integral role in defining what bohemia could (and could not) mean for emerging conceptions of the American counterculture, as well as for the discourse surrounding women's rights.

In 1860, Ada Clare, a Pfaff's regular and the universally acknowledged "Queen of Bohemia," defended the figure of the bohemian against charges that this new, French-derived social type "must take pleasure in keeping his boots and cheese in the same drawer," insisting instead that "the principles

Figure 12. Frank Bellew, The Bohemians ("As they were said to be by a knight of The Round Table"), *New York Illustrated News* (February 6, 1864). *The Round Table* had recently published a scathing criticism of the bohemian excesses at Pfaff's.

of good taste and feeling" always guided the bohemian revolt against traditional manners and mores.[3] In 1904, while recognizing that the word bohemian was still often "used as a term of reproach" and that "the person so spoken of, especially if a woman, would be supposed to have no home belongings, no domestic habits," Julia Ward Howe nonetheless echoed Clare's earlier defense: "Bohemia nowadays . . . desires to conform to all the healthful decencies of life, to all social ordinances that are truly refining."[4] Conversely, Howe admitted that bohemians "gave little heed to senseless social ordinances," and she retrospectively acknowledged her own participation in the "moral and intellectual advance" that the term "bohemian" had come to signify.[5] The poet who dedicated herself to such reform movements as women's suffrage and abolitionism and who defied her husband's opposition to her active engagement in public life (including her pursuit of a literary career) came to recognize that she was part of the vanguard of bohemianism.

But which social ordinances were "refining"? Which were "senseless"? A bracing moral certitude animated Howe's famous Civil War poem "Battle-Hymn of the Republic" (1862), but other social issues, even in

Figure 13. Frank Bellew, The Bohemians ("As they are – described by one of their own number"), *New York Illustrated News* (February 6, 1864).

the hands of self-professed bohemians, generated more ambivalence and ambiguity. This was especially true with respect to "the woman question" and attitudes toward normative gender roles and sexual morality. Bohemia – a liminal terrain between the public and the private, the traditional and the modern, propriety and license, the fictive and the real – offered an experimental space in which to negotiate these shifting social expectations. As Jerrold Seigel has argued, "Bohemia grew up where the borders of bourgeois life were murky and uncertain. It was a space where newly liberated energies were continually thrown up against the barriers that were erected to contain them, where social margins and frontiers were probed and tested."[6] From the underground beer halls of New York to the salons of San Francisco, nineteenth-century American women poets drew on the emerging discourses of bohemianism to critique gender norms in both mainstream culture and within bohemian circles themselves.

Antebellum Bohemia

Like their male counterparts, the women poets associated with the bohemian scene in antebellum New York wrote about bacchanalian revels, dark and tragic love, the redemptive power of art, and the vagaries of literary fortune. Many of them, such as Anna Mary Freeman Goldbeck, contributed poetry to the bohemians' house organ, the *New York Saturday Press*, which is best known for being the periodical that helped to revive Walt Whitman's floundering career when the poet published the third edition of *Leaves of Grass* in 1860.[7] Goldbeck's "Night Song" is a paean to the Manhattan nightlife, eschewing the "childlike mornings" and "noon-like evenings" that pass "silently and slow," and celebrating instead "the queenly midnights" that "Pour life's richest wine for me."[8] She wrote poems about the intensity of romantic love – in one she writes that she and her lover "could do without the sunlight" because "I am warmth to his spirit, / And he is light to mine!" – and the equally intense feelings of artistic inspiration:

> Just now my frame felt full of fire,
> As if a poet's soul possess'd it,
> And every nerve was thrilled, like wire
> Of harp, when minstrel's hand has press'd it.[9]

In addition to being one of the women who joined in the predominantly male gatherings at Pfaff's beer cellar, Goldbeck was also part of what A. L. Rawson called, in a retrospective from the 1890s, "the galaxy of bright young women who, like stars about the moon, made a beautiful group around Ada Clare" at the Queen of Bohemia's West Forty-second Street home.[10]

Clare regularly hosted a gathering in her apartment that was, like the late-century women's salons Mary Loeffelholz describes, a "site of literary production and performance."[11] As the actress Rose Eyting recalled, "There, of a Sunday evening, could be found a group of men and women, all of whom had distinguished themselves in various avenues, – in literature, art, music, drama."[12] While only a minor poet herself, Clare was a recognized tastemaker in poetry, as evidenced by her defense of the free-verse form of Whitman's "Out of the Cradle Endlessly Rocking," which was published as "A Child's Reminiscence" in the *Saturday Press* in 1859 ("it could only have been written by a poet," she wrote, "and versifying would not help it").[13] Clare established an environment that fostered a spirit of camaraderie and creativity among bohemian women and men alike.

One account of this spirit of collaboration among the women of bohemian New York revolves around Dora Shaw, an actress and "golden woman of poetical tendencies," who is described as not only a "genius," but also "a sort of Aladdin who could bring help when needed," suggesting that her power to create art was as great as her power to foster community. "She had the ideas of [a] poem," Rawson recounted in 1896, from a letter by an unnamed friend,

> and fancied she could not write it as it should be, and so got me interested, and I wrote the lines to clothe her ideas.... I wrote down her brilliant improvisations as she walked to and fro in the room; verbatim sometimes, and at others, when she flew over the words, I drove in a tack, "the" or "I," etc., to keep the poem just below the clouds.[14]

Shaw is depicted here as magical ("a sort of Aladdin") and ethereal ("just below the clouds"), both as a poet and as the catalyst for creativity among the members of the salon who participate in transcribing ("I wrote down her brilliant improvisation"), copyediting ("I drove in a tack"), and even writing the poem itself ("I wrote the lines to clothe her ideas"). And while the story of the composition of Shaw's poetry is that of a supportive and collaborative environment, Shaw and other bohemian women also wrote numerous poems on the figure of the fallen woman who is abandoned by her community as a result of her sexual indiscretions.

Women such as Dora Shaw could join with the men at Pfaff's in raising a glass to *la vie bohème* (and to the libidinal excesses of both drink and sex that it implied), but they registered the consequences of their sexual adventures in ways that bohemian men did not. Since at least the eighteenth century, the figure of the fallen woman has been part of what Nina Auerbach calls a "cultural mythology" that serves either to generate sympathy for the plight of women in a patriarchal culture or to discipline women for their sexual excesses.[15] The women in Ada Clare's circle adapted the figure of the fallen woman in response to the images of *bohémiennes* that had recently made their way to the United States in translations of Murger's *Scènes de la vie de bohème.*[16] Their efforts to do so underscore how bohemian women such as Clare put the discourses of bohemianism and feminism into productive conversation.[17]

The *Saturday Press* published several "fallen woman" poems, such as Margaret Eytinge's "Unto the Pure All Things Are Pure," which tells of a woman with "a bold, defiant face" marred by "lines of hard and stern despair" who silently suffers the scorn of the women who pass her on the street.[18] Men, too, call out to the woman with "bitter mocking, / Careless laughter, heartless jest" as they look upon the "painted roses" on her cheek and the flowers "faded in her hair" as the tell-tale signs of a licentious woman. While the freedoms of bohemia promise a safe haven for sexual experimentation, poems such as these suggest that bohemian women faced a double standard for their sexual choices. Eytinge in particular was scrutinized for her open sexuality by Thomas Butler Gunn, a British writer living in New York who kept a detailed diary about the exploits of the antebellum bohemians. Gunn avers that Eytinge frequented an underground "'Free Love' haunt" during "her Bohemienne days, when she was hawking her writings, and a more vendible commodity, about the low newspaper offices in New York." Gunn accuses Eytinge of "hawking" her sexuality (the "more vendible commodity" he refers to with a wink and a nudge) in an effort to see her poetry into print, and goes so far as to say that Henry Clapp, Jr., the editor of the *Saturday Press* and the "King of Bohemia" at Pfaff's, "affected to admire her verses" because he expected to be repaid with sexual favors for publishing her work. When Margaret's husband Sol Eytinge intervened, however, Gunn records that "No more of [Margaret's] writings appeared henceforth in the saturday press [*sic*]."[19] If Gunn is to be trusted, the sexual double standard of antebellum culture that Eytinge lamented in her poetry persisted among the bohemians as well.

Ada Clare, in contrast, found that the male and female courtiers who surrounded her as the Queen of Bohemia helped to ameliorate the stigma of being an unwed mother. When Clare returned from a sojourn in Europe with a young child in tow, she unabashedly introduced herself as "Miss Ada Clare and Son," and her son became known as the "infant Prince of Bohemia."[20] Similarly, the actress and poet Adah Isaacs Menken found in her brief association with the bohemians a community that supported and validated her multiple marriages and sexual adventures. The women of bohemia also provided Menken with a sense of community that gave an added dimension to her famously public persona. Clare and Menken left New York in the 1860s to work as actresses in San Francisco, and with Californian bohemians such as Ina Coolbrith, Renée Sentilles writes, "Menken enjoyed a female cohort unlike any she had experienced back east, and her decision to publicly claim such friendships indicates that she wanted them to shape her celebrity image. Just as she was claiming masculine freedoms, she was also publicly displaying female friendships."[21]

This public display of female friendship continued when Menken moved to England and published a poem in the *New York Clipper* titled "Reply to Dora Shaw. Westminster Palace, London, Aug. 29, 1864." It is unclear what, precisely, Menken was replying to as Shaw doesn't appear to have published anything about Menken in either the *Clipper* or any other New York paper at the time.[22] The very public nature of the response, however, is perfectly suited to the celebrity identity that Menken had crafted for mass consumption. The poem, which issues a vow of loyalty to Shaw at a time when both women's acting careers were on the rise, promises that neither "Fashion and Ease" nor "Ambition" will alter in any way the bond that the two women share. "There comes no change upon my heart," Menken swears. "I pledge again in Woman's Truth; / I am no changeling – doubt me not!"[23] Menken's claim to be "no changeling" should raise the eyebrow of anyone familiar with her biography: she went by six different names throughout her life, claimed at least as many racial or ethnic identities, and built an entire career around continually reinventing her public persona.[24] The fans she left behind in New York would have noted this as well, which only serves to underscore that the "changeling" Menken has one constant anchor: her relationships with other women.

While "Reply to Dora Shaw" articulates a strong and public connection to a community of bohemian women, the poems from Menken's 1868 collection *Infelicia* focus instead on the impossibility of human connection and the voices that no one is willing to hear. As Eliza Richards has recently argued, Menken patterned *Infelicia's* poems after the free-verse form and polyvocality of fellow bohemian Walt Whitman, but Menken replaces Whitman's ability to contain a multitude of voices with her own *inability* to speak for herself, let alone anyone else. [25] In poems such as "Resurgam," Menken frames this voicelessness within the tropes of bohemianism, setting a scene of unrestrained revelry complete with wine and passionate embraces that, ultimately, leaves her feeling empty and alone: "But the purple wine that I quaff sends no thrill of Love and Song through my empty veins," she writes. "I feel neither pleasure, passion nor pain." Similar to the women whose sojourns in bohemia result in verses on fallen women, Menken turns a saturnalia into a funeral: "Leave me dead in the depths!" she demands. "Leave me dead in the wine! / Leave me dead in the dance!" And like the fallen woman of Victorian poetry whose transgression is never seen but only presumed, Menken tantalizes her readers with the crime of passion that has brought her low: "How did I die? / The man I loved – he – he – ah, well!"[26] Menken's elliptical refusal to acknowledge either sin or seduction while simultaneously hinting at foul deeds done by "The man I loved" stands as a testament to the complex ways that she and other women poets drew upon the discourses of bohemianism to comment on the gendered imbalances of American culture.

In addition to Menken, poet and novelist Elizabeth Barstow Stoddard wrote some of the most sophisticated poems on women's experiences in antebellum bohemia. Stoddard and her husband, Richard Henry, hosted a Manhattan literary salon that put them into frequent contact with Pfaffians such as Thomas Bailey Aldrich, Launt Thompson, and Edmund Clarence Stedman.[27] While not a regular at Pfaff's herself, Stoddard claimed the title of "bohemian" in an 1857 letter, writing that "New York. . . .. is the place for literary vagabonds. I too am a Bohemian and I love my fellow tinkers."[28] According to Lillian Woodman Aldrich, belonging to the Stoddard salon was a "solemn thing," and receiving a personal invitation from Elizabeth "was to this company what a ribbon is to a soldier, and prized accordingly."[29] Stoddard contributed to the two periodicals that were born around the tables at Pfaff's – the *Saturday Press* and *Vanity Fair* – and in the poetry she wrote during this period she joins with Menken, Shaw, Eytinge, and Goldbeck in teasing out the implications of *la vie bohème* for emerging conceptions of women's rights.

In an 1861 poem Stoddard turns a meditation on the regrets of the past into a bohemian revel in the court of "The Sensual." Despite being welcomed as "A courtier; deep I drain his wine," and enjoying the freedom to celebrate "hot among the rioters," the speaker's full participation in the proceedings is limited by the premium put on youthful feminine beauty:

> What then is my ignoble grief?
>   I am a woman, and my dower
> Of Beauty spent; is all this wail
>   Of *Why* and *Wherefore* vanished power?[30]

Conversely, in "A Woman's Dream" from 1857, Stoddard longs for "Some ideal passion," greater than what she experiences as a wife and mother, wondering why domestic joys are not enough to satisfy her. (At one point, the speaker of the poem forces herself to look at her infant child in an effort to cool her desire for an extramarital affair.) She asks,

> It is a woman's province, then,
> To be content with what has been?
> To wear the wreath of withered flowers,
> That crowned her in the bridal hours?[31]

In both poems, the sexual and vinous excesses associated with bohemianism are either too much or not enough for their speakers, which allows Stoddard to register in gendered terms – the phrases "a woman's province" and "a woman['s] . . . dower" are the hinges upon which the poems' heartaches bend – what bohemia offers and what it takes away.

It is appropriate that this complex relationship with what bohemia could and couldn't give to women should come from Stoddard, given that she claimed bohemianism entirely on her own terms. In 1865 she wrote a friend from the relative quiet of Massachusetts: "At heart I believe I am a Literary Bohemian and the city suits me – but I like to be a Bohemian in good society. Nice things suit me. . . . Everything that is beautiful, graceful, full of luxury."[32] In the latter half of the nineteenth century multiple variants of bohemianism continued to develop along similar lines as genteel versions of bohemianism flourished alongside more raucous forms.

Postbellum Bohemia

Late nineteenth-century women poets and writers were well aware of bohemia's liminal social positioning – or, in the words of Ella Wheeler Wilcox, its "unatlassed borders." The poet of the popular and controversial *Poems of Passion* (1883), Wilcox followed her *succès de scandale* with *Mal Moulée: A Novel* (1885), among the first novels by an American woman to venture into bohemianism. Featuring her poem "Bohemia" (later republished in her collection *Poems of Reflection* [1902]), the novel praises this mythic cultural space:

Bohemia, o'er thy unatlassed borders
  How many cross, with half-reluctant feet,
And unformed fears of dangers and disorders,
  To find delights, more wholesome and more sweet
Than ever yet were known to the "*elite*."

Herein can dwell no pretence [*sic*] and no seeming;
  No stilted pride thrives in this atmosphere,
Which stimulates a tendency to dreaming.
  The shores of the ideal world, from here,
Seem sometimes to be tangible and near. . . .

We call no time lost that we give to pleasure;
  Life's hurrying river speeds to Death's great sea;
We cast out no vain plummet-line to measure
  Imagined depths of that unknown To Be,
But grasp the *Now*, and fill it full of glee.

All creeds have room here, and we all together
  Devoutly worship at Art's sacred shrine;
But he who dwells once in thy golden weather,
  Bohemia – sweet, lovely land of mine –
Can find no joy outside thy border-line.[33]

Throughout the late nineteenth century, similar idealizations of bohemia would appear in poems, novels, and plays; on the mastheads of periodicals;

and in the by-laws of bohemian clubs. With increasing frequency, the once scandalous domain of bohemia emerged as the paradoxically "wholesome" and genteel land where "Art's sacred shrine" transcended more worldly social distinctions and allowed for the truest forms of pleasure and good fellowship.[34] This too was the bohemia that Isabella T. Aitken evoked in the title poem of her only published book, the collection *Bohemia and Other Poems* (1891):

> Who are the natures who haunt true Bohemia?
>   Those whose high souls from society rebel;
> Those whom the earth-hovering, narrow, vain natures
>   Cannot control, yet they cannot dispel.[35]

In Bohemia, these poems insisted, narrow-minded definitions of respectability and propriety would yield to more capacious understandings of human possibility. And yet, when bohemian rebellions assumed a more specific and concrete shape than these poetic generalities allowed, then the "unformed fears of dangers and disorders" referenced in Wilcox's "Bohemia" were less easily dismissed.

As in the antebellum bohemian scene, free love remained one such danger. Even in the context of *Mal Moulée*, the novel in which Wilcox's "Bohemia" is embedded, *la vie bohème* and its informal sexual relationships devolve into a toxic substitute for domestic happiness – for the "Kingdom of Love," in the words of another poem inserted into the narrative.[36] Nevertheless, in keeping with the carpe diem ethos of bohemianism – "the *Now*" of Wilcox's "Bohemia" – the early Wilcox was best known for her idealization of fleeting moments of passionate intensity. In *Mal Moulée*, the male protagonist becomes sickened by his "rank growth of wild oats," but in "The Duet" from *Poems of Passion*, Wilcox adopts the voice of a male speaker whose visions of a bygone bohemia and lost love, the "pretty grisette" named "Lisette," soon overtake the "sweet home air" and present reality of his respectable wife, "Stately Maud, with her proud blond head":

> You were so full of a subtle fire,
>   You were so warm and so sweet, Lisette;
> You were everything men admire,
> And there were no fetters to make us tire,
>   For you were – a pretty grisette.[37]

In 1857, Stoddard had allowed her female speaker to question her contented married life and long for "some ideal passion." Later in the century, Wilcox's married speaker remembers an actual love affair, but that speaker is, significantly, male. Other contemporary female poets also used male speakers to romanticize unfettered bohemian love. Fully compatible with male privilege and double standards of sexual morality, this subject position allowed for the expression of bohemian desire. For example, Eve Brodlique – who had successfully entered into a predominantly male profession, becoming an editor for the Chicago *Times-Herald* – inhabited another masculine social space in one of her poems, writing (seemingly without irony) of "Bohemia's Land" as a place where "a man may smoke at his ease" and "sing of the pretty girls we've kissed": "Let others shorten in dull home lives / Their hair and their liberty, / And be constrained at the word of their wives – / Bohemia's land for me!"[38]

From "The Duet" and "Bohemia's Land" to *Mal Moulée*, the "unatlassed borders of Bohemia" alternately led to sexual danger or fulfillment, to moral corruption or transcendence. The question of how to achieve a stable equilibrium between individual freedom and moral order – the perfect balance found in genteel versions of bohemia and in such seemingly paradoxical figures as the "good bohemian" and the "conventional bohemian" – proved to be especially challenging for women who were caught within ongoing double standards.[39] In her personal correspondence with her future husband, for instance, Ella Wheeler Wilcox carefully mediates between modern and traditional, bohemian and bourgeois personas. She relies on a variety of euphemisms to state that she will only go so far toward having a sexual relationship with him outside of marriage:

> No I am not puritanical in my ideas of right and wrong. I am very liberal – though not as liberal as you had hoped. . . . I think I have a fairly good light – it gives me a good deal of room in which to roam about and enjoy this palpitating life – but it does not quite extend to the latchkey. . . . We can never be the "comrades" that you wish.[40]

Though some critics dismissed her *Poems of Passion* as "SCARLET POEMS IN SCARLET BINDING," others maintained that she successfully managed the sort of balancing act that she sought in her correspondence with Robert Wilcox: according to *Cosmopolitan*, "she combines peculiarly the art of Swinburne and the boldness of Whitman with the genius and moral purpose of Jean Ingelow."[41] *Cosmopolitan* maintained that this was a fruitful combination for Wilcox, but the critic for *Literary World* was far more skeptical of Aitken's efforts to draw upon diverse sensibilities and literary models in her *Bohemia and Other Poems*: "Her models appear to include impartially Byron and Mrs. Sigourney, and her style is as if these poets had exchanged goblets at a feast, Byron imbibing

Mrs. Sigourney's weak tea, and she unfortunately elated by his bowl of Samian wine."[42] *Lippincott's*, however, touted Aitken's "waywardness in the selection and treatment of subjects," insisting her book had "a decided dash of originality."[43] "Bohemia" implicitly emerged from just such collisions between pre-existing poetic styles and discourses.

The borders of bohemia may have afforded women a range of liminal positions between opposing social forces, poetic styles, and subject positions, but how secure a foothold could a female poet have within this ever-shifting territory? For Ina Coolbrith, California's first poet laureate and one long associated with various phases of bohemian life in San Francisco, the "Cloudless Clime" of "Bohemia" offered an escape from the "aimless fret of household tasks" and a portal to what Coolbrith memorably referred to as "the man-life grand – pure soul, strong hand, / The limb of steel, the heart of air!"[44] And yet, despite her "longing" for this "man-life grand," her status as an honorary – but not full – member of the all-male Bohemian Club of San Francisco serves as a telling metonym, revealing some of the overarching tensions between women and men that, more broadly, shaped nineteenth-century women's relationships to *la vie bohème*.[45]

The Bohemian Club first formed in 1872, announcing that "The object of the Club shall be the promotion of social and intellectual intercourse between journalists and other writers, artists, actors and musicians, professional or amateur, and such others not included in this list as may by reason of knowledge and appreciation of polite literature and the fine arts be deemed worthy of membership."[46] But full membership did not extend to women, and, when Ina Coolbrith and Margaret Bowman became honorary members of the Club in 1874, the master of ceremonies apparently told the two women that they had achieved this distinction because they had sewn the Club's curtains. Despite this chauvinist joke, the Bohemian Club no doubt knew that Coolbrith deserved recognition for artistic productions that extended well beyond the curtains. Just a few months before her initiation, the Club had held a "complimentary testimonial," raising six hundred dollars for Coolbrith (who was at the time in acute financial need due to familial responsibilities) and enumerating her accomplishments.[47] As Club members must have realized, Coolbrith had a privileged claim to the land of bohemia. *La vie bohème* had been linked to literary San Francisco ever since Bret Harte first used "The Bohemian" as his pseudonym in his early *Golden Era* columns.[48] In the 1860s, Harte became editor of *The Overland Monthly* (the periodical that, for a time, defined the literary west), and Coolbrith – together with Harte and Charles Warren Stoddard – became part of the *Overland's* "Golden Gate Trinity." Of the seventeen poems in the first volume, all but one were written by members of the literary threesome.[49] They regularly met in Coolbrith's parlor on Taylor Street, and Stoddard later reminisced about "the exquisite atmosphere of the small salon," characterizing Coolbrith as the "mistress of this enchanting retreat."[50] Harte, however, made it clear that he saw her less as hostess/muse for the male bohemians than as one who actively "uses the Muses / Pretty much as she choses – this dark-eyed, young Sapphic divinity."[51]

"In Quest of Bohemia," a later writer for the *Overland*, E.P. Irwin, writes: "weary mortals, straining at the leashes of ennui, struggling to escape from the deadly monotony of life-emptiness, set forth in search of the fair land of Bohemia."[52] Irwin does not identify Coolbrith by name in the "Quest," but in "San Francisco Women Who Have Achieved Success" he recognizes that her poetry exhibits this urgency: "A plaintive strain runs through some of the poems, a longing expressed in a minor key. The poetic genius cramped by the stern restrictions of Fate cries out for freedom." Still, Irwin carefully insists that Coolbrith managed to achieve the precarious balance between propriety and license that other female bohemians of the era sought to maintain: on the one hand, "her poems breathe the highest and purest ideals, the truest womanhood, the most patient resignation," and, on the other, "at times one may catch a glimpse of a wild bird beating its wings against the cage that holds it back . . . from flight into its native element."[53] Based on this tension, Cheryl Walker has placed Coolbrith within the "nightingale tradition" of nineteenth-century women's poetry.[54] And yet, in their collective yearning for the "Unattained" (the title of another Coolbrith poem), it is important to recognize that certain nightingale poets, such as Coolbrith, looked toward bohemia – whether it took shape in verse, salons, editorial rooms, beer cellars, or clubrooms – as a liberating space in which they could begin to claim their rights and imagine a wider sphere of action and possibility.

Notes

1. Walt Whitman, *Notebooks and Unpublished Prose Manuscripts*, 6 vols, Edward Grier (ed.), (New York: New York University Press, 1963), vol. 1, 454.
2. See Joanna Levin, *Bohemia in America, 1858–1920* (Stanford: Stanford University Press, 2010) and Daniel Cottom, *International Bohemia: Scenes of Nineteenth-Century Life* (Philadelphia: University of Pennsylvania Press, 2013).
3. Ada Clare, "Thoughts and Things," *New York Saturday Press* 3 (February 11, 1860), 2. Available online: *The Vault at Pfaff's*. http://lehigh.edu/pfaffs [accessed December 15, 2015].

4. Julia Ward Howe, "What and Where is Bohemia," *Bohemia: A Symposium of Literary and Artistic Expressions*, Alexander K. McClure (ed.), (Philadelphia: The International League of Press Clubs, 1904), 394–395.
5. Howe, "What and Where is Bohemia," 395.
6. Jerrold Seigel, *Bohemian Paris: Culture, Politics, and the Boundaries of Bourgeois Life, 1830–1930* (New York: Penguin Books, 1986), 11.
7. Amanda Gailey, "Walt Whitman and the King of Bohemia: The Poet in the *Saturday Press*," *Walt Whitman Quarterly Review* 25 (Spring 2008), 143–166, rpt. in *Whitman among the Bohemians*, Joanna Levin and Edward Whitley (eds.), (Iowa City: University of Iowa Press, 2014), 19–36.
8. Anna Mary Freeman [Goldbeck], "Night Song," *Living Age* 51 (July 31, 1858), 332. Available online: *Making of America*. http://ebooks.library.cornell.edu/m/moa [accessed December 15, 2015].
9. Mary Freeman Goldbeck, "My Love and I," New York *Saturday Press* 4 (December 23, 1865), 332; Anna Mary Freeman [Goldbeck], "Transition," *New York Saturday Press* 2 (January 1, 1859), 4. Available online: *The Vault at Pfaff's*. http://lehigh.edu/pfaffs [accessed December 15, 2015].
10. A. L. Rawson, "A Bygone Bohemia," *Frank Leslie's Popular Monthly* 41 (January 1896), 103–04. Available online: *American Periodicals Series Online*. www.proquest.com [accessed December 15, 2015].
11. Mary Loeffelholz, *From School to Salon: Reading Nineteenth-Century American Women's Poetry* (Princeton: Princeton University Press, 2004), 162.
12. Rose Eytinge, *The Memories of Rose Eytinge: Being Recollections & Observations of Men, Women, and Events, during Half a Century* (New York: Frederick A. Stokes, 1905), 21. Available online: *Harvard University Library Digital Initiative*. http://hul.harvard.edu/ois/ldi/ [accessed December 15, 2015].
13. Ada Clare, "Thoughts and Things," *New York Saturday Press* 3 (January 14, 1860), 2. Available online: *The Vault at Pfaff's*. http://lehigh.edu/pfaffs [accessed December 15, 2015].
14. Rawson, "A Bygone Bohemia," 103.
15. Nina Auerbach, "The Rise of the Fallen Woman," *Nineteenth-Century Fiction* 35 (June 1980), 29.
16. Carl Benson [Charles Astor Bristed], "The Gypsies of Art: Translated for The Knickerbocker from Henry Murger's 'Scenes de La Boheme'," *The Knickerbocker* 41 (January 1853): 12–23.
17. See Joanna Levin, "'Freedom for Women from Conventional Lies': The 'Queen of Bohemia' and the Feminist Feuilleton," in *Whitman among the Bohemians*, 75–97.
18. M[argaret] E[ytinge], "Unto the Pure All Things Are Pure," *New York Saturday Press* 2 (April 23, 1859), 1. Available online: *The Vault at Pfaff's*. http://lehigh.edu/pfaffs [accessed December 15, 2015].
19. Thomas Butler Gunn, *Diaries, 1849–1863*, vol. 14 (1860): 102, Missouri History Museum. Available online: http://collections.mohistory.org/ [accessed December 15, 2015].
20. Quoted in Levin, "'Freedom for Women from Conventional Lies,'" 78.

21. Renée M. Sentilles, *Performing Menken: Adah Isaacs Menken and the Birth of American Celebrity* (New York: Cambridge University Press, 2003), 190.
22. Five years earlier, Shaw published the poem "Shadow and Sunshine" in the *New York Clipper* 7 (October 22, 1859), 216. Available online: *Illinois Digital Newspaper Collections*, http://idnc.library.illinois.edu [accessed December 15, 2015]. Menken joined the bohemians at Pfaff's in the summer of 1859, and the poem's lament for an absent friend or lover (the speaker addresses "my darling child") makes it tempting to read the poem as the precursor to Menken's "Reply to Dora Shaw."
23. Adah Isaacs Menken, "Reply to Dora Shaw. Westminster Palace, London, Aug. 29, 1864," *Infelicia and Other Writings*, Gregory Eiselein (ed.), (Peterborough: Broadview Press, 2002), 164–165.
24. Menken claimed African American, French, Irish, Spanish, and Jewish parents, and went by the names Marie Rachel Adelaide de Vere Spenser, Dolores Adios Fuertos, Adelaide McCord, Adah Bertha Theodore, and Rachel Adah Isaacs. See Sentilles, *Performing Menken*, 1–21.
25. Eliza Richards, "Whitman and Menken, Loosing and Losing Voices," *Whitman among the Bohemians*, 205.
26. Menken, "Resurgam," *Infelicia and Other Writings*, 43–45.
27. Lynn Mahoney, *Elizabeth Stoddard and the Boundaries of Bourgeois Culture* (New York: Routledge, 2004), xii–xv. A list of Stoddard's published poems (in addition to short fiction for the *Saturday Press* and *Vanity Fair*) is available in Regula Giovani, *"I Believe I Shall Die an Impenetrable Secret": The Writings of Elizabeth Barstow Stoddard* (New York: Peter Lang, 2002), 221–251.
28. Elizabeth Stoddard, *The Selected Letters of Elizabeth Stoddard*, Jennifer Putzi and Elizabeth Stockton (eds.), (Iowa City, IA: University of Iowa Press, 2012), 44.
29. Lillian Woodman Aldrich, *Crowding Memories* (Boston: Houghton, Mifflin, 1920), 15.
30. E. D. B. Stoddard, "Still Unknown," *Harper's New Monthly Magazine* 24 (December 1861), 83. Available online: *Making of America*. http://ebooks.library.cornell.edu/m/moa/ [accessed December 15, 2015].
31. "A Woman's Dream," *Harper's New Monthly Magazine* 15 (June 1857), 77. Available online: *Making of America*. http://ebooks.library.cornell.edu/m/moa/ [accessed December 15, 2015].
32. Stoddard, *Selected Letters*, 116. William Dean Howells commented that the Stoddards "were frankly not of that Bohemia which I disliked so much" in "First Impressions of Literary New York," *Harper's New Monthly Magazine* 91 (June 1, 1895), 73. Available online: *Making of America*. http://ebooks.library.cornell.edu/m/moa/ [accessed December 15, 2015].
33. Ella Wheeler Wilcox, *Mal Moulée: A Novel* (New York: G.W. Carleton and Co. 1885), 127–128.
34. On the bohemian vogue, see Levin, *Bohemia*, 125–284.
35. Isabella T. Aitken, *Bohemia and Other Poems* (Philadelphia: J.B. Lippincott Company, 1891), 7.
36. Wilcox, *Mal Moulée*, 246.

37. Wilcox, *Mal Moulée*, 265; Wilcox, "The Duet," *Poems of Passion* (Chicago: W.B. Conkey Company, 1883), 39.
38. Eve Brodlique, "Song: Bohemia's Land," *The New Bohemian: A Modern Monthly* 2 (1896), 42. Brodlique's success as an editor is mentioned in Margherita Arlina Hamm, "Some Women Editors," *Peterson's Magazine* 6 (1896), 613.
39. On this figure, see Levin, *Bohemia*, 125–128, 154–155.
40. February 3, 1883, Wilcox Papers, quoted in Angela Sorby, "The Milwaukee School of Fleshy Poetry: Ella Wheeler Wilcox's Poems of Passion and Popular Aestheticism," *Legacy* 26 (2009), 85.
41. E.D. Walker, "Ella Wheeler Wilcox," *The Cosmopolitan: a Monthly Illustrated Magazine* 6. (1888), 47.
42. "Bohemia," *The Literary World* 22 (1891), 130.
43. *J.B. Lippincott's Monthly Bulletin of New Publications* (Philadelphia: J.B. Lippincott Company, 1891), 13.
44. Ina Coolbrith, "Bohemia," *Wings of Sunset* (Boston: Houghton Mifflin Co., 1929), 28; Ina D. Coolbrith, "Longing," *Overland Monthly* 1 (1868), 17.
45. A fuller discussion of bohemianism and nineteenth-century American women poets would include the work of Louise Guiney. On Guiney and the Boston decadents, see David Weir, *Art and Literature Against the American Grain, 1890–1926* (Albany: State University of New York Press, 2008), 50–85.
46. *Annals of the Bohemian Club*, Vol. 1, 1872–1887 (San Francisco: Press of the Hicks-Judd Co., 1898), 26–27.
47. Josephine DeWitt Rhodehamel and Raymund Francis Wood, *Ina Coolbrith: Librarian and Laureate of California* (Provo: Brigham Young University Press, 1973), 125.
48. Levin, *Bohemia*, 70–121.
49. Ibid., 94.
50. Charles Warren Stoddard, "Ina D. Coolbrith," *The Magazine of Poetry and Literary Review* 1 (1889), 313 and Charles Warren Stoddard, "In Old Bohemia II," *The Pacific Monthly* (1907), 268.
51. Bret Harte, quoted in Rhodehamel and Wood, *Ina Coolbrith*, 95.
52. Edwin P. Irwin, "In Quest of Bohemia," *Overland Monthly and Out West Magazine* 48 (1906), 91.
53. E. P. Irwin, "San Francisco Women Who Have Achieved Success," *Overland Monthly and Out West Magazine* 44 (1904): 513.
54. Cheryl Walker, "Ina Coolbrith and the Nightingale Tradition," *Legacy* 6.1 (1989), 27–33.

PART III

1865–1900, Experiment and Expansion

CHAPTER 17

Women Poets and American Literary Realism

Elizabeth Renker

American literary histories have long presented realism as the "major" or "great movement" of the postbellum period. According to this narrative, William Dean Howells, Henry James, and Mark Twain towered over the era as its "major realists," with the year 1885 standing as the "annus mirabilis" that saw the publication of *The Rise of Silas Lapham, The Bostonians* (serialized that year in *The Century Magazine*), and *Adventures of Huckleberry Finn*. (Designating 1885 to be "a year of wonders" itself speaks to the chronological exceptionalism that undergirds this narrative.) In more recent decades, scholarship has turned to extending the story of realism backward in time (e.g., to Rebecca Harding Davis) and simultaneously to expanding its canon to include a more diverse array of writers, including women (especially regionalists such as Sarah Orne Jewett and Mary E. Wilkins Freeman) and writers of color (such as Zitkala-Ŝa). Nevertheless, realism has remained a mostly genre-exclusive conception that leaves poetry out of the story.[1] My argument here breaks with the long scholarly tradition of dissociating poetry from realism. I argue that an active strain of realist writing not only by women, but by women *poets* in particular, evolved in the decades following the Civil War. Common in print culture by the 1870s, women's realist poems helped to shape the literary climate for the later and better-known projects of their fellow realists working in fiction.

The term "realism" is one of the most troubled keywords in American literary history, rendering terminological ground-clearing especially necessary. Michael Davitt Bell argues that the term "realism," both during the postbellum era and in twentieth-century scholarship about it, is consistently plagued by problems of definition.[2] Nancy Glazener demonstrates that culturally authoritative magazines promoted "realism" as a literary quality that readers should "read for," even though any precise definition remained slippery at best.[3] For present purposes, I adopt a necessarily brief working gloss that incorporates key points of consensus in both postbellum discourses and in twentieth-century scholarship: realism is a mode of literary writing that seeks to represent contemporary social reality in a way that entails accurate observations of commonplace events, characters, and settings and that does so without recourse to transcendental frames of reference as a foundation.[4] I present a selected group of realist poems by four women, published between 1872 and 1889.[5] Read both individually and as a limited sample from a large and heterogeneous data set, these poems challenge the chronological, gender, and genre boundaries that restrict formulations about American literary realism.

Sarah Morgan Bryan Piatt, 1836–1919

One of our most profound realist poets is the Kentucky-born Sarah Morgan Bryan Piatt, who married into the Ohio Piatt family on the brink of the Civil War. Her husband, J.J. Piatt, co-authored *Poems of Two Friends* with Howells in 1860, the first book publication for both of them. Widely known in postbellum literary circles, often as poets of the "West" (in an era before the term "Midwest" entered the national imaginary), the Piatts' work routinely appeared in periodicals, as single-authored poetry books, and in anthologies. They held a certain cachet as married poets, akin in this regard to the celebrity-poet couple Elizabeth Barrett and Robert Browning.[6] Sarah Piatt fell from view in the twentieth century – as indeed did American women poets more generally, with the notable exception of Emily Dickinson.

The more general recovery of Piatt's extensive body of work now in progress presents a significant opportunity to revise our understanding of the position of realist poetry in postbellum US literary history. Her poems plunge into what Paula Bennett calls "the real," the "everyday dramas of family and social life and the life of the nation."[7] Extending Robert Browning's innovations in the dramatic monologue, Piatt frequently wrote dramatic lyrics that depict the complex and layered perspectives of multiple speakers, a method through which she explored the psychological disjunctions that cut through scenes of daily life. (In this regard, her work shares an epistemology with realist works by Herman Melville and Henry James.) As startling, arresting, or devastating as these "daily life" disjunctions are in her poems, it is part of their force to treat them as, in human fact, "commonplace," a term that would become a touchstone in postbellum debates about how to identify realist writers.

Her poems often render such commonplace disjunctions formally in ways that readers found challenging in her own time, as they still do in ours. For example, in a single poem Piatt might simultaneously depict multiple unidentified voices without marking them clearly. In addition to her complexities of voice and shifting perspective, she experiments with ruptures in time, fragmented speech, and evasions and omissions. Her interest in dramatic voice tapped into the popular arena of poetic taste that fired enthusiasm for Robert Browning, whom American readers praised for epistemological inquiry and aesthetic complexity.[8]

Two poems that she published in the early seventies, "Mock Diamonds (At the Seaside)" (1872) and "Two Veils" (1874), work with dramatic frames that place idealist and realist perspectives in counterpoint – a counterpoint that became one of Piatt's realist signatures. For her, as for other writers developing practices of literary realism, idealism (roughly synonymous with the term "romance" at the time) was a cultural formula that had become ripe for challenge, critique, sarcasm, and, more generally, aesthetic take-down. Both "idealism" and "romance" functioned as widely circulating cultural keywords that denoted an imagined set of traditional, uplifting aesthetic practices grounded both philosophically and morally in a transcendental sphere of "Truth." It would become common for realist writers to write against the grain of these idealist formulae in order to undercut the romance position. Perhaps the most famous example of the contrapuntal realist scenario is Howells' fake romance novel *Slop, Silly Slop* in *The Rise of Silas Lapham*, a meta-reference to the imagined romance antagonist for Howells' own realist novel.[9] Antecedent texts such as Piatt's demonstrate just how familiar these concerns would have been by the time Howells' novel was published.

"Mock Diamonds (At the Seaside)" appeared in the Washington, DC, newspaper *The Capital*. Donn Piatt, her cousin by marriage, founded and then edited this paper from its first issue in March 1871 until 1880. *The Capital* took as its purpose aggressive, independent, and critical coverage of Washington politics, and Donn was legendary for his "unsparing" attacks on lawmakers.[10] At the same time, *The Capital* aimed to include "literary features of a high order of excellence."[11] He published numerous poems by Piatt, often on the front page. An 1893 biography of Donn recalled that the paper ran tales by Harriet Prescott Spofford and poems by "Mrs. S.M.B. Piatt, whose delicate verses have found recognition abroad, and who is one of the sweetest poets of this generation."[12] The unsurprisingly tone-deaf account of Piatt's verses as "delicate" speaks to the larger misreading of her realist poetics, filtered through gendered perceptions of women poets that would continue to flatten their voices throughout the twentieth century. For present purposes I simply flag and bracket the problem of reception as one with larger implications for the status of women's realist poetics, both then and now.

A dramatic dialogue in which a husband and wife visit the seaside in the Reconstruction-era South, the poem explores the fantasies of romance operative both in heterosexual love and sociopolitics. Although Bennett's edition of Piatt indicates that "Mock Diamonds" was an unsigned poem, *The Capital* in fact ran it on the front page with the byline "By the author of *A Woman's Poems*," a clear attribution to Piatt's 1871 volume by that title. *A Woman's Poems* received wide recognition, and its title concept of poetry uniquely suited to "a woman" poet led to some of the gender stereotypes of her sweet delicacy.[13] In "Mock Diamonds," as in other poems, Piatt crafted a domestic scenario imbricated in a larger social and national dynamic of *political* romance. The semantic juxtaposition in the two words of the title – "mock" and "diamonds" – frames the poem's central realist trope: glittering idealizations, in both love and politics, whose foundation turns out to be deception – with devastating consequences at personal, domestic, and political levels.

The plot of the poem is one in which a former Southern belle returns to a vacation resort in the South with her Northern husband after the war, where she somewhat uncomfortably encounters antebellum suitors and must address her husband's questions about who they are and what they meant to her. Although the poem never explicitly identifies her spouse as Northern, his outsider curiosities and questions about the South suggest that a North/South distinction is one of the many perspectival disjunctions at work both in their marriage and in the poem. Her tactical tale for her husband works in part because of his somewhat clueless distance from the social world she describes to him in partial and evasive terms. Recalling her youth, she presents a lush scene of "orange flowers," "rich plantation[s]," "Beauty," "kisses," "bud-scents," "dreamy" eyes, and "diamonds." She now dismisses this antebellum scene of romantic intrigue as a time "Before the South laid down / Her insolent false glory," a time that allegedly has no relevance to the couple's domestic present – and that her husband therefore need not be jealous about. (In its larger frame, the poem metaphorically aligns the South's "false glory" with the "mock diamonds" of the title.)

An alternative story whose emotional force she cannot so easily contain percolates up through the romantic tale that she manages so carefully for her husband's hearing. Of the former suitors they see on the beach, one in particular, a former Confederate soldier, quickly comes to dominate the present scene as well as her recollections. Her husband remarks that he looks like a member of the Klan – a suspicion she counters, perhaps too quickly. Her story of her antebellum affair with him is dreamy with romance but simultaneously cut through – in ways she only partially acknowledges, to her husband or to herself – with her admission that she was partly motivated to acquire his plantation wealth. The dramatic conclusion to their love story as she summarizes it is that he ultimately leaves her for an heiress who in turn "flash'd him blind" with diamonds.

The wife's posturing evasions as she crafts this tale for her husband indicate that she is only pretending to have recovered from the consequent heartbreak. For example, she refers to her former lover as a "guerilla from – the dead?", and the question mark is her own. The word "guerilla" speaks to his military past as a Confederate soldier and his possible paramilitary "guerilla" present in the Klan. He is also a "guerilla" in his emotional effect on her now, ambushing her in the present moment in a way that will leave her reeling by the poem's end. Her rising inflection and her question mark signify that this former suitor is a kind of time guerilla (as indeed former lovers sometimes are) who has not, in emotional fact, been "dead" to her. In the poem's larger frame, the troubled boundary between past and present and between what is and is not "dead" also characterizes the antebellum South as such – an allegedly lost world whose uncanny power continues to unsettle the present.

These time problems at the heart of the poem reach their apex at its conclusion. In the final two stanzas, this guerilla walks across the beach from the (physical, temporal, emotional, and psychic) distance from which she has first spotted him to confront her in the poem's present real-time. Losing the composure she maintained while telling her husband her carefully crafted tale, her perceptions suddenly grow shadowy and dim, and she hovers on the verge of fainting. The former lover who suddenly stands before her speaks only one sentence, without preamble, as if, indeed, their antebellum conversation could pick up right where they left it years before: "*She wore Mock-Diamonds.*" In this final turn, the wife learns only in the present that she had long misunderstood her own story. All three figures in the Southern love triangle turn out to have been scheming for wealth while jockeying for love. And although she claims in the final line that her lover now walks away (again) and passes "to the Past forever" (again), the entire poem belies the tidy resolution claiming that the past can ever, in fact, be "dead." Romantic idealizations threaten to reappear, uncanny, altered, and scarred, to wreak their damage in new scenarios. Most crucially, those idealizations have not lost their power or their aesthetic appeal for this woman who otherwise claimed all along to have moved ahead.

Two years later, Piatt's poem "Two Veils" appeared in the *Atlantic Monthly*; William Dean Howells had taken over as editor in 1871.[14] According to Edwin H. Cady, Howells was not yet a "realist" when he took over at *The Atlantic*, although "[h]ints of realism or of what would someday become realism were very much in the air."[15] While Cady was not thinking about poetry as part of this "air" in his 1958 study, it's easy to see from the poems Howells was publishing that women realist poets, including Piatt and Lucy Larcom (to whom I'll turn in the next section), were already exploring that terrain. As their editor, Howells was, of course, a careful reader of their work. The fact that he does not appear to have understood their realism is one sign that they were carving out artistic terrain that he did not yet fully comprehend; indeed, his own poetry would not go in this direction until the 1890s. In the July 1874 issue of *The Atlantic*, Howells positively reviewed both Piatt's book *A Voyage to the Fortunate Isles* and a book of poems by transatlantic realist George Eliot, *The Legend of Jubal and Other Poems*.[16] A month before the review appeared, Howells sent it to J.J. Piatt, noting, "I'm pledged by my praises, to show Mrs. Piatt always at her best hereafter."[17] Howells' friendship, correspondence, and work with J.J. Piatt dated back to their 1860 volume together. Sarah's work was familiar to Howells across many years, including the period of her Reconstruction poems of the 1870s. Scholarship has yet to parse the influence of her realist poetics on Howellsian realism as it would develop later, a particularly clear instance of one of the conceptual fissures in standard accounts of American literary realism.

"Two Veils," which Howells published the month after his review of Piatt and Eliot, also places idealist and realist orientations in counterpoint, juxtaposing characters (two women), time frames (past and present), female social roles (nun and girl), and regions (North and South). As in "Mock Diamonds," Piatt depicts the romance attributes of a lost South, tied again to social identities for women who are bound up in the economy of mating. Both poems are historically particular to the Reconstruction moment, situated amidst larger Reconstruction discourses about the meaning of the South and the North as political spaces as well as heavily charged locations in the national imaginary.

A dramatic dialogue in nine quatrains, "Two Veils" presents two speakers, a "nun" and a "girl," one wearing the veil of the nun's vocation and the other planning to take the veil of her pending marriage. A third unidentified speaker serves as narrator and frames the other two voices. Like the female speaker in "Mock Diamonds," the nun reaches into a painful past, recalling a lost world of "Love and beauty." When she, too, tells the story of her former lover, her heart still beats "fierce." Explaining that she has taken refuge in "Faith in God" because of her forsaken "Faith in man," she portrays her experience of lost love through a metaphorics of the "Tropic" South. Like the wife in "Mock Diamonds," she recalls "music in the dewy distance / And the whole land flowering at my feet." Whether this South is literal or merely imagistic, the tropical scenario of romantic idealization is one that the idea of the "North" comes to disrupt:

> "Tropic eyes too full of light and languor,
> Northern soul too gray with Northern frost:
> Ashes – ashes after fires of anger –
> Love and beauty – what a world I lost!"

While the literal alignment of the lovers with regions ultimately remains indeterminate, she parses their *break* through tropes of North–South difference. The luxurious and passionate past is metaphorically Southern, and losing that world leaves her with her nun's frosty "Northern soul."

The girl laughs at the nun's memories as a form of "envy" for her own present happy romance, and here the bifurcation of two female figures (girl/nun, young/old) opens out into Piatt's characteristic disjunction between idealist and realist perspectives. The girl mocks the nun's tedious counting of rosary beads and gloats over the "jewels worth the wearing / Waiting in the sunny world for me!" For this young bride dreaming of that figuratively Southern tropic scene, the jewels will turn out to be "mock diamonds." In the final ironic turn of the poem, she returns many years later, renouncing those "jewels" and seeking to swap her veil with that of the "Sister" she had mocked, now become a "Sister" in suffering.

In both "Mock Diamonds" and "Two Veils," the realist tropes of deception and duality interrogate forms of romance that nevertheless maintain psychological, political, and social force. Neither the Northern matron nor the nun recalls the past from a space of distant neutrality. In Piatt's terms, romance is the thing that won't stay dead – *even under the realist gaze* that sees through it. Piatt's construction of the realist perspective thus entails insight but certainly not objectivity or superiority. Indeed, one of Piatt's major contributions to realism more generally is her insistence that – unlike Howells' romance straw man *Slop, Silly Slop* – romance, as a realist subject, is no laughing matter.

Lucy Larcom, 1824–1893

In September 1874, Lucy Larcom's poem "Goody Grunsell's House" also appeared in the *Atlantic Monthly*, once again under the editorship of

Howells. Larcom works here in a romantic poetic style – gothic fantasy – that she converts to a realist mode. A narrative poem of ten stanzas, "Goody Grunsell's House" frames itself as an archaic tale. Its protagonist, weary and old, bears the title "Goody," an outdated designation for a married woman. The first two stanzas introduce her and her house as analogous gothic figures. Her "weary old face," "craggy forehead," "long, lean fingers," and black hat ("black mutch") paint a picture of Goody as crone.[18] Her "dreary old house" is surrounded by plants that have displaced the former garden, including witch-grass, nettle, rag-weed, nightshade, and henbane, all of which literally or figuratively suggest witchcraft and magical or poisonous brews. The gothic botanicals lurk about the dreary old house "Like demons that enter in / When a soul has run waste to sin." The house itself weeps, with "drew that forever dripped and crept / From the moss-grown eaves."

The gothic scenario evolves, like any good gothic narrative, to reveal the secrets of the haunted house. In this case, the secrets are so oppressive that, "inch by inch, as the cold years sped, / She was burning the old house over her head." Literally tearing strips of "worn and weather-stained oak" from her own dwelling to kindle her fires, she burns her own domicile bit by bit, a sign of how trapped she remains by this haunted dwelling. Although she lives alone, she "conceal[s]" the torn strips before she burns them. Her impulse to conceal serves no ostensible purpose, since no other characters are present except for the house itself. The concealed strips of the literal house serve as figures for other kinds of domestic concealment. Stanza six reports that "not a memory glad / Illumined bare ceiling or wall" – only "cruel shadows." The gothic specters here are her memories of the domestic violence of which she was both agent and victim: "For she had not been a forbearing wife, / Nor a loyal husband's mate; / The twain had been one but in fear and hate." The "horror" also included child abuse, as children "blighted grew" and died, likely by Goody's own hand. The poem remains equivocal on Goody's particular actions as an abusive mother also bound up in a violent marriage, but the children "cried / From their graves, to denounce her a homicide." Their cries suggest that, at best, she failed to protect or neglected them; more likely, she murdered them herself. She attacks this house, "a lair of pain and shame," piece by piece, making "wound after wound" in its physical structure. Her literal exercise of "domestic" violence thus functions both as repetition compulsion and as exorcism.

Larcom undercuts the romance elements of gothic fantasy with the realist nightmare of domestic abuse. In the final stanza, she initially summarizes Goody's story as "pictures out of a long-lost book," returning to the archaic tropes that open the poem. She then quickly switches frames to the present commonplace social world. There, the speaker reminds us, "many a human," like Goody, is haunted by a "dwelling-place" that is "not love's home." Piatt's realism in "Mock Diamonds" and "Two Veils" turns on ironic juxtaposition, a mode that Bennett calls "the organizing principle of her verse."[19] Working in a distinct realist mode, Larcom writes the gothic as the real and vice versa. These particular realist poems by Piatt and Larcom, contemporary to one another, remind us that realist poetic practices at this time were divergent and heterogeneous rather than monolithic in form, content, or style.

Susan Coolidge [Sarah Chauncey Woolsey], 1835–1905

Susan Coolidge, well known in her own time although unknown today, carves out her realist poetics in the domain of what she calls "earthly" or "real" things. The title of her poem "Shadow-Land," published in *The Christian Union* in 1880, semantically evokes the common poetic landscape of the idealist dreamland. Her intervention is to pull out of such romantic otherworldly spaces into the realm of specifically bodily experience. Of her "shadow-land," she writes,

> That is the land where baby dwells:
> All things are shadows to his blue eyes,
> Houses and trees and flowers and shells
> And men and women and butterflies.[20]

The sphere of alterity that she describes is not an otherworldly realm or dreamscape, but specifically the physiological realm of infant perception. The "shadows to [baby's] blue eyes" are his literal perceptions of phenomena: "The moon is a shadowy, yellow thing" that he reaches to grasp and "the birds are shadows that flit and sing." The baby cannot yet distinguish or discriminate among the shadows: "All, all alike are the large and the less; / Alike to baby are near and far." Also working within the long tradition of mother–child poems founded on a Christian promise of baby's direct connections to a heavenly otherworld, Coolidge offers instead a bodily ground:

> One only thing is real and nigh,
> The touch of the mother [*sic*] close embrace,
> The mother's breast, with its sweet supply,
> And the mother kiss on his soft, soft face.

This poem stakes the ground of the "real" in the earthly primacy of the mother's physical body.

In her 1881 volume, *Verses*, Coolidge uses the term "earthly" to characterize her explicitly anti-idealist poetic project.[21] In contrast with Piatt and Larcom, Coolidge defines her anti-idealist poetics in terms of audience. Published by Roberts Brothers, who would publish Emily Dickinson a decade later to great popularity, Coolidge's volume opens with a poem titled "Prelude."[22] As in "Shadow-Land," "Prelude" presents idealist conventions about poetry in order to recast them. She begins with the definition of "poems" itself:

Poems are heavenly things,
And only souls with wings
May reach them where they grow,
May pluck and bear below,
Feeding the nations thus
With food all glorious.

Here Coolidge appears to endorse the commonly circulating cultural definition of poems as inherently idealist. (Lines by Oliver Wendell Holmes in 1889 present one representative example: the poet is he "Who drinks the waters of enchanted streams / That wind and wander through the land of dreams / For whom the unreal is the real world."[23]) But Coolidge sets up this familiar formula in order to say that what she is writing does not conform to it:

Verses are not of these;
They bloom on earthly trees,
Poised on a low-hung stem,
And those may gather them
Who cannot fly to where
The heavenly gardens are.

Verses thus offers not the idealist stuff of wings, souls, and glories, but the "bloom" of "low-hung," "earthly trees" for a different group of readers who cannot or prefer not to "fly to where / The heavenly gardens are." Indeed, Coolidge talks back to the familiar cultural discourse about poetry as inherently idealist, going so far as to insist that what she is writing must not even *be* poetry but something else entirely.

Emma Lazarus, 1849–1887

Emma Lazarus' "August Moon" poses the explicit question of poetry's relation to the domain of the notional "real." The poem frames that question as one that her readers will recognize as a subject of contemporary social and aesthetic debate, a debate she represents formally through a dramatic play of voices. She dated "August Moon" "1877" in her notebook, where she indicates that she published it in a newspaper that year.[24] Published again posthumously in an 1889 collection, it garnered attention yet again in *Poet Lore* in 1897, a decade after Lazarus' death, as a "modern" poem that "dare[s] to challenge" old forms.[25] The chronological arc of the poem's composition and reception indicates its active cultural engagement, across two decades, with evolving debates about poetry and realism.

Three voices, framed by an unidentified narrator, speak about poetry and its place in the "modern" moment. As the title indicates, the debate in the poem centers on the issue of "poetic" interpretation of the natural world. The question hovering over the poem is whether or not poetry will remain or can remain adequate to a newly scientific, modern worldview.[26] It is for this reason that the specifically romantic idea of the moon metapoetically hangs over the poem, in title and content. Contemporary to Lazarus' poem, influential critic and anthologist Edmund Clarence Stedman had, like others skeptical of or hostile to realism, construed realism to be poetry's primary opponent within the literary field. In his 1875 *Victorian Poets*, Stedman wrote that "the old position of art in relation to knowledge" held that "the imagination, paradoxical as it may seem, has been most heightened and sustained by the contemplation of natural objects, *rather as they seem to be* than as we know they are."[27] Poetry's relation to the natural world was thus a primary battleground for the epistemic shifts that so threatened Stedman and his like-minded contemporaries.

As the argument defending poetic idealism worked itself out, poetry faced extinction by realism's insurgent forces. For example, Stedman still hoped, in *Poets of America* in 1885, that "the phase of minute realism and analysis through which modern literature is passing" would come to an end, leaving idealist poetry to rebound.[28] In 1894, William R. Thayer, only one of many voices in the debate, excoriated realism in general and Howells in particular, noting among realism's more general offenses that "Poetry, of course, could no more exist in its presence than frost before a blow-pipe." The vogue for realism, he claimed, meant that poetry had "had its death-warrant signed."[29] Thayer was not unique; he was recapitulating a common cultural formula about poetry as inherently idealist and therefore antithetical to realist projects as such.

The scene of "August Moon" is late summer, when the impending harvest signals ripeness and the natural cycle soon to move toward death.

An unidentified initial speaker recounts the monologues of three male "friends," the first of whom is "Ralph, the artist." For him, the "weird orb" of the moon "unroll[s] / Scenes phantasmal," peopling the "vacant air" with the stuff of fables and myths: mermaids, trolls, elves, and "all the shapes by poet's brain / Fashioned," disporting themselves in "this spiritual light." His "romantic," "waking dream" is one he marks as past its time:

> Ah! no modern mortal sees
> Creatures delicate as these.
> All the simple faith has gone
> Which their world was builded on.
> Now the moonbeams coldly glance
> On no gardens of romance.

For Ralph, modernity marks the demise of "the Beautiful," sacrificed to "prosaic senses dull" of modern times.

Claude, the next speaker, contests Ralph's claim that poetry and the Beautiful are dead. He sides with modernity: "I am one / Who would not restore that Past, / Beauty will immortal last, / Though the beautiful must die." While Ralph claims that "Fables, myths alone are real" and invisible to "modern mortal," Claude counters him forcefully. Indeed, Claude's first utterance is to tell Ralph – in Latin – to shut up. Claude's rhetoric focuses on the "new," on redefinitions of "Truth," and on "the marvels of the real." When he announces that he awaits the bard who "the baseless feud shall heal / That estrangeth wide apart / Science from her sister Art" and whips out his telescope for ready viewing of the heavens, he marks himself an astronomer or other scientist.

The next (and final) speaker is "Poet Florio," silent during the disagreement between art and science. Florio's monologue embraces Claude's scientific approach: "Widening knowledge surely brings / Vaster themes to him who sings." Ralph's framework of fables and myths has expired, he explains, giving rise to a "naked sky" in which "the heavens like a scroll / Stand revealed." The revelation, however, is not that of simple material objects. Ralph the artist had seen nothing through the telescope but barren planets. Far from destroying the role of the poet, widening scientific knowledge, according to Florio, calls for mortal poets to "embrace" – in the sense of "take in with the eye or the mind" – the new heavens of a cosmos in ceaseless change, "World on world" in endless cycles of ice and fire.[30]

Lazarus importantly situates the poet as a modern rather than conventional thinker about the state of poetics. Indeed, she gives Florio the poem's literal final word. "August Moon" embraces science and "the real" as a new domain that will necessitate a new kind of poetic encounter with "natural objects." In this sense the poem stood opposed to the hegemonic constructions and laments by Holmes, Stedman, Thayer, and their like-minded contemporaries. The 1897 article about Lazarus in *Poet Lore* makes it very clear how effective and on-point the poem was in addressing evolving cultural conceptions of poetry during this time: "the 'August Moon' of Emma Lazarus dares to challenge the old beauty with beauty fed anew with modern knowledge."[31] Like the other poems by women poets that this brief essay has presented, Lazarus embraces a realist project for poetry that cuts against hegemonic conceptions that "poetry" was, a priori, synonymous with romantic idealism.

Even in our own moment of reception, the women realist poets of the postbellum era still have to cut against that grain. For example, the most recent edition of the *The Princeton Encyclopedia of Poetry & Poetics* – published in 2012 – holds that "realism" denotes styles and methods of a period in literary history "during which poetry is at best of secondary importance." It also repeats the claim, familiar from the postbellum debates traced here, that "realistic poetry" as a concept entails principles that "would, of course, bring about the desiccation of poetry."[32] In this regard, even very recent treatments of poetry in relation to realism repeat the authoritative literary discourses of the postbellum period that conceived of "poetry" as inherently "idealist," "romantic," and "unreal." Twentieth-century literary histories accepted these ideological accounts as if they described "poetry" as such. But those debates were a part of their time; they were scenes of contest, not tales of truth. Challenging the genre-exclusive definition of American literary realism points to an alternative history of realism, of poetry, of the postbellum era more generally, and of the pioneering contributions of women realist poets to all three.

Notes

Many thanks to Paula Bernat Bennett and Karen L. Kilcup for their engaged responses to an early draft of this essay.

1. Cheryl Walker points out that poetry's exclusion from conceptions of American literary realism is a product of history, since scholarly accounts of realism included some poetry through the 1930s (Cheryl Walker, "Nineteenth-Century Women Poets and Realism," *American Literary Realism* 23.3 (1991), 25, 39). In an emblematic example of such genre exclusions, the headnote to Zitkala-Ŝa in the eighth edition of the *Norton Anthology*, amidst its nine paragraphs detailing her life and career, contains the following parenthetical note: "(She also wrote poetry.)"

(*The Norton Anthology of American Literature*, Nina Baym and Robert S. Levine (eds.), (New York: W.W Norton, 2012), 8th edn., vol. C, 1085.)

2. See Michael Davitt Bell, *The Problem of American Realism: Studies in the Cultural History of a Literary Idea* (Chicago: University of Chicago Press, 1993).
3. See Nancy Glazener, *Reading for Realism: The History of a U.S. Literary Institution, 1850–1910* (Durham: Duke University Press, 1997).
4. See, for example, René Wellek, *Concepts of Criticism*, Stephen G. Nichols, Jr. (ed.), (New Haven and London: Yale University Press, 1963), 228–229; Brook Thomas, *American Literary Realism and the Failed Promise of Contract* (Berkeley: University of California Press, 1997), 13, 14; and Donald Pizer (ed.), *Documents of American Realism and Naturalism* (Carbondale and Edwardsville: Southern Illinois University Press, 1998), 3–4.
5. My book in progress, *American Realist Poetics, 1866–1911*, presents the larger archive.
6. Emily Corey, "Married Poets and Marriage Poems: The Brownings and the Piatts," *Salon at Mac-O-Chee, Public Humanities Program at Piatt Castles*, May 25, 2015.
7. Paula Bernat Bennett (ed.), *Palace-Burner: The Selected Poetry of Sarah Piatt* (Urbana: University of Illinois Press, 2001), xxviii, xxxiii.
8. Nancy Glazener, "The Browning Society in US Public Literary Culture," *Modern Language Quarterly* 75.2 (2014), 175, 177. Yopie Prins shows that Browning's avid American readership generated popular reprintings such as those on railway timetables in 1872–1874. Yopie Prins, "Robert Browning, Transported by Meter," *The Traffic in Poems: Nineteenth-Century Poetry and Transatlantic Exchange*, Meredith L. McGill (ed.), (New Brunswick: Rutgers University Press, 2008), 208.
9. William Dean Howells, *The Rise of Silas Lapham* (New York: Penguin, 1980), 183.
10. Charles Grant Miller, *Donn Piatt: His Work and His Ways* (Cincinnati: Robert Clarke & Co, 1893), 233.
11. Miller, *Donn Piatt*, 229.
12. Ibid.
13. Bennett, *Palace-Burner*, 166 n 19; Sarah Piatt, "Mock Diamonds," *The Capital* 2.19 (July 14, 1872), 1.
14. Sarah Piatt, "Two Veils," *Atlantic Monthly* 34.202 (August 1874), 215; Ellery Sedgwick, "The Atlantic Monthly," *American Literary Magazines: The Eighteenth and Nineteenth Centuries*, Edward E. Chielens (ed.), (New York: Greenwood Press, 1986), 57.
15. Edwin H. Cady, *The Realist at War: The Mature Years, 1885–1920, of William Dean Howells* (New York: Syracuse University Press, 1958), 156.
16. George Eliot, *The Legend of Jubal and Other Poems* (Boston: J.R. Osgood, 1874).
17. W.D. Howells, letter to J.J. Piatt (June 13, 1874), typescript, William Dean Howells Papers, Special Collections and University Archives, Rutgers University Libraries.

18. Lucy Larcom, "Goody Brunsell's House," *Atlantic Monthly* 34.203 (September 1874), 279–280.
19. Paula Bernat Bennett, *Poets in the Public Sphere: The Emancipatory Project of American Women's Poetry, 1800–1900* (Princeton: Princeton University Press, 2003), 139.
20. Susan Coolidge, "Shadow-Land," *The Christian Union* (December 8 1880), 493.
21. Susan Coolidge, "Prelude," *Verses* (Boston: Roberts Brothers, 1881), 5–6.
22. Ibid., 5–6.
23. "To James Russell Lowell, at the Dinner Given in His Honor at the Tavern Club, on His Seventieth Birthday, February 22, 1889)," *Atlantic Monthly* 63 (Boston: Houghton Mifflin, 1889), 556–558.
24. I have not yet been able to locate this newspaper printing. Emma Lazarus, "August Moon," Manuscript Notebook from the Emma Lazarus collection, 1877–1887, 111, Emma Lazarus papers, American Jewish Historical Society, New York and Boston, digital.cjh.org, [accessed June 3, 2015].
25. "Lazarus, Emma," *Poet Lore* 9 (January 1, 1897), 419.
26. Emma Lazarus, August Moon *The Poems of Emma Lazarus: Narrative, Lyric, and Dramatic* (Boston and New York: Houghton, Mifflin and Company, 1889), 1, 186–191.
27. Edmund Clarence Stedman, *Victorian Poets* (Boston: Houghton, Mifflin, 1889), 18.
28. Edmund Clarence Stedman, *Poets of America* (Boston: Houghton, Mifflin, 1875), xiii.
29. William R. Thayer, "The New Story-tellers and the Doom of Realism," *Forum* (December 1894), 472, 474.
30. "embrace, v.2." OED Online, Oxford University Press http://www.oed.com/ [accessed March 20, 2015]. In the last four lines of the poem, Florio suddenly waxes theological, asserting the "One" whose "will" at the heart of Nature we are charged to conceive, a moment that I group more generally with what Bennett has called Lazarus' penchant for "hollow" idealizations (*Poets in the Public Sphere*, 101). Dorothea Steiner argues that Claude's monologue is Lazarus' own plea "for poetry . . . to become realistic" at a time when poetry and realism were construed to be antithetical (Dorothea Steiner, "Women Poets in the Twilight Period," *American Poetry Between Tradition and Modernism*, Roland Hagenbuchle (ed.), (Regensburg: Verlag Friedrich Pustet, 1984), 181).
31. "Lazarus, Emma," *Poet Lore* (January 1, 1897), 419.
32. M. Winkler, "Realism," *The Princeton Encyclopedia of Poetry and Poetics*, 4th edn., Roland Greene and Stephen Cushman (eds.), (Princeton: Princeton University Press, 2012), 1148–1149.

CHAPTER 18

Verse Forms

Cristanne Miller

Those who write about mid- to late-nineteenth-century American poetry tend to say very little about verse forms or about formal characteristics of verse, yet it is widely accepted that the modernist poetry of the 1910s differs strikingly from its nineteenth-century predecessors in its forms.[1] Consequently, understanding the shifting preferences for particular verse forms from the mid- to late nineteenth century provides useful information for understanding both late-nineteenth-century taste and the beginnings of modernist poetry in the United States. At stake is not just the transition from metered to free verse but a more basic conception of the poetic line and poetic rhythms. This essay focuses on a few elements of formal practice that shift during this period and on ways that some women poets manipulated syntax and rhythm within metered forms anticipating the more idiomatic rhythms of modernist poetry.

No change in a period's formal preferences or practices occurs at a particular moment. As Christopher Hager and Cody Marrs suggest in "Against 1865," there are no simple dividing lines or sharp moments of transition in uses of literary form.[2] In the nineteenth century, many poets wrote through more than one literary era, as scholars typically delimit them: the 1840s and 1850s, the Civil War, the late nineteenth-century, and early modernism. Nonetheless, one can distinguish some shifts in aesthetic preferences and formal practices between the 1860s and the 1890s.

My perception of these changes is based upon years of reading in this period and, for the context of this essay, primarily upon the poetry collected in two anthologies from the second half of the nineteenth century, one early twentieth-century anthology that adheres primarily to late nineteenth-century verse norms, and two late twentieth-century anthologies: Ralph Waldo Emerson's *Parnassus: An Anthology of Poetry* (1874); Edmund C. Stedman's *An American Anthology, 1797–1900* (1900); Bliss Carman's *Oxford Book of American Verse* (1927); John Hollander's *American Poetry: The Nineteenth Century* (1993); and Paula Bernat

Bennett's *Nineteenth-Century American Women Poets: An Anthology* (1998).[3] These texts provide a relatively thorough survey of the period and give a surprisingly consistent sense of what is valued in poetry written between the late 1860s and 1900. Each of these anthologies also includes a large number of poems by women.[4] Emerson's and Stedman's anthologies were the most influential of the second half of the century. Although Carman's appeared in 1927, he had established his reputation as an astute critic of new poetry over more than three decades before its publication, and his selections were based in large part on a late-nineteenth-century aesthetic. Hollander's and Bennett's anthologies reveal the extent to which forms valued during this period continue to dominate anthologies a century later – although often in a different choice of poems. Although not every poet or poem I discuss here appeared in these anthologies, the shifts in form I discuss are well represented there.

In the decades following the war, women wrote with increasing frequency in longer-lined forms – that is, longer than eight syllables – particularly in rhymed iambic pentameter. While they continued to use ballad meters, such meter increasingly appeared in lines of four, five, six, or even seven beats rather than in lines of two, three, or combinations of three and four beats, forms that were popular during the 1840s and 1850s.[5] Shorter forms continued to be used in the late nineteenth century, as did ode-like forms of varying line and stanza lengths, but women showed an increased preference for longer lines. In the 1880s and 1890s, poets also increasingly wrote short poems – perhaps a reason why the sonnet remained popular for women writers.

These tendencies are consistent in all but one of the anthologies I examined, suggesting that the increased representation of long-lined forms and of poems fourteen lines or shorter is not simply a matter of individual editors' preference.[6] For example, although Emerson's *Parnassus* would logically be least likely to show this tendency (both because it cannot represent any poetry beyond its 1874 date of publication and because Emerson's taste was so clearly formed by antebellum standards), among the eleven antebellum poems by women he selected only three in pentameter (27 percent), whereas eleven of the fifteen post-war poems by women use this form (over 75 percent). In the early-nineteenth-century sections of Stedman's anthology, approximately 27 percent of the poems by women are wholly or largely in pentameter; in the following sections, approximately 40 percent of the poems are in pentameter or include primarily pentameter lines.[7] In Carman's anthology, all eight poets who began writing before the 1860s are represented exclusively by short-lined verse (including Emily Dickinson) whereas the fifty-eight later poems include twelve entirely or mostly in pentamenter (21 percent). Bennett's anthology includes less than 30 percent poems in pentameter from women writing mostly before the war, and nearly 50 percent in the later period. Hollander's anthology includes approximately 30 percent poems in pentameter by writers publishing before the war and 72 percent in pentameter in the later sections.[8] In each case, the increased number of pentameter poems accompanies a general increase in poems containing more than, or predominantly more than, 10 syllables per line.

Stedman's "Close of the Century: 1890–1900" section also contains shorter poems by female poets than in previous sections: sixteen poems of eight or fewer lines, sixteen poems of ten to twelve lines, and fifteen sonnets – making for approximately 34 percent poems with fourteen or fewer lines. Bennett's anthology similarly includes several short poems from this decade, and she refers elsewhere to the "quatrain craze" of the late 1880s and 1890s.[9] These patterns do not mean that late nineteenth-century women wrote exclusively in short poems with long lines. Far from it. Women continued to use short-lined forms, but there was either a marked increase in the proportion of long-lined verse published after the mid-1860s, or anthology editors particularly valued pentameter and other longer-lined forms – or both. Similarly, the majority of collected poems were longer than fourteen lines, but an increasing number of short poems appeared toward the end of the century.

The general conception of post-war nineteenth-century verse is that it became not longer-lined or shorter, but formally more innovative, leading progressively toward the formal originality of modernism.[10] I do not find this to be the case. The most innovative nineteenth-century period for verse was the 1840s through the mid-1860s, although the concision of the shorter poems toward the end of the century does anticipate one aspect of modernist poetry and there was some tendency toward writing in more idiomatic rhythms, as I discuss later. The popularity of ballads as a model for poetry of authenticity and true feeling encouraged irregularities in rhythm and form during the antebellum and war-time periods.[11] Later in the century, it was not the syllabically irregular ballad – associated with ordinary lives and a humble speaker – but the more formal iambic pentameter, with its long tradition of epic, Shakespearean drama, and neoclassical commentary, that drove the preferred norm.

Criticism and reviews of the 1890s typically praised a poem's beauty, spiritual qualities, or elevation rather than the concision and formal originality or irregularity that characterize modernism. Following his collection of all reviews of Dickinson's poetry published in the 1890s, Willis Buckingham concludes that reading expectations for poetry "moved toward increased intimacy, mystery, and sacred personalism"; poetry readers expected a representation "at the farthest remove from rational explanation."[12] In 1893, D. Dorchester, Jr. asserts that "in poetry, the sensible is courted, that the idea may be married to a beautiful form and stir the feelings. The thought of the poet, like that of the philosopher, must be elevated and self-consistent, but does not, like his, become satisfied with the truth alone; ... it covets the beautiful."[13] Stedman writes of the "taste, charm, and not infrequent elevation" of the verse in "the second portion of this compilation"; its "force" is of "beauty and enlightenment."[14] Criticizing this assumption, Martha Shackford writes in 1913 that "tradition still animates many critics in the belief that real poetry must have exalted phraseology."[15] Such elevation and mystery were, in turn, typically conveyed through forms associated with the great poets or poems of the past – primarily iambic pentameter or long-lined ballad forms reminiscent of medieval verse.[16]

The association of poetry with effeminacy and the subsequent turn away from sentimentalism following the war also may have encouraged women in particular to write in a more formally measured vein and in longer lines. Poetry leaning too far in the direction of sentimental affect, especially that using short-lined beat-based forms, was belittled as lowbrow and feminine – most famously in Mark Twain's 1876 portrayal of Emmeline Grangerford, a poet who "didn't ever have to stop to think" before whipping off a bathetic morbid verse in 7676 meter and predictable rhyme. Ambitious female poets particularly felt the need to distance themselves from sentimental discourse, verbal excess, and pathos. In 1890, Louise Chandler Moulton was criticized by a female editor for, in effect, echoing too closely the pathos of sentimentality: Helen Clarke praised her "faculty of artistic expression" but regretted that her sonnets were all "in the same [morbid] key," "echo[ing] these woful strains."[17] Male and female poets were praised for writing with masculine force and style. As Clarke continues, "graceful, flowing diction and smooth rhythm everywhere abound" in the poetry of 1889, but "through its frequently unvirile expression our sense of fitness is rudely offended."[18] Carman writes in 1894 that "The true artist ... in these qualities of courage and hope must be distinctly the most manly of his fellows, and there is no more manly note in American letters to-day than that which rings through the lyrics" of Louise Guiney; "a single lyric like 'The Wild Ride,' has virility enough to furnish the ordinary minor poet with lyric passion ten times over."[19] "The Wild

Ride" is unrhymed and written in triplets with five beats per line – markedly different from the short-lined rhymed quatrains popularly associated with female poets.

While emotion remained central to poetry, its expression was increasingly dictated as poetry-appropriate, or not. In 1904, Oscar Firkins noted that "The poet's first duty is to reject all matter that is not beautiful," then classified "matter unavailable for poetry" into five divisions: "First, the repulsive . . . Second, the arid, comprising the plain, the homely . . . the technical, the general, and the abstract. . . Third, the humorous. Fourth, the utilitarian [and] . . . Fifth, the conventional."[20] Firkins' references to "the plain, the homely," and "the humorous" have direct implications for poetic form, although he does not mention them: poetry about the everyday is most apt to use plain language, and comic verse is particularly likely to be disruptive of conventional norms. The professionalization of literary study also encouraged poets to write in ways increasingly distinct from the sometimes raucous energy of comic or popular verse or song – typically written in 8-syllable or shorter lines.[21] Consequently, despite widespread condemnation of verse that was merely "correct" and praise for creative genius, originality was for the most part a lesser criterion for excellence than "beauty"; moreover, it was typically associated with thought rather than form. Originality of form was apt to be considered whimsical and associated with lack of seriousness, immaturity, or even crudity – categories associated in other contexts with the feminine and to which women were especially vulnerable. Dickinson's first editors, Thomas Wentworth Higginson and Mabel Loomis Todd, understood this fact and immediately threw up the white flag of form when publishing the first volume of her verse in 1890, admitting that it was open to criticism at the level of meter and rhyme and arguing instead for the appeal of her extraordinary astuteness and naturalness: as Higginson put it in his "Preface," the poems' "wholly original and profound insight . . . set in a seemingly whimsical or even rugged frame" will make the poems seem "torn up by the roots, with rain and dew and earth still clinging to them."[22] In "American Poetry of the Past Year," published in 1901, Clarke praises Josephine Peabody's "The Wingless Joy" for its "strength and originality," "striking both in form and subject-matter," but this dramatic monologue in blank verse contains no formal irregularities.[23] Formal irregularity was sometimes acknowledged as contributing to a verse's power, but it was rarely praised as such.

The criticism of the period distinguished the desired qualities in poetry from those desired for fiction primarily through the lack of reference to realism in verse.[24] Nonetheless, within the standards of increasingly elevated and long-lined verse, and despite the continuation of poeticized diction and syntax, poetry by women in the late nineteenth century does manifest experiments in its speech rhythms – a move commensurate with realism.[25] Both Dickinson and Sarah Piatt are well-known for the speech-like attributes of their idiomatic and dialogic poetry. There has been little attention, however, to ways that other female poets of this period also introduce effects of spoken syntax or rhythms within conventional verse forms. The rest of this essay will focus on relatively long-lined (and, in two cases, short) poems experimenting with rhythmic idiom written by women poets in the last half of the century.

A striking example of an imposed spoken syntax within conventional form occurs in Frances Harper's one experiment with a long-lined poem – "Moses: A Story of the Nile" (1869) – which was not anthologized during her lifetime, probably in part because of its length and in part because few poets of color were included in nineteenth-century anthologies. Often described as Miltonic, this poem is written in a very loose form of blank verse – almost as though Harper applied the rules of syllable substitution or omission common in ballads to this more precise meter. Harper's loosening of the expected metrical standards of blank verse in "Moses" may have enabled her turn in 1872 to the more fully conversational idiom of her three- and four-beat quatrains in the Aunt Chloe poems. Varying from eight to thirteen syllables and using extensive enjambment, Harper's lines in "Moses" undercut the stately measure assumed to be appropriate for both blank verse and epic. Such disruption occurs at points of emotional tension in her story. For example, as the Pharoah's daughter Charmian tells her adopted son Moses that "thou art / Doubly mine" because she has saved his life twice, Harper moves into indeterminate rhythms.[26] In a line of thirteen syllables, Charmian accuses Moses of rejecting her, and Moses responds with silence:

	syllables	beats
With rásh and cáreless hánd, thou dost thrúst asíde that lóve.	13	6
Thére was a páinful sílence, a sílence	10	4
So húshed and stíll that you míght have álmost	10	4
Héard the húrried bréathing of óne and the quíck	11	5
Thróbbing of the óther's héart: for Móses,	10	5
He was slów of spéech, but shé was éloqúent	11	5 or 6

	syllables	beats
With wórds of ténderněss and lóve, and had bréathed	11	5
Her fúll héart ínto her líps; but thére was	10	4 or 5
Fírmness in the yóung man's chóice, and he béat báck	11	5 or 6
The ópposítion of her líps with the cálm	11	5
Grándeur óf his wíll, and agáin he essáyed to spéak.	13	6

In these lines, it is the exception rather than the rule that a line follows an iambic pentameter rhythm, and at times the rhythm within the line is so irregular that it is hard to know which grammatically accented syllables to promote as taking metrical stress (e.g., with the sequences "her full heart into" and "he beat back"). The rhythms are not conversational, but the syntax is prosaic, and its idiomatic flow creates a tension with the expected verse rhythm. The phrase "a silence," for example, follows a syntactic break that prevents elision of the consecutive unaccented syllables ("silence, a silence") and the line ends prematurely with a falling rhythm, never reaching its expected fifth beat. The following line ends similarly, its meager four beats interrupting the expected interplay of stresses by interposing what is functionally a four-beat ballad line. The uneasiness of rhythmic patterns is extreme enough that one is tempted to call this a patch of free verse with lines hovering around a ten-syllable norm.

Harper might have avoided such disruption by altering a few words to allow fuller coincidence of syntax and blank-verse rhythms. For example, changing the syntactic order and a few words produces six lines of far more regular iambic pentameter than Harper's at the beginning of the passage quoted above:

	syllables	beats
Thére was a páinful sílence, húshed and stíll –	10	5
A sílence so you míght have álmost héard	10	5
The húrried bréathing of the óne and quíck	10	5
Thróbbing of the óther's héart: for Móses,	10	5
Hé was slów of spéech, but shé was éloqúent	11	6
With wórds of ténderněss and lóve, and bréathed	10	5

This slight rearrangement makes word rhythms and syntax coincide much more closely with blank-verse meter while maintaining the "throbbing" trochees of the fourth line and required eleven-syllable, six-beat following line to reinstate the iambic rhythm, effectively suggesting Charmian's strained effort to persuade her adopted son.

In other passages, Harper writes fully polished blank verse. Toward the end of Chapter I we read of Charmain: "With silent lips but aching heart she bowed / Her queenly head and let him pass, and he / Went forth to share the fortune of his race." Here Harper's skilled use of enjambment maintains every expectation of blank verse while also powerfully moving the narrative forward and suggesting the finality of Moses's decision, with its line-final emphases on "she bowed" and "and he / Went forth." A practiced public speaker and poet, Harper could not have constructed such disruptive rhythms accidentally. She is also unlikely to have been careless in a poem written on a theme so important to her and in her only departure from short-lined verse.[27] Mary Loeffelholz interprets Harper's post-war verse as anti-heroic, middle-brow, and anti-monumentalist; Harper, she argues, constructs an accessible space for African American letters.[28] Her foray into pentameter both supports this thesis and complicates it in that Harper's prosody is more difficult and irregular than one would expect in popular verse. Yet Harper's choice of unrhymed pentameter and its occasional roughness seem appropriate to the poem's tale. Moreover, the dramatic tensions created by her complex rhythms would be difficult to achieve in short-lined verse.

Although Emma Lazarus wrote some free verse, she wrote primarily in iambic pentameter or lines of eight syllables.[29] In 1890, Clarke and Charlotte Porter gave Lazarus as their single example of a female poet "with Emerson and Whitman in the front rank of genuinely original American writers," and in 1893 they published a lengthy laudatory essay on Lazarus by Mary M. Cohen.[30] Lazarus is also the only female poet Stedman praises in his introduction, where he calls her a "star," "the western beacon of her oriental race."[31] While Lazarus's work is now best known for its frank support of Jews and of immigrants to the United States, it is also notable for its idiomatic rhythms. Especially in her pentameter poems, Lazarus uses hyphenated noun phrases and combined monosyllables to create sequences of emphatic stress. The result is an almost syncopated rhythm playing across and within her metrically regular lines, resembling in mild form her contemporary Gerard Manley Hopkins' sprung rhythm.

"The New Year. Rosh-Hashanah, 5643" (1882), for example, begins with the line "Nót while the snów-shróud róund déad éarth is rólled," which contains a remarkable seven grammatical stresses within its ten syllables, stresses underlined by the chiastic assonance of *o ou ou o* (snow-shroud round . . . rolled).[32] The third stanza contains six instances of strong sequential stress:

Blow, Israel, the sacred cornet! Call
  Back to thy courts whatever faint heart throb
With thine ancestral blood, thy need craves all.
  The red, dark year is dead, the year just born
Leads on from anguish wrought by priest and mob,
        To what undreamed-of morn?

Such combinations ("faint heart throb . . . need craves all . . . red, dark year . . . year just born") dominate the stanza's rhythm without overthrowing the iambic norm. These consecutive stresses are particularly emphatic when crossing a syntactic break or line ending: "cornét! Cáll / Báck" and "yéar júst bórn / Léads" seem almost trumpet-like in calling forth the new "morn." In the following stanza this urgency is even more pointed:

For never yet, since on that holy height,
  The Temple's marble walls of white and green
Carved like the sea-waves, fell, and the world's light
  Went out in darkness, – never was the year
Greater with portent and with promise seen
        Than this eve now and here.

Here the verse fluctuates between lines of precisely patterned successions of unstressed and stressed grammatical rhythms and lines of loaded stress. The sequence "yet, since" in the stanza's first line, made more emphatic by the caesura, marks the tension of Lazarus's claim that 1882 "promise[s]" to be the most remarkable year for Judaism in centuries. The verse rhythms build to this climax. Lazarus's exclusive use in this stanza of two-syllable words with falling rhythms (never, holy, Temple's, marble, darkness, never, greater, portent, promise) while maintaining the rising metrical beat creates a powerful sense of movement. Lines three and four in particular promote the intensity of her claim that this is the year of greatest promise since the ancient's temple's cataclysmic destruction: "[the Temple] whíte and gréen / Cárved like | the séa- |wáves, féll, | and the | wórld's líght / Wént óut | in dárk |ness,–né |ver wás | the yéar / Gréater." The patterned sequence of stresses and tension of word boundaries crossing foot boundaries in these lines builds to the concluding "never," which in turn surprisingly leads to celebration of the current year ("never was the year / Greater than [this one]") rather than the anticipated "never again" lament. The turn on "never" is also emphasized through its unusual position, beginning after a mid-foot caesura and crossing another foot boundary. The falling rhythm of "never" heralds "Greater," "portent," and "promise" in the following line, all leading to the emphatically monosyllabic "this eve now and here." Mid-poem, we stand on the cusp of change, and its radical claim for the "morn" of Judaism's future in the United States is articulated as powerfully by the poem's rhythms as by its language. Lazarus fulfills so completely the conventions of iambic pentameter that one does not immediately notice how artfully she uses syntax and word rhythms to give a plain-spoken urgency to her lines.

Helen Hunt Jackson, like Lazarus, was highly praised in her day. Emerson describes her poems as having "rare merit of thought and expression," and Jackson is the only woman Higginson included in his 1880 *Short Studies of American Authors.*[33] In 1895, Mary J. Reid opines that "some half dozen of her poems," including "the famous sonnet on 'Thought,' will doubtless live as long as . . . [Christina Rossetti's] 'The Goblin Market.'"[34] In "Thought" (1870), Jackson uses the archaic "thee" and verb forms such as "art" or "dalliest," poetic spellings such as "stand'st" and "lay'st" (to ensure the reader's metrical pronunciation), and the unidiomatic exclamations "lo" and "Ah," but a markedly prosaic syntax:

O messenger, art thou the king, or I?
Thou dalliest outside the palace gate
Till on thine idle armor lie the late
And heavy dews: the morn's bright, scornful eye
Reminds thee; then, in subtle mockery,
Thou smilest at the window where I wait,
Who bade thee ride for life. In empty state
My days go on, while false hours prophesy
Thy quick return; at last, in sad despair,
I cease to bid thee, leave thee free as air;
When lo, thou stand'st before me glad and fleet,
And lay'st undreamed-of treasures at my feet.
Ah! messenger, thy royal blood to buy,
I am too poor. Thou art the king, not I.[35]

This sonnet contains more line-internal than line-end caesurae, or conclusions of clauses indicating a completed thought or turn in thought, marked by punctuation. Some of these endings even occur mid-foot, the most rhythmically disruptive spot for caesurae – for example, in line 5, where the line's second foot ("thee; then,") is broken by a semi-colon; or in line 9, where the comma in "thee, leave" marks the beginning of a new major clause. Especially given its medieval images and archaic diction, this sonnet has a strikingly unaffected rhythm. Jackson's enjambments artfully represent the element of uncontrollability and surprise in the relationship she depicts between will (the "I" of conscious ego) and "Thought." There is no element of disruption or awkwardness, but a powerful and vital mesh of subject, syntax, and the sonnet form. As with Harper's and Lazarus's poems, here the iambic pentameter allows a greater flexibility with complex rhythms and syntax than is easily achieved in short-lined forms while meeting expectations of poetry's elevated status.

As a final example of women's verse forms in the late nineteenth century as both adhering to long-lined meter and pushing toward a more syntactically or idiomatically defined rhythm, I turn to Louise Imogen Guiney, who was well-represented by all the later anthologists of my sample. In a twelve-page essay on Guiney's significance, Clarke and Porter summarize the poetry's value as including "a passion of beauty, in form and spirit; an intermingling of imagination and fancy in deft proportion ... [and] a poetic sureness of touch and phrase," describing one poem as "perfection in choice of rhythm."[36] Harriet Prescott Spofford writes of her in 1894 that "The warmth of genius everywhere suffuses her crystal clarity of line when at her best" and describes her verse as having "enormous power."[37] Bennett describes Guiney as "among the most significant women poets of the *fin de siecle* ... her subtle dependence on cadence (as opposed to the metronome) helped pave the way for free verse."[38] Indeed, Guiney writes in various beat-based and accentual syllabic rhythms, combining lines of four, six, eight, and ten or more syllables in unusual combinations as well as writing sonnets and other pentameter verse. "The Wild Ride" (1887), extolled by Carman for its virility, as previously noted, is a five-beat poem mixing iambs and anapests, and its lines frequently conclude with an unaccented syllable. The poem is also relatively short, and a refrain appears twice in its fifteen lines:

> I hear |in my heart, |I hear |in its om |inous pul |ses,
> All day,| on the road,| the hoofs |of invi |sible hor |ses;
> All night,| from their stalls,| the impor |tunate tramp |ing and neigh |ing. [39]

As this marking for (beat-based) foot boundaries indicates, in the refrain there is a pattern of successive 2- and then 3-syllable feet at least once within each line; the first foot of each line is iambic, although one might read both syllables as taking interpretive and grammatical stress, like a spondee. Similarly, lines of the verses begin with uncharacteristically strong phrases for a poem written primarily in anapests: "Let Cowards ... Straight, grim ... What odds? ... We spur ... We leap ... Thou leadest, O God!" The final stanza contains both emphatic line beginnings and the hyphenated phrases and sequence of monosyllables seen in Lazarus's verse:

> We spur |to a land |of no name, |out-rac |ing the storm-|wind;
> We leap |to the in |finite ark,| like the sparks |from the an |vil.
> Thou lead |est, O God!| All's well |with Thy troop |ers that fol |low.

Here Guiney uses an almost Anglo-Saxon verse rhythm, with its heavily stressed long lines and mid-line breaks, without disrupting the pulse already established in her earlier lines.

This poem represents the forms of women's verse becoming more popular by the 1890s: in its medieval images of knighthood, final religious turn, and use of a refrain; in its irregular, heavy-stressed but clearly beat-based rhythm; in its relatively long lines and short length; and in its combination of plain and elevated diction ("Thou leadest" yet "All's well . . . troopers"). Uncharacteristically, it does not rhyme, which contributes to its tone of forthrightness. And it anticipates some of Ezra Pound's and Marianne Moore's early medieval-themed, roughly metered poems.

Like their male peers, women writing poetry in the late nineteenth century attempt to balance the conservative cultural pressures pushing poetry toward greater elitism (hence longer-lined, rhyming forms) and the socio-economic pressures pushing all cultural aesthetics toward greater realism and plainness (perhaps, interestingly, also pushing verse toward longer-lined forms). The meter, rhymes, and renewed enthusiasm for archaic diction and poeticisms can make such poetry seem circumscribed by norms. Some women, however, seem to have found in longer-lined forms a greater flexibility to use more idiomatic rhythmic patterns and syntax than that facilitated by the previously more popular short-lined quatrain. Regardless of topic and diction, their use of such rhythmic variation contributes to the move during these decades toward a more idiomatic and modern verse.

Notes

1. To take a recent example, Elizabeth Renker analyzes labor poetry as different from elitist in subject matter, not form, in "The 'Twilight of the Poets' in the Era of American Realism," *Cambridge Companion to Nineteenth-Century American Poetry*, Kerry Larson (ed.), (Cambridge: Cambridge University Press, 2012), 135–156. John Timberman Newcomb also focuses primarily on subject matter and ideology in *Would Poetry Disappear: American Verse and the Crisis of Modernity* (Ohio State University Press, 2004).

2. Christopher Hager and Cody Marrs, "Against 1865: Reperiodizing the Nineteenth Century," *J19: The Journal of Nineteenth-Century Americanists* 1 (2013): 259–284.
3. Ralph Waldo Emerson (ed.), *Parnassus: An Anthology of Poetry* (Boston: Houghton, Osgood and Co., 1874); Edmund C. Stedman (ed.), *An American Anthology, 1797–1900* (Houghton Mifflin, 1900); Bliss Carman (ed.), *American Verse* (New York: Albert and Charles Boni, Oxford University Press, 1927); John Hollander (ed.), *American Poetry: The Nineteenth Century* (New York: Library of America, 1993); Paula Bernat Bennett (ed.), *Nineteenth-Century American Women Poets* (Malden and Oxford: Wiley-Blackwell, 1998).
4. A survey of verse published across these decades in a single periodical, or a variety of periodicals, might well complicate this portrait. In providing this analysis, I hope further to open, not close, a conversation about shifts in verse form as they relate to an understanding of the century's changing poetic practices. A more thorough analysis of this subject would compare male and female poets' formal choices.
5. By ballad meter, I mean beat-based meter, combining iambs and anapests in irregular sequence. It is the irregular inclusion of either one- or two-syllable units to fill an unaccented metrical slot that distinguishes this verse; where such substitution is rare I consider the verse to be accentual syllabic. Long meter (8-syllable lines) was the most popular beat-based post-war form, whereas earlier in the century shorter lined forms were used more frequently: 8686, 6686, 76s, 64s, and so on.
6. I also looked at John J. Piatt, *The Union of American Poetry and Art: A Choice Collection of Poems by American Poets* (Cincinnati: W. E. Dibble & Co., 1882), but his selections were not in sync with those of the other anthologists. Piatt represents the thirty-one poets writing primarily in the late 1860s and '70s and the thirty-seven earlier poets with approximately the same number of pentameter poems.
7. Pentameter stanzas including an occasional 6-syllable line were popular: for example, Elizabeth Pullen's "The Sea-Weed," Alice Brown's "Cloistered," and Charlotte Stetson (Gilman)'s "The Beds of Fleur-de-Lys"; poems by Harriet Monroe include poems in 6464 (essentially a pentameter couplet), 10–6–10–6, 11–4–11–4, and 14s. These were all typical in the 1890s.
8. Hollander, *American Poetry: The Nineteenth Century* includes no iambic pentameter poems for the male poets of the 1840s through mid-1860s and approximately 58 percent for those publishing in the second half of the century – including a few poems that function as pentameter but were not written precisely in this form.
9. Paula Bernat Bennett, *Poets in the Public Sphere: The Emancipatory Project of American Women's Poetry, 1800–1900* (Princeton: Princeton University Press, 2003), 190–192.
10. In particular, see Mary Louise Kete, "The Reception of Nineteenth-Century American Poetry," *Cambridge Companion to Nineteenth-Century American*

Poetry, Kerry Larson (ed.), (Cambridge: Cambridge University Press, 2012), 15–35. In Bennett, *Poets in the Public Sphere*, she associates several female poets of the 1890s as "imagist forerunners" or "early modernist" (xliii). In Karen Kilcup, "Scarlet Experiments: Dickinson's New English and the Critics," *Emily Dickinson Journal* 24.1 (2015): 22–51, Kilcup agrees with this characterization, noting that the Dickinson publications of the 1890s "coincided with – and advanced – increased openness to innovation" (43).

11. Such generalization is relative. The majority of published verse throughout the century was in regular metrical forms.
12. Willis Buckingham, "Poetry Readers and Reading in the 1890s: Emily Dickinson's First Reception," *Readers in History: Nineteenth-Century American Literature and the Contexts of Response*, James L. Machor (ed.), (Baltimore: Johns Hopkins University Press, 1992), 164–179, 175, 173.
13. D. Dorchester, Jr., "The Nature of Poetic Expression," *Poet-Lore* 5 (1893): 81–90, 85.
14. Stedman, *An American Anthology*, 20.
15. Martha Shackford, "Emily Dickinson's Poetry," *Atlantic Monthly* 11.1 (1913): 93–97, 96.
16. See Newcomb, *Would Poetry Disappear*, 120–122, on late-nineteenth-century insistence on standard forms and perfect rhymes except in the work of already-famous poets such as Shakespeare and Robert Browning.
17. Helen Clarke, "Recent American Poetry," *Poet-Lore* 2 (1890): 427–435, 430.
18. Ibid., 428. In *An American Anthology*, Stedman also writes that "in a time half seriously styled 'the woman's age,' . . . [t]he work of their brother poets is not emasculate, and will not be while grace and tenderness fail to make men cowards, and beauty remains the flower of strength" (23).
19. Carman, "Louise Imogen Guiney," *Chap-book* 2.1 (15 November 1894). www.canadianpoetry.ca/confederation/Bliss%20Carman/13.htm, n.p. [accessed September, 22, 2014]. See also Helen Tracy Porter, "Characteristics of the Work of Louise Imogen Guiney," *Poet-Lore* 13 (1902): 287–299; 292, where Clarke and Porter (writing under the joint pseudonym "Helen Tracy Porter") also describe Guiney's lines as having "a virile, objective treatment."
20. Oscar Firkins, "Poetry and Prose in Life and Art," *Poet-Lore* 15 (1904): 77–87, 77–79.
21. On poetry as distinct from song in the 1880s and 1890s, see Newcomb, *Would Poetry Disappear*, 91–102; on the loose boundaries between poetry and song in the antebellum and war periods, see Faith Barrett, *To Fight Aloud is Very Brave: American Poetry and the Civil War* (University of Massachusetts Press, 2012); on literary professionalization, see Stedman, *An American Anthology*, 22, and Mary Loeffelholz, *From School to Salon: Reading Nineteenth-Century American Women's Poetry* (Princeton University Press, 2004).
22. Thomas Wentworth Higginson, "Preface," *Poems by Emily Dickinson* (Boston: Roberts Brothers, 1890), iii–vi; v.
23. Helen Clarke, "American Poetry of the Past Year," *Poet-Lore* 13 (1901), 123–140; 123.

24. In Willis Buckingham's *Emily Dickinson's Reception in the 1890s: A Documentary History* (Pittsburgh: University of Pittsburgh Press, 1989), such reference occurs only three times (63, 258, 524).
25. By poeticisms I mean archaic usage such as "thee/thou," abbreviations such as "tho'" or "'tis," stylized exclamations, such as "lo" and "alas," and frequent use of inverted syntax.
26. Frances Ellen Watkins Harper, "Moses: A Story of the Nile," *A Brighter Coming Day: A Frances Ellen Watkins Harper Reader*, Frances Smith Foster (ed.), (New York: The Feminist Press, 1990), 138–165.
27. "Moses" is the only poem in *Brighter Coming Day* written in lines longer than four beats.
28. Loeffelholz, *From School to Salon*, 120.
29. Her *Selected Poems* includes three translations in free verse; one translated poem and one drama (*The Dance to Death*) in blank verse with occasional irregularities such as those in Harper's "Moses"; and one free verse poem, the sequence "By the Waters of Babylon: Little Poems in Prose." Stedman represents Lazarus by four pentameter poems (two are sonnets) and one in 8s. Carman includes two poems in 8s. Bennett's anthology includes Lazarus poems in pentameter, in 8686, a free-verse translation, and an excerpt from "By The Waters of Babylon." All six of Hollander's inclusions are in pentameter.
30. Helen Clarke and Charlotte Porter, "Notes and News," *Poet-Lore* 2 (1890): 666–668, 668. Mary M. Cohen, "Emma Lazarus: Woman; Poet; Patriot," *Poet Lore* (1893): 320–331.
31. Stedman, *An American Anthology*, 21.
32. Lazarus, "The New Year. Rosh-Hashanah, 5463," *Selected Poems and Other Writings*, Gregory Eiselein (ed.), (Orchard Park: Broadview Press, 1985), 175.
33. Emerson (ed.), *Parnassus*, x. Higginson adds Louisa May Alcott to his *Short Studies of American Authors* (Boston: Lea and Shepard, 1880) in its 1888 edition, but Jackson remains the only female poet.
34. Mary J. Reid, "Julia Dorr and Some of Her Poet Contemporaries," *Midland Monthly* 3 (1895): 499–507; 442.
35. Emerson (ed.), *Parnassus*, 91.
36. Helen Tracy Porter, "Characteristics of the Work," 295, 289.
37. Harriet Prescott Spofford, "Louise Imogen Guiney," *Harper's Bazaar* 27.42 (October 1894), 836.
38. Bennett, *Nineteenth-Century American Women Poets*, 317, 318.
39. Guiney, The Wild Ride, *The White Sail and Other Poems* (Boston: Ticknor and Company, 1887), 126–127.

CHAPTER 19

Braided Relations: Toward a History of Nineteenth-Century American Indian Women's Poetry

Robert Dale Parker

Perhaps the first thing that needs saying about nineteenth-century poetry by American Indian women from within the boundaries of what is now the United States is both the least and the most interesting thing to say: that it is there. Except for the relatively recent and still-emerging discussions of the poetry (and other writings) of Jane Johnston Schoolcraft, Olivia Ward Bush, and Ann Plato, poetry by nineteenth-century American Indian women has received almost no scholarly attention and almost never shows up in the classroom.[1] This essay identifies all the known poems by nineteenth-century American Indian women and reads them both as individual poems and collectively, as a related group of poems.

I know of thirteen American Indian women who wrote poems in the nineteenth century. Here they are chronologically, with "B" indicating a boarding-school student and "P" indicating a pseudonymous poet:

Jane Johnston Schoolcraft, Ojibwe, approximately 50 poems, 1815–1840
Ann Plato, Long Island or Southern New England Algonquian, 20 poems, 1840–41
Corrinne, Cherokee, "Our Wreath of Rose Buds," 1854, B, P
Lily Lee, Cherokee, "Literary Day Among the Birds," 1855, B, P
Lelia, Cherokee, "We have faults, to be sure," 1855, B, P
Emma Lowrey Williams, Cherokee, "Life," 1855, B
Wenonah, Cherokee, "Thanksgiving," 1886, P
Elsie Fuller, Omaha, "A New Citizen," 1887, B
Olivia Ward Bush, Montaukett, 14 poems, 1890–1900 (and more poems later)
Cora Snyder, Seneca, "The Frequent Showers of April," 1895, B
Melinda Metoxen, Oneida, "Iceland," 1896, B
Zitkala-Ša/Gertrude Simmons, Sioux, "Ballad" and "Iris of Life," 1897–1898 (and several poems about 20 years later)
Mabel Washbourne Anderson, Cherokee, "Nowita, the Sweet Singer," 1900[2]

From the array of poets and poems on this list, which presumably does not represent all the poems that were written, several patterns emerge. The most prolific poets – Schoolcraft, Plato, and Bush – open and close this historical sequence. Beyond those three poets, the record includes eleven poems by ten different women, six of them Cherokees and six of them boarding-school students at the time of their writing. At least five of the six Cherokees attended the Cherokee Female Seminary, either at the time of writing or earlier. And four poems, all by Cherokees, including three of the boarding-school poems, are pseudonymous (assuming that first names without family names are pseudonyms).

While this may seem like a fairly large number of poets and poems for an area that literary history has mostly ignored, most Indian women poets in the nineteenth century did not have access to each other's poetry. Schoolcraft's poetry was not published in her lifetime, and only barely and obscurely published in the decades after her death. The early Cherokee poets who published in *Cherokee Rose Buds*, their school magazine, would have read each other's poems, but there could not have been many copies of the *Rose Buds* for other poets to read. The other poets published mostly in local newspapers and school outlets. No American Indian woman that we know of published a full-length book of poetry in the nineteenth century – but two came close. Ann Plato published a small volume of essays and poems in Connecticut in 1841, but her book was erased from Native literary history because readers did not recognize her as Indian. Olivia Ward Bush published *Original Poems* in Rhode Island in 1899, a book (or pamphlet) with ten poems in nineteen pages and a small enough print run that only three copies survive in catalogued libraries. But for the most part, *Original Poems*, like Plato's book, presented its author as African American and not as Native.

Although the various poets mostly did not read or even know about each other, we may still gain from reading their work together. This essay on literary history seeks to constellate patterns of congruence across poems that more traditional literary history might render as separate. Such connections live outside the minds of the poets who produced the poems. A project like this could converge with what has recently come to be called *distant* or *surface reading*, but I do not oppose distant or surface reading to interpretive, close, or deep reading. Instead, I seek to braid a reading of the poems together with a reading of what Ojibwe/Anishinaabe theorist and literary writer Gerald Vizenor has called *survivance*.[3] Building on these contexts, I will propose connections and analogies between or among:

Plato and Bush, from the beginning and end of the sequence; the boarding-school poets; the Cherokee poets; and, finally, Schoolcraft and Anderson, from the beginning and end of the sequence again. Thus, I set out to privilege relations across the group, relations both in the sense of intertextuality and in the sense of the American Indian expression "all our relations" – that is to say, the sense of cultural and historical connection.

Ron Welburn has brilliantly argued that Plato, whose slender volume appeared when she was 17–21 years old, was Indian as well as African American, from one or more of the Algonquian peoples of the Long Island Sound Basin, most likely eastern Long Island. Welburn shows that the peoples from eastern Long Island, including the Montaukett, Shinnecock, Yennicock, and Corchaug nations, who often had Black and Indian mixed heritages, generated a diaspora across Southern New England, including Hartford, where Plato (and other Black and Indian people named Plato) lived when we have records of her. Plato rarely addresses politics or race, but her book includes one poem about emancipation (a poem that Welburn reads as distant and unimpassioned) and a more emotionally intense, first-person poem titled "The Natives of America." There, a daughter asks her father to "Tell me a story," and he responds in "words of native tone" that tell "how my Indian fathers dwelt, / And, of sore oppression felt; / And how they mourned a land serene." While the interest in storytelling fits well with Native traditions, Welburn notes that it is not exclusive to Native traditions. But the focus on family storytelling as a repository and sustainer of Native history seems much more centrally Native, and distinctively so in New England, where people survived by keeping invisible, as Indians, to non-Indians, minimizing the public and print performance of Native life, and thus putting a premium on the oral and familial transmission of identity and heritage.[4] The father's story focuses on joined commitments to history and land, which for many Native peoples fuse together, especially in oral history.

From the perspective of our own time, written nineteenth-century Native characterizations of Native history often seem corrupted by the dominant culture's mythologies, even when they also resist those mythologies. In that vein, Plato's poem, like many other Native poems from before the 1960s Red Power resurgence, can seem complicit with the myth of the vanishing Indian, preoccupied with its own mournfulness and pain, and given to idealizing the pre-contact past and reducing the present to victimization. When such patterns show up in indigenous writing – as they do in several of Schoolcraft's poems, in many poems by nineteenth-century Indian men, and in such later but still early Native novels as John Joseph

Mathews' *Sundown* (1934) and D'Arcy McNickle's *The Surrounded* (1936) – they can offer a form of cultural assertion and agency that is hard for our own age to see. Such cultural claims take hold all the more when embedded, as in Plato's poem, in an homage to and act of familial transition across generations and relations. Thus, when Plato idealizes precontact history, writing such lines as "We all were then as in one band, / We join'd and took each others hand," she misrepresents the past in one sense, but in another sense she highlights a genuine contrast between precontact Native life and post-contact war, disease, dispossession, and genocide. Even when she apologizes for traditional architecture – "Our houses were of sticks compos'd; / No matter, – for they us enclos'd" – her defensiveness speaks back to colonialist condescension and insists on angles of thought that run outside what the colonizing culture takes for granted as superior. In such ways, while Plato can seem so swept up into colonialist assumptions that she denies the history of Native agriculture ("Our food was such as roam'd that time"), she also resists those same assumptions later in the poem: "strangers destroy'd / The fields which were by us enjoy'd." After all, by the time Plato wrote this poem, the Algonquian peoples of Long Island and Southern New England had a long, fiercely contested history of whites driving them off their agricultural lands.[5]

From almost every direction – storytelling, architecture, agriculture, war – the history comes back to land. Recounting the history of dispossession, the father says "We sold, then some bought lands, / We altogether moved in foreign hands. Wars ensued." Since the "we" are moving from white-controlled territory, the foreign hands seem to be the hands of other Indian peoples, an implication that depends on recognition of Native sovereignty. Still more, it depends on the Native sovereignties (plural) of diverse Native nations and thus seems unlikely to be heard or recognized by non-Indian readers, which in turn suggests an Indian-specific language and frame of reference for the poem. In these ways, Plato's poem recognizes the multiplicity of Indianness. It acknowledges that Indians in Southern New England and Long Island often had to sell their land, and that they sometimes bought land from other Indians. They found themselves displaced not only among non-Indian settlers, but also among other Indian peoples.

The provocatively metonymic bodily intimacy of the unexpected rhyme between *lands* and *hands* calls on touch to compress the corporeal into the earthly, into the source of food, shelter, and national continuity. Such a bond between body and earth has fractured, except for the possibility of what transgenerational memory and storytelling can recover and sustain.

Memory and storytelling sustain the bond between body and land orally, in the family, or through a surreptitious rising to the surface in poetry masked by the distancing persona of an Indian other. When readers see Plato as an African American trying to voice what a hypothetical Indian other might think, as trying out a merely speculative hypothesis, they assume that all African Americans share a singular identity, at least in the sense that no African Americans can also be Indian. Such an assumption makes invisible the possibility that when Plato writes in a first-person Indian voice, she writes as herself, trying to archive her own father's story.

We have a far larger record for Bush than for Plato, a record that, as Bernice F. Guillaume notes, shows lifelong identifications with and recognition by both African American and American Indian communities.[6] Neither Bush nor Plato is less of either identity because she is also the other identity. For the worlds they lived in, and for many people before them and after them, living as both is part of living as either, so that to diminish either side of their identification is also to diminish the other side. We might argue that by acknowledging both identities Bush takes her simultaneous blackness and Indianness, which others see as a contradiction, and rewrites it as non-contradictory. Still, depending on the context, she sometimes focuses more on one or the other identity. While her readiness to vary her identifications may go against expected practice, which pressures people to define themselves by one identity only, it might also help define the conditions of living with two identities that have different cultural histories.

Bush's larger body of surviving poems, even more than Plato's, rings with poignant variations that we might read, or misread, as internal contradictions. She opens her 1899 pamphlet with a dedication "TO THE PEOPLE OF MY RACE,/THE AFRO-AMERICANS," and with a poem called "Morning on Shinnecock." Readers may pass by "Shinnecock" as just another dead metaphor in the settler-colonial use of indigenous place names, names that grow so familiar that their Indian meanings no longer get heard. Such readers will not recognize that "Shinnecock" refers to a specific Native community that overlapped culturally, genealogically, and politically with Bush's Montaukett world.

In 1890, Bush published a broadside poem, "On the Long Island Indian," which she left out of her 1899, more African-American-centered pamphlet. But she served as the Montauk tribal historian and reprinted the poem in the 1916 Montauk annual report.[7] "On the Long Island Indian" is rife with competing characterizations of Indians. It reviews a romanticized history of Long Island Indians that includes such oversimplifications as "warlike," "noble," and "beauteous," and then recounts how "a paler nation . . . / Robbed him of his native right," leaving "a scattered remnant" that "Now remains" but can "find no home, / Here and there in weary exile." The final words lament that "today a mighty people / Sleep within the silent grave." These lines describe Long Island Indians as warlike but peace-loving, "Savage" and "crude" but also wise and lawmaking, remaining "Now" while sleeping in death. Bush shows pride in the poem by publishing it as a broadside, but then indicates a reluctance to let it blur the African American specificity of her pamphlet of poems. Meanwhile, she opens the pamphlet with "Morning on Shinnecock," visible as Native to those who recognize "Shinnecock" as the name of a Native community. She also continues to assert her Native poetic vision by reprinting both poems in the later annual report issued for fellow tribal members.

The 1899 pamphlet also includes a poem called "Crispus Attucks," which never acknowledges that Attucks was Indian as well as African American. Though the key historical work describing Attucks as both African American and Indian appeared a generation earlier, in 1872, he remained an African American icon, rarely recognized as Indian, and so Bush may not have known that, like her, he was both Indian and African American.[8] On the other hand, as a devotee of Indian history, she may well have known and may have chosen to mask his Indianness for her more African-American-centered pamphlet. But I see no hint in the poem that might parallel the hint of Indianness in the title of "Morning on Shinnecock." The poem seems to represent Attucks as exclusively African American:

> A Negro's blood was flowing free.
> His sable hand was foremost
> To strike the blow for liberty.
>
> . . .
>
> Naught but a slave was Attucks.

And yet, in a context where disguising New England Native identity was often a strategy for helping that identity to survive, we cannot help wondering. The point is not to figure out what Bush really thought about Attucks' identity or what she was really trying to do in her poems. Instead, the point is to see how when Bush writes about Attucks without showing that he was Indian, or when she feels a need to mask that knowledge, her poem – beyond anything she may have known or thought personally – offers a metaphor for the ongoing pressure to render New England Natives as invisible.

By calling attention to this metaphor, I am drawing a line – albeit not a straight line – from Plato to Bush, a line that circles the history of New England Native survivance before and after Plato and Bush and thus portrays a set of conditions that color Native New England public creative expression, including public poetry. Plato and Bush were the two most prolific nineteenth-century American Indian poets from New England and the Long Island Basin, and the only known nineteenth-century American Indian women poets from their region. Both were Black as well as Indian, and both were circumspect about their Indianness in their poems. We can see their poetry, then, and the strategies available for reading it, as caught up, perhaps unfairly, in a dialogue between the possibility of living as Black and Indian without diminishing either identity, and the pressure to make any one person's simultaneous blackness and Indianness invisible.

By comparison, although Schoolcraft was both Irish American and American Indian, the simplifying pressures of cultural clichés have urged us to see Schoolcraft as primarily Indian. Just the opposite holds for Plato and Bush, whose blackness had the effect, for their readers, of overwhelming their Indianness. These examples do not allow us to isolate one variable. Instead, they blur two variables together: region (Southern New England and Long Island, compared to Schoolcraft's Northern Michigan) and race or ethnicity (African American, compared to Schoolcraft's Irish). Nevertheless, this constellation of examples suggests that Indianness trumps Euro-Americanness, following the ideological dictates of hypodescent, which make the perception of non-white ancestry overrule any perception of white ancestry. It also suggests that African Americanness trumps Indianness, because the ideology of hypodescent paints blackness as even more defining than Indianness. In these contexts of cultural expectations and pressures, the analogy between Plato and Bush yields its coincidences as signs of a pressure to silence New England Native and Native women's expression, visible in the meagerness of response to their poems, and in the similarly constrained and calculated expression of the poems themselves.

With the wide gap in years between some of the poets, and the limited circulation of their poetry, Plato and Bush would not have read or been read by the Cherokee or boarding-school poets. But since three of the four Cherokee boarding-school poets – Corrinne, Lily Lee, and Lelia – published in the same school magazine in 1854–1855, they surely read each other and were read by their fellow student-poet, Emma Lowrey Williams (who could even have written one of their poems). Their magazine could also have been read by, or at least heard of by, the later nineteenth-century Cherokee poets, Wenonah and Mabel Washbourne Anderson. We might also find connections between the Cherokee boarding-school poems and the other boarding-school poems.

Student poets may have felt constrained, politically, by what their teachers allowed them to say, though they may also have internalized those constraints. Only one or two boarding-school poems by girls seem especially weighted politically, most notably Elsie Fuller's response to the Dawes Act of 1887. The Dawes Act, named after its sponsor, Senator Henry Dawes, called for redistributing communally owned Native lands by "allotting" parcels of land to individual Indians and selling "surplus," unallotted lands. The individual owners could, in turn, sell their land, and they often had to sell in order to pay taxes. The Dawes Act devastated Indian sovereignty by obliterating Indian jurisdiction, ending communal land ownership, and massively transferring Indian lands to whites. At the same time, its focus on individuality led many white "friends of the Indian," and not a few Indians who saw themselves as "progressives," to support allotment. In that context, the 16- or 17-year-old Fuller (Omaha) published the following poem in an 1887 publication of her boarding school, the Hampton Institute:

> Now I am a citizen!
> They've given us new laws,
> Just as were made
> By Senator Dawes.
>
> We need not live on rations,
> Why? there is no cause,
> For "Indians are citizens,"
> Said Senator Dawes.
>
> Just give us a chance,
> We never will pause.
> Till we are good citizens
> Like Senator Dawes.
>
> Now we are citizens,
> We all give him applause –
> So three cheers, my friends,
> For Senator Dawes!

It is hard to tell whether Fuller genuinely thanks Senator Dawes for disavowing treaty obligations and destroying Indian sovereignty and communal land ownership, or, dripping with sarcasm and cleverly defying the views of her school newspaper, scorns Dawes and everything that he and the conquering government that he represents have foisted on Indian peoples. As with Bush's "Crispus Attucks," the point is not to figure out what Fuller really thought – which even she might not entirely have known. Instead, the point is to observe how a single poet or poem can occupy multiple positions at the same time amidst the combined languages of political and poetic debate and student subjection, especially the subjection of many Indian boarding-school students, who were often forcibly taken from their homes, families, peoples, and lands. As readers, then, we can sometimes do better by mapping a poem's indeterminacy than by shrinking it into a single, settled meaning. While the possibility that Fuller saw her own poem as sarcastic may seem far-fetched, it also seems risky to underestimate students' capacity for clever cynicism, especially when pointed at the teachers and schools that hold authority over them. Nor are obsequiousness and cynicism necessarily mutually exclusive. For such a poem, any interpretation will risk reducing it to too few readings or expanding it to too many readings. In such cases, there is no risk-free reading, just as there may have been no risk-free writing.

We might face a similar impasse in interpreting a poem by Melinda Metoxen, a student at Carlisle, the most famous federal boarding school. Metoxen wrote her poem in the voice of a visitor from Iceland. The visitor interrupts her own cheerful description of Iceland to speak directly to Carlisle students, "here" at their school, in the commanding second-person:

> You should e'er remember here,
> Iceland's voyageurs, so bold,
> First discovered, in days drear,
> America, – so we're told.

Much as we must recognize the risk of reading too confidently through the eyes of a later age, it is hard to see these lines as sarcasm-free, and therefore hard to see them as entirely compliant with the expectations of Carlisle authorities. As an Oneida from Wisconsin, Metoxen would have had contact with other Wisconsin Indians. Their families lived in the region before the Oneida moved there from New York State in the 1820s and 1830s, and had close ties to the western Great Lakes fur trade, a shaping force in the local culture from the late seventeenth century to the early nineteenth century. In that setting, the word "voyageurs" (especially with the *u*) suggests the French voyageurs of the fur trade, who left a vexed heritage. They fathered many children with Indian women, and they also passed along a cultural legacy, and so, culturally and often genetically, they were among the ancestors of most of the region's Indians. But when Metoxen calls Leif Erikson and his crew "voyageurs," she also ties them to the voyageurs' history as intruders. Whether or not Metoxen thought about her spelling, the force of the word sharpens her seemingly sarcastic resistance to the idea that either Erikson or Columbus discovered America, an idea that masks conquest and genocide under a metonymy of heroism and adventure.[9]

The Cherokee Female Seminary (1851–1909), like the Cherokee Male Seminary, differed from boarding schools such as Hampton (founded in 1868) and Carlisle (1879–1918). It was not free from overvaluing the wider, assimilating culture, but as a Cherokee school – rather than a federal school such as Carlisle or a missionary school such as Hampton – it was far more respectful of Indian peoples and concerns. In the established Cherokee tradition of literacy and school education, it also provided a far better education.[10]

The three pseudonymous poems from the *Cherokee Rose Buds* mix demure modesty, such as we might expect from properly schooled girls, with understated assertion, such as what later feminist and post-Red Power readers might hope to find. In an essay titled "Critics and Criticism," Lelia laments that "no writer can put his thoughts before the public, but what his work is pounced upon by some merciless *critic*, who takes delight in bringing out, not the beauties of a piece, but its defects.... Even our poor little *Rose Bud* cannot escape, but has to receive its full share of criticism" from readers who call the contributions "copied," complain about a "slight grammatical blunder," or complain that they strive too hard for "sublimity" and "the upper regions." In response, Lelia writes a modest quatrain about modesty into her prose lament:

> We have faults, to be sure,
> We very well know it;
> We don't expect to vie
> With proser and poet.
> [That *poetry* was not stolen from anyone.]

In the same essay and lines where she claims not "to vie / With proser and poet," she winks at us poetically to vie with them nevertheless.

In "Literary Day Among the Birds," Lily Lee describes how one spring day the "Bird Nation" assembles for "a literary feast, / Where only Birds were invited guests." The birds "from every tree in the land" include (as the poem renders their names) Mrs. DOVE, Mr. CANARY, the MARTINS, and

Mr. Woodpecker. Their voices "United," they sing "a scientific song" and then listen to the orations of Squire RAVEN, Master WHIP-POOR-WILL, "Eight pretty green Parrots," Mr. Quail, and Sir Blackbird. With its sense of a distinct nation and a comfortable division of labor (with no hint of the slavery still continuing among Cherokees), the poem nudges against the possibility of a national allegory of the Cherokee Nation, itself made, like any nation, of many alliances among smaller groups. It honors the collective action of literary expression and reception, including their capacity to bring different groups together without eroding individual histories, even if at the cost of denying the Cherokee status of enslaved Blacks, repressing a debate over Black Cherokees that continues to the present day.[11]

The national pride of these poems, while mixed with modesty, looms more largely and blends with feminine self-awareness in Corrinne's lyrical "Our Wreath of Rose Buds," which opens the first issue of the *Cherokee Rose Buds* by proclaiming that "our simple wreath" of flowers

> is twined
> From the garden of the mind;
> Where bright thoughts like rivers flow
> And ideas like roses grow.

Despite faults and blemishes, "Their petals fair will soon unclose, / And every bud become – a Rose." The Female Seminary is "our *garden* fair, / And *we*, the *flowers* planted there."

> And o'er our home such beauty throw
> In future years – that all may see
> Loveliest of lands, – the Cherokee.

With Corrinne and her readers living on newly Cherokee land, so soon after forced removal from their homelands in the Southeast, the vulnerable status of Cherokee sovereignty and nationality merges with the vulnerable status of young Cherokee women whose intellectuality, mindfulness, cultivation, and domestic talents may all look suspect to the critics resented by Lelia. They may even look suspect to Cherokees, including Seminary students and their families, who, under the pressures of a partly colonialist education, may internalize the skepticism of outsiders. The metaphor of roses responds by bringing together the cultivation of manner and mind with the cultivation of femininity and Cherokee land. The last lines proclaim the domestic spaces of home and school as workshops where young women's aesthetic imagination can help uphold national and feminine pride.

Mabel Washbourne Anderson graduated from the Cherokee Female Seminary in 1883, and her long narrative poem "Nowita, the Sweet Singer" (published in 1900 in the *Indian Chieftain*, an Indian Territory newspaper) tells the story of a gullible Female Seminary student courted by a white teacher from the Male Seminary. Here are the opening lines:

> Should you ask me whence this story,
> Whence this romance and tradition
> Of the sad-eyed Indian maiden,
> Of Nowita, the sweet singer,
> I should answer, I should tell you
> Of a pale and handsome stranger
> Teaching at an Indian college
> In the village of Tahlequah
> At the time that you shall hear of;
> I should speak up, I should tell you:
> How this fair and fickle stranger
> Trifled with this child of nature.

Eventually, the teacher abandons Nowita, leaving her heartbroken and "wedded" only to "mem'ry." By contrast, Zitkala-Ša's nearly contemporaneous "Ballad" tells of a romance between an Indian man and an Indian woman, Winona, which eventually ends in a happy reunion. Much more politically, Anderson draws an analogy between the teacher's abuse of Nowita and the federal government's theft of Cherokee lands.

With clichéd wit, the poem's prose prologue introduces the teacher's sweetheart waiting at home as "the accusing memory of a pair of blue eyes among the green mountains of New Hampshire." But we might see the cliché as free indirect discourse, for its patronizing metonymy evokes not only the exterior narrator's description, but also the teacher's reductive memory. His fear of accusation shows his recognition of guilt. He defends against the guilt by shrinking his deserted white lover to parts of her body and, from his safe distance, implicitly chuckling at his wit with self-satisfied superiority. But the guilt for betraying his faraway sweetheart displaces his guilt for betraying Nowita. The similarity between the two women's positions implies an unrealized potential for cross-racial female solidarity, making the analogy between the abusive teacher and the abusive federal government suggest a conflict between genders as well as a conflict between whites and Indians.

When the teacher tells Nowita "I have come to know your people, / Learn your language, customs, habits, / Learn your legends and traditions," his insincere, opportunistic appropriation treats indigenous culture as trivial, as a plaything that he abusively trades on to make himself attractive to Nowita. Nowita puts her parents' and grandparents' distrust of her lover in the context of prejudice against whites. But in this poem, that is not a bad prejudice, because whites have driven the Cherokees from their lands and may yet drive them again from their new lands. Nowita's freedom from that prejudice comes across as naïve rather than humane.

As a scholar of Cherokee history who would later publish a biography of Stand Watie, the famous Cherokee Confederate brigadier general and her distant cousin, Anderson may have seen the *Cherokee Rose Buds* poems. As an admiring niece of John Rollin Ridge/Yellow Bird, a major Cherokee poet, she would also have taken note of Cherokee poetry.[12] Whether she read the *Rose Buds* poems or not, she returned her poem and its melancholy heroine to the scene of their writing. In that way, "Nowita" pays homage to some of the first known poems by American Indian women. Moreover, Anderson's poem also harks back to Schoolcraft, the first-known American Indian woman to write poetry, even though Anderson would not have read Schoolcraft's poems. For "Nowita" repeats a common story of white men abandoning Indian women, which was also the topic of an Ojibwe song that Schoolcraft transcribed and translated into English in both prose and poetry. Here is Schoolcraft's poetic translation, which survives in a not entirely legible copy made (and possibly revised) by her white husband Henry.[13] (x's indicate illegible words, while question marks – after the first line – indicate uncertainly legible words.)

American, what ails thee now?
A soft remembrance or a vow!
That stream, so often crossed before
With joy thy bark shall cross no more
Tears glisten in thy manly face
Because thou seest th'Ojibwa maid
Run? away? and depart the place?
xxxxx xxxxx a noble breast inviol.
Thou seest her with her trim white sail
Waiting to catch the xxxxxx gale
That bears her off. Nor shall thy? sighs,
Long for that forest maid arise
But she, as soon as out of sight,
Shall be by him forgotten quite.

In a familiar pattern for the fur-trade world that Schoolcraft grew up in, the white man abandons the Indian woman. In this case, instead of explicitly deserting her, he merely declines to go with her. His self-serving evasion anticipates the teacher who abandons Nowita by telling her he must leave, vowing he will return, and then never returning. In each case the American man spares his Indian supposed beloved – and spares himself – any direct statement of his decision to abandon her.

The opening lines of "Nowita" also connect to Schoolcraft in ways at once more circuitous and more direct by playing off the beginning of Henry Wadsworth Longfellow's 1855 *The Song of Hiawatha.* Here are the celebrated opening lines of *Hiawatha:* "Should you ask me, whence these stories? / Whence these legends and traditions," followed twice by "I should answer, I should tell you." These lines are the undisguised source for the opening of "Nowita" quoted above, written in the same famous trochaic tetrameter, which explains why Anderson's prologue describes her poem as following "parodical form." As it turns out, for both Longfellow and Anderson, these opening lines ask good questions, because the stories and legends in *Hiawatha,* and in part of Longfellow's famous *Evangeline* (1847), rely heavily on writings from Henry Schoolcraft, which in turn often derive from manuscripts by Jane Johnston Schoolcraft and her brother William Johnston.[14] In the prologue to "Nowita," Anderson quotes (without attribution) the famous opening words of *Evangeline*: "This is the forest primeval." And the opening lines of *Hiawatha* even claim to repeat the stories "From the lips of Nawadaha, / . . . the sweet singer," presaging Anderson's title: "Nowita, the Sweet Singer."

For *Hiawatha,* though not for *Evangeline,* Longfellow's notes frequently (though not comprehensively) acknowledge Henry Schoolcraft. As a historian, Anderson might well have noticed that Henry Schoolcraft married into an Indian family, and thus might have suspected that a good deal of his material – and, thus, of Longfellow's material – came from an Indian woman and her family, even though too little information was available for Anderson to know much about Jane Schoolcraft. "Nowita" seems as much an homage to Longfellow as a parodical putting of Longfellow in his place. By connecting her poem to Longfellow's poems, Anderson lets the heavy cultural weight of *Hiawatha* hang over her poem as a canonical vision of Indian culture and story, a vision that any Indian poet of the time might feel compelled to confront, even apart from its partly troubling and partly honoring appropriation of Jane Schoolcraft's writing.

In these ways, Anderson lands, in 1900, in a loop that closes the history of nineteenth-century Indian women's poetry. Collectively, these poems merge the reclaiming of literature (Corrine, Lily Lee, Zitkala-Ša, Anderson) with the reclaiming of land or the lament for its loss (several poems by Schoolcraft, plus the poems discussed here by Plato, Corrinne, Lelia, Fuller, Bush, Metoxen, and Anderson). Thus, even as Anderson salutes Longfellow, she returns Indian poetry and Indian women's poetry to where it began, doing what she modestly could to reclaim Native literary traditions – and the lands they represent, memorialize, and enshrine – from their appropriation by white settler writers and culture.

Notes

1. See Jane Johnston Schoocraft, *The Sound the Stars Make Rushing Through the Sky: The Writings of Jane Johnston Schoolcraft*, Robert Dale Parker (ed.), (Philadelphia: University of Pennsylvania Press, 2007); Olivia Ward Bush-Banks *The Collected Works of Olivia Ward Bush-Banks*, Bernice F. Guillaume (ed.), (New York: Oxford University Press, 1991); Ron Welburn, *Hartford's Ann Plato and the Native Borders of Identity* (Albany: SUNY Press, 2015).
2. These poems are available in Robert Dale Parker (ed.), *Changing Is Not Vanishing: A Collection of Early American Indian Poetry to 1930*, (Philadelphia: University of Pennsylvania Press, 2011) and/or Schoolcraft, *The Sound the Stars Make Rushing Through the Sky*; Ann Plato, *Essays*, 1841, Kenny J. Williams (ed.), (rpt. New York: Oxford University Press, 1988); Lelia, "Critics and Criticism," *Cherokee Rose Buds*, 1 (August 1855); Cora Snyder, "The Frequent Showers of April," *Red Man* 12 (May 1895), 5; Zitkala-Ša, *Dreams and Thunder: Stories, Poems, and "The Sun Dance Opera,"* P. Jane Hafen (ed.), (Lincoln: University of Nebraska Press, 2001).
3. Gerald Vizenor, *Manifest Manners: Narratives on Postindian Survivance* (Lincoln: University of Nebraska Press, 1999).
4. For the growing scholarship on the often surreptitious (until recently) persistence of New England Indians, see, for example, Daniel R. Mandell, *Tribe, Race, History: Native Americans in Southern New England, 1780–1880* (Baltimore: Johns Hopkins University Press, 2008); Jean M. O'Brien, *Firsting and Lasting: Writing Indians Out of Existence in New England* (Minneapolis: University of Minnesota Press, 2010); and Siobhan Senier (ed.), *Dawnland Voices: An Anthology of Indigenous Writing from New England*, (Lincoln: University of Nebraska Press, 2014).
5. See O'Brien, *Firsting and Lasting*, and John A. Strong, *The Montaukett Indians of Eastern Long Island* (Syracuse: Syracuse University Press, 2001).
6. Guillaume, "Introduction," *Collected Works*, 3–22.
7. Rpt. in *The History and Archaeology of the Montauk*, Gaynell Stone (ed.), 2nd edn. (Stony Brook: Suffolk County Archaeological Association, Nassau County Archaeological Committee [1993]), 470–472.
8. J. B. Fisher, "Who Was Crispus Attucks?" *American Historical Record* 1 (1872), 531–533.
9. For more discussion of Fuller's and Metoxen's poems, and of boarding-school poems by boys, see Parker, *Changing Is Not Vanishing*.

10. Devon A. Mihesuah, *Cultivating the Rosebuds: The Education of Women at the Cherokee Female Seminary, 1851–1909* (Urbana: University of Illinois Press, 1993); see also Daniel Heath Justice, *Our Fire Survives the Storm: A Cherokee Literary History* (Minneapolis: University of Minnesota Press, 2006) and James W. Parins, *Literacy and Intellectual Life in the Cherokee Nation, 1820–1906* (Norman: University of Oklahoma Press, 2013).
11. The Martin family, for example, whose name the poem echoes, was a major Cherokee slaveholding family. See Parker, *Changing Is Not Vanishing*, 38–40, 152–154.
12. Anderson's biography of Stand Watie concludes with a short biography of Ridge: Mabel Washbourne Anderson, *The Life of General Stand Watie*, 2nd edn. (Pryor, OK, 1931).
13. The song survives in nine versions, including Ojibwe texts, a musical score, and two prose translations into English published during Schoolcraft's lifetime, which Anderson could have seen but probably did not see. Schoolcraft's poetic translation, quoted here, was first published in 2007 in Schoolcraft, *The Sound the Stars Make Rushing Through the Sky*. For full details, see *Sound*, 201–204, 248–249.
14. Parker, "Introduction: The World and Writings of Jane Johnston Schoolcraft," *The Sound the Stars Make Rushing Through the Sky*, 25–27, 57–59, 161–164. Three years after Anderson's "Nowita," in 1903, Laura Cornelius (Oneida) published another long poem in trochaic tetrameter, including lines from *Hiawatha*; see Parker, *Changing Is Not Vanishing*, 253–257. Longfellow is quoted from *Poems and Other Writings*, J. D. McClatchy (ed.), (New York: Library of America, 2000).

CHAPTER 20

Frances Harper and the Poetry of Reconstruction

Monique-Adelle Callahan

In his seminal work *The Underground Railroad* (1871), abolitionist William Still identified Frances Ellen Watkins Harper as the "leading colored poet in the United States."[1] Indeed, Harper was a prominent poet and orator, an avatar of literary activism whose widespread popularity and fierce commitment to postbellum social reform make her a unique figure in American literary history. In this essay, I examine a specific phase of Harper's poetics, focusing on the era known as Reconstruction beginning with the end of the Civil War and ending in 1877. As the country recovered from the trauma of civil war, the "problem" of slavery and then of emancipated blacks became as much a legal and political dilemma as an existential one. The legal question of black citizenship carried with it the existential question of black humanity. These questions complicated the pursuit of a new definition of American citizenship. For blacks, creative, articulate literary endeavor was a way of contending for recognition as legitimate constituents of a changing American body politic. Werner Sollors and Maria Diedrich remind us how the beginnings of American consciousness asserted themselves at the intersection of race and place: the "New World" became "truly new only when the European Columbiad was redefined by the African diaspora, when the European inventions of America encountered the inventions of America that were manufactured by the involuntary African pioneers."[2] This legacy of invention and manufacturing came to characterize African American participation in nation-building.

Scholars have examined Harper's work in light of Romantic sentimentalism, the post-abolition literature of racial uplift, and women's suffrage. My critique builds on these approaches and recasts Harper's work as pioneering in its poetic treatment of a national–transnational dialectic in American history. More specifically, I examine this dialectic as it plays out in African American poetry, a poetic corpus that I believe stands at the nexus of American national and global discourse. I argue here that Harper's Reconstruction poetry reflects an American consciousness deriving from a radical tension between a legacy of slavery that informs black identities and an evolving national ethos in dialogue with a global enterprise. In its expression of a national consciousness that is both transatlantic and transhemispheric in scope, Harper's poetry exemplifies a kind of literary transnationalism. By "literary transnationalism," I mean the phenomenon of "reaching across or extending beyond predefined national boundaries" and thereby offering "an alternative to a nation-based understanding of literature and history and an alternative way of theorizing literary texts."[3] Harper's understanding of the collaborative workings of race and gender, both nationally and transnationally, predates W.E.B. DuBois' pan-Africanism and Langston Hughes' "black world" ideology by over half a century.

In addition to publishing in a number of journals and newspapers during this period, Harper published the collections *Poems* (1871), *Sketches of Southern Life* (1872), and *Moses: A Story of the Nile* (once in 1868 and again in 1869).[4] *Sketches of Southern Life* specifically reflected her observations of southern life during Reconstruction and features the figure of Aunt Chloe. Michael Stancliff examines Harper's participation in the "reform rhetoric" of the Reconstruction period, defining her as an "innovator" of the "craft" of "nineteenth-century African American rhetorical pedagogy."[5] Designating Harper a "Reconstruction poet," however, presents its own ironies. The word "reconstruction" contains within it both the implication of loss and the promise of re-creation through recovery of what was lost in a concerted effort to build again. Harper rejected this reconstructive theory when it came to American national identity and ethics. Her poetry exposed the cracks in America's foundational ideologies and unveiled the internal hypocrisies of its use of biblical interpretation. Ultimately, Harper's global consciousness is evident in her appropriation of biblical narratives, her use of iconic figures, and her strategic use of versification and poetic form. Combining an appropriation of Jewish historical narratives and a challenge to biblical justifications of slavery, Harper's poetry aligns biblical literacy with a global consciousness.

Well before Reconstruction, Harper had already established herself as a biblical revisionist and avid critic of biblical justifications for slavery. For instance, she concludes the six-stanza "Bible Defense of Slavery" (1857) with this indictment:

A "reverend" man, whose light should be
The guide of age and youth,
Brings to the shrine of Slavery
The sacrifice of truth!

For the direst wrong by man imposed,
Since Sodom's fearful cry,
The word of life has been unclos'd,
To give your God the lie.

Oh! When ye pray for heathen lands,
And plead for their dark shores,
Remember Slavery's cruel hands
Make heathens at your doors![6]

Harper's strict adherence to the traditional British ballad form enacts a tension with the thematic content of the poem. She plays by the rules aesthetically with the intention of rewriting them ideologically, thereby undermining the legacy of racial inequity through the uncensored critique of a biblical defense of American slavery. By personifying slavery Harper distinguishes between the legacy of slavery and the implied audience of the poem – American citizens – thereby opening the door for a reconciliation of black and white in the larger context of American nationhood. Central to Harper's critique is the "word of life," an allusion to the Bible. As opposed to an infallible truth, this "word" appears to God in the form of a lie. Through her emphasis on the role of active interpretation of the "word" and its propensity to communicate untruths, Harper underscores the potential for deleterious interpretive error of biblical content.

The final stanza shifts from the national to the transnational, marking the heightened intensity of Harper's critique. Harper insists her readers consider the extent to which the American religious project extended itself beyond the shores of American nationalism. Her imagery of "dark shores" refers to those colonized "lands" considered "heathen" for their cultural and religious *otherness*, including countries in Africa and South America colonized as extensions of European imperialism. These "dark shores" also implicitly allude to the Middle Passage, an aperture in the geographically and ideologically delineated boundaries of the New World. Harper's poem enacts movement from "heathen lands" to the "doors" of American nationhood, thus highlighting the transnational network established by American slavery.

Harper's poetic corpus reflects an awareness of the dialectical interdependence of the domestic and the global. She acknowledges her own identity position at the intersection of race and gender, an intersection at the very heart of an evolving African American national citizenship. As Harper's work negotiates race and gender, it simultaneously aims to articulate the larger, transnational context of American identities.

Recognizing the Bible as a quintessentially national and transnational text whose interpretation was at the center of American politics, we can acknowledge how Harper's literary transnationalism and biblical revisionism aligns with her poetic treatment of race and gender. Harper's transnational vision also manifested in her understanding of herself as a poet in the United States. In her address to the 1866 National Women's Rights Convention, Harper asserted: "I, as a colored woman, have had in this country an education which has made me feel as if I were in the situation of Ishmael, my hand against every man, and every man's hand against me."[7] The son of Abraham but not Sarah, Ishmael is the outsider within. He is both kin and marginal to a lineage of the chosen. He is a son of God's chosen but denied the promise of inheritance. Both included by law and excluded in practice, African Americans – black women doubly so – were the American *seed* excluded from the *promise* of equality. Like Ishmael, Harper is both at home and exiled, both inside and outside of the national body politic.

The interchange between national and transnational poetics in Harper's work manifests in the figures and tropes she chooses. It is at this particular intersection of national and transnational that Harper develops the figure of "Aunt Chloe," a highly politically conscious figure whose ethos ingratiates the reader while at the same time offering a shrewd critique of America's political realities. Through Aunt Chloe, Harper reconfigures black femininity in service of a national project of racial uplift and national unity. In "Aunt Chloe's Politics" (1872) Harper introduces Chloe as a rhetorical figure, quintessentially marginal by virtue of race and gender. Elizabeth Petrino notes that the figures Aunt Chloe and Uncle Jacob "revise plantation myths and assume the role of prophets."[8] Mark Sanders comments on how Harper's rhetoric "implicitly constructs the black female poet as national prophet, the quintessential American capable of revealing (and excoriating) the soul of the nation."[9] From this marginal position, Harper offers a critique of the political ethics of American governance:

> Of course, I don't know very much
> About these politics,
> But I think that some who run 'em,
> Do mighty ugly tricks.[10]

Not only does Harper employ a rhetorical eunoia – a strategy for establishing goodwill between speaker and audience – but she also uses the Aunt Chloe figure to enter a discursive arena. Aunt Chloe is a kind of alter-ego for Harper – a woman outside of politics who offers an ethical compass and whose intuitive knowledge challenges the political status quo. In Aunt Chloe, Harper creates a marginal voice that can master the art of liminality, similar to the way in which Harper herself had to toe the line in her "performance of gentility" and her "commitment to political activism."[11]

Continuing her ethical critique of American politics, Chloe exposes the corrupt elements of an election process driven by capital:

> And this buying up each other
> Is something worse than mean,
> Though I thinks a heap of voting,
> I go for voting clean.

By speaking through the voice of Chloe, Harper assumes a different class identity, aligning herself – an educated, free black – with an uneducated, emancipated slave. The performance of class alignment across class further demonstrates Harper's Reconstruction ethic. This ethic appears also in a letter Harper composed while on a speaking tour in the South, in which she writes: "After all whether they encourage or discourage me, I belong to this race, and when it is down I belong to a down race; when it is up I belong to a risen race."[12]

In other instances Harper assumes a masculine voice, transforming the poem into a space in which she can project her voice into a predominantly male discursive arena. The poem "Lines to Miles O'Reiley" (1871) is a direct response to a series of articles written by Irish immigrant and former Union officer Charles Halpine, who wrote under the pen name Miles O'Reilly. In this poem Harper addresses a distinctly racialized war politics:

> You've heard no doubt of Irish bulls,
> And how they blunder, thick and fast;
> But of all the queer and foolish things,
> O'Reiley, you have said the last.
>
> You say we brought the rebs supplies,
> And gave them aid amid the fight,
> And if you must be ruled by rebs,
> Instead of black you want them white.
>
> . . .
>
> And when we sought to join your ranks,
> And battle with you, side by side,
> Did men not curl their lips with scorn,
> And thrust us back with hateful pride?[13]

Harper identifies the racial biases that corroded interaction between blacks and whites during the American Civil War. Her rhetorical play with the term "Irish bull" refers, in its denotation, to a foolish statement made by a speaker and also draws attention to O'Reilly's "otherness" as a member of a group characterized by its history of immigration to America. This reference to the Irish, then, also draws attention to the fundamentally transnational character of American identities. The transnationalism of a "melting pot" ideology meets a growing American nationalism steeped in racial segregation. Harper calls out O'Reilly's racist bias by highlighting the willingness of blacks to "battle . . . side by side" with men in O'Reilly's "rank," and the unwillingness of O'Reilly's men to do the same. In doing so, Harper advocates for an identity politics that transcends the black–white binary passed down by the legacy of slavery and segregation in America.

Harper simultaneously advocates for the assertion of black male legitimacy and black female agency in an era in which, as one writer suggests, "[p]roslavery and anti-suffrage lecturers and propagandists promulgated a version of the Eden story in which the snake was a black man and Eve was an unruly activist woman who transgressed race and gender boundaries through her illicit relationship with the snake."[14] Harper's poetry both reflected and incited a radical transformation of thought about African Americans in general, and African American women in particular.

Aligning race and gender politics, "An Appeal to the American People" (1871) chronicles African American solidarity with Union troops and allegiance to the cause of a united American nation. An appeal to a collective American people, Harper identifies "the traitor" who stands

> With the crimson in his hands,
> Scowling 'neath his brow of hate,
> On our weak and desolate,
> With the blood-rust on the knife
> Aimed at the nation's life.[15]

The trochaic feet here, a falling meter, reinforce the imminent "fall" of the nation at the hands of "traitors" who are insensitive to the plight of the disempowered constituents of its citizenry. In the final stanza of this appeal, Harper infers a particular brand of masculinity that would protect the interests of a fledgling national project with "the name of freedom" at its ideological, legal, and political core.

> To your manhood we appeal,
> Lest the traitor's iron heel
> Grind and trample in the dust

All our new-born hope and trust,
And the name of freedom be
Linked with bitter mockery.

Harper's position regarding the role of black men in the national project caused a divide between her and many of her white feminist counterparts. Harper criticized white suffragists for "letting race occupy a minor position" and focusing only on gender.[16] For Harper, race and gender were inextricably linked in American politics.

Harper's Reconstruction poetry proposed a particular brand of African American citizenship, in part by applying biblical typology that aligned African American experience and the figure of Christ. Her proscription for a post-abolition racial ethics of citizenship for blacks reflected a doctrine of racial uplift that twentieth-century black intellectuals would adopt in their efforts to secure a stake in the national project. In "Fifteenth Amendment" (1870), an apostrophe to African Americans, Harper articulates this vision of racial uplift:

Shake off the dust, O rising race!
Crowned as a brother and a man;
Justice to-day asserts her claim,
And from thy brow fades out the ban.

With freedom's chrism upon thy head,
Her precious ensign in thy hand,
Go place thy once despiséd name
Amid the noblest of the land.[17]

Harper's diction and form reinforce her politicized, reconstructive poetics. The "rising" iambs in each tetrameter line echo her call for racial uplift. The language of nobility ("crowned as brother and man," "chrism upon thy head," "ensign in thy hand") suggests a chiasmic reversal of the social and ideological positioning of African Americans from slave to lord. The "rise" of the race is Christic in its ascent ("chrism" referring to the Greek word for anointing). What "Justice" offers is an opportunity for reinvention and revision. Harper renders the race Christ-like in its crowned head ("freedom's chrism upon thy head") and its ultimate ascension above the thrall of slavery. Furthermore, the race "rises" from the "dust" in a kind of second Genesis creation; within this poetic space, the race is recreated and encouraged to engage in the re-naming process that will establish its place among the free.

The Christian biblical tradition has its own doctrine of crowns. In Timothy 4:8, the "crown of righteousness" is a reward after judgment given on "that day." The believer is crowned after a redemptive, salvific process that is ultimately transformative. Harper draws on this biblical metaphor to provide a poetics of redemption and transformation during Reconstruction. She imagines a transformed race, crowned after being judged. How had it responded to the challenge of reforming and of becoming an active participant in a post-abolition American nation? The poem is a clarion call for participation in a vision of reconstructed racial and national identity. Harper couches the African American struggle for socioeconomic progress in biblical language and typology. During a time when increased violence between blacks and whites in the South, particularly through the racial agitation and violence of the Ku Klux Klan, induced fear of another civil war between whites and blacks, Harper encouraged a vision of a race ennobled by its participation in the activation and cultivation of its recently acquired legal freedoms.[18]

To further consider the figure of Aunt Chloe in this context, we see that reading the Bible not only distinguishes Chloe from the larger community of formerly enslaved peoples, but it also represents an act of agency that enables her to carve out a space in which she can achieve independence and social mobility. Biblical literacy and social mobility intertwine in "Learning to Read," which appeared in the 1872 edition of *Sketches of a Southern Life*:

> And, I longed to read my Bible,
> For the precious words it said;
> But when I begun to learn it,
> Folks just shook their heads,
>
> So I got a pair of glasses,
> And straight to work I went,
> And never stopped till I could read
> The hymns and Testament.
>
> Then I got a little cabin –
> A place to call my own
> And I felt as independent
> As a queen upon her throne.[19]

Chloe's biblical literacy is transformative. Beginning with seeing the text through a pair of glasses that she herself procures, Chloe instructs herself in independent thinking through the biblical text. She changes its meaning through her reading, and is changed into an independent citizen through her active engagement with the text. The fact that she gains literacy late – seemingly too late – speaks to her as a representative of formerly enslaved peoples denied the right to read. Rather than passively accepting the terms of her illiteracy, Chloe fights back, achieves literacy, and is thereby empowered to do the reconstructive work of reimagining herself and her racial and national communities. Through Chloe, Harper offers a theory of re-reading the very texts that informed American ethics and racial politics.

In addition to her use of the Aunt Chloe figure, Harper offers another form of Bible "reading" that enacts a form of literary transnationalism through its appropriation of the Jewish scriptures and its iconic fathers. In "Moses: A Story of the Nile" (1869), Harper's poetic vision is transatlantic – it is essentially pan-African in scope – and transliterary. It works across texts in its presentation of the biblical narrative of the enslaved Israelites and the modern narrative of enslaved Africans. Harper's construction of Moses in this poem is a strategic literary transnationalism of which we see echoes and various iterations in her other Reconstruction poetry.

For Harper's Moses, the burden of racial oppression manifests as a legacy unchanged by the particular circumstances of his freedom. Echoing the relationship Harper herself had to the cause of abolition and post-abolition racial uplift, this Moses figure identifies with the suffering of his "kindred race":

> Within those darkened huts my mother plies her tasks,
> My father bends to unrequited toil;
> And bitter tears moisten the bread my brethren eat.
> And when I gaze upon their cruel wrongs
> The very purple on my limbs seems drenched
> With blood, the warm blood of my own kindred race;
> And then thy richest viands pall upon my taste,
> And discord jars in every tone of song.
> I cannot live in pleasure while they faint
> In pain.[20]

Here, the oppression of slavery enters the intimate, nuclear space of family life. The speaker's body is "drenched with blood, the warm blood of [her] own kindred race," suggesting that the body itself bears the proverbial stain of generational oppression – perhaps a definition of race itself as it functions on the bodies of African Americans. Born free herself, Harper chose a life of advocacy for blacks, free and enslaved, thereby choosing to "not live in pleasure while they faint in pain."

For Harper, Moses is a paradoxical figure. He is at once "a Hebrew child" (and therefore *other*) and he is heir to the Egyptian throne. His national and ethnic affiliations are in conflict, indicative of a legacy of

African descent as well as a legacy of Judaic promise. In this sense, Moses' condition is emblematic of the African American post-reconstruction condition. Stancliff notes Harper's use of Moses in this epic poem as a "pedagogical model for practical politics, one designed for the Reconstruction moment."[21] Of the figure of Moses, Harper said:

> I like the character of Moses. He's the first disunionist we read of in the Jewish Scriptures. The magnificence of Pharaoh's throne looked up before his vision, its oriental splendors glittered before his eyes; but he turned from them all and chose rather to suffer with the enslaved, than rejoice with the free. He would have no union with the slave power of Egypt.[22]

The Reconstruction "moment" was one in which blacks of various experiences aligned themselves with a common goal of sociopolitical progress, an exigency produced by the systematic exclusion of blacks from positions of power and influence. The legacy of African descent placed African Americans in a precarious position vis-à-vis the "throne" of American capitalism, while at the same time blacks wrote themselves into the legacy of American freedom through appropriation – or adoption, if you will – of biblical notions of redemption and freedom.

Perhaps Harper's boldest appeal to a global literary aesthetic during the Reconstruction "moment" appears in her poem "Death of Zombi" (1871), a transhemispheric glance toward South America. In this poem, Harper recounts the story of "Zombi" (also written Zumbi), the chief of a *quilombo* – a community of escaped slaves – in seventeenth-century Brazil. The poem narrates the demise of The Republic of Palmares, perhaps the most famous *quilombo* in modern history, and Harper places her reader in the middle of the attack. Her speaker is a member of the community of escaped slaves, facing their imminent destruction at the hands of Portuguese slavers. The "inhuman and fierce" slavers in Brazil offered only one choice – "freedom in death or the life of a slave" – and so the escaped Africans fight "[t]ill, broken and peeled, we yielded at last / And the glory and strength of our kingdom were past":[23]

> But Zombi, our leader, and warlike old chief,
> Gazed down on our woe with anger and grief;
> The tyrant for him forged fetters in vain,
> His freedom-girt limbs had worn their last chain.
>
> Defiance and daring still flashed from his eye;
> A freeman he'd lived and free he would die.
> So he climbed to the verge of a dangerous steep,
> Resolved from its margin to take a last leap;

For a fearful death and a bloody grave
Were dearer to him than the life of a slave.

Nor went he alone to the mystic land –
There were other warriors in his band,
Who rushed with him to Death's dark gate,
All wrapped in the shroud of a mournful fate.

Zumbi is a God-like figure; he gazes down and has the ability to transcend the body. The agency he exercises in taking his own life establishes him as an iconic, mythic figure whose martyrdom produces admiration and praise from the larger community for its principled motivation.

Harper's use of Zumbi here in the context of African American slavery and of postbellum Reconstruction initiatives demonstrates again her understanding of the national project in conjunction with a larger transnational context. During a time when Brazil had yet to abolish slavery – and would not do so for almost two decades – Harper appropriates a narrative of slave liberation in Brazil for an American audience. She conjures an icon of resistance and a community of Africans in diaspora who carved out a space to thrive outside of the boundaries of legal slavery.

Harper's glance toward Brazilian history mirrors her glance toward biblical history – or, more specifically, toward a history of biblical interpretation. Like a modern midrashist, Harper mediates the scriptures with an eye for interpretation; her moves are strategic and artful, and her incisions into the text are performed loyally as an act of love. In *The Nakedness of the Fathers* (1994), Alicia Ostriker writes:

> In midrash, ancient tales yield new meanings to new generations. Not surprisingly, many midrashists today are women; we should expect many more in the future. How could it be otherwise? The texts plainly beg and implore women to read them as freshly, energetically, passionately – and even playfully – as they have been read by men. "Turn it and turn it," the rabbis say of Torah, "for everything is in it."[24]

Harper's midrash is a kind of transnationalism. Harper borrows from a tradition outside of the boundaries of the United States to construct a narrative of African American and American national and racial identities. Furthermore, in her poetic reconstructions of blackness and Americanness, Harper proposes a particular brand of black femininity and masculinity to serve the larger project of racial uplift and national unification. In this process, black identity serves as a metonymical figure for national identity – a nation, albeit, in ideological crisis. Through the figure of Aunt Chloe in particular, Harper adds a gendered component to the growing tradition of African American biblical reinterpretation that followed a period of countrywide Evangelicalism and made the Bible, as one scholar asserts, "the most accessible literature in America."[25] Both Black politicians and preachers imagined emancipated blacks as the modern "children of Israel," at times specifically referencing the Book of Joshua and even using the story of Haman to decry the persecution of blacks through racially oppressive legislation. Freed blacks referred to slavery as "Paul's Time" and Reconstruction as "Isaiah's Time." Eric Foner speculates that this was because Paul preached obedience where Isaiah prophesied a violent, sudden change.[26]

Direct evidence of Harper's tendency to reconstruct African American identity through Jewish narratives can be found in her 1886 poem "The Jewish Grandfather's Story":

Come, gather around me, children,
  And a story I will tell.
How we builded the beautiful temple –
  The temple we love so well.

I must date my story backward
  To a distant age and land,
When God did break our fathers' chains
  By his mighty outstretched hand

Our fathers were strangers and captives,
  Where the ancient Nile doth flow;
Smitten by cruel taskmasters,
  And burdened by toil and woe.[27]

When Harper published this poem, Jews were experiencing waves of migration, including to the United States and Latin America, as a result of shifting politics and economic conditions in Europe. During this time Jewish peoples endured increasing marginalization. Assuming the voice of a Hebrew patriarch, Harper highlights the parallels between African American and Jewish narratives of slavery and freedom. The rhetorical gesture here aligns the two narratives and thereby interprets one communal identity through another. The poem proceeds through the history of Babylonian captivity, beginning with "a day of doom" and leading into a period of enslavement:

And we were captives many years,
  Where Babel's stream doth flow;
With harps unstrung, on willow's hung,
  We wept in silent woe.

We could not sing the old, sweet songs,
  Our captors asked to hear;
Our hearts were full, how could we sing
  The songs to us so dear?

The allusion to Babylonian captivity and the songs of captivity echo what W.E.B. DuBois would name the "sorrow songs" in his canonical work, *The Souls of Black Folk*, at the turn of the century. The "Negro folk-song – the rhythmic cry of the slave," wrote DuBois, was "the singular spiritual heritage of the nation and the greatest gift of the Negro people."[28] A precursor to the evolution of an African American poetics, these Negro spirituals sampled from biblical stories and applied them to the ideological crises of the nation. Harper's transhemispheric leanings toward Brazil demonstrated a transnational poetics; furthermore, by appropriating the biblical Exodus, she employs a rhetorical strategy used by a number of nineteenth-century African American writers and scholars. According to Allen D. Callahan, African Americans "heard, read, and retold the story of the Exodus more than any other biblical narrative. In it they saw their own aspirations for liberation from bondage in the story of the ancient Hebrew slaves."[29] Engaging the enslavement of the Israelites and the biblical Exodus as metaphors through which to read African American experience is both a transnational gesture and poetic act.

The global vision Harper demonstrates in her Reconstruction poetry also appears in her later work. The Civil War in America coincided with the momentous emancipation of the serfs in 1861 by Tsar Alexander II. During the first half of the nineteenth century America had good diplomatic ties with Russia because Russia had offered its support during the Civil War. Within the next few decades, however, Russia experienced a series of wars and political turmoil and its relationship to the United States changed. Accordingly, American liberals and radicals possessed an increased awareness of Russian politics. In "The Vision of the Czar of Russia" (1899), Harper demonstrates an awareness of the interconnectedness of American and Russian politics and of the American "gaze" on Russian soil. Harper projects a vision of peace in Russia that echoes her vision of a unified nation in the United States:

To the Czar of all the Russia's
Came a vision bright and fair,
The joy of unburdened millions,
Floating gladly on the air.

The laughter and songs of children,
Of maidens, so gay and bright,
Of mothers who never would tremble,
Where warfare and carnage blight.[30]

In the ninth of thirteen stanzas, we find echoes of biblical prophetic writings and the end-time prophecy of the Book of Revelation. The vision of the poem expands beyond Russia to a more global, apocalyptic vision of world peace:

And Earth, once so sorrow laden,
Grew daily more fair and bright;
Till peace our globe had enfolded,
And millions walked in its light.

'Twas a bright and beautiful vision,
Of nations disarmed and free;
As to heaven arose the chorus
Of the world's first jubilee.

How long shall the vision tarry?
How long shall the hours delay,
Till war shrinks our saddened Earth,
As the darkness shrinks from day?

In these stanzas, biblical allusions to John the Revelator's vision of a "new heaven and a new earth" meet Levitical law and Judean prophecy. Of this apocalyptic moment, John writes: "And God shall wipe away all tears from their eyes; and there shall be no more death, neither sorrow, nor crying, neither shall there be any more pain: for the former things are passed away."[31] Harper echoes this post-tribulation moment described by John in the longing for the delayed "vision" of the "bright and beautiful vision" in which nations as "disarmed and free," walking in the new "light" of a new earth for which the former things of war are passed away. In the stanza that follows, Harper articulates a worldwide "jubliee," referencing the Levitical year of jubliee that called for the mandatory release of persons in bondage or debt. This appeal to global freedom extends Harper's legacy of abolitionism beyond the boundaries of the nation-state.

The next line links Judean prophecy of the Babylonian era to contemporary global conflict at the turn of the century. Harper references the book of the prophet Habbakuk, a figure known for decrying the oppression and injustice imposed on an international level by Judah's Chaldean enemies.[32] "How long shall the vision tarry? / How long shall the hours delay" echoes Habbakuk's sentiment implicitly and God's response directly: "And the Lord answered me, and said, Write the vision, and make it plain upon tables, that he may run that readeth it. For the vision is yet for an appointed time, but at the end it shall speak, and not lie: though it tarry, wait for it; because it will surely come, it will not tarry."[33] Like Habbakuk, Harper's speaker laments the delay of a vision of peace; the written word comes as a solution, a precursor to the realization of this vision. In this sense, Harper offers an ars poetica of sorts – poetry is the pitocin that induces the birth of the vision.

By no means parochial in scope, Harper's poetry imagines an interconnected world for which national lines are at once boundaries and bridges. Ultimately, understanding Harper's work in the context of literary transnationalism encourages us to consider how literary transnationalism functioned in its various iterations in the work of early African American writers. It also prompts us to investigate how that legacy manifests in contemporary African American writing. More generally, Harper's work leads us to interrogate poetry as a form of transnational (i.e. global) currency – an art form whose emphasis on imagery and linguistic precision provides the building blocks for a restructuring of the symbolic and ideological constructs of national histories. If Mariano Siskind offers us the "novelization of the global" – a theory examining the "production of images of a globalized world as they are constructed in specific novels" – then I suggest a *poeticization of the global* – a production of images of a globalized world as they are constructed in specific poems.[34] In her poeticization of the global, Harper destabilizes the nation-state ideological main stage and projects a global worldview, acknowledging a world of interdependent political, economic, and social bodies.

Notes

1. William Still, *The Underground Railroad* (Philadelphia: William Still Publisher, 1871), 755.
2. Werner Sollors and Maria Diedrich (eds.), *Defining Moments in African American Literature and Culture* (Cambridge: Harvard University Press, 1994), 3.
3. Monique-Adelle Callahan, *Between the Lines: Literary Transnationalism and African American Poetics* (New York: Oxford University Press, 2008), 6.
4. This second edition of *Moses: A Story of the Nile* is the earliest extant copy. Historians speculate that Harper published the original a year prior. See Harper, *A Brighter Coming Day: A Frances Ellen Watkins Harper Reader*, Frances Smith Foster (ed.), (New York: Feminist Press, 1990), 135.
5. Michael Stancliff, *Frances Ellen Watkins Harper: African American Reform Rhetoric and the Rise of a Modern Nation State* (New York: Routledge, 2011), xiii.
6. Harper, "Bible Defense of Slavery," *Brighter Coming Day*, 60.

7. Harper, "We Are All Bound Up Together," *Brighter Coming Day*, 218.
8. Elizabeth Petrino, "'We are Rising as a People': Frances Harper's Radical Views on Class and Racial Equality in *Sketches of Southern Life*," *American Transcendental Quarterly* 19.2 (June 2005), 149.
9. Mark Sanders, "Toward a Modernist Poetics," *The Cambridge Companion to African American Literature*, Maryemma Graham and Jerry Ward, Jr. (eds.), (Cambridge: Cambridge University Press, 2011), 227.
10. Harper, "Aunt Chloe's Politics," *Brighter Coming Day*, 204–206.
11. Petrino, "'We are Rising as a People,'" 139.
12. Harper, "I Visited One of the Plantations," *Brighter Coming Day*, 128.
13. Harper, "Lines to Miles O'Reiley," *Brighter Coming Day*, 192–193.
14. C.C. O'Brian, "'The White Women All Go for Sex': Frances Harper on Suffrage, Citizenship, and the Reconstruction South," *African American Review* 43.4 (Winter 2009), 606.
15. Harper, "An Appeal to the American People," *Brighter Coming Day*, 167–168.
16. Eric Foner, *Reconstruction: America's Unfinished Revolution* (New York: Perennial Library, 1989), 448.
17. Harper, "Fifteenth Amendment," *Brighter Coming Day*, 189–190.
18. Douglas R. Egerton, *The Wars of Reconstruction: the Brief, Violent History of America's Most Progressive Era* (New York: Bloomsbury Press, 2014), 298.
19. Harper, "Learning to Read," *Brighter Coming Day*, 205–206.
20. Harper, "Moses: A Story of the Nile", *Brighter Coming Day*, 138–166.
21. Stancliff, *Frances Ellen Watkins Harper*, 57.
22. Harper, "Our Greatest Want," *Brighter Coming Day*, 103–104.
23. Harper, "Death of Zombi," *Brighter Coming Day*, 172–173.
24. Alicia Ostriker, *The Nakedness of the Fathers: Biblical Visions and Revisions* (New Brunswick: Rutgers University Press, 1994), xiii.
25. Allen Dwight Callahan, *The Talking Book: African Americans and the Bible* (New Haven: Yale University Press, 2008), 6.
26. Foner, *Reconstruction*, 94.
27. Harper, "The Jewish Grandfather's Story," *A Brighter Coming Day*, 244–49.
28. W.E.B. DuBois, *The Souls of Black Folk* (New York: Dover, 1994), 156.
29. Callahan, *The Talking Book*, 83.
30. Harper, "The Vision of the Czar of Russia," *Brighter Coming Day*, 381–382.
31. Revelation 21:4 KJV.
32. Abraham Heschel describes Habakkuk's "world" as a "place in which 'justice never goes forth' (1:4) except in perverted form." *The Prophets* (New York: Harper Perennial, 2001), 178.
33. Habakkuk 2:2, 3 KJV.
34. Mariano Siskind, "The Globalization of the Novel and the Novelization of the Global: A Critique of World Literature (2010)," *World Literature Reader: A Reader*, Theo D'haen, César Domínguez, and Mads Rosendahl Thomsen (eds.), (New York: Routledge, 2013), 331.

CHAPTER 21

"hear the bird": Sarah Piatt and the Dramatic Monologue

Jess Roberts

For much of the latter half of the nineteenth century, American poet Sarah Piatt wrote and published poems that gave voice to women and children, that grieved the loss of loved ones and moral certainty, and that revealed an unnerving inclination for self-conscious complexity. Some of the most culturally influential periodicals of her time – *Atlantic Monthly, Harper's Weekly, Scribner's* – circulated hundreds of her poems, as well as reviews of the many collections of these poems in book form. These reviews were, by turns, delighted and discomfited by what they called Piatt's "distinctiveness," heralding her as one of America's geniuses even as they cautioned her against apparently unbecoming subtlety and obscurity.[1]

Among the things that distinguished Piatt was her obvious interest in the contextual dynamism of spoken language and the poetic genre that seemed particularly well suited to capitalize on and examine it: the dramatic monologue.[2] Over the course of her career, Piatt wrote more dramatic monologues than any other nineteenth-century American poet.[3] Though many Piatt scholars have addressed dramatic monologues in the context of essays about Piatt's irony or ambivalence, and in terms of her place among Confederate poets or in postbellum magazine culture, no one has yet read her dramatic monologues primarily through the lens of genre.[4] That is what I do here. In the pages that follow, I describe the generic conventions of the dramatic monologue that are integral to Piatt's experiments with it, building an interpretive framework out of the doubleness inherent to the genre.[5] I ground that analysis in Piatt's fifth collection, *Dramatic Persons and Moods* (1879), because it provides the poems I address with a shared print context, the very title of which directs the reader's eye to genre.[6] What emerges is a clear picture of how Piatt manipulated the particular conventions of the dramatic monologue in order to anatomize the way women maintained and disrupted the very conventions that restricted their range of experience and expression in their roles as mothers and daughters, readers and writers.

Like all genres, the dramatic monologue is a fluid one, existing as it does somewhere between so-called lyric and narrative poetry, making use of dramatic conventions without relying on or anticipating actual performance.[7] Whatever other characteristics dramatic monologues may have, they are first-person poems that present themselves as spoken utterances and that draw attention to themselves as acts of speech. These two generic features – the first-person point of view and the pronounced spoken-ness – produce the genre's most distinctive effect: its signature doubleness. Though all poems mean in multiple ways, dramatic monologues always mean in at least two different ways simultaneously: they mean according to their status as a subject's spoken utterance and as a printed object. On the one hand, the dramatic monologue represents the expression of a speaking "I" often, though not always, directed at a listening "you." That expression draws its meaning from the poem's internal context, which includes not just the relationship between the "I" and "you," but also the fictive world in which they exist together, a world to which the reader has only limited access. On the other hand, the dramatic monologue is an object created and read by people who exist external to the poem itself. Exceeding the intentions and comprehension of its speaking subject, the poem's objective meaning is created by and within a much larger and more complicated external context of which the reader and writer are a part. That context includes both the world in which the poem is read and through which it circulates as well as the very page on which it is manifest.

The subjective/internal and objective/external dimensions of the poem invite and reward different reading strategies. The objective dimension (experienced by author and reader) focuses attention on aspects of the poem that its subjects (the speaking "I" and the implied "you") have no access to or conception of: its visual components (the way line-breaks and typographical marks create meaning), its intertextuality (allusions that fall outside the ken of the poems' characters), and its relationship to its external context (the world in which it circulated, the page on which it appeared). By contrast, the subjective dimension of the poem requires that readers attend to the interaction between a poem's "I" and "you" and the poem's internal context. The speaking subject and the world that implicitly surrounds her are, of course, constructed fictions that gesture to but do not possess the material reality of the text itself. As a result, though it can be richly productive to maintain a kind of separation between the objective and subjective dimensions of the poems, the former ultimately subsumes the latter.

One thing that distinguishes the dramatic monologues in *Dramatic Persons and Moods* is the striking generality of their speakers. Unlike, say, the duke in Robert Browning's "My Last Duchess" or Eulalie in Augusta Webster's "The Castaway," Piatt's "speakers" do not represent particular characters embedded in specific narratives. Instead, Piatt's speakers are what Glennis Byron would call "only vaguely particularised."[8] That is, though they bear certain markers of identity (race, class, and gender), they are not characterized by details that distinguish them as individuals. Piatt's speakers are, for the most part, white middle-class mothers, as Piatt herself was. But they are not specific mothers of specific children whose individual selves emerge out of and within a set of experiences presented as particular to them. Even the word "speaker" seems somehow inaccurate insofar as it suggests a more specific centralized self than Piatt's poems, in fact, offer up. This lack of specificity likewise characterizes the poem's "you's." They are either girls who believe in the myths and promises of domestic bliss that, according to the "I's," leave women unprepared for the lives they find themselves trapped within later, or they are the men who perpetuate and rely on those myths and promises.

Like Piatt herself, the "I's" in her poems actively stress the gender identity of men and women over and above their individuality. In the dramatic monologue entitled "After the Quarrel," for instance, a maternal "I" attempts to soothe her apparently jilted daughter by assuring her that "There are men, and men, and men – / And these men are brothers all! / Each sweet fault of his you'll find / Just as sweet in all his kind."[9] In "A Pique at Parting," one of Piatt's most fascinating dramatic monologues, the "I" begins by addressing a singular "you" but quickly expands her addressees to include the "lords – and gentlemen" that, to her mind, the "you" represents.[10] In "Her Word of Reproach," the speaking "I" accuses the "you" of "talking in a man's great way" when he apparently claims that "love would last though the stars should fall."[11] Men and women alike, it seems, abide by particular and predictable patterns: the former make promises they cannot keep; the latter, by turns, both believe those promises and cease to believe those promises and, in both cases, find themselves trapped.

This pattern of generalized subjects suggests Piatt's interest in examining not individuals but categories, not subjectivities but the roles men and women play and how they play them. Though the "I's" and "you's" may lack particularity, the poems they inhabit do not lack precision. That precision shows itself in Piatt's manipulation of the dramatic monologue as a genre to expose how women – as mothers, daughters, lovers, and *poets* – might maintain and, perhaps more importantly, how they might disrupt the conventions and expectations that restrict them. That manipulation is made visible by the interplay between the poems' subjective and objective planes, between their status as spoken utterances and as printed objects.

Such interplay is on full display in her playful and understated poem "A Lesson in a Picture." This dramatic monologue stages an interaction between a mother and daughter, a maternal "I" and a filial "you." They, like many of Piatt's "I's" and "you's," are "only vaguely particularised." The poem offers them neither names nor a specific location nor a particularly detailed past. Their interaction is, it seems, prompted by the "you" having recently become the object of a young man's admiration and by the "I's" suspicions regarding that admiration and its attendant promises. By way of its subjective and objective planes, the poem not only scrutinizes and undermines youthful promises of romantic love, which the "I" finds dubious, but also draws attention to its own generic features in ways that make visible Piatt's agency as a poet and thereby the poet's role in maintaining or disrupting gendered expectation. I quote the poem in full:

So it is whispered here and there,
　　That you are rather pretty? Well?
(Here's matter for a bird of the air
　　To drop down from the dusk and tell.)
Let's have no lights, my child. Somehow,
The shadow suits your blushes now.

The blonde young man who called to-day
　　(He only rang to leave a book?—
Yes, and a flower or two, I say!)
　　Was handsome, look you. Will you look?
You did not know his eyes were fine?—
You did not? Can you look in mine?

What is it in this picture here,
　　That you should suddenly watch it so?
A maiden leaning, half in fear,
　　From her far casement; and, below
In cap and plumes (or cap and bells?)
Some fairy tale her lover tells.

Suppose this lonesome night could be
　　Some night a thousand springs ago,

Dim round that tower; and you were she,
　　And your shy friend her lover (Oh!)
And I — her mother! And suppose
I knew just why she wore that rose.

Do you think I'd kiss my girl, and say:
　　"Make haste to bid the wedding guest,
And make the wedding garment gay,—
　　You could not find in East or West
So brave a bridegroom; I rejoice
That you have made so sweet a choice"?

Or say, "To look forever fair,
　　Just keep this turret moonlight wound
About your face; stay in mid-air; —
　　Rope-ladders lead one to the ground,
Where all things take the touch of tears,
And nothing lasts a thousand years"?[12]

I want to focus first on the poem's status as a mother's spoken utterance to her daughter. Doing so requires attending to the imaginative game that the speaking "I" initiates in the fourth stanza, a game in which she imagines a narrative for a picture that ostensibly appears in the "book" the young man has left behind for her daughter. Though short on details, the correspondence between the picture and the poem's implied backstory seems plain enough: both include a young man paying attention to a young woman. Responding to her daughter's apparent fixation on the picture, the "I" tells the "you" to imagine that they are themselves players in the scene the "picture" captures and so instructs her to do what we (the readers) have reason to believe she (the daughter) is doing already – namely, mapping herself and the "blonde young man" onto the picture. In that picture, presumably, the daughter/"you" sees a version of her own experience – or, more precisely, her experience as she would like to imagine it. The parenthetical "(Oh!)" that appears in line twenty-two presents itself as evidence for just such a reading. Though spoken by the "I," the exclamation seems to register the "you's" recognition of her own interior act in her mother's game and, maybe more importantly, of her mother's apparent (and, to her, apparently surprising) knowledge of that act. The "I's" final command to "suppose / I knew just why she wore that rose" seems designed to emphasize her own understanding of both the maiden in the picture and the one who fixes her eyes on her.

By way of the game she initiates, the "I" adapts the "you's" implied act of reading (her reading herself into the picture) to complicate and question her desires and the narratives that perpetuate and affirm them. Though we do not know exactly what goes on in the mind of the "you," it seems reasonable to assume that "I's" game makes the "you's" identification with the "maiden" in her casement a more difficult matter. By inserting herself into the picture ("And I — her mother!"), the "I" resituates the "maiden" and her "lover" within a network of relationships that the picture seems designed to avoid – namely, the maiden's relationship with her mother. With the mother suddenly an agent in the drama, multiple plotlines and competing desires now come into play, among them the "I's" desire to disrupt the "fairy tale" the picture tells. If the final stanza is any indication, the "I" believes that the scene of youthful love simply cannot hold: boys and girls grow to be men and women, love grows worn, and "nothing lasts a thousand years." These are ideas to which Piatt returns over and over again, with a more and less gentle hand. Here, the "I" relies on humor to instruct the "you," advising her that to maintain her beauty and, by implication, her lover's affections requires nothing less than defying the inexorable forces of time and gravity. "Just keep this turret moonlight wound / About your face," she says, and "stay in mid-air." Let the pictures and poems say what they will, the "I" implies, the ground that waits below that balcony is made up of stone and tears.

Reading the poem with a focus on what is being communicated internally between the poem's characters suggests that mothers complicate things, particularly those mothers who ask questions, who fail to accept prevailing narratives as inevitable, and who imagine other possibilities, presumably (but not necessarily) based on their own lived experiences. Importantly, the "I's" willingness to ask those questions and imagine those possibilities is not anchored in a highly particularized subjectivity. We hear nothing of specific lovers who made her promises they failed to keep, of a specific mother who failed to warn her, of specific books from her girlhood that told in print the fairy tales that life belies. More important than that type of particularity is the pattern the poem suggests and the way the "I" disrupts it. In the context of an ordinary interaction that involves an act of reading, the maternal "I" recognizes the daughter's reading strategy and uses it to insist on the fantasy as fantasy. The "I" and "you" find themselves in a recursive narrative, one that leads women into relationships that trap and restrict them, and the "I" knows it. She transforms the very thing that might have encouraged and perpetuated that narrative (the picture) into the thing that disrupts it.

If the subjective dimension of the poem demonstrates the "I's" canny awareness and adaptation of how the "you" "reads" the picture, the objective dimension of the poem – that is, the dimension that derives from the poem's status as a printed object – draws attention to the genre in which Piatt is working and to her own awareness of it. The poem announces that awareness by having the speaking "I" engage in one of the defining acts of a dramatic monologue: namely, to present the voice of a person who is obviously not its author. The voice the poem's "I" fashions in the last two stanzas is that of a person she imagines into a work of art. Though not identical, the creative act that produces these embedded monologues is similar to the creative act that produced Augusta Webster's Medea and Alfred Lord Tennyson's Ulysses. In these poems, the authors, like Piatt's speaking "I," create an imagined voice born out of an extant narrative or image.

Rather than settle on a single monologue, the "I" presents two possibilities, one that plays by the rules (stanza five), so to speak, and the other that breaks them (stanza six). When I say that the penultimate stanza "plays by the rules," I mean not only that the sentiments of that monologue are consistent with the spirit of the narrative implied by "the picture," but also that the monologue itself maintains its verisimilitude. The imperatives – "Make haste to bid the wedding guest, / And make the wedding garment gay" – do nothing to draw attention to their theatricality beyond being a spoken utterance. That is not the case in the final stanza. There the language shifts, in effect, from that of an actor to that of a director, drawing attention to the artificiality of the scene: "To look fair forever, / Just keep this turret moonlight wound / About your face." Here, Piatt uses the demonstrative adjective "this" to draw attention to the moonlight as a constituent aspect of the scene that might be controlled to particular effect. In doing so, she (Piatt) bids us as readers to recognize it as a convention: that is, moonlight is not simply the reflection of the sun's light on a sphere of rock, but an image that recurs in literary and visual texts and carries with it various accumulated associations.

The description of the moonlight as "*wound* / About your face" (emphasis mine) not only intensifies the imperative's strangeness, but also underscores the poem's generic self-awareness. The verb "wind" tends to describe the action of something rope-like. Moonlight that is "wound / About" a person's face does not simply cover it but coils about it, much like the fair "maiden's" hair in Browning's famous dramatic monologue "Porphyria's Lover," which was first published in 1836. In that poem, the murdering "I" explains how he asphyxiated his lover by winding her hair about her neck: "all her hair / In one long yellow string I *wound* / three times her little neck around / And strangled her" (emphasis mine).[13] The word "wound" alone might seem tenuous grounds for an intertextual reading; however, in both dramatic monologues that winding is associated with remaining "forever fair." Porphyria's lover kills her so that she might remain "mine, fair, / Perfectly pure and good." The "I" in "A Lesson in a Picture" commands the "you" to "keep this moonlight wound / About your face" in order to "look forever fair." Piatt's imperative is not murderous, but her odd use of the past participle "wound" suggests something vaguely suffocating, as though the "you" risks being smothered not literally by her own hair, but figuratively by desires that cannot be realized. Moreover, just as Porphyria did not recognize her own hair as the weapon that would end her life, the "you" in Piatt's poem may not recognize the moonlight as a convention of narratives that perpetuate unfulfill-able fantasies. But Piatt certainly does.

These embedded monologues not only bid us to recognize convention for what it is – a tool that might be used, rather than an inevitability – but they also bid us to recognize Piatt's poetic agency. The overlapping subjective and objective planes of the poem together suggest a striking degree of control and intentionality. Just as the "I" on the subjective plane of the poem suggests a game that bespeaks her knowledge of how the "you" is reading, that same "I" on the objective plane of the poem is the tool that Piatt uses to bespeak her knowledge of the genre in which she is working. By having the "I" construct additional voices within the context of the poem, voices that enact the same gender role differently, Piatt bids the reader to consider the nature of the poem's "I" and of the choices Piatt made in crafting her. Piatt puts herself in the poem – *not* by expressing her own thoughts or ideas through the voice of the speaking "I," but by making her authorial presence felt through the manipulation of generic convention. The point isn't so much that Piatt inserts her own particular self, possessed of a specific history and set of motivations, into the poem. The point is that she externally reveals her poetic presence in the crafting and shaping of the poem itself. The "I" does not express her ideas so much as it allows Piatt to perform the fact of her own artistic agency and intentionality.

Such performed agency and intentionality are particularly important to a history of American women's poetry insofar as they contradict the pervasive notions that women lacked the instinct and capacity to craft. Even at the end of the nineteenth century, one half century after Rufus Griswold's *Female Poets of America* (1849), readers continued to imagine and value women's poetry not as the product of intellect and skill, but as a manifestation of spirit and effusion.[14] You can see a version of this impulse clearly in Katharine Tynan's 1894 portrait of Piatt in her essay

"Poets in Exile." In a passage that fuses Piatt's person and her poems, Tynan stresses Piatt's "extreme womanliness" and characterizes Piatt's husband as the "methodical" one who takes "most tender care of his wife's poetry."[15] Piatt is, she insists, "a living contradiction of inked fingers and slipshod disarray that used to be the common idea of the woman poet."[16] What exactly Tynan finds contradictory about Piatt is unclear. What I find contradictory is Tynan's own insistence on Piatt's alleged disarray given the manifest order and deliberation in the poems themselves. Whatever Tynan's motivations in writing – to distinguish herself as a more modern woman poet, to prime readers to purchase Piatt's two-volume *Poems*, which was published that same year – her language provides important insight into the culture in which Piatt circulated and to which, however inaudibly to Tynan, Piatt's poems respond.

My reading of "A Lesson in a Picture" stresses Piatt's visible agency in the poem and clear engagement with the dramatic monologue as a genre. But as she was deeply aware, she was not the only agent in the meaning-making process. That process involved numerous other agents, among them the reader and the page on which the poems travelled. Several of her dramatic monologues bid her readers to recognize and consider their own role in that process by bidding them to see the page itself. Those poems do so in part by way of their visual dimension, which generates meaning beyond the ken of the poems' subjects. One of the most striking ways that Piatt's poems insist on their status as visual artifacts is by way of typographical marks – long and short dashes, ellipses, and parentheses. It is not particularly surprising that marks such as these, which were at once visibly significant and interpretively indeterminate, proved frustrating to contemporary reviewers. One reviewer of *Dramatic Persons and Moods* bemoaned that "a thread of delicate thought [was] mixed up in a tangle of parenthetical ejaculations," while another lamented that "in certain cases her thought is completely beclouded by a dexterous use of parentheses, dashes, and marks of interrogation."[17]

Rather than "becloud" her thought, her "dexterous use of parentheses, dashes, and marks of interrogation" signals a particular kind of thought: thought about the role that the reader plays, about the decisions the reader makes in the act of reading. Encountering such marks – particularly when reading aloud, as dramatic monologues seem to impel us to – forces readers to acknowledge the difference between the aural and the visual dimensions of the poem, between what the "I" can presumably see and what the reader can, between the subjective and objective dimensions of the poem. What, the reader may wonder, are the parentheses in the first stanza of "A Lesson in a Picture" – "(Here's a matter for a bird of the air / To drop down from the dusk and tell)" – intended to signify? An aside? A silent thought? A shift in tone? All, or none, of the above? Whatever they may mean in a particular instance, these marks remind readers that the poem's "I" and "you" share two spaces. As subjects or characters, they share an unseen landscape ostensibly full of material referents to which they gesture and to which readers only have partial access. As printed language the "I" and "you" share the landscape of the page, of which the poem's subjects, represented by the first- and second-person pronouns, are entirely unaware.

The dramatic monologue "Her Word of Reproach" contains a notably rich line in which the poem's typographical marks signify a particular interest in how the reader reads. The poem stages an interaction between a female speaking "I" and a male "you" regarding the promise of romantic love. Like the subjects in "A Lesson in a Picture," the "I" and "you" possess few, if any, characteristics that would distinguish them as specific individuals. The poem represents the "I's" response to the "you's" apparent and multiple attempts to persuade her of love's ability to withstand even the world's end. She remains dubious, fairly certain that love cannot endure life much less outlast death. The fifteenth line of that poem is a parenthetical command – that is, an imperative set off by parentheses – that appears as part of the "I's" response to the "you's" apparent minimization of death and that breaks in half a sentence that insists on the limitations of human knowledge:

> Ah, death is nothing! It may be so.
> Yet, granting at least that death is death
> (Pray look at the rose, and hear the bird),
> Whatever it is – we must die to know!
> Sometime we may long to say one word
> Together – and find we have no breath.[18]

As is always the case with imperatives, "you" is the implied subject: (you) look at the rose and (you) hear the bird. And like all pronouns, "you" draws its meaning from its referent. Obviously the second-person pronoun in this poem refers most often to the "I's" interlocutor, but this particular command is framed by typographical marks that only the reader can see and so bids the reader to see the imperative as looking up, so to speak, at the eyes that look down. Simply put, while the "I" is talking to the "you," the poem is talking to us, commanding us as readers to "look at the rose and hear the bird."

But what would it look like for the reader to do as the poem instructs? It can't be to look, as the internal "you" might, at the material world that presumably surrounds them. That world is largely invisible to readers. One thing the reader might do is track the birds and roses that share the poem's print context: here, the pages of *Dramatic Persons and Moods.*[19] Such tracking certainly yields: roses and birds, it turns out, abound in the book's pages as they do in nineteenth-century women's poetry more generally.[20] Though an analysis of both the rose and the bird falls outside the scope of this essay, the pattern that emerges by considering just the bird suggests the richness of such an exercise. In *Dramatic Persons and Moods*, birds are consistently associated with the speaking "I's" of dramatic monologues. "A Lesson in a Picture" refers to itself (parenthetically) as a "matter for a bird of the air / To drop down from the dusk and tell" and so implicitly aligns the "I" with the bird (given that she is the one, in fact, who tells the matter). In "After the Quarrel," another maternal "I" attempts to soothe her daughter's grief at lost love and says, "Voice like his was never heard? / No – but better ones, I vow; / Did you ever hear a bird? – / Listen, one is singing now!"[21] Whatever else the "you" is hearing in that moment, she is certainly hearing the "I's" voice. The "I" in "A Wall Between" uses the same verb – "moan" – to describe what she and the doves do. In "A Pique at Parting," the "I" accuses the male "you" of "leav[ing]" women with "the bird in the cage to sing."[22] In this particular line, the bird might be read as both the subject and the direct object of the infinitive "to sing": men leave women with a bird that sings to them and leave them the image of the bird to sing. To hear the bird, then, at least in part, is to hear the speaking "I's," to listen to what they say and how they say it.

But, as I hope my reading of "A Lesson in a Picture" makes clear, hearing the speaking "I" is a tricky matter. Any one of these "I's" functions not only as an expressive subject but also as a linguistic object, a tool that Piatt herself uses to turn conventions associated with particular genres (here, the dramatic monologue) and particular categories of writers (e.g., women poets) just so. To hear only the expressive subject is not to hear the bird. If the poems themselves are songs, as they were often described as being, then to hear the bird is, in some way, to hear the being that created it – namely, Piatt. But hearing Piatt requires that we not confuse Piatt (the maker) with the "I" (a tool she uses). We hear Piatt in the songs not because she speaks in or through the voices of these poems but because she creates the tension between the visual and the audible, the subjective and objective, that energizes and animates the poems.

To some extent, this entire essay has been my attempt to "hear the bird" in and through Piatt's dramatic monologues. Grappling with the relationship between the subjective and objective planes of the poem is one generically specific way of doing so. When applied to these poems, such a method reveals Piatt's careful consideration of how as mothers and daughters, as readers and writers, women possess and might exert agency to maintain or disrupt the things that restrict them. Piatt turns the "I," the bird, the rose, the moonlight, and the "you" just so, and suddenly we see differently how they might mean. I will confess that my experience of reading Piatt's poems – those I have addressed here and others – is not unlike the daughter's experience in "A Lesson in a Picture." The poem, like the "I," seems to have anticipated my act of reading and understood it long before I have.

Notes

1. See, for instance, "Art vs. Heart," Rev. of *A Voyage to the Fortunate Isles, Scribner's Monthly* 8.4 (August 1874), 501–502; William Dean Howells, "Some New Books of Poetry," Rev. of *That New World, Atlantic Monthly* 39 (January 1877), 87–90; "Mrs. Piatt's Poems," Rev. of *That New World, Scribner's Monthly* 14.1 (May 1877), 118–119; and "Current Poetry," Rev. of *Dramatic Persons and Moods, Literary World* 11 (January 1880), 11–12. Paula Bennett led the way in the recovery of Sarah Piatt's poetry, publishing *Palace-Burner: The Selected Poems of Sarah Piatt* (Urbana: University of Illinois Press), 2001. *Palace-Burner* collects a disproportionate number of poems that are overtly and aggressively political. The fact that many of Piatt's books are now available via Google Books may make possible a critical engagement with a wider selection of her work.
2. The moniker "dramatic monologue" was not used consistently until late in the century. According to Cornelia D. J. Pearsall, "Intermediary terms used by poets, often as titles for collections, such as 'Dramatic Lyrics,' 'Dramatic Romances,' 'Dramatic Idylls,' 'Dramatic Studies,' ... indicate their own attempts to place and even formalize literary production that was for some time unnamable." Cornelia D. J. Pearsall, "The Dramatic Monologue," *Cambridge Companion to Victorian Poetry*, Joseph Bristow (ed.), (Cambridge: Cambridge University Press, 2000), 69–70.
3. Nineteenth-century American poets are virtually absent from the literary history of the dramatic monologue. Interestingly, the absence is so complete that critical works tend not even to make note of it.
4. See, for instance, J. Zachary Finch, "The Ethics of Postbellum Melancholy in the Poetry of Sarah Piatt," *ESQ* 58.3 (2012), 415–445; Faith Barrett, *To Fight Aloud is Very Brave: American Poetry and the Civil War* (Amherst: University of Massachusetts Press, 2012), 187–251; Matthew Giordano, "'A Lesson From' the Magazines: Sarah Piatt and the Postbellum Periodical Poet," *American Periodicals* 16.1 (2006), 23–51; and Paula Bernat Bennett, *Poets in the Public Sphere: The Emancipatory Project of Women's Poetry, 1800–1900* (Princeton: Princeton University Press, 2003), 135–158.

5. As will become clear, my thinking about the dramatic monologue has been significantly influenced by Herbert Tucker and Isobel Armstrong in particular. See Herbert Tucker, "Dramatic Monologue and Overhearing the Lyric," *The Lyric Theory Reader*, Virginia Jackson and Yopie Prins (eds.), (Baltimore: Johns Hopkins University Press, 2014), 144–156, and Isobel Armstrong, *Victorian Poetry: Poetry, Poetics, and Politics* (New York: Routledge, 1993).
6. Dramatic monologues appear in Piatt's early collections, and contemporary readers associated her with that form. One reviewer of *A Masque of Poets*, which published Piatt's dramatic monologue "Her Word of Reproach" anonymously, declared he would be "surprised to learn" she was not its author, suggesting this poem's aesthetic consistency with her earlier poems. Rev. of *A Masque of Poets, Sunday Afternoon* 3 (January–September 1879), 191.
7. For a history of thinking about the dramatic monologue, see Glennis Byron, *The Dramatic Monologue* (New York: Routledge, 2003), 1–29.
8. Byron, *Dramatic Monologue*, 13. For other examples of "vaguely particularized speakers," see Elizabeth Barrett Browning's "The Runaway Slave at Pilgrim's Point" and Robert Browning's "Any Wife to Her Husband." For an example of a Piatt poem that contains a more "clearly particularised speaker," see "A Wall Between," which appears in Sarah Piatt, *Dramatic Persons and Moods* (Boston: Houghton Mifflin, 1880), 25–35.
9. Piatt, "After the Quarrel," *Dramatic Persons and Moods*, 48.
10. Piatt, "A Pique at Parting," *Dramatic Persons and Moods*, 14. For an extended reading of this particular poem, see Jess Roberts, "Sarah Piatt's Grammar of Convention and the Conditions of Authorship," *The Cambridge Companion to Nineteenth-Century American Poetry*, Kerry Larson (ed.), (Cambridge: Cambridge University Press, 2012), 172–192.
11. Piatt, "Her Word of Reproach," *Dramatic Persons and Moods*, 17.
12. Piatt, "A Lesson in a Picture," *Dramatic Persons and Moods*, 41–42.
13. Robert Browning, "Porphyia's Lover," *The Poetical Works of Robert Browning*, G. Robert Stange (ed.), (Boston: Houghton Mifflin 1974), 286.
14. For a particularly anxious description of the difference between male genius and female spirit, see Rufus Griswold, "Preface," *The Female Poets of America* (Philadelphia: Carey and Hart, 1849), 7–8.
15. Katharine Tynan, "Poets in Exile," *The Critic* 21 (24 February 1894), 628.
16. Ibid.
17. Rev. of *Dramatic Persons and Moods, National Quarterly Review* 6.12 (April 1880), 498–499; "Current Poetry," Rev. of *Dramatic Persons and Moods, Literary World* 11 (January 1880), 11–12.
18. Piatt, "Her Word of Reproach," *Dramatic Persons and Moods*, 17–18.
19. Thus far, when scholars address the relevance of print context in reading Piatt's poetry, they tend to focus on magazine culture. See Bennett, *Poets in the Public Sphere*; Giordano "'A Lesson from' the Magazines"; and Elizabeth Renker, "The 'Twilight of the Poets' in the Era of American Realism, 1875–1900," *The Cambridge Companion to Nineteenth-Century American Poetry*, Kerry Larson (ed.), (Cambridge: Cambridge University

Press, 2012), 135–153. While Piatt's poetry certainly enriches and is enriched by an understanding of that particular medium, her book publications represent a rich material incarnation of her poetry that exerted considerable influence in the nineteenth century.

20. Birds were so commonly associated with women poets that Cheryl Walker called her survey of nineteenth-century women's poetry *The Nightingale's Burden: Women Poets before 1900* (Bloomington: Indiana University Press, 1983).
21. Piatt, "After the Quarrel," *Dramatic Persons and Moods*, 49.
22. Piatt, "A Pique at Parting," *Dramatic Persons and Moods*, 14.

CHAPTER 22

Women Writers and the Hymn

Claudia Stokes

Though it seldom receives attention from literary scholars, the hymn was the most popular poetic form of the nineteenth century, as it was the primary medium in which a great many Americans engaged with and experienced poetry. Though hymns had long been acceptable reading material for private religious devotions, they were for centuries prohibited from inclusion in mainline congregational worship on the grounds that lay-authored religious lyric might promote questionable doctrines and undermine clerical authority. This ban became increasingly tenuous in the early nineteenth century amid the meteoric rise of Methodism, a denomination that attracted an enormous following in part because of its promotion of congregational song as well as its populism, lively revival meetings, and rejection of the Calvinist doctrine of predestination. After losing both cultural relevance and thousands of members to Methodism, mainline Protestant denominations attempted to remain viable by reluctantly sanctioning the inclusion of hymns in public worship – a decision that did little to prevent the ascent of Methodism but that nevertheless imparted new legitimacy and respectability to hymnody. Following this official benison, hymns flourished throughout the nineteenth century, a period that became a veritable golden age for this devotional poetic form.

Authored by amateurs and professionals alike, hymns circulated in both conventional and unconventional literary venues. Hymn lyrics were often first published as poems in periodicals or poetry collections, where they were discovered by hymn editors, and they were frequently interpolated in nineteenth-century religious novels, as with the inclusion of hymn lyrics in such novels as Susan Warner's *The Wide, Wide World* (1850) and E.P. Roe's novels *Barriers Burned Away* (1872) and *The Earth Trembled* (1887). Hymns circulated most widely, however, in such religious venues as the hymn book, the denominational hymnal, and the hymn collection, which was among the most popular printed forms of the century and which sold in astounding numbers unrivaled in the world of mainstream literary publishing. For example, Ira Sankey and Philip Bliss's famed collection *Gospel Hymns and Sacred Songs* (1875) sold well over a million copies in the United States alone; together with its sequels, it sold over 50 million copies.[1] Beyond the world of print, hymns circulated through oral performance in worship services, and in that setting they reached those who otherwise had little contact with published poetry: the working classes, rural and frontier people, slaves, and the illiterate. Widely disseminated in both print and public performance, hymn lyrics saturated daily life in the nineteenth century, for they were habitually included in conversation, epistolary correspondence, and chapbooks, as well as such domestic activities as family worship and recreation.[2] In her memoir of her 1820s childhood, Lucy Larcom, for instance, describes how the recitation of hymn lyrics was a normal accompaniment to her mother's domestic labors, her work "baking or ironing" regularly supplemented by the cadences of devotional verse.[3] It was through her childhood immersion in hymnody, Larcom insists, that she first came to love poetry and understand the workings of metaphor and prosody.

Despite its prominence in nineteenth-century American culture, hymnody has remained unintegrated in scholarly considerations of nineteenth-century American poetry. It may be tempting to presume that hymns operated in a parallel lyric world, with its own array of writers, venues, and distribution conduits, but the largely fallow archive of nineteenth-century hymnody confirms the strong presence of this form in the literary mainstream. This was particularly the case in the careers of nineteenth-century American women writers, whose professional bodies of work often included forays into the newly fashionable genre of the hymn. Indeed, in overlooking one of the major poetic forms of the nineteenth century, we have disregarded a genre of momentous import to the period's women writers. Though Mary De Jong has shown that women never numbered more than a fraction of published hymnists, estimating that female contributors to hymn books comprised about 9 percent in the 1870s and 12 percent in the 1890s, June Hadden Hobbs has argued that the late nineteenth century nevertheless saw the "feminization of American hymnody," the female gendering of this devotional lyric form, regardless of the actual number of women hymnists.[4] Outside the circles of sectarian publishing and religious music, the hymn form became particularly popular among established American women writers, who proportionally authored many more hymns than their male counterparts. While a handful of mainstream male writers – such as Fireside Poets William Cullen Bryant, Henry Wadsworth Longfellow, and John Greenleaf Whittier – composed hymns, the corresponding number of women is far greater and constitutes a veritable Who's Who of nineteenth-century American women writers. Among the better-remembered products of this new literary enthusiasm for hymnody are Julia Ward Howe's 1861 "Battle Hymn of the Republic" and Emily Dickinson's use of such hymn forms as the fourteener (in which lines of eight syllables alternate with lines of six) and allusions to eighteenth-century hymnist Isaac Watts.[5] Less remembered are the many hymns by Louisa May Alcott, Margaret Fuller, Helen Hunt Jackson, Lucy Larcom, Lydia Sigourney, and Susan Warner. In some instances, these professional women writers crafted poems that were clearly demarcated as hymns, whether through their employment of established hymn forms or through titles that announced their genre; in other cases, however, they wrote devotional poems that would be adapted and set to music by hymn editors. Through both channels, hymn contributions by women writers saturated the nineteenth century, and a few examples illustrate the wide range of women writers who made important contributions to the form. The nineteenth-century literary reputation of Pheobe Cary derived not from the regionalist writings recently rediscovered by scholars but from such hymns as "Nearer Home" and "One Sweetly Solemn Thought." Harriet Beecher Stowe's hymns "Still, Still with Thee" and "Abide in Me" nearly rivaled *Uncle Tom's Cabin* in their fame and popularity, and are still included in hymnals across denominations. Novelist Anna Warner – Susan Warner's sister – was a celebrated hymnist and hymn editor who authored "Jesus Loves Me," the world's most famous children's hymn, which she first published in the pages of her novel *Dollars and Cents* (1852). Mary Mapes Dodge, author of the children's novel *Hans Brinker* (1865) and editor of the periodicals *Hearth and Home* and *St. Nicholas*, authored numerous hymns, including the children's hymn "Can a Little Child Like Me?" Activist and suffragist Frances Willard wrote several hymns, including the temperance hymns "Write It on the Workhouse Gate" and "List to the Tread of Many Feet." Elizabeth Stuart Phelps not only authored such hymns as "Thine the Bearing and Forbearing," but her bestselling novel *The Gates Ajar* (1868) also inspired such contributions to hymnody as Lydia Baxter's hymn "The Gates Ajar for Me" and the 1885 hymn collection *Gates Ajar*, edited by J.H. Kurzenknabe.

As these many examples attest, the hymn reigned as one of the era's major poetic genres available to women. However, the hymn was not merely another lyric genre in the range of possible forms. It was opposed by clergy for so long because it imparted extraordinary religious authority to common people, enabling them to influence the religious beliefs and practices of worshippers and to offer scriptural interpretation, and for this reason it was promoted by populist, egalitarian movements such as seventeenth-century nonconformists and eighteenth-century Methodists. At the time hymnody became popular in the nineteenth century, women in most denominations were still prohibited even from speaking in church, with an outright ban on preaching for women, and they typically acquired public religious authority through charitable work in benevolence organizations or Sunday school instruction.[6] Hymnody provided an alternate route for women to acquire public religious authority while still complying with normative expectations about female respectability. Hymns were typically composed within the confines of the home, a setting that blunted any concerns about female public ambitions, and, as devotional works of poetry, they provided ample confirmation of the authors' piety, refinement, and sensibility. It is for this reason that female hymnody achieved its first flowering amid mid-century sentimentalism, for this register provided an acceptable literary discourse of female public religious instruction tempered by normative assurances of feminine modesty, sensibility, and domesticity; unsurprisingly, most of the major figures of sentimentalism – such as Alcott, Stowe, and Warner – actively participated in the thriving new culture of hymnody, both incorporating hymn lyrics into their novels and trying their own hands at this newly acceptable devotional form.[7] Conventional femininity thus served as an asset in the world of hymnody, providing both opportunities and justification for women's participation in this form. For instance, women's traditional supervision of childrearing justified their involvement in, and eventual control of, the sub-genre of children's hymnody, a form charged with particular importance: it was believed that hymns were better suited than scripture to the religious education of children because of their capacity to simplify doctrine and package it in the memorable devices of prosody.

But even while hymnody capitulated to these conservative standards, it nevertheless imparted an authority to female hymnists that far exceeded anything otherwise available to women poets more generally. While to the undiscerning eye hymns may appear to be mere devotional poems, these works enabled women writers to evade traditional restrictions and proffer public religious counsel, circulate their own exegetical interpretations of scripture, and influence the religious ideas of readers and worshippers. Though hymns were expected to be conventional in their form and prosodic technique, their contents may propound tendentious doctrines and scriptural interpretations, and in so doing influence the beliefs and practices of worshippers. For instance, Unitarian hymnist Eliza Lee Follen's anti-slavery hymn, "Lord Deliver, Thou Canst Save," advocates numerous contentious political and religious beliefs, among them a belief that the deity virulently opposes slavery, despite the many references to slavery in scripture, and a post-millennialist belief in the perfectibility of the social world, with human beings playing a central role in the fulfillment of divine prophecy. In this respect, hymns functioned in ways akin to the sermon, a public medium forbidden to women, though female hymnists avoided censure by using the voices of the singing congregation to articulate their words for them. But, unlike the sermon or even other poetic genres, the hymn was regarded as a sacred form rooted in divine inspiration, and it was the sole lyric genre to retain the ancient perception of the poet as a vessel of divine communication. Anna Warner articulated this opinion in the first verse of her 1864 hymn, "How Can I Keep from Singing":

> My life flows on in endless song;
> Above Earth's lamentation,
> I catch the sweet, tho' far-off hymn
> That hails a new creation;
> Through all the tumult and the strife,
> I hear the music ringing;
> I find an echo in my soul –
> How can I keep from singing?

Warner here depicts hymns as a providential gift from the deity and an important instrument of divine communication. In addition, hymnody serves as the poem's chief figurative trope for piety: amid life's difficulties, the hearing of hymns provides the speaker with continued inspiration, and the singing of hymns likewise reflects the speaker's full, joyful embrace of Christian belief.

Against the long-standing opposition of clergy, hymns were popularly regarded as a legitimate source of religious instruction, their contents often studied by readers in lieu of scripture itself. Henry Ward Beecher, the mid-century's most prominent celebrity minister, summarized the elevated status of hymnody with his assertion that "with a Bible and a hymn-book a man has a whole library; and if he knows how to use those two things, he knows enough to be a missionary, or to be a minister anywhere."[8] Hymns, it was widely believed, possessed the power to instigate religious conversion and inculcate virtue, and children across religious denominations were encouraged to memorize hymns on the grounds that such texts could lay a strong moral foundation built to last throughout life.

Advocates repeated anecdotes recounting how the timely recollection of a hymn verse memorized in childhood could prevent adults from committing sinful acts.[9] Their reading thus functioned not as an act of aesthetic engagement, literary pleasure, or leisure, as was more typically the case with poetry in general, but as an act of religious piety: to read hymns was to participate in religious devotion, and to recite or sing them was to engage in an act of prayer.

In all these ways, hymns imparted genuine religious authority to women writers: the power to offer public religious instruction, to serve as a prophetic instrument of the divine will, to compose poems regarded as sacrosanct, and to minister to the multitudes. Though it would be many years before women would be ordained in Protestant denominations, hymnody offered the first public, liturgical setting for the execution of female priestly authority, and in this way poetry provided the earliest precedent for the clerical consecration of women. However, hymnody was a deeply conflicted enterprise for nineteenth-century women, and it imparted this authority only on the condition that women publicly renounced it, whether through assertions of modesty, the use of pseudonyms, or even anonymity. In a contradiction that such critics as Nina Baym, Mary Kelley, and Jane Tompkins have shown to be endemic to women's literature of the period, women proved their worthiness of such authority by their refusal of it, a condition that imparted distinguished religious standing in the short term but that also contributed directly to their exploitation at the hands of religious publishers, to their disappearance from the archive, and to scholarly inattention to the most potent of all female poetic forms.[10]

Beyond the ranks of celebrated female writers well remembered in mainstream literary history, hymnody also attracted thousands of women who penned devotional poems that were set to music, included in hymn collections, and sung by congregations, among them Mrs. E. W. Chapman, Mamie P. Ferguson, Mary C. Bishop Gates, Lucia F. W. Gillette, Minnie B. Johnson, Priscilla Jane Owens, Phoebe Palmer, Sybil F. Partridge, Emily C. Pearson, Ida L. Reed, Harriet R. K. Spaeth, and Maria Straub, to name just a few of the countless female hymnists who contributed to the period's flowering of hymnody. De Jong has shown that women's contributions to hymnals increased as the century wore on, and this increase may be due to the mounting successes of sentimentalism in confirming the respectability of hymnody for women or to the growing amenability of hymn editors to the merits of female-authored hymns.[11] By the late century, female hymnists were so well established that the period saw the publication of several specialized hymn collections, among them Eva Munson Smith's mammoth, nearly 1,000-page anthology *Woman in Sacred Song* (1888), Emma Pittman's *Lady Hymn Writers* (1892), and Nicholas Smith's *Songs from the Hearts of Women* (1903), which acknowledges "Woman's [particular] relation to Church hymnody" and asserts that women hymnists have "given the Church many of the tenderest and sweetest of the world's best hymns."[12]

Most women hymnists published only one or two works, and the few women who successfully created an esteemed corpus of hymns did not tend to be diffident, retiring women confined to the domestic space – as they were implicitly expected to be and as their hymns often suggested – but were instead accomplished, well-connected women with ready access to the literary public sphere. The career of Emily Huntington Miller (1833–1913) is an illustrative one. A prolific writer who authored numerous poems, short stories, and collections, she also wrote dozens of hymns in wide circulation in the nineteenth century. As the daughter of a Methodist minister, Miller was reared in a denominational setting known for its commitment to both congregational song and female religious leadership, for Methodism was the first mainstream denomination to permit women to perform clerical duties.[13] For these reasons, Methodism yielded many of the period's most eminent female hymnists, among them Eliza Hewitt, Mary Artemisia Lathbury, and Fanny Crosby. Miller was highly educated, and she spent much of her career in women's higher education, working for nearly a decade as the Dean of Northwestern University's women's college. She also spent many years as editor of *The Little Corporal*, a children's periodical based in Chicago, and she used that setting as a venue for the initial publication of lyrics that would soon become children's hymns. For instance, in 1867 she printed her own children's poem, "I Love to Hear the Story," in the pages of *The Little Corporal*; by the 1880s it had been set to two different musical arrangements and appeared in more than 150 different hymnals and hymn collections, including the distinguished English hymn collection *Hymns Ancient and Modern* (1861), where it was one of the few American works.[14]

However, in marked contrast with the authority and prominence of hymnody in this era, social convention dictated that female hymnists demonstrate Christian humility and avoid avidly promoting themselves and their hymns for material gain or careerist ambition. Desire for public recognition was particularly unseemly for women and could undermine their reputations and legitimacy as hymnists, though this expectation did not prevent prominent literary women, such as Miller, from using the literary media at their disposal to position their lyrics to advantage. The inconspicuousness of the female hymnist was achieved through a confederation of various circumstances, chief among them the basic religious demands of the form. Though these poems were expected to derive from the authors' own personal experiences, the central figure of these poems was expected to be the deity alone, with the hymnist renouncing his or her own ego and stepping aside in deference to the deity. This presumption is evident, for instance, in the 1896 assertion of *Atlantic Monthly* editor Horace E. Scudder that his kinswoman Eliza Scudder had been an effective hymnist because of her "self-effacement in the larger life of a spiritual reality outside of and beyond herself": the perception of hymnody as a form of divine communication necessitates that the hymnist resign any personal ambition or vanity in the spirit of Christian service.[15] Common practices of religious publishing contributed further to the relative public invisibility of the female hymnist, for, in saturating the market with cheap, disposable hymn collections, publishers inadvertently prevented individual hymns from acquiring longevity and hymnists from achieving renown.[16] Hymn editors did their part, too, by meticulously expunging stylistic or theological traces of hymnists out of concern that these authorial remnants would inhibit reader identification.[17] After passing through the hands of editors, hymns shed some of the distinguishing hallmarks of their authors and, in this more simplified state, often became the copyrighted property of religious publishers, who controlled their distribution and earned the lion's share of revenue from their sale. In this respect, an insistence on pious modesty worked to the financial advantage of religious publishers, who could use this perception of hymnody as a form of Christian service in order to justify their low pay rates and exploitative practices, especially in their dealings with women writers. Hymnists were not expected to write for reasons other than piety, and any expectation of public attention or fair payment would necessarily throw into question the hymnist's motives and sincerity.

The only acceptable instances in which women were exempted from these expectations were when their celebrity derived from the public prominence of their husbands or families, as with the public status of hymn composer Phoebe Palmer Knapp (1802–1874), whose husband, Joseph Knapp, was an enormously successful businessman and the founder of the Metropolitan Life Insurance Company, and whose home served as one of the central cultural salons of New York elite. Elizabeth Payson Prentiss (1818–1878), author of the bestselling religious novel *Stepping Heavenward* (1869) and such hymns as "More Love to Thee, O Christ," also had acceptable public standing due to the prominence of her father, Congregationalist minister Edward Payson, and husband, George Prentiss, who was minister at New York's Mercer Street Presbyterian Church. After her death, her husband issued a collection of her private writings that, though it exposed to public view her personal religious life, nonetheless corroborated her compliance with the normative standards of modesty, domesticity, and refinement expected of the ideal Christian woman and of the female hymnist in particular. A journal entry dated to 1841, for instance, evidences her preference for private religious reflection over unseemly public avowals of faith: "I do dislike the present style of talking on religious subjects," she wrote. "Let people pray – earnestly, fervently, not simply morning and night, but the *whole day long*, making their lives one continued prayer; but, oh, don't let them tell others, or let others know *half* how much of communion with Heaven is known to their own hearts."[18] Restraint, decorum, and a modest refusal of public life affirm the legitimacy of the female hymnist's faith, the emotional sincerity of her hymns, and her suitability for service as a vessel of divine communication.

No examination of nineteenth-century American hymnody would be complete without a consideration of Fanny Crosby (1820–1915), who was without question the most prolific and widely-known American hymnist, male or female, of the nineteenth century but whose vexed reputation demonstrated the consequences of diverging from the genre's expectations of gentility, education, and pious anonymity. She was a dedicated professional writer who, by contractual agreement, wrote three hymns a week for religious publisher Biglow and Main, and she is credited with the authorship of approximately 9,000 hymns, many of which are still in wide circulation today, among them such songs as "Blessed Assurance," "Jesus, Keep Me Near the Cross," and "Safe in the Arms of Jesus."[19] Crosby was a genuine celebrity in the late century, and in her memoir, *Memories of Eighty Years* (1906), she recounted several incidents of being publicly recognized by strangers. However, Crosby received criticism on numerous fronts, and these comments amply illustrate the social conditions women hymnists were expected to follow. Her extraordinary output was no doubt motivated in part by genuine financial exigency: she was blinded during infancy, and, in the long-standing nineteenth-century tradition of impoverished female writers, she supported herself through her writing, living separately from her estranged husband, about whom little is known. Her financial reliance on hymn writing, her productivity, and her public renown proved problematic in the socially conservative world of hymnody, and she was accused of being a careerist motivated less by piety than by ambition and financial greed. Though Crosby's productivity might be perceived as evidence of her work ethic, a compulsion to sanctify the deity, or the boundless depths of her faith (let alone the onerous contractual demands of her publisher), it was instead received as evidence of an opportunistic insincerity and unseemly vulgarity, a criticism that was by no means levelled at her male peers in the world of religious music. Though in her memoir she described her poverty and the limitations imposed by her disability, she publicly disavowed being in any way motivated by financial necessity, declaring that she donated all her royalty revenue – modest though it was, thanks to the terms of her publishing agreement – to charitable causes, despite her own significant needs.[20] And in response to questions about the emotional sincerity of hymns produced with such frequency, she insisted that all her poems derived from personal experience, and she even claimed to serve as a medium of divine communication, as with her assertion, "That some of my hymns have been dictated by the blessed Holy Spirit I have no doubt; and that others have been the result of deep meditation I know to be true."[21] As these criticisms suggest, the female hymnist was implicitly expected to be financially secure, either born among the elite or married to a man capable of providing a stable living; in this way, she was expected to have normative, conventional domestic arrangements, which could both finance her hymn writing and provide a respectable setting to which she could modestly recede from public view. Furthermore, she was also expected to be unconcerned by the economic value of the hymn, which was one of the most lucrative literary commodities of the period in an era with a seemingly inexhaustible appetite for new religious music.

These financial expectations were concomitant with parallel expectations of a superior education and refined sensibilities, both of which Crosby lacked and which provided the grounds for enduring criticisms of her hymns. Due to her disability, Crosby received a limited formal education, beginning school at the advanced age of fifteen, and she composed by dictation. This combination resulted in a poetic style characterized by simple phrasings, vernacular rhetoric, and repeated refrains, and which inadvertently showcased her lack of advanced literary learning or command of the finer points of prosody. Perhaps to compensate for this deficit, Crosby made literacy a central component of her public image, insisting that she be photographed holding a book – which she was of course unable to read. In her memoir she claimed that she always composed hymn lyrics while holding a book, asserting that "somehow or other the words seem to come more promptly when I am so engaged. I can also remember more accurately when the ... volume is in my grasp."[22]

Her lack of education was coupled with a distinctive hymn style that yielded immense popularity as well as widespread criticism. Though she was descended from New England Puritans, in 1850 she converted to Methodism at a revival meeting, a setting that gave rise to a genre of hymnody known as the "gospel" or revival style that would become Crosby's own signature style. Following the conventions of this hymn style, Crosby's hymns were often of a simple, earthy character and often openly broke ranks with the standards of modesty and decorum that governed women hymnists, as with the lyric in which she proclaimed "the children of the Lord have a right to shout and sing."[23] One of her most famous hymns, "We Are Going" (1858), is typical of the colloquial, unadorned style of her verses and of revival hymnody in general:

> We are going, we are going,
> To a home beyond the skies,
> Where the fields are robed in beauty,
> And the sunlight never dies.
>
> We are going, we are going,
> And the music we have heard,
> Like the echo of the woodland,
> Or the carol of the bird.[24]

These lines rely on repetition, simple diction, and uninventive metaphors, and they are thus readily accessible to an oral, listening audience. But in violation of the standard conventions of mainstream hymnody, her hymn does not examine a scriptural verse, narrate a spiritual epiphany, or proffer a theological tenet – features that require greater education and lyrical sophistication.

Generations of critics have assailed Crosby for the seemingly low caliber of her verse, attributing their style and content to a dearth of craftsmanship, a lack of education, and to the rapidity with which she composed hymns. Underlying this criticism is the suggestion that, had she possessed more pride in her work or greater piety, she would have devoted more time to her hymns and thereby infused them with greater lyric sophistication or theological substance. Venerable hymnologist John Julian dismissed her hymns with the pronouncement that, "with few exceptions, [her hymns are] very weak and poor," and he attributed their popularity to "the melodies to which they are wedded."[25] More recently, critic J.R. Watson bluntly denounced Crosby's hymns as "crude," and her most recent biographer,

Edith Blumhofer, conceded that her hymns cannot be recognized as "serious."[26] As is evident in Julian's suggestive use of the economic term "poor" in describing Crosby's hymns, these recent critics cleave to some of the same standards and expectations that characterized female hymnody of the nineteenth century, conflating literary quality with the trappings of elite social class and denouncing hymnists who fell short of this standard. Missing in these assessments is an attempt to understand Crosby's immense popularity, which was enabled rather than undermined by her unaffected, simple style. Unlike the sophisticated prosody of such august hymnists as Isaac Watts or Charles Wesley, Crosby's hymns were accessible to the listening audiences of revival meetings, who could readily pick up and join in on their simple repeated refrains. Furthermore, amid the religious cynicism and doubts of the late century, Crosby's hymns suggestively invoke a prior era of unquestioning religious faith and project a nostalgic image of piety that is unconflicted and assured, unencumbered by qualifications or hesitations.[27] Her hymns, that is, fashioned an appealing image of Christian faith as unpretentious and straightforward. Though superior education, refinement, and elite standing were expected of female hymnists, Crosby's style implicitly conveyed to countless worshippers that these traits were by no means requisite for membership in the Christian fold, and her hymns were successful because they presented Christianity as inclusive and down-to-earth.

Though women-authored hymnody in no way declined after Crosby's death in 1915, her hymn corpus serves as the genre's high-water mark, reaching unparalleled heights of popularity, productivity, and influence. Little remembered outside the fields of hymnology or American religious history, Crosby – and, to a lesser degree, her cohort of nineteenth-century women hymnists – was an important transitional figure in the ascension of women to official positions of religious leadership. Despite the criticism she endured, her hymns shaped the religious lives of millions of Americans, and she was without question one of the period's most influential, recognizable religious public figures. Her career coincided with a number of important developments that indicated shifting attitudes toward female religious leadership, among them the 1878 resolution of the National Woman Suffrage Association denouncing religious patriarchy as well as the publication of Elizabeth Cady's Stanton's feminist work *The Woman's Bible* (1895, 1898), which assailed the sexism of Christianity and called for women's liberation from the strictures of religious law. Though Crosby, a devout evangelical, likely would not have condoned these events, her prominence nevertheless helped the American public adapt to the presence of women in public religious life, and her hymns, as well as those of her female contemporaries, would pave the way for such unapologetic female religious leaders as Mary Baker Eddy, Aimee Semple McPherson, and Carry Nation. Less fortunate, however, is the possibility that Crosby's public prominence also contributed to an elite perception that woman-authored hymnody was lesser in quality and thus undeserving of attention. In some senses, Crosby's hymns epitomized some of the literary traits – such as mawkishness, unambitious artistry, and unoriginality – that, in the twentieth century, would become standard summary judgments of nineteenth-century women's writing as a whole and that would be used to justify their exclusion from study or scholarly attention. Though over the last fifty years critics have successfully rehabilitated nineteenth-century women's literature from this critique, female hymnists still await a similar recovery and admission into the canons of nineteenth-century American women poets and of American literature writ large.

Notes

1. Sandra S. Sizer, *Gospel Hymns and Social Religion: The Rhetoric of Nineteenth-Century Religion* (Philadelphia: Temple University Press, 1978), 5; Candy Gunther Brown, *The Word in the World: Evangelical Writing, Publishing, and Reading in America, 1789–1880* (Chapel Hill: University of North Carolina Press, 2004), 211.
2. Mary De Jong, "'Theirs the Sweetest Songs': Women Hymn Writers in the Nineteenth-Century United States," *A Mighty Baptism: Race, Gender, and the Creation of American Protestantism*, Susan Juster and Lisa MacFarlane (eds.), (Ithaca: Cornell University Press, 1996), 141–142.
3. Lucy Larcom, *A New England Girlhood: Outlined From Memory* (Boston: Houghton, Mifflin, 1890), 58.
4. De Jong, "Theirs the Sweetest," 144; June Hadden Hobbs, *"I Sing For I Cannot Be Silent": The Feminization of American Hymnody, 1870–1920* (Pittsburgh: University of Pittsburgh Press, 1997).
5. See, for instance, Carolyn Lindley Cooley, *The Music of Emily Dickinson's Poems and Letters: A Study of Imagery and Form* (Jefferson: McFarland, 2003); Benjamin Lease, *Emily Dickinson's Readings of Men and Books* (New York: St. Martin's, 1990), 50–54; Shira Wolosky, "Rhetoric or Not: Hymnal Tropes in Emily Dickinson and Isaac Watts," *The New England Quarterly* 16 (June 1988): 214–232.
6. See Anne M. Boylan, *Sunday School: The Formation of an American Institution 1790–1880* (New Haven: Yale University Press, 1988); Lori D. Ginzberg, *Women and the Work of Benevolence: Morality, Politics, and Class in the Nineteenth-Century United States* (New Haven: Yale University Press, 1990).

7. For more on the involvement of sentimentalism in the rise of female hymnody, see Claudia Stokes, "My Kingdom: Sentimentalism and the Refinement of Hymnody," *ESQ* 58.3 (2012): 294–337, and chapter 2 of Claudia Stokes, *The Altar at Home: Sentimental Literature and Nineteenth-Century American Religion* (Philadelphia: University of Pennsylvania Press, 2014).
8. Henry Ward Beecher, "Relations of Music to Worship," *Yale Lectures on Preaching*, vol. 2, 1893 (New York: Ford, Howard, Hurlbert, 1896), 137.
9. For instance, Fanny Crosby included many such anecdotes in her memoir, the final chapters of which are dedicated to recounting stories of the effects of her hymns on suffering, anguished people in need of help. See Fanny Crosby, *An Autobiography, 1906* (Grand Rapids: Baker House, 1986).
10. Nina Baym, *Woman's Fiction: A Guide to Novels By and About Women in America 1820–1870*, 2nd edn. (Urbana: University of Illinois Press, 1993), 44; Mary Kelley, *Private Woman, Public Stage: Literary Domesticity in Nineteenth-Century America* (New York: Oxford University Press, 1984); Jane Tompkins, *Sensational Designs The Cultural Work of American Fiction 1790–1860* (New York: Oxford University Press, 1985), 122–146.
11. De Jong, "Theirs the Sweetest Songs," 144.
12. Nicholas Smith, *Songs from the Hearts of Women: One Hundred Famous Hymns and Their Writers* (Chicago: A.C. McClurg, 1903), ix.
13. For a history of this phenomenon, see Catherine A. Brekus, "Female Evangelism in the Early Methodism Movement, 1784–1845," *Methodism and the Shaping of American Culture*," Nathan O. Hatch and John H. Wigger (eds.), (Nashville: Kingswood, 2001), 135–173; Catherine A. Brekus, *Strangers and Pilgrims: Female Preaching in America, 1740–1845* (Chapel Hill: University of North Carolina Press, 1996).
14. Edward S. Ninde, *The Story of the American Hymn* (New York: Abingdon, 1921), 16.
15. Horace E. Scudder, "Introductory Note," *Hymns and Sonnets*, Eliza Scudder, (Boston: Houghton, Mifflin, 1896), xiii.
16. Edith L. Blumhofer, "Franny Crosby, William Doane, and The Making of Gospel Hymns in the Late Nineteenth Century," *Sing Them Over Again To Me: Hymns and Hymnody in America*, Edith L. Blumhofer and Mark A. Noll (eds.), (Tuscaloosa: University of Alabama Press, 2006), 158.
17. De Jong, "Theirs the Sweetest Songs," 149.
18. George Prentiss (ed.), *The Life and Letters of Elizabeth Prentiss* (New York: Anson D.F. Randolph, 1882), 55. This journal entry was written on January 1, 1841.
19. Henry Wilder Foote, *Three Centuries of American Hymnody* (Cambridge: Harvard University Press, 1940), 267.
20. Brown, *Word in the World*, 197–198.
21. Crosby, *An Autobiography*, 187.
22. Ibid.

23. Quoted in *Songs of Joy and Gladness*, W. McDonald, Joshua Gill, et al. (eds.), (Boston: McDonald, Gill, 1888), 74.
24. Quoted in Ninde, *Story of the American Hymn*, 347.
25. A *Dictionary of Hymnology*, revised edition, John Julian (ed.), (London: John Murray, 1925), 1204.
26. J.R. Watson, *The English Hymn: A Critical and Historical Study* (Oxford: Clarendon, 1999), 496; Edith L. Blumhofer, *Her Heart Can See: The Life and Hymns of Fanny J. Crosby* (Grand Rapids: Wm. B. Eerdmans, 2005), 252.
27. Jackson Lears, *No Place of Grace: Antimodernism and the Transformation of American Culture 1880–1920* (New York: Pantheon, 1981), 24, 42; Ferenc Morton Szasz, *The Divided Mind of Protestant America, 1880–1930* Tuscaloosa University of Alabama Press, 1982), 21.

CHAPTER 23

Women Poets, Child Readers

Angela Sorby

Almost all nineteenth-century women poets – from Lucretia Davidson to Emily Dickinson, from Frances E. W. Harper to Charlotte Perkins Gilman – wrote at least some verses for children.[1] Why? In part, there were cultural pressures at work: women faced obstacles in most professional fields, but writing for children was viewed as acceptable and even natural. As Sarah Josepha Hale put it, "the department of Juvenile literature is peculiarly appropriate to female writers" who wish to be "useful to others" rather than "shining themselves."[2] Writing children's poetry could be understood as a natural outgrowth of maternal nurturing instead of as a form self-expression. Moreover, writing for children also afforded women poets creative advantages, pressing them to produce poems that were intensely audience-oriented and that were shaped – formally and thematically – by the (perceived) needs of their readers.

In 1839 M. Gurney (who calls herself "A Mother") prefaced her *Rhymes for My Children* with an account of its origins that made her attention to readers explicit:

> The writer of the simple "Rhymes" which it contains, intended them solely for the use of her own children, to whom she wished to convey, with amusement, such rhymes as their tender minds were capable of receiving. As they seem to have answered the purpose for which they were designed, she is induced to offer them to other parents and the little inhabitants of their nurseries.[3]

Gurney's preface resembles many other antebellum women's paratexts in its modest insistence on the private roots, and hence the legitimacy, of her published work. More significantly for my purposes, her orientation is audience-based; it is invested in a feedback loop that includes her children, who apparently helped her verify the worth and use-value of her rhymes. Indeed, as I will argue, pedagogical relationships organized women's juvenile verse formally and functionally, and these relationships generated intense, sustained engagement with questions of interdependence, autonomy, and power.

According to Virginia Jackson's influential historicization of lyric reading, nineteenth-century poetry reflected an eclectic set of social practices and expectations.[4] Verses, including verses for children, did not necessarily circulate as author-centered expressive lyrics; instead, they were called ditties, "bits of talk," songs, jingles, or rhymes. Gurney's insistence on the primacy of audience over author, then, is not just sentimental self-deprecation; it reflects a structural feature of children's literature – which is, as Peter Hunt has argued, the only major literary genre defined by its audience.[5] Even lexically, then, the idea of women's juvenile poetry resists lyricization, because it posits not a single self-expressive author but two people, locked in a socially contingent relationship with one another: the adult woman and the child.

To tell the story of women's juvenile poetry in America chronologically, with attention to major authors and works, would be to reinscribe the process of lyricization in ways that are inappropriate to the material. Instead, in this essay, I will focus on the ways that children's poems emerged from, and also helped to forge, pedagogical relationships that complicate and enrich the bonds between readers and writers. Two distinct types of poetry can be seen through this lens: poetry that reflects and promotes the interdependence of women and children, and poetry that idealizes childhood autonomy. I will thus traverse the nineteenth century twice: first, I will follow the thread of what I'll call "interdependent" children's verse, as practiced by many poets but explored here through the work of Lydia Sigourney, Lucy Larcom, and Sarah Piatt. Next, I will trace a second thread of what I'll call "self-governing" children's verse – again widely practiced, but represented here by Eliza Follen, Emilie Poulsson, Mary Mapes Dodge, and Agnes Lee. Taken together, these two discourses index issues that fueled women's imaginations throughout the nineteenth century: What is childhood, and what is adulthood? Are people more free as adults (per Locke) or as children (per Rousseau)? What is inside, to use Gurney's terms, the "tender minds" of children, and what forms of language are "peculiarly appropriate" to them? Children's poetry was an expanding concern in the nineteenth century, and it gave women a chance to respond to these questions, not just through abstract philosophical musings, but through a medium that could shape the lived experiences of readers.

Interdependent Poetry

Lydia Sigourney knew what was inside the tender minds of children – namely, whatever mothers put there. In her *Letters to Mothers*, she makes this point, using language that blurs the line between writing and child-rearing: "Write what you will, upon the printless tablet, with your wand of love . . . Now, you have over a newborn immortal, almost that degree of power which the mind exercises over the body."[6] Interdependent juvenile poetry assumes an intimate and constitutive connection between parent, child, and text. Even as the writer (with her "wand of love") exerts sentimental power over the child, the tabula rasa child also empowers the mother/writer, who finally has something to write about, or on. Interdependent poetry, as my examples from Sigourney, Larcom, and Piatt will show, generally has the following characteristics: 1) its texts are, to use U.C. Knoepflamcher's term, cross-written for both adults and children – often in "household editions" aimed at entire families; 2) it assumes that the child must be redeemed, spiritually or psychologically, by the adult; and 3) because the adult has "almost that degree of power which the mind exercises over the body," interdependent poetry often imagines the child as a construct and plays, quite self-consciously, with the porous boundaries between writers, readers, and listeners.[7]

Lydia Sigourney's 1835 *Poems for Children* opens with a poem that was cross-published the same year as a hymn in a hymnal.[8] A fictive child poses the italicized title/question *Who made me?*, and the mother's voice replies:

He, who spread out the sky,
That broad blue canopy;
 Who made the glorious sun,
The moon to shine by night,
The stars with eyes so bright,
 He made thee, little one.[9]

Sigourney's evangelical (and patriarchal) message is clear: God makes children. However, the preface to *Poems for Children* posits a more matrifocal origin story:

> It is believed that poetry might be made an important assistant to early education . . . Feeling and Fancy, put forth their young perceptions, even before they are expected, and Poetry, more successfully than the severer sciences, bends a spray to their embrace, or a prop for their aspirings . . . It is the natural ally of the mother.[10]

As in *Letters to Mothers*, Sigourney stresses that poetry can mold the child's heart while also encouraging the emergence of individual ambitions, or "aspirings." The *tabula rasa* child might get its body from God, but its powers and its sense of self come from its mother.

"Who Made Me?" is directed at children who are, as the headnote to the hymnal version puts it, "past the stage of prattling infancy," but who can presumably not yet read. It is thus written to be voiced – and as a voiced text, the fiction of dialogism breaks down. "Who made me?" becomes a question posed by the mother-reader in a voice that answers itself, implicitly locating the Creator's omniscience, omnipotence, and omnibenevolence in her own person. This is not, however, a romantic genius fantasy, because by the time the refrain comes ("*He made thee, little one*") Sigourney's presence no longer registers. Instead, the poem works as what Mary Louise Kete has called "a utopian promise of emotional cohesion which dissolves disruptive differences into amiable unity."[11] One voice (the sentimental mother's) encloses all other voices (the child's, the poet's, God's). What matters is the relationship that the poem, not the poem's author, forges.

As "Who Made Me?" nurtures the child through language, the poem also satisfies what Sigourney sees as a mother's central need: the need to see the child, always living under the threat of early death, as eternal, not contingent. All of the metaphors in the first stanza – sky, sun, moon, and stars – are fixed features of nature. Cross-writing through mothers to children and through children to mothers, Sigourney provides a script that posits the child as safe from the ravages of time, whether it ultimately lives, dies, or disappears into adulthood. Ultimately, the poem (like the stars) is fixed, and among the things it "fixes" is the perilous relationship between the mother and the child.

Interdependent poetry also allows women poets to explore the notion of childhood persisting into adulthood, although in ways that are more pragmatic than romantic because of the imperatives of the genre. In the preface to *Childhood Songs* (1874), Lucy Larcom makes her assumptions about interdependence explicit: "In naming these little poems 'Childhood Songs,' one especial thought was that not all of them were written from the child's point of view, but as one may write who in mature life retains a warm sympathy with childhood, through a vivid memory of her own."[12] For Larcom, readers are always multiple ages at once, and so she cross-writes: some of her poems are for small children; some are more sophisticated, for older readers; and many, including the beautiful opening poem, "In Time's Swing," are clearly for adults and children.

"In Time's Swing" begins as an apostrophe, spoken by a child to Father Time:

Father Time, your footsteps go
Lightly as the falling snow.
In your swing I'm sitting, see!
Push me softly; one, two, three,
Twelve times only. Like a sheet
Spreads the snow beneath my feet.
Singing merrily, let me swing
Out of winter into spring.[13]

As the poem continues, however, the voice ages, and the speaker grows ambivalent about the passage of time:

Frosty-bearded Father Time,
Stop your footfall on the rime!
Hard your push, your hand is rough;
You have swung me long enough.
"Nay, no stopping," say you? Well,
Some of your best stories tell,
While you swing me – gently, do! –
From the Old Year to the New.

Who, exactly, is trapped on the swing? The speaker is not so much a fixed age as a series of ages; indeed, in the final metaphor, the child who is growing older swings paradoxically out of an old year and into a young one. In Sigourney's poetry, child mortality always hovers as a threat; in Larcom's later (but still interdependent) verse, the child's mortality is prefigured by the inevitable and progressive "death" of year after year. At the same time, though, the swinging meter of the poem frames the "best stories" as a product of precisely this intergenerational, interdependent dynamic. In many of Larcom's poems, tension and pathos are created as adults see or remember themselves as former children even as they address readers who are (still) children.

Sarah Piatt's *Poems in Company With Children* (1877) pushes the interdependent mode into even more self-conscious territory, interrogating the very foundations of children's poetry and the relationships that organize it. Paula Bennett, Piatt's twentieth-century editor, insists that her poems are *about*, not *for*, children.[14] However, in the tradition in which Piatt is writing – one that deliberately mixes child and adult audiences and voices – it is precisely this blurry distinction (*about* or *for*?) that interests Piatt. Piatt's speakers are often acutely aware of their creative powers; but, unlike

Sigourney's republican mothers, Piatt's postbellum speakers are not emboldened by the ideology of Christian sentimentalism. Zachary Finch has pointed out that Piatt's mother–child dialogues follow the pattern of sentimental education poems, but at the same time make "a space that has become dangerously unmoored from the moral certainty of antebellum sentimentalism."[15] Piatt loves her children, but she also knows she is using them for her own creative (and sometimes selfish) purposes.

So are these children's poems? In the very first poem in her collection, "A Book About the Baby," Piatt wrestles self-consciously with the question of apostrophe versus address:

> If I could write a book for you
>   What a pretty book it would be! –
> And the prettiest things would all be true.
>   But *can* I? Ah, you shall see.[16]

This poem was first published in an 1877 issue of *Wide Awake: An Illustrated Magazine for Young People*, so its (part-)child audience was structurally in place. Still, Piatt wonders: *can I write a book for you?* Interdependence, and the power of mothers (and poets), preoccupies her as a problem. *Poems in Company With Children* suggests that Piatt is drawing on the authority that "real" children were believed to add to nineteenth-century women's verse. Unlike Gurney and Sigourney, however, Piatt questions her own authority. She is not sure that her relationship with her children (and the poet's relationship with the reader) is like that of a mind and a body. Rather, her poems admit that cross-writing might produce not a single, unified reader/listener pair, but, rather, half-failed attempts at communication.

That said, Piatt remains a compelling practitioner of interdependent poetry precisely because, like Sigourney, she takes children seriously as readers who can share profound questions, and poems, with adults. This was increasingly rare in the 1870s, as it became unfashionable to discuss death with children. In his review of *Poems in Company With Children*, William Dean Howells complains about Piatt's morbidity:

> Nothing is more noticeable in children than their propensity to play at funerals and grave-digging and dissolutions; but when they are caught at these dismal dramas, they are very properly and very promptly stopped, with more or less abhorrence on the part of the spectator; and it is not good art, however true, to celebrate in verse for children the caprices and fancies of these infantile undertakers.[17]

Howells assumes that "infantile undertakers" are making light of a topic that they don't understand, but in Piatt's poems, death is properly shared with children because *nobody* understands it and yet nobody is exempt from it.

Moreover, in the interdependent mode, the function of a poem is to meet the mother's psychological needs as well as the child's, because the two are assumed to be inextricably linked. Thus, for instance, "Five and Two" begins as a poem addressed to a child:

> You have cherry-trees to climb,
> Lambs to look at, doves to coo;
> I can kiss you any time;
> Butterflies will fly from you.
> You are five and they are two.[18]

Those who "are two" turn out to be the child's dead siblings who (ambiguously) either died at two years old, or are two in number. Rather than reassuring the child, as Sigourney might do, Piatt can only conclude:

> They are dead. This is the most
> I can know of them, ah me!
> . . . No, I never saw a ghost. –
> Nor an angel. There must be
> Somewhere things I cannot see.

I would argue that this is children's poetry precisely because it uses the tools of sentimentality – what Sigourney pictures as a "wand of love" – to make a space that, if it has become "dangerously unmoored" from certainty, nevertheless forges a bond between a mother and a child. By refusing to be omniscient, Piatt's speaker can participate in exchanges that are rooted in deeply secular and psychologically complex ideas about what counts as child's play (including ghosts and angels) and what counts as children's poetry.

To return to the big picture: Many, if not most, women poets working in the sentimental mode wrote interdependent poetry for child and adult readers, and it is tempting to see the conflation of women, mothers, and child readers as a symptom of restrictive and infantilizing separate spheres of ideologies. Karen Sanchez-Eppler suggests that nineteenth-century children worked as test-cases for liberal democratic ideals, since some of them (white males) would grow into autonomous citizens and some (people of color, girls) would not.[19] Writers who explored childhood were thus exploring how, and whether, non-autonomous subjects were fully human. However, Anna Mae Duane has questioned the assumption that dependence is always problematic: "If scholars are to do the work of engaging people whose experiences necessitate allowing for authentic interdependence, rather than an illusory independence, whose literature speaks with mediated voices rather than through romantic authorship, we can no longer stand on the crumbling ground that assigns partial, dependent, mediated subjectivity *only* to childhood."[20] Women poets were often closely identified with children, not least because – as Sanchez-Eppler points out – they could never be legal, voting adults. At the same time, this position gave them a vantage point from which to write verses that articulate vulnerabilities – to death and to time – that ultimately make all humans, as Duane insists, interdependent.

Self-Governing Poetry

Interdependent poetry emerged gradually in response to the many needs and interests of writers, parents, and children. Self-governing American children's verse, by contrast, had an inventor with an agenda: Eliza Lee Follen. As my examples from Follen, Emilie Poulsson, Mary Mapes Dodge, and Agnes Lee will show, such verses tend to share the following traits: 1) they are written directly to children, not cross-written; 2) they assume that the child is naturally redeemed; 3) they valorize non-teleological play; and 4) they imagine that adults should not – or at least, should not *appear to* – exercise too much direct power over children.

In 1833, Eliza Lee Cabot Follen published *Little Songs*, a collection of unpretentious rhymes that became, as *Harper's Magazine* put it in 1875, "childhood classics . . . almost as well-known among children as any of the ancient melodies of Mother Goose herself."[21] Follen's poems endured because they embodied qualities that came to be associated with childhood: playfulness and the need to be isolated from – or even *protected* from – the adult world. When Howells complained about Piatt's "infantile undertakers," he was marking a discourse of age-appropriateness that was commonplace by the 1870s: the notion that children's texts, spaces, and activities should be free of what were defined as adult concerns. When Follen published *Little Songs* these assumptions were new, and even strange, but her book established a set of assumptions that would, by the end of the century, dominate most children's verse.

In Follen's preface, she appeals directly to children: "The little folks must decide whether the book is entertaining. To them I present my little volume, with the earnest hope that it will receive their approbation. If children love to lisp my rhymes, while parents find no fault in them, I ask no higher praise."[22] For Sigourney and other interdependent poets, the relationship between parent and child is the raison d'etre for the poem, but in Follen the parent's role recedes: her "little" volume is for "little" folks, who will (she hopes) love them enough to voice them. Its form thus follows its function, and its function is aesthetic pleasure. Follen had helped produce the American edition of Friedrich Schiller's work, and she was profoundly influenced by his theory that children must acquire a taste for beauty (which reconciles the sensuous and the rational) before they can emerge as fully moral beings.[23]

Toy-books were nothing new on the American market, but Follen's *Little Songs* was different because it was not a purely commercial venture. Indeed, *Little Songs* is just as didactic, in its way, as Sigourney's *Poems for Children*, but more covertly. While Sigourney's poems bind children and mothers together, Follen's stress children's autonomy. They are didactic not because they teach moral lessons directly, but because they steer children into a circumscribed and ideologically freighted space – the space of "childhood innocence" – and keep them there. For Follen, the child is born good and is only corrupted by outside influences; thus, while mothers can promote development, they are neither better nor more powerful than the child him- or herself.

Little Songs begins with a child alone, in a garden:

> In little Annie's garden
> Grew all sorts of posies;
> There were pinks and mignonettes
> And tulips, and roses.[24]

No parent figure ever appears; rather, "every day" little Annie goes to play "in her own pretty garden." In the volume's second poem, "The New Moon," a mother appears, but she is the *object* of her child's clever and original (because innocent) "teaching":

> Dear mother, how pretty
> The moon looks tonight!
> She was never so cunning before;
> Her two little horns
> Are so sharp and so bright,
> I hope she'll not grow any more.[25]

This is not a Lockean object-lesson about the moon; rather, it displays the power and value of the child's imaginative self-expression. The child is his or her own final authority – and indeed, very remarkably for a child's book from this period, God doesn't appear even once to steal the child's clouds of glory.

Follen's romantic assumptions affect the form and language of her poetry. Instead of positing a poem as a shared conversation between an adult and a child – with rewards for both – she tailors her words and syntax to her readers' "natural" (primitive, innocent) life-stage:

> Swing swong,
> Here we go;
> Sing a song,
> Hurrah ho![26]

Compared to Larcom's "In Time's Swing," the swinging here is not intergenerational – and neither is the language. Indeed, by distinguishing child and adult diction Follen often ends up depicting child-speech as closer to pet-speech. Thus, in one poem, little Fanny and Lucy talk to a sheep ("How's your mama?"), to which the sheep replies "ba-a!," and in another poem a child tries to teach his dog, Trusty, the A-B-Cs.[27] The animal noises in *Little Songs* mark Follen's distance from Calvinists and evangelical Christians, who tended to take children seriously because their souls were in peril; here, children are natural, but sometimes perhaps trivialized as they are lumped with other cute but loud creatures. Indeed, Follen's most famous contribution to American poetry is the "Three Little Kittens," a folk-rhyme that she transcribed and modified. Are these mitten-washing, pie-eating kittens stand-ins for human children, or are they actual animals? Their "speech" suggests that they are both; first they make animal sounds, then they segue seamlessly into child sounds: "Purr-r, purr-r, purr-r / O let us have the pie."[28]

Follen's aim, of course, is not trivialization but age-appropriateness: *Little Songs* is meant to appeal to children, so that they will want to "lisp" it themselves. Formally, Follen's poems are scaled to fit young children – a strategy that becomes necessary only when children are imagined not as inferior or less-developed beings but as agents with their "own" bodies, rights, needs, and words. Follen's assumptions here anticipate later ideas about children's rights, and no doubt emerged from her oft-articulated dedication to universal human rights and her involvement in the antislavery movement.[29] There can be no question – as there is in Sigourney, Larcom, and Piatt – about the extent to which *Little Songs* are children's poems: if anything, they engage in a utopian individualist fantasy that a child's garden (of flowers, of verses) can be entirely separate from the sullied world of adulthood.

After the Civil War, Follen's vision of self-governing childhood became a mainstream assumption, less utopian and more infused with the forces of consumer capitalism. Children needed their own gardens, but more importantly, they needed their own market-niche, their own magazines, and their own toys. Janet Gray describes this transition in children's poetry as a retreat, from "childhood as a time of introduction to physical, social, and theological dangers" to childhood as a space of protection "from danger through deferral of contact with the real."[30] While I agree that the broad trend in women's poetry for children was toward more demographically targeted juvenile verses, and that this reflects the evolving market economy, it is not clear that playing with a toy, or reading a poem about a toy, or reading a poem *as* a toy, necessarily defers the real. Instead, ludic or even nonsensical poems for children often reflect the thinking of pioneering educators such as Susan Blow, who argued in 1908 that play constitutes a child's reality.[31] As Blow put it, "The value of work is that it subordinates the self; the value of play is that it creates the self."[32] For Blow, play is ideally process-oriented rather than aimed at some productive goal; this, ironically, is what makes it so productive.

To encourage play, the inheritors of Follen's self-governing aesthetic drew on folk motifs and on an emerging proto-modernist preference for concrete images. Emilie Poulsson's 1889 *Finger-Plays for Nursery and Kindergarten*, for instance, combines poems, illustrations, music, and children's physical bodies. Poulsson reprises Follen's "garden" motif, but with a twist; as the child recites or sings, "In my little garden bed, / raked so nicely over," she first cups her hands to make a bed, then rakes the ground with her "rake"-shaped fingers. Poulsson explains that the effect is not just amusing, but productive: "By their judicious and early use, the development of strength and flexibility in the tiny lax fingers may be assisted, and dormant thought may receive its first awakening call through the motions which interpret as well as illustrate the phase of life or activity presented by the words."[33] In other words, the poem's meaning is realized only when the child *makes it real* with her own hands.[34]

At its best, self-governing poetry allows readers to embrace poetry's mediating materiality. In her book *Rhymes and Jingles* (1874), for instance, Mary Mapes Dodge uses "The Alphabet" to call attention to – precisely – *the alphabet* as a series of lines and loops. Dodge thus modifies the (old) pedagogical tradition of the alphabet poem; instead of turning the letters into, say, animals or emblems, she emphasizes their qualities as print. Her alphabet concludes:

W ought
To be called double V;

X is a cross,
As you plainly can see;

Y is just formed
Like a V on a stand;

Z is the crookedest
Thing in the land![35]

X is not a Christian cross, but literally two intersecting lines; its importance lies in its shape, not its moral or meaning. The poem is self-governing because it embraces the self-directed, process-oriented logic of play, rather than the other-directed, message-oriented tendencies of interdependent verse.

In other poems in *Rhymes and Jingles*, however, trivialization creeps in; for instance, when Dodge uses baby-talk:

Poor little Toddlekins,
All full o' skeeter-bites –
Bodder him awful,
Can't even sleep o' nights![36]

On the one hand, the poem pretends to speak in a child's voice, with a child's diction. On the other hand, the baby's discomfort emanates from an outside perspective that makes light of the baby's suffering. "Toddlekins" is a pet-name, and here – as in some Follen poems – the child veers closer to pet status than to human subjectivity. Freed from the need for sentimental salvation, Dodge's children are less imperiled, but also risk becoming merely entertaining, or even laughable.

Self-governing poetry is, of course, still poetry written for children living in the hierarchical power structure of the family. As Richard Brodhead has argued, nineteenth-century reformers advocated self-governance as a form of "disciplinary intimacy" meant to help (or force) children to internalize hegemonic race, class, gender, and economic relations through bonds of love rather than through corporal punishment.[37] However, perhaps the practical orientation of nineteenth-century women poets – who were so often working on the ground as educators and mothers – can offer perspective: capitalist hegemony was a real threat in the nineteenth century, but so was the threat (especially to girls) of illiteracy. Must education always be a form of domination? This was not a settled question in the nineteenth century; indeed, it is one of the major questions that women poets for children continually explored.

Moreover, even though women were often subtly pressured to write juvenile verses, it seems evident that their work for children, like other marginal genres, enabled them to write past the sometimes stultifying conventions of the mainstream "poetess" mode. While I hesitate to recapitulate the narrative in which all the best nineteenth-century poetry is best because it anticipates modernism, it is true that children's poetry, with its simple (even "primitive") and functional forms, helped craft an emerging modernist aesthetic even as it pursued – quite effectively – its own aesthetic aims and cultural functions. Women poets – including Emily Dickinson, whose cross-writing practices deserve more attention – were at the fore of this aesthetic, since they so frequently chose (or were strongly encouraged) to work with children in mind.

In closing, then, I want to examine the work of Agnes Lee, whose one children's poetry collection, *The Round Rabbit*, appeared in 1898, just before Lee made the leap from juvenile to adult verse (a line that had been codified by the end of the century), from *St. Nicholas* (edited by Mary Mapes Dodge) to *Poetry* (edited by Harriet Monroe). Just as Piatt thematizes the reciprocal, interdependent perspectives of mother and child, so Lee takes, as her primary theme, the self-governing time and space of childhood. Almost every poem in *The Round Rabbit* hinges on a child who misunderstands, or objects to, the laws of physics: a "little man of Michigan" grows bigger as the child approaches him, changing her visual perspective; a clock strikes "three ones in a row," suggesting that it's always one o'clock; a child imagines that when her mother was small, she herself must have been even smaller and thus perhaps a doll. Lee's poems do not condescend to a child who makes such observations; rather, they draw on an aesthetic that privileges unexpected angles of vision. Lee's speakers frequently fix on the concreteness of language, as in "Sometime":

> When I ask my father when
> We shall leave the town again,
> Where the houses hide the sky,
> "Sometime" is his one reply.
> . . .
> And I wonder where they are,
> Sometime lands, so dim and far;
> For to wait I scarce know how!
> Oh! is SOMETIME never Now?[38]

Rather than simply delivering a message, the words on the page call attention to themselves as words: what is the relationship between "sometime" and time, between the adult's sense of language and the child's? The child refuses to admit abstraction, imagining "sometime lands," insisting that there are no ideas but in things.

In another poem, "The Moon in the Pond," a speaker allows space to collapse, so that the sky falls:

> Pebbles light as little kisses
> To the water moon I throw,
> And in pleasant, cool abysses
> Sinking down the sky they go.[39]

The child depicted does not necessarily literally believe that the pond and the sky are one, but the conventions of self-governing poetry allow such leaps, without the encumbrance of metaphorical or apostrophic frames. Lee's poems insist that the reality of childhood, while different from that of adulthood, can produce specific effects and images that are less available to poets writing for adults.

Childhood, as imagined by Agnes Lee, is a valuable and generative life-stage defined by process-oriented play. However, throughout the nineteenth century, children's literature was dismissed as a "minor" genre. Thus, in the headnote to Lee's selections in the 1919 modernist anthology *Our Poets of Today*, Howard Cook remarks genially: "While in Boston Miss Lee wrote verses for children that appeared in St. Nicholas and other juvenile periodicals, and these were gathered together and published by Copeland and Day under the title of 'The Round Rabbit.' Then work of a more serious sort from her pen began to appear in magazines."[40] One could conclude that *The Round Rabbit* prepared Lee to write modernist verse of a "more serious sort." I contend, however, that *The Round Rabbit* was itself serious (not just because it was proto-modernist), and that, throughout the nineteenth century, women poets understood that writing for children was – like other forms of writing, and like mothering and teaching – real work.

When they wrote interdependent poetry, poets such as Sigourney, Larcom, and Piatt generated complex, cross-written poems for children who (they assumed) needed to be spiritually awakened by adults. When they wrote self-governing poetry, poets such as Follen, Poulsson, Dodge, and Lee produced concrete, simple poems for children who (they assumed) thought concretely and needed to learn through play. In identifying two through-lines in the history of children's poetry, I do not want to over-state the division: many poets wrote both interdependent and self-governing poems. Moreover, all children are simultaneously autonomous and dependent to varying degrees, and all children's literature is co-created by a mix of adult writers, editors, publishers, illustrators, parents, teachers, and child readers. By capturing and using the genre's shifting, intersubjective power dynamics, nineteenth-century women writers produced an important body of collaborative, popular – and yes, serious – poetry.

Notes

1. Space constraints prohibit a comprehensive list of nineteenth-century women's poetry for children, but some of the better-known names include – in addition to those mentioned above – Louisa May Alcott, Alice and Phoebe Cary, Lydia Maria Child, Rose Terry Cooke, Mary McNeill Fenollosa, Mary Wilkins Freeman, Hannah Flagg Gould, Sarah Josepha Hale, Helen Hunt Jackson, Sarah Orne Jewett, E. Pauline Johnson, Louise Chandler Moulton, Elizabeth Stuart Phelps, Lizette Woodworth Reese, Laura E. Richards, Harriet Prescott Spofford, Margaret Vandergrift, Anna Bartlett Warner, Anna Maria Wells, and Ella Wheeler Wilcox. All appear in Karen Kilcup and Angela Sorby (eds.), *Over the River and Through the Wood* (Baltimore: Johns Hopkins University Press, 2014).
2. Sarah Josepha Hale, "Literary Miscellany," *Ladies Magazine* 1 (July 1828), 336.
3. [M. Gurney], "A Mother", *Rhymes for My Children* (New York: Colman and Collins, Keese & Co., 1839), 1.
4. See Virginia Jackson, *Dickinson's Misery: A Theory of Lyric Reading* (Princeton: Princeton University Press, 2005).
5. See Peter Hunt, "Children's Literature," *Keywords for Children's Literature*, Philip Nel and Lissa Paul (eds.), (New York: New York University Press, 2011), 43.
6. Lydia Sigourney, *Letters to Mothers* (Hartford: Hudson & Skinner, 1838), 10.
7. For more on cross-writing, see U.C. Knoepflmacher and Mitzi Myers, "From the Editors: 'Cross-Writing' and the Reconceptualizing of Children's Literary Studies," *Children's Literature* 25.1 (1997), vii–xvii.
8. Lydia Sigourney, "Who Made Me?," *The Mother's Nursery Songs*, Thomas Hastings (ed.), (New York: John P. Haven, 1835), 43.
9. Lydia Sigourney, "Who Made Me?" *Poems for Children* (Hartford: Canfield & Robins, 1836), 13.
10. Sigourney, *Poems for Children*, 5–6.
11. Mary Louise Kete, *Sentimental Collaborations* (Durham: Duke University Press, 2000), 105.
12. Lucy Larcom, *Childhood Songs* (Boston: James Osgood, 1874), vii.
13. Larcom, "In Time's Swing," *Childhood Songs*, 19.
14. See Paula Bernat Bennett, "Introduction," *Palace-Burner: The Selected Poetry of Sarah Piatt* (Champagne-Urbana, University of Illinois Press, 2005), xxxii.
15. Zachary Finch, "The Ethics of Postbellum Melancholy in the Poetry of Sarah Piatt," *ESQ* 58:3 (2012), 416.
16. Sarah Piatt, "A Book About the Baby," *Poems in Company with Children* (Boston: D. Lothrop, 1877), 11.

17. William Dean Howells, "Some Recent Volumes of Verse," *The Atlantic Monthly* 41 (May 1878), 632.
18. Piatt, "Five and Two," *Poems in Company with Children*, 108.
19. See Karen Sanchez-Eppler, *Dependent States: The Child's Part in Nineteenth-Century American Culture* (Chicago: University of Chicago Press, 2005).
20. Anna Mae Duane, "Introduction," *The Children's Table* (Athens: University of Georgia Press, 2013), 6.
21. "Editor's Literary Record," *Harper's New Monthly Magazine* 50 (1875), 601.
22. Eliza Lee Follen, "Preface," *Little Songs* (Boston: Lee and Shepard, 1856 [1833]).
23. See Elizabeth Maddock Dillon, "Sentimental Aesthetics," *American Literature* 76:3 (2004), 495–523.
24. Follen, "Annie's Garden," *Little Songs*, 9.
25. Follen, "The New Moon," *Little Songs*, 11.
26. Follen, "Swing Swong," *Little Songs*, 65.
27. Follen "Nothing But Ba-a," *Little Songs*, 37; Follen, "Trusty Learning A B C," *Little Songs*, 50–51.
28. Follen, "The Three Little Kittens," *Little Songs*, 92.
29. Follen edited a volume of lectures that addresses the issue of human rights at length; one passage declares, for example: "The essence of right is liberty, that is, the power of man to be determined in his conduct by his own choice. It belongs to each human being, from the first moment of his existence to the last, whether he be able to exercise it or not." See Eliza Lee Follen (ed.), *The Works of Charles Follen* (Boston: Hillyard Gray, 1841), 262.
30. Janet Gray, *Race and Time* (Iowa City: University of Iowa Press, 1994), 203.
31. See Barbara Beatty, *Preschool Education in America* (New Haven: Yale University Press, 1995).
32. Susan Blow, *Educational Issues in the Kindergarten* (New York: D. Appleton, 1908), 247.
33. Emilie Poulsson, "The Little Plant," *Finger-Plays for Nursery and Kindergarten* (Boston: Lothrop & Co., 1889), 21.
34. Poulsson cites Susan Blow in Emilie Poulsson, *Love and Law in Child Training* (Springfield: Milton Bradley, 1900).
35. Mary Mapes Dodge, "The Alphabet," *Rhymes and Jingles* (New York: Scribner, 1874), 126.
36. Dodge, "Poor Little Toddlekins," *Rhymes and Jingles*, 134.
37. See Richard Brodhead, *Cultures of Letters: Scenes of Reading and Writing in Nineteenth-Century America* (Chicago: University of Chicago Press, 1993).
38. Agnes Lee, "Sometime," *The Round Rabbit* (Boston: Copeland & Day, 1898), 8.
39. Lee, "The Moon in the Pond," *The Round Rabbit*, 50.
40. Howard Cook, *Our Poets of Today* (New York: Moffat, Yard, 1919), 228.

CHAPTER 24

Emma Lazarus Transnational

Shira Wolosky

Emma Lazarus's Statue of Liberty poem, "The New Colossus," stands out as one of the few texts by a nineteenth-century woman to have remained in circulation after the death of its author.[1] It defies long-held assumptions about women's writing: it is not domestic, it is not private, it is not psychological or directly biographical or confessional. These categories mark the continued force of what in the nineteenth-century itself was called the "woman's sphere," the "narrow circle" Alexis de Tocqueville described American women to inhabit.[2] "The New Colossus" is a directly public poem, projecting a vision of America original to Lazarus herself: not only is the nation made up of plural identities, but being American means being multiply constituted.

This multiplicity is registered in the poem's own textuality. The representation of America as archetypal hostess offering "world-wide welcome" to the "homeless" registers Lazarus's own gendered identity. Indeed, it presents a gendered America in the image of the female benevolent societies that served the poor and the immigrant throughout the century.[3]

> A mighty woman with a torch, whose flame
> Is the imprisoned lightning, and her name
> Mother of Exiles. From her beacon-hand
> Glows world-wide welcome; her mild eyes command
> The air-bridged harbor that twin cities frame.[4]

This "mighty woman" is directly contrasted with the Greek brazen male Colossus, posing his conquering gigantism against her specifically feminized, restrained strength, rendered through a series of oxymora: imprisoned/lightning, Mother/exiles, mild eyes/command, cries/silent lips, indeed mighty/woman itself. But woven through this feminized America are other identities: obviously the varied "masses" who are here incorporated into American life as its very purpose, but also Lazarus's own particular identity as a Jew. Reflecting the Hebrew Lazarus was then studying, the poem braids events of Jewish history into the very fabric of American history. The "mighty woman with a torch" recalls Deborah as "*eshet lapitdoth*," the "woman" of the "torch" whose husband was named "*Barak*," meaning lightning. "Mother of Exiles" evokes Rachel weeping for her children. The concluding lifted "lamp" correlates with a series of lamps in Lazarus poems associated with the Maccabees, who, in defense of the existence of their own ethnic culture, rebelled against the Greeks – against whom America too has been contrasted in the opening lines, thus aligning America itself with ethnic difference, not in mutually exclusionary ways but rather as negotiated multiplicity.

In this and other Lazarus poems, issues of identity – or, as I will argue is a better term, of membership – are central to her textuality in ways that directly engage what has emerged as a core topic in contemporary American Studies: the question of transnationalism. Lazarus's treatment of membership affiliations, locations, commitments, and tensions point, however, in directions that differ from those of most contemporary discussions. Instead of privileging a dissolution of borders that suspends identity, Lazarus's texts open the possibility of multiple memberships as an ongoing unfolding of the self and its commitments.

Post- or Transnational?

Transnationalism in American Studies contexts is largely aligned with other essentially post-nationalist terms: diasporism, hybridization, border-crossing, nomadism, transculturalism, translocalism, and, most generally, cosmopolitanism.[5] All of these are intended to point to the dissolution, or at least subordination of national as well as other bounded "identities" – not only, or even mainly, in descriptive ways, but as a normative ideal for new geographic, political, social, cultural, and economic realities. Thus, as against national and other identities, Homi Bhabha proposes the transnational as a cultural space that is "in-between" or "interstitial," crossing borders where contemporary demographics, communication practices, and political and civil-social trends verge into globalization.[6] This border-crossing penetrates into subjectivity as well, producing what Arjun Appadurai calls the "transformation of everyday subjectivities across borders" into and through "diasporic public spheres."[7] Consistent with the post-structuralist critique of reified categories of subject, group, and culture, both subject and social formation are theorized as fluid, displaced, and dislocated, overturning cultural definitions which privilege centers over margins, unified identities over constructed, destabilized ones.

As Janice Radway put it in the first of a series of Presidential Addresses to the American Studies Association centered on transnationalism, the Americanist focus should be on "cultural negotiations ... that do not recognize national borders but flow across – focusing on exchanges, crossings, and mutual influences, placing the idea of the transaction rather than that of the boundary or limit." This border-crossing, in turn, implies a post-structuralist notion of the subject, a "fluidity and flexibility in a mobile, always changing subject," "a flexible individual no longer tied to any subject position that may define and trap her."[8]

In the discourses of American Studies, transnationalism is thus taken to mean a dissolution of identities, particularly national ones. Winfried Fluck, through a series of essays, has traced this Americanist usage as pointing "to border regions and intercultural spaces," to "space or territory of border zones, diasporas, intermediate spaces which force inhabitants to adopt several identities" in an effort "to evade subjection by America."[9] Identity is subjection; liberation is then resistance to and release from identity, with the goal of attaining an "alternative oppositional perspective" of a pure revolutionary subject.[10] American cultural study thus pursues transatlantic border-crossing against notions of closed American boundedness. But this often devolves into rigid oppositions between what are denounced as "essentializing modes" and, as Vikki Bell puts it, notions of performative and rhetorical selfhood proposing "identity without that affect implied ... by the term identification." Based in Michel Foucault and developed by Judith Butler, performativity proposes "the production of selves as effects."[11]

The problem, however, then becomes how to "retain social and political consequence" against an assumption of purely "fluid, forever changing identities." Bell proposes "belonging" as a way to overcome this divide between the social and the performative. Yet this version of "belonging," while rejecting the self as "essentialized," nonetheless remains suspended between accounts of the self as – in a radical inconsistency – at once socially determined and performatively emancipated. Here the "performative" is a "sensorial, unself-conscious response to the social conditions that define one's selfhood" in a "socially enacted agenda or ideology" that at once dissolves into a collective agenda and yet also, somehow, is radically free of it.[12] The selfhood that emerges is on one side "a chronically unstable productivity," and on the other purely "situational" as "realized in the course of culturally patterned interactions," which results in "reliquishing the skin-bound individual as its primary site of moral control."[13]

A different approach to transnationalism can circumvent this rigid binary by re-theorizing identity in ways that do not simply oppose a socially determined fixed self against a radically free one. A counter-account of the formation of the self would not oppose radical performative discontinuity against determinative processes of regulation, the first leaving the self without commitments or indeed definition, the second rendering any social organization oppressive.

A revision of transnationalism offers ways to recognize the complexity, fluidity, and multiplicity of identity while respecting a sense of agency in which the self can act with commitment to others. Such a transnationalism would conceive the self as multiple and negotiated, not as dissociated from communities but rather as participating in more than one of them. The self, that is, emerges through multiple *memberships*, rooted in while also constructing community – a selfhood and community which need not and should not be conceived as either unitary and "essentialist," nor as radically discontinuous in subversive resistance to the coercive power of society as power regimes. To speak of memberships instead recognizes how selves emerge from and participate in communities, indeed more than one of them, while each community in turn arises out of the shared cultures and actions of its members. Neither a coercive collective nor merely an atomistic collection of autonomous individuals, community engenders the members who in turn shape it. The self is neither determined by social power structures nor utterly free of them in perfomative fluidity – both of which are inconsistently claimed in Butlerian theory – but acts out of its own unique conjunction and negotiation of memberships as it participates in multiple communities in varying ways, degrees, priorities, and situations. Indeed, instead of "identity," selfhood can be cast in terms of memberships: not as fixed, but as changing. The self would then be seen as the unique intersection and negotiation among different memberships. The focus is, then, turned from identity as a determined "subject" either as essentialist or coerced, toward selves who participate in social worlds. Such a shift to the language of membership rather than identity is significant. The fixation implied in "identity" would give way to the activism of participation. The notion of membership moves from a self-referential model of selfhood to a relational one, which, by definition, can never be fixed and enclosed since self and others are all involved in continuous and ever changing circumstances and interchanges.

This structure – or, rather, event – of plural memberships can be seen in the work of Emma Lazarus. Lazarus's writing is situated in a specific moment in American culture after the Civil War, when multiple identities – which had always been an actuality of American demography – emerge as a recognized notion of pluralism for the first time. Prior to that, what might be called the grammar of American identity was essentially singular, albeit in two forms.[14] Inclusive singularity permitted assimilation through conformity to what defined the standard model: British white Protestantism. Exclusive singularity, the model of Nativism, denied the option of such assimilation: only British white Protestants could be American, and others could not be incorporated. A third option, what later came to be called (by Israel Zangwill in his 1908 play of that title) "the melting pot," in fact closely resembled singular inclusive identity: whoever melted into the pot came out looking very like the original British American. The Civil War, however, disrupted earlier identifications, as the destruction of the sections of South and North gave way to a new federalism and new regionalism. New senses of local, gendered, and racial selfhood emerged, in complex combinations and alignments. Diversity itself was embraced as an American value, leading to what Michael Walzer calls "hyphenated Americanism."[15]

Lazarus was among the first American poets to theorize and conceive herself in such "hyphenated" terms, making conscious and central for the first time a multiple American identity (or American identity as multiple). Consciousness of gender had already penetrated women's poetry, alongside other strands of self-definition and presentation including region, religion, and class. In Lazarus's case, her sense of herself as an American woman poet became transformed in light of her ethnicity in transnational senses. Born in 1849 into a New York family of Portuguese and German Jewish descent, Lazarus was tutored at home. By the time of her first published volume – *Poems and Translations* (1866) – at the age of seventeen (printed privately by her father), she was well-schooled in classics and modern languages and literatures, including German, Italian, and French. Lazarus's verse remains throughout structured not only by her extraordinary education, but also by her sense of cross-cultures derived in this wide-ranging exposure to world languages and literatures, as well as in her own increasingly conscious mixed identities. Lazarus's work registers gender from the start, if mainly in the apologist, hesitant claims with which women poets negotiated their emergence into publication (Lazarus had her Statue of Liberty poem read aloud by someone else).[16] Judaism came rather later in her short life, which ended in 1887 when she died of Hodgkins lymphoma.

It is not quite correct to say that Lazarus had no Jewish involvement through her girlhood. Her family attended the Portuguese Synagogue, but were not devout. Summers were spent in the elite society of Newport, Rhode Island, where the first American Synagogue had hosted George Washington, subsequent to receiving his famous "Letter" assuring Jews that America was a place where "all possess alike liberty of conscience and immunities of citizenship."[17] Lazarus's own "In the Jewish Synagogue at Newport" was meant to change focus to the living Synagogue, in contrast to Henry Wadsworth Longfellow's "The Jewish Cemetery at Newport" where it is the "cemetery" that locates and defines "Hebrews in their graves."[18] In the 1870s, Lazarus's New York Rabbi enticed her, apparently against some resistance, to translate Jewish poets from Medieval Spain, working from German versions.

Still, Lazarus's girlhood was largely spent defining herself as an American poetess. Then, Lazarus discovered more or less radically (how sudden or gradual this "conversion" was has been variously argued) her identity as a Jew. Rabbi Gottheil convinced her, in 1882, to accompany him to Ward Island, to witness the mass immigration of Jews fleeing pogroms in Russia. From an elite and sheltered lady, Lazarus was transformed politically into an activist of Jewish identity and poetically into a visionary prophetic voice, in complex address to both Jewish and American history. She thus embarked on remaking the map for understanding each and the constitution of identity itself. Not only in substance but more strikingly in structure, the very notion of identity comes to be altered: how it is defined and what defines it. Lazarus began to formulate a sense of selfhood as multiple, participating in more than one culture and history. This does not assume the co-presence in a culture of different unitary identities, each conceived or claimed as exclusive, essential, or fixed, as often is implied in discourses of multiculturalism.[19] Rather, what Lazarus affirmed is a self who is composed of multiple strands; or, rather, of plural memberships: as belonging to multiple communities, each of which is invested in its history and culture but never in rigid fixation, since each is indeed historical and hence changing, made up by members who may also be members of more than one community.

What Lazarus became is the first American Zionist. She began to write polemical essays and poems on Jewish persecution, history, and cultures for both Jewish and secular American journals. She accordingly confronted issues of the multiple distribution of Jewish communities, each in different political contexts, ranging from the pogroms of Russia to the nascent resettlement in Israel to American Jewish communities in their various locations. This is not to contradict, but to extend what has always been the character of Jewish affiliations, which have in fact always been composite, and have been so on a number of different axes: religion, which was never centralized; ethnicity; languages; and cultures. Jews always belonged to more than one community: the specific Jewish community they were members of, but always within some other polity to which they also had a relationship, however strained, precarious, or oppressive. They had further relationships with other Jewish communities situated in other polities, and also with Israel, where a Jewish community always survived with emissaries keeping them in contact with other Jewish sites, not least for economic support.

This multiplicity of Jewish cultures is described by Moshe Rosman in terms of shared cultural bases and polysystems of constant interaction and multiple intersection. Yet this does not deny identity altogether. He warns that "to retain meaning, Jewish culture, while highly variegated, malleable, and multi-faceted, cannot be infinitely protean."[20] Identifications shift in terms of priorities, intensities, and relationalities, belying both rigid structures and sheer structurelessness. These may (and do) include national identifications while also extending beyond them, through multiple attachments. Emma Lazarus's representation of "identity" is multiple in this sense. She has membership in more than one community, each of which – the American, the Jewish – is itself multiple rather than unitary.

Lazarus identified with but also very clearly distinguished among these varieties of situations and memberships. She links herself to the plight of the Russian Jews, but is herself very staunchly American. Caught up in the vision revealed to her by George Eliot's *Daniel Deronda* of the return to a Jewish homeland and other contemporary Zionist discourses, she calls for a Jewish "repatriation" to the Holy land as a "nation for the denationalized."[21] Her vision is secular and national, imagining strong ties of support among the various Jewish communities but not their direct consolidation, certainly not with those in America. *Epistle to the Hebrews*, Lazarus's series of articles arguing for a Jewish homeland in Israel (published in the *American Hebrew* in 1882–1883), insists: "There is not the slightest necessity for an American Jew, the free citizen of a republic, to rest his hope upon the foundation of any other nationality soever," nor need he decide whether he himself "would or would not be in favor of residing in Palestine." All that is required is a "patriotic and unselfish interest in the sufferings of his oppressed brethren of less fortunate countries, sufficient to make him promote by every means in his power the establishment of a secure asylum."[22]

Lazarus's essay on "The Jewish Problem" circulates among a variety of senses of exile, diaspora, and homecoming. It describes the ancient Israelite world as one of expanding culture, then disrupted through expulsion into a "landless, denationalized people" yet "bound together by a purely spiritual tie." Lazarus remained purely secular in her notion of peoplehood.

Nor did she call for any total reunion of the different Jewish communities in her contemporary times. Yet she spoke of establishing "an independent nationality," supported by those remote from each other in place through "mutual cooperation and aid," to "knit Jew to Jew" in "patriotism and sympathy." Thus, Lazarus's vision included migration, purchase of land, and "Restoration" as "again forming a united nation." She even spoke of a "central government." But she concluded her essay by stating: "I would not have all Jews congregate in a single community." Yet this "new life" on a transnational level is to be "instilled" when "once more incorporated as a fresh and active nation."[23]

Lazarus was far from settling the tensions, counter-pulls, even contradictions of this rather vague Zionism, whose political formation is completely unspecified, whose ties to Jews elsewhere are more assumed than clearly grounded, and whose relation to other loyalties and self-definitions remains unexamined. Just how unstable these multiple pulls are can be seen in Lazarus's remarkable use of Pauline language, stating that from "consolidation of the Jews as a nation," American Jews are to be excluded, since they "have lost color and individuality and are neither Jew nor Gentile."[24] This passage echoes her sonnet "1492." As in "The New Colossus," Lazarus in this sonnet casts Jewish history as American and American history as Jewish:

> Thou two-faced year, Mother of Change and Fate,
> Didst weep when Spain cast forth with flaming sword,
> The children of the prophets of the Lord,
> Prince, priest, and people, spurned by zealot hate.
> Hounded from sea to sea, from state to state,
> The West refused them, and the East abhorred.
> No anchorage the known world could afford,
> Close-locked was every port, barred every gate.
> Then smiling, thou unveil'dst, O two-faced year,
> A virgin world where doors of sunset part,
> Saying, "Ho, all who weary, enter here!
> There falls each ancient barrier that the art
> Of race or creed or rank devised, to rear
> Grim bulwarked hatred between heart and heart!"[25]

1492 is a "Two-faced year" containing both the expulsion of the Jews from Spain and the discovery of America as haven for them, making the latter an event in Jewish history. The invocation of "Prince, priest and people" constitutes a complete national formation, from sovereignty to religious culture (which is what religion represents to Lazarus) to peoplehood. But if the Spanish expulsion recalls the one from Eden – "cast forth with flaming sword" – the fall here is fortunate. It inaugurates a new revelation, as the year "unveil[s]" a "virgin world" – feminized like the Statue of Liberty but now perhaps suggesting Mary. The promise that here will fall "each ancient barrier that the art / Of race or creed or rank devised" recalls, as in "The Jewish Problem," Paul's vision of Galatians 3:28: "There is neither Greek nor Jew." But, as in Paul, the question remains: how does such universalist fusion allow for difference?

In "1492," as in so much of her writing, Lazarus displays a recognition close to today's that identity has fissures as well as connections; that it is neither unitary nor enclosed; that it unfolds in history in multiple ways, across multiple sites, with varying priorities. Identity emerges as volatile and unstable rather than static, tied to historical events and not mere personal reference. It cannot be reified, but rather alters and changes as its component elements are renegotiated. Yet the different identity components do not thereby dissolve. They instead engage each other, mutually defining each other in ways that sustain ongoing memberships even as these evolve. Among others, nationhood as political self-government constitutes one membership identity as community organization, linked to others but not absorbing or displacing them.

Plural Memberships

Lazarus's poetic texts are events negotiating her plural identities as American-born (she was not an immigrant), Jewish, and female, as well as regional, class, and other affiliations. The poem "The New Year. Rosh-Hashanah, 5643" offers an extended enactment of these multiple identities.[26] The poem is dated in Jewish calendar enumeration as 5643, correlating to 1882: the year of Jewish mass immigration to the United States and Lazarus's encounter with it when she visited Ward Island with Rabbi Gottheil. During this momentous visit, what changed was a complex set of orientations and their interrelationships, including class and gender roles, historical interpretation and memory, the very frames of reference for understanding history and politics. The result, as registered in her textuality, is not a fluid, performative selfhood of dissolved parameters, but, rather, an historical self, engaged with social groups and situated in relation to them, with lines of attachment as well as division and difference. It is of these multiple memberships that her texts are woven.

The poem opens by placing the Jewish New Year (September) in a winter that is not Middle-Eastern, but North American; the stanzas that follow closely interweave liturgical as well as historical and cultural Judaic references into this "unsunned West." The poem's final stanza affirms the liturgical energy of the poem, in a cascade of ritual times and objects:

> Kindle the silver candle's seven rays,
> Offer the first fruits of the clustered bowers,
> The garnered spoil of bees. With prayer and praise
> Rejoice that once more tried, once more we prove
> How strength of supreme suffering still is ours
> For Truth and Law and Love.

The "silver candle's rays" of the Temple Menorah again evokes the lamp imagery so persistent in Lazarus and associated, as here, with Jewish history. The "first fruits of the clustered bowers" refer to the Feast of Tabernacles that follows the New Year; the "garnered spoil of bees" to the honey that is customary in hope that the year will be a sweet one. The poem's last line is polemical, identifying "Law" with "Love," that is letter with spirit, rather than their opposition as in traditional arguments of Christianity superseding Judaism. Yet "supreme suffering" also introduces a Christic note, in a syncretism that in the course of the poem is complex with both inter-reference and tension.

Lazarus's own self-representation enters into this liturgical scene in ways that also cut across it. As a woman she was not given to lead or conduct a service. Yet in this poem this is what she does. Indeed, she emerges as more than Rabbi. Hers is a prophetic voice, the voice of the "sacred cornet" *shofar* itself which she, the poet, summons to trumpet its call to the people to return, a call at once to the past and to the future:

> Blow, Israel, the sacred cornet! Call
> Back to thy courts whatever faint heart throb
> With thine ancestral blood, thy need craves all.
> The red, dark year is dead, the year just born
> Leads on from anguish wrought by priest and mob,
> To what undreamed-of morn?

As in the reading of Hosea 14 scheduled for the Sabbath of the New Year, where the Israelites are summoned to "Return," Lazarus herself acts to "Call / Back" Israel, evoked as a people through "ancestral blood," yet very expressly situated in an immediate and contemporary history of "priest and mob" carrying out the persecution of the Jews of Russia.

Lazarus's Judaism is here firmly transnational: across the geographic locations and indeed the polities of America and Russia, each a specific and demarcated if also ongoing and volatile history, each defining membership differently. Indeed, these different constructions of membership define each history, as well as Lazarus's transnationalism in a further sense, as Jewish and American herself. The Russia of that time had disallowed non-Christians from inclusion in their nationhood. But America, in complex, uneven ways, left open the possibility of entry into membership, while sustaining other affiliations. For Lazarus, the American/Jewish braid has multiple strands. The prophetic tradition is shared by both through genealogies of Puritan typological identification with the Old Testament. And, in her experience, both the American and the Jewish are already multiple communities, telescoped together in a trope of immigration that opens paths for and between both.

This at least is Lazarus's construction. Lazarus's work enacts these new possibilities for both American and Jewish pluralism and nationalism, including strains, contradictions, and reversals that they carry. Hers is less a symphony of voices than moments of harmony or conjuncture that occur within ongoing syncopation, missed beats, and dissonance. In this poem, address, audience, imagery, and geography begin to multiply, sometimes as overlay, sometimes as parallel, sometimes as contest, to the Jews of the past now fulfilling ancient prophecy in multiple directions, not least the American West:

> Even as the Prophet promised, so your tent
> Hath been enlarged unto earth's farthest rim.
> To snow-capped Sierras from vast steppes ye went,
> Through fire and blood and tempest-tossing wave,
> For freedom to proclaim and worship Him,
> Mighty to slay and save.
>
> High above flood and fire ye held the scroll,
> Out of the depths ye published still the Word.
> No bodily pang had power to swerve your soul:
> Ye, in a cynic age of crumbling faiths,
> Lived to bear witness to the living Lord,
> Or died a thousand deaths.
>
> In two divided streams the exiles part,
> One rolling homeward to its ancient source,
> One rushing sunward with fresh will, new heart.
> By each the truth is spread, the law unfurled,
> Each separate soul contains the nation's force,
> And both embrace the world.

Lazarus, albeit a woman, aligns herself with the "Prophet," her own textuality recalling the Torah "scroll" that "published still the Word" and, through her writing, still does. "Tent" signals an Israelite speaker and audience. But "snow-capped Sierras" are located in America (the steppes are Russian). The poem in fact registers an immigrant group that made its way west to an agricultural life in Texas. "Tempest-tossing wave" again invokes the Statue of Liberty poem's invitation to "send these, the homeless, tempest-tossed to me," conjoining immigrant and American, immigrant as American. But the "freedom to proclaim and worship Him" has a specifically American ring, even while, as so often in American ideology, it at the same time invokes and restages Hebrew Scripture. The Exodus from Egypt to worship God who is "mighty to slay and save" was adopted by the Puritans, who applied it to their own venture from the Old World to the New promised one.

But here there seem to be two paths of Exodus. The next stanza's imagery of "two divided streams" has attracted much comment, but often as opposition. Thus, it has been interpreted as "bifurcated" between a "nationalism of territorial homeland and cosmopolitanized diaspora," as "conflicting yearnings for universalism and nationalism, cosmopolitanism and tribalism."[27] Yet these are the very divisions Lazarus is re-writing, and not as a "millennial" or "utopian bond to distant myth" that "replaces the link to the historical immediate past."[28] Lazarus directly addresses immediate history. As she writes in "The Jewish Problem," the urgent question in Judaic tradition is "what provision is here made for the world as it is?"[29] In the poem, the "divided stream" at once registers differentiation and rapprochement. "Homeward" and "sunward" are not the same direction, despite the poetic parallelism. But the poem affirms each as renewal; each, indeed, as "truth." This is to confirm that truth is plural. Likewise, the poem affirms each individual's "separate soul," but also "nation," through each one's participation in "the nation's force." Further, "nation" itself has multiple references, Jewish and American both at once, distinct yet "embrac[ing] the world."

Conclusion

Jewish diaspora repeatedly serves as both instance and paradigm for contemporary discourses of border-crossing nomadism. Paul Gilroy notes that it is with "Jewish histories [that] the term diaspora is most deeply intertwined."[30] James Clifford similarly calls the Jewish diaspora the "ideal" type, although he then urges differentiation among diasporic models.[31] The Jew as paradigm in discourses of identity is not new. Always a challenge to definitions of identity and yet seeming to necessitate them, the Jew emerges as the contested figure on both sides of any identity question. In today's post-nationalist discourses, the Jews are cosmopolitan to nationalists, but essentialist to post-identarians; to racists a race; to leftists, racist. The oppositions in a sense require each other. Both sides assume a binary choice: either total identity (racism) or no identity, in which case any identity is a racist one. But identities need not be defined as merely unitary. Arguments against essentialism are in some sense straw ones, since essentialism need not be assumed for identity as membership(s).[32]

Lazarus's poetics points "transnationalism" away from the border-crossing dissolution of boundaries that makes it indistinguishable from post-nationalism, and toward relationship between individuals in communities that remain distinct from each other, each bounded although in necessarily porous and permeable ways, overlapping and interlocking in relationship to each other. Such a multiplied rather than dissolving transnationalism emerges in discourses outside American Studies, where, as Sieglinde Lemke notes, transnationalism has an ideological slant "that rejects the parochial, nationalist stance of American exceptionalism" in favor of a "cultural radicalism" of "in-betweenness." But transnationalism is elsewhere taken to mean "global flow" that "extends beyond a single nation-state" but still assumes each nation's continued existence.[33] Khachig Tölölyan similarly speaks of national identity as a form of "collective identity that may coexist with sub, or . . . other forms of collective identity." Distinct from a "global nation," the "trans-nation" would not posit a uniformity of "identity across the globe," but would "include homeland and variously territorialized diaspora communities" in which the "center" would be a "node in a network that has other [locations]." The nation state itself is "part of a larger collectivity" but would "leave the homeland as still essential, but not as the center and source of the ethical imperatives of nationalism." Such a notion of "diasporic transnationalism" refuses the "centrality of claims of the old center [but] does not result in assimilation."[34] A similar complex interchange is suggested in what Peggy Levitt and Nina Glick Schiller call "simultaneity" in a "transnational social field," where it is possible for people to "feel a sense of belonging to both their country of origin and their host country." In this model, the "incorporation of individuals into nation-states and the maintenance of transnational connections are not contradictory social processes."[35]

Lazarus's multiplicities do not involve the erasure of memberships but an embrace of them. For her, claiming membership is not focused on herself as a solitary performance or even subject or subjectivity. Nor, in Foucauldian terms, is subjectivity a mode of coercive subjection. There is positive identification, adoption, and adaptation, while also friction and divergence, allowing critical resistance as well as correction among the different memberships and their interrelationships. Against a performativity that ultimately isolates the self even as it dissolves him and her – for where in this performative model are other people and the possibility of obligations and commitment to them? – her texts ask: without membership, who would a self even be? Discourses of transnationalism that, despite their claims to historicist, materialist, political engagements, dissolve and transcend location and community – the very conditions history and politics entail and require – ultimately also dissolve any sense of obligation to others. Lazarus instead in her textuality proposes and enacts both difference and commitment, in multiple memberships that constitute unique selves.

Notes

1. For a fuller discussion of the Statue of Liberty poem as a multiple discourse, see Shira Wolosky, *Poetry and Public Discourse in Nineteenth-Century America* (New York: Palgrave Macmillan, 2010), 139–142.
2. Alexis de Tocqueville, *Democracy in America* Volume II section 45, http://xroads.virginia.edu/~hyper/DETOC/toc_indx.html [date of access not available].
3. See Shira Wolosky, *Feminist Theory Across Disciplines: Feminist Community and American Women's Poetry* (New York: Routledge, 2013).
4. Emma Lazarus, "The New Colossus" *Selected Poems and Other Writings*, Gregory Eiselein (ed.), (Orchard Park: Broadview Literary Texts, 2002), 233.
5. See James Clifford, "Diaspora: Further Inflections: Toward Ethnographies of the Future," *Cultural Anthropology* 9.3 (August 1994), 302–338.
6. Homi Bhabha, "Culture's In-between," *Questions of Cultural Identity*, Stuart Hall and Paul Du Gay (eds.), (London: Sage, 1996), 57.
7. Arjun Appadurai, *Modernity at Large* (Minneapolis: University of Minnesota Press, 1996), 10.
8. Janice Radway, "What's in a Name," *American Quarterly* 51.1 (1999), 22.
9. Winfried Fluck, "A New Beginning? Transnationalisms," *New Literary History* 42.3 (Summer 2011), 365; Winfried Fluck, "Inside and Outside" *American Quarterly* 59.1 (2007), 26.
10. Winfried Fluck, *Romance with America? Essays on Culture Literature and American Studies* (Heidelberg: Winter Pub., 2009), describes how

essentialism was replaced by the figure of in-betweenness that can be found in border theory, postcolonial studies, and now also in transnational studies (99), with the goal to "transcend a coercive national identity and thus open up new perspectives for resistance" (71).

11. Vikki Bell, "Introduction," *Performativity and Belonging*, Vikki Bell (ed.), (London: Sage, 1998), 1–2.
12. Ibid.
13. Deborra Battaglia, "Problematizing the Self: A thematic introduction," *Rhetorics of Self-Making*, Debborra Battaglia (ed.), (Berkeley: University of California Press, 1995), 3, 5, 8, 7.
14. For fuller discussion, see Wolosky, *Poetry and Public Discourse in Nineteenth Century America*, 125–127.
15. Michael Walzer discusses hyphenation in "What it means to be an American," *Social Research* 71:3 (Fall 2004), 638.
16. Esther Schor, *Emma Lazarus* (New York: Schoken, 2006), 190.
17. George Washington, "Letter to the Hebrew Congregations of Newport, Rhode Island" (August, 1790) www.tourosynagogue.org/history-learning/gw-letter [accessed January 16, 2015].
18. Lazarus, *Selected Poems*, 49. Henry Wadsworth Longfellow, "The Jewish Cemetary at Newport" www.gutenberg.org/cache/epub/1365/pg1365-images.html [date of access not available].
19. Stuart Hall, for example, in an interview ("Cultural Composition," in an interview with Julie Drew, *JAC: A Journal of Composition Theory* 18.2, 1998) sees the ethnic definition of groups as still "essentialist" within each group, and thus still pluralist in an old sense, as against "mongrelized" open borders between groups (187).
20. Moshe Rosman, *How Jewish is Jewish History* (Portland: Litman Library, 2007), 93, 101.
21. Cf. Saul Friedman, *A History of the Middle East* (Jefferson: McFarland & Co, 2006), 68. Also Schor, *Emma Lazarus*, 62–65. On Eliot's influence on Zionism, see Gertrude Himmelfarb, *The Jewish Odyssey of George Eliot* (New York: Encounter Books, 2012).
22. Emma Lazarus, "Epistle to the Hebrews VII," *Epistle to the Hebrews* (Centennial Edition NY Jewish Historical Society of New York, 1987), 41.
23. Emma Lazarus, "The Jewish Problem," *Emma Lazarus*, Gregory Eiselein (ed.), (New York: Broadview, 2002), 265–266, 270–271, 280–281.
24. Lazarus, "Jewish Problem," 280.
25. Lazarus, "1492" *Selected Poems*, 233.
26. Lazarus, "New Year: Rosh Hashanah, 5643," *Selected Poems*, 175.
27. Max Cavitch, "Lazarus and the Golem of Liberty," *American Literary History* 18.1 (2006), 6–7 and Ranen Omer-Sherman, *Diaspora and Zionism in Jewish American Literature* (Lebanon, NH: Brandeis University Press, 2002), 56.
28. Cavitch describes Lazarus's reference as millennial (9); Omer-Sherman as millennial and utopian (29, 42); as well as describing Lazarus's "alienation from the communal," which is far from the case (55).

29. Lazarus, "Jewish Problem," 276.
30. Paul Gilroy, "Diaspora and the Detours of Identity," *Identity and Difference*, Katherine Woodward Sage (ed.), (London: Sage Publications Ltd., 1997), 330. On the case of Jewish diaspora as exemplary, see Anthony Smith, "Diasporas and Homelands in History: The Case of the Classic Diasporas," *The Call of the Homeland: Diaspora Nationalisms, Past and Present*, Allon Gal, Athena S. Leoussi, and Anthony D. Smith (eds.), (Leiden: Brill, 2010), 3.
31. Clifford, "Diaspora," 305–306.
32. See Bhabha, "Culture's In-between," 53, where he concedes that anti-essentialism has become the normal assumption. Arguments for multiple identities thus need not exclude the possibility of nationhood as betraying the multiplicity of transnational membership, as Daniel Boyarin does. See Daniel Boyarin, "Introduction: Purim and the Cultural Poetics of Judaism-Theorizing Diaspora," *Poetics Today* 15.1 (1994) and Jonathan and Daniel Boyarin, "Diaspora: Generation and the Ground of Jewish Identity," *Critical Inquiry* 19 (Summer 1993).
33. Sieglinde Lemke, "Liberty: A Transnational Icon," *Re-Framing the Transnational Turn in American Studies*, Winfried Fluck, Donald Pease, John Carlos Rowe (eds.), (Hanover: Dartmouth College Press, 2011, 193–218, 212.
34. Khachig Tölölyan, "Beyond the Homeland: From Exilic Nationalism to Diasporic Transnationalism," *The Call of the Homeland: Diaspora Nationalisms, Past and Present*, Allon Gal, Athena S. Leoussi, Anthony D. Smith Leiden (eds.), (Brill, 2010), 29, 37–38.
35. Tölölyan, "Beyond the Homeland," 40; Peggy Levitt and Nina Glick Schiller, "Conceptualizing Simultaneity: A Transnational Social Field Perspective on Society," *International Migration Review* 38.3 (Fall 2004), 1003.

CHAPTER 25

The Creation of Emily Dickinson and the Study of Nineteenth-Century American Women's Poetry

Mary Loeffelholz

In the July 1893 issue of the *Atlantic Monthly*, an aspiring woman poet published one late contribution of many to the nineteenth-century American vogue for sonnets – the writer's first and, as it turned out, her last notice by Boston's aging grande dame of nineteenth-century high literary culture:

GHOST-FLOWERS

(***Monotropa uniflora.***)

In shining groups, each stem a pearly ray,
Weird flecks of light within the shadowed wood,
They dwell aloof, a spotless sisterhood.
No Angelus, except the wild bird's lay,
Awakes these forest nuns; yet, night and day,
Their heads are bent, as if in prayerful mood.
A touch will mar their snow, and tempests rude
Defile; but in the mist fresh blossoms stray
From spirit-gardens, just beyond our ken.
Each year we seek their virgin haunts, to look
Upon new loveliness, and watch again
Their shy devotions near the singing brook;
Then, mingling in the dizzy stir of men
Forget the vows made in that cloistered nook.[1]

The author of this unimpeachably correct Petrarchan sonnet was Mary Potter Thacher Higginson, previously the author of *Seashore and Prairie, Stories and Sketches* (1877); an occasional contributor of poetry to *Harper's Magazine, Harper's Bazaar, Cosmopolitan*, and other periodicals; and the second wife of the reformer, author, and editor Thomas Wentworth Higginson. In the summer of 1893, she and her husband were in the thick of negotiating with Thomas Niles, of the Boston-based publishing firm Roberts Brothers, for the rights and illustrations for a joint collection of their poetry; the July printing of "Ghost-Flowers" in the *Atlantic* served as a small advance notice for *Such as They Are: Poems* by Thomas Wentworth Higginson and Mary Thacher Higginson, which would be issued by Roberts Brothers in late 1893. The fate of the Higginsons' joint volume, however, was predicted by its self-deprecatory title: *Such as They Are* sank into obscurity without drawing significant popular or critical notice.

The *Atlantic*'s printing of "Ghost-Flowers," followed in short order by the chastening of its author's hopes for her published volume of poetry, tells one typical story – reasonably typical at least with respect to her race and class stratum – of women's access to authorship in late nineteenth-century American poetry. Mary Higginson was one of many writers, male and female, who gained a narrow foothold in periodical verse in the burgeoning American literary marketplace of the 1890s without crossing over to the more stable and prestigious recognition of successful book publication. Like many women poets of her generation, Mary Higginson published both in women's magazines and in venues not marked as belonging to a separate sphere of women's culture. The middlebrow, general interest journals that brought out Mary Higginson's work, like her joint venture in publishing her poetry alongside that of her husband's, testify to what Monika Elbert calls the "gender convergence" of nineteenth-century American letters – the emergence of shared spaces in which women's and men's "interactions created a national culture in flux."[2] Although she never ceased to be a woman poet in the eyes of those contemporaries who read her, Mary Higginson was equally a poet marked by her region, by her class, by her race, and by her negotiation of the American cultural field's growing divisions between the "elite humanistic culture" represented by the *Atlantic Monthly* and the "rising tide of mass culture" identified with journalism, allied with fictional realism, and frequently prepared to outbid the *Atlantic* for literary talent.[3]

"Ghost-Flowers" is both a document of this moment in the history of American women's poetry and a document in the creation of Emily Dickinson.[4] Mary Higginson's *Monotropa uniflora* is more widely known by its popular name, "Indian pipes"; and, as most of her readers in the *Atlantic* would have recalled, the inaugural volume of Dickinson's poems, edited by Mabel Loomis Todd and Thomas Wentworth Higginson and released by Roberts Brothers in 1890, reproduced on its cover a painting of Indian pipes that Todd had made and given to Dickinson early in their acquaintance. The volume's production values were much admired even by those reviewers mystified by the poems themselves, and the cover's "strange blanched blossom, the Indian Pipe, the flower of shade and silence," as one early notice called it, quickly became an icon amalgamating the weird aesthetic appeal of Dickinson's poems with her strangely sheltered, reclusive life.[5] Todd's edition of Dickinson's *Letters* (1894) would confirm the status of this icon, and at the same time bolster Todd's claims to ownership of the Dickinson brand, by reprinting Dickinson's warm letter of 1882 thanking Todd for her gift:

> DEAR FRIEND,–That without suspecting it you should send me the preferred flower of life, seems almost supernatural, and the sweet glee that I felt at meeting it I could confide to none. I still cherish the clutch with which I bore it from the ground when a wondering child, an unearthly booty, and maturity only enhances mystery, never decreases it. To duplicate the vision is almost more amazing, for God's unique capacity is too surprising to surprise.[6]

Although Thomas Wentworth Higginson had, by 1893, withdrawn from his active collaboration with Todd in editing Dickinson's writings for publication, he supported Todd's project to publish the letters and was in the midst of sorting out his own correspondence with Dickinson for her edition when "Ghost-Flowers" appeared.[7] Building upon the cultural capital accrued by the couple's other literary enterprises, Mary Higginson's poem thus tacitly allied her own debut in the *Atlantic*'s pages with one of the more sensational literary debuts in recent American memory.

As an interpretation of Dickinson's life and work, however, "Ghost-Flowers" is markedly ambivalent. Mary Higginson's rendering of the Indian pipes "dwelling aloof" in their "virgin haunts" echoes Thomas Wentworth Higginson's famous introduction of Dickinson to the reading public, in his preface to the 1890 *Poems*, as "[a] recluse by temperament and habit, literally spending years without setting her foot beyond the doorstep . . . as invisible to the world as if she had dwelt in a nunnery." Mary Higginson's insistence on the ghost-flowers' virginal fragility, though, represses her husband's acknowledged wonder at Dickinson's "power"—his praise for what he called the "extraordinary grasp and insight" and "uneven vigor" of the poems, the "rugged frame" Dickinson found for her thought, and her compressed depiction of "the very crises of physical and mental struggle." To Thomas Wentworth Higginson, Dickinson's poems read "like poetry torn up by the roots, with rain and dew and earth still clinging to them" – an invasive mode of aesthetic apprehension, but one that Dickinson's own letter of thanks to Mabel Loomis Todd for her painting of Indian pipes seems to endorse.[8] For Dickinson, the adult's "sweet glee" along with the greedy "clutch" of the child snatching her "unearthly booty" are part and parcel of the flower's weird beauty. Near the end of her life,

Dickinson still revels in the proximity of beauty to booty, much as she had in an early poem about a similarly invasive, acquisitive act of reading:

So bashful when I spied her!
So pretty – so ashamed!
So hidden in her leaflets
Lest anybody find –

So breathless till I passed her –
So helpless when I turned
And bore her struggling, blushing,
Her simple haunts beyond!

For whom I robbed the Dingle –
For whom betrayed the Dell –
Many, will doubtless ask me –
But I shall never tell![9]

Both Dickinson's poem and Thomas Wentworth Higginson's metaphors describing her work imply that female expressive power can survive some degree of uprooting, displacement, and rough handling. Mary Higginson's "Ghost-Flowers," by contrast, yokes Dickinson's "preferred flower of life" to a stereotypical construct of female identity as virginal, a fugitive and cloistered virtue that touch can only "mar" or "defile." Ostentatiously refusing to "betray[ ] the Dell" – unless by her forgetfulness of its "shy" beauties when she returns to "mingling in the dizzy stir of men" – Mary Higginson appreciates its cloistered "spirit-gardens" without attempting to bear these blooms beyond their "virgin haunts." Where Mabel Loomis Todd and Thomas Wentworth Higginson selected "So bashful when I spied her!" for inclusion in their first volume of Dickinson's poems, as if to defend their posthumous revelation of Dickinson in her "leaflets," "Ghost-Flowers" suggests that Mary Higginson politely demurred from her husband's efforts to bring his recluse into the public eye.

Mary Higginson's implicit reservations may have extended beyond Dickinson to a wider "sisterhood" of nineteenth-century women's poetry. The title and subtitle of "Ghost-Flowers / Monotropa uniflora" (its Latin botanical name describes the plant as *once turned* and *single-flowered*) declare the subject of Mary Higginson's poem to be at once plural and singular. Single, singular, virginal, how does *monotropa uniflora* reproduce? – for reproduce it does, most efficiently, year after year colonizing its space "near the singing brook" and sending forth "fresh blossoms / From spirit-gardens, just beyond our ken." The ghost-flower's virginal prolixity invokes not only the emerging biographical myth attached to

Dickinson in the 1890s (and perhaps Mary Higginson's privileged awareness of how dauntingly many blossoms and scraps Dickinson left behind her) but also the historical type of the poetess, copiously reproducing herself and her ilk on paper and in print. The speaker of "Ghost-Flowers" seeks some distance from this type, using a generic first-person plural rather than a singular voice and asserting her own prerogative to leave the cloister behind, to go "mingling in the dizzy stir of men"; the speaker is a connoisseur of the "spotless sisterhood," but is not eager to be construed as one of their number. "Ghost-Flowers" frames a familiar mode of women's writing as pallid, fragile, and aloof, and in doing so gestures toward a modernity that the poem seems unable to define or practice, except by negation.

With the advantage of historical hindsight, readers today may be more inclined to see Mary Higginson's sonnet as one more late turn in the asexual, print-mediated reproduction cycle of the poetess than as a decisive break with this figure. For most educated readers of American poetry today, it is of course Dickinson herself, not Mary Higginson, who represents that break; it is Dickinson who is singular and Mary Higginson who has been absorbed into the pallid sisterhood. "Ghost-Flowers" demonstrates that Dickinson's writing emerged into public view at a time when American women poets – and their male readers, critics, and champions – were deeply engaged in contests over what kind of writing by women would define literary modernity. As Paula Bennett has argued most forcefully, these contests often took the form of generational struggles among women: "When, between 1890 and 1910, 'the sentimental' became nascent modernism's 'Other,' the pole against which literary modernity defined itself, female modernists no less than their male counterparts, participated in an auto da fé that sent hundreds, perhaps thousands, of earlier women poets into the fire."[10] For all its repressive pallor, "Ghost-Flowers" is a document of that struggle. Although Mary Higginson's poems would be consigned in short order to that great turn-of-the-century bonfire, at least one question posed by "Ghost-Flowers" remains alive for Americanist literary studies to this day: do we read Emily Dickinson as one, or as one of many?

As the position of this essay in this volume underlines, my answer to this Dickinsonian riddle is "yes." In the words of Pierre Bourdieu, the late French sociologist of culture: "social history cannot understand anything about a work of art, least of all what makes its *singularity*, when it takes as its object an author or a work in isolation." For Bourdieu, the object of understanding and inquiry is, famously, the literary or cultural field, even or perhaps especially in the instance of the most singular among the field's authors – concerning whom "analysis of the structure of the field would show that certain positions . . . may only have *place for one*."[11] By the time Harvard University Press issued Thomas H. Johnson's edition of Dickinson's *Poems* (1955), followed by Johnson's and Theodora Ward's edition of her *Letters* (1958), Dickinson had come to occupy this kind of singular place, with room but for one woman poet, in American literary history. That place stood at the apex of a nineteenth-century literary field drastically reconstructed, in retrospect, by the advent of literary modernism and the institutional success of the New Criticism in the US literary academy. Other nineteenth-century American women poets appeared in this literary history, if they appeared at all, only as foils to her accomplishment – as illustrations of what Dickinson was not.

In more recent years we have seen increasingly rich critical accounts, authored by many hands, of how Dickinson's singularity within the field of American poetry – her *place for one* – was produced over the course of her posthumous publication and reception. Tracing a line that runs from Thomas Wentworth Higginson's early portrait of Dickinson as "the perfect figure of the lyric poet" issuing her "unseen birdsong," through "the modernist version of Dickinson's voice as distinct from the public voice of mass culture," to "the alienated personal voice essential to the New Critical reception of Dickinson," Virginia Jackson proposes that the constant element in the posthumous creation of Dickinson is her definition "as a private – and therefore transcendent – lyric voice," American poetry's most irresistible exemplar of "the poetics of the single ego."[12] The "poetics of the single ego" chimed with the nationalist strand in the creation of Dickinson's singularity, where she became the lone nineteenth-century woman poet routinely paired with Walt Whitman. In Adrienne Rich's trenchant 1993 summary of this coupling as psychodrama, she argues that "our categories have compressed the poetic energies of the nineteenth-century United States into a gendered opposition: a sensual, free-ranging, boastful father, and a reluctant, elusive, emotionally closeted mother – poetic progenitors, neither of whom had children of the flesh."[13] At another intersection of literary nationalism with literary form and the ideologies surrounding literary form, Timothy Morris finds that "Dickinson emerged as a feminine version of Whitman" in the 1890s, accused along with him of formlessness and praised along with him for what Rupert Hughes, in 1896, called "their unbending comradery with God and humanity . . . our best realizations of the distinctively American spirit" in poetry.[14] As Morris observes, this formation is alive to this day:

Martha Nell Smith, writing almost a century after Rupert Hughes, yokes Dickinson with Whitman along much the same lines, identifying Whitman's dream of the "truly American poet" with Dickinson's experiments in merging poetry with personal letters, both of them projects in "the ultimate democratization of poetry" – and yet both of them set apart, in this influential formulation, from the huddled masses of nineteenth-century poets who failed, or never tried, to represent democracy's formal avant garde.[15]

These powerful and necessary critical narratives (and many others like them) typically focus on the creation of Dickinson's singularity after her death, beginning with the circumstances in which her manuscript writings were edited and circulated in print. Those exceptional circumstances were – and remain – of absorbing interest. And yet this focus on Dickinson's posthumous editing and reception runs the risk of amplifying the very singularity it analyzes: Dickinson's contemporaries continue to recede from view while Dickinson's posthumous figure organizes critical thinking about poetry within the literary field of the twentieth and twenty-first centuries. As Bourdieu emphasizes, however, the relational logic of the cultural field operates at the point of production as well as reception, even for the field's most singular producers. Eliza Richards, replying to Virginia Jackson, argues in this vein that the "lyric reading" into which Dickinson's writings were conscripted after her death did not begin there: "Dickinson herself received and arguably worked within these understandings of lyric practice . . . Dickinson may have helped write the terms of her own reception."[16] Dickinson contributed to producing her own singularity, in the only way that singularity can ever be produced – in relation to a surrounding literary culture. For Dickinson, this was one in which women poets were extraordinarily important, both individually and as a type.

Women poets were a well-established constellation in Anglo-American letters, both a recognized empirical fact and a symptom of the spread of literacy and the democratization of print, from the earliest years of Dickinson's life as a writer. She grew up and was educated in the awareness that "poetical," as she wrote to a friend at age fourteen, is "what young ladys aim to be now a days."[17] A few years later, Henry Wadsworth Longfellow's popular novel *Kavanagh* (1849), which "went the rounds" among the Dickinson siblings and their set soon after its publication, confirmed the association between "young ladys" and the "poetical."[18] *Kavanagh* presented Dickinson with contrasting modes of women's access to authorship, public and private: on the one hand, Clarissa Cartwright, "the poetess, whose delightful effusions" have graced the nation's periodicals and who seeks a publisher and advance publicity for her "Symphonies of the Soul"; and, on the other hand, the novel's devoted pair of female friends, Alice Archer and Celia Vaughn, who carry on an erotically charged, self-consciously literary correspondence that parallels Dickinson's correspondence with Susan Gilbert, begun at almost the same time.[19]

A few years later, Emily Dickinson and Susan Dickinson also shared their reading of Elizabeth Barrett Browning's *Aurora Leigh* (1856). By contrast with *Kavanagh, Aurora Leigh* and its eponymous poet-heroine provided Dickinson with what Betsy Erkkila calls "a compelling model of poetry as a serious vocation for women," a vocation apparently compatible with ambitions for publication.[20] Yet *Aurora Leigh*, like *Kavanagh*, represents its approved model of women's writing by negation, setting it against less noble and more widely available kinds of women's cultural production. In a famous passage underlined in Dickinson's copy of the poem, Aurora declares that "The works of women are symbolical. / We sew, sew, prick our fingers, dull our sight / Producing what? . . . at best, a cushion, where you lean / And sleep, and dream of something we are not."[21] Women's painstaking craft labor churns out objects destined to be consumed without thought in the domestic setting: *Aurora Leigh* in these lines anathematizes not only embroidery but also other feminized forms of cultural production – such as the "Spun glass, stuffed birds, and modelled flowers in wax" of Aurora's youthful education – undertaken for no higher purpose than to demonstrate women's "Potential faculty in every thing / Of abdicating power in it."[22]

For all their differences, both *Kavanagh* and *Aurora Leigh* may have given Dickinson important lessons in the production of singularity at significant junctures in her career as a poet. *Kavanagh* satirizes the democratization of American letters and the increasing eagerness displayed by consumers of literature, both male and female, to enter the marketplace as its producers. "There are so many poets now-a-days!" sighs one character in *Kavanagh* when confronted by yet another newspaper poet; in Longfellow's fictional village, as in Dickinson's Amherst, "Every little girl from the Academy" wants to see herself in print.[23] Declining to represent this sororal competition directly, *Aurora Leigh* maps out for its heroine a place for one in the poem's cultural field: Aurora undertakes her poetic apprenticeship in comparison with those of Keats, Byron, and Pope, but not with the career in mind of any other woman writer, whether real or fictional. *Kavanagh* idealizes the writing created and circulated by women in the domestic sphere, while *Aurora Leigh* disdains it; but both books converge in disavowing writing "done for popularity . . . for praise or hire," especially when authored by women.[24] Erkkila goes so far as to suggest that Aurora Leigh's distaste for the literary marketplace "may have played a more determining role than Higginson in persuading Dickinson not 'to print'."[25] I suspect, though, that Dickinson was more able to distinguish Aurora Leigh from her creator, and more alive to the irony of disavowing the literary marketplace in a book that sold briskly on both sides of the Atlantic, than Erkkila's reading quite allows. Virginia Jackson and Yopie Prins argue that *Aurora Leigh* "narrates the paradigmatic career of a poetess, in order to meditate on the production of that generically gendered figure"; it seems likely that Dickinson was drawn to *Aurora Leigh* by Barrett Browning's strenuous and at times self-canceling efforts to transmogrify that paradigmatic, generic, all-too-common figure into something singular and rare.[26]

Sometime after her reading of *Kavanagh*, and around the time of her reading of *Aurora Leigh*, Dickinson seemingly began to take concrete steps toward producing her own rarity within this crowded field. Surveying the gaps in the documentary record of the 1850s, Ralph Franklin surmises that Dickinson may have carried out in 1858, if not earlier, "a major stocktaking . . . a sifting and winnowing of her entire corpus."[27] Destroying the manuscript record of her earlier efforts in album and newspaper verse (evidence of which survives in the first two poems printed in Franklin's variorum edition), Dickinson began to copy some of her poems on sheets and assemble them into the home-stitched manuscript booklets that Mabel Loomis Todd christened her "fascicles." As Alexandra Socarides demonstrates, Dickinson's fascicles were both like and unlike the scrapbooks, commonplace books, and albums – both handmade and ready-bound – by means of which her contemporaries produced and consumed poetry. Dickinson could have marked her self-dedication as a poet by producing folios like Clarissa Cartwright's large, limp, velvet-bound "Symphonies of the Soul," in its "dainty manuscript, with its delicate chirography and crimson cover"; apparently she elected not to do so.[28] The material format of Dickinson's manuscript books, as Socarides argues, embodies "the tension between convention and experimentation, between making a new form and living in the shadow of an old form."[29]

Thematically as well as materially, Dickinson's earliest fascicles repeatedly probe the conventions of reading and writing attached to women poets in her time and place. The first fascicle's extended variations on the album genre of the floral offering – its gentians, roses, columbines, and daisies – experiment with using this feminine tradition to frame a more ambitious kind of poetry.[30] In the second fascicle, Dickinson explicitly pokes fun at women's album verse:

By such and such an offering
To Mr So and So –
The web of life is woven –
So martyrs albums show![31]

Several poems of the third fascicle return again to the floral offering tradition for the means of reflecting on the conditions under which Dickinson wrote and circulated her poetry. "I hide myself within my flower" begins one poem that Dickinson may have used in other contexts to accompany the gift of a bouquet or a blossom.[32] In a contrasting poem, Dickinson imagines ravishing just such a conventionally demure poetess figure, drawing her forth "blushing" and "struggling" from where she lies "hidden in her leaflets," as if to pin Clarissa Cartwright down as a specimen in the leaves of Dickinson's own manuscript book.[33] Considered together, the early fascicles even more than their individual poems showcase what Bennett describes as Dickinson's drive "to stretch the boundaries of what it meant . . . to write in a womanly way" and "to handle the traditional genres of women's verse in ways that they had never been handled before."[34]

When Dickinson contacted Thomas Wentworth Higginson in 1862 to ask, famously, if he might tell her whether her verse was "alive," her self-presentation notably avoided the kind of embodied, overtly feminine appeal exerted by Clarissa Cartwright's "liquid" eyes and "delicate, trembling hand" in her approach to publication.[35] Higginson opened Dickinson's letter to find a short note, four poems transcribed in ink, and an envelope containing a card with her name written on it in pencil, as if to suspend the question of the author's gender for at least the space of Higginson's initial reading and to underscore the provisional quality of her social identity as compared to the poems.[36] In crafting her approach, Dickinson had little reason to assume that Higginson would be prejudiced against an unknown woman poet; Higginson's published writings declared him to be not only a sympathetic editorial patron of young would-be writers, as in his "Letter to a Young Contributor" (1862) that prompted Dickinson's outreach, but also a forceful advocate for women's education and women's writing. His *Atlantic* essay of 1859, "Ought Women to Learn the Alphabet?," identified "the genius of women" with the renovating spirit of "the present epoch" and its growing "empire of the higher reason, of arts, affections, aspirations."[37] Yet Dickinson's letter declines to personify "the genius of woman" for

Higginson, referring instead to her "mind" and her "Honor" in the neuter third person: "The mind is so near itself – it cannot see distinctly – ."[38]

Of the two authors, it would always be Higginson more than Dickinson who was intensely interested in advancing American women writers as a group, and in linking Dickinson to the American women poets of her own day. However disappointing his reaction to Dickinson's poetry in other respects, Higginson did make efforts to introduce her to his considerable network of American women poets, recommending Julia Ward Howe's poetry to Dickinson following one of his visits to Amherst and sharing her poems with his friend and neighbor Helen Hunt (later Helen Hunt Jackson). By his own lights, Higginson was trying to connect Dickinson with the most advanced embodiments of the female literary accomplishment available to him.[39] Jackson's poetry, Higginson thought, successfully split the difference between poems aimed at "the popular heart" and those appealing to sophisticated readers with "the most condensed and deepest ... obscurity." Less convinced of Jackson's popular appeal, another contemporary reviewer complained of the same qualities in Jackson's work that Higginson praised, noting "the remote and unfamiliar way in which [her] subjects are often handled" and her address to an audience of "the educated, the refined."[40] Contemporaries similarly distinguished Howe's poetry by its pursuit of "the azure flower of high aesthetic art" coupled with obscure, abstract imagery and formal knottiness.[41] In the eyes of their contemporaries, and in their different ways, Jackson and Howe personified a new kind of aesthetic singularity and rarity for women writers; in this context, Higginson's attempt to draw Dickinson toward their work made perfect sense.

Dickinson managed her distance from Higginson's proffered network of American women poets, but did not withdraw from it altogether. Higginson's exchange of Dickinson's poems with Jackson opened the way to a correspondence that brought Dickinson closer to the possibility and reality of print publication, in the late 1870s, than she had been since the end of the Civil War. Jackson's well-known solicitation of Dickinson's "Success" for her anonymous volume *A Masque of Poets* (1878) brought Dickinson's poetry to the attention of Jackson's editor Thomas Niles, at Roberts Brothers in Boston; Niles was intrigued enough by Jackson's enthusiastic praise to ask Dickinson to share more of her work with him.[42] Like Higginson, Niles was an important editorial patron of American women writers. Over the next several years, Dickinson forwarded Niles copies of several poems. Notably, she also queried him closely about forthcoming biographies of George Eliot and attempted to make a gift to

Niles of her personal copy of the Brontë sisters' poems – a gesture so extravagant that Niles returned the "very rare book" to her while volunteering one more time that he would "take instead a M.S. collection of your poems, that is, if you want to give them to the world through the medium of a publisher."[43] Dickinson's correspondence with Niles underlined her identification with British women writers of high ambition while for the most part observing silence on her American contemporaries.

The first poem Dickinson chose to send Niles, like the first letter she sent to Higginson, assumed a neuter or even masculine persona – that of a "little Stone / That rambles in the Road alone," indifferent to worldly "Careers":

> Whose Coat of elemental Brown
> A passing Universe put on
> And independent as the Sun
> Associates or glows alone
> Fulfilling absolute Decree
> In casual simplicity[44]

Dickinson also sent Higginson a copy of this poem, around the same time, in summer 1882.[45] In the context of both correspondences, Dickinson's sun-browned vagrant seems intended to establish its sender's distance from the pallid, sheltered sisterhood of the poetess stereotype. Perhaps she was heeding Higginson's earlier advice that she should become more like the strong American women writers that Higginson most admired. "[C]ultivate the ruddy hues of life," Higginson had urged Dickinson in 1874, recalling for her the concluding vaunt of Howe's poem "Rouge Gagne" – "I stake my life upon the red" – and recommending to Dickinson both Helen Hunt's latest poems and her appreciation for Colorado's "out-door climate."[46] Certainly her choice of poem proclaimed to Niles her indifference, like that of Aurora Leigh, to writing "for praise or hire." While her cover letter to Niles graciously acknowledged her desire to earn his and Jackson's good opinion, her poem solicited Niles' professional interest in her poetry by disclaiming her need for it.

Niles was not sufficiently engaged by this poem or the others Dickinson sent him to pursue the question of publication. Higginson, however, kept up his efforts to connect Dickinson with her American contemporaries throughout her life, and in the posthumous afterlife of her writings. When Higginson and Todd edited the first volume of Dickinson's poems, he gave some of them titles evoking the most aesthetically ambitious American women writers of his and Dickinson's generation: Howe, after whose

"Rouge Gagne" Higginson titled two of Dickinson's poems, "Rouge Gagne" and "Rouge et Noir"; and Harriett Prescott Spofford, whose story "The Amber Gods" contributed another of Higginson's poem titles, "Astra Castra."[47] When at last a selection of her poems appeared in print, Dickinson was introduced to the public sphere of American letters as a flowering of that distinctive mid-century generation of American women poets: belated, but very much of her time.

What came next in the posthumous creation of Emily Dickinson may be seen as either a rise or a fall: in the words of Theo Davis, either "the rise of modern academic critical methods capable of understanding Dickinson's greatness," or the fall that "eras[ed] the network of personal affiliations in which Dickinson's manuscripts circulated" and, along with it, the network of women poets surrounding her.[48] My wager, however, is that we cannot understand the creation of Emily Dickinson during her lifetime, as well as after her death, without also coming to understand more clearly how generational tension and innovation and modernization structured the wider canon of nineteenth-century American women poets – and, through them, the entire Anglo-American literary field. In this perspective the creation of Emily Dickinson is not the story of a rise or fall, of one woman poet or many women poets, so much as it is the story of what Bourdieu calls the literary field's ongoing "struggle to produce time itself."[49] In Dickinson's own words, "The Admirations – and Contempts – of Time" require of readers both magnifying and distancing perspectives, both "Convex – and Concave Witness –," to distinguish what cannot be seen without her "Compound Vision."[50]

Notes

1. Mary Thacher Higginson, "Ghost-Flowers," *Atlantic Monthly* 72 (July 1893), 60.
2. Monika M. Elbert (ed.), *Separate Spheres No More: Gender Convergence in American Literature, 1830–1939* (Tuscaloosa: University of Alabama Press, 2000), 2.
3. Ellery Sedgwick, *A History of the Atlantic Monthly, 1857–1909* (Amherst: University of Massachusetts Press, 1994), 203; see also John Timberlake Newcomb, *Would Poetry Disappear? American Verse and the Crisis of Modernity* (Columbus: Ohio State University Press, 2004), 58–63.
4. Katharine Rodier suggestively links Mary Higginson's sonnet to the intertextual triangle between Dickinson, Thomas Wentworth Higginson, and Harriet Prescott Spofford, whose brief essay in the June 1892 number of *Harper's Bazar*, "Pomegranate Flower and Apple Blossom," catalogs "the Indian pipe" among

New England's spring flowers and recalls its appearance on Dickinson's *Poems*. "'Astra Castra': Emily Dickinson, Thomas Wentworth Higginson, and Harriet Prescott Spofford," in Elbert (ed.), *Separate Spheres No More*, 50–72. As Rodier observes, Spofford's association of this "pallid," "ghastly" plant with Dickinson is "ambiguous" (61).

5. Qtd. in Willis J. Buckingham, *Emily Dickinson's Reception in the 1890s: A Documentary History* (Pittsburgh: University of Pittsburgh Press, 1989), 16.
6. Mabel Loomis Todd (ed.), *The Letters of Emily Dickinson, 1845–1886* (Boston: Roberts Brothers, 1894), 430. See also letter 769 in Thomas H. Johnson and Theodora Ward (eds.), *The Letters of Emily Dickinson*, 3 vols. (Cambridge, MA and London: The Belknap Press of Harvard University Press, 1958), hereafter cited by the Johnson and Ward (L) letter number.
7. Millicent Todd Bingham, *Ancestors' Brocades: The Literary Debut of Emily Dickinson* (New York and London: Harper & Brothers, 1945), 217–224.
8. Thomas Wentworth Higginson, "Preface," *Poems by Emily Dickinson*, Mabel Loomis Todd and Thomas Wentworth Higginson (eds.), (Boston: Roberts Brothers, 1890), iii–vi.
9. Unless otherwise noted, Dickinson's poems are from Emily Dickinson, *The Poems of Emily Dickinson*, Variorum Edition, 3 vols., R. W. Franklin (ed.), (Cambridge, MA and London: The Belknap Press of Harvard University Press, 1998), hereafter cited by the Franklin (Fr) poem number. Fr 70, copied about 1859, in Fascicle 3.
10. Paula Bernat Bennett, *Poets in the Public Sphere: The Emancipatory Project of American Women's Poetry, 1800–1900* (Princeton: Princeton University Press, 2003), 202.
11. Pierre Bourdieu, *Sociology in Question* (1984), trans. Richard Nice (London: Sage, 1993), 142.
12. Virginia Jackson, *Dickinson's Misery: A Theory of Lyric Reading* (Princeton: Princeton University Press, 2005), 128–129.
13. Adrienne Rich, "Beginners," *The Kenyon Review*, New Series, 15.3 (Summer 1993), 15.
14. Timothy Morris, *Becoming Canonical in American Poetry* (Urbana and Chicago: University of Illinois Press, 1995), 54, 62, 67.
15. Martha Nell Smith, *Rowing in Eden: Rereading Emily Dickinson* (Austin: University of Texas Press, 1992), 111; Morris, *Becoming Canonical*, 143.
16. Eliza Richards, Review of *Emily Dickinson's Shakespeare* by Paraic Finnerty and *Dickinson's Misery: A Theory of Lyric Reading* by Virginia Jackson, *New England Quarterly* 80.3 (Fall 2007), 511–512.
17. R. W. Franklin, "Emily Dickinson to Abiah Root: Ten Reconstructed Letters," *Emily Dickinson Journal* 4.1 (Spring 1995), 15.
18. Richard Sewell, *The Life of Emily Dickinson* (New York: Farrar, Straus and Giroux, 1974), 683.
19. Henry Wadsworth Longfellow, *Kavanagh: A Tale* (Boston: Ticknor, Reed, and Fields, 1849). See also Elizabeth Petrino, *Emily Dickinson and Her Contemporaries: Women's Verse in America, 1820–1885* (Hanover: University

Press of New England, 1998), 39–41, and Mary Loeffelholz, "Really Indigenous Productions: Emily Dickinson, Josiah Holland, and Nineteenth-Century Popular Verse," *A Companion to Emily Dickinson*, Martha Nell Smith and Mary Loeffelholz (eds.), (Malden and Oxford: Blackwell Publishing, 2008), 193–196.

20. Betsy Erkkila, *The Wicked Sisters: Women Poets, Literary History, and Discord* (New York and Oxford: Oxford University Press, 1992), 74.
21. Elizabeth Barrett Browning, *Aurora Leigh* (1856; New York: C. S. Francis & Co., 1857), 16.
22. Ibid., 15.
23. Longfellow, *Kavanagh*, 121, 145.
24. Browning, *Aurora Leigh*, 172.
25. Erkkila, *Wicked Sisters*, 75.
26. Virginia Jackson and Yopie Prins, "Lyrical Studies," *Victorian Literature and Culture* 27.2 (1999), 523.
27. Franklin (ed.), *Poems of Emily Dickinson*, 11.
28. Dickinson's effusive offer, early in their correspondence, to have Susan Gilbert's journal bound at her own expense (L 88, April 1852) indicates Dickinson's awareness of the book-making alternatives she did not pursue in compiling her fascicles.
29. Alexandra Socarides, *Dickinson Unbound: Paper, Process, Poetics* (New York: Oxford University Press, 2012), 35.
30. See Fr 18, 19, 20, 22, 25 32, 34, 35.
31. Fr 47.
32. Fr 80.
33. Fr 70.
34. Paula Bernat Bennett, *Emily Dickinson: Woman Poet* (Iowa City: University of Iowa Press, 1990), 18; on Dickinson and women's floral verse see also Petrino, *Dickinson and Her Contemporaries*, 129–160.
35. Longfellow, *Kavanagh*, 141, 143.
36. L 260; Thomas Wentworth Higginson, "Emily Dickinson's Letters," *Atlantic Monthly* 68 (October 1891): 444–456.
37. Thomas Wentworth Higginson, "Ought Women to Learn the Alphabet?" *Atlantic Monthly* 3 (February 1859), 146.
38. L 260.
39. Mary Loeffelholz, "U.S. Literary Contemporaries: Dickinson's Moderns," *Emily Dickinson in Context*, Eliza Richards (ed.), (New York: Cambridge University Press, 2013), 131–32.
40. Qtd. in Mary Loeffelholz, *From School to Salon: Reading Nineteenth-Century American Women's Poetry* (Princeton: Princeton University Press, 2004), 149, 151.
41. Bayard Taylor, "The Diversions of the Echo Club," *Atlantic Monthly* 30 (July 1872), 78; see also Gary Williams, *Hungry Heart: The Literary Emergence of Julia Ward Howe* (Amherst: University of Massachusetts Press, 1999), 137.

42. "Success," *A Masque of Poets* (Boston: Roberts Brothers, 1878), 174. Dickinson's correspondence with Helen Hunt Jackson has accumulated a rich critical commentary: see Erkkila, *Wicked Sisters*, 86–98; Sewell, *Life*, 779; and Petrino, *Dickinson and Her Contemporaries*, 161–200. For Niles' letter to Dickinson, see L 749b.
43. L 749a, 813a, and 813b.
44. Fr 1570E; L 749.
45. See Fr 1570F.
46. L 405a.
47. See Rodier, "Astra Castra," and Loeffelholz, "Dickinson's Moderns."
48. Theo Davis, "Critical History I: 1890–1955," *Dickinson in Context*, Eliza Richards (ed.), 311.
49. Pierre Bourdieu, *The Rules of Art: Genesis and Structure of the Literary Field* (1992), trans. Susan Emanuel (Stanford: Stanford University Press, 1996), 157.
50. Fr 830.

Suggested Further Reading

Argersinger, Jana L. and Phyllis Cole, eds. *Toward a Female Genealogy of Transcendentalism*. Athens: University of Georgia Press, 2014.

Armstrong, Isobel. *Victorian Poetry: Poetry, Poetics, and Politics*. New York: Routledge, 1993.

———, Joseph Bristow and Cath Sharrock, eds. *Nineteenth-Century Women Poets*. Oxford and New York: Oxford University Press, 1996.

Backscheider, Paula R. *Eighteenth-Century Women Poets and Their Poetry: Inventing Agency, Inventing Genre*. Baltimore: Johns Hopkins University Press, 2005.

Bailey, Brigitte, Katheryn P. Viens, and Conrad Edick Wright, eds. *Margaret Fuller and Her Circles*. Durham: University of New Hampshire Press, 2013.

Barrett, Faith. *To Fight Aloud Is Very Brave: American Poetry and the Civil War*. Amherst: University of Massachusetts Press, 2012.

Bauer, Dale M. and Philip Gould, eds. *The Cambridge Companion to Nineteenth-Century American Women's Writing*. Cambridge: Cambridge University Press, 2001.

Beam, Dorri. *Style, Gender, and Fantasy in Nineteenth-Century Women's Writings*. Cambridge and New York: Cambridge University Press, 2011.

Bennett, Paula Bernat. "Laughing all the Way to the Bank: Female Sentimentalists in the Marketplace, 1825–1850." *Studies in American Humor* 3 (2002): 11–25.

———, ed. *Nineteenth-Century American Women Poets: An Anthology*. Malden and Oxford: Wiley-Blackwell, 1998.

———, ed. *Palace-Burner: The Selected Poetry of Sarah Piatt*. Urbana: University of Illinois Press, 2001.

———. *Poets in the Public Sphere: The Emancipatory Project of American Women's Poetry, 1800–1900*. Princeton: Princeton University Press, 2003.

———. "'Pomegranate-Flowers': The Phantasmic Productions of Late-Nineteenth -Century Anglo-American Women Poets." *Solitary Pleasures: The Historical, Literary, and Artistic Discourses of Autoeroticism*. Paula Bennett and Vernon A. Rosario II, eds. New York: Routledge, 1995. 189–213.

———. "Was Sigourney a Poetess? The Aesthetics of Victorian Plenitude in Lydia Sigourney's Poetry." *Comparative American Studies* 5 (2007): 265–289.

———, Karen L. Kilcup and Philipp Schweighauser, eds. *Teaching Nineteenth-Century American Poetry*. New York: Modern Language Association of America, 2007.

Boggs, Colleen G. *Transnationalism and American Literature: Literary Translation, 1773–1892*. New York: Routledge, 2007.

Boyd, Melba Joyce. *Discarded Legacy: Politics and Poetics in the Life of Frances E. W. Harper, 1825–1911*. Detroit: Wayne State University Press, 1994.

Brooks, Joanna. "Our Phillis, Ourselves." *American Literature* 82.1 (2010): 1–28.

Callahan, Monique-Adelle. *Between the Lines: Literary Transnationalism and African American Poetics*. Oxford and New York: Oxford University Press, 2011.

Carretta, Vincent. *Phillis Wheatley: Biography of a Genius*. Athens and London: University of Georgia Press, 2011.

———, ed. *Unchained Voices: An Anthology of Black Authors in the English Speaking World of the Eighteenth-Century*. Lexington: University of Kentucky Press, 2003.

Carruth, Mary, ed. *Feminist Interventions in Early American Studies*. Birmingham: University of Alabama Press, 2006.

Cavitch, Max. *American Elegy: The Poetry of Mourning from the Puritans to Whitman*, Minneapolis: University of Minnesota Press, 2007.

———. "Lazarus and the Golem of Liberty." *American Literary History* 18.1 (Spring 2006): 1–28.

Chapman, Alison, ed. *Victorian Women Poets*. Cambridge: D. S. Brewer, 2003.

Cherciu, Lucia. "Parody as Dialogue and Disenchantment: Remembering Phoebe Cary." *American Transcendental Quarterly* 20.1 (March 2006): 325–341.

Cohen, Lara Langer and Jordan Alexander Stein, eds. *Early African American Print Culture*. Philadelphia: University of Pennsylvania Press, 2012.

Cohen, Michael. *The Social Lives of Poems in Nineteenth-Century America*. Philadelphia: University of Pennsylvania Press, 2015.

Coultrap-McQuin, Susan. *Doing Literary Business: American Women Writers in the Nineteenth-Century*. Chapel Hill: University of North Carolina Press, 1990.

Diehl, Joanne Feit. *Women Poets and the American Sublime*. Bloomington: Indiana University Press, 1990.

Dillon, Elizabeth Maddox. "Sentimental Aesthetics." *American Literature* 76.3 (September 2004): 495–523.

Dobson, Joanne. "Reclaiming Sentimental Literature." *American Literature* 69.2 (June 1997): 264–288.

Elbert, Monika M. *Separate Spheres No More: Gender Convergence in American Literature, 1830–1939*. Tuscaloosa: University of Alabama Press, 2000.

Erkkila, Betsy. *The Wicked Sisters: Women Poets, Literary History, and Discord*. Oxford and New York: Oxford University Press, 1992.

Ferry, Anne. *Tradition and the Individual Poem: An Inquiry into Anthologies*. Stanford: Stanford University Press, 2001.

———, Donald Pease, and John Carlos Rowe, eds. *Re-framing the Transnational Turn in American Studies*. Lebanon: Dartmouth College Press, 2011.

Finch, Annie. "The Sentimental Poetess in the World: Metaphor and Subjectivity in Lydia Sigourney's Nature Poetry." *Legacy* 5.2 (Fall 1998): 3–18.

Foster, Frances Smith, ed. *A Brighter Coming Day: A Frances Ellen Watkins Harper Reader*. New York: Feminist Press of CUNY, 1990.

———. *Written By Herself: Literary Production by African American Women, 1746–1892*. Indianapolis: Indiana University Press, 1993.

Gardner, Jared. *The Rise and Fall of Early American Magazine Culture*. Urbana: University of Illinois Press, 2012.

Ginzberg, Lori D. *Women and the Work of Benevolence: Morality, Politics, and Class in the Nineteenth-Century United States*. New Haven: Yale University Press, 1990.

Golding, Alan. *From Outlaw to Classic: Canons in American Poetry*. Madison: University of Wisconsin Press, 1995.

Graham, Maryemma and Jerry W. Ward, eds. *Cambridge History of African American Literature*. Cambridge and New York: Cambridge University Press, 2011.

Gray, Janet. *Race and Time: American Women's Poetics from Antislavery to Modernity*. Iowa City: University of Iowa Press, 2004.

———, ed. *She Wields a Pen: American Women Poets of the Nineteenth Century*. Iowa City: University of Iowa Press, 1997.

Gruesz, Kirsten Silva. *Ambassadors of Culture: The Transamerican Origins of Latino Writing*. Princeton: Princeton University Press, 2002.

Hagenbuchle, Roland, ed. *American Poetry Between Tradition and Modernism*. Regensburg: Verlag Friedrich Pustet, 1984.

Hager, Christopher and Cody Marrs. "Against 1865: Reperiodizing the Nineteenth Century." *J19: The Journal of Nineteenth-Century Americanists* 1 (2013): 259–284.

Henderson, Desirée. *Grief and Genre in American Literature, 1790–1870*. New York: Ashgate, 2011.

Hollander, John, ed. *American Poetry: The Nineteenth Century*. New York: Library of America, 1993.

Homestead, Melissa. *American Women Authors and Literary Property, 1822–1869*. Cambridge: Cambridge University Press, 2010.

Jackson, Virginia. "American Victorian Poetry: The Transatlantic Poetic." *Victorian Poetry* 43 (2005): 157–164.

———. *Dickinson's Misery: A Theory of Lyric Reading*. Princeton: Princeton University Press, 2005.

——— and Yopie Prins. "Lyrical Studies." *Victorian Literature and Culture* 7 (1999): 521–530.

Kelley, Mary. *Private Woman, Public Stage: Literary Domesticity in Nineteenth-Century America*. Oxford and New York: Oxford University Press, 1984.

Kete, Mary Louise. *Sentimental Collaborations: Mourning and Middle-Class Identity in Nineteenth-Century America*. Durham: Duke University Press, 2000.

Kilcup, Karen and Angela Sorby, eds. *Over The River and Through The Woods: An Anthology of Nineteenth-Century American Children's Poetry*. Baltimore: Johns Hopkins University Press, 2014.

Klotz, Sarah. "A Flight From Home: Negotiations of Gender and Nationality in Frances Osgood's Early Career." Bailey, Brigitte, Lucinda Damon-Bach, and Beth L. Lueck, eds. *Transatlantic Women: Nineteenth-Century Women Writers and Great Britain*. Durham: University of New Hampshire Press, 2012. 3–20.

Kohler, Michelle. *Miles of Stare: Transcendentalism and the Problem of Literary Vision in Nineteenth-Century America*. Tuscaloosa: University of Alabama Press, 2014.

Larson, Kerry ed. *The Cambridge Companion to Nineteenth-Century American Poetry*. Cambridge and New York: Cambridge University Press, 2011.

———. *Imagining Equality in Nineteenth-Century American Literature*. Cambridge: Cambridge University Press, 2008.

Lawrence, Kathleen. "The 'Dry-Lighted Soul' Ignites: Emerson and His Soul-Mate Caroline Sturgis as Seen in Her Houghton Manuscripts." *Harvard Library Bulletin* 16.3 (2005): 37–67.

———. "Soul Sisters and the Sister Arts: Margaret Fuller, Caroline Sturgis, and Their Private World of Love and Art." *ESQ: A Journal of the American Renaissance* 57.1 (2011): 79–104.

Lehuu, Isabelle. *Carnival on the Page: Popular Print Media in Antebellum America*. Chapel Hill: University of North Carolina, 2000.

Leighton, Angela. *Victorian Women Poets: Writing Against the Heart*. Charlottesville: University Press of Virginia, 1992.

Leonard, Keith. *Fettered Genius: The African American Bardic Poet from Slavery to Civil Rights*. Charlottesville: University of Virginia Press, 2006.

Levin, Joanna. *Bohemia in America, 1858–1920*. Stanford: Stanford University Press, 2010.

——— and Edward Whitely, eds. *Whitman among the Bohemians*. Iowa City: University of Iowa Press, 2014.

Loeffelholz, Mary. *Dickinson and the Boundaries of Feminist Theory*. Urbana: University of Illinois Press, 1991.

———. *From School to Salon: Reading Nineteenth-Century American Women's Poetry*. Princeton: Princeton University Press, 2004.

Mandell, Laura, ed. "The Transatlantic Poetess." *Romanticism on the Net* 29–30 (February–May 2003). www.erudit.org/revue/ron/2003/v/n29/index.html.

Martin, Wendy, ed. *The Cambridge Companion to Emily Dickinson*. Cambridge: Cambridge University Press, 1992.

McGill, Meredith L. *American Literature and the Culture of Reprinting, 1834–1853*. Philadelphia: University of Pennsylvania Press, 2003.

———, ed. *The Traffic in Poems: Nineteenth-Century Poetry and Transatlantic Exchange*. New Brunswick: Rutgers University Press, 2008.

Mellor, Anne K. *Romanticism and Gender*. New York: Routledge, 1993.

Miller, Cristanne. *Reading in Time: Emily Dickinson in the Nineteenth Century*. Amherst: University of Massachusetts Press, 2012.

Morris, Timothy. *Becoming Canonical in American Poetry*. Urbana and Chicago: University of Illinois Press, 1995.

Newcomb, John Timberlake. *Would Poetry Disappear? American Verse and the Crisis of Modernity*. Columbus: Ohio State University Press, 2004.

Okker, Patricia. *Our Sister Editors: Sarah J. Hale and the Tradition of Nineteenth-Century American Women Editors*. Athens: University of Georgia Press, 1995.

Ostriker, Alicia. *Stealing the Language: The Emergence of Women's Poetry in America*. Boston: Beacon, 1986.

Parker, Robert Dale, ed. *The Sound the Stars Make Rushing Through the Sky: The Writings of Jane Johnston Schoolcraft*. Philadelphia: University of Pennsylvania Press, 2007.

Petrino, Elizabeth A. *Emily Dickinson and Her Contemporaries: Women's Verse in America, 1820–1885*. Lebanon: University Press of New England, 1998.

———. "'We are Rising as a People': Frances Harper's Radical Views on Class and Racial Equality in Sketches of Southern Life." *American Transcendental Quarterly* 19.2 (June 2005): 133–153.

Putzi, Jennifer. "'Some Queer Freak of Taste': Gender, Authorship, and the 'Rock Me to Sleep' Controversy." *American Literature* 84.4 (2012): 769–795.

Richards, Eliza, ed. *Emily Dickinson in Context*. Cambridge and New York: Cambridge University Press, 2013.

———. *Gender and the Poetics of Reception in Poe's Circle*. Cambridge and New York: Cambridge University Press, 2004.

Roberts, Jess. "'The Little Coffin': Anthologies, Conventions, and Dead Children." *Representations of Death in Nineteenth-Century US Writing and Culture*. Lucy Frank, ed. Burlington: Ashgate, 2007. 141–154.

Rubin, Joan Shelley. *Songs of Ourselves: The Uses of Poetry*. Cambridge: Harvard University Press, 2007.

Shields, David S. *Civil Tongues and Polite Letters in British America*. Chapel Hill: University of North Carolina Press, 1997.

———. *Oracles of Empire: Poetry, Politics, and Empire in British America, 1690–1750*. Chicago: University of Chicago Press, 1990.

Socarides, Alexandra. *Dickinson Unbound: Paper, Process, Poetics*. Oxford and New York: Oxford University Press, 2012.

Sorby, Angela. "The Milwaukee School of Fleshy Poetry: Ella Wheeler Wilcox's Poems of Passion and Popular Aestheticism." *Legacy* 26.1 (2009): 69–91.

———. *Schoolroom Poets: Childhood, Performance, and the Place of American Poetry, 1865–1917*. Durham: University of New Hampshire Press, 2005.

Stabile, Susan. *Memory's Daughters: The Material Culture of Remembrance in Eighteenth-Century America*. Ithaca: Cornell University Press, 2004.

Stancliff, Michael. *Frances Ellen Watkins Harper: African American Reform Rhetoric and the Rise of a Modern Nation State*. New York: Routledge, 2011.

Steele, Jeffrey. *Transfiguring America: Myth, Ideology, and Mourning in Margaret Fuller's Writing*. Columbia: University of Missouri Press, 2001.

Steiner, Dorothea. "Women Poets in the Twilight Period." *American Poetry Between Tradition and Modernism*. Roland Hagenbuchle, ed. Regensburg: Verlag Friedrich Pustet, 1984. 169–190.

Tompkins, Jane. *Sensational Designs: The Cultural Work of American Fiction, 1790–1860*. Oxford and New York: Oxford University Press, 1985.

Vietto, Angela. *Women and Authorship in Revolutionary America*. Aldershot: Ashgate Publishing, 2006.

Vincent, Patrick H. *The Romantic Poetess: European Culture, Politics, and Gender, 1820–1840*. Hanover: University Press of New England Press, 2004.

Walker, Cheryl, ed. *American Women Poets of the Nineteenth Century: An Anthology*. New Brunswick: Rutgers University Press, 1995.

———. "Ina Coolbrith and the Nightingale Tradition." *Legacy* 6.1 (1989): 27–33.

———. *The Nightingale's Burden: Women Poets before 1900*. Bloomington: Indiana University Press, 1983.

———. "Nineteenth-Century Women Poets and Realism." *American Literary Realism* 23.3 (1991): 24–41.

Watt, Emily Stipes. *The Poetry of American Women from 1632 to 1943*. Austin: University of Texas Press, 1977.

Wendorff, Laura C. "'The Vivid Dreamings of an Unsatisfied Heart': Gender Ideology, Literary Aesthetics, and the 'Poetess' in Nineteenth-Century America." *American Transcendental Quarterly* 15 (2001): 109–129.

Weyler, Karen A. *Empowering Words: Outsiders and Authorship in Early America*. Athens: The University of Georgia Press, 2013.

Williams, Gary. *Hungry Heart: The Literary Emergence of Julia Ward Howe*. Amherst: University of Massachusetts Press, 1999.

Williams, Susan S. *Reclaiming Authorship: Literary Women in America, 1850–1900*. Philadelphia: University of Pennsylvania Press, 2006.

Wolosky, Shira. *Feminist Theory Across Disciplines: Feminist Community and American Women's Poetry*. New York: Routledge, 2013.

———. *Major Voices: 19th-century American Women's Poetry*. New Milford: The Toby Press, 2003.

Index